BUSINESS REVIEW BOOKS

Business Law

SIXTH EDITION

Robert W. Emerson

JD, Harvard Law School
Huber Hurst Professor of Business Law, University of Florida
Affiliate Professor, Center for European Studies
Advisory Editor-in-Chief, *American Business Law Journal*
Academic Board Member and Reporter, International Association of Judicial Officers
Seven-Time Winner, Best Paper Award, Academy of Legal Studies in Business
Thirteen-Time Winner, Annual Teaching Award, University of Florida
Member of Maryland State Bar and U.S. District Court Bar

BARRON'S

Library of Congress Catalog Card No. 2015938004

ISBN: 978-1-4380-0511-9

PRINTED IN CANADA
9 8 7 6

10%
POST-CONSUMER
WASTE
Paper contains a minimum
of 10% post-consumer
waste (PCW). Paper used
in this book was derived
from certified, sustainable
forestlands.

CONTENTS

COMMERCIAL RELATIONS

BUSINESS FORMATIONS

PREFACE

• *PURPOSE AND SCOPE OF THE BOOK*

This book presents both students and other interested persons with a simple and readily understandable explanation of essential and related business law and legal environment subjects.

For the citizen, corporate executive, and business manager, the book should serve as an independent explanation of fundamental law in both a practical and a technical setting. For the student, this overview should serve as a guide through the complex maze of the literally thousands of legal principles tossed out in a typical course on the law or legal environment of business.

Business law, including the legal environment of business, is a broad field; nearly every law school subject is covered or touched upon in this book. However, as an experienced teacher and practicing attorney, I have attempted to treat, in particular detail, the legal subjects that actually engage the attention of businesspersons and that are covered in university and college courses.

Legal theory is important in the "everyday business world" inhabited by corporate managers and all other persons making major business decisions, as well as buying and selling supplies and services. We expect businesspeople to know about tort responsibility and their duty to the public. Moreover, the modern business world now requires a general knowledge of governmental relations and activities, including the societal obligations described in the criminal and other statutory or regulatory law. This book deals with all of these concerns. For example, persons involved in production and transportation will find extensive information about contracts, environmental law, product liability, and international law. Those in marketing and sales will see much relevant material on contracts, consumer protection, antitrust laws, and torts. Personnel specialists can read much on contracts, employment law, and labor law, while finance or accounting concerns are often addressed in contracts, credit regulation, and securities regulation. Research and development (R & D) questions can be answered in torts and product liability law as well as intellectual property law.

• *CONTENTS OF THE BOOK: BOTH LEGAL ENVIRONMENT AND BUSINESS LAW*

This book covers all of the material in the general business law course offerings (usually two semesters). Among these subjects are (a) an introduction to the law, (b) crimes and torts, (c) contracts, (d) business organizations (especially corporations and partnerships), (e) commercial paper, (f) agency, (g) property, (h) creditor rights and obligations, and (i) a full review of the Uniform Commercial Code (including relevant international law concepts).

The text has been updated and expanded to include all relevant new topics and trends, as well as revisions of existing legislation, regulation, and case law. I examine the legal environment of business and delve at length into the conduct of litigation, the nature of governmental powers and individual rights, and specific areas of law with a strong impact on business. These include—in addition to "standard" business law topics—administrative and constitutional law, securities regulation, antitrust law, labor and employment law, consumer protection law, computer law, international law, insurance, attorneys and accountants, tax law, environmental law, and the general moral and social duties of business. Furthermore, the book contains an in-depth glossary of over 2,350 words, much more comprehensive than the glossaries of other books on business law or the legal environment of business. The glossary is a major asset of the book in that it can serve as an independent dictionary of legal terminology useful in the business world. Along these lines, a very thorough index also helps readers to find and understand legal topics in their overall context.

• *VALUE TO TEACHERS AS WELL AS STUDENTS AND BUSINESSPERSONS*

The material presented is designed to prepare all students, including accounting students, for their future profession. It is in keeping with American Institute of Certified Public Accountant (AICPA) education requirements. All AICPA law course topics are included, and the book should serve as an excellent review for practicing accountants.

For the more general business law or legal environment student, my breakdown of the subject by chapter ties in with standard textbook treatment. This, and the comprehensive glossary and index, should be of help to the student who may need to key the class lectures or work assignments into explanations developed here.

Second only to my desire that readers receive a practical education in law suitable for the everyday business world is my desire that this book be eminently "teachable." I have tried to design a primary or supplementary text for the busy professors and lawyers who teach business law and the legal environment of business. The text presentation is easy to summarize and readily tied to related legal concepts. It is flexible enough to cover all subjects required in any current study of business law or the legal environment of business.

• *CONCLUSION AND ACKNOWLEDGMENTS*

This book embodies my teaching philosophy and experience, years of legal research and writing, and day-to-day advice to businesspersons. I welcome the comments and suggestions of my readers.

I am extremely grateful to my late father-in-law, the Honorable John W. Hardwicke, the coauthor and instigator of this book in its initial version. He was a constant source of ideas and inspiration, both professionally and personally, for nearly three decades as my second father.

I also thank my students for their support, their ideas and, most importantly, their questions. I have received helpful suggestions from many individuals. Finally, I especially thank, for all her assistance, the love of my life—my muse, my wife, Heidi Hardwicke Emerson.

Gainesville, Florida   Robert W. Emerson
September 2015

THE LAW AND SOCIETY

1
ORIGIN AND NATURE OF LAW

THE ORIGIN OF LAW

The origin of law is as obscure as the origin of society, since the existence of law is a precondition of society. In its most primitive, unreasoned form, law rests on brute power—the ability of one individual to control other individuals through strength. The *lex talionis*, the law of retaliation (an eye for an eye, a tooth for a tooth), arose from the natural impulse of individuals. As societies formed, this impulse was sanctioned by government as law. The law of damages is the substitution of monetary compensation for blood or retribution in kind.

As time passed, however, it became necessary to adopt rules governing the conduct of individuals toward one another and the conduct of a single individual toward the body of individuals as a whole (society). Certain laws were enacted, or evolved and developed, for different purposes:

1. To proscribe certain kinds of behavior that society finds objectionable. This is *public law* and concerns a citizen's relationship with society constituted as government. Public law includes constitutional, administrative, and criminal law and many forms of antitrust law, environmental law, labor law, and securities regulation.

2. To make an injured party (citizen, corporation, or other entity) whole. This is *private law* and concerns an individual's relationship with another individual. In this sense, private law includes tort, agency, contract, corporation, partnership, and property law.

3. To end disputes. This is again private law, specifically contract law, the law governing agreements. (If law is knowable, reasonable, fairly certain, and yet flexible, it may *prevent* disputes.)

YOU SHOULD REMEMBER

The origin of law is obscure; society cannot exist without law. Individual power and cunning constituted the first law, and primitive governments merely presided over the *lex talionis*, or law of private retribution.

As societies became complex, it became necessary to adopt rules of conduct for various purposes (for example, to forbid objectionable behavior, to make an injured party whole, and to end disputes).

DEFINITIONS OF LAW

Only if the total collective, the society, enforces its rules can they have any meaning, or serve any purpose, in the regulation of conduct. One school of thought, sometimes called the school of American legal realism, considers **law** to be that which a judge will decide concerning matters properly brought before him/her; thus, in a broader sense, this approach defines law as any rule that society will enforce. For our purposes, we prefer this definition of law. During the course of this book we will refer to law in terms of judicial decisions as well as statutory enactment.

However, there are other widely accepted definitions of law. A school of thought sometimes called "legal positivism" defines law as the command of a constituted political authority; "natural law" theorists argue that there is a higher law grounded in absolute moral rules and that any law contrary to such natural law is not law. The English jurist Blackstone (see page 8) defined law as "a rule of civil conduct prescribed by the supreme power in a state, commanding what is right, and prohibiting what is wrong."

Schools of Jurisprudence

Critical Legal Studies
Describing the legal system as using manipulable concepts to preserve the socioeconomic status quo while maintaining the fiction of a just decision-making process, adherents of this school often argue for more arbitrary, but less malleable rules tied to community values, egalitarianism, and actual fairness.

Historical School
The law is shaped by events, traditions, and customs; the past helps us to discern the principles of contemporary law.

Law and Economics
The link between law and economics cannot be severed; market efficiency is, or at least should be, the law's prime focus.

Natural Law
Law is tied to morals and ethics, including some principles that are immutable.

Positivism
The law is a set of rules developed and enforced by the governing authority.

Utilitarianism
More a social or economic philosophy than simply jurisprudence, this approach to life and law is often reduced to the phrase, "the greatest good for the greatest number," with law therefore judged by how much pleasure or pain it creates—how much it produces a net "plus" in terms of societal progress.

LAW AND MORALITY

Law generally represents the developing, common **morality** of human beings. Government almost always seeks to ally itself with prevailing customs, to proclaim as right only that which most citizens already perceive to be right, and to impose as law the rules considered by the majority or by more powerful or vocal minorities to be moral and therefore just. Thus, no matter how law is defined, there is a close, although imprecise, relationship between morality and any rule that society will enforce.

Since law is, or should be, reflective of prevailing morality, rigid societal control over all members of society should be unnecessary. The goal is self-control, based on the individual's own moral philosophy or "instincts." Indeed, the law's typically majoritarian and moral origins (described on page 5) serve to promote its enforcement, the ease or practicability of which depends on the acquiescence of a large preponderance of the population.

The relationship between law and morality is not mere speculation. Contracts may be found illegal if in violation of "public policy," that is, contrary to the "public good," and some case law even refers to lawful action as consistent with that of "right-thinking members of the community." Juries are considered to be made up of ordinary people reflecting prevailing morality.

Important Principle: Conduct that a reasonable person conscientiously deems moral and just is unlikely to collide with law.

Even if supposedly moral conduct proves illegal, that is, in violation of a rule that society will normally enforce, society's enforcement in a specific case may be muted, otherwise restrained, or even suspended.

Example: Relationship Between Law and Morality

In criminal law (see Chapter 19), even when an action is criminal, a good motive is considered in mitigation of punishment. "Bad" motives can have the opposite effect, such as leading to punitive damages in tort cases.

YOU SHOULD REMEMBER

There is a close relationship between law and morality. Law not only has its origin in morality, but also is easier to enforce when citizens yield to government for moral reasons.

DEVELOPMENT OF CIVIL LAW

As society became increasingly complex, various "lawgivers" attempted to provide orderly systems of laws that would promote security and justice. There are four landmark "codes," each of which represents distinct progress in the development of law:

Lawgiver	Date	Noteworthy Aspects
Hammurabi (Babylonian)	1792–1750 B.C.	Designed to promote "justice" but based on the *lex talionis*. A well-ordered system of 285 laws, arranged by titles.
Solon (Athenian)	594 B.C.	Established a stable government operating under a system of rules imposed by a consenting citizenry. "Citizens" were equal under the law.
Justinian (Roman)	A.D. 533	Summarized and systematized the civil law of Rome; remains the basis for the laws of most of Europe and Latin America and for parts of Asia and Africa.
Napoleon (French)	A.D. 1804	Preserved many democratic achievements of the French Revolution, such as civil equality and jury trial. Influenced modern law, for example, the modern law of the state of Louisiana.

    Civil Law, or code law, is one of two major legal systems currently in use in the Western world. It is based primarily on the written codes of Justinian and Napoleon. The predominant feature of civil law is the attempt to establish a body of legal rules in one systematized **code**, a single comprehensive legislative enactment. In this system, judicial decisions, case law, are not a source of law, although judicial precedents may be useful in the decision of cases. Civil Law remains the basis of the legal system not just throughout Europe, but also in many other parts of the world once under European colonial influence (e.g., Latin America and many nations in Africa and Asia). Indeed, non-Western countries such as China have, on their own, adopted much of the Civil Law system as a move to modernize and encourage business growth and international commerce. The two most important modern streams of Civil Law jurisprudence emanate from France and Germany, with the French tradition going back to the Napoleonic Code and the elaborations since, and the German doctrine dating to the German Civil Code of 1896. France's Code not only influenced almost all of Europe and Latin America, but also many countries in sub-Saharan Africa, the Maghreb, the Middle East, Southeast Asia, Oceania, and Francophone enclaves from North America (e.g., Quebec and Louisiana) to India. The French in fact heavily influenced Germany's system, and in turn the German approach to Civil Law has been adopted comprehensively by Japan. The German Code has also influenced legal systems in Scandinavia, the Baltics, Greece, Ukraine, China, South Korea, Taiwan, Thailand, Taiwan, and Brazil. These dominant doctrines for Civil Law traditions have caused many to refer to them as the Franco-Germanic Civil Law.

YOU SHOULD REMEMBER

The progress of law through the centuries can be traced through the activities of four "lawgivers" who attempted to state the law in keeping with their perceptions of evolving civilization and to provide remedies for those wronged.

The laws of certain countries are still based on the principles set forth in these codes.

DEVELOPMENT OF COMMON LAW

One country did not follow the comprehensive code approach to law. In England, disputes were resolved on a case-by-case basis, binding the arbiter of a dispute to the rule elicited from the determination of an earlier, similar dispute—hence **common law**. Common law is the second of the two major legal systems currently in use in the Western world.

Today England (together with the United States, Canada, Australia, New Zealand, and—to a lesser extent—India and other Asian, African, and Caribbean countries colonized by the British) follows the common law. An understanding of the concepts underlying the common law of England is thus vital to any discussion of American law, including American business law. Sir William Blackstone's **Commentaries**, published just before the American Revolution, are generally considered to be the best statement of English common law as it existed when the United States became an independent nation.

According to Blackstone, the common law is that "ancient collection of unwritten maxims and customs" which have "subsisted immemorially in this kingdom." These principles are revealed by the courts of law "through experience in the rendering of judicial decision." Common law is, therefore, the overall accumulation of judicial decisions, known as **case law**.

England has no written constitution. The basis of its constitution is the common law, derived mainly from precedent and incorporating also certain landmark documents, such as the Magna Carta (1215) and English Bill of Rights (1689).

American common law includes not only the "ancient maxims and customs" inherited from England, but also all subsequent and modern case law as developed and pronounced from time to time.

PRECEDENT AND COMMON LAW; *STARE DECISIS*

As common law developed, a judge confronted with a puzzling new case would search the literature for a similar case to determine whether a precedent had been established. If so, the judge would follow the prior decision.

Stare Decisis

The requirement that courts follow their own precedents is based on the legal principle of *stare decisis* or "stand by the decision." *Stare decisis* binds all of the lower courts of a jurisdiction to determinations rendered by the highest court in that same jurisdiction.

Stare decisis is not absolute; a decision of the highest court can be amended either by this court's changing its mind or by legislative mandate.

If a case arises for which no modern American or English precedent can be found, the court sometimes bases its decision on the Justinian code, from which some areas of the common law are derived. In the absence of a precedent, a court may follow its own sense of justice or fairness, with due regard for prevailing custom or morality.

LEGISLATION AND COMMON LAW CODES

Unless changes are constitutionally prohibited, Congress or the state legislatures may enact laws (**statutes**) that modify the common law. These statutes, also subject to judicial interpretation, are collected into codes: along with case law, the codes form the law generally applied in court. Unlike Civil Law codes, common law codes are not intended to be entire statements of the whole law; in fact, they often are meant to be supplemented by judicial opinions and also, for some areas of law, by administrative regulation.

EQUITY AND COMMON LAW

After the conquest of England by William the Conqueror (A.D. 1066), Norman kings created an independent, but parallel, system of justice alongside the developing common law, with ultimate judicial responsibility residing in the king himself. This system, the **equity** system, had exclusive jurisdiction over injunctive relief (court-ordered action) and the specific performance of a contract as well as certain contract modifications. Since the kings were not learned in the common law, they based their decisions on sensible principles of fair play (equity) embodied in "maxims" or commonsense rules of Solomon-like justice. As the equity system functioned alongside the common law courts, the two systems of law gradually merged. Equity maxims—"He who comes to equity must come with clean hands (courts may consider the past behavior of the claimant)," "Equity regards as done that which ought to be done," "Equity considers substance, not form," "Whoever seeks equity must do equity (behave fairly)," "Equality is equity (if there is no contrary evidence, equity favors the equal division of property [funds] to which more than one person is entitled)," "Do not sleep on your rights (delay may indicate acquiescence)," "Equity suffers no wrong without a remedy," and many other "fair play" principles—were adopted by the common law and are currently cited in judicial decisions.

Starting in the sixteenth century, before the equity courts merged into the common law system, the equity courts received responsibility for matters previously vested in the ecclesiastical (church) courts. Thus equity absorbed a number of functions involving the family (divorce, annulment, adoption). These equity responsibilities became part of the general legal system—and part of the common law—that developed in the United States.

Although law and equity are today merged into a common system in which equity principles are cited freely, the old equity domain (injunctive relief, specific performance of contract, contract modification, family law, divorce) is particularly influenced by the idea of fairness and is deliberately more relaxed in its concept of justice. Also, jury trial is not available in an equity-type proceeding, the jury having been a feature of the common law courts. Thus, although the equity court as a separate system of justice has ceased to exist, equity principles permeate all of the common law but are most diligently applied to traditional equity subject matter.

YOU SHOULD REMEMBER

England, the British Commonwealth, and the United States follow the common law. Whereas Civil Law attempts to state the whole law in a comprehensive code, the common law is found in the collected cases of the various courts of law. American common law began with the common law of England as summarized by Blackstone in his *Commentaries*. It includes the English common law and all subsequent legal developments, including the principle of *stare decisis*.

Common law codes should not be confused with Civil Law codes. In the common law, a code is a collection of statutes passed by a legislature; a

Civil Law code is intended as a full and comprehensive statement of the whole law.

Equity began as an independent legal system based on concepts of fair play. It covers injunctive relief, specific performance of contract, and certain contract revisions, as well as parts of family law. Many of the principles and maxims of equity have been merged into the common law. There is no jury trial in an equity case.

SUBSTANTIVE LAW AND PROCEDURAL LAW

Substantive law refers to any body of law creating, defining, and regulating rights and obligations within the framework of a single subject, such as contracts, torts, crimes, or property.

Procedural law pertains to operating rules for obtaining substantive rights or defining substantive obligations in a court of law. Procedure may be as important as substance in obtaining justice, since access to the court and proper statement of the cause of action (basis for a lawsuit) are controlled by the rules of an orderly society.

In the federal legal system and in most state systems, procedural rules are promulgated by the judiciary, adopted after public hearings, and published along with editions of the various codes. The rules of procedure are intended to promote justice and are to be interpreted flexibly and broadly, in the interest of fairness. A trial attorney's basic skills center around his/her mastery of procedure.

Lesser courts, such as small claims courts or probate courts, have developed simplified procedures so that citizens may handle their own cases without benefit of attorneys.

YOU SHOULD REMEMBER

Substantive law defines legal rights and obligations in regard to a specific subject.

Procedural law is concerned with the enforcement of substantive law in a court of law.

LAW, ETHICS, AND ATTORNEYS

Ethics and law are not the same, but there is an overlap, with enormous influence of one on the other. *Law is easier to enforce when viewed as moral*, when almost everyone agrees with it, when many people follow the law without even really thinking about it because they support the underlying rationale for the law.

If a law is perceived as having no ethical component, then people tend to have little respect for the law; perhaps they have just a "fear of getting caught." However, we usually want the law to lag somewhat behind ethics; law—more conservative force (not way out ahead), but subject to gradual conservative change (trailing ethics, as becomes well understood and generally supported).

Knowledge Is Only the Start Toward Wisdom

Be wary of simply noting the details and adopting a strictly technical view of the law, if doing so flies in the face of the spirit of the law and of common sense and decency. Do not get absorbed in details and miss the "big picture" of societal or attitudinal changes. Businesses sometimes wrongly assume that law and ethics are far apart. They thus stick with a technical, literal interpretation of the law that worked a decade ago, but ignores the trends and moral notions recently imbued in the law.

CODES OF ETHICS

The Sarbanes and Oxley Act (2002) at Section 406 mandates that all corporations whose stock is publicly traded have a code of ethics for their upper-level financial officers. Even without that requirement, nearly every publicly held business (e.g., a large corporation) has adopted a "Code of Ethics" for all of its employees to follow. Likewise, almost all professional associations, such as the American Institute of Certified Public Accountants, the American Bar Association, the National Society of Professional Engineers, and the American Medical Association, have ethics codes for their members. These codes may require specific conduct in particular situations—more likely, disclosure to the employee's superior—but most codes are general statements of values more than anything else: (1) honesty; (2) transparency; (3) loyalty; (4) being respectful; and (5) obedience to the law. Some codes, especially those of professionals, create standards that courts may cite when interpreting contracts, professional norms, or industry customs. Many codes of ethics, especially professional codes, provide sanctions for noncompliance even though they do not constitute criminal penalties.

THE ATTORNEY'S MANY ROLES AND ETHICAL DUTIES, LEGAL FEES, ATTORNEY/CLIENT CONFLICT, AND THE BUSINESSPERSON'S ROLE

THE ATTORNEY'S ROLES

Businesses increasingly rely on attorneys not only when they are sued or encounter other crises, but also to prevent problems. The hope is to improve business practices and thus reduce the risks of lawsuits, fines, or other legal penalties or expenses.

Lawyers do not so much "know the law" as they are familiar with general legal principles and able to find specific cases, statutes, or other law applicable to a particular set of facts. A lawyer often has several functions: investigator, drafter, negotiator, advisor, and advocate. A lawyer has a duty to advise against illegal actions, but also must maintain confidences shared with him/her during the course of the attorney/client relationship.

THE ATTORNEY'S ETHICAL RESPONSIBILITIES

Although U.S. Supreme Court decisions permit advertising by lawyers, there still are restrictions on an attorney's individual solicitation of clients. Therefore, except for "in-house" counsel (lawyers who are employees of a business, perhaps in a company's "legal department"), the businessperson usually contacts an attorney rather than vice-versa. Only if a business has already had dealings with outside counsel can it sometimes expect these attorneys to take the initiative concerning new legal problems.

The **attorney/client privilege** permits clients to keep confidential matters discussed by or with their attorneys. This privilege can be waived by the client; for instance, he/she may subsequently disclose attorney/client communications to a third party. Also, because the attorney/client privilege depends on *confidential* communications, it does not extend to statements made in the presence of, or letters sent to, persons in addition to the attorney and client. Nor can confidentiality protections ordinarily extend to nonclients. Thus, what an employee tells the corporate employer's lawyer may not be protected because the attorney is not the *employee's* lawyer, but the corporation's; even if there is such confidentiality, the corporation may choose to waive any confidentiality.

> **International Comparison:** Most European countries do not extend the attorney-client privilege to cover any communications with in-house attorneys.

In extreme cases, lawyers may reveal to the court a client's spoken criminal intent. Most states have adopted the American Bar Association's (ABA's) Model Rules of Professional Conduct, in which Rule 1.6 says, "a lawyer *may reveal* [emphasis added] such information to the extent the lawyer reasonably believes necessary: to prevent the client from committing a criminal act that the lawyer believes is likely to result in imminent death or substantial bodily harm . . ." When that rule was adopted, some lawyers argued for a mandatory disclosure rule, but the ABA made it optional. As for corporate fraud, lawyers tend to be free—under state law—to act in the corporation's best interests as the lawyer sees it. Critics, however, say lawyers have been hesitant to expose paying clients, and that shareholders thus have suffered. The Sarbanes-Oxley Act of 2002, as well as Securities and Exchange Commission rules, impose certain whistleblowing requirements on lawyers that exceed anything under state law. (See Chapter 18.)

> For lawyers to do their work, they must be able to work with a certain degree of privacy. Only if extreme necessity is shown, such as hardship and injustice toward the other party, may work-related material be obtained. The **work-product doctrine** is broader than the attorney-client privilege. For example, in cases where the attorney-client privilege has been waived, a lawyer's notes, or those of his/her assistant, have remained protected under the work-product doctrine.

Each state has ethical codes of conduct governing lawyers. These concern the attorney's responsibilities, sometimes conflicting, both to the client and to the legal system. In general, the attorney must:

(a) only take cases that he/she can handle competently;

(b) zealously advocate the client's cause, while remaining faithful to the attorney's own obligation, as an officer of the court, not to undermine the overall purposes of the system itself;

(c) keep the client reasonably informed (e.g., concerning settlement offers);

(d) abide by the restrictions of attorney/client privilege; and

(e) when withdrawing from a case, take measures to protect the client's interests (e.g., try to obtain new counsel for the client).

These rules help to delineate duties in specific situations. Published opinions of courts and bar association panels, as well as telephone "hotline" services, may also furnish lawyers with guidance. Violation of the rules can result in disciplinary action, with punishment ranging from reprimand to disbarment.

Businesses' Social Responsibility

The ethical duties of businesspersons are not as firmly or as long established as the duties for lawyers, medical doctors, accountants, and others with extensive training and testing accompanied by specialty credentials and, in effect, exclusive or near-monopoly licenses to practice a particular profession. However, the development and elaboration of standards for business—both in particular fields and generally—is growing rapidly.

One approach is to recognize that, regardless of whether there are actual laws requiring certain behavior, businesses have certain duties to society. The traditional view is that a business' dominant, if not only, duty is, as long as it acts lawfully, to maximize profits—hence, to maximize the owners' (e.g., corporate shareholders) return on their investment. Three other approaches expect more social awareness and thus more activity in line with a general duty to the public. A business should consider its overall impact on society (perhaps comparable to, in terms of environmentalism, how persons should measure and then seek to reduce their carbon "footprint"). Effects, both long-term and immediate, both intended and entirely coincidental, should be understood and, if deleterious, corrected or at least mitigated.

The stakeholder-interest approach to businesses' social responsibility compels businesspersons and entities, such as corporations, to consider the effects that their actions have on all stakeholders (constituents), not just the business owners (the shareholders). These other stakeholders include employees, customers, suppliers, creditors, and the community as a whole. Benefit corporations (discussed on page 365) are a recent example of stakeholder interests in action.

Another approach is to demand of a business that it meet a moral minimum. This is, at the very least, a "do no harm" or a "clean up your mess" standard. The business is free to earn as much profit as is lawful so long as it avoids causing harm to other, innocent third parties. Under laws concerning the environment, occupational safety, product liability, consumer protection, business competition (antitrust), and other fields, a business may not be judged so as to blame as much as it is expected to rectify its errors. That is, the business must pay for any iniquity it causes, often with damage awards and also corrective measures meant to make injured parties whole and to prevent future harm (e.g., to clean up a toxic spill, to correct a product defect, to warn consumers of helpful safety or health measures they should take).

The highest of the approaches typically is one concerning corporate citizenship.

ATTORNEY'S FEES

Ordinarily, unless a statute provides that a winning party may recover **attorney's fees** or a claim or defense was outrageously wrong, the parties pay their own counsel. So it is still somewhat unusual that a loser must pay the winner's attorney's fees. In Britain and many other countries, though, the loser must customarily pay the winner's attorney's fees. (That occurs to discourage and punish risky litigation.)

Legal ethics and consumer protection concerns generally require professional clarity about legal fees. For example, the fee arrangement should be put *in writing* and explained *in-depth* before a client hires a lawyer (a requirement in most states, particularly for contingency-fee arrangements). **Retainers** are often requested, and sometimes attorneys will not represent a client without them. Clients may see the retainer as assurance that, if work is needed, the lawyer will be available. Actually, it is instead an assurance to the lawyer that the client is able and willing to pay for the lawyer's services, with the retainer simply being advance payment. If there is any unused, but paid for, lawyer's time, the lawyer is obliged to return that portion of the retainer to the client.

As legal costs have soared, a growing number of states have relaxed the centuries-old, common law ban on outsiders (nonlawyers, nonparties) investing in lawsuits (financing the costs in return for a percentage of the winnings if there is a victory). Moreover, bar associations, private firms, and the states increasingly have pushed for lawyers to engage in reduced-fee or pro bono (free) legal representation for those who need legal counsel in *civil* (*noncriminal*) matters but cannot afford to hire a lawyer.[1]

ATTORNEY/CLIENT RELATIONS: CONFLICT AND THE BUSINESSPERSON'S INPUT

As a professional, the attorney cannot always be expected to do the client's bidding; the attorney may believe that the client's interest would

---

[1] At the criminal level, constitutional protections are in place for people facing criminal charges and possible incarceration but unable to pay for defense counsel; these people are entitled to a public defender. *Gideon v. Wainwright*, 372 U.S. 335 (1963) (interpreting the U.S. Constitution's Sixth Amendment).

best be served by another course of action. But occasionally attorney/ client differences stem from what the attorney perceives to be his/her professional, ethical obligations. Whenever differences arise, no matter what the reason, frank discussions are usually necessary and may, in fact, resolve the differences.

The businessperson, armed with some knowledge of the legal system, the role of lawyers, and the substantive and procedural law, can play an active role in the lawyer's endeavors to resolve problems and/or prepare cases for litigation. Although taking a few courses, reading law books, and participating in past cases are no substitute for professional advice, the businessperson's basic, if limited, knowledge of the law should help him/her to realize when the services of a lawyer are necessary, and what assistance the attorney and the client can provide one another. Although businesspersons may turn to published legal guides and form books for specific answers to some basic, obvious problems, often the most valuable service lawyers perform is noticing potential difficulties that the client did not even consider.

YOU SHOULD REMEMBER

Attorneys can be used not only to resolve problems, but also to prevent them. Familiar with general legal principles, the lawyer directs his/her knowledge toward finding and applying the law to a particular set of facts.

A lawyer may have several roles: investigator, drafter, negotiator, advisor, and advocate. Each state's code of attorney conduct governs the lawyer's duties to his/her client and to the legal system.

The attorney/client privilege protects communications between attorney and client. The client may waive the privilege, and it arises only for confidential communications (ones not shared with third parties).

UNIFORM LAWS

Theoretically there would be 50 bodies of common law (combined case and statutory law) among the 50 states. Actually, however, there is great interdependence, as well as conscious parallelism, among the various federal and state court systems. Moreover, there has long been a disciplined effort to develop uniform legislation, with states enacting the same set of statutes so as to reduce uncertainty about the laws of sister states, particularly in commercial law.

The **Uniform Commercial Code** (UCC—adopted in 49 states and partly in Louisiana) is the most successful of the proposed uniform laws. This comprehensive statute covers numerous subjects within the framework of substantive commercial law, including sales, commercial paper, and secured transactions. The UCC is thoroughly discussed in Chapters 9–13.

Summary of the Coverage of the Uniform Commercial Code (UCC)

Article	Coverage
Article 1 General Provisions	General principles, rules of interpretation, and definitions applicable to the entire UCC
Article 2 Sales	Contracts for the sale of goods
Article 2A Leases	Leases of goods
Article 3 Negotiable Instruments	Negotiable instrument payable in money, primarily promissory notes and checks
Article 4 Bank Deposits and Collections	Bank collection process and the legal relationship between a bank and its checking account customers
Article 4A Funds Transfers	Wholesale wire transfers
Article 5 Letters of Credit	Rights and obligations of parties to a letter of credit, a financing device used primarily in international trade
Article 6 Bulk Sales	Protection for creditors of a merchant who sells his entire stock in trade not in the ordinary course of business (most states have dropped Article 6 of the UCC, but— even if they have—these states have other laws dealing with bulk transfers)
Article 7 Documents of Title	Rights and duties of parties to documents of title issued in exchange for the carriage or storage of goods
Article 8 Investment Securities	Rules for transfer of stocks, bonds, and other securities traded on exchanges or in other organized markets
Article 9 Secured Transactions	Security interests in personal property created by agreement of the parties and all sales of accounts, chattel paper, payment intangibles, and promissory notes

The UCC has not achieved complete uniformity, however. As with any such enactment, the various state legislatures can make changes, and courts are free to give varying interpretations to the same words and phraseology. Nevertheless, there is a general consistency (if not uniformity) of subject matter, sufficiently definite and ascertainable for the businessperson operating within several states.

The **National Conference of Commissioners on Uniform State Laws** (NCCUSL) proposes new uniform laws, and changes to existing laws, for states to adopt. The NCCUSL spends years drafting and reaching consensus on uniform proposals that can then be submitted to state legislatures. The NCCUSL commissioners tend to be judges, professors, legislators, and practicing lawyers appointed by each state. The commission holds open drafting meetings so the public can comment on proposals.

Another enormously influential organization is the American Law Institute (ALI), a group of prominent lawyers, judges, and academics that studies laws, issues reports, and sometimes recommends legal reforms. The ALI is responsible for, among other things, the Restatements of Law, described on page 20.

RESEARCHING THE LAW

Modern attorneys operate in two main areas: the law office and the courtroom. All practicing attorneys bring to their profession a general working knowledge of legal principles. In addition, both sound office advice and courtroom skill require the *ability to find specific and detailed application of legal principles* within the large body of case law and statute law. Therefore a student of business law should have a general understanding of the kinds of legal materials needed to research the law.

Statutory law is found in a state code or in the federal code. These codes are published with annotations, footnotes, and cross references to other statutes and to key cases interpreting and applying the statute in question. A lawyer will instinctively turn to the statutes, whether online or in books, for information about criminal law, taxation, and governmental regulation of all kinds. Moreover, familiarity with the Uniform Commercial Code is essential for the student of commercial law.

Case law is collected in the opinions of the appellate courts of the states and of the United States. Opinions of trial courts are usually not published, except for federal trial courts. (Even those courts that do publish opinions, such as federal appeals and trial courts, often issue unpublished decisions.)

Besides the statutory annotations, case law may be found in legal encyclopedias, textbooks, treatises, case digests, Internet sites, and computer data banks. All law books are based on principles developed and enunciated in the cases. Indeed, the cases themselves follow, distinguish, and discuss other cases, all of which are meticulously referenced and cited. Finally, most law books include comprehensive tables of contents and indices.

Restatements of Law do not bind the courts, but serve as guidance to which the courts often give great weight. Restatements contain general points of law, accumulated by legal scholars; these points "restate" the case law generally found in the United States. The Restatements typically delineate trends in the common law, and they also occasionally put forth what scholars and practitioners believe is the "best" law (the optimal approach to an area where the law is unclear or the courts disagree). Although courts do not have to follow an approach adopted in a Restatement, many often do.

A REVIEW OF CATEGORIES OF LAW, VIA SIX EXAMPLES

Which category of law applies to the following six examples?

- A prominent athlete is accused of rape. The accuser goes to the local prosecutor, who begins formal proceedings against the athlete. CRIMINAL (not civil).

- Ultimately, charges against the athlete are dismissed. However, his accuser wants to sue him for battery. CIVIL (not criminal).

- Esmeralda enters into a contract with her neighbor, Neddie, to clean Neddie's garage for $50. Esmeralda cleans the garage, but Neddie refuses to pay. Esmeralda sues Neddie for breach of contract. PRIVATE (not public).

- A defendant's attorney files a pleading asking the court to dismiss the complaint against her client because the client was not served with process (given the proper notice). PROCEDURAL LAW (not substantive).

- The Uniform Commercial Code §2-201 details, for the sale of goods, a statute of frauds provision (requiring a writing for the sale of goods costing more than $500). STATUTORY LAW (not case law).

- A lawyer cites *MGM Studios, Inc. v. Grokster, Ltd.*, 545 U.S. 913 (2005), a U.S. Supreme Court decision concerning online file sharing, as a controlling precedent showing how strong copyright is to be protected, even on the Internet. CASE LAW (not statutory law).

Note: One category may not exclude another category. For example, most lawsuits, such as that brought by Esmerelda, above, involve not just civil law but also private law, moreover, the law a court applies for its decision will likely have both substantive and procedural aspects.

KNOW THE CONCEPTS
DO YOU KNOW THE BASICS?

1. In what major way does the common law differ from the Civil Law?

2. Why should a definition of law emphasize enforcement?

3. When we say that law "improved" or "progressed" from Hammurabi to Napoleon, what is meant by "improved" or "progressed"?

4. Are there any circumstances under which society could exist without law?

5. If the law requires that a person take some action (salute the flag, report or spy on an unpopular minority group or person) he/she considers immoral, should the person obey the law? Give other examples of such a conflict.

6. Why is it difficult to make law "uniform" by enacting uniform statutes?

7. Which is more important, procedural law or substantive law?

8. Why is it likely that the common law system will produce a greater number of lawyers than the Civil Law system?

9. Is it easier to know your "rights" in a Civil Law country or in a common law country?

10. Which of the following may waive the attorney/client privilege: (a) the attorney; (b) the client; (c) a third party; (d) a judge?

11. Name at least four general, ethical duties of an attorney.

TERMS FOR STUDY

attorney/client privilege
attorney's fees
case law
Civil Law
code
common law
equity
law
lex talionis

morality
procedural law
Restatements of Law
retainers
stare decisis
statute
substantive law
Uniform Commercial Code
Work-product doctrine

PRACTICAL APPLICATION

1. If you were a citizen in the following societies at the times indicated, how would you conduct yourself in regard to a conflict between personal morality and the law?
    (a) Nazi Germany in 1937.
    (b) Boston, Massachusetts, at the time of the Boston Tea Party (1773).
    (c) A slave owner in a Southern state in 1850.

2. The right of appeal to a higher court usually expires 30 days after a decision is rendered in a trial court. Suppose that your lawyer forgets to "note" your appeal within that period of time, although you have instructed her to do so. Under the law, you lose your right to appeal under these circumstances. Do you agree with the law?

3. Under what circumstances would an American court consider the Justinian code in deciding a case?

4. Bernhard Goetz shot and wounded four young men who apparently were attempting to rob him in a New York subway in 1984. He had been robbed before under similar circumstances. Discuss the morality and legality of Goetz's conduct.

5. In what sense is the "constitution" of England a "creature" of the common law?

ANSWERS
KNOW THE CONCEPTS

1. The common law emphasizes precedent; Civil Law emphasizes the wording of the applicable code. Common law codes are collections

of statutes and do not try to set out the entire law on a particular subject.

2. If law is not enforced, it has no effect on society—it is ignored, a "dead letter" without meaning. If government passes many laws but does not attempt to police them, the citizenry loses its respect for government and law, and society is greatly weakened.

3. "Improvement" and "progress" are relative terms and must be evaluated in accordance with principles or criteria. If our evaluations are based on democracy or self-determination, then clearly there has been "improvement" and "progress." If, however, the criterion is order or governmental control, Justinian's code may have been the best of the codes.

4. To the extent that society necessarily involves several persons or millions of persons, it is hard to imagine common existence without enforced rules. Insofar as individuals are "self-enlightened" or "self-controlled," friction may be minimized, but will not be eliminated.

5. When the law conflicts with personal morality, the individual has a hard choice. When a person has strong feelings about the moral principle involved and enforcement of the conflicting law is weak, the individual may (at his/her peril) choose to ignore the law. However, there are many variations in regard to these conflicting forces, and no simple rule can be stated. Be wary of unlawful conduct that implies a gain or profit from the act, even though disobedience to the law (draft evasion; nonpayment of unjust, oppressive taxes) may be stated in moral terms.

6. Each of the 50 states is a "sovereign" state with the right to judge its own citizens and to define and carry out its own laws, subject, of course, to constitutional limitations. Also, even when uniform laws are uniformly enacted, judges may interpret them differently.

7. Substance is probably more important, but incorrect or improper procedures can deprive the individual of his/her substantive rights and remedies. Procedural law is (or should be) more flexible, but this flexibility is not without limits.

8. The fact that there are many precedents in the common law system, and hence, much scope for argument and disagreement, encourages litigation, which produces a need for lawyers.

9. The Civil Law, written in more comprehensive detail, may seem more definitive as to "rights." However, a clear code may not lead to strong, understandable rights in actual practice. A society's willingness to sustain rights as well as the actual trial of cases involving rights both may be more uncertain in Civil Law countries.

10. (a) No; (b) Yes; (c) No—if a communication was made in the presence of a third party, then no confidentiality existed and no privilege ever arose in the first place; (d) No (a very rare exception might be an emergency in which a lawyer's client posed immediate danger of inflicting deadly force on others and the lawyer's revelation of confidential information could be narrowly tailored to the prevention of such harm, not building a case against the client).

11. An attorney should: handle cases competently, zealously advocate the client's cause, remain true to his/her duties as an officer of the court, keep the client reasonably informed, abide by the strictures of attorney/client privilege, and try to protect a client from problems caused by the attorney's withdrawal from a case.

PRACTICAL APPLICATION

1. For the individual, the three situations presented involve moral conflicts between society and law, and many answers are possible. In your answer, consider the morality of (a) acquiescence, (b) feigned or actual ignorance of the law, (c) patriotic activity that is unlawful, (d) the "right" to rebel against unjust government (note the Declaration of Independence), and (e) profit making in an immoral but "legal" situation.

2. The loss of the right to appeal after passage of a specified time is fairly rigid. The reason is that cases must end; it is unfair to the winning side to leave appeals open and unresolved. This is one of many examples of procedure superseding substance.

3. If there are no modern American or English precedents for a specific case, our courts can, and sometimes do, consider Justinian's code. Some areas of the common law, such as the law of negotiable instruments, are derived from Roman law.

4. This classic case of "taking the law into one's own hands" was the subject of much discussion. As noted in this chapter, if Goetz acted in a way that seemed to him "moral" or "right," this may be considered in assessing his punishment, but guilt of the crime is still a fact. Even if society is failing in its duty to protect its citizens, a return to the *lex talionis* does not seem to be a workable solution.

5. The "constitution" of England is unwritten and is largely based on precedent; hence it is a true creation of the common law. Several documents, such as the Magna Carta and the English Bill of Rights, are incorporated into the precedent.

2 GOVERNMENT UNDER LAW

KEY TERMS

constitution a nation's or state's supreme set of laws, outlining the basic organization, powers, and responsibilities of the government and guaranteeing certain specified rights to the people

statute a law passed by the U.S. Congress or a state legislature

ordinance a law passed by a governmental body below the state level and dealing with a local concern

rule a regulation issued by a federal state, or local administrative agency (or court) and governing procedure or conduct in a specific field

---

SOURCES OF U.S. LAW

There are eight important sources of law in the United States:

1. The U.S. Constitution.

2. Federal statutes, executive orders, and treaties (including customs, conventions, and international law).

3. The 50 state constitutions.

4. State statutes and executive orders.

5. Local ordinances.

6. The rules and rulings of federal, state, and local agencies.

7. Decisions by federal and state courts.

8. Private laws and custom (e.g., contracts, leases, internal company "rules," and business traditions as practiced in an industry).

> The first six sources are roughly in the order of importance. Agency and court actions, however, are found throughout the hierarchy, from interpretations of constitutions to statutes to rules and regulations, and from federal to state to local laws.

THE U.S. CONSTITUTION

The U.S. Constitution (also known as "the federal constitution") outlines the organization, powers, responsibilities, and limits of the federal government. Federal and state judges are bound by the U.S. Constitution; any law that violates the Constitution is null and void.

> The **supremacy clause**—in the second sentence of Article VI of the U.S. Constitution—states that the federal constitution, laws made in pursuit of the Constitution, and treaties are "the supreme law of the land." If the federal government has the right to regulate in a particular subject area (e.g., interstate commerce), then its laws in that area may expressly or implicitly cover the subject so completely that the states are barred from making their own laws on the subject. That effect is termed *preemption*.

DIVISION OF POWERS AMONG THE FEDERAL BRANCHES OF GOVERNMENT

The U.S. Constitution sets forth a division of powers among the three major branches of government: legislative, executive, and judicial. Each branch of government has a *major area of responsibility:*

- Congress (the federal legislature) makes the laws. A bill may be introduced in either the Senate or the House of Representatives, where it is referred to the appropriate committee. After consideration and sometimes public hearings, the committee returns the bill with pro and con recommendations. The bill is then debated on the floor, often amended, and brought to a vote. A bill passed by both houses goes to a conference committee of the Senate and the House of Representatives to resolve any differences. If both houses approve the compromise bill, it is then sent to the President. If he signs it, the bill becomes a law. A bill vetoed by the President may become a law if repassed by a two-thirds vote of both houses.

- The President (the chief executive) enforces the laws. The modern President has broad powers in both domestic and foreign affairs. Domestically, he may sign or veto bills, issue pardons for federal crimes, and remove executive officials (e.g., cabinet officers) without legislative or judicial approval. Subject to the majority consent of the Senate, he makes appointments to the executive branch, to ambassadorships, to federal regulatory commissions, and to federal judgeships.

  In foreign relations, the President may recognize or withdraw recognition of foreign governments, enter into executive agreements with other nations without obtaining congressional approval, make treaties with the approval of two thirds of the Senators voting, and—as commander-in-chief—oversee military affairs.

- The courts (judiciary) pass on the constitutionality of laws enacted by Congress or a state legislature. They also interpret the law, using as guidelines:

  (a) the "plain meaning rule," that is, the obvious or customary meaning of the words in a law;

  (b) the legislative history of the bill, that is, the purpose for which it was enacted.

  Finally, the courts make law in the sense that, under the principle of *stare decisis,* judicial decisions in cases for which no legal precedent exists become binding, or at least serve as precedent, when similar cases arise.

In a very important U.S. Supreme Court case, *Marbury v. Madison,* 5 U.S. 137 (1803), Chief Justice John Marshall announced the doctrine of *judicial review: the courts can declare federal or state actions to be in violation of the Constitution (unconstitutional).* Although state courts may base decisions upon the U.S. Constitution, when opinions conflict, it is the federal judiciary, led by the Supreme Court, whose interpretations control.

Of course, there are many more limits and areas of overlapping powers. Some are not part of the constitutional, statutory, or common law framework, but are nevertheless universally recognized. For example, Senators from the President's party have long held a *de facto* power to veto the confirmation of executive appointments to federal positions within their home states. As another example, courts traditionally refuse to decide cases that they believe present predominantly political questions (such as foreign policy). This is a form of self-limitation.

Rather than simply declaring a statute unconstitutional, the judiciary is to construe a statute narrowly enough so as to render it constitutional, if that is possible. In fact, if there is an adequate and independent basis in state law for a decision, the federal courts are not to reverse the state court holding even if the constitutional issues were decided erroneously.

In conclusion, courts are to presume that governmental action is constitutional. Courts are not even supposed to consider constitutional issues if the facts of the case can support alternative grounds for disposition.

U.S. constitutional rights do not protect American citizens if they are subject to legal action in another nation. Similarly, U.S. constitutional rights generally do *not* cover noncitizens who are outside the United States. For example, in *United States v. Verdugo-Urquidez*, 495 U.S. 259 (1990), the Supreme Court held that the Constitution's Fourth Amendment does not apply to American agents' search and seizure of property owned by a non-U.S. citizen and located outside the United States. The Constitution should protect people in the United States against arbitrary governmental action; it typically does not restrain the federal government's actions against aliens outside U.S. territory.

THE SYSTEM OF CHECKS AND BALANCES

Fearing the accumulation of excessive power in any one person or group, the Founding Fathers established a system of **checks and balances**. Overlapping powers impinge upon each area. The President can veto bills passed by Congress and is responsible for selecting federal judges. Congress may override the President's veto, it may conduct hearings and compel the attendance of witnesses from the executive branch, and the Senate may refuse to confirm the President's nominees for federal judgeships or for certain high-level positions in the executive branch. The judiciary may limit or invalidate laws or other actions by Congress or the President. In turn, Congress may limit the scope of judicial review or increase the number of federal judges, including the number on the U.S. Supreme Court.

As with all other civil officers of the United States (including federal judges), the President may be impeached by a majority vote of the House of Representatives and removed from office via conviction by a two-thirds vote of the Senate. Grounds for such impeachment are "Treason, Bribery, or other high Crimes and Misdemeanors."

Each state government also has three branches, with powers and checks and balances similar to those found at the federal level.

International Comparison: In parliamentary forms of government, the legislature tends to predominate. The executive and his cabinet are usually members of the legislature, and the courts' power to strike down parliamentary actions (exercise *judicial review*) is generally nonexistent or highly limited. In short, there are fewer checks and balances (hence, more concentrations of power) in the Parliament itself. (Among the relatively few countries with strong courts exercising judicial review are Australia, Canada, Germany, India, Israel, the Philippines, South Africa, and the United States.)

YOU SHOULD REMEMBER

The U.S. Constitution is the supreme law of the land. There are three branches of government: the legislative, executive, and judiciary. Each has certain powers, and there is a system of checks and balances among the three branches.

Judicial review permits courts to declare governmental actions unconstitutional. Courts may avoid deciding issues in a case (particularly constitutional issues) because of a policy of judicial self-restraint.

FEDERAL STATUTES

Congress has only such legislative powers as are granted to it by the U.S. Constitution, either expressly (enumerated powers) or implicitly; other powers (reserved powers) are granted to the states.

ENUMERATED AND IMPLIED POWERS

Article I, Section 8, of the U.S. Constitution expressly authorizes a number of Congressional legislative powers, including to tax, to coin money, to establish roads and post offices, to control immigration and naturalization, to regulate foreign and interstate commerce, to govern bankruptcy proceedings, and to provide for the nation's defense and general welfare. Section 8 also states that Congress may make laws "necessary and proper" for carrying out any of the government's enumerated powers under the Constitution. The implied powers under this **necessary and proper clause** have been interpreted to include any law not prohibited by or violative of the letter and spirit of the Constitution, so long as the law advances a legislative goal within the scope of the Constitution.

Such a broad reading of the "necessary and proper" clause first occurred in *McCulloch v. Maryland*, 17 U.S. 316 (1819), a key decision written by the great Chief Justice John Marshall. In *McCulloch,* the U.S. Supreme Court held that Congress had the power to incorporate the

Bank of the United States; although such an incorporation is not an enumerated power under the Constitution, it is, the Court found, appropriate to Congressional exercise of its enumerated fiscal powers.

Since the 1930s, the implied powers have been interpreted as permitting all kinds of federal powers.

• *POWER TO REGULATE INTERSTATE COMMERCE*

Congress has passed **statutes** that bar discrimination, regulate even small businesses, or are otherwise directed toward local commercial activities. In almost all cases, courts have refused to probe Congressional motives and have upheld the legislation under the **affectation doctrine**: as long as the activity sought to be regulated affects interstate commerce, it is within Congressional regulatory authority.

The term "affects" has been quite broadly interpreted. For example, the Supreme Court has upheld (1) a federal ban on racial discrimination even in a small restaurant whose out-of-state purchases and customers were minimal (*Katzenbach v. McClung,* 379 U.S. 294 (1964)); and (2) federal regulation of wheat production even when a particular crop was not placed in interstate commerce. (In the latter case, *Wickard v. Filburn,* 317 U.S. 111 (1942), the Court found that, in effect, this crop freed another crop to be used in interstate commerce.)

STATES' RIGHTS

However, for the first time in 60 years, the U.S. Supreme Court in *U.S. v. Lopez,* 514 U.S. 549 (1995), declared a federal law unconstitutional on the grounds that the law exceeded Congressional powers over commerce. The decision voided the 1990 Gun-Free School Zones Act, a statute prohibiting the possession of a gun within 1,000 feet of a school. The legislation failed to include findings showing a link between education, safety, and the economy. *Lopez* signals that, at the very least, Congress needs to articulate clearly how a bill touches upon matters of interstate commerce. Even then, its regulation may fail, as the high court has since ruled several times. In *U.S. v. Morrison,* 529 U.S. 598 (2000), for example, the Supreme Court ruled 5-4 that Congress lacked authority under the Constitution's Commerce Clause to enact civil remedies in the 1994 Violence Against Women Act because "gender-motivated crimes of violence are not, in any sense of the phrase, economic activity." Rejecting the notion that Congress can regulate any crime as long as it has substantial effects on employment, production, transit, or consumption, the Court spoke of the need to maintain the Constitution's "carefully crafted balance of power between states and the national government." (Along these lines, the Constitution's 11th Amendment bars citizens of one state from suing another state in federal court. Moreover, in a series of rulings since 1999 upholding states' rights, the Supreme Court has also held that Congress cannot give state workers the power to sue their state employer for some types of employment discrimination (e.g., based on age or disability), nor can Congress extend to citizens the power to sue states for alleged fraud, patent infringement, or overtime violations.)

• *POWER TO TAX*

Courts generally uphold any taxing measure, even one that serves to regulate an activity, so long as the measure purports to be and is, in fact, revenue-producing. For example, the Supreme Court, in *National Federation of Independent Business* v. *Sebelius* (2012), rejected a constitutional challenge to the 2010 Patient Protection and Affordable Care Act (ACA, often called Obamacare). The 5–4 decision to uphold the ACA was not made on the grounds of Congress' power to regulate interstate commerce, but rather on the grounds that the ACA's individual penalties could be deemed a tax (thus, within Congressional authority). If, however, the measure is intended to punish rather than to raise money, it is likely to be judged an invalid penalty rather than a valid tax.

Example: Invalidating a Tax Law Passed for the Wrong Purpose

A statute placing a substantial tax on employers using child labor was found to be an invalid penalty because it applied only to employers who *knowingly* hired under-age children. (A valid tax would have applied to all employers of children rather than just the intentional wrongdoers whom Congress wished to punish.)

• *POWER TO SPEND FOR THE GENERAL WELFARE*

With its power to levy taxes for the general welfare, Congress has the implicit right to spend money for any general welfare purpose. In implementing this spending power, Congress may impose reasonable conditions on state and local governments, corporations, and individuals; failure to meet such conditions precludes participation in that spending program. Hence Congress can often induce compliance with a regulatory scheme by using a "carrot and stick" tandem: revenue-sharing and eligibility requirements.

While the U.S. Constitution's Tenth Amendment reserves to the states or the people all powers not delegated to the federal government, this amendment has not barred the use of national regulation ancillary to (meaning, "that comes along with") valid spending or taxing measures.

LEGISLATION TO PROTECT CIVIL LIBERTIES

Two fundamental rights in the U.S. Constitution are found in the Fourteenth Amendment: due process and equal protection. The amendment not only restricts governmental acts ("state action") infringing these rights, but also expressly authorizes Congressional legislation to enforce its provisions. Such authorization has been broadly interpreted to permit any legislation Congress rationally concludes is appropriate for enforcing the amendment. Probably the most important "enforcement" role, though, has been played by the courts. U.S. Supreme Court decisions have served to "incorporate" almost all of the fundamental rights in the Bill of Rights (U.S. Constitution, First through Tenth Amendments) into the due process clause of the Fourteenth Amendment, thus making these rights applicable to the states as well as the federal government.

Bill of Rights Provisions
Amendment 1
   Establishment Clause—freedom from governmental establishment of
      religion
   Free Exercise Clause—freedom to exercise one's religious beliefs
   Freedom of Speech and
   Freedom of the Press
   Right to Assemble and Petition the government
Amendment 2
   Well-regulated militia and right to bear arms
Amendment 3
   Restrictions on quartering soldiers
Amendment 4
   Warrants requirements
   No unreasonable searches and seizures
Amendment 5
   Grand jury indictment or presentment needed for a federal capital or
      infamous crime
   No compulsory self-incrimination
   No double jeopardy
   Due process must be provided before taking life, liberty, or property
   Eminent domain—compensation for taking private property
Amendment 6
   For criminal cases, the right to counsel, to a speedy and public trial, to
      confront witnesses, and to a jury trial
Amendment 7
   Right to a jury trial in civil, common law cases
Amendment 8
   No excessive bail or fines
   No cruel and unusual punishment
Amendment 9
   Rights of the people not limited to those stated in the Constitution
Amendment 10
   Powers the Constitution does not delegate to the national government
      are reserved to the people and the states

The **due process** provision, and its case-law progeny, protect persons from being "deprived of life, liberty, or property, without due process of law" and outline the steps that must be followed to ensure a "fundamentally fair" process. Under the **equal protection** provision no person may be denied "the equal protection of the laws"; "equal protection" does not prohibit all differences in the treatment of persons but rather requires that, at the very least, any distinctions be *reasonable,* not arbitrary or invidious. Corporations, as well as individuals, are covered under the due process and equal protection provisions. Moreover, via the Fifth Amendment's "due process" provision, the federal government also must not violate due process or equal protection.

Due Process and Equal Protection

Due process requires *procedural* protections: a fundamentally fair process including notice, a hearing, an unbiased factfinder, presentation of evidence and cross-examination, and appeals. Due process also encompasses fundamental *substantive* rights, including, but certainly not limited to, some of the "incorporated" Bill of Rights provisions. From roughly the 1880s to the 1930s, courts used "substantive due process" to invalidate numerous state and federal laws regulating commercial, industrial, and labor conditions. This approach, in business or economic areas, has been replaced by a much more relaxed standard: As long as the government (state or federal) does not violate some other provision of the Constitution, it is free to regulate economic activity in any manner it so chooses.

For most cases involving regulation of business and for other "ordinary" cases, *equal protection* simply requires that differential treatment be reasonable and related to a legitimate, governmental purpose (the "rational basis" test). For cases involving "suspect" classes (particularly racial, religious, or nationality minorities) or fundamental rights (voting, marriage, privacy, interstate movement, access to the courts), equal protection is violated unless the differential treatment is as narrow as possible and is necessary to achieve a compelling governmental interest (the "strict scrutiny" test).

In cases involving sex, geography, age, or illegitimacy classifications, the class is not "suspect," but courts often require more than a mere rational basis for differential treatment. Although a "compelling" governmental interest (the "strict scrutiny" test) is unnecessary, the differential treatment must be substantially related to achieving an important governmental goal. This "intermediate scrutiny" test is perhaps most difficult for predicting court outcomes, whereas the other two tests lean heavily toward one party or the other: (1) strict scrutiny leaves governmental action highly vulnerable to a finding of unconstitutionality; and (2) rational basis is highly deferential to (prone to support the constitutionality of) governmental action.

Some important U.S. Constitutional rights for businesses, as well as individuals, are these:

1. Due process. For example, in *State Farm Mutual Automobile Insurance Co. v. Campbell*, 538 U.S. 408 (2003), plaintiffs had won a case against their auto liability insurer for bad-faith failure to settle a claim. The Supreme Court ruled that, inasmuch as due process prohibits grossly excessive or arbitrary punishment on a tortfeasor (someone who commits a tort) and that it is rarely constitutional for a punitive damages award to be ten times or more higher than the compensatory damages award, a punitive damages award of $145 million on a $1 million compensatory judgment violated due process, as it was neither reasonable nor proportionate. However, the law remains murky. More recent court decisions, including those of the Supreme Court, indicate that the *State Farm* standard is hard to apply and that, in practice, judgments far above the ten-to-one, punitive damages to compensatory damages ratio may often be upheld on appeal.

2. Equal protection. Three famous equal protection cases are *Brown v. Board of Education*, 347 U.S. 483 (1954) (outlawing state-mandated racially segregated public schools); *Baker v. Carr*, 369 U.S. 186 (1962) (holding that legislative districts should be of equal size so that each person's vote is of equal value); and *Bush v. Gore*, 531 U.S. 98 (2000) (in the disputed 2000 presidential election, ruling that the Florida Supreme Court's order favoring manual vote recounts, without specific standards to discern a voter's intent, failed to satisfy the Equal Protection Clause's requirement of nonarbitrary treatment of voters.)

3. Freedom of expression (First Amendment). Commercial speech (e.g., advertising) is not as well protected as political speech. However, governments may not prohibit commercial speech that accurately presents information unless there is a substantial state interest in doing so **and** the governmental prohibition is as narrowly drawn as possible, i.e., the least burdensome method of accomplishing the state's interest. (Also, courts have upheld restrictions on speech deemed obscene, defamatory, posing a "clear and present danger" to public safety, or going beyond speech into unprotected conduct.)

   There are four key factors that courts consider when assessing the harm that the government seeks to prevent when it suppresses expression: (1) the speaker's state of mind, (2) the likelihood that harm will result, (3) the nature of the harm, and (4) the gravity of the harm. The Supreme Court increasingly has turned to an empirical, fact-based assessment of these four factors.

   For speech as expressed through political campaign expenditures independent of the candidates themselves, the Supreme Court held, 5–4, in *Citizens United v. Federal Election Commission*, 558 U.S. ___ (2010), for federal laws and 5–4 in *American Tradition Partnership,*

Inc. v. Bullock, 567 U.S. ___ (2012), for state and local laws. The Court wrote that "independent expenditures, including those made by corporations, do not give rise to corruption or the appearance of corruption"; therefore, "[n]o sufficient governmental interest justifies limits on the political speech of non-political or for-profit corporations."

Employees who set up blogs or otherwise communicate via Internet websites have a direct method of communicating with the public about their employer; customers, competitors, and others can easily find these communications. The employees may wrongly use trademarked or copyrighted materials, post information about yet-to-be-released products, or defame someone (e.g., a coworker). Many companies have instituted policies to protect the business, such as requiring these employees to disclaim any company involvement, to not engage in harassing, libelous, or otherwise tortious posts, and to not disclose any proprietary information or violate anyone's privacy. That employers can require the employees to agree to these and other policies, can use the violation of these policies as grounds for an employee's dismissal, and can monitor the employee's Internet activities is not a free speech issue, ordinarily, in that the First Amendment protections are from governmental restrictions, not those by private organizations.

4. Protection from laws impairing contractual obligations (Article I, Section 10).

5. Compensation for the public taking of private property—eminent domain (Fifth Amendment). The Supreme Court has held that when a regulation (a) denies the property owner of all "economically viable use of his land" (*Lucas v. South Carolina Coastal Council*, 505 U.S. 1003 (1992)), or (b) requires a property owner to dedicate for public use a disproportionate share of his land considering the probable impact of land developments the owner is permitted to make (*Dolan v. City of Tigard*, 512 U.S. 374 (1994)), fair compensation must be paid. However, in *Tahoe-Sierra Preservation Council v. Tahoe Regional Planning Agency*, 535 U.S. 302 (2002), the Supreme Court ruled that a government-imposed moratorium on property development, even one that lasts for years, does not automatically amount to a taking of private property for which taxpayers must compensate the landowners.

As for a governmental purpose permitting eminent domain, the Supreme Court in *Kelo v. City of New London,* 545 U.S. 469 (2005), held that the U.S. Constitution lets local governments seize (and, of course, pay for) people's homes or businesses to use that seized property for tax-producing projects such as shopping malls. In response, though, almost all states enacted laws denying themselves, or their local governments, the right to follow the broad *Kelo* interpretation: These states forbid the use of eminent domain to transfer land from one private party to another private party for economic development purposes.

6. Protection against some state regulations, including taxes, that discriminate against interstate commerce in favor of local businesses.

A few constitutional provisions that apply to individuals, such as the Fourteenth Amendment's privileges and immunities clause and the Fifth Amendment's protection against self-incrimination, do not extend to business entities.

YOU SHOULD REMEMBER

Legislative power must be expressly or implicitly delegated to Congress by the U.S. Constitution, or else it belongs solely to the states.

Many such Congressional powers are stated in Article I, Section 8, of the Constitution, including three whose expansive interpretation has permitted national regulation of numerous activities. These three powers are (1) to regulate interstate commerce, (2) to tax, and (3) to provide (spend) for the general welfare.

The Fourteenth Amendment authorizes Congress to pass any legislation necessary to enforce the due process and equal protection provisions of the amendment.

THE STATE CONSTITUTIONS

Each of the 50 states has a constitution that establishes the general organization, powers, responsibilities, and limits of the state's government. The state constitution is the supreme law of the state, but it cannot contain any provision that violates a provision of the U.S. Constitution. Under this system of governance, *federalism*, the state governments have their own spheres of power and do not look to the federal government as the source of their authority.

INTERNATIONAL COMPARISON OF FEDERALISM, UNITARY SYSTEMS, AND CONFEDERACIES

1. Argentina, Australia, Austria, Belgium, Bosnia, Brazil, Canada, Ethiopia, Germany, India, Iraq, Malaysia, Mexico, Nepal, Nigeria, Pakistan, Russia, South Africa, Spain, Switzerland, Tanzania, the

United Arab Emirates, and Venezuela each have—at least to a certain extent—a **federal** system like that of the United States (spheres of power for both the national government and the states/provinces). These and a few other federal nations, although still a minority of the world's total, are growing in number and represent about 40% of the world's population. The powers of the states or provinces vary from one federal system to another, but in all such systems, the national government—while typically superior to the states in core areas such as foreign relations and territorial integrity (e.g., no secession)—is not absolute, and power must be shared with the state/provincial sovereigns. Because the division of powers between the two levels of government is embodied within the national constitution and is formally guaranteed, any significant change must be mutually agreed upon (as constitutional amendments require the consent of both levels).

2. Bangladesh, Bulgaria, Colombia, Chile, China, Egypt, France, Indonesia, Iran, Japan, the Netherlands, Norway, the Philippines, Poland, Romania, Sweden, Thailand, Turkey, Vietnam, and a very large majority of countries have a **unitary** form of government. Unlike a federal system, the unitary system is centralized, with only one true zone of power—the national government. There may be some powers granted to local authorities, but these regional officials serve in that role only because the national, unitary government permits them to do so; whenever it wants, the national government may eliminate or reconfigure regional governments in any way it desires because governments below the national level exist only as a matter of administrative efficiency or convenience in implementing national programs.

3. In a **confederacy**, the member-states are, ultimately, supreme. A province within a nation—or, in a multinational arrangement such as the European Union, the national membership—has the greater powers, whether directly stated or not, such as to secede from (leave) the larger governing structure. Some prominent past confederacies have included the early United States under the Articles of Confederation (1781–89) and the Confederate States of America (1861–65), or, more recently, Senegambia (1982–89) and Serbia-Montenegro (2003–06). Also, there are current supranational organizations, such as the European Union (EU), with confederacy characteristics. In the EU, for example, the national members have ceded to it some powers, but these members retain so much control over foreign policy, national defense, and other aspects of sovereignty that the entity is not a federal system. Confederation thus may be a step between federalism and independent statehood as a federal system disintegrates (e.g., the former Soviet

Union, Czechoslovakia, and Yugoslavia); or confederation can be a step in the opposite direction, as independent nations move toward federalism.

STATE STATUTES

State statutes constitute another important source of U.S. law. Just as some legislative powers are exclusively federal, others (reserved powers) remain exclusively or primarily within the domain of the states—for instance, divorce law and the common law of torts and contracts.

Examples of Regulatory Responsibilities

Federal Regulatory Power:	Overlapping Power:	State Regulatory Power:
Aviation	Securities	Agency
Foreign trade	Environmental law	Contracts
Patents	Taxation	Insurance
Copyrights	Consumer protection	Corporations
		Property

A third class of powers is shared by the state and federal governments. Sometimes the absence of Congressional action in regard to a shared power permits the states to act, even though Congress could preempt (bar) state action. (Preemption can be express, or it can arise implicitly from a Congressional legislative scheme intended to have uniform, national application.) *Regulation of commerce* tends to be such a shared power.

So long as a nonpreempted state regulation: (a) does not directly regulate interstate commerce, (b) concerns essentially local matters, (c) does not discriminate against out-of-state commerce, and (d) is the least burdensome method for achieving legitimate state objectives, it will usually be permitted *if* the state interest in maintaining the regulation outweighs any burdens imposed on interstate commerce. The courts ultimately make this determination.

Exception: Courts sometimes hold that even without federal regulations, the commerce clause bars certain state legislation because an area requires national uniformity or is otherwise unsuited to state action. However, just as Congress may preempt state actions, so it may overturn these "negative implications" of the commerce clause and allow state regulation.

DETERMINING THE VALIDITY OF STATE STATUTES

In determining the validity of a state law involving a shared power, the court must first determine (1) whether the state law conflicts with a federal law, that is, whether a person obeying the state law would violate a federal law, and (2) whether Congress intended to preempt state legislation in that area. If the answer to either question is "yes," the state law is void.

TWO TYPES OF LAWS THAT CANNOT BE PASSED BY CONGRESS OR THE STATES

In addition to rights discussed previously, two other fundamental rights stated in the U.S. Constitution apply to the states as well as the national government. These rights, specifically set forth in Article I, Sections 9 and 10, are individual freedom from (1) ***ex post facto*** laws (laws making criminal past actions that were not defined as criminal when they occurred), and (2) **bills of attainder** (laws intended to single out an individual and/or punish him/her without benefit of a trial).

YOU SHOULD REMEMBER

Major legislative powers are divided between the state and federal governments. They are exclusively federal, exclusively or primarily state, or shared. Congress may preempt some areas that would otherwise be shared with the states.

The power to regulate commerce is an important example of a shared power, although certain areas are barred from state regulation.

Neither Congress nor the state legislatures may pass an *ex post facto* law or a bill of attainder.

LOCAL ORDINANCES

An ordinance is an enactment by a legislative body below the state level (a city council, a county legislature, a town board, etc.). Ordinances deal with local concerns such as zoning, on-street parking, area speed zones, and littering, and are designed to promote the safety and general welfare of the community to which they apply.

RULINGS OF FEDERAL, STATE, AND LOCAL AGENCIES (ADMINISTRATIVE LAW)

Legislation or case law cannot cover every actual or potential problem that arises in a dynamic, increasingly complex society facing numerous social, economic, and technological issues. Also, legislatures or courts cannot develop or retain the expertise to handle all specialties. Therefore administrative agencies have been created by legislative acts known as **enabling acts**, whereby the government—federal, state, or local—**delegates** some of its **authority** to the agency.

> A typical *enabling act* sets forth the objectives and standards by which an agency is to administer the law in a particular field. The agency then develops technical expertise in order to fill legislative gaps with detailed rules and to render sound decisions in individual cases.
>
> Agencies can monitor regulated industries continuously, whether or not there have been violations. While still bound by constitutional protections (e.g., due process), agencies can proceed more quickly and informally than ordinary judicial processes entail.

The courts have usually upheld even very broad delegations of authority. However, Congress may not completely abdicate its legislative responsibilities; before delegating authority to an agency, Congress must first determine the basic legislative policy and state some standards for the agency to follow. The standards may simply be to do what is just, reasonable, fair and/or equitable.

Most important federal agencies have a mixture of legislative, judicial, and executive powers. (Administrative agency judicial proceedings are discussed in Chapter 3, pages 82–83.) Agencies perform some or all of seven functions, with certain functions being more important in some agencies than in others: (1) advising, (2) reviewing, (3) supervising, (4) rule making, (5) investigating, (6) prosecuting, (7) adjudicating. Enforcement powers may include fines, prohibitions, restrictions on or revocation of licenses, and the threat of public exposure.

Some agencies are directly under the supervision of one of the three branches of government, usually the executive. However, a large number are *independent* agencies, and their legislative hearings and the rules they make are generally free from outside control. Examples of independent federal agencies include the Federal Communications Commission, Federal Reserve Board, Federal Trade Commission, International Trade Commission, National Labor Relations Board, and Securities and Exchange Commission.

The federal Government in the Sunshine Act (1976) requires that most agencies have open public meetings with agendas published in advance. Meetings concerning national defense, trade secrets, foreign policy, law enforcement, or personnel matters need not be public. All federal rules can be viewed in the U.S. Code of Federal Regulations (the CFR).

The **Freedom of Information Act (FOIA)** requires federal agencies to disclose information that the agencies have in their possession. A citizen's proper, narrowly worded request for information may not be refused. However, while Congress cannot be denied information, there are ten areas in which agencies are exempt from FOIA requirements (i.e., do not have to turn over information to private parties): (1) national defense, (2) foreign policy, (3) trade secrets or other commercial or financial information that was obtained from an outside source and should be deemed privileged or confidential, (4) bank examiners' reports and other material in the reports of agencies responsible for regulating financial institutions, (5) geological or geophysical data (including maps) concerning wells, (6) personnel, medical, and similar files whose disclosure would clearly be an unwarranted invasion of personal privacy, (7) investigatory records compiled for law enforcement purposes, (8) interagency or intra-agency memoranda or letters, (9) an agency's internal personnel rules and practices, (10) subjects on which another federal statute specifically allows the agency to keep information secret.

The actions of an administrative agency must conform with:
(a) constitutional law,
(b) relevant general acts governing administrative procedure (e.g., the federal Administrative Procedure Act),
(c) requirements in the agency's own enabling act, and
(d) rules of the agency itself.

When exercising its legislative (rule-making) powers, the typical agency does not need to hold a hearing. However, the *agency's own rules,* or *general statutes* such as the federal Administrative Procedure Act, *may require* that the agency give *notice of a proposed rule* (e.g., through publication of the proposed rule in the Federal Register) and afford interested parties the opportunity to submit written or oral comments. The federal Negotiated Rulemaking Act (1990) is intended to foster cooperative rulemaking—rules negotiated between agencies and affected parties. Also, the Regulatory Flexibility Act of 1980 (RFA), as strengthened via several amendments (e.g., the Small Business Regulatory Enforcement Fairness Act of 1996), requires agencies to consider their proposed regulations' impact on small entities, to analyze alternatives that minimize such impacts, and to make these analyses available and subject to public comment. The covered "small entities" are small businesses, nonprofit enterprises, and governments for municipalities or for school or other special districts for a population of under 50,000. Nearly every state has enacted a similar law meant to make regulations proportionate to the size of affected entities.

Courts have the power to review rules promulgated by regulatory agencies in much the same way as they are empowered to review legislative enactments. However, with respect to areas in which an agency presumably has expertise, its decisions (executive, legislative, or judicial) generally are overturned only if found to be clearly erroneous, arbitrary, based on bias, or exceeding the agency's authority.

YOU SHOULD REMEMBER

Certain legislative, judicial, and/or executive powers have been delegated to federal, state, and local administrative agencies. Many agencies are not directly supervised by the legislature or executive; they are independent agencies.

An administrative agency may have to give interested parties both notice and an opportunity to comment before making a rule or regulation.

DECISIONS BY FEDERAL AND STATE COURTS

In the United States, as in England, decisions handed down by federal and state courts, that is, case law, constitute a primary source of the common law. New cases requiring the interpretation of statutes arise continually. When no precedent can be found, the judge's decision will produce a new legal principle.

A case may originate in either a federal or a state court, depending on the nature of the suit.

Under Article III of the U.S. Constitution, the federal courts' power is limited to actual "cases or controversies." This provision has prevented federal courts from furnishing advisory opinions, even if requested by another branch of government. (Many state courts can and do issue advisory opinions.) The case must be a real dispute between opposing parties with actual interests in the case (standing to sue, because of direct and immediate injury from, or other such connection with, the matter at issue). The proceeding must be in an adversarial format. Federal district courts have **original jurisdiction** (meaning that proceedings commence there) over federal criminal cases and certain specified civil cases.

The U.S. Supreme Court has original jurisdiction when the parties include ambassadors or other foreign officials, or when two states are the opposing parties. However, almost all of the cases heard by the Supreme Court arise out of its **appellate jurisdiction**: the power to hear appeals from other courts' decisions. Appeals generally involve interpretation of constitutional law and/or federal statutes.

The various types of courts and the cases they handle are discussed more fully in Chapter 3.

YOU SHOULD REMEMBER

Decisions by state and federal courts are a primary source of U.S. common law.

To originate in a federal court, a case must involve a real dispute between opposing parties.

The U.S. Supreme Court has original jurisdiction over certain cases, but its main function is to review lower court decisions that have been appealed.

KNOW THE CONCEPTS

DO YOU KNOW THE BASICS?

1. For each of the three branches of the federal government, describe the system of checks and balances on the powers of the other branches.

2. Name three Congressional powers specifically enumerated in the U.S. Constitution.

3. By what constitutional provision does Congress have the implied powers to take legislative action not specifically mentioned in the U.S. Constitution?

4. State the general test for determining whether a tax is constitutional.

5. How does Congress use its power to spend as a method for national regulation?

6. What two types of bills may neither Congress nor a state legislature pass?

7. Name the seven general functions that may be performed by an administrative agency.

8. State the two major standards for review in equal protection cases, including the type of cases that fall under each standard.

9. Name three independent federal agencies.

10. Over what types of cases does the U.S. Supreme Court have original jurisdiction?

11. Name two fundamental rights set forth in the Fourteenth Amendment to the U.S. Constitution.

TERMS FOR STUDY

affectation doctrine
appellate jurisdiction
bill of attainder
Bill of Rights
checks and balances
commercial speech
confederacy
constitution
delegated authority
due process
eminent domain
enabling act
equal protection

ex post facto law
federalism
judicial review
"necessary and proper" clause
ordinance
original jurisdiction
preemption
rule
states' rights
statute
"supremacy" clause
unitary system

PRACTICAL APPLICATION

1. Commerce-in-Claus is an interstate shipper of Santa Claus outfits. A neighboring state has passed a law raising fees on its toll roads for all trucks with out-of-state registration, but no one else. Is this constitutional? Discuss. What bearing does Santa Claus have on your answer?

2. Suppose that a dissatisfied customer brings his complaint against XYZ, Inc., to the state legislature, which passes a law making illegal XYZ's sales arrangement with the customer. Effective 30 days after the law's enactment, XYZ's sales license is to be suspended for 3 months. What should XYZ do? What arguments should XYZ make?

3. Congress has enacted a broad statutory scheme covering most aspects of labor/management relations. Fearing that unionization would increase operational costs for the town's private employers, Poor Town's board of commissioners wants to keep a national union from organizing any of the workers. What legislation may the commissioners enact?

4. A state statute prohibits businesses from contributing to election campaigns. This statute is challenged in court by a group of law students. What will be the outcome?

5. In Problem 4, on what grounds should the law be challenged?

6. Scott Sneaky wants the state legislature to pass a law that would provide his business with a series of windfall profits. A friend has persuaded him to go to a state administrative agency to obtain a rule that would serve essentially the same purpose and, Scott hopes, would avoid the publicity that would probably kill the chance for a new law in his favor. Assuming that there are no constitutional problems with Scott's plan, will it succeed?

ANSWERS

KNOW THE CONCEPTS

1. *Executive:* veto legislation, appoint federal judges.
   Legislative: override veto, compel executive official's attendance at hearings, refuse to confirm appointments, limit scope of judicial review, increase the number of federal judges, impeach executive or judicial officials.
   Judiciary: limit or invalidate laws or executive actions.

2. To regulate foreign and interstate commerce, to tax, and to provide for the nation's defense and general welfare.

3. The "necessary and proper" clause of Article I, Section 8.

4. A tax may serve to regulate an activity. However, the more a tax acts as a punishment rather than as a source of revenue, the more likely it is to be judged an invalid penalty.

5. By placing conditions (compliance with a regulatory framework) upon participation in a federal program. Without compliance, the would-be participant—be it a state or local government, a corporation, or an individual—cannot receive the federal money.

6. An *ex post facto* law and a bill of attainder.

7. Advising, reviewing, supervising, rule making, investigating, prosecuting, and adjudicating.

8. "*Strict scrutiny*" (differential treatment constitutional only if (1) drawn as narrowly as possible, and (2) necessary to achieve a compelling governmental interest): cases involving adverse impact on racial, religious, and nationality minorities.

"*Rational basis*" (differential treatment constitutional when reasonable and related to a permissible governmental goal): cases involving business regulation or "nonsuspect" classes.

A third, intermediate standard for review is sometimes used for differential treatment based upon sex or illegitimacy. There, the differential treatment must be substantially related to achieving an important governmental goal.

9. Federal Communications Commission, Federal Trade Commission, National Labor Relations Board. For other agencies, see page 40.

10. Cases involving ambassadors or other foreign officials and cases in which two states are adversaries.

11. Due process and equal protection.

PRACTICAL APPLICATION

1. No. The state's action violates the commerce clause by purposely imposing a greater burden on interstate commerce than on local interests. Moreover, Congress may have preempted such state legislation.

   The state's action also appears to violate the Fourteenth Amendment's guarantee of equal protection. The court may not believe that the state had a reasonable justification (rational basis) for the law.

   Re: Santa Claus

   A claim based on religious freedom, or one asking for the equal protection clause's "strict scrutiny" test because there is a suspect class (religion), would probably fail. Regardless of whether the Santa Claus aspect of the company gives it a religious affiliation, the legislation does not discriminate based on religion; the basis of the discrimination is whether or not a vehicle is an out-of-state truck.

2. Challenge the law in the courts. It seems to be both an *ex post facto* law and a bill of attainder, which are prohibited by Article I, Sections 9 and 10, of the Constitution.

3. None. The commissioners must follow the federal law. Inasmuch as the subject of unionizing has been preempted, no state, let alone a local government, can pass laws in this area (e.g., an ordinance prohibiting or limiting union activities).

4. The law students will be dismissed as plaintiffs. They are not members of the class affected by the statute (businesses), and therefore do not have standing to sue. The businesses themselves should be able to have the same statute declared an unconstitutional infringement of *their* right to free speech.

5. Violation of equal protection: the law treats businesses, including individuals and corporations, differently from other persons, and

this differential treatment is neither reasonable nor related to a permissible, governmental purpose.

Violation of due process: The Fourteenth Amendment's due process clause incorporates the First Amendment of the Bill of Rights, and thus protects persons from a state's infringement of their right to free speech. In *First National Bank of Boston v. Bellotti*, 435 U.S. 765 (1978), the Supreme Court held unconstitutional a Massachusetts statute that prohibited most corporate spending on political referendum proposals.

6. It is difficult to say. The agency rule-making process may indeed be less publicized, and thus Scott may be able to get a new rule promulgated. However, either of two factors may keep Scott from succeeding: (1) since this is an area apparently still open to the state's customary legislative oversight, it may *not* have been delegated to the agency in the enabling act; (2) the rulemaking process usually requires notice to the public and an opportunity for comment. Thus publicity and/or opposition is, in fact, possible.

3
THE U.S. COURT SYSTEM AND THE LEGAL PROCESS

KEY TERMS

jurisdiction the power to hear and decide the issues in a case (subject-matter jurisdiction) and to bind the parties (personal jurisdiction)

pleadings the papers filed in court, with copies to other parties concerned, in preparation for bringing or defending a lawsuit before the court

discovery pretrial procedures by which the parties to a lawsuit obtain information from other parties and from potential witnesses

trial the proceedings before a competent tribunal in which a civil or criminal case is heard and adjudicated

Most of this book focuses on *substantive law*, such as contracts, business associations, and commercial paper. This chapter, though, concerns the places and methods for resolving disputes and applying the substantive law to individual cases.

THE TWO MAJOR U.S. JUDICIAL SYSTEMS

There are two main court systems in the United States, the federal and the various state systems.

STRUCTURES OF THE FEDERAL AND STATE COURT SYSTEMS

The hierarchical structure of federal courts is comparable to that of the various state court systems. Therefore, by way of example, we will look at the federal court system.

At the bottom rung are 94 U.S. *district courts*, with 677 judges altogether. These are trial courts. In each state there is at least one federal district court. Each district court may include any number of judges, one of whom will hear a particular case.

If a party wishes to appeal the district court's judgment, he/she brings the case before the *appeals court*, the circuit court, for that district. Besides the U.S. Court of Appeals for the Federal Circuit, a specialized court based in Washington, D.C. for specific subject matter such as patents, trade, and government contracts, there are 12 geographic circuits. Altogether, there are 179 circuit judges, 12 of whom serve on the federal circuit. These are the geographic circuits, their principal court locations, and the states or territories from which federal district court appeals are heard:

First Circuit—*Boston*; Maine, Massachusetts, New Hampshire, Rhode Island, and also Puerto Rico

Second Circuit—*New York City*; Connecticut, New York, and Vermont

Third Circuit—*Philadelphia*; Delaware, New Jersey, Pennsylvania, and also the Virgin Islands

Fourth Circuit—*Richmond*; Maryland, North Carolina, South Carolina, Virginia, and West Virginia

Fifth Circuit—*New Orleans*; Louisiana, Mississippi, and Texas

Sixth Circuit—*Cincinnati*; Kentucky, Michigan, Ohio, and Tennessee

Seventh Circuit—*Chicago*; Illinois, Indiana, and Wisconsin

Eighth Circuit—*St. Louis*; Arkansas, Iowa, Minnesota, Missouri, Nebraska, North Dakota, and South Dakota

Ninth Circuit—*San Francisco*; Alaska, Arizona, California, Hawaii, Idaho, Montana, Nevada, Oregon, Washington, and also Guam and Northern Mariana Islands

Tenth Circuit—*Denver*; Colorado, Kansas, New Mexico, Oklahoma, Utah, and Wyoming

Eleventh Circuit—*Atlanta*; Alabama, Florida, and Georgia.

D.C. Circuit—*Washington, D.C.* (Because of its heavy volume of work, for example, in administrative law, the District of Columbia—with just one district trial court [for Washington, D.C., of course]—has its own circuit.)

Lastly, appeals from circuit court decisions (or from holdings of the highest court of the state) *may* be heard by the *U.S. Supreme Court*. In a few cases, a party has an absolute right of appeal. *Supreme Court review by appeal* is a matter of right when:

(1) a state court declares a treaty or federal statute invalid or holds that a state law does not violate a treaty, the U.S. Constitution, or federal statutes; or

(2) a federal court
  (a) decides that a state law violates federal law; or
  (b) if the federal government or its employees are parties, rules that a Congressional statute is unconstitutional.

In most cases, however, it is within the sole discretion of the Supreme Court whether to hear an appeal. Usually the case must involve a federal question (e.g., about the U.S. Constitution and/or a federal statute). Only if four of the nine Justices agree to it is a *writ of certiorari* granted so that a discretionary appeal is heard by the U.S. Supreme Court. Instead, although the Supreme Court issues about 75 to 100 opinions annually, it refuses to hear an appeal (states "cert. denied") for some 7,000 to 8,000 petitions each year.

Federal judges—appointed for life (at age 70, a judge may go on "inactive status" at full pay).

State judges—usually for a set, renewable term and with a mandatory retirement age; sometimes appointed but usually elected; some elections are "contested" elections (between different candidates); some elections are "retention" elections (voters vote "yes" or "no" on whether to retain a judge); sometimes a mixed approach—first appointed, then subject to retention elections.

Of course, there are other types of courts. For instance, many federal and state administrative agencies have their own judicial systems. There are specialized courts (e.g., federal bankruptcy courts), and states generally have special courts (ones without juries) for cases involving small amounts or special litigants, such as orphans or landlords and tenants. However, the general trial courts, with juries available, remain the crucial arena for most important cases.

The following diagrams show the structures of the federal court system and a typical state system.

JURISDICTIONS OF THE FEDERAL AND STATE COURT SYSTEMS

As discussed in Chapter 2, the national and state governments have different, but sometimes overlapping, spheres of power. This holds true also for their court systems. The power of a court system to hear and decide a case is called its **jurisdiction**.

• *SUBJECT-MATTER JURISDICTION*

Subject-matter jurisdiction: judicial power to decide the issues in a case.

THE FEDERAL JUDICIAL SYSTEM

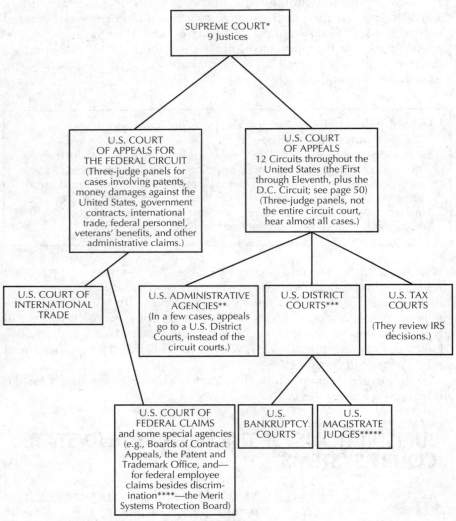

* Appeals from the highest state court also may be heard by the U.S. Supreme Court.
** Although federal administration agencies are not part of the federal judiciary, they are included here because appeals from their decisions go to the federal courts.
*** In rare cases, appeals from U.S. District Courts go to the U.S. Court of Appeals for the Federal Circuit.
**** Those cases are appealed to either the Equal Employment Opportunity Commission or the U.S. District Courts.
***** These officials—over 600 in all—are appointed to terms (usually 8 years) by votes of a particular District Court's judges. They generally oversee the processing of criminal cases and other administrative tasks.
Note: Although they are courts, often with long judicial terms of office (e.g., 15 years), these courts above—U.S. Tax Court; U.S. Courts of Federal Claims; U.S. District Courts in Guam, the Virgin Islands, and Northern Mariana Islands; and U.S. Bankruptcy Courts—are not courts under Article III of the Constitution. Article III courts have lifetime appointments for judges who are subject to removal only through impeachment. These courts are the U.S. Supreme Court; the Court of Appeals (12 Circuits and the Federal Circuit); U.S. District Courts in the 50 states, the District of Columbia, and Puerto Rico; and the U.S. Court of International Trade (which has 9 judges).

A TYPICAL STATE JUDICIAL SYSTEM

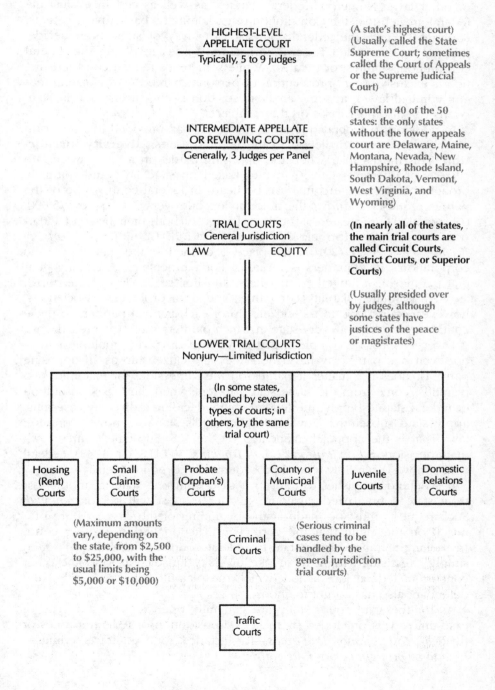

HIGHEST-LEVEL APPELLATE COURT
Typically, 5 to 9 judges

(A state's highest court)
(Usually called the State Supreme Court; sometimes called the Court of Appeals or the Supreme Judicial Court)

INTERMEDIATE APPELLATE OR REVIEWING COURTS
Generally, 3 Judges per Panel

(Found in 40 of the 50 states: the only states without the lower appeals court are Delaware, Maine, Montana, Nevada, New Hampshire, Rhode Island, South Dakota, Vermont, West Virginia, and Wyoming)

TRIAL COURTS
General Jurisdiction
LAW   EQUITY

(In nearly all of the states, the main trial courts are called Circuit Courts, District Courts, or Superior Courts)

(Usually presided over by judges, although some states have justices of the peace or magistrates)

LOWER TRIAL COURTS
Nonjury—Limited Jurisdiction

(In some states, handled by several types of courts; in others, by the same trial court)

| Housing (Rent) Courts | Small Claims Courts | Probate (Orphan's) Courts | County or Municipal Courts | Juvenile Courts | Domestic Relations Courts |

(Maximum amounts vary, depending on the state, from $2,500 to $25,000, with the usual limits being $5,000 or $10,000)

Criminal Courts

(Serious criminal cases tend to be handled by the general jurisdiction trial courts)

Traffic Courts

The federal courts are limited to hearing cases specifically placed within their power (subject-matter jurisdiction) by the U.S. Constitution or other laws. Numerous federal statutes, as well as certain exclusively federal areas under the Constitution (e.g., admiralty, bankruptcy, patents, copyrights), give the federal courts a vast array of subjects to decide: these areas are called **federal questions** (cases involving the federal constitution, statutes, or treaties). While sometimes federal court jurisdiction is exclusive (e.g., prosecution of persons charged with violating federal criminal laws), in some areas jurisdiction is concurrent, that is, state courts can also hear cases on these subjects.

In addition to federal questions, Congress has provided another form of subject-matter jurisdiction to the federal courts: **diversity jurisdiction**. This means that, when the opposing parties in a civil lawsuit are citizens of different states, a matter based on state law (and normally brought before a state court) can be heard in federal court *if* one of the parties requests it *and if* the amount in controversy is above $75,000. (Corporations are treated as being "citizens" of both their place of incorporation and their principal business location. Under *Hertz Corp. v. Friend*, 559 U.S. 77 (2010), that place is defined as the state where the corporation's headquarters is located.) For partnerships (including general partnerships, limited partnerships, and limited liability partnerships), as well as limited liability companies and unincorporated associations, however, courts look to the citizenship of each general partner; so those entities are citizens of every state in which partners/members are citizens.

Diversity must be complete; that is, in cases involving multiple parties not even one party may have the same state citizenship as an opposing party. (It does not matter if parties on the same side, for example, two plaintiffs, come from the same state.) Except when the U.S. Constitution or federal statutes apply, the federal courts deciding a diversity case must apply state substantive law—both the state's statutes and its common law. That is the approach mandated by the U.S. Supreme Court's landmark decision in *Erie Railroad Co. v. Tomkins*, 304 U.S. 64 (1938). Federal courts, however, follow federal procedural law, even in diversity cases.

If a defendant wishes to transfer a case from one state to another, or from state court to federal court, his/her request will be for *removal*. Such requests must be made at the beginning of the case and are premised on the claim that the correct jurisdiction lies in another court. In seeking a transfer from state to federal court, the defendant is often simply exercising a right to invoke diversity jurisdiction, or some other concurrent federal jurisdiction, which the plaintiff failed to use but the defendant also has a right to choose.

As for the state courts, they are generally open to hear any type of case unless it is precluded by the U.S. Constitution or federal statutes or treaties. *Most common law areas—for instance, torts, contracts, crimes—tend to be brought before state courts.*

• *PERSONAL (IN PERSONAM) JURISDICTION*

In addition to subject-matter jurisdiction, for each particular case a court needs jurisdiction over the litigants themselves.

> **Personal (*in personam*) jurisdiction:** judicial power over the parties in a case.

By filing a lawsuit the *plaintiff* voluntarily submits to the court's personal jurisdiction. Personal jurisdiction over the *defendant* depends on: (1) his/her being properly served with the complaint and summons; and (2) his/her having sufficient ties to the state in which the lawsuit was filed. Obviously, if the defendant resides or works in the state (or a business is incorporated or has an office in the state), personal jurisdiction is well founded. Also, states have passed **"long-arm statutes,"** *which extend personal jurisdiction* over people or corporations that do business in the state, own real property there, or (in cases involving a tort or contract) committed the alleged tort in the state or entered the contract in the state.

There are many other grounds for "long-arm" personal jurisdiction. For each case, the *key constitutional question is whether the defendant has had enough "minimal contacts" within the state* so that requiring him/her to defend the lawsuit in that state does not violate due process of law (Fifth and/or Fourteenth Amendments) by offending "traditional notions of fair play and substantial justice" [*International Shoe Co. v. Washington*, 326 U.S. 310, 316 (1945).] Any presence in a state, other than a passive Internet site accessible there,[1] may leave a firm subject to personal jurisdiction.

But the possibility of personal jurisdiction often depends upon whether it is specific or general. *Specific personal jurisdiction* arises from the defendant's contacts with the state where the case has been

---

[1] For example, a New York business that has an interactive, informational web site, even one allowing customers to download order forms and to e-mail with inquiries, does not subject that business to personal jurisdiction in any other state where a plaintiff thereby accessed the site. However, once sales occur over the Internet, even relatively minor transactions, those "contacts" outside of New York may subject the New York seller to jurisdiction where the plaintiff-buyer was when he/she placed his/her order(s). Resolving this jurisdictional issue may depend on whether the buyer initiated the order(s). If the defendant's marketing efforts did not lead the buyer to the defendant's web site but the buyer found the site on his/her own, then that may undermine the rationale for personal jurisdiction outside of New York if the resulting sales were quite small.

Between business parties, courts usually let the parties—including those who contract over the Internet—stipulate their choice of jurisdiction, venue, and substantive law. Inasmuch as consumers often lack adequate bargaining power to negotiate effectively the terms proposed in a seller's click-wrap agreement, consumers may receive special protection: perhaps being permitted to sue in their home states under local law, especially when a nonresident defendant knowingly and repeatedly uses the Internet to transact business in that state.

filed (the forum) *and* how the case relates to issues (e.g., an accident, a contract) arising from those contacts. As stated in *International Shoe*, 326 U.S. at 318, *general personal jurisdiction* occurs when "continuous corporate operations within a state [are] so substantial and of such a nature as to justify suit against [the defendant] on causes of action arising from dealings entirely distinct from those activities." In other words, an out-of-state corporation's "affiliations with the State [must be] so 'continuous and systematic' as to render [it] essentially at home in the foreign state" (and thus it is fair to subject it to a lawsuit having nothing specifically to do with the corporation's in-state conduct). *Goodyear Dunlop Tires Operations, S.A. v. Brown*, 564 U.S. __ (2011).

As a further refinement of personal jurisdiction concepts, the Supreme Court's decision in *Daimler AG v. Bauman*, 571 U.S. __ (2013), rejects the notion that it reaches a corporate defendant whenever a party related to that corporation performed a function, in the forum state, "important" to the corporation. Such logic would mean that anything a corporation does through an agent, distributor, independent contractor, subsidiary, or other relations could subject the corporation to general jurisdiction—a "sprawling view of general jurisdiction." The *Daimler* holding's main effect is to maintain the distinction between specific and general personal jurisdiction first established in *International Shoe*.

A defendant who does not challenge the court's personal jurisdiction over him/her is deemed to have consented to that court's determination of his/her rights and obligations. However, the defense, that *subject matter* jurisdiction is lacking, cannot be waived.

VENUE, CONFLICT OF STATE LAWS, AND FULL FAITH AND CREDIT

• *VENUE*

When a court has authority over the subject matter and parties of a lawsuit, it has jurisdiction. However, there still may be problems with **venue**, that is, the place (usually the county) where the case will be tried.

Generally, a lawsuit is to be brought in the judicial district where the parties work or reside, where the disputed interest in land is located, or where the occurrence leading to the lawsuit took place. Proper venue is defined by statute, and is usually based on the notion of convenience to the parties, especially the defendant. If there is to be a change in venue, it usually must be requested at the outset of the case. In rare instances, pretrial publicity or other factors may force a change of venue later in the case.

• *CONFLICT OF STATE LAWS*

Obviously, the law varies from state to state. The doctrine of *stare decisis* (see Chapter 1) does not require one state to follow another state's precedents.

What makes matters even more confusing is that disputes often arise out of transactions occurring in more than one state. Which state's substantive laws are to govern the resolution of such a dispute? This question is covered by a body of law known as **conflict of laws** (or choice of laws).

Although a court will almost always apply its own *procedural law* (rules about form of pleadings, discovery, and the like), it must look to conflict-of-laws principles to choose between differing *substantive laws* (e.g., on contracts, torts, agency). The forum jurisdiction (where the dispute is being tried) determines that most basic question: whether something is a matter of procedure or of substance. The following matters usually are classified as *procedural* (hence, governed by the trial court's rules) when a conflict of laws occurs: (1) whether a claim is actionable (ripe; a legally sound claim in front of the appropriate court); (2) identity of the proper parties able to sue or to defend a suit; (3) admissibility of evidence; (4) relative priority of protected interests; (5)set-off claims and rights; (6) the nature and extent of remedies; (7) methods of enforcing a judgment; and (8) the right to appeal.

Example: Conflict of Laws

A Colorado court is deciding a case involving a contract executed in New York, performed in Missouri, and involving Delaware corporations with principal offices in Colorado. So long as the lawsuit remains before a Colorado court, it will be governed by Colorado rules of procedure. However, interpretation of the contract may be based on the law of another state, such as New York or Missouri.

For *torts*, the applicable law is usually the *law of the state where the injury occurred*.

For *contracts*, the courts usually look to the *law intended by the parties*. A court ordinarily honors an express stipulation in a contract that the contract is to be governed by a particular state's laws. Even if no such express statement is made, courts will often look to the parties' *implied* intentions. At that point, though, the courts may turn to an earlier approach (still followed in some states) governing conflicts of law in contract cases: use of the law where the contract was made or performed. (In very complex tort or contract cases, some courts seek to determine, and then apply, the law of the state with the most significant ties to the parties and the matter in dispute.)

Usually the parties' choice-of-law provision controls. But there are some exceptions to the idea that a contract's "choice of law" provision governs. Sometimes a court finds that its state's laws overcome a choice-of-law clause favoring the law of another state. A survey of decisions indicates that courts have found the following laws embody public policies that warrant overriding the contractual choice-of-law clause: (1) prohibitions of covenants not to compete; (2) unconscionability doctrines; (3) fair dealership laws; (4) boxing licensing schemes; (5) state bankruptcy laws; (6) contractor licensing schemes; (7) statutes of frauds; (8) usury statutes; and (9) insurance laws barring suicide exception clauses.

In *criminal cases*, conflicts of law simply do not arise. Courts apply their own substantive as well as procedural laws, even for acts committed elsewhere. Of course, if another jurisdiction's interests are paramount (i.e., because the crime took place on its soil), then the alleged criminal can be **extradited** (sent, via a legal process, to the other jurisdiction). Thus the accused is almost always tried in the place where the crime supposedly occurred.

Extradition (to send the accused to the jurisdiction in which the crime was committed) is usually an easy formality between states within the United States; but extradition can be difficult between foreign countries, depending on:

1. treaty obligations (or lack thereof),

2. the status of the accused (e.g., diplomatic immunity, or powerful business interests),

3. the two nations' substantive law and culture concerning the alleged crime(s), and

4. the similarities and differences between the two nations' criminal law procedures—e.g., what sort of trial; what rights to have counsel, subpoenaing of witnesses, and cross-examination; what sorts of presumptions for or against the defendant; what range and likelihood of punishment; and what type of decision-maker—e.g., an independent judge, a jury, a bureaucrat, or a "political flunky."

• *FULL FAITH AND CREDIT*

Article IV, Section I, of the U.S. Constitution states, "full faith and credit shall be given in each State to the public acts, records and judicial proceedings of every other State." This **"full faith and credit" clause** does not mean that other states must adopt the reasoning on which a decision was based; one state's precedents are *not* binding on another state. It simply means that other states must recognize the validity of a civil or criminal judgment as it specifically affects the rights and duties of the parties subject to that judgment (i.e., involved as parties in the original case), provided, however, that the original court had personal and subject-matter jurisdiction.

YOU SHOULD REMEMBER

Although there are many types of courts, the main state and federal judicial systems involve general, trial courts, with appeals taken to one or more higher courts.

Federal courts have *particularized subject-matter jurisdiction*, usually based on "federal questions" or diversity jurisdiction.

State courts have *general subject-matter jurisdiction*.

Personal (in personam) jurisdiction requires that the defendant reside or work in the state in which the lawsuit was filed, or have other clear-cut ties to the state. *Long-arm statutes* grant courts power over out-of-state individuals and corporations in certain specified circumstances.

Courts follow their own procedural law. However, in some cases, they may apply the substantive law of another state.

For *torts*, the applicable law is usually that where the injury occurred.

For *contracts*, courts generally look to the law intended (expressly or implicitly) by the parties to the contract.

In *criminal cases*, courts apply their own substantive and procedural laws, regardless of where the acts were committed; however, almost all criminal prosecutions take place in the same state where the alleged crime occurred.

Once a court with jurisdiction renders a judgment, the U.S. Constitution's "full faith and credit" clause requires that, as between the parties to the lawsuit, the judgment must be honored by other states' courts.

TAKING A CASE TO COURT

Assume that Paul Plaintiff decides to sue Doris Defendant for breach of contract. Paul must file his lawsuit in an appropriate court and thereafter, since this is a civil case, meet the procedural rules governing civil litigation.

Procedural law is very complex and varies from court to court. There are federal rules of procedure, and each state court system also has its own set of procedures. Appellate courts have different rules from trial courts, and even the same type of courts, in the same jurisdiction (e.g., the same state), may have different local rules for each court. Moreover, criminal and civil cases follow different rules.

Nevertheless, it is also fair to say that, despite the differences, most cases follow a general pattern of procedure. In our case (*Paul Plaintiff v. Doris Defendant*), we will follow the general procedural pattern usually found in any American court of law. (For all cases, settlement can come at any point in the process.)

THE PARTIES TO A LAWSUIT

The person who initiates a lawsuit is called the **plaintiff**. The person sued is the **defendant**. In equity cases (see Chapter 1), these parties are instead often called the **petitioner** and the **respondent**, respectively. In a criminal case, there is no "plaintiff"; rather, the criminal defendant is opposed by the state itself, often called "the prosecution" or even "the people." (Criminal cases are brought on behalf of the public as a whole.)

THE PLEADINGS

The papers required to bring the issues in a lawsuit before the court are termed the **pleadings**. Paul's lawsuit (action) against Doris starts when he or his lawyer files a complaint (sometimes called a declaration, petition, or bill of complaint) with the clerk of a trial court having proper jurisdiction and venue. The complaint should include a statement of facts, the basis of the suit (in this case, alleged breach of contract), and a request for one or more remedies (e.g., damages or an injunction). Often a complaint must also include information showing that the court has jurisdiction and venue. Paul's complaint might be as follows:

Example: Plaintiff's Complaint

Paul Plaintiff,	*	In the Circuit Court
Plaintiff	*	For Our County
v.	*	State of Bliss
Doris Defendant,	*	Civil Action No. AA-000
Defendant		

* * * * *

COMPLAINT

The plaintiff, Paul Plaintiff, by his attorney, Lucretia Lawyer, sues the defendant, Doris Defendant, and says:

1. Paul Plaintiff (hereinafter, "Plaintiff") and Doris Defendant (hereinafter, "Defendant") are both residents of the State of Bliss. This action concerns a contract entered into in Bliss between Plaintiff and

Defendant. The amount due and owing to Plaintiff by Defendant is more than $10,000.00.

2. Based on the facts stated in paragraph 1, jurisdiction over this subject matter and over the person of Defendant is found upon Bliss Code, Courts Article, Sections 21 and 22.

3. Defendant resides in Anytown, Our County, State of Bliss. Venue is thus founded upon Bliss Code, Courts Article, Section 31.

4. At various times in or around August, September, and October, 2015, Plaintiff, at the request of Defendant, delivered certain XYZ computers and ABC software programs to Defendant. The price agreed upon by Defendant was $29,000.00, and Defendant has made only one payment of $2,000.00.

5. Payment was to be made within thirty (30) days of delivery. Despite Plaintiff's repeated demands for payment, Defendant has refused and continues to refuse to pay the remaining amount owed.

WHEREFORE, Plaintiff demands judgment against Defendant for damages in the sum of Twenty-Seven Thousand Dollars ($27,000.00), plus prejudgment interest, costs of suit, attorney's fees, and such other relief as the Court deems just and equitable.

Lucretia Lawyer
Attorney for Paul Plaintiff
100 Lawyers Lane
Big City, Bliss

The sheriff or other such official then serves a **summons** and a copy of the complaint on Doris Defendant. Alternative methods of "service of process" include using a private process server or sending the summons and complaint by certified mail (receipt returned to sender); in either case, an affidavit is usually filed attesting to the fact that the defendant received the summons and complaint. In a case involving land or certain corporate defendants, service may be made by publishing notices in a newspaper or elsewhere and/or serving the summons and complaint upon an authorized state official, such as the state secretary of state or other registrar of corporations. There are many other variations on these procedures, which differ from state to state. Electronic service of process (e-service) and, even more so once the case has been filed, electronic filing of pleadings (e-filing) increasingly are used.

International Law: The Hague Service Convention (1965) established procedures for serving process in another country, whether by using

1. a central governing authority in that other country;

2. diplomatic channels; or

3. any other method of service permitted by the laws of that other country (even just via mail, although some nations have chosen not to permit that type of service).

The Convention's signatories encompass about 70 countries, including **every** European nation other than Austria and a few microstates (e.g., Andorra). Of the top twenty trading or producing nations worldwide, only three—Brazil, Indonesia, and Saudi Arabia—are not signatories.

The Convention's language indicates that its purpose is to give notice to a party, not grant jurisdiction. In fact, the Convention provides no basis for personal jurisdiction, which must first be established through a long-arm statute or other domestic law. Thus, the Convention does not replace, but instead supplements, the domestic law requirements for jurisdiction.

Direct mail, fax, or Internet transmissions are typical methods for filing and exchanging documents once the lawsuit has been answered, but—at the initial stage—service of process usually requires more, such as use of a government agency and providing the defendant with a translated copy of the complaint and the summons.

The summons notifies Doris Defendant that she must file her **answer** to the complaint with both the court and the plaintiff's attorney within a certain time period (usually 20 or 30 days, though often longer for out-of-state defendants). The summons also tells the defendant that failure to file an answer will lead to a judgment by default for the plaintiff.

An answer, though, is not Doris Defendant's only choice. She may file a **motion to dismiss**, sometimes called a **demurrer**, in which she contends that, even if the complaint's allegations are true, there is no legal basis for finding the defendant liable.

Major Reasons Why Dismissals May Be Granted

1. The court lacks subject-matter jurisdiction.

2. The time period to sue (statute of limitations) has expired.

3. The allegations do not set forth a breach of contract, tort, or whatever else could lead to a judgment for the plaintiff.

In most jurisdictions, as in Doris's case, a motion to dismiss may be raised in lieu of an answer. Only if the court rules that part or all of the complaint remains viable, must the answer be filed.

The answer generally admits or denies each of the various allegations set forth in the complaint. It also may include **affirmative defenses**, that is, allegations of facts that, if proved by the defendant, defeat the plaintiff's claim.

Since the court does not uphold Doris's motion to dismiss, she files the following answer:

Example: Defendant's Answer

Paul Plaintiff,	*	In the Circuit Court
Plaintiff	*	For Our County
v.	*	State of Bliss
Doris Defendant,	*	Civil Action No. AA-000
Defendant		

* * * * *

ANSWER

Doris Defendant, by her attorneys, Atilla Attorney and Dewey, Cheatham & Howe, answers Paul Plaintiff's Complaint, and says:

1. Defendant admits the allegations in the first sentence of paragraph one of the Complaint, and denies the allegations in the second and third sentences.

2. Paragraph two of the Complaint is a legal conclusion rather than a factual allegation, and thus Defendant need not admit or deny said paragraph.

3. Defendant admits the allegations in the first sentence of paragraph three of the Complaint. Defendant need not admit or deny the second sentence, which is a legal conclusion.

4. Defendant acknowledges that, after she paid plaintiff $2,000.00, some computers and software were delivered to defendant by plaintiff on one occasion in or around September 2015. In all other respects, defendant denies the allegations stated in paragraph four of the Complaint.

5. Defendant admits that she has refused and continues to refuse to pay additional money to plaintiff. Defendant denies all other allegations in paragraph five of the Complaint, including any inference that defendant owes money to plaintiff.

Affirmative Defenses

1. There was no contract between the parties.

2. In the alternative, the contract was not as alleged by plaintiff.

3. Plaintiff failed to deliver goods promised.

4. Plaintiff delivered defective goods.
5. The court lacks jurisdiction over the subject matter.

Atilla Attorney
Dewey, Cheatham & Howe
5 Esquire Court
Big City, Bliss

(Generally, a complaint or answer may be amended unless a statute or rule specifically bars such amendment or unless the amendment is made at such a late date that its acceptance as a new pleading would be grossly unfair to another party.)

When answering the complaint, or shortly thereafter, a defendant generally has the option to file a *counterclaim*, which is, in effect, a "reverse" complaint: one by the defendant against the plaintiff. Two other claims are *cross claims*, brought by a plaintiff against one or more coplaintiffs or, more likely, by a defendant against one or more codefendants, and *third-party claims*, whereby a defendant brings a new party into a lawsuit. In addition, large numbers of similarly situated plaintiffs may join together in a **class action**.

CLASS ACTIONS

Class actions are lawsuits in which a few persons represent a group of similarly situated persons, perhaps huge in number (the "class"). Lawyers usually gather the representatives and file an action either in the federal courts under Federal Rule of Civil Procedure 23 or in a state court where the procedural rules are similar. Class action status is only to be granted if the plaintiffs are similarly situated, and thus having one large case is a fair and efficient use of court resources. For the court to grant the required class certification, the plaintiffs must show, under Rule 23(a): (1) claimants too large in number for affected persons joining together as plaintiffs in a single, traditional lawsuit (numerosity); (2) questions of law or fact common to the class (commonality); (3) representatives fairly and adequately protecting the class' interests (adequacy); and (4) claims and defenses typical for the class (typicality).

Assuming the four elements of commonality, adequacy, numerosity, and typicality[1] are present, then under Rule 23(b), a class action can proceed if:

---

[1] The first letter of each of these four terms, in order, spell the acronym, *CANT*.
Note: Denial of class-action status does not necessarily end a dispute. The denial may have that *practical* effect if there is no logical or economic way for individual parties to pursue claims. However, as a legal matter the denial ordinarily means that claims still can be brought, but individually, not as one large class action.

(1) individual lawsuits, rather than a class action, would create a risk of inconsistent decisions (e.g., requiring the employer to treat an employee in a way that might undermine the employer's ability to treat other employees equally) or would impair the interests of other class members (e.g., in cases with large potential damage awards and limited funds for payment, the first to collect damage awards may end up with the lion's share of the total payout); or

(2) the defendant's actions or inaction were on grounds applicable to the whole class, thereby making an injunction or other declaration of relief appropriate for the entire class; or

(3) questions of law or fact common to the class members predominate, with a class action superior to all alternatives for dealing with the issues in the case.

Most class actions fall under this last category of "predominance" and "superiority," and it is only this form of class membership that is not mandatory. For this last category, notice must be given to potential class members, who can opt out of the class—thereby preserving their right to sue individually and waiving any right to whatever recovery the class members may receive.

In a case alleging sex discrimination against female employees, *Wal-Mart Stores, Inc. v. Dukes*, 564 U.S. ___ (2011), the U.S. Supreme Court overturned certification for a class of present and former Wal-Mart workers from more than 3,400 stores in a multitude of varying jobs and time periods involving thousands of different supervisors. There was, the court held, little evidence of commonality in terms of the plaintiffs' circumstances or a corporate-wide practice—only that supervisors at each store had their own discretion concerning employment decisions. Furthermore, the court held that the Wal-Mart employees' claims for back pay should have been interpreted as the type of claim requiring predominant, common questions of law or fact (not simply relief that might come with an injunction under Rule 23(b)(2)). So, even assuming the case could have proceeded as a class action, it should have featured notice to class members along with their ability to opt out.

The *Class Action Fairness Act of 2005* (CAFA) shifts most large class-action lawsuits involving parties from different states to federal courts, removing them from the jurisdiction of state courts that historically have been more receptive to such suits. Under CAFA, class-action suits seeking more than $5 million are in federal court if fewer than a third of the plaintiffs are from the same state as the primary defendant. If the primary defendant and more than a third of the plaintiffs are from the same state, the case can still be heard in state court. CAFA also may limit the fees of class-action lawyers in that their fees from settlements must be based on rewards plaintiffs actually received (e.g., coupons redeemed), not just those issued.

Class Actions in Europe

Some countries, such as Australia, China, India, Israel, Japan, and South Africa, have followed America's lead and now permit class actions. However, a class action or something akin thereto is a foreign concept in many nations, including much of Europe. For example, while the United Kingdom and Sweden generally allow class actions, in France and Spain class actions tend to be limited to consumer rights cases.

Without calling it a class action, many countries (e.g., Germany, the Netherlands) let settlements in some cases, such as shareholder suits against corporations, have the same effect as class action compromises. A representative case binds all plaintiffs, so that individual plaintiffs share the costs of litigation, allow one case to proceed to a resolution, and agree to have all interested parties bound to the result of that one case.

In our hypothetical case, Doris Defendant might file a counterclaim against Paul Plaintiff for return of the $2,000.00 already paid. The grounds for such a counterclaim would probably be the same as the third and fourth affirmative defenses raised in the answer: plaintiff breached the contract by failing to deliver goods and/or by delivering defective goods.

Besides the motion to dismiss, many other types of **motions**, that is, requests to the court, may be made before the case goes to trial. Such motions may ask for rulings on evidence, or may seek orders compelling a party or witness to provide discovery (see the next section). In fact, each party is generally free to make any motion that he/she wishes.

The most important motion is probably the motion for **summary judgment**, which is based on the pleadings, discovery, disclosure materials on file, and any affidavits. This motion may be filed at any time, by either party.

In the federal courts, there is a little more leeway for the court to reduce caseloads by entering a summary judgment than is the case in state courts. The U.S. Supreme Court has elaborated on the summary judgment standard found in Federal Rule of Civil Procedure 56(c)(2) by noting that summary judgment must be granted if there can be only one reasonable conclusion as to the verdict. So, for example, an opposing party cannot simply deny the facts or assert uncorroborated inadmissible hearsay statements. That is because, before a judge denies a properly asserted, factually and legally supported, summary judgment motion, the judge must find sufficient evidence that a jury could reasonably rely upon in reaching a verdict for the party opposing summary judgment.

> Summary judgment is to be awarded if the judge decides that
>
> (1) there is no genuine issue as to material (potentially determinative) facts, *and*
>
> (2) when the law is applied to these facts, one party is entitled to a verdict in his/her favor.

Summary judgment may be granted on all or part of a lawsuit. For instance, if a complaint sets forth different theories of liability (e.g., negligence and breach of warranty), the defendant may be able to get one of them stricken, even if the judge will not grant summary judgment on all counts. The summary judgment process may also be used to limit or eliminate certain types of damages, such as punitive damages. Of course, plaintiffs may also gain a partial summary judgment.

The party seeking to avoid trial (summary judgment), to take a case away from the jury (directed verdict; see page 73), or to overturn a jury verdict (J.N.O.V.; see page 76) must meet the same high standards.

The "Virtual" Courtroom of the Internet

The cybercourtroom increasingly found in state and federal courts includes teleconferences from scattered locations, Internet court filings, computer-simulated exhibits and digital evidence, electronically stored documents, and transcripts stored on CD-ROM. More and more courts now accept electronic filing of lawsuits and paperless record keeping. Additionally, almost every court has a website where the public can look up real estate assessments, civil cases, deed information, judges' opinions, and other matters.

Representing Oneself (Proceeding *pro se*)

A small but growing number of lawyers agree to let some clients do part of the work themselves. For example, a lawyer may let clients draft letters, conduct research, file certain documents with courts or government agencies, and deal with expert witnesses. A lawyer may limit his/her work to simply appearing in court, reviewing correspondence, helping out with the procedures for an appeal, or acting as a "court coach" for people who want to represent themselves in minor disputes: everything else is handled by the client. Problems include: (1) the lawyer still may be subject to malpractice claims, even for matters handled by the client on his own; and (2) judges may consider lawyer "ghost-writing" of court pleadings or other legal documents an unethical subterfuge (making it look like the party is *pro se* (acting on his/her own) when he/she actually is not). But some who have reviewed the process view the hiring of a legal "coach" as a welcome middle ground as opposed to going completely *pro se*.

Many state and local courts offer services to people who are proceeding *pro se,* or who otherwise are in search of some legal self-help (often especially related to family law).

DISCOVERY

Before there is a trial, each party is entitled to obtain information from other parties and from other potential witnesses. These pretrial procedures are known as **discovery**.

Ordinarily, the discovery process requires little, if any, direct judicial involvement. However, courts can order parties to comply with discovery requirements. If noncompliance continues, courts can issue an array of sanctions, including not just fines but—in extreme cases (e.g., a corporate defendant's deliberate policy of withholding important evidence)—a default judgment for the other party.

The scope of discovery is far broader than what is permitted at trial. Going beyond what is usually allowed in the courtroom, discovery operates under rules that allow for more flexibility in questioning and in other requests for information: probing into all evidence that is admissible in court *and all other information that could lead to admissible evidence.*

Discovery may serve several purposes:

1. By providing parties with access to evidence that might otherwise be hidden, it prevents surprises at the trial.
2. It may narrow the issues at trial (i.e., some questions may be resolved).
3. It preserves witnesses' testimony prior to trial (important when witnesses may be unavailable at trial, their memories may fade, or their testimony may change).
4. It may place the case in a posture suitable for summary judgment.
5. It may lead to a pretrial settlement, as opposing parties come to see their strengths and weaknesses.

The main methods of discovery are depositions, interrogatories, requests for admissions, and the production of documents. Other methods include physical and mental examinations and, in cases involving land, inspections of premises.

A **deposition** is sworn testimony, by one of the parties or any other witness, usually recorded and transcribed by a notary public. The testimony is ordinarily taken in response to oral questions from the parties' attorneys, although it also can be in response to written questions.

Under the federal rules, one side—no matter how many parties there are (whether co-plaintiffs or co-defendants) on that side—may call only 10 oral depositions. For more, or to depose someone a second time, one needs court permission.

"Apex" Corporate Officers

Most courts will accede to a corporation's request that plaintiffs conduct less intrusive discovery—depose only high-level company officials—if (1) these "apex" officers have specific, direct knowledge of relevant facts, and (2) the subordinate company employees (who normally could be expected to answer questions at depositions and furnish documents if need be) actually are less informed about the particulars of the case. The apex corporate officials may be insulated from depositions when affidavits (prepared by corporate counsel and signed by these apex officers) contained express denials that these people had any "unique," "superior," or "personal" knowledge of relevant facts. Sometimes, a court may even require the use of interrogatories before permitting the scheduling of the deposition of an apex corporate employee (e.g., the CEO).

Interrogatories are written questions, to be answered in writing, and under oath, by another party (generally, the opposing party). Unlike depositions, interrogatories can be directed only toward the parties themselves. Their usefulness is further limited by the fact that the answering party's attorney can, in effect, prepare the answers. However, interrogatories usually cost less (both in legal fees and other expenses such as transcripts) than depositions, and their scope can be broader.

Requests for admissions are, like interrogatories, made and answered in writing and can be directed only toward another party. The requesting party asks the other side to admit particular facts or acknowledge the genuineness of certain documents. Admissions are conclusive. Thus the requests, with the admissions they elicit, can save trial time because the parties have already agreed on some matters.

Finally, parties may be required to *produce*, for inspection and copying, all their *documents* that may be relevant to the case. Likewise, a deposition may include document production by the witness.

• *E-DISCOVERY*

In **electronic discovery** ("**e-discovery**"), parties seek or provide information in *electronic format* (*Electronically Stored Information*—"ESI"). This data evidence could be text, images, databases, spreadsheets, websites, animation, audio files, instant messaging chats, calendar files, computer programs, and even malware (e.g., viruses, spyware, and Trojan horses). Probably the most frequent and valuable ESI is electronic mail (e-mail), as people are often less careful with this correspondence than with postal letters, memoranda, faxes, or other writings. Computer forensics ("cyberforensics") is an investigation of a computer's hard drive.

The Federal Rules of Civil Procedure (FRCP) address e-discovery and "legal hold." Organizations must retain all paper and electronic records until each legal matter has been formally settled. The duty remains even if an organization only reasonably anticipates litigation. The FRCP explicitly names, among other things, e-mails and instant message (IM) chats as electronic records to be archived and produced when relevant. Systems must prevent changes to or deletions of original messages, with archived records kept in a form allowing efficient and timely production. The failure to meet ESI retention and management requirements puts parties at risk of claims for spoliation of evidence, summary judgment, adverse inferences about the missing evidence, and sanctions, including attorneys' possible suspension or disbarment.

• *SANCTIONS FOR DISCOVERY ABUSES*

Federal Rule of Civil Procedure 37, as well as comparable rules in most states, permits judges to impose numerous sanctions for discovery abuses (e.g., for a party's failing to provide documents or other information). Sanctions may include judicial orders (1) mandating that certain facts at issue are deemed conclusively established against the abusive party; (2) forbidding the abusive party from making or opposing certain claims or defenses; (3) prohibiting the abusive party from putting certain matters into evidence; (4) striking certain pleadings or parts of pleadings; (5) suspending all proceedings until a violation is rectified; (6) dismissing an abusive plaintiff's action, or entering a default judgment against an abusive defendant; and (7) requiring the abusive party to pay the reasonable expenses, including attorneys' fees, incurred by the other parties as a result of the discovery abuse. Other sanctions could be (1) a contempt of court finding, and (2) informing the jury of the abusive party's violation.

Comparative Law on Discovery

Many other nations, particularly those with inquisitorial traditions (e.g., France, Germany), provide for little, if any, pretrial discovery by parties or their attorneys. (Any such discovery would be by the court itself.) Even countries such as the United Kingdom, with a legal system similar to the U.S. system, permit only limited discovery. Also, other countries often require a judge to be present at depositions, making the procedure more formal and controlled than it is in the United States, where only lawyers and witnesses are present.

INFORMAL DISCOVERY

Informal discovery techniques are distinct from "formal" discovery (e.g., depositions, interrogatories, requests for admissions or documents, e-discovery). Litigators also perform these informal tasks: (1) Internet searches concerning everyone pertinent to the case, such as all parties and witnesses; (2) reviewing credit, stock, or other reports (e.g., medical reports, with the patient's permission), as well as all public filings (e.g., 10-K and 10-Q filings under the securities laws; see page 425); (3) reading news articles and government records; and (4) interviewing third parties (e.g., neighbors, acquaintances, current and former co-workers or employers). Rules, if any, are scattered, and new developments—e.g., growing and changing social media—make informal, often Internet-related discovery likely to receive much future attention by courts and regulators. So far, for instance, other than some privacy norms and regulations, there are few well-established institutional rules governing social network sites.

There are some basic rubrics for informal discovery as to witnesses and Internet searches. *Ex parte* interviews with **witnesses** are largely unrestricted by the federal rules and in most state litigation. Typically, no party to litigation has a proprietary right to a witness's evidence; unless a privilege (e.g., attorney-client) is affected, one side in litigation cannot restrict the other side's access to a witness. Indeed, while the Federal Rules of Civil Procedure and many state rules provide specific means for parties to compel the taking of testimony or other evidence from recalcitrant sources, this does not preclude the use of informal discovery techniques such as interviews of a willing witness. That witness may demand compensation for his/her reasonable expenses (e.g., travel costs) as well as, for experts, their time.

As for **Internet searches**, collecting information from online sources such as social media websites may violate professional disciplinary standards. For example, bar standards may find an attempt to deceive, and thus grounds for disciplining (e.g., censuring or even disbarring), the lawyer who uses "friending" as an investigative tool—sending a Facebook friend request to a represented party. While lawyers representing a client in litigation can access the public pages of another party's social networking website to obtain material to impeach that party, they are not permitted to access social networking websites under false pretenses, whether directly or through agents.

THE PRETRIAL CONFERENCE

The trial issues can be narrowed via a pretrial conference. Except for some smaller cases, such conferences may be called by the parties or the court itself; they are routinely held in most federal civil cases.

Although judges may use these conferences to encourage settlement, the main purpose is to ensure that the trial will proceed as smoothly as possible: witnesses, exhibits, areas of dispute, and agreed upon facts are all identified ahead of time.

THE TRIAL

Aside from any pretrial motions (discussed previously), the next step is the trial itself.

Jury trial is available in criminal cases and most civil lawsuits. Major exceptions:

1. Certain types of cases (e.g., divorce) historically based on equity.

2. Administrative agency proceedings.

Plaintiff or defendant can ask for trial by jury; this right is usually waived if not requested in plaintiff's complaint or defendant's answer. A contract clause waiving the parties' right to a jury is generally upheld in business-to-business or other commercial dealings, but much less so for employment contracts, particularly if the clause is inconspicuous or not in conjunction with an arbitration clause.

A jury trial involves a **petit jury** (12 members ordinarily in federal court and some state courts, although many states have as few as 6). The petit jury decides whether the defendant is guilty in criminal cases or is liable in civil cases; in federal courts and most state courts, the jury's decision must be unanimous. [The federal courts and most states also have **grand juries** (around 18 to 24 jurors), which, under the guidance of prosecutors, decide whether a person should be charged with a crime (indicted).]

In *jury selection*, the first step in the trial, prospective jurors are questioned by the attorneys for both sides and by the judge. This examination is known as **voir dire**. Any number of potential jurors can be kept off the panel "for cause" (e.g., bias), and the attorneys for each side also have the right to reject a few (generally about three) without offering a reason, that is, by *peremptory challenge*. The Supreme Court has ruled, though, that a peremptory strike may not be used to remove a potential criminal or civil juror simply because of his race or sex.

Most other nations do not have juries. Of those that do, a jury trial tends to be rare when compared with its use in the United States. In England, for example, jury trials are available only for criminal cases. Even in the United States, where juries are common, only about one in seven civil trials is before a jury.

After the jury has been selected, the next step is the presentation of *opening statements*. These provide each attorney with the opportunity to indicate what he/she expects to prove.

The *plaintiff's* case is then presented. Witnesses, called by the plaintiff's attorney, testify in response to the attorneys' *questions: first, direct examination* by the attorney that called them, and then *cross-examination* by the opposing attorney. Also, exhibits, documents, and other evidence that may advance the plaintiff's cause are offered. At the close of the plaintiff's case, the defendant may file for dismissal of the case or for a **directed verdict**, that is, a judgment rendered by the court, in his/her favor.

Federal Rule of Civil Procedure 50 calls both the motion for a directed verdict and the motion for a judgment notwithstanding the verdict (see page 76) a motion for a judgment as a matter of law.

The standard for granting these motions is generally the same as for granting a summary judgment motion.

If the trial is to continue, the next step is to present the *defendant's case*, following the same procedures as above but offering witnesses and evidence for the defense. The plaintiff may submit rebuttal evidence; then, in turn, the defendant may submit rebuttal evidence. When the defendant's case has been completed, the plaintiff may move for a directed verdict in his/her favor. Also, in jury trials this may be the proper time for the defendant to request a directed verdict.

In the *summation* (the *closing argument* or *final argument*), each attorney has the opportunity to review the testimony and other evidence and make his/her closing arguments.

Throughout the trial, the judge makes legal rulings on evidence or other matters. Generally, only after the summations does he/she *instruct* the jury concerning the law that is applicable to the case and the various verdicts that the jury may render.

The jury then retires and attempts, in its deliberations, to resolve all factual (not legal) issues. As stated previously, in federal courts and in most states, it is only when all members agree that the jury renders a *verdict*. In a nonjury trial the judge makes the decision.

In reaching a verdict, consideration of evidence is governed by the *burden of proof*. This refers to:

1. A party's obligation, when asserting a fact, to *come forward* with evidence establishing this fact.

Example: Come forward

If party A alleges fact *x*, party A must produce evidence in support of *x* before opposing party B is expected to disprove *x*.

2. The necessity for one party (in civil cases, almost always the plaintiff) to *persuade* the trier of fact (judge or jury) that a preponderance of the evidence supports his/her contentions—that his/her version of the facts is, at the very least, slightly more credible than the opposing party's. If dead-even, the opposing party (generally the defendant) wins. ("Persuasion," not "coming forward," is the more common usage of the term "burden of proof.")

A few special types of allegations (e.g., fraud) may demand a higher standard of persuasion, such as "clear and convincing" proof; and, of course, in a criminal case, the prosecution has a much higher burden of persuasion: "beyond a reasonable doubt." (See Chapter 19.)

EVIDENCE

The two types of evidence generally presented during a trial are *direct evidence* and *circumstantial evidence*. **Direct evidence** is testimony from someone (e.g., an eyewitness) who claims to have *actual knowledge* of one or more facts. **Circumstantial evidence** constitutes the proof of a chain of circumstances indicating the existence of one or more facts. In other words, circumstantial evidence, if true, leads to an inference about the existence of other facts. While the layperson may assume courts require a higher degree of certainty to introduce or use circumstantial evidence than direct evidence, that is not so. The law does not distinguish between the two types of evidence as to the degree of proof for admissibility in court, or as to the weight or the value to be given such evidence by a judge or jury.

Categorization of evidence (whether direct or circumstantial) is dictated not by set rules, but by the particular aspects of a case and—if it is a jury trial—by the judge's jury instructions. Some rules, however, do affect the admissibility of certain types of evidence. For example, the use of documentary evidence is governed in federal court proceedings by Federal Rule of Evidence 1002, which ordinarily requires parties to use as evidence the original document, not a copy—the "Best Evidence Rule."

Demonstrative evidence is placed directly before the jury without requiring testimony. The use of physical objects is either "real" or "demonstrative" evidence, with use of such evidence allowed when the object is relevant to an issue in the case *and* the evidence in effect helps to explain something important for a judge or jury to understand. The trial judge normally has wide discretion in deciding the admissibility or not of demonstrative evidence, with a decision to bar such evidence as irrelevant, not explanatory, or misleading (e.g., an inaccurate model or picture).

THREE TYPES OF WITNESSES

Eyewitnesses are the most important type of witness, in most cases. The primary utility of eyewitnesses may be their memory of what they saw, read, heard, or otherwise experienced.

Character witnesses generally are only used for criminal cases, such as the sentencing stage. In the civil context, character witnesses are just used for a special type of civil case, one in which character is actually a main issue in the case (e.g., defamation).

Expert witnesses testify not so much about what the facts are, but what the facts *mean*. There are many different types of experts, such as economists, architects, accountants, plumbers, medical doctors, and accident reconstruction specialists. The U.S. Supreme Court and other federal and state courts typically demand that there be some scientific or other support as a prerequisite for expert testimony. Among the basic criteria that an expert's testimony must meet are relevance, reliability, and helpfulness to the trier of fact. To testify, the witness must have sufficient knowledge of the pertinent field (e.g., a medical specialty) and of the facts in the case itself so as to enable the expert to express a reasonably accurate conclusion.

EXPERT WITNESS RULES

Federal Rule of Evidence 702 presents the basic qualifications a witness must have to be qualified as an expert: "knowledge, skill, experience, training, or education." Federal Rule of Evidence 703 lays out what information may form the basis of an expert opinion ("facts or data in the case that the expert has been made aware of or personally observed"). These two categories (facts and data *made aware of* and those that arise from *personal knowledge*) in effect describe three bases for expert testimony: firsthand knowledge, facts learned at trial, and outside information (facts on which others in the field can reasonably rely). Rule 703 often allows experts to rely on otherwise inadmissible evidence to reach their conclusions.

Federal Rule of Evidence 704 allows experts to do something they could not do under earlier rules: give an opinion on an ultimate issue in a case, such as whether the defendant is liable. One limitation exists in Rule 704(b), which prohibits an opinion on a criminal defendant's mental state if that mental state is an element of the criminal charges or defenses.

Federal Rule of Evidence 706 allows judges to appoint expert witnesses who are to be made available to both sides, to work for the court, or otherwise to assist the judge in reaching a just outcome. This practice has seen limited use in the United States but is commonly practiced in many nations, especially civil law countries such as France.

As for nonexperts, Federal Rule of Evidence 701 limits a lay witness' opinion testimony to statements "(a) rationally based on the witness's perception; (b) helpful to clearly understanding the witness's testimony or to determining a fact in issue; and (c) not based on scientific, technical, or other specialized knowledge within the scope of Rule 702" (a true expert is, of course, the witness best suited for offering testimony based on any special knowledge). Rule 701 recognizes that facts and opinion are not completely separable, so a lay witness can testify in the form of an opinion as long as such testimony is based on his/her own perceptions and is necessary for the jury or judge to understand the testimony.

For their court proceedings, most states have rules of evidence similar to the federal rules.

MOTIONS AFTER TRIAL

Under rare circumstances, in civil cases the judge may grant a *motion for judgment notwithstanding the verdict* (sometimes called **"J.N.O.V.,"** for **judgment** *non obstante veredicto*); there, after the jury has rendered a verdict for one party, the judge finds that there was insufficient evidence to support the jury's conclusions, and *enters a judgment for the other side*. This is a serious measure, and the judge's interpretation of evidence at the trial must meet very high standards.

Either attorney can request that the trial court grant a *new trial*, usually for one or more of the following reasons: (1) erroneous interpretations of the substantive law, (2) erroneous admission or exclusion of evidence, (3) insufficient evidence and/or a verdict contrary to law, (4) excessive or inadequate damages award, (5) jury misconduct or other irregularities, and (6) newly discovered evidence. Often these grounds, particularly (1) through (4), serve as the basis for an appeal requesting reversal or a new trial.

THE APPEAL

Each party to a lawsuit generally is entitled to one **appeal**, which is held in an appellate court. Consideration of further appeals (e.g., to the state or U.S. Supreme Court) is usually discretionary: such appeals can be, and often are, summarily denied (without any hearing).

Appellate courts do not hold trials. There are no witnesses or juries. The court simply reviews the record of the trial and the briefs submitted by the parties' attorneys. In an especially important case, a nonparty (usually a governmental or other institutional group) may file an *amicus curiae* ("friend of the court") brief.

A **brief** is a written argument supported by citations of prior court decisions, statutes, or other authorities. (Alas, briefs often are not brief.)

The attorneys may present oral arguments, which are usually not so much polished speeches as short statements of key points. They must also answer searching questions from the judges. When the court reaches a decision, it issues a written opinion that can provide future guidance in similar cases.

Opinions—in whole or in part—may affirm the original judgment, reverse it, instruct the lower court to issue a new judgment, and/or remand (i.e., send back) the case to the lower court for further proceedings. Appellate courts rarely reverse the trial court for its factual findings; to do so requires that the findings be unsupported or contradicted by the evidence. (Mere belief that the lower court, or jury, did not draw the right factual conclusions is insufficient grounds for reversal.) Any holding other than affirmance almost always must be based on errors of law.

ENFORCEMENT OF A JUDGMENT

A monetary judgment is a debt. If the losing party does not pay the judgment, the judgment creditor (winning party) may collect by using one or more of the debt-collection methods discussed in Chapter 13.

YOU SHOULD REMEMBER

Some of the more important pleadings are the complaint, answer, motion to dismiss, counterclaim, and motion for summary judgment.

There are four major types of discovery: *depositions, interrogatories, requests for admissions,* and *document production.* Each has its advantages and limitations.

The scenario for a lawsuit is as follows:

1. Alleged injury to plaintiff.

2. Complaint filed by plaintiff or his/her attorney.

3. Answer and/or preliminary motions by defendant or his/her attorney.

4. Discovery and pretrial motions.

5. Pretrial conference.

6. Trial.

7. Posttrial motions.

8. Appeal.

Summary judgment motions can occur from the time the complaint is filed until the trial. Attempts to settle the case are almost always possible, from before the case is filed through the appeals stage.

In a jury trial, the jury decides the factual disputes, while the judge interprets the law and instructs the jury on the law.

The plaintiff generally has the burden of proof (persuasion). In civil cases, he/she need only have a preponderance of evidence in his/her favor; criminal cases require that the prosecution produce proof of guilt beyond a reasonable doubt.

A trial judge can overturn a jury verdict, but to do so requires much more than simply a belief that the jury drew the wrong factual conclusions.

An appeal does not entail a new trial. The appellate court must consider the law as a whole; its function is to furnish future guidance, not simply resolve an individual dispute.

An appellate court usually affirms the lower court's judgment. However, if the appeal is well founded in law, not merely a claim that the facts are different from what was decided by the jury or trial judge, an appeals court may reverse, instruct the lower court to issue a new judgment, or remand for further proceedings.

OUT-OF-COURT PROCEDURES FOR SETTLING DISPUTES

The vast majority of disputes are settled out of court. Most do not even reach the point where a suit is actually filed. If a complaint is filed, settlement usually occurs before trial.

Several factors may spur compromise, including (1) anxiety about going to court (more broadly, the psychological costs of bringing or defending legal claims), (2) the time and expense of lawsuits, (3) concern about bad publicity, (4) the need for a speedier resolution, (5) uncertainty as to outcome, (6) the amount of potential damages awards, including any prejudgment interest, and (7) a desire to maintain good business or personal relationships with the other party.

Alternative Dispute Resolution (ADR)—rather than going to court—is a fast-growing phenomenon featuring such *private* approaches as using "early neutral evaluations" of the case, "renting" retired judges, or holding summary (expedited and nonbinding) jury trials or "minitrials." (The Judicial Improvements Act (1990) and the Alternative Dispute Resolution Act (1998) encourage and in some cases require the use of ADR by federal district courts. Many states have comparable laws for their courts. Also, ADR is often sought in administrative disputes—e.g., the Administrative Dispute Resolution Act (1990) authorizes federal agencies to use ADR.)

The two most frequently used out-of-court methods of dispute resolution are mediation and arbitration. Both involve neutral third parties who often are familiar with, or even experts in, the contested subjects.

MEDIATION

In **mediation**, a third party (mediator) helps the disputing parties to settle the case. *Mediators cannot impose a settlement* on the parties, but often, by such means as separate, private consultations with each party and neutral recommendations to both sides, mediators can effect a compromise. Besides possibly leading to a settlement agreement between the disputants, mediation can also assist them in investigating the facts, defining and clarifying issues, understanding others' perspectives, identifying common interests, and evaluating potential solutions.

Mediation is increasingly used in settling labor disputes (the function of the Federal Mediation and Conciliation Service) and in resolving consumer complaints (via state or local government agencies or such private groups as the Better Business Bureau). Indeed, some laws mandate the use of mediation; for instance, when a business has an informal dispute-resolution system for complaints about its product warranties, an amendment to the Federal Trade Commission Act requires that parties first attempt mediation before filing a lawsuit for breach of warranty.

ARBITRATION

Of course, mediation can accomplish little when the parties themselves are unwilling to compromise. In such cases, **arbitration** may work. *Unlike a mediator, an arbitrator has the power to make a final, binding decision.* Arbitration is usually a shorter, cheaper version of litigation. Both sides present evidence and arguments, although often in a more informal manner than in court trials.

A dispute usually goes to arbitration because a contract either requires it or permits a party to request it. In certain instances (e.g., medical malpractice), a state law may mandate arbitration. Parties seeking to avoid arbitration, despite a contractual provision requiring it, may run headlong into either the Federal Arbitration Act (1925) (FAA) or the Uniform Arbitration Act (adopted by most states). Both acts broadly support arbitration, and **courts almost always will compel parties to keep their agreements to arbitrate**. For example, in *CompuCredit Corp. v. Greenwood*, 565 U.S. __ (2012), the U.S. Supreme Court held that since the Credit Repair Organizations Act (1996) is silent on whether claims can proceed in an arbitration forum, the FAA requires the parties' arbitration agreement to be enforced against consumers according to that agreement's terms. Likewise, in cases where plaintiffs were employees, clients of talent agents, consumers, or franchisees challenging arbitration clauses, the U.S. Supreme Court has routinely overturned as superseded by the FAA various state laws lodging primary jurisdiction in any other nonarbitration forum, whether judicial or administrative.[2] Also, in *14 Penn Plaza LLC v. Pyett*, 556 U.S. 247 (2009) the U.S. Supreme Court upheld contract clauses that required arbitration rather than litigation, for age discrimination claims, per a collective bargaining agreement.

The arbitrator's power may extend to transactions between foreign and American businesses and to the establishment of policy related to contracts. In *Mitsubishi Motors Corp. v. Soler Chrysler-Plymouth*, 473 U.S. 614 (1985), the U.S. Supreme Court significantly bolstered the use of arbitration when it upheld a contract clause requiring arbitration abroad, even though that meant certain claims or defenses recognized under American law might not be available to the parties. In *Nitro-Lift Technologies, LLC v. Howard*, 568 U.S. __ (2012), the U.S. Supreme Court held that an employee's non-compete agreement with the employer was to be interpreted by an arbitrator, not state courts, per the employment agreement's arbitration clause. The FAA rendered the arbitrator's decision-making power superior to that of state law.

Most arbitration decisions are binding throughout almost all of the world under the UN Convention on the Recognition and Enforcement of Foreign Arbitral Awards (ratified by the United States and 153 other nations).

---

[2] A typical case is *AT&T Mobility LLC v. Concepcion*, 563 U.S. __ (2011). The U.S. Supreme Court concluded that states must enforce arbitration clauses in consumer contracts even if a state law would deem unenforceable the clause's waiver of class action rights. For these cases, the FAA trumps state law and requires individual arbitration rather than allowing class action litigation. In *American Express Co. v. Italian Colors Restaurant*, 569 U.S. __ (2013), the Supreme Court held that the FAA does not permit courts to invalidate a contractual waiver if such arbitration requirements are enforceable even when the cost of a plaintiff's pursuing an individual claim is likely to exceed the damage recovery.

State Approaches to Arbitration Legislation

1. A few states have no legislation; they just have the common law. A final arbitration award is enforceable, but until that point the agreement to arbitrate likely is revocable.

2. Some state statutes provide only a method for enforcing arbitration awards. An agreement to arbitrate remains, for the most part, revocable until arbitration has actually occurred.

3. Most states have comprehensive statutes covering all aspects of submission to arbitration, the issuance of an award, and enforcement. A party cannot unilaterally revoke his/her agreement to arbitrate if that submission to arbitration has followed the statutory rules (otherwise, it is treated as common law arbitration, thus remaining revocable, like the first two approaches).

4. Some states make their state statutory provisions exclusive. Submission to arbitration, the proceedings, any award, and enforcement must all follow the state legislation. If not followed, the arbitration agreement and any award are a nullity; if followed, the agreement is irrevocable and the award is enforceable.

Most states require that arbitration agreements must be in writing to be binding. Except for the exclusive approach of the fourth approach, above, a failure to follow the state statute (e.g., to not have the arbitration agreement in writing) does not necessarily doom an attempt to arbitrate, as the parties may still pursue any form of arbitration allowed under the common law.

Once arbitration is completed, grounds for appeal are extremely limited. Courts are to overturn an arbitration award only *if* (1) it went beyond the matters submitted to the arbitrator(s), or (2) the arbitrator(s) failed to follow statutory requirements (e.g., acted in complete disregard of evidence), or (3) the award arose out of fraud, partiality, or corruption. Clearly, an *arbitration award is even less susceptible to reversal than is a court judgment.* Because arbitration usually saves money and time, often promotes less hostile relations than litigation, and can, when necessary, submit complex issues to experts, arbitration clauses are routinely placed in many business contracts. Information about arbitration clauses, as well as experienced arbitrators, can be obtained from the American Arbitration Association, a nonprofit, private organization founded in 1926 to improve and promote arbitration techniques.

YOU SHOULD REMEMBER

The vast majority of cases never come to trial; they are settled before-hand. *Mediation* and *arbitration* entail the out-of-court use of third persons (mediators or arbitrators) to resolve disputes. A mediator cannot impose a settlement, but an arbitrator's decision is final (subject only to very narrow grounds for appeal).

ADMINISTRATIVE AGENCY PROCEEDINGS

All government, both state and federal, operates through agencies which are generally legislatively created. These agencies are given carefully drawn duties and responsibilities among which are the duties to promulgate rules and regulations, a quasi-legislative function. The agency may also exercise a quasi judicial function since due process under the Fifth and Fourteenth Amendments requires that notice be given and a hearing held whenever a person is to be deprived of "life, liberty or property." Generally, this hearing must be held before the agency.

Examples: Administrative Deprivations of Liberty or Property (thus requiring a hearing)

- Revocation or suspension of a license to operate a motor vehicle.
- Revocation of a professional or business operating license.
- Cessation or reduction of welfare.
- Cessation or reduction of unemployment or social security benefits.
- Firing of a tenured teacher or—in most instances—a public employee.
- Revocation of parole.
- Termination of parental custodial rights.

The adoption of rules and regulations, as well as the holding of hearings, is governed by federal and state Administrative Procedure Acts. Under these Acts, the rules of evidence are relaxed (even hearsay evidence may be given some weight) and the hearing officer may play a more active, inquisitive role than is customary in U.S. courts. Nevertheless, basic fairness may not be disregarded. For instance, as in a court trial, each party has a right to counsel and is entitled to state his/her case and to cross-examine opposing witnesses. Moreover, although an agency may have considerable discretion in outlining the format of its hearings, it must, like a court of law, render decisions based only on the evidence presented. In cases involving administrative law, there is no right to a trial by jury. However, a dissatisfied party may appeal for judicial review of the case on the hearing record.

Many agencies have a staff of *administrative law judges* (hearing examiners) who are separate from the investigatory or prosecutory personnel. Most important federal agencies provide for intraagency appeals from the rulings of the administrative law judges to the board or commission at the top of the agency; some agencies also have intermediate review boards. Many states have created independent offices of administrative hearings; this completely separates the judicial function from a particular agency's executive, enforcement function and assures the citizen of an unbiased due process hearing.

Exhaustion of remedies: The doctrine whereby court appeals are not permitted until administrative remedies are exhausted. Before complaining to a court of law, the appellant must use all available agency procedures that are required by statute or regulation.

The exhaustion of remedies doctrine may be discarded in certain rare circumstances:

1. An administrative procedure is unconstitutional, illegal, or otherwise exceeds agency authority.
2. The case involves fundamental constitutional guarantees (e.g., free speech).
3. The agency is deadlocked or hopelessly behind in its docket schedule.
4. Irreparable harm is likely to occur if court relief is not permitted.
5. An appeal within the agency is not required by agency rule or by statute.

THE INQUISITORIAL APPROACH AND THE ADVERSARIAL MODEL

Most Civil Law nations follow the inquisitorial approach for their trials. This means there is an inquiry into the facts, directed from above, by the judge or magistrate.[3] As a result, inquisitorial judges have a strong role in

---

[3] In France and many other countries following the French legal tradition, judicial officers—*huissiers*—may conduct extensive inquiries, including the examination of documents, the viewing of premises, and the questioning of witnesses; these legally-trained officials then draft statements of facts for the court to use in deciding the case. These statements (*constats*) supplant much of the discovery and eyewitness testimony that occurs in the United States. This neutral, inquisitorial approach even extends to matters of expert testimony, where the judge often appoints experts in that field to compile a comprehensive report summarizing the relevant facts and providing an opinion about those facts.

finding and developing the facts, not just applying the law to the facts. In Germany, for example, the judge, not the lawyers, (1) decides which witnesses to call, and (2) interrogates the witnesses.

In the United States and the countries following the adversarial model (basically, the common law nations), the judge's role is usually limited to applying the law to the facts of the case. However, there is a similarity to the inquisitorial system, although rarely used: Since 1975 the Federal Rules of Evidence have permitted federal trial judges to appoint independent experts to help them assess the expert testimony or otherwise sort through the evidence. The American judge typically makes such an appointment, if he/she ever does, only for highly complex, scientifically challenging cases. (For example, it was done in a silicone breast implant federal class-action case.)

Especially since 2003, Federal Rule of Civil Procedure 53 affords to federal judges broad rights to appoint special masters (people with broad judicial power for a particular case). The master's work could be on any or all aspects of a case: pretrial, trial, and post-trial. State rules may also provide for court appointment of masters or neutral experts, but that, too, is not the tradition. In contrast, Civil Law judges, such as in France, routinely rely upon such assistance.

Common law judges generally have far more of a role developing the law than do Civil Law judges. On the other hand, as part of an adversarial system, common law judges usually have a much lesser role developing the facts than do the Civil Law judges presiding under an inquisitorial system. *In the adversarial system, the attorneys and parties develop and present the facts.* The idea is that as the opposing sides clash, the truth will arise. These parties have the time and incentives to find the facts much better than a judge or magistrate (the inquisitorial model) might.

However, how events are described often depends drastically on who is telling the story. Lawyers thus have been criticized as *hired guns* practicing "the tricks of the trade." Increasingly, for big adversarial system trials with well-heeled parties, a battery of consultants may help to choreograph the trial. The concern is that lawyers' actions and personalities may come to dominate how juries decide cases, and—for close cases—the adversarial system may exacerbate the potential for unfair results due to inequality of resources and/or experience.[4] So, whereas the inquisitorial process often resembles a routine business meeting, American trials, perhaps the most adversarial in the world, often are compared to theater.

---

[4] The adversarial system can be quite advantageous to those with more money or other resources. One may, for example, "paper the other side to death"; if a party does not have enough money, then it cannot respond on certain points and it cannot hire that effective-but-expensive expert. Unlike criminal cases, there tend to be no constitutional issues associated with having an inadequate civil lawyer.

An argument for the adversarial system is that its lawyers often serve as strong advocates for individual rights. The system may be *better* for ferreting out the truth and for bringing fully developed cases than the inquisitorial approach *if* both sides have competent counsel and there is no gross disparity in resources. It also probably reflects a free-market, individualistic culture better than does the government-centered inquisitorial approach.

YOU SHOULD REMEMBER

Due process under the Fifth and Fourteenth Amendments generally requires that notice be given and a *hearing* held before an administrative agency can render a decision that deprives a person of liberty or property. Administrative hearings are usually more informal than court cases but must be conducted fairly. In almost all cases, courts will not review an agency's decision until the administrative remedies have been exhausted.

HOW CASES ARE CITED

For the key case of *Marbury v. Madison*, 5 U.S. 137, 2 L. Ed. 60 (1803), in which Chief Justice John Marshall announced the doctrine of judicial review of federal and state actions, the citation means the following: 5 stands for the fifth volume of the United States Reports (the official record of the rulings, orders, case tables, and other U.S. Supreme Court proceedings), and 137 is the page number of that volume on which the case begins; 2 stands for the second volume of the Lawyers Edition (L. Ed.), and 60 is the beginning page number for the case; 1803 is the year of the decision. To identify a quotation or point taken from a case, a second page number may be added to show the page(s) from which the quotation or point is derived. For instance, if a point in *Marbury v. Madison* were taken from page 176 of the United States Reports and page 73 of the Lawyers Edition, the citation would be 5 U.S. 137, 176, 2 L. Ed. 60, 73 (1803).

Federal circuit court of appeals cases are found in the *Federal Reporter*, 1st, 2nd, or 3rd series (F., F.2d, or F.3d, respectively, with cases from the years 1880–1924 (F.), 1924–93 (F.2d), and 1993–present (F.3d)). Also, the *Federal Supplement* (F. Supp. and F. Supp. 2d—the latter from late 1997 onward) and the *Federal Rules Decisions* (F.R.D.) contain federal district court opinions.

Cases from the state appellate courts, including the District of Columbia, are found in the National Reporter System of the West Publishing

Company. The states are divided among seven regional reports: Atlantic (Atl. or A.), North Eastern (N.E.), North Western (N.W.), Pacific (Pac. or P.), South Eastern (S.E.), South Western (S.W.), and Southern (So.). Each of these reports has reached a second series (cited as A.2d., N.W.2d, S.E.2d, etc.) containing more recent cases, and three—the Pacific, the Southern, and the Southwestern—have reached a third (P.3d, So.3d, S.W.3d).

YOU SHOULD REMEMBER

Published opinions by the U.S. Supreme Court, federal circuit courts of appeals, federal district courts, and state appellate courts are cited in U.S. Supreme Court Reports, the Federal Reporter, the Federal Supplement, and the National Reporter System, respectively.

KNOW THE CONCEPTS
DO YOU KNOW THE BASICS?

1. State the three main levels of courts in the federal system.

2. Describe the differences between the functions of a trial court and an appellate court.

3. What is the key constitutional question concerning "long-arm" personal jurisdiction?

4. Distinguish jurisdiction from venue.

5. What state's substantive laws usually govern a tort case?

6. (a) State the general order of pleadings filed before a trial.

(b) What are the four main methods of discovery?

7. (a) Who usually has the burden of persuasion?

(b) Who has the burden of coming forward?

8. Name at least four reasons why disputes are compromised.

9. What is the most important difference between mediation and arbitration?

10. Give at least four examples of administrative deprivations of liberty or property (thus requiring a hearing).

11. Explain what each part of this citation means: *Brown v. Board of Education*, 347 U.S. 483 (1954).

TERMS FOR STUDY

Administrative Procedure Act
adversarial model
affirmative defenses
alternative dispute resolution
answer
appeals
arbitration
brief
certiorari
circuit court
class action
complaint
conflict of laws
counterclaim
cybercourtroom
defendant
demurrer
deposition
direct verdict
discovery
district court
diversity jurisdiction
exhaustion of remedies
extradite
federal questions
"full faith and credit" clause

grand jury
huissiers
inquisitorial approach
interrogatories
J.N.O.V. (judgment *non obstante
veredicto*)
jurisdiction
"long-arm statutes"
mediation
motions
motion to dismiss
opening statements
personal (*in personam*)
 jurisdiction
petitioner
petit jury
plaintiff
pleadings
requests for admissions
respondent
summary judgment
summation
summons
trial
venue
voir dire

PRACTICAL APPLICATION

1. Susie Sharp wants to sue Hap Hapless for breach of contract. Susie lives in New York, and Hap lives in Massachusetts. The contract was signed at a business meeting in Boston. Hap has not been outside Massachusetts for years, nor has he done any business elsewhere.
    (a) In what court can Susie sue?
    (b) In what court does Susie's right to sue depend on the amount in controversy?
    (c) Why is Susie unlikely to be able to sue elsewhere?
    (d) What happens if the contract specifies that it is to be governed by New York law? Discuss both personal jurisdiction and conflict of laws.

(e) Assume that New York gives defendants a longer time to answer a complaint than does Massachusetts. Which time period can Hap use?

2. Hap refuses to answer Susie's complaint. Susie obtains a judgment, including a damages award, by default. Hap moves to another state, one that generally does not enforce the type of contract that Susie and Hap had. May Susie use the new state's courts to collect her money (damages) from Hap?

3. Hap does not leave Massachusetts. He answers and files a motion for summary judgment, with an affidavit saying that he has never met anyone named Susie Sharp, that there was no contract, and that the signature on the alleged contract is not his. Will he win? What is the standard for granting summary judgment?

4. On Monday, a dissatisfied customer files a complaint about Dew Processing, Incorporated (Dew). On Tuesday, an official at the State Board of Business calls the president of Dew and informs him of the complaint. On Wednesday, Dew receives notice that its consumer sales license has been suspended. What preliminary request for relief should Dew make? Discuss the problems of administrative procedure presented by this case.

5. At an administrative hearing, the Administrative Law Judge (ALJ) bases his decision on inadmissible evidence, unauthenticated records, and the ALJ's own knowledge of customs in the industry. He also talked about the case while on the telephone with one of the parties.

The ALJ permitted testimony from all witnesses but allowed cross-examination of only the witnesses who were also parties. In an oral opinion announcing his holding, the ALJ did not clearly state the reasons for his decision. What problems, if any, are there with the ALJ's conduct of the case?

6. A case is cited as follows: 63 A.2d 221. Where would you find that case?

ANSWERS
KNOW THE CONCEPTS

1. District courts, circuit courts, U.S. Supreme Court.
2. In a jury trial, the trial judge interprets the law and instructs the jury on the law. He/she makes rulings on evidence and any motions. In a nonjury trial, the trial judge also assumes the jury's role and decides factual disputes.

An appellate court does not retry the case. It does not hear witnesses. Rather, it reviews the lower court case for errors of law. Factual findings can be overturned only if they are not at all supported by the evidence.

3. The key question is: Has the defendant had enough "minimal contacts" within the state so that requiring him/her to defend a lawsuit there does not violate due process of law?

4. Jurisdiction involves a court's power to decide the issues in a case (subject-matter jurisdiction) and to bind parties (personal jurisdiction). Once jurisdiction has been established, the question of venue is merely a matter of deciding whether a particular locale (e.g., county) is the proper place to bring suit.

5. The state where the injury occurred.

6. (a) (1) Complaint, (2) motion to dismiss (optional), (3) answer, (4) counterclaim (optional). At any time, until shortly before trial, discovery requests, summary judgment motions, and other motions are possible.

(b) Depositions, interrogatories, requests for admissions, and document production.

7. (a) The plaintiff.

(b) Whichever party alleges the fact in question.

8. (1) Anxiety about going to court, (2) time and expense of lawsuits, (3) worries about bad publicity, (4) need for a speedy resolution, (5) uncertainty as to outcome, (6) desire to maintain personal or business relationship with other side.

9. Mediation cannot force a settlement; arbitration can. Arbitration, in essence, substitutes for a court trial.

10. Revocation of a professional or business operating license, cessation or reduction of welfare, cessation or reduction of unemployment or social security benefits, firing of a tenured teacher or (in most cases) another public employee, revocation of parole, termination of parental custodial rights.

11. Brown was a plaintiff and the Board of Education was the defendant. The U.S. Supreme Court opinion is in Volume 347 of the United States Reports, starting at page 483. The case was decided in 1954.

PRACTICAL APPLICATION

1. (a) Massachusetts state court.

(b) Susie can sue in the federal court in Massachusetts if the alleged contract was worth more than $75,000 (diversity jurisdiction).

(c) It does not appear that Hap would be subject to another state's (e.g., New York's) long-arm jurisdiction; thus, no personal jurisdiction.

(d) This probably would have no effect on personal jurisdiction. However, it should mean that the Massachusetts court must interpret the contract according to New York law, as that is the law intended by the contracting parties.

(e) The one allowed by the court where he has been sued (presumably, Massachusetts). This is a matter of procedure, not substantive law.

2. Yes. The Massachusetts judgment is entitled to "full faith and credit."

3. Most unlikely because summary judgments can be granted only if there is (1) no genuine issue about the material facts, and (2) entitlement to judgment on the law applicable to the material facts.

Susie's complaint probably sets forth enough facts to show that there is a material factual dispute between the parties as to whether there was a contract and whether Hap was a party to it. To be on the safe side (especially since Hap asserts that he never met Susie), Susie should probably file her own affidavit countering Hap's contentions and/or showing why his points are irrelevant (e.g., she acted through her agent and hence never met Hap).

4. Request that the suspension be lifted until a hearing has taken place. The State Board's action in suspending Dew's license without a hearing and perhaps without proper notice (telephone call enough?) may supersede agency authority and/or due process.

Dew has a property interest in the license. Generally, administrative deprivations of property (or liberty) can only follow due notice and a hearing. The main exception is an emergency situation, which does not appear to be the case here.

Dew may attempt to exhaust its administrative remedies before going to court, although on these facts some courts would not let the exhaustion of remedies doctrine operate to bar judicial relief.

5. ALJs usually have much more discretion than courts of law with respect to rules of evidence and the overall conduct of a trial. The improper activities were (1) talking about the case with one party while the other party was not present, and (2) not permitting cross-examination of all witnesses. Due process and, more likely, the enabling act and/or agency regulations would require that the ALJ's findings of fact (reasons for his decision) be stated to the parties.

6. In volume 63 of the Atlantic Reports (second series), starting on page 221.

CONTRACTS

4

NATURE, CLASSIFICATION, AND FORMATION

KEY TERMS

contract a legally enforceable agreement, express or implied

agreement a meeting of the minds

consideration something (a promise, an action, forbearance) a party provides in exchange for something from the other party (a promise, an act, forbearance)

statute of limitations a statute setting forth the period during which a lawsuit must be brought after a right to sue arises

---

NATURE OF CONTRACTS

Contract law is a foundation upon which is built many other areas of business law, such as corporations, agency, employment, partnerships, sales, commercial paper, and secured transactions. The law of contracts is a framework to ensure that lawful expectations are met or that remedies are provided.

WHAT IS A CONTRACT?

A **contract** is a legally enforceable agreement, express or implied. There are four essential elements of a valid contract:

1. Capacity of the parties.
2. Mutual agreement (assent) or meeting of the minds (a valid offer and acceptance).

3. Consideration (something of value given in exchange for a promise).

4. Legality of subject matter.

Just as law is a rule that society will enforce, so a contract is also an enforced rule of society. That the rule to be enforced is derived from voluntary agreements between individuals does not make it any less a rule, or any less enforceable. Once a contract has been made, that contract is as binding upon the parties as any statute or any other law, and one party cannot withdraw without additional agreement by the other party or parties.

Most people make a number of contracts during each day. Every cab ride, purchase of a grocery item, use of a soft drink machine, or appointment with a doctor involves a contractual relationship. It does not matter that these contracts are oral, or are based on gestures or even on a course of conduct. Mere informality does not render a contract less binding.

As defined above, a contract is a legally enforceable agreement; an agreement is a meeting of the minds. Since courts and juries are not mind readers, the existence of this mental condition must be manifest in words, oral or written, or in actions. ("Verbal" is not a synonym for "oral"; *verbal* includes all words, written as well as oral.) The mental condition that forms the agreement should be distinguished from the words or actions giving evidence of the mental condition. Although we sometimes call a written document a "contract," the document is only evidence of the mental agreement that constitutes the actual contract.

HOW MAY INTENT BE DETERMINED?

Let's assume that the words used, the action taken, or both the words and the actions would convince a reasonable person, such as a member of a jury, that there is a meeting of the minds and hence a contract. But suppose that there is trouble determining precisely what the agreement is, that the *intent* is clouded by ambiguity, contradiction, or vagueness. How can an observer arrive at an understanding of the real agreement existing in the minds of the parties? The **basic principle of contract interpretation** is to determine the *intent* of the parties from words or actions taken as a whole, not from isolated words, actions, or events.

Certain commonsense rules may be used to resolve contradictions and uncertainties. Fine print, obscurely placed, is given less weight than large, boldface type; handwritten interlineations, especially if initialed, are strong evidence of firm intention. Formal documents, diligently executed, may yield to conduct of the parties if that conduct clearly shows a mutual intent contrary to the written document.

YOU SHOULD REMEMBER

The four essential elements of a contract are competent parties, mutual agreement, consideration, and legality.

Contracts arise out of agreements that are purely mental; hence a contract really exists in the mind. This mental condition is shown by actions, by oral or written words, and rarely, by silence or inaction.

In interpreting a contract, a court tries to determine the *intent* of the parties from words and actions considered in their entirety.

CLASSIFICATION OF CONTRACTS

Contracts can be classified in several different ways.

BY TYPE OF FORMATION: EXPRESS VERSUS IMPLIED

An **express contract** is stated in words, written or oral, or partly written and partly oral. The express contract is overtly, consciously, and specifically arrived at.

There are two types of implied contracts: those implied in fact and those implied in law.

The existence and the terms of an **implied-in-fact contract** are manifested by conduct, rather than words. The proof of the contract lies in the conduct of the parties; a reasonable person aware of this conduct, including words, if any, would infer that a contract exists.

An **implied-in-law** or **quasi contract** is created by operation of law (i.e., a court implies a contract) in order to avoid *unjust enrichment* of one party at the expense of another. *There is no agreement, no meeting of the minds*; one party has rendered a benefit to another under such circumstances that fairness and equity require compensation.

Example: A Quasi Contract

Stanley Samaritan, M.D., renders assistance to an unconscious person on a city sidewalk. When the patient recovers, he receives a bill for these services.

Since the patient received and benefitted from the services, he may be required to pay on grounds of quasi contract.

The amount of compensation due under a quasi contract is the current market price (called *quantum meruit*, "as much as he/she earned"), not a special price or even the performer's usual rate. In the example above, Dr. Samaritan is entitled to the ordinary rate of pay of a general physician rendering these services, even if Samaritan is a specialist ordinarily receiving thousands of dollars for his work.

BY TYPE OF PERFORMANCE

• *BILATERAL VERSUS UNILATERAL*

A **bilateral contract** is based on an exchange of promises—a promise for a promise.

Example: A Bilateral Contract

Roommate Robert offers to make for Lodger Louise a deluxe grilled cheese sandwich in return for Louise's promise to clean the kitchen after she eats the sandwich. Louise agrees to those terms. There is an exchange of Robert's promise (to make the sandwich) for Louise's promise (to clean the kitchen).

A **unilateral contract** involves a promise by one party and an act by the other. If, however, the person receiving the offer promises to act before doing so, the contract may become bilateral.

Example: A Unilateral Contract

If a homeowner offers a man $25.00 to mow her lawn, this is an offer to make a unilateral contract. The offer is a promise (to pay $25.00) in exchange for the performance of an act (mowing the lawn).

• *EXECUTED VERSUS EXECUTORY*

An **executed contract** is one that has been fully performed by both parties; all promises have been fulfilled.

In an **executory contract** something remains to be done by one or both parties.

BY ENFORCEABILITY: VALID VERSUS UNENFORCEABLE, VOID, AND VOIDABLE CONTRACTS

A **valid contract** meets all legal requirements and can be enforced by either party.

An **unenforceable contract** does not meet one or more legal requirements and cannot be enforced by either party. Examples are promises to make a gift (no consideration), promises made in jest (no contractual intent), agreements that fail to meet Statute of Frauds requirements (see pages 141–147), and past breaches of contract now beyond the statute of limitations.

A **void contract** has no validity and cannot be enforced by either party. Examples are illegal agreements made under threat of physical force.

A **voidable contract** is binding on only one of the parties. The other party has the option to withdraw from the contract or enforce it. Examples are contracts made by minors and contracts made under mental duress.

YOU SHOULD REMEMBER

Contracts may be classified by type of formation (express or implied), performance (unilateral or bilateral, executed or executory), or enforceability (valid or unenforceable, void, or voidable).

NEGOTIATION

The word "negotiation" is derived from the Latin *negotium*, meaning "business" or, literally, "the absence of leisure." Since a contract (except a quasi contract) arises out of an agreement, and an agreement is a meeting of the minds, it is clear that most minds meet through the transaction of business, or through **negotiation**.

STEP-BY-STEP FORMATION OF AN AGREEMENT BETWEEN TWO PARTIES

1. Negotiations begin with discussion or exchange of comments to determine mutual interest in making a deal.
2. Mutual interest is clarified and refined in terms of both parties' basic objectives, such as description of goods to be sold, work to be performed, and price for goods or services.
3. The contract subject is defined, with a price agreed upon.
4. The deal is now worked out in detail (e.g., method of payment, guarantees, delivery place, and date).
5. The contract is formally accepted—a written agreement is prepared and executed, or the parties shake hands or otherwise express an intention to be bound.

Implied contracts are far more informal in their negotiation than are express contracts. Implied contracts may arise entirely from actions, but these actions must be so clear that no reasonable person (member of a jury, for example) would doubt the existence of a meeting of the minds. In the case of an implied contract, the performer is entitled to receive his/her current rate of pay for services rendered, since it is implied that the other party should have expected to pay that price. Under a quasi contract, as mentioned previously, the compensation is *quantum meruit*, the current market rate.

Express contracts are usually formal; certainly the fact that the contract exists is more formally expressed.

The express contract is often revealed through *words of contract*: "agree," "agreement," "promise," "offer," "accept," or even the very word "contract."

Most legal writers treat the negotiation of an express contract as though it invariably transpires through a formal offer and the acceptance of that offer. As a matter of fact, however, it may be difficult to say which party extends the offer (is the *offeror*) and which accepts the offer (is the *offeree*).

Example: Negotiation as Flirtation

> Brown: "I like your car."
> Jones: "Yes, Smith offered me $5,000 for it last week."
> Brown: "That sounds like a good price. You should have sold it."
> Jones: "I would not take less than $7,000."
> Brown: "I would give you $6,000."
> Jones: "It's yours for $6,200."
> Brown: "Sold."

If the transaction is concluded at this point, most courts would construe the agreement as an express contract, *even without contract words*. In reality, it makes no legal difference that the offer and acceptance are not formally stated, or that the offeror or offeree cannot be identified or separated.

The Uniform Commercial Code defines an "agreement" as the bargain of the parties. This bargain is *always* derived from mutual assent, proved by outward actions or by spoken or written words. Subjective intent, not manifested by words or action, counts for little or nothing in a court of law.

YOU SHOULD REMEMBER

Most contracts are reached through negotiation, which may be formal or informal. Once there is a meeting of the minds on the fundamentals (an agreement), the parties are bound and neither party may withdraw without consent of the other.

FORMING A CONTRACT

Each of the four essential requirements—capacity of the parties, mutual agreement or assent, consideration, and legality—must be met in the formation of a valid contract.

CAPACITY OF THE PARTIES

Under the law, only a person who is legally competent has the power to make a binding contract and can be held to any promises contained therein. Persons who may be considered to be legally incompetent include minors, insane persons, and, sometimes under specified circumstances, intoxicated persons. This subject is discussed in detail in Chapter 6.

MUTUAL AGREEMENT (ASSENT): THE OFFER AND THE ACCEPTANCE

The mutual assent of the parties to a contract is manifested in two legal concepts, the offer and the acceptance.

• *THE OFFER*
The simplest way to form an express contract begins with a formal **offer**. This offer is transmitted directly to the offeree by acts or by words, whether spoken or written, through any medium whatsoever.

Requirements of an Offer

1. It must indicate a clear *intent* to make a contract.
2. It must be sufficiently *definite* so that a court can determine the actual intent of the parties.
3. It must be *communicated* to the other party.

The offer should contain the fundamental ingredients of the contract; then acceptance by the offeree will bind the deal. In communicating the offer, use of the word "offer" helps, but is not necessary, to show intent to make a contract. Even if the word "offer" is used, circumstances, actions, or other words may indicate that there is no real intent to enter into a valid contract. "Offers" made in obvious jest or under great emotional stress, for example, do not possess the requisite intent.

WHEN IS AN ADVERTISEMENT AN "OFFER"?

Things generally *not offers* are: opinions, plans, requests for bids, circulars, price quotations, invitations to deal, social invitations, price lists, preliminary negotiations, and statements of future intent ("I plan to sell my stock"). Similarly, general advertisements, agreements to agree, catalogs, brochures, and announcements are usually *not* offers because:

(a) they are not sufficiently definite,

(b) they are not communicated to a specific person or persons, *or*

(c) the circumstances of publication indicate lack of contractual intent.

Advertisements are usually considered to be "invitations to deal," that is, invitations to the public to make offers to the advertiser.

In the following circumstances, however, an advertisement *can* be construed to be an offer: *it is so specific to an identified or identifiable person or group* that contractual intent can be inferred.

Example: An Advertisement Construed to Be an Offer

A store places an ad in a newspaper that reads: "The first person in our store on Washington's Birthday will receive $100 toward the purchase of an appliance."

Courts would probably hold this to be an offer because it is addressed to an identifiable individual, not the general public. Therefore the first person in the store on the holiday named would be entitled to receive $100 toward his/her appliance.

Businesses generally should uphold *advertisements* as a matter of ethics and of maintaining goodwill (sustaining short-term losses rather than a long-term diminution of business because of fewer "repeat" customers). Businesses also often must honor their advertisements in order to comply with consumer protection laws (e.g., laws against "bait and switch" tactics). Egregious cases could even subject a business to fraud claims and possible punitive damages.

HOW DEFINITE MUST THE OFFER BE?

Although an offer must state the essential terms of the proposed contract, modern common law, as well as the Uniform Commercial Code, assumes that many unstated terms may be understood by the parties, may be implied, or may be matters of common sense. With respect to the sale of goods, Article 2 of the Uniform Commercial Code specifically provides that one or more terms (including even the proposed price) may be left open so long as there is a clear intention to make a contract. Under the present common law also, if the offeror offers to sell his hat for $20, it is implied, or understood, (a) that the price is payable in cash, and (b) that delivery is to occur, and payment to be made, with reasonable promptness.

HOW LONG DOES AN OFFER LAST?

If an offer does not specify a period of time during which it is to remain open, it expires after the passage of a reasonable time. What constitutes a reasonable time depends on the implied intention of the offeror as shown by the property or goods offered, customs of the trade or business, and the like. An offer to sell or buy perishable goods, such as fresh fruit or vegetables, or goods having an unstable or fluctuating market, such as stock or other securities, is generally held not to remain open as long as an offer to sell or buy real estate, a far more stable item.

When the time during which the offer is to remain open is specified, that time then becomes the expiration date. An offer may expire at an earlier time than stated, however, because of *rejection, counteroffer*, or the *death* or *incompetency* of either offeror or offeree.

WHEN CAN AN OFFER BE REVOKED?

Fundamental Principle of Contract Law
An offer may be withdrawn at any time before it is accepted.

An offer is like an outstretched hand—it may be pulled back at any time before it is clasped by the outstretched hand of the offeree. Even a firm offer, that is, one expressly stated to remain open for a specified time, may generally be withdrawn. Thus a person who makes a firm offer to sell his hat for $20 and promises to leave the offer open for one week may withdraw the offer immediately, or any time before acceptance. If not accepted within one week, the offer will have expired.

There are four exceptions to the easy right to withdrawal.

Option contracts: The **option contract** (usually referred to as an "option") commits the offeror to keep his/her offer open in return for a specified price. In other words, the offeror makes a contract to hold the offer open for some specified period, and is paid a consideration for this agreement.

Example: An Option Contract

An offeror offers to sell a farm for $100,000, agrees to hold this offer open for 7 days, and is paid $100 for this agreement to be held open.

In this example, if the offeror withdraws the offer by selling the farm to some other person within the 7-day period, this would be a breach of contract. The offeree (also called the "optionee") has no obligation to buy; he has paid $100 for the right to accept the offer within the 7-day period. If he does not buy, his $100 is not refunded; if he does buy, the $100 is not credited to the purchase price unless the option contract expressly so provides.

An option is an excellent legal device to provide the opportunity to think a proposition over, investigate a deal, or raise money to go through with the deal.

Unilateral contracts: Since a unilateral contract depends on the performance of an act by the offeree, some courts consider that the offer can be revoked unless there has been substantial performance. According to this view, in the example on page 96, the homeowner could revoke the contract even though the youngster had already mowed half the lawn. Other courts, however, hold that the offer cannot be revoked once the offeree has clearly commenced to perform; the commencement is treated as *consideration*. (See further on pages 105–110.)

The Uniform Commercial Code exception: Section 2-205 of the Uniform Commercial Code provides that a merchant's firm *written offer* to buy or sell goods cannot be revoked during the term specified in the offer, or, if no time is specified, for a reasonable period (but in either case the period of irrevocability shall not exceed 3 months).

Promissory estoppel: Described on page 109—if the offeree reasonably relies on the offer's being held open, and will suffer injustice if it is revoked, then the offer is deemed irrevocable.

YOU SHOULD REMEMBER

An offer must meet three requirements: it must be *communicated*, it must indicate a clear *intent* to make a contract, and it must be *definite*. However, many terms may be left unstated or may be implied or understood by the parties.

An advertisement is not an offer unless it is addressed specifically to an identified or identifiable person or group.

An offer lasts for the period of time stated or, if no time is stated, for a reasonable time. It may also expire by reason of rejection, counteroffer, or the death or incompetency of one of the parties.

> Generally, an offer may be withdrawn at any time before it is accepted. There are four exceptions: option contracts, the UCC exception stated in Section 2-205, promissory estoppel, and, according to some courts, unilateral contracts if clear commencement to perform has occurred.

• *THE ACCEPTANCE*

Acceptance of the offer clinches the contract. However, the acceptance must meet certain standards.

First, the acceptance must be *clear* and *unqualified*; an "acceptance" that modifies the offer or attempts to get a better deal is treated in the law as a **counteroffer**, that is, a rejection of the original offer and the making of a new offer. Thus, if an offeror offers to sell his hat for $20, and the offeree says, "I can't pay $20, but I will give you $12," the offeree becomes the offeror for $12. If the original offeror rejects the $12 offer, the original offer is "dead" and cannot be revived by the original offeree.

Second, the offeree *must accept in any manner required by the offer*. If the offer states, "I must have your answer by 1 P.M. on December 1," then failure to have the answer in the hands of the offeror by that time is fatal to the contract.

HOW MAY AN ACCEPTANCE BE TRANSMITTED?

Prior to the Uniform Commercial Code, the common law gave special status to acceptance by the same medium as was used to transmit the offer. Thus, if the offer was mailed, the acceptance was good upon being *placed* with the mail carrier or in the post office—effective, as a matter of fact, more speedily than if made by wire, in which case the acceptance had to be received to bind the contract. According to UCC 2-206(1)(a), however, acceptance in any manner or by any medium, so long as reasonable and meeting the requirements of the offer (if any), is as effective as any other method.

WHAT CONSTITUTES ACCEPTANCE OF A UNILATERAL OFFER?

We have defined a unilateral contract as a promise in exchange for an act. Thus an order for 100,000 steel widgets to be shipped for a price of $100,000 is unilateral: upon delivery of the widgets the contract will have been made. Under UCC 2-206(1)(b), an offer to buy goods to be shipped may be accepted either by performance (shipment of the goods) *or by a promise to act*; the latter effectively converts a unilateral offer to a *bilateral* contract, something the common law would not permit.

Since some courts, as well as the Uniform Commercial Code, Section 2-206(2), take the view that failure by the offeree to notify the offeror of acceptance of the order or offer gives the offeror the right to withdraw, good business dictates that the offeree of a unilateral offer transmit an acceptance *before commencing to act*, particularly when fulfillment of the contract will be expensive and laborious. Equitable principles of fair play may operate in many courts to favor an innocent party who has acted in good faith in reliance upon the unilateral offer and has clearly *begun* to do the requested act before the offer was withdrawn. Of course, substantially performing or completing the requested act constitutes acceptance in all courts.

DOES SILENCE CONSTITUTE ACCEPTANCE?

Generally, silence is not acceptance, nor can the offeror impose a duty upon the offeree to speak. This principle is found not just in American law, but also in international law. Article 18(1) of the Convention on Contracts for the International Sale of Goods (the CISG, discussed in later chapters) states, "Silence or inactivity does not in itself amount to acceptance."

"If I do not hear from you, I will assume that you have accepted my offer" does not operate to impose a duty of any kind on the offeree. Indeed, if such a statement, in writing or otherwise, accompanies goods that have not been ordered, no duty arises to pay, even if the goods are not returned and are consumed. There is no implied-in-fact contract because the circumstances do not give rise to the inference of an agreement; there is no quasi contract because there is no unjust enrichment.

There are, however, certain circumstances under which silence may give rise to acceptance.

1. If the offeror observes the offeree acting in response to the offer, and says nothing, there may be a contract.

2. The parties may mutually agree that silence will constitute acceptance by the recipient of goods that are shipped to him/her (record and book clubs use this approach).

3. If the parties, by previous dealings, have considered silence to be acceptance, the silent party must reject the offer if he/she wishes to change the customary practice.

Good business (if not good law) indicates that a written rejection should be sent to the offeror when silence could be reasonably considered ambiguous or the outcome doubtful.

YOU SHOULD REMEMBER

The acceptance of an offer should be clear and unconditional. A conditional acceptance is treated as a counteroffer, and is a new offer and, hence, a rejection.

Some courts hold that a unilateral offer is accepted by a clear commencement to perform the act requested. Since the offeror may withdraw his/her offer (and promise), however, the offeree should confirm acceptance and thereby bind the contract as a bilateral contract.

Silence does not constitute acceptance unless (1) the offeror, observing the offeree acting in response to the offer, says nothing; (2) the parties mutually agree that silence means acceptance; or (3) in previous dealings, the parties have considered silence to be acceptance.

• *LACK OF MUTUAL ASSENT*

Mutual assent may be lacking for a variety of reasons, including mistake, misrepresentation, duress, and undue influence. This topic is discussed in detail in Chapter 5.

CONSIDERATION

Consideration is any lawful alteration of responsibilities that is given in exchange for the other person's consideration ("his/her lawful alteration of responsibilities"). Consideration is based on the idea of *quid pro quo* ("something for something"): some action, forbearance, or promise. In almost all contracts, consideration is required for enforceability.

It is not necessary that the thing promised be affirmative; it may be refraining from acting or promising not to act (his/her lawful alteration of responsibilities). A promise made to give $1,000 to a friend if she does not smoke (a negative unilateral contract) is mutual and binding.

A contract cannot be one-sided; it exists only if there is a promise or an action (or nonaction) on each side.

Comparative Law: Consideration

The Civil Law tradition does not require an exchange of consideration. A contract, in Civil Law (e.g., in Germany) requires only offer, acceptance, and mutual consent about the contract's essential content. (That is somewhat like the older common law of centuries past, in which consideration was not yet an essential element of contracts.)

• *WHAT IS ADEQUATE CONSIDERATION?*

Usually a court will not evaluate the adequacy of consideration. In other words, if two parties make a deal, it will not be struck down because the court feels that the consideration is inadequate or unequal.

Indeed, if a person contracts to buy a pencil or a piece of ordinary paper for $500, the agreement is enforceable, provided, of course, that there is intent to make a contract, the parties are competent, and there is no fraud or violation of other contract principles.

However, the agreement to pay a small amount of money in return for a larger amount of money is *not* enforceable; this is merely an agreement to make a gift of the difference. Thus, if a person were to agree to accept $10 for a $100 debt immediately due, the agreement would be to make a gift of $90. Usually a promise to make a gift is not consideration.

Suppose, however, that a property owner agrees to pay a contractor $150,000 to build a house in accordance with specifications. Suppose further that a dispute arises over the price after an agreement that the contract is to be modified by certain changes. The owner pays $145,000 "as full payment," which the contractor accepts. If there had been no dispute, the contractor could recover the remaining $5,000 since he received no consideration for this "gift"; here, however, since for $5,000 the owner gave up her disputed claim, the contract is considered real, and the benefits mutual.

1. Adequacy of consideration is not an issue for the court *unless* (a) there was no consideration at all, or (b) *in equity cases*, there was grossly inadequate consideration.

2. Adequacy of consideration always can be part of the evidence that assent may not have been genuine (e.g., a party was defrauded, under duress, etc.)

3. *IRS Issues:* While adequacy of consideration is generally unimportant in determining whether a valid contract exists, agencies, such as the Internal Revenue Service, will look at the value of a so-called bargained-exchange when the "contract" at issue has tax implications. For example, even if a contract is okay under the law of contracts, it does not mean that the IRS will accept it for purposes of permitting one to take a tax benefit for business losses or other deductions or credits. The IRS is likely to look at the real, objective value of a "deal."

• *WHEN DOES CONSIDERATION EXIST?*

Consideration entails a bargained for exchange: a "legal detriment" (or benefit), not necessarily an economic or material loss or benefit but *any lawful alteration of responsibilities (e.g., giving up one's right to sue) can be consideration.*

There are *a number of reasons why consideration may be absent.*

ILLUSORY PROMISES

The mutual promises must be real. An *illusory promise* is not an actual promise; the promiser offers to do something only if he/she "wishes" or "needs" to.

Example: Illusory Promises

An employment agreement whereby the employee agrees to work for one year at a salary of $25,000, provided the employer has need of her services, is not a contract because the employer has no real obligation.

Commodity agreements to buy all of one's requirements, or to sell all of one's output, may be illusory if no requirement or output has been established, typically through past usage or production. Thus, if a homeowner heats his house with gas and expects to convert to fuel oil, the agreement to buy all of his fuel oil requirements from a particular supplier may be considered illusory, since no requirement for fuel oil has been established.

DOING WHAT ONE IS BOUND TO DO

An agreement to do one's duty is not consideration. If a person already has a contract, an additional agreement to perform this same contract is lacking in consideration. An airline pilot who promises to land the plane safely for a frightened passenger who offers him $1,000 cannot claim the reward; he is already contractually obligated to land the plane safely. For the same reason, a sheriff is usually not entitled to a reward for capturing a wanted criminal—he is merely doing his duty, for which he is being paid.

Exceptions to the Preexisting Duties Rule

1. Modified duties of both parties; and

2. Rescission and a new contract meant to cancel the old contract.

UCC 2-209(1) states, "An agreement modifying a contract within this Article needs no consideration to be binding." However, under UCC 1-203, every contract imposes an obligation of good faith. Thus, modifications must also be in good faith. This means no "low-balling," in which a party enters into a contract and then seeks the modifications that the party had all along intended (e.g., insisting on a higher price than the "low-ball" amount).

MORAL OBLIGATION

A moral obligation (what a person ought to do) has no *legal* substance; it is not measurable and not commercial. Under this heading are agreements to pay the obligations of others or agreements to provide for relatives. In addition, love and affection, as such, will not support a contract, although they may be of the highest moral nature.

Ordinarily, there is no consideration in such cases. However, some courts have recognized one or more special situations in which a moral obligation may be consideration: (1) it arises from a preexisting legal liability acknowledged by a new promise; (2) a party obtained a benefit or suffered a legal detriment; and (3) the agreement supported by moral consideration has been wholly or partially executed.

PAST CONSIDERATION

Past consideration is something that was performed without expectation of obtaining something in return from the other party. If the latter party should afterward promise some compensation for the benefit received, the traditional rule is that this promise would not be enforceable because it was not bargained for in the current transaction.

Example: Past Consideration

Susanna Swimmer rescues drowning Larry Landlubber, who thereupon promises to give Susanna $500 for her courageous act. Under the common law's traditional interpretatation, Larry's promise is not contractually binding because the act for which it was made—Susanna's rescue of Larry—has already been completed.

A Minority View

In a minority of states, including Colorado, Idaho, Louisiana, Maryland, Missouri, New York, Oregon, and South Dakota, the traditional rule against past consideration has been relaxed: a promise based on past consideration is enforceable if (a) the promise is based on a material benefit (typically, but not exclusively, economic) that the promisee had previously provided to the promisor, and (b) the benefit triggered a duty (even if only a moral duty) to pay compensation. Of course, the key question is what type of past benefits actually triggers such a duty. Some states holding to this minority approach have a fairly broad interpretation of what would qualify as a trigger, while a few states (e.g., New Jersey, Washington) may, for their exceptions to the traditional "no past consideration" rule, narrowly limit those exceptions to benefits related to providing a mortgage or conveying real estate.

STATUTE OF LIMITATIONS

Sometimes a contract is barred (no longer subject to legal action) by the statute of limitations. Periods of limitations vary from state to state but generally run from 3 to 6 years, except for sales contracts under the Uniform Commercial Code (4 years). An agreement to pay made years later, after the original obligation to pay is no longer binding, results, however, in a valid contract. No new consideration is needed; the old consideration is revived by the new promise to pay. Thus the law has arbitrarily created an exception to the "illusion" principle since concepts of fair play and equity do not favor the statute.

• *REQUIREMENTS AND OUTPUT CONTRACTS*

Consideration is found by the courts in rather vague contracts calling for the purchase of one's requirements or for the sale of a manufacturer's output. Frequently, a manufacturer will agree to buy all of his requirements for a material from a specified source, or he may agree to sell all of his output of a certain product to a single customer. Even though the quantity to be bought or sold is not specified, these contracts are good under modern case law, as well as under the Uniform Commercial Code, unless one side acts in bad faith or attempts to take advantage of the other by padding or understating the requirements or output.

Requirements and output contracts should be accompanied by an estimate of the quantities to be bought or sold. In most cases the facility buying or selling should have a record of needs or production so that contractual intent can be ascertained in the event of a dispute. If there is no such record, the contract could be "illusory," that is, no obligation to buy or sell could be demonstrated.

• *PROMISSORY ESTOPPEL*

Consideration may also be found where there is total reliance on the promise of another. This reliance gives rise to estoppel, which is a holdover from equity principles and appears in modern law in a number of different contexts. The word generally describes a situation in which a person, by reason of his/her actions, cannot assert certain legal defenses that are in contradiction of these actions.

Promissory estoppel occurs when a promise is made without any consideration, but the promisee, relying upon the gratuitous promise, takes certain action, or fails to take action, to his detriment. It is not sufficient that the gratuitous promise be made carelessly or thoughtlessly; the promisor should know, or reasonably expect, that the promisee will act in reliance. Unjustified reliance on a promise does not give rise to promissory estoppel.

Example: Promissory Estoppel

The promise to make a charitable contribution to a church, followed by expenditures or actions taken by the church in reliance upon the promise, would create a binding contract. Reliance should be expected and is surely reasonable, even though this simple promise to make a gift would ordinarily be unenforceable as lacking consideration.

YOU SHOULD REMEMBER

Consideration means "something for something"—one party promises to do something, or refrain from doing it, and the other party promises to give something of value in return.

The mutual promises must be real, not illusory.

A promise to do what one is already bound to do (one's duty) or to carry out a moral obligation is not consideration.

Usually the court is not concerned with the adequacy of consideration. An exception occurs when a small amount of money is given for a larger amount.

Past consideration is something that was done without expectation of receiving something in return. A subsequent promise of compensation for a benefit received in the past is not binding.

Promissory estoppel, a holdover from equity law, requires that a person who has made a gratuitous promise be held to it when the promisee, to his/her detriment, justifiably relied upon the promise.

LEGALITY OF SUBJECT MATTER

Contracts that are in violation of common or statutory law or are against public policy are generally held to be illegal. This topic is discussed in Chapter 6.

THE SEAL

Under the early English common law, consideration was not required for a contract. To be binding, a contract had to be in writing and under seal. The seal was placed on the contract in heated wax, either on the signature or at the place of execution. Later, as wax seals fell into disuse, the word "Seal," *Locus Sigilli* (Place of the Seal), or the abbreviation "L.S." was substituted. Such "sealed" contracts did not require consideration, and the laws of many states extended the period of limitation for these agreements. Modern court cases, as well as the Uniform Commercial Code, have abolished the seal as a consideration substitute, but many states still permit seals to extend limitation periods. However, a notary seal, corporate seal, or personal seal (including "Seal" and "L.S."), is still required for certain formal documents (e.g., deeds to real estate).

KNOW THE CONCEPTS
DO YOU KNOW THE BASICS?

1. In what sense is it incorrect to refer to a written document as a contract?
2. How would you go about proving (a) an express contract, (b) an implied-in-fact contract, (c) a quasi contract?
3. Why is a lawsuit based on an implied contract more likely to produce greater damages and a larger verdict than one based on a quasi contract?
4. How can a unilateral offeree convert the contract into a bilateral contract? When should he/she do so?
5. When is an advertisement an offer?
6. What are the four exceptions to the rule that an offer can be withdrawn at any time before it is accepted?
7. What is the effect of a conditional acceptance?
8. What is the meaning of the term "adequacy of consideration"?
9. What does it mean to say that a contract must have "consideration"?
10. What is the consideration for the promise in a unilateral contract?

TERMS FOR STUDY

acceptance	option contract
agreement	past consideration
bilateral contract	promissory estoppel
consideration	quasi contract
contract	seal
counteroffer	statute of limitations
executed contract	unenforceable contract
executory contract	unilateral contract
express contract	valid contract
implied-in-fact contract	void contract
negotiation	voidable contract
offer	

PRACTICAL APPLICATION

1. You enter an expensive restaurant and are seated by the hostess. A waiter brings you plates, knives and forks, napkins and other "setups" for dinner, including bread and butter, which you partly

consume. When you read the menu, you realize that the prices far exceed what you can afford, and you then make it clear that you do not intend to order a meal. What kind of contract (obligation) do you have, if any?

2. In Problem 1, you read the menu and place an order. Nothing is said about agreement to pay. Is there a contract?

3. In Problem 1, there is fine print at the bottom of the menu: "15% gratuity, $25.00 cover charge." What is the effect, assuming that you order dinner but do not see the fine print?

4. You receive a letter from the General Moose Company containing an offer and concluding: "... and we will pay you for your services $50,000 for your first year." You respond by saying, "I like your offer, and would accept for $55,000." You hear nothing in response, so after 10 days you write and say, "I accept your offer of $50,000." Is there a contract? Suppose you hear nothing in response to this second letter. What is the result?

5. If a farmer agrees, in writing, to pay his wife $100 a month to keep farm accounts and perform farm chores "as you have always done," is this an enforceable contract?

ANSWERS
KNOW THE CONCEPTS

1. A contract is a mental condition expressed in a written document. The written document is only evidence of the mental condition.

2. (a) An express contract should be easy to prove since it is stated in words and generally in contract language.

   (b) An implied-in-fact contract is implied by the facts of the case. These facts include proof of the circumstances, actions of the parties, and their words, if any. All of these together should lead a "reasonable person" to believe that there was an agreement.

   (c) A quasi, or implied-in-law, contract involves proof of unjust enrichment, that is, proof of a benefit to an individual under circumstances requiring payment for the benefit. A quasi contract generally does not include benefits imposed upon someone who may or may not want them.

3. The implied contract is for the *usual charge* for services rendered, whereas the quasi contract is for the *going price* for such services in the marketplace. On the assumption that usual charges are higher than those in the marketplace, the implied contract is preferable.

4. If the offer is to buy goods that are to be shipped, the unilateral offeree can say, "I accept your offer and hereby agree to perform the requested services." This should be done before the offeree expends money and effort.

5. An advertisement is an offer only when definite and made very specifically to an identifiable person or group of persons.

6. The option contract, promissory estoppel, the unilateral contract after substantial performance has taken place, and the UCC exception relating to a merchant's firm agreement to hold his offer open for the period specified or, if no time is specified, for a reasonable period (in either case, no more than 3 months).

7. A conditional acceptance is a counteroffer and a rejection of the original offer.

8. "Adequacy of consideration" relates to the value of the consideration or to its weight when compared with the consideration offered by the other party to the contract. Ordinarily, courts do not test the value or weight of consideration.

9. All contracts require "something for something," that is, a contract cannot be a "one-way street." There must be consideration on both sides.

10. In a unilateral contract, the consideration for the promise is the performance of the requested action.

PRACTICAL APPLICATION

1. There is a quasi contract for the food that you have consumed; the value of this food should be a subject of some discussion. Also, it could be argued that there is an implied unilateral contract for the price of a dinner, since you may have entered the restaurant knowing the kind of establishment it purported to be. However, a unilateral offer can be withdrawn before it is accepted if no substantial performance has occurred. Some courts, however, hold that clear commencement to perform constitutes acceptance.

2. Yes. Ordering food from the menu creates an implied-in-fact contract to pay the menu price.

3. In case of conflict between fine print and express contract language that contradicts the fine print, the fine print would be ignored. In this case the fine print is uncontradicted and becomes part of the contract. If the fine print is illegible or hidden in some manner, it could be argued that it is not part of the agreement and therefore not a part of the contract obligation. The fact that you did not see

the fine print does not excuse your obligation if a "reasonable man" would have seen it.

4. Your response would probably be viewed as a counteroffer and a rejection of the General Moose offer. Consequently, your subsequent letter attempting to accept the rejected offer does not create a contract for the job in the $50,000 offer. However, failure of the original offeror to respond may lead a reasonable person to believe that General Moose has accepted the second reply. Usually, silence is not an acceptance, but there are exceptions to this rule, one of which relates to circumstances creating a duty to speak. Such a duty may arise when the first party opened the transaction by the original offer, and General Moose should now make some kind of response. This question should provoke discussion both pro and con.

5. If a person agrees to do what she already has a duty to do, there is no consideration for the agreement. Whether the wife has a duty to keep accounts and perform chores is the central question in this case. The fact that she has always done so without being paid, or as part of her wifely responsibilities, suggests that such a duty exists, and the new contract is not enforceable.

5
REALITY OF THE CONTRACT: DID THE MINDS REALLY MEET?

KEY TERMS

material mistake a mistake that goes to the very heart of the agreement

fraud intentional misrepresentation of a material fact, made knowingly, with intent to defraud, that is justifiably relied upon by the other party and causes injury to him/her

undue influence taking advantage of another by reason of a position of trust in a close or confidential relationship

duress coercion, either physical or mental, that deprives a person of free will

unconscionability gross unfairness brought about by the superior position of one of the parties to the contract

As explained in Chapter 4, a contract is a legally enforceable meeting of the minds—a mental condition. This mental condition is manifested by words—oral or written—by actions, or by both words and actions. This chapter is concerned with situations where there is not really an agreement, even though words or actions seem to prove otherwise.

A meeting of the minds—mutual assent or agreement—is a necessary element of a contract. Without it, the contract may be void or voidable.

There are six reasons why mutual assent may be lacking: mistake, fraud, innocent misrepresentation, undue influence, duress, and unconscionability.

MISTAKE

> The most frequent circumstance barring a real meeting of the minds is mistake.

MATERIAL OR INCIDENTAL?

> A mistake concerning an incidental or trivial detail or insignificant matter will not affect the fact of agreement so long as there is agreement on the basic or material features of the transaction.

What is "incidental" or "trivial," and what is "material" or "basic"?

A basic or **material mistake** generally goes right to the heart of the matter; indeed it usually pertains to the existence or nature of the subject matter. If, for example, the parties agree that one will sell and the other buy a horse that, unknown to them, has died, the mistake is material and there is no contract.

In the preceding example, the parties believe that they know the facts—there is a live horse to be bought and sold—but both parties are mistaken. However, if the facts are not known *and* both buyer and seller take their chances, each believing that he/she has some advantage, there will be a contract. Purchase of land or chattels that prove to be more valuable, or less valuable, than anticipated by either party fall within this category. Such a contract is based, not on a common fallacy, but on judgments about value. Such differing judgments and opinions about the bargain are present in practically all contracts, are considered incidental mistakes, and do not affect the validity of the contract.

MUTUAL OR UNILATERAL?

In general, there is no binding contract if a material mistake or fallacy is **mutual**. The contract is binding, however, if only one party is mistaken, that is, if the mistake is **unilateral**, except when the other party knows, or should have known, of the mistake.

> ### Basic Philosophy of the Unilateral Mistake Principle
> A person should not be allowed to benefit from his/her own ignorance or carelessness.

Persons who carelessly fail to read what they sign, fail to observe defects that are readily apparent, or fail to examine that which is displayed before them should not be able to claim lack of agreement in order to abandon contracts they do not like. In other words, a unilateral mistake usually does not provide the mistaken party with grounds for rescinding the contract.[1]

But this result does not apply if the nonmistaken party either caused the mistake or knows of or suspects the mistake. Thus, if the buyer believes that a property contains 100 acres when in reality it contains only 65 acres, the seller should correct the buyer's misapprehension, if the seller is aware of it, even though the buyer might be able to discover the exact acreage without assistance from the seller. In such a case of *palpable unilateral mistake*, the contract may be voidable. (Also, if the effect of a mistake is to make an agreement unconscionable (extremely unfair), then the agreement may be voidable.)

In the earlier common law, the principle of *caveat emptor* ("let the buyer beware") required buyers to inspect fully and carefully. Failure to do so was at their peril. Modern law, influenced by the equity concepts of fairness and the consumer-friendly provisions of the UCC, is more generous to unobservant or careless buyers and imposes on sellers a higher duty of speaking out. Indeed, it is sometimes argued that the law now enforces *caveat venditor* ("let the seller beware"). Mere failure by the seller to speak, in cases where he should have spoken, may permit the negligent, unobservant buyer to withdraw from the contract.

An agreement made as a result of a mutual mistake regarding a material fact can be made void by either party in the equitable action of **rescission** (cancellation). (Rescission is unavailable, though, to a person who expressly takes the risk of a mistake—e.g., someone who buys an item "as is.") In this action, the supposed contract is rescinded, and the parties are restored to the respective positions existing before the agreement was formed, that is, any monies paid are returned and any goods delivered are restored to the original owner. Thus we say that all such contracts are *voidable*—they can be made void by the action of rescission.

Example: Rescission Due to Mutual Mistake of Fact

Sheila Steinway agrees to sell a painting generally thought to be a genuine Rembrandt to Angus Artlover for $2 million. Later a panel of experts

---

[1] To undermine further any potential claims of overlooking the terms in a contract, the document should be in an easily read font and type size, and any significant nonadjacent terms (e.g., conditions found on the reverse side of the page or in an addendum) should be boldly identified with a phrase such as, "This contract is subject to terms and conditions in Addendum A." Key terms should be accompanied by blanks for the parties to sign their initials indicating clear assent to those contract terms specifically.

determines that the painting was done by a pupil of Rembrandt, not by the master himself. The contract is voidable because of a mutual mistake of fact.

YOU SHOULD REMEMBER

A material mistake usually pertains to a fact, not to a matter of value or opinion.

In general, mutual mistake of a material fact is grounds to cancel a contract. Unilateral mistake by one party, however, is not grounds for cancellation unless the other party knew about the mistake and said nothing.

A voidable contract may be rescinded. Unless rescission occurs, the contract remains in effect.

FRAUD

If a person enters into a contract as a result of the **intentional misrepresentation** or deceit of the other party to the contract, there is no meeting of the minds, no agreement, and hence no legal obligation. In most cases of mistake, both parties are innocent of wrongdoing—the minds simply did not meet. In the case of fraud, however, the minds not only do not meet, but one party is guilty of deceptive, dishonest conduct.

REQUIREMENTS FOR A FINDING OF FRAUD

Five Requirements for a Finding of Fraud
(all five must be present)

(1) Misrepresentation of a *material* fact,

(2) made *knowingly*,

(3) with *intent to defraud*,

(4) justifiably *relied upon*,

(5) *causing injury* to the other party.

• *MISREPRESENTATION OF A MATERIAL FACT*

To prove a case of fraud, the misrepresentation must concern a material (important) fact.

Examples: Misrepresentations of **Material Facts**

1. A painting is by a specified artist.
2. An air conditioner will adequately cool a certain-size room.
3. An automobile will pass state inspection.
4. Turkey poults are healthy and free from disease.

Matters pertaining to *value* and matters asserted as *opinion* are generally not factual in nature and are not grounds for fraud.

As stated concerning incidental mistakes, the parties to a contract usually have different perceptions of the value of the chattel, land, or other object being bought or sold. Moreover, it is customary for the seller to "huff and puff" and to exaggerate the value of his/her goods, and many buyers, in turn, seek to diminish or deprecate the value of the goods in order to lower the price. Opinions are, of course, statements of judgment, not of fact, and do not constitute grounds for fraud.

There is, however, one major exception to this principle: an "opinion" by an expert—for example, a physician, an accountant, a lawyer, an engineer, a financial advisor—or one claiming to be an expert may be the basis for fraud. The law treats the expert as a master of the facts; his/her judgments are to be relied on as skilled—and factual.

• *MADE KNOWINGLY*

The party misrepresenting the material fact must do so knowingly.

Scienter is the legal word for "guilty knowledge." Nonlawyers frequently believe that they can claim ignorance of the falsity of a statement and thus defeat a claim for fraud. However, *scienter* goes beyond actual knowledge—it includes careless indifference to the truth, a lack of belief by the declarer in his/her statements. Whether *scienter* is present is a question for a properly instructed jury, and juries can be cynical about persons who "unintentionally" lie to gain an advantage.

• *WITH INTENT TO DEFRAUD*

The misrepresentation of a material fact must be made with intent to defraud. Obviously, every defrauding party will claim he/she had no intention to deceive, that the falsehood was innocent and not willful. *Unfortunately for such persons, the intent to defraud is presumed if the false statement is made knowingly—if* scienter *is present.*

• *JUSTIFIABLY RELIED UPON*

The party to whom the misrepresentation was made must rely on it. This requirement is of the greatest importance. *If the seller lies, knowingly and intentionally, and the buyer recognizes* (or should recognize) *the lie, but buys anyway, there is no fraud.* Thus, if the salesman says, "This pesticide will kill beetles on roses," but the container has a clear statement that the product will kill aphids and slugs but not beetles, an argument can be made that there is no reliance. (Some recent cases, however, have held that reliance is justified under these circumstances, and hence there may be fraud.)

A Warning to Liars! One cannot lie, thinking that a lack of justifiable reliance will prevent one's liability for fraud; the court may determine that reliance was reasonable. Although potential plaintiffs should investigate the facts (be careful), potential defendants must understand that the modern trend is not to presume that cheated people should have found out about a lie. As caveat emptor ("buyer beware") has become a less important legal doctrine, so an assertion of unreasonable reliance has become more circumscribed.

• *CAUSING INJURY TO THE OTHER PARTY*

The party to whom the misrepresentation was made must have suffered injury as a result. Frequently, however, the false statement or concealment does not cause injury. In this case, there is no fraud.

Example: Misrepresentation That Does Not Cause Injury

Sam, the seller, tells Bill, the buyer, that Sam is the original and only owner of the 1985 Mustang Bill is purchasing. In fact, Sam bought the Mustang from his next-door neighbor.

In this case the car is in excellent condition, and there is doubt that any injury will result from the falsehood. Hence, there would be no basis for a claim of fraud.

As a matter of fact, many misrepresentations, although intentional and deceptive, are not bases of fraud, particularly if they pertain to other matters than the *use* intended of the goods by the buyer.

CONSEQUENCES OF FRAUD

In the case of fraud, the defrauded party can rescind the contract. However, he/she has an alternative remedy: to affirm the contract and bring an action in tort to recover damages for the deceit. For example, if a seller misrepresents the expired mileage of a second-hand automobile by turning back the odometer, the buyer may rescind the contract. Alternatively, she may keep the automobile and recover damages for the lessened value of the automobile.

Fraud is a grave offense in the eyes of the law. In any case where it can be proved, the victim has a real advantage over the perpetrator. Our analysis of business torts and crimes (Chapter 19) points out that not only is fraud a tort, it is also a crime. If the fraud is particularly aggravated, malicious, or oppressive, it can give rise to punitive damages (see Chapter 8).

Failure to keep up with common professional, industrial, or other business practices could become a legal problem—perhaps fraud or unconscionability (see pages 124–125). Assume that those practices represent a consensus on the ethical standards for a particular field— that they are not simply seen as aspirational (a goal) but instead are viewed as the lowest common denominator of behavior (required conduct). Therefore, typically through court decisions but also possibly through legislation or regulation, these ethical standards may be incorporated into public policy and thus into law. This process transforms "mere" custom or ethics that were optional (e.g., something that a businessperson may like to do, but may decided he/she cannot afford to do so) to obligatory (no longer simply a choice).

YOU SHOULD REMEMBER

Fraud is intentional misrepresentation of a material fact, made knowingly, with intent to defraud, that is justifiably relied upon by the other party and causes injury to him/her.

A defrauded party has two choices: (1) rescind the contract and get back any consideration paid, or (2) retain the goods or value obtained and sue in tort for damages (the lessened value because of the fraud).

INNOCENT (NONFRAUDULENT) MISREPRESENTATION

Misrepresentation that lacks element 2 (knowing) and element 3 (intent to defraud) will result in a contract *voidable* by the innocent party.

Unlike fraud, however, **innocent misrepresentation** is not a tort and does not give rise to a claim for damages. The only remedy available to the plaintiff is rescission of the contract.

Example: Innocent Misrepresentation

Alice bought a rug for $1,000 at auction and was given a certificate stating that the rug was a genuine Aubusson. Shortly thereafter, Alice sold the rug, as an Aubusson, to Betty, whose insurance agent called in an appraiser. The expert pronounced the rug a fake worth at most $200.

Since Alice had been assured that the rug was an Aubusson and had innocently misrepresented it as such, with no intent to defraud, Betty could not win damages. The contract, however, could be rescinded; Betty returned the rug and Alice refunded the money.

UNDUE INFLUENCE

Undue influence occurs when one party takes advantage of another by reason of a superior position in a close or confidential relationship.

A contract entered into as a result of undue influence, although having the form and shape of an agreement, is *not* enforceable over the objection of the victim.

There are many confidential relationships that may give rise to undue influence, in which the dominant party exercises control over the dominated person's will for the former's benefit. Attorney and client, doctor and patient, clergyman and parishioner, trustee and beneficiary, principal and agent, husband and wife (or wife and husband), guardian and ward—these are examples of such relationships. In each case, the person occupying a superior position, that is, one of trust, should be acting in the interest of the other person; hence any contract that is in reality for the former's benefit, and not for the latter's, is presumed to be tainted with undue influence and therefore voidable.

Examples: Undue Influence

A client wins a large judgment in a lawsuit and then lends a portion of the award to her attorney.

A dying patient deeds over valuable property to his doctor.

A husband, hospitalized because of a serious illness, signs insurance releases for the sole benefit of his wife, and upon her advice.

All these transactions would be suspect.

To overcome suspicion, the party in a position of trust should make full disclosure of his private interest and potential gain (in writing or before independent witnesses) to the other party, and if possible should assist him/her in obtaining independent advice concerning any proposed contract or gift.

When a transaction may have occurred because of undue influence, we are concerned about use of excessive pressure by the dominant person (e.g., the professional over his/her patient or client), and we recognize the susceptibility of the subservient person. If strong enough, any one of these characteristics of "overpersuasion" may prove undue influence took place, or—even if one factor is not overwhelming—the combination of these factors may have a cumulative effect indicating undue influence:

1. Discussion of the transaction at an unusual place or time.
2. Consummation of the transaction in an unusual place.
3. Insistent demand that the business be finished at once.
4. Extreme emphasis on the untoward consequences of delay.
5. The use of multiple persuaders (e.g., several people) by the dominant side.
6. Absence of third-party advisers to the servient party.
7. Statements that there is no time to consult with advisers.

DURESS

A contract that is in valid form and to all appearances is an agreement may be voided because of duress.

> **Duress** is coercion, either physical or mental, that deprives a person of free will and leaves that person with no reasonable alternative other than to accept the contract terms as imposed on him/her.

A contract made at gunpoint or under other compelling *physical* force is simply *void*. No mental condition of agreement ever existed.

The more typical case of duress arises out of mental coercion. A contract made under mental coercion is *voidable*. Such coercion may come about by threats—a kind of blackmail. However, the threat must be *improper* or *wrongful*. A threat to sue in civil court on a just debt, thereby inducing a promise to pay, is not duress.

Five kinds of threats are generally considered duress in contract law:

1. Threat of physical violence or harm to the individual or to his/her family or property.
2. Threat of criminal prosecution.
3. Threat of a lawsuit, but only if the threat is made with actual knowledge that the suit would be without any basis.

4. Threat of personal or family social disgrace.
5. Threat of economic loss *if* the party claiming duress can show that the loss may occur because of actions of the one accused of coercion. *Note*: It is not wrong to threaten suit to recover a valid debt or even a supposedly valid debt.

UNCONSCIONABILITY

A contract in valid form may be voided because of gross inequality in the respective positions of the parties during the contract process. "Unconscionable" describes special situations in which an overbearing party in a superior position (e.g., a merchant) imposes outrageously unfair terms on some other party (e.g., a consumer) through fine print and "fast talk." (UCC 2-302 covers unconscionable sales contracts.) An **adhesion contract**, for example, often is unconscionable because it is a standardized agreement tendered to a consumer on a "take it or leave it" basis, leaving him/her no opportunity to bargain or to obtain the desired goods or services without signing the printed form.

Unconscionability is not an "easy out" from contract obligations. The burden of proof is high; the law imposes a heavy duty to resist such high-handed, aggressive tactics before entering into the contract. Moreover, even if a court finds part of the contract to be unconscionable, the court may enforce the rest of the contract; the court even may choose to enforce the unconscionable clause, but limit its application so as to avoid an unconscionable result. UCC 2-302 thereby grants judges wide-ranging remedial discretion.

Courts often describe two categories of unconscionability, procedural and substantive. **Procedural unconscionability** concerns contract formation. It may be present when there is inequality in bargaining power (generally, a very high degree of inequality) or unfair surprise caused by to "hidden" terms in a contract that is lengthy, confusing, or both. **Substantive unconscionability** concerns the fairness of a contract; it may exist when there is an unjustified and overly harsh allocation of risks or costs or a great price disparity (e.g., a contract price three to four times higher than fair market value).

Other countries may be more energetic in intervening to protect parties from a supposedly unfair contract. For example, Germany's closest equivalent to the UCC, its Law on General Business Terms (the German acronym is AGBG), prohibits any clause that violates good faith by imposing an "unfair burden" on the other party. It forbids certain contract terms quite common in U.S. commercial contracts, such as (1) a bargained-for disclaimer that the parties are not liable for lost profits as a result of problems that arise and (2) clauses that give the seller the right to increase prices, except in limited circumstances. In general, the AGBG does not look favorably on enforcing boilerplate terms in a contract "imposed" by a large firm on a smaller firm. German judges even may void contracts they deem to be for unusually long periods of obligation.

KNOW THE CONCEPTS
DO YOU KNOW THE BASICS?

1. Explain the circumstances under which it may be possible to rescind a contract because of unilateral mistake.

2. Name a situation in which an opinion statement would give rise to rescission of a contract.

3. How have the old equity doctrines influenced the law of contract mistake?

4. How does the penalty for contract fraud differ from the right of recission in cases of simple mutual mistake?

5. Can a person's careless statements give rise to fraud when the person does not know for a fact that he/she is lying?

6. Name four confidential relationships where undue influence could exist.

7. When does duress cause a contract to be (a) void or (b) voidable?

8. Define "unconscionable contract."

TERMS FOR STUDY

adhesion contract	material mistake
caveat emptor	mutual mistake
caveat venditor	rescission
duress	*scienter*
fraud	unconscionability
innocent misrepresentation	undue influence
intentional misrepresentation	unilateral mistake

PRACTICAL APPLICATION

1. Fred Farmer is the owner of a 100-acre farm near a large city. Consider the following two situations:
   (a) An employee of the State Roads Department tells a friend, Lester Listener, that the state plans a major road relocation through Fred's property, including a cloverleaf and commercial interchange on the property. Lester persuades Fred to sign an option contract to sell him the farm for $125,000, a fair price for farm land.
   (b) Lester knows that XYZ Chemical Company is seeking a plant site near the city, and he gets an option contract from Fred, as before, for $125,000.

   If Lester says nothing to Fred about the plans outlined in (a) and (b), in either case is there mistake? Fraud?

2. Bruce Brown is seriously ill. While heavily sedated, he is persuaded by his wife Betty to sign some "papers" so she can pay the hospital bills. These "papers" include a bill of sale on Bruce's cabin cruiser. Actually, the hospital bill is amply covered by insurance, and Betty sells the boat to purchase expensive jewelry for herself. Is Betty's action lawful?

3. Marian Merchant discovers that her bookkeeper has embezzled $50,000 while working in Marian's store. Marian agrees not to report this theft if the bookkeeper will sign a 3-year, interest-free promissory note. Is the note valid?

4. Nellie Naive is an elderly, naturalized American citizen with a marginal knowledge of English and a meager education. She owns a boarding house but is having trouble making ends meet. One of her boarders, Sam Slick, a traveling salesman, is aware of her difficulties. He offers to lend her $10,000 "on her home" if she will sign a "paper." The "paper" turns out to be a deed, and Nellie now seeks to have an equity court set aside the conveyance. Should she be successful?

ANSWERS
KNOW THE CONCEPTS

1. Generally speaking, a unilateral mistake does not provide ground for rescinding a contract. The major exception covers situations where the other party is aware of the mistake and should have spoken up.

In today's consumer-minded world, the unilaterally mistaken party has a substantial chance of rescinding the contract if (a) he/she could not easily have learned the facts, and (b) the other party had full control of the situation.

2. In a case involving fraud, an opinion given by a professional, such as an attorney or a physician, is a statement of fact giving rise to grounds for rescission. In addition, you should consider that opinions given by tradespeople, such as plumbers, electricians, and hairdressers (in cases concerning shampoos or brushes), will be given greater weight and should be discussed.

3. The equity concept of fairness controls the law of contract mistake. The old idea of *caveat emptor* favored an unscrupulous seller. The modern law tries to "balance the equities," so that neither side should be able to take unreasonable advantage of the other. This is basic equity law.

4. Contract fraud permits the defrauded party either to keep the contract and receive damages in tort (perhaps even punitive damages) or to rescind the contract; simple mutual mistake permits only the right of rescission.

5. Merely careless statements can give rise to fraud if they are made recklessly. The law does not protect those who show disregard for the truth, whether the disregard is shown by outright lying or lack of interest in presenting the facts accurately.

6. Undue influence can exist in the relationship of husband/wife, minister/parishioner, lawyer/client, doctor/patient, parent/child, trustee/beneficiary, political office holder/constituent and others involving trust and potential conflict of interest.

7. (a) Duress causes a contract to be void if it is the result of a physical threat, such as pointing a gun. (b) A contract is voidable when it is the result of mental coercion.

8. "Unconscionable" means grossly unfair. Gross unfairness occurs generally when one party is in an advantageous position in relation to the other party, because of either superior knowledge and power, or the inferior knowledge and power of the other. Disparities in skill, education, professional background, and economic status would be factors in determining unconscionability.

PRACTICAL APPLICATION

1. (a) This is an example of unilateral mistake on the part of Fred, where such mistake is known to the other party. Therefore Fred would have the right to rescind the contract. An argument could

also be made that fraud exists since Lester has inside information that a judge or jury might hold he has a duty to share with Fred.

(b) There is neither mistake nor fraud in this situation. XYZ Chemical Company may or may not be interested in Fred's property according to the statement of facts, and therefore Lester's failure to disclose this information is not nondisclosure of a material fact.

2. This is an example of undue influence practiced by a wife upon a husband. Betty is acting in her own self-interest while leading her ill husband to believe that she is acting either for him or for both parties.

3. The bookkeeper can rescind the obligation. The promise not to report a crime as consideration for a contract is duress. (*The promise not to sue generally would be okay.*)

4. This is a prime example of an unconscionable contract that will be set aside in an equity court. The one-sided nature of the bargain, combined with the lack of equality between the parties, is the essential characteristic of unconscionability. In addition, it could be argued that this is a case of fraud (check each of the five fraud elements) or even of undue influence (is there a relation of trust?).

6

CAPACITY OF THE PARTIES AND LEGALITY OF SUBJECT MATTER

KEY TERMS

capacity a legally defined level of mental ability sufficient to reach an agreement

insanity mental impairment sufficient to prevent one from appreciating the nature of an agreement or the consequences of his/her actions

public policy concepts of prevailing morality used by courts to determine the legality or illegality of contracts

Preceding chapters have dealt with consideration and mutual assent, two of the four elements necessary for a valid contract. In this chapter we consider the other two: capacity of the parties and legality of subject matter.

CAPACITY OF THE PARTIES

The technical requirement of capacity arises out of common sense. **Capacity** is a legally defined level of mental ability sufficient to reach an agreement. If one (or both) of the parties has a mind so immature or childish, so befuddled by mental illness or disease, or so stupefied by alcohol or other drugs that it cannot form an intent or know what is going on, the party (or parties) thus lacking capacity may opt to disavow their agreement.

Three categories of people may lack capacity to make a contract: minors, insane persons, and intoxicated persons.

MINORS

In most states both parties must be at least 18 years old to make a legally binding agreement; a few states set the minimum age at 21.

• *DISAFFIRMANCE BY A MINOR*

> A person who deals with a minor does so at his/her peril. The adult party to the contract is bound by the bargain; the minor is not.

If one of the parties is under the age of 18—is a **minor**—that party has the right to declare the contract void. **Disaffirmance** is the cancellation or rejection of a contract made during one's minority. Disaffirmance may consist of returning goods bought (if they still exist or have not been consumed), in whatever condition they then may be, or of some other express or implied action of cancellation or rejection made known to the adult party. *This action must occur during minority or within some reasonable period after the minor reaches 18.*

If the minor has sold the goods in question to an innocent *third party*, that party will have acquired a good title with respect to third parties, but the minor can also disaffirm the contract and recover the goods. As for the original contract, if the minor still has the goods in his/her possession at the time of disaffirmance, most courts hold that the minor must return the goods to the other party; if the goods are damaged, these courts hold that the damaged goods must be returned.

In a departure from the traditional rule that the adult party, in effect, takes all of the risk when contracting with a minor, some states now require that the minor reimburse the other party for the use or depreciation of its property.

> State law often prevents minors from disaffirming transactions such as marital agreements, child support obligations, educational loans, duties concerning financial transactions (e.g., bank accounts, stock and bond transfers), life and health insurance policies, transportation contracts, court-approved contracts (e.g., to employ a child actor), and medical care or psychological counseling. In most states, *emancipation* (termination of a parent's right to control a child, e.g., because of the minor's marriage or full-time employment) does not, by itself, give a minor the capacity to contract.

• *MINOR'S LIABILITY FOR FRAUD*

> **General Rule:** A minor is responsible for his torts down to a very tender age; however, a parent is not responsible for the torts of a minor child.

Some state courts hold that a minor who represents him/herself to be an adult is estopped from disaffirming the contract that he/she made with the other party. Other courts, while allowing disaffirmance would permit the other party to sue the minor for fraud. Damages would be the loss sustained by the adult because of the minor's disaffirmance. Of course, if the minor is of such obvious youth that the adult party could not reasonably have *relied* on his/her misrepresentation of age, there would be no estoppel or fraud (see Chapter 5).

Caution: Some courts, albeit decreasing in number, do not follow the estoppel or fraud principle set out above since they see it as a subterfuge for circumventing principles of law designed to protect minors.

• *CONTRACTS INVOLVING NECESSARIES*

Necessaries are items required to sustain existence, such as food, shelter; clothing, medical services, and some types of schooling (e.g., vocational training). A car may or may not be a necessary, depending on the minor's circumstances and intended use of the car. Indeed, the concept of "necessary" is flexible and may be defined in accordance with circumstances and the minor's station in life.

A minor is legally liable for necessaries that he/she has used or consumed and that were provided by another person at the minor's request.

This liability is based on the quasi-contract (unjust enrichment) principle since a minor does not have the mental ability to make an express or implied-in-fact contract. Since the obligation is based on a quasi contract, the liability is for the *reasonable* value of the goods, which may or may not be the agreed-upon value. Moreover, a quasi contract does not exist if the minor is living at home under the care of a parent or guardian.

Note that the unjust enrichment *is for goods used or consumed.* This principle does not apply to an executory contract (an exchange of promises not yet performed).

Example: Contract for Necessaries

If a 17-year-old enters into a 6-month lease agreement, at an exorbitant rental of $1,000 per month, and if she occupies the premises for 3 months, she would be responsible for the 3 months of actual usage but at a *reasonable* rental.

The express contract of lease is not relevant to the quasi-contractual obligation and is not binding on the minor. Of course, the minor has no liability for the unexpired 3-month remaining period in the lease.

• *RATIFICATION BY A MINOR*

Once a minor reaches the age of 18, he/she may accept the contract, and thus ratify it **ab initio** (from the beginning). *Such ratification may be express or implied*—an understanding of the kind required to have made a contract in the first place.

The courts sometimes differ on what actions constitute implied ratification. In general, however, making payments when due, continuing to enjoy the benefits of the agreement, or other clear, unambiguous action within the scope of the contract usually implies acceptance.

INSANE PERSONS

By "insanity" the law does not necessarily mean insanity in the medical or extreme sense. Any temporary, oppressive condition affecting the mind and the ability to understand may amount to legal **insanity**, particularly if this condition is apparent to the other party.

A person who enters into a contract while unable to appreciate the nature of the agreement or the consequences of his/her actions may, upon recovery, declare the contract void. Such a person is in the same position as the minor (the contract is voidable) with one exception: *If the sane party acted in good faith, upon disaffirmance of the contract the mentally impaired party must restore whatever he/she received.*

If a person is "insane" in the medical sense *and* has been adjudicated insane (declared insane, upon medical evidence in a court of law), his/her agreements are void *ab initio* and of no effect. Such a person cannot contract for anything, and a guardian handles his affairs.

INTOXICATED PERSONS

For *intoxication* by drugs or alcohol to operate as a defense to a claim based on contract, the intoxication must (a) be such as to deprive the subject of the ability to understand the nature of his/her agreement, and (b) be apparent to the other party. If these two conditions are present, the contract is voidable, but the person under disability must restore the other party to the status quo by returning any goods or other consideration received. (A court may declare a person who cannot control his/her appetite for alcohol a "habitual drunkard," and he/she is therefore without any capacity, similar to a person who has been adjudicated insane.)

YOU SHOULD REMEMBER

A minor, a person under the age of 18, lacks capacity to make a contract. Therefore a minor can cancel a contract at any time during minority and for a reasonable period of time after his/her eighteenth birthday. A minor is, however, responsible for necessaries consumed.

Although minors cannot be held to their contracts, they are responsible for their torts (down to a tender age), including frauds. Consequently, some courts hold a minor responsible for losses to the adult party to a contract because of the misrepresentation of age (fraud).

If a minor accepts the contract after reaching the age of 18, he/she is then bound by it because of ratification.

Insanity is grounds for cancellation of a contract. If, however, the "insane" person has not been adjudicated insane and if the other party acted in good faith, the mentally impaired party must restore value received if he/she wishes to cancel.

A contract made by a person so intoxicated by alcohol or drugs that he/she did not understand the nature of the agreement is voidable if the intoxication was apparent to the other party.

LEGALITY OF SUBJECT MATTER

If the subject matter of an agreement is not legal, the agreement is not enforceable in court. *The illegal agreement is considered void.* Generally, neither party can obtain court assistance for any aspect of a void agreement.

There are two reasons why a contract's subject matter may be illegal: statute and public policy. Statutes are legislative acts; **public policy** is a judicial determination of prevailing morality.

In Chapter 1 we explored the close relationship between law and morality. We shall now see how law as statute and law as morality ("public policy") play identical roles in the law of contracts.

AGREEMENTS THAT VIOLATE STATUTES

Criminal statutes such as those dealing with murder or arson, and the criminal provisions of the antitrust laws, prohibit certain conduct. Any contract in furtherance of such activity (e.g., a wife's contract with a hired killer to murder her husband) would have no legal effect and be unenforceable.

In addition there are other statutes—for example, statutes requiring professionals or tradesmen to be licensed, statutes prohibiting betting or wagering, "blue laws" prohibiting purchases on Sundays, usury laws prohibiting exorbitant interest—that indirectly affect a contract and may render it unenforceable. Thus a person who is not a lawyer cannot enforce an agreement to be compensated for legal advice, and a faith healer cannot recover in contract for medical advice. For the same reason, an unlicensed person cannot collect in contract for a real estate commission, nor can an unlicensed contractor collect for home improvements in states where a license is required. Because these licenses are regulatory measures mainly meant to protect the public from unqualified practitioners (e.g., in medicine, law, accounting), the service recipient need not uphold his end of the bargain. However, revenue licenses (intended to tax licensees, not prescribe practice standards for them) can be enforced.

Betting and wagering contracts are generally illegal except where such activities are permitted by statute. (Insuring of risks is permissible, and is discussed in Chapter 21.) *Public attitudes* (prevailing morality) *in these areas of the law, however, are influencing statute law*, so that many gambling activities, such as the bingo games conducted by churches or charities, are now lawful where only recently prohibited. Similarly, **blue laws**, prohibitions of trading contracts on Sunday, seem to be yielding to a more liberal morality in many states. However, one should be aware that Sunday sales of nonnecessity items are illegal in many states and contracts to pay consideration for such transactions may not be enforceable.

Usury is an unlawful rate of interest. Ceilings, set by statute, vary from state to state. A usurious contract is thus void, or enforceable only as to principal, or enforceable as to principal plus interest up to the legal rate. (The standard varies from state to state, and according to the type of contract involved.) "Interest" is usually defined as a charge for the use of money and does not extend to carrying charges or finance charges related to the sale of goods.

AGREEMENTS THAT VIOLATE PUBLIC POLICY

In this second ground for illegality of subject matter, general morality again gives rise to public policy, but *this illegality is judicially declared* in cases before the courts.

• *RESTRAINT OF TRADE*

Before the enactment of any antitrust laws, the common law found agreements that unreasonably restrained trade to be illegal. *Typical of such agreements were those unduly restricting a person in the pursuit of his/her livelihood.*

Example: Agreements Restricting Persons in Pursuit of Their Livelihoods

If a chemist agreed that, after any termination of her employment by a chemical manufacturer, she would not work for any other chemical manufacturer for an unlimited period of time, this agreement not to be employed would be found unduly restrictive and unenforceable.

If a barber sold his business and the agreement of sale provided that the seller would not thereafter work as a barber at any place in the state, such an agreement might be found unduly restrictive and unenforceable.

In determining the illegality of such restrictions (covenants), the courts consider the legitimate interests of the party that the agreement seeks to protect as well as the negative effect on the party being restricted. If, in the examples above, there is a likelihood that the chemist may know technology and trade secrets useful to a competitor, or that the barber may be planning to work in a nearby shop, a court may be sympathetic to a restriction upon her/his activity. Conversely, an undue hardship on the chemist or barber may cause the court to refuse enforcement of the restriction.

In *all* cases, however, the parties should refrain from total restriction—a person should be able to continue to make a living by practicing a trade, profession, or skill. Thus the restriction should be limited as to time (e.g., 2 or 3 years), place (miles or a region), and specialty (e.g., organic chemist, woman's hair stylist). Otherwise, it may be vulnerable to attack as unreasonable.

A covenant not to compete must be ancillary to some other legitimate agreement, such as employment, sale of a business, partnership, or franchise contract. Some limit—by time, place, and subject matter—should be placed on a covenant not to compete.

How do courts treat non-compete clauses if they are unreasonably broad?

1. Throw out entirely.
2. Winnow down to a reasonable level; make reasonable, e.g., in time, in geographic scope.
3. Blue-Pencil Doctrine—judicial removal of parts of the clause, but enforcement of the rest.

The second and third approaches have been criticized for encouraging the drafters of non-compete clauses to make the clauses overbroad: such clauses may have an *in terrorem* effect (severely discouraging competition), yet still be enforceable, to a lesser extent, if challenged in court.

• *EXCULPATORY CLAUSES*

Many agreements contain **exculpatory clauses**, that is, provisions that disclaim liability for negligence or other actions. Thus a sign in a restaurant may warn customers that the restaurant has no responsibility for lost coats or a sign in a parking garage may deny liability for damages to vehicles. Exculpatory clauses are not against public policy *per se*, and disclaimers such as those in the restaurant or parking garage may genuinely warn the public or another party to a contract that one uses the premises at his/her own risk.

If, however, the parties are not in equal bargaining positions, or if the exculpatory clause attempts to excuse a party from his/her own negligence, such a clause may be against public policy and be illegal and unenforceable.

Such unequal bargaining positions are held, for example, by individual travelers with respect to public carriers, whose exculpatory clauses on tickets and claim checks may be found to be contrary to public policy and thus unenforceable.

In the case of the restaurant or parking garage mentioned above, the public has other options for obtaining the services offered and may refuse to be subjected to the risk implied by the disclaimer or denial of liability.

Courts in California and other states have found six criteria necessary to deem an exculpatory clause against public policy and thus unconscionable:

1. It concerns a business of a type generally thought suitable for public regulation.

2. The party seeking exculpation is engaged in performing a service of great importance to the public, which is often a matter of practical necessity for some members of the public.

3. The party holds him/herself out as willing to perform this service for any member of the public who seeks it, or at least any member coming within certain established services.

4. As a result of the essential nature of the service, in the economic setting of the transaction, the party invoking exculpation possesses a decisive advantage of bargaining strength against any member of the public who seeks his/her services.

5. In exercising a superior bargaining power the party confronts the public with a standardized adhesion contract of exculpation, and makes no provision whereby a purchaser may pay additional fees and obtain protection against negligence.

6. Finally, as a result of the transaction, the person or property of the purchase is placed under the seller's control, subject to the risk of carelessness by the seller.

• *OTHER PUBLIC POLICY ILLEGALITY*

Some other types of contracts that are contrary to public policy and therefore illegal are those that would

- Obstruct justice.

- Corrupt public officials.

- Impair public morality.

- Offend public concepts of decency.

- Discriminate because of race, religion, color, or national origin in the sale or rental of property or the use of public facilities.

EFFECT OF ILLEGALITY

As a general rule, a court of law will not admit into evidence any matter pertaining to an illegal agreement. Such agreements are not actionable and *do not even have legal existence* except as possible evidence of a crime or tort.

Exceptions to this general rule are primarily equitable in nature: the innocent public, the disadvantaged party, a repentant party, a party not as guilty of wrongful intent as the other party—all may be permitted to sue on the illegal agreement, and in many cases may obtain restitution and return of the status quo.

YOU SHOULD REMEMBER

An agreement may be illegal because it violates a statute.

An agreement may also be illegal because it violates public policy, that is, it is contrary to general morality as declared by a court of law. Two examples of such illegality are contracts in restraint of trade and contracts between parties not in equal bargaining positions that contain exculpatory clauses.

KNOW THE CONCEPTS
DO YOU KNOW THE BASICS?

1. State how the term "capacity" applies to minors, insane persons, and sometimes users of alcohol or drugs.

2. Discuss the pros and cons of permitting a suit against a minor for fraud if he misrepresents his age.

3. Name a specific instance in which contract law attempts to protect general morality.

4. Why is an intoxicated person not given the same right to disaffirm his/her contract that a minor is given?

5. Does the warning on cigarette packages that "Smoking by Pregnant Women May Result in Fetal Injury ..." operate as an exculpatory clause to the cigarette company?

6. If an action (e.g., murder) is a crime by reason of a statute, will it usually also be a crime by reason of public policy?

TERMS FOR STUDY

ab initio	intoxication
blue laws	minor
capacity	necessaries
disaffirmance	public policy
exculpatory clause	usury
insanity	

PRACTICAL APPLICATION

1. Just after his seventeenth birthday, Murdock Minor signs a contract with Scholarship Books, Inc., for a correspondence course in geology. The cost of this course is $1,000, payable in 20 monthly installments of $50.00 each. There are 20 units, each completed monthly. Murdock completes 14 units and makes monthly payments promptly. In the fifteenth month, he seeks to rescind the contract. Can he do so?

2. Fran Flighty, the 17-year-old daughter of wealthy parents, is visiting an aunt in Honolulu. While there, she signs a contract with the ABC Dancing School whereby she is to be taught "all sophisticated

modern dances for young and old alike" in "12 easy lessons." Fran takes no lessons, makes no payments, and seeks to rescind the contract when the ABC Company threatens to sue.

(a) What will be the result?

(b) What would happen if she took the lessons and refused to pay just after her eighteenth birthday?

3. Dan Diver is a 22-year-old student at Ambiance Air Academy in Smalltown, Any State. He joins a parachute diving club to "experience the exhilaration of diving" and to "engage in the world's most exciting sport," according to a contract he signs with the club, Live-Long Divers, Inc. The contract also contains an exculpatory clause releasing the club for damages due to any reason whatsoever, "including negligence by the Club." While descending via parachute on his first jump, Dan collides with electric power lines and is seriously injured. Would the exculpatory clause excuse Live-Long Divers, Inc., if it should be found negligent?

ANSWERS
KNOW THE CONCEPTS

1. The term "capacity" relates to the ability of one mind to meet another mind. This ability may not yet be developed in a minor and may be clouded or confused by insanity or alcohol/drug use.

2. A reason for permitting such a suit is that fraud is a tort, and minors are responsible for this kind of tort if all other requirements of fraud are met. A reason not to permit such a suit is that it indirectly permits the adult party to obtain the same benefits he/she would have received for the minor's breach of contract.

3. Public policy is "grounded" in common morality. Thus, an agreement contrary to public policy is simply one that is contrary to general morality. Restraint of trade is contrary to fairness and good morals. The same is true of an excessively broad exculpatory clause, as well as other illegality.

4. An intoxicated person becomes intoxicated by reason of his/her own freedom of action and is not within a class of persons whom society seeks to protect. Thus, unless the intoxication is evident to the other party, he/she is bound by a contract made while intoxicated.

5. Cigarette companies have attempted to use the Surgeon General's warning as an exculpatory clause. However, such a clause does not excuse harm caused by their gross negligence, recklessness, or active, intentional misconduct (e.g., fraud).

6. Actions made criminal by statute are usually contrary to prevailing morality and, hence, contrary to public policy. Murder, arson, robbery, and so forth are contrary to public policy. Some crimes—speeding, failure to file income tax returns, failure to register securities being offered to the public—arguably are criminal only because they are in violation of a statute.

PRACTICAL APPLICATION

1. No. Murdock has ratified the contract by continuing to take the course and making payments after his eighteenth birthday.

2. (a) This contract by a minor is not enforceable as an express or implied-in-fact contract. The dance studio might argue that it is a contract for necessaries and that there is a liability in quasi contract. However, since the lessons were never taken and no benefit has been received, there is no such liability.

   (b) If Fran had taken the lessons, she might be required to pay in quasi contract if the lessons could be considered necessaries. Whether "sophisticated modern dancing" lessons are "necessary" for the teen-age daughter of wealthy parents is a jury question.

3. Dan Diver does not have to take parachute diving lessons, and even if he did he could choose some other club—thus the parties are in equal bargaining positions. However, the clause should not operate to excuse the club from its own negligence, even though Dan proceeded to take the lessons at his own risk.

7

THE STATUTE OF FRAUDS; PAROL EVIDENCE RULE; PRIVITY

Up to this point we have emphasized the mental nature of contracts—in fact, we have stated that written and oral words are mere evidence of the mental condition comprising the contract. However, some contracts require more than a provable mental condition.

THE STATUTE OF FRAUDS

In 1677, the British Parliament passed "An Act for the Prevention of Frauds and Perjuries," generally referred to as the **Statute of Frauds.** *This act was designed to prevent the perpetration of frauds arising out of purely oral agreements.* It required that there be specified evidence in writing (called a "memorandum") about certain kinds of contracts that the Parliament considered particularly subject to perjury, abuse, and frauds.

When the various states adopted the common law of England in 1776, this common law included the English statute law then in effect, including the Statute of Frauds. All 50 states, to this very day, follow the old English Statute of Frauds as part of their common law, and in addition follow the Uniform Commercial Code statute of frauds provision relating to sales contracts. The British, however, have repealed the original Statute of Frauds.

The Statute of Frauds has two features: (1) it covers certain categories of contracts, and (2) it requires that there be a written memorandum about contracts within these stated categories.

SCOPE OF THE STATUTE OF FRAUDS

The Statute of Frauds relates to six kinds of contracts that require written evidence:

1. A contract calling for the sale of land or an interest therein.
2. A contract not to be performed within one year.
3. A contract to sell goods for $500 or more (UCC 2-201) or to lease goods for total payments (excluding payments for options to renew or buy) of $1,000 or more (UCC 2A-201).
4. A promise by one person to pay the debt of another.
5. A promise made in consideration of marriage.
6. A promise by the executor or administrator of an estate to pay a debt of the estate out of his/her own funds.

The meanings of specific words and phrases in contracts within these six categories are, of course, subject to judicial interpretation.

A brief explanation of each of these various contract categories follows.

1. **A contract for the sale of land or an interest in land.** This category covers real estate contracts, mortgages, life estates, leases, and easements (rights of way and the like), as well as buildings, growing crops, trees, and other property attached more or less permanently to real estate. There is one important exception to the written evidence requirement: most states, by statute, provide that an oral lease for one year or less is valid.

2. **A contract not to be performed within one year.** If it is possible for a contract to be performed within a year, a memorandum is not necessary.

A contract made January 1 for 2 years must have a written memorandum; a contract made January 1 for 1 year may be oral since the contract can be performed within a year. A contract to do work "for life" may also be oral, since the law acknowledges that a person may

THE STATUTE OF FRAUDS

die within a year and thus fully perform the contract. Similarly, a contract for 5 years terminable at any time upon 90 days prior notice (or some other notice provision of 1 year or less) is a valid oral agreement.[1] Finally, under UCC 8-113, sales of securities may be oral regardless of whether the one-year rule could apply—i.e., no statute of frauds extends to securities sales even when such sales could not be performed within one year of being agreed upon.

3. **A contract to sell goods for $500 or more (UCC 2-201) or to lease goods for $1,000 or more (UCC 2A-201).** UCC 2-201(3)(c) and 2A-201(4)(c) make it clear that the statutes cover only fully executory (unperformed) contracts. Once the goods have been delivered, the money can be recovered on an oral agreement; likewise, if the money has been paid, the goods can be demanded, again on an oral contract.

4. **A promise by one person to pay the debt of another.** This provision generally relates to *contracts of guaranty,* and is sometimes called the "suretyship provision." The contract; of guaranty actually involves two contracts: (1) X is indebted to Y on a contract; and (2) as part of a separate contract between A and Y (with consideration going from each party to the other), A assures Y that, if X does not pay, A will pay. It is this second contract, a guarantee of one person's performance by another person, that is subject to the Statute of Frauds. Such contracts are generally not enforceable if oral.

5. and 6. **A Promise made in consideration of marriage** and **executors' contracts.** These two categories are somewhat archaic and narrowly technical. The category relating to marriage was not intended to be applicable to the promise to marry, that is, it does not involve an engagement to marry, which itself is not a legally binding contract. Rather, it was intended to involve **dowry**—the agreement of a woman (or her father) to pay consideration (money or land) to the intended husband. Although dowry agreements are not common in the United States, *prenuptial (or antenuptial) agreements are covered by the Statute of Frauds since such agreements usually involve a division of property upon death or separation and are made in consideration of marriage.*

---

[1] This possibility test states that if the terms of the contract do not require completion to occur more than one year after the contract was entered into and if it is at all possible for the contract to be completed within that first year, then the contract does not fall under the Statute of Frauds. However, a minority of states, including Alabama and Florida, require that more contracts evince a writing than does this possibility test. Instead of just looking for possibilities of performance within a year, however remote, this minority approach is as follows: (1) When a contract does not provide any agreed upon time period, the court is to examine the contract's purpose and the surrounding circumstances to decide whether the parties must have intended for the contract period to extend longer than a year; (2) If it clearly appears that a longer period was intended, although less than a year was possible, then the contract (under this minority approach) must meet the Statute of Frauds. If there is no reasonable possibility of completing the contract within a year, this minority view is that the Statute of Frauds applies.

The executors' contract relates to the promises of administrators or executors (sometimes called "personal representatives") to pay the estates' debts from their own pockets. This promise is like the agreement to pay the debts of another, and the memorandum in writing is required.

THE MEMORANDUM IN WRITING

> **Caution:** It is misleading to say that the Statute of Frauds requires that certain contracts be in writing.

The Statute of Frauds requires, not that the entire contract be reduced to a written document, but only that there be some written evidence of the agreement. Several documents, letters, or notations may be read together as a memorandum if all clearly pertain to the disputed transaction.

The memorandum in writing must meet the following minimum requirements:

1. It must identify all the essential parts of the transaction. (This requirement is satisfied if only the *quantity of goods* is referred to in a sales contract subject to exceptions made by the Uniform Commercial Code.)

2. It must have been signed by the party being charged (sued) in case of a dispute.

3. It must identify the other party to the agreement.

The contents of item 1 may vary from circumstance to circumstance, but usually a description of the price or consideration, as well as the nature or identification of the items being sold or the work to be done, is required. Note in items 2 and 3 that, although both parties must be identified, both parties do not have to sign; only the party against whom suit is being brought or against whom the claim is being made must have signed. Many legal writers and courts are critical of this one-sided requirement, since only one party (the signer) may be sued, not the other party. Moreover, in this rule, as well as most other rules of law pertaining to signing, *any* signing is sufficient: initials, a stamped or typed signature, a nickname, and the like.

Since the common law favors the enforceability of agreements, *the Statute of Frauds is strictly applied;* that is, if possible, a court will permit an agreement to stand if there is reasonable evidence that the written memorandum is adequate (or, in some cases, if a party asserting the statute has admitted there was in fact a contract, e.g., under UCC

2-201(3)(b), an admitted oral sales contract is enforceable up to the quantity of goods admitted). Moreover, the statute of frauds will not bar enforcement of a contract for specially-made goods, even though it is a sale for $500 or more and lacks the necessary written evidence. UCC 2-201(3)(a) states that such a contract is enforceable "if the goods are to be specially manufactured for the buyer and are not suitable for sale to others in the ordinary course of the seller's business and the seller, before notice of repudiation is received and under circumstances which reasonably indicate that the goods are for the buyer, has made either a substantial beginning of their manufacture or commitments for their procurement."

THE UETA AND ESIGN

The **Uniform Electronic Transaction Act** of 1999 (**UETA**), a model state law enacted in 47 states (all but Illinois, New York, and Washington, although even those states have electronic commerce, authentication, or signature laws), and the federal **Electronic Signatures in Global and National Commerce Act** of 2000 (**ESIGN**) both try to bolster enforcement of electronic contracts. They are procedural statutes that defer to existing substantive law but remove any barriers in those substantive laws that are based upon the method of transaction. For example, UETA permits notary publics to act electronically, thus eliminating stamp or seal requirements.

The UETA strives to eliminate obstacles that the Statute of Frauds might impose by stating four basic principles, at §7: (a) A record or signature may not be denied legal effect solely because it is in electronic form; (b) A contract may not be denied legal effect solely because an electronic record was used in its formation; (c) If a law requires a record to be in writing, an electronic record satisfies the law; and (d) If a law requires a signature, an electronic signature satisfies the law. Pursuant to these principles, electronic records and signatures (e.g., with passwords, digital formats, website click-through processes, or other technologies) may take the place of traditional paper and ink. "The medium in which a record, signature, or contract is created, presented or retained does not affect its legal significance," UETA §7, comment 1. ESIGN likewise counters any Statute of Frauds defense. Under UETA or ESIGN, people can buy insurance, open bank or brokerage accounts, buy securities or mutual funds, get a new mortgage, or take other online actions without signing a piece of paper.

UETA and ESIGN do not mandate the use of electronic records or signatures and thus apply only if the parties agree to conduct transactions by electronic means. The documents offered electronically to consumers must be transmitted "in a manner that reasonably demonstrates that the consumer can access information in the electronic form," the Federal Trade Commission has held.

If a law outside the UETA requires a person to provide, send, or deliver information in writing to another, that information may be communicated in an electronic record that the recipient is able to retain. To be effective, the electronic record must follow any formatting, type size, or other requirements imposed by the law requiring the information. If, however, the law explicitly requires that the information be communicated by a specific method (e.g., registered U.S. mail), that method must be used. (The UETA even provides that, in a legal proceeding, evidence of a record or signature may not be excluded solely because it is in electronic form, UETA §13.)

ESIGN protects customers in the following six ways. (1) A customer cannot be forced to use an e-signature—the company has to offer the option of a paper contract, although it can charge extra for it. (2) A customer must be told how to withdraw his/her consent for an electronic account and have notices sent by mail, instead. (3) E-signature deals have to be confirmed by computer to prove that the customer understood the rules. (4) All notices about an account will arrive by e-mail so that the company also has to confirm that the customer's system can open the electronic envelopes. (5) The electronic contract is to be saved via a method that renders the document unalterable. (6) Critical notices (e.g., utility shutoffs, evictions, foreclosure notices, terminations of health insurance, and most product recalls) must still be sent via the U.S. mail.

Neither UETA nor ESIGN applies to the writing requirements for UCC articles 3 through 9 (every article but 2 and 2A) and/or for the creation of wills, codicils, or testamentary trusts. Because the UETA and ESIGN are similar, it usually does not matter which law applies. Also, ESIGN specifically provides that *if a state has enacted UETA, then UETA rather than ESIGN governs* the exceptions to the state's Statute of Frauds.

OTHER COMMENTS ON THE STATUTE OF FRAUDS

The Statute of Frauds relates only to executory contracts. Once an oral agreement has been carried out by both parties, the court will not nullify the performed agreement. Moreover, if the oral agreement has been partly or fully performed by one party, a quasi-contract action may be brought for the value of benefits rendered.

With regard to real estate contracts subject to the Statute of Frauds, an oral contract may be enforceable by the buyer even without the memorandum in writing if he/she has paid some or all of the purchase price *and* has taken possession of the property.

> **Practical advice:** Regardless of whether the Statute of Frauds applies, put agreements in writing.
>
> **1.** While writing, one often thinks of things that should be covered.
>
> **2.** The writing process helps to clarify terms, hence making the contract better.
>
> **3.** The written document serves as (a) evidence that there was a contract, and (b) evidence of the agreement terms. Memories fade, but written evidence remains.

PAROL EVIDENCE RULE

The **parol evidence** *rule prohibits either of the parties from contradicting or invalidating a fully written contract by means of evidence prior or contemporaneous to the contract and external to the contract.* If the parties have reduced their agreement to writing, why should they be permitted to introduce other evidence contrary to their own written understanding?

Although the word "parol" is derived from a Latin word meaning "oral," the rule prohibits *any* outside (extrinsic) evidence that contradicts or alters the written agreement. Great care should be used, however, in attempting to apply this broadly stated rule, because (1) there are many exceptions and (2) judges often are reluctant to exclude evidence of clear understandings freely assented to by both parties.

Here is a *four-part test* for deciding whether to apply the parol evidence rule:

1. Have parties reduced their contract to *a written document* (put it in writing)?

if yes, then

2. *Is the contract "integrated"* (a final expression of all contract terms)? This is sometimes also referred to as "merging" the terms into a written document.[2] An example of an integration or merger clause (which makes the contract "integrated" or "merged") is the following:

---

[2] *Partial integration* occurs when contracting parties reduce some provisions of their contract to written form and leave other parts unwritten. If the parties meant to leave the latter items to oral expression only, these unwritten provisions may be proven by parol evidence consistent with (e.g., merely adding to, not contradicting) the written portion of the contract.

> "This agreement contains and constitutes the parties' entire agreement and supersedes all prior agreements, contracts, and understandings, whether written or otherwise, between the parties relating to the subject matter hereof."

if yes, then ·

3. Is the proposed evidence to be introduced at court as *evidence of a prior or contemporaneous agreement*?

if yes, then

4. Does the evidence *conflict with or substantially add to* the terms of the integrated contract?

If the answer is "yes" to all four questions, then the parol evidence rule bars the introduction of that evidence. If there is a "no" to any of the questions, the inquiry stops and the determination is that the parol evidence rule does not apply.

The following types of evidence are considered exceptions to (or simply are not covered by) the parol evidence rule, and therefore may be introduced concerning matter *outside* the written contract:

1. *Evidence explaining,* clarifying, or elaborating upon the agreement.

2. *Evidence concerning later dealings* between the parties, particularly if there was mutual consideration, or reliance by either party, with respect to such dealings.

3. *Evidence tending to prove* that the parties did not intend the writing to be a contract, or that the transaction was signed under duress or tainted by fraud, or that other factors would render the agreement void *ab initio*.

4. *Evidence completing* an incomplete written agreement.

5. Evidence that a condition was to occur before the contract was to be enforced, and that condition did not happen.

6. For a sale of goods, explanatory or supplemental evidence of a custom (trade usage) or of the parties' prior repeated actions (course of dealing, course of performance) in similar situations (UCC 2-202).

Because parties have limited time and resources, they often decide to, or simply feel compelled to, not gather all of the relevant information for their decision making. Instead, they only bargain over a small portion (what they consider the key clauses) of a large, complex, and formulaic contract. The economic and public policy premise behind the parol evidence rule thus is undermined because a long, written agreement contains many terms the parties did not discuss and that even the attorneys may have spent very little time reviewing. If a party has otherwise reasonable notions of what the contract involves, but some "buried," non-negotiated point conflicts with these notions, the rule tells judges to bar evidence of those notions. Perhaps the best example of the parol evidence rule's potential to exclude evidence is the complex approach it takes to alleged fraudulent inducement of the agreement. Evidence of the inducement, if it varies from terms in the written agreement, is not admissible. Moreover, the promisee must reasonably have relied on the promisor's promises to perform, with those promises having been false when made. In other words, the promisor not only failed to perform his promise, but also—when he made his promise to perform—already knew that he would or could not perform. Statements that turn out to be merely unfulfilled promises or statements of future events cannot form the basis for a claim of fraud, and thus there is no exception to the parol evidence rule based on alleged fraud. Also, if the false promise does not concern something other than the written terms of the document but instead contradicts terms in that document, the falsehood is inadmissible. Note, however, that according to some state courts, a party is not bound by its signed statement that it (a) received no representations of fact outside the scope of the written agreement, and (b) only relied on representations of fact within the contract. Other courts have honored such clauses and thus barred parties who sign such statements from introducing evidence in conflict with those disclaimers of reliance on extra-contractual representations, particularly if the signing party is "sophisticated" (e.g., an experienced, knowledgeable businessperson, or one represented by counsel).

YOU SHOULD REMEMBER

The Statute of Frauds requires that there be written evidence (called a "memorandum") for certain kinds of contracts: a contract for the sale of land or an interest in land, a contract not to be performed within a year, a provision by one person to pay the debts of another, a promise made in consideration of marriage, an executor's promise to pay a debt of the estate from his/her own funds. In addition, the Uniform Commercial Code requires written evidence for a contract for the sale of goods for $500 or more.

The memorandum in writing does not have to be a fully written contract, but it must (1) include all the essential parts of the transaction, (2) have been signed by the party being sued, and (3) identify the other party to the agreement.

The parol evidence rule prohibits extrinsic (outside) evidence that contradicts or alters a written agreement. Exceptions to the rule, however, are broad and numerous.

PRIVITY

Privity is the old common law requirement that *for a person to have a legal interest or right in a contract he/she must be a party to the contract.*

Exceptions to the Privity Doctrine
Modern common law has grafted two very important exceptions onto the privity doctrine: first, one party to the contract can assign his/her rights to someone else; second, sometimes an outside party intended to benefit by the contract may sue on the contract in order to obtain his/her benefit.

ASSIGNMENT OF RIGHTS

Each party to a contract enjoys a right but is also burdened with a duty. If A agrees to sell his hat to B for $20 and B agrees to buy A's hat for $20, A has a right (to receive $20) and A also has a duty (to deliver the hat); B has a right (to receive the hat) and B also has a duty (to deliver the $20).

Rights are freely assignable. Thus A could assign his right to receive the $20 to C; B could assign his right to receive the hat to D.

Example: Assignment of Rights

Smith gives Thompson an option contract to purchase his property, known as Blackacre, for $100,000. Thompson can freely assign the option (the right to buy Blackacre) to Sanders, and Sanders can show up at the place of sale and purchase the property in the place of Thompson.

Whenever rights are assigned, the party to whom they are assigned (called the **assignee**) is simply substituted for the person making the assignment (called the **assignor**). In the example above, Thompson is the assignor, and Sanders is the assignee. This substitution of parties gives the assignee precisely the same rights and duties as the assignor, that is, the assignee is said "to stand in the shoes of the assignor."

This "standing in the shoes" principle is one of the most important rules of contract law and of commercial law generally.

Suppose that one purchases a boat and signs a contract of sale calling for making certain payments. If the seller of the boat assigns to any third party, such as a bank, the right to receive the payments under the contract, the assignee is substituted for the seller (assignor). If a dispute arises, *any defense (breach of contract, defects in the boat, or other claim of any kind) is good against the assignee to the same extent as against the seller* (assignor).

• *TWO RIGHTS THAT CANNOT BE ASSIGNED*

The right to receive personal services cannot be freely assigned. Thus, if Employee X agrees to perform clerical services in Y's store, and Y sells her store to Z, Z cannot claim the services of Employee X even though Y may have attempted to assign this employment agreement to Z.

Also, *the right to purchase goods on credit* generally cannot be assigned because it is based on a credit rating of the original party.

• *PROHIBITION OF ASSIGNMENT*

The contract *may expressly forbid assignment* by one or by both parties. A milder prohibition may require that the person wanting to assign must obtain the consent of the other party. To this requirement of consent is sometimes added the phrase "which consent shall not unreasonably be withheld."

In case of doubt, if you do not want your contract assigned, place a prohibition in the contract, or require consent of both parties for an assignment.

DELEGATION OF DUTIES

Whether duties to be performed under a contract can be delegated to someone else must be examined on a case-by-case basis. Routine duties, that is, duties that do not require any personal skill or reliability, can be delegated. On the other hand, if the performing party was chosen because of talent, skill, reputation, standing, credit, or the like, such a performing party cannot assign or delegate the duty to perform to some other party. The person contracting to receive this performance is entitled to the work of this skilled or highly regarded person, be he/she a lawyer, doctor, engineer, artist, musician, actor, cabinetmaker, electrician, or other such person; this performer cannot delegate his/her duties to another.

A delivery service, messenger service, meter reader, storekeeper, or other party may perform routine duties that *can* be delegated, but a provision can be made in the contract prohibiting delegation.

NOVATION

A **novation** is an agreement among the two contracting parties and a third party whereby all parties agree that this third party shall perform the duties of one of the original parties to the contract. For example, if a patient agrees that a new doctor may assume the duties of a prior doctor under an original contract, and the new doctor accepts the delegation of these duties, this three-way agreement is a novation and the first doctor is relieved of the obligation.

THIRD-PARTY BENEFICIARIES

The rights of an assignee in a contract constitute one exception to the privity requirement; the other exception is the right of a third-party beneficiary in a contract. A **third-party beneficiary** is a person for whose benefit a contract is made but who is not an actual party to the contract. Two categories of such beneficiaries can bring suit on a contract even though they are not parties to the contract: the creditor beneficiary and the donee beneficiary.

A **creditor beneficiary** is a person who is owed the performance of a contract. If X owes Y $1,000, which X agrees to pay by having Z pave Y's driveway, Y is the creditor beneficiary of the paving contract between X and Z. Y can sue Z to compel him to perform the paving agreement between Z and X. Of course, if Z cannot or does not perform, Y can still sue X for the $1,000 original debt.

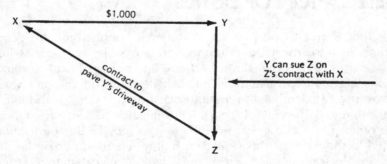

A common third-party creditor beneficiary is a bank holding, say, a mortgage of M that is assumed by a new party, A. Under the assumption contract, A agrees with M that she will take over (pay) M's mortgage. The bank is the creditor beneficiary of this assumption agreement and may bring suit against A even though the bank is not in privity with M and A on their contract. Of course, the bank may also sue the original mortgagor, M, if A does not pay.

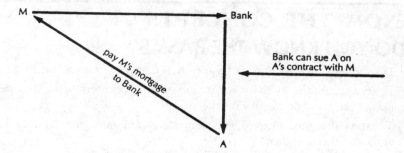

A **donee beneficiary** is the recipient, by gift, of a contractual performance agreed to by two other parties. Thus, if Mr. Smith makes a contract with an insurance company whereby Mrs. Smith will be given certain benefits upon the death of Mr. Smith, Mrs. Smith is a third-party donee beneficiary who can bring suit directly on Mr. Smith's contract with the company if payment is refused upon the death of Mr. Smith.

Beneficiaries of contracts other than creditor or donee beneficiaries cannot sue on the contracts of other parties. These **"incidental" beneficiaries** do not have a substantial interest in the contract. Although such a person may show a benefit under the contract, the contract was not made expressly *for* him/her or *for* his/her benefit. Thus, if a landlord were to employ security guards for an apartment complex and through the negligence of these guards a tenant's apartment was burglarized, the tenant would have no cause for action (under the lease) against the guards.

YOU SHOULD REMEMBER

Privity is the requirement that a person must be a party to the contract to bring suit on the contract. There are two major exceptions: the assignment of rights and third-party beneficiaries.

Most rights can be assigned, but as a rule certain others (e.g., the right to receive personal services) cannot.

Routine duties can be delegated, but duties requiring personal skill or reliability generally cannot.

Novation is a three-party agreement permitting one of the parties to be excused and another person to take his/her place.

There are two important types of third-party beneficiaries: creditor beneficiaries and donee beneficiaries.

KNOW THE CONCEPTS
DO YOU KNOW THE BASICS?

1. Does the Statute of Frauds require that certain contracts be in writing?
2. Is an agreement to work for a person for the lifetime of that person subject to the Statute of Frauds?
3. What is the meaning of the sentence "The assignee stands in the shoes of the assignor"?
4. Would the right to enter another person's property and pick fruit from fruit trees be subject to the Statute of Frauds?
5. Explain why an incidental beneficiary cannot sue on contracts to which he/she is a party.

TERMS FOR STUDY

assignee
assignor
creditor beneficiary
donee beneficiary
dowry
ESIGN
"incidental" beneficiary

novation
parol evidence
privity
Statute of Frauds
third-party beneficiary
UETA

PRACTICAL APPLICATION

1. Evan Eager telephoned the Ardent Cosmetic Company asking for a job as manager of sales. Ardent had advertised this job in a trade publication, stating, in part, as follows: "Exciting opportunity for sales manager with leading cosmetics manufacturer. $99,000 per year; 2 years to make good."

   The president of Ardent, Amy Ardent, agreed on the telephone to employ Evan, and he reported for duty the following Monday. Amy also wrote Evan, stating, "Glad you saw our ad in *Cosmetics World*; welcome aboard!"

   Amy fires Evan after 6 months, and he sues for 18 months' compensation. What will be the result?

2. Guana Fertilizer Company made a written contract with Rufus Rural to mine phosphate from the "Rural farm in Boise County, Idaho."

The contract required Guana to pay a royalty of $35 per ton for all mineable phosphate taken from the property.

(a) Discuss whether parol evidence can be introduced for each of the following purposes: (1) to describe the location of the farm; (2) to define phosphate; (3) to state the depth to which Guana must dig to remove phosphate subject to the royalty.

(b) Decide whether the royalty can be paid in Guana Company stock as opposed to cash.

3. Irene Instructor made an agreement to teach at a well-known university for a period of one year for a salary of $80,000 per year.

(a) Discuss (1) Irene's right to delegate her teaching position to her friend, Smith, a highly qualified and respected teacher in the same field; (2) The university's right to assign this contract to a nearby university.

(b) Discuss Irene's right to assign her salary to a bank as collateral for a large farm.

ANSWERS
KNOW THE CONCEPTS

1. The Statute of Frauds requires that there be written *evidence* of certain contracts. This written evidence is a so-called memorandum, not a full contract.

2. No. It is possible for this contract to be performed within one year.

3. The sentence simply means that the assignee has exactly the same rights as did the assignor. The other party to the contract does not have a better or worse position because the contract has been assigned.

4. Yes. Since the fruit is attached to trees, which are in turn attached to the real estate, and since the right to enter property is a right affecting real estate, a memorandum should be prepared as evidence of the agreement.

5. An incidental beneficiary's benefit is too indirect and too remote. When persons make a contract, they should not have to expect that any person in the world can bring suit on their private agreement.

PRACTICAL APPLICATION

1. This 2-year contract is covered by the Statute of Frauds. There is probably a good memorandum, since the ad contains the basic terms

of the contract and Amy's letter is a signed document that can be read with the ad, thus meeting the requirements of the Statute of Frauds.

2. (a) Items (1), (2), and (3) are definable in court by parol evidence, since they do not contradict the terms of the contract. (b) Since the use of a dollar value suggests cash or the equivalent, Guana stock does not meet these requirements and would, therefore, contradict the writing.

3. (a) (1) The teaching position cannot be delegated, since teaching is a personal service and substitution is not permitted. (2) The same answer is true of the right to receive the teaching skill, since again the relationship between the employer and the employee is personal. (b) Irene can assign her salary, however, since this is the mere right to receive money.

8

DISCHARGE; DAMAGES AND OTHER REMEDIES

KEY TERMS

discharge termination or completion of the contract

condition a fundamental requirement that must be met by one party before the other party has an obligation under the contract

damages the compensation owed to the nonbreaching party to recover any financial loss or injury caused by a breach of contract

---

DISCHARGE

Discharge is a general legal term describing the termination or completion of a contract. This word is much broader than "performance," which denotes only one of several ways in which a contract is brought to an end.

DISCHARGE BY PERFORMANCE

When a contract is performed by both parties, it is said to be discharged by performance. By "performance" is meant substantial performance, not necessarily performance to the very last detail. To determine whether the essential parts of the contract have been performed, one must usually look at the main provisions of the contract; if these have been achieved, the contract has been substantially performed. Thus, if a contract to build a house and to grade and prepare the lot and lawn is fulfilled except for grading the lot, the contract is "performed," but the cost of completing the work can be subtracted from the agreed-upon price. On the other hand, if the contract is not substantially performed, that is, if the house itself is not completed, the contractor can recover, not on his unperformed express contract, but only in quasi contract for the quantum meruit ("going market value"; see Chapter 4) of his limited performance. Of course, the contractor is responsible for his unperformed express contract. Moreover, in many states, a contractor who willfully departs from the contract cannot recover even in *quantum meruit*.

Tender of Performance: occurs when a party tenders (presents) an unconditional offer to perform, and the party is truly ready, willing, and able to perform. If the other party rejects the tender, it is as if the first party **performed.**

CONDITIONS

Conditions are events whose occurrence or nonoccurrence changes, limits, precludes, gives rise to, or terminates a contractual obligation. ***Conditions are distinguished from promises.*** There is breach of contract liability for broken promises, but with non-completed conditions, there simply is no contract (rather than a breached contract).

There are a number of ways to classify conditions: by formation, there are (1) express conditions and (2) implied conditions; by timing, there are (1) conditions precedent, (2) conditions concurrent, and (3) conditions subsequent.

• *EXPRESS CONDITIONS*

Express conditions are conditions that the contracting parties *deliberately* create as such in making the contract. Usually, such phrases as "under the following conditions," "on condition that," "of the essence," and "subject to" are used to describe the agreed-upon essentials of the contract. In making a contract, each party should carefully state as essentials or conditions the things that must be done in order to call forth his/her obligation to perform.

• *IMPLIED CONDITIONS*

Most contracts, whether oral or written, contain **implied conditions,** some implied in fact or by the nature of the agreement, others implied by law (constructive).

Example: Implied Condition

If Arnold agrees to sell his hat to Bert for $25, it may be implied that the hat to be sold is the hat Arnold is wearing. This would be a condition implied in fact. The law implies that the $25 is to be cash and not a check.

The conditions set out in the example are implied from the nature of the transaction even though they are not expressly or consciously stated by the parties.

• *TIME OF PERFORMANCE*

Time of performance is usually not an implied condition; if one of the parties strictly requires performance at a certain time, express words of condition should be used. Thus, if a contract to have a house built for A provides "completion to be on or before September 1," failure to add such a phrase as "time being of the essence," or other words of condition, will require A to accept late completion, that is, September 20 or even October, as substantial performance. On the other hand, in the sale of highly perishable goods or of stocks and bonds having rapidly fluctuating values, time of performance could be implied as a condition because of the unusual or peculiar circumstances.

If time of performance is not specifically stated, courts will ordinarily enforce a contract, and find performance timely, as long as the contract's terms are performed in any reasonable time frame.

• *SATISFACTORY PERFORMANCE*

Satisfactory performance may be called for in the contract. Whether satisfaction is guaranteed as a condition depends on whether the "satisfaction" called for is subjective (a matter of personal taste) or whether the "satisfaction" can be objectively proved. If the satisfaction is subjective, the performer is saying, in effect, "I guarantee that the contract will be completed to your taste," and satisfaction *is* a condition. Thus, an agreement by painter P to paint C's portrait "to the satisfaction of C" sets up a subjective condition that must be met by P before C is obligated to pay under the contract.

On the other hand, an agreement by B to build a club basement for H "as per plans and specifications attached hereto, to the satisfaction of H," sets up an objective satisfaction for H. In other words, if the plans and specifications are complied with, H cannot unreasonably claim that he is not satisfied. In this case, satisfaction is not a matter of taste, and not a condition.

• *CONDITIONS PRECEDENT, CONCURRENT, AND SUBSEQUENT*

A **condition precedent** is one that must be complied with, or must occur, before the other party becomes obligated for his/her performance.

Example: A Condition Precedent

Tom agrees to buy certain property for commercial purposes, provided that Sheila, the seller, obtains proper zoning by an agreed-upon date. The zoning must be obtained before Tom becomes obligated.

Conditions concurrent require that performance by both parties take place at the same time. Most conditions fall within the concurrent category: the deed will be delivered when the price is paid or tendered, or the bank will make a mortgage loan when the buyer presents proof of credit.

A **condition subsequent** may abolish liability or obligation: for example, a clause that the seller will be liable for defective goods provided that the buyer gives notice within 30 days of delivery that the goods are defective. Failure to give such notice absolves the seller of any obligation for the defective goods.

DISCHARGE BY BREACH

If one party to a contract *fails* in a material way *to perform*, the other party has no obligation on the contract—the contract is discharged by breach. Bear in mind, however, that if the contract is substantially performed it is not materially breached. Also, remember that, even when the contract is not substantially performed, the nonbreaching party is responsible for value received (*quantum meruit*) in quasi contract. This value received may be subtracted from damages recovered from the breaching party.

• *BREACH OF CONTRACT AND INTERNATIONAL LAW: THE NACHFRIST NOTICE*

Unless the UCC's perfect tender rule applies (see page 192), only a material breach, or under Civil Law a "fundamental breach," permits the nonbreaching party to cancel the contract. However, CISG Article 49(1) lets a nonbreaching party ("N") issue a Nachfrist notice (taken from German law), which notifies the other, breaching party ("B") that B has been given an additional specific period of time to comply with the N-B contract. If B still fails to comply, N may void the contract because it now has been fundamentally breached. The Nachfrist notice thus lets the innocent (nonbreaching) party do more than just sue for damages. It permits the innocent party to declare a breach to be a fundamental breach that, if not corrected, gives the innocent party the right not to have to perform anymore.

Nachfrist Notice: Example

Anna Agro Machinery (AAM) of Jacksonville, Florida, makes mechanized harvesters and agrees to sell eight to a buyer, Svensson Farm Cooperative ("Svensson") of Goteborg, Sweden. The order calls for the harvesters to be painted blue and gold, Sweden's colors. Svensson learns that the harvesters to be delivered were being painted orange and blue instead. A Nachfrist notice demanding that AAM obey the contract specifications (here, a possible "minor" breach) within a specific time period would establish for Svensson a right to terminate the contract for a "fundamental breach" under Article 49(1) of the CISG, if AAM does not comply.

DISCHARGE BY ANTICIPATORY BREACH

If one of the parties to a contract clearly states or implies that he/she cannot or will not perform as agreed, the other party does not have to sit idly by and await the due date of performance before declaring the contract breached and therefore discharged. Such a statement of non-performance creates an **anticipatory breach**. Anticipatory breach may be implied by some clear, unambiguous action on the part of one of the parties: sale of goods under contract to the other party to some other person; failure to commence construction of a residence within several days or weeks of the date of completion.

When breach appears probable, but is not certain, the innocent party should demand assurance from the other party that the contract will be performed. For sales contracts, if no assurance is given within a reasonable time (no more than 30 days), repudiation has occurred. UCC 2-609.

Basic Principle of Anticipatory Breach
An anticipatory breach occurs if one party to a contract clearly states or implies that he/she cannot or will not perform as agreed, even though the time of performance has not yet arrived.

DISCHARGE BY AGREEMENT OF THE PARTIES

• *MUTUAL RESCISSION*
Since a contract comes into being by mutual agreement, it can be ended at any time by mutual agreement or mutual rescission. **Mutual**

rescission *is a contract to end a contract*. If the contract is wholly executory, the mutual rescission requires no additional consideration.

Parties may orally agree to end a written agreement, regardless of the formality with which the written contract was made. Indeed, most courts hold that a written agreement providing "This contract shall not be modified except in writing, duly executed by a corporate officer of each of the parties hereto" may nevertheless be orally cancelled provided that the parties effecting the cancellation have the authority to do so.

• *ACCORD AND SATISFACTION*

Accord and satisfaction discharge a contract in that the parties agree to substitute a new performance in place of, and in satisfaction of, an existing obligation. An essential element is acceptance of the new performance, frequently the doing of an act, as full satisfaction for an obligation to pay money. The **accord** is the agreement to accept the substitution; the performance of the accord is the **satisfaction**.

Example: Accord and Satisfaction

Arthur owes Beth $1,000, which he cannot pay. Arthur agrees to repair the roof on Beth's house in lieu of paying the $1,000. The agreement to accept the repair is the accord; performance of the repair is the satisfaction.

Acceptance of a new performance in satisfaction of an existing obligation discharges the old obligation and operates as an accord and satisfaction.

• *A "PAYMENT IN FULL" CHECK*

If there is an unliquidated debt (e.g., a partly or totally contested bill), with a colorable (real) dispute, then payment of part of the alleged debt with a conspicuous statement that payment is "in full," usually discharges the debtor from any remaining amounts allegedly owed.

But what if the debtor cannot prove that, within a reasonable time before the creditor tried to collect on (receive payment from) the check, the creditor knew the check was tendered as a payment in full? Then, under UCC 3-311, the creditor's claim for the remainder of the amount supposedly owed is *not discharged* (despite the cashing/depositing of a "payment in full" instrument), *if*

1. the creditor is an organization, and the debtor was informed reasonably prior to his/her tendering the instrument that all communications about disputed debts, including attempted "payments in full," are to be sent to a designated person, office, or place; and the instrument or accompanying communication was not received by the designated person, office, or place; or

2. the creditor is an individual or (assuming no payment went to the organization's designated person, office, or place) is an organization and the creditor proves that, within 90 days after payment of the alleged "payment in full" instrument, the creditor tendered to the debtor repayment of the amount that the creditor received on that instrument.

• *RELEASE*

Another type of discharge of contract by agreement of the parties is a release. A **release** is an agreement by one party to excuse the other party from performance of his contract. If A and B have a contract, and A is unable to perform or is in breach of contract, he may obtain a release from B by the payment of consideration, usually money, although anything of value will support the discharge. A release is valuable protection when a person has, or may have, breached a contract and wishes to avoid any possibility of suit.

In the case of claimed breaches by both parties, with claims and counterclaims by the contracting parties, mutual releases should be obtained in order to ensure the full discharge of the contract by both parties.

• *WAIVER*

Section 1-107 of the Uniform Commercial Code provides that "Any claim or right arising out of an alleged breach can be discharged in whole or in part without consideration by a written waiver or renunciation signed and delivered by the aggrieved party." A **waiver** is the voluntary relinquishment of a party's rights in a contract. A waiver may result in acceptance of defective or incomplete performance.

One should be careful, therefore, to object to incomplete performance and to serve notice that one's rights are *not* being waived when additional time is granted for performance or a defaulting party is afforded an opportunity for correction.

DISCHARGE BY OPERATION OF LAW

Four categories of occurrences will operate to discharge a contract as a matter of law: subsequent illegality, impossibility, bankruptcy, and the statute of limitations.

• *SUBSEQUENT ILLEGALITY*

Subsequent illegality is a rather narrow category of discharge. The principle applies to contracts that are legal when made, but become illegal by the subsequent passage of a statute. The example usually given pertains to alcoholic beverages; contracts to buy and sell become illegal by reason of the passage of prohibition laws.

Generally, legislation making certain acts or conditions illegal contains a **grandfather clause**, an exemption for conditions or circumstances (including contracts) existing before the legislation was enacted. Typical of such clauses are those found in zoning statutes: uses in existence before enactment of a law may continue thereafter as "nonconforming" uses even though contrary to the new statute.

A very real, but also narrow, subsequent illegality occurs with the declaration of war. Statutes making "trading with the enemy" illegal would nullify any executory contract requiring commerce with the enemy or even with a neutral if the "enemy" could be shown to benefit. There is a distinction, however, between executed and executory contracts: if the enemy had delivered goods or licensed patent rights (an executed contract as to him) but money was owing or not yet paid (an executory contract as to the buyer or licensee), payment would be suspended until the cessation of hostilities. After the war was over, the former "enemy" could collect!

• *IMPOSSIBILITY*

If performance becomes *"impossible,"* the contract is discharged by operation of law. There are a number of occurrences that may render performance impossible:

- In a personal service contract (e.g., services of a professional such as a lawyer or teacher), the death or incapacitating illness of the performer.

- Destruction of the subject matter of the contract (the property or goods being bought or sold).

- A law or administrative act of government (such as environmental controls prohibiting disposal of wastes or regulating the chemical or toxic content in goods to be manufactured and sold under a contract) that makes performance illegal.

- Acts of God (natural occurrences such as floods or hurricanes that render performance impossible).

"Acts of God" are frequently addressed in contract provisions called *force majeure* clauses. These clauses may excuse nonperformance (or permit delayed performance) because of a *force majeure*, that is, a superior force operating beyond the control of either party to the contract. Such clauses are highly desirable in contracts where performance is vulnerable to natural occurrences or to strikes, inability to obtain raw materials, or other outside "supervening" interferences. Reliance on the general legal principles of impossibility may not suffice, in that simple discharge of contract by the affected party would leave the other party in an unprotected, precarious position. It is best to define in the contract the *force majeure* occurrence in question and to anticipate possible delays and necessary make-up work, the need to purchase elsewhere, and other events occurring because of superior force intervention.

Some courts follow the principle of *strict impossibility*: the only impossibility excusing performance is absolute factual impossibility—the contract could not be performed *at any cost by anyone* under any circumstance. Other courts follow a rule of *commercial impracticability*, that is, if the contract cannot be performed except at excessive and unreasonable cost, the party subject to such cost is excused under the doctrine of impossibility. Courts following the impracticability rule require, however, that some unforeseen contingency occurred, that such contingency was not bargained for in the agreement, and that custom or usage in the business or trade of the contracting parties did not require that one of the parties assume the risk of the contingency.

Example: Commercial Impracticability

An excavator agrees to excavate a cellar under an existing building for a specified price. Upon commencing work, the excavator finds that underground springs at the site disproportionately multiply the anticipated costs. Even though it might be possible to do the job at enormous loss, many courts would excuse the contractor from performance on the grounds of economic impracticability, or impossibility.

The Uniform Commercial Code (see Section 2-615) also adopts the rule of commercial impracticability with regard to sales contracts.

• *BANKRUPTCY*

The Bankruptcy Act provides that certain contracts are discharged by compliance with the act (see Chapter 13). After a proceeding in a bankruptcy court, the debtor is released from all contractual obligations to his/her creditors.

• *STATUTE OF LIMITATIONS*

The statute of limitations was discussed in Chapter 4. It should be emphasized that, if the promise to perform is renewed *in writing* following the period of limitation, the contract obligation is revived.

YOU SHOULD REMEMBER

"Discharge" means termination or completion of a contract.

A contract may be discharged by *substantial performance* of the obligation (i.e., it may be "performed" even though minor aspects have not yet been completed). The performing party may bring suit on the contract, but the court will deduct the cost of completion.

A contract may be discharged by meeting the fundamental *conditions* of the agreement. These conditions may either be agreed to in the contract specifically as conditions or be implied. It is important in making a contract to use words of condition to describe the things that are fundamental to the parties.

A contract may be discharged by *breach* if one party fails in a material way to perform his/her obligations.

If a contract is not working out to the satisfaction of both parties, it can be ended by *agreement*. In mutual rescission, this agreement may be written or oral: the only requirement is that there be a meeting of the minds to cancel.

In accord and satisfaction, the parties agree to substitute a new performance in place of, and in satisfaction of, the existing obligation. When one party has failed to perform a contract, or if there is dissatisfaction with his/her performance and fear of a suit by the other party, it is recommended that a release be obtained as protection from a later lawsuit. In a waiver one party voluntarily relinquishes his/her rights in a contract.

A contract may be discharged by *operation of law*. Four kinds of occurrences will operate to discharge a contract as a matter of law: subsequent illegality, impossibility, bankruptcy, and the statute of limitations.

Since the meaning of "impossibility" is subject to argument (e.g., strict impossibility versus commercial impracticality), it is helpful to put into a contract a *force majeure* clause, which defines impossibilities that may occur during the life of the contract and states the consequences for the person claiming the impossibility. Generally, *force majeure* clauses relate to things beyond the control of the parties to the contract.

DAMAGES

The word **damages** refers to the compensation due the nonbreaching party to recover any financial loss or injury caused by a breach of contract. Damages are an essential ingredient in every contract case in a court of law.

> ## Essential Elements of Plaintiff's Case in a Contract Action
>
> 1. Proof of the existence of a contract.
> 2. Proof that the contract was breached by the defendant.
> 3. Proof that, as a result of defendant's breach, the plaintiff has been injured or damaged.

Whether the contract action is brought by the plaintiff *pro se* (acting as his own lawyer) in a small claims court, or is a multimillion dollar suit between giant corporations in federal court, these three elements of proof are required.

Sometimes the injury or damage to the plaintiff is negligible, that is, the financial loss to the complaining party is so small as to be practically immeasurable. In that case, the plaintiff will receive only *nominal damages* ($1 or some other token amount), or plaintiff's case may be dismissed altogether for lack of proof of injury. *De minimis non curat lex* ("the law does not concern itself with trifles"), frequently abbreviated simply as *de minimis*, is an important principle of the law and should be carefully considered before a person goes to court to avenge some perceived violation of principle, hurt feelings, or embarrassment.

COMPENSATORY DAMAGES

If there has been a material breach of contract and this breach has caused measurable damages to the plaintiff, the court will try to compensate the plaintiff by awarding a sum of money sufficient to make him/her "whole." This sum of money is called **compensatory damages**. In Hammurabi's Code, society compensated the injured party by permitting him to injure the other party in the same manner; modern law places a money value on the injury and takes that money from the wrongdoer as compensation to the injured party.

Example: Compensatory Damages

Smith agreed to sell a new automobile, model X, to Jones for $30,000. If Smith fails or refuses to sell that automobile to Jones, or for any reason cannot deliver, and if Jones must pay $32,000 to some other seller for model X, the injury to Jones is $2,000, and that amount of money from Smith will make him "whole," or will compensate him.

Three principles operate to limit compensatory damages.

Limitations on the Ability to Be Legally Compensated for Damages

1. Damages must be proved to a *reasonable certainty.*

2. Defendant is liable only for damages that were *reasonably foreseeable* at the time the contract was made or at the time the breach occurred.

3. Plaintiff must use every reasonable effort to *mitigate*, that is, avoid or minimize, the damages.

Because of these three principles, proof of damages may be the most difficult part of the contract case.

• *CERTAINTY*

The first principle, *certainty*, eliminates speculative losses. Suppose, for example, that ABC Contractors, Inc. has a contract with Glass Manufacturing Company to build and have operative a glass factory by February 1, time being of the essence. Suppose that the factory is not completed on time, and the Glass Company claims that it would have made profits of over $1 million during the period of delay in completion. These profits are generally considered too speculative to support an award of damages.

• *FORESEEABILITY*

The second principle, *foreseeability* of damage when the contract was made or breached, is a reasonable guide for a party about to breach his/her contract: What will it cost to breach? This question can be answered only in terms of foreseen consequences. Suppose, for example, that a manufacturing company has a breakdown in its operations. It orders certain machinery parts from X Machine Company, such parts to be delivered in 24 hours. If the Machine Company is 3 days late in delivering the machine parts, the manufacturing company would have no basis for lost profits during the 3-day period if loss of these profits would not have been reasonably foreseeable by X Machine Company at the time of the breach.

• *MITIGATION*

The requirement of *mitigation* is the third limitation on compensatory damages. **Mitigation** means reduction to a minimum. It is the requirement that the injured party use reasonable efforts to minimize his/her loss. *If the plaintiff fails to mitigate damages, such failure may operate as a partial or complete bar to his/her ability to recover in a breach of contract suit.*

Suppose a tenant has a valuable piano under a leaking roof in a rented apartment. If the tenant has the opportunity to move the piano from the leaking area, failure to do so will defeat a contract case (for damages to the piano) against the landlord for breach of the lease provision requiring the roof to be kept in good repair.

Examples: Mitigation Requirement

1. The duty of a wrongfully fired employee to find comparable employment at the best salary possible.
2. The duty of a landlord to find a new tenant to replace a tenant who broke her lease by moving before the end of the lease period.

Of course, the mitigating plaintiff is entitled to compensation for the cost of mitigation. The fired employee is entitled to reasonable moving expenses to his new job; both the fired employee and the landlord whose tenant moved are entitled to reasonable advertising expenses. These direct costs of mitigation which can reasonably be anticipated by the parties are called **incidental damages** and are generally allowed to plaintiffs as part of their loss.

CONSEQUENTIAL DAMAGES

Consequential damages are also allowed as part of the compensatory damages if the breaching party knew or had reason to know that losses would result from the breach. These indirect damages *can* include injury and lost profits caused by faulty performance *if* the principles of foreseeability and certainty are met. If, for example, an automobile with defective brakes is delivered to a buyer pursuant to a contract, injuries to that buyer and other persons caused by this defect may be the responsibility of the seller. Lost profits may be allowed if the breaching party knew or should have known that the other party expected such profits at the time the contract was made.

However, consequential damages are examined carefully under both the certainty and foreseeability tests; their inclusion in a specific case is usually a matter for the fact finder jury (or, if a bench trial, the judge) to decide. For some special types of contracts where the nature and purpose of the agreement make reasonably foreseeable the mental anguish or anxiety associated with a breach, courts have awarded damages related to psychological or economic distress. Such special types of contracts have included insurance policies, funeral arrangements, transportation, hotel stays, weddings, plastic surgery, and other "personal" contracts.[1]

---

[1] Many civil law nations permit a broad form of compensation—often termed "moral damages"—intended to cover not just outrageous contract-related misconduct, but sometimes extending to a broader class of almost any purposeful breach. That makes for potential damage awards that would not be available in common law jurisdictions and also some civil law nations. See pages 477–478.

LIQUIDATED DAMAGES

The question of damages is not always a simple one. *It is a good idea, therefore, to consider the inclusion of a damage clause in the contract itself as part of the meeting of the minds.* It is perfectly acceptable to insert a provision that the performing party shall (or shall not) be responsible for damages. A clause creating responsibility may be preceded by a statement that the parties understand and agree that profits in certain amounts are expected and are dependent on timely completion of performance.

Clauses specifying the dollar amount due upon breach are called **liquidated damage** clauses. When these clauses reflect reasonable efforts by the parties to calculate damages, they are enforced by the courts, particularly if the subject matter is such as to make the actual assessment of damages difficult. However, if the clause is found to be a *penalty* (i.e., an unreasonable or arbitrary amount) for nonperformance or breach, it is not judicially enforceable.

Comparative Law: America, Brazil, and Foreseeability

In the United States, the foreseeability rule limits the award of damages to those damages that were predictable.

In Brazil, on the other hand, the foreseeability rule differentiates a total breach from mere tardiness (a delay but not an outright, absolute breach). For mere delay, liability awards are only for the recovery of foreseeable losses, whereas for the total breach Brazilian law permits the additional recovery of even unforeseeable losses. Generally, the Civil Law is more forgiving about late performance than is U.S. contract law.

PUNITIVE DAMAGES

Punitive damages (to punish), sometimes called **exemplary damages** (to serve as an example), are recoverable in tort cases as punishment for the outrageous, malicious, and oppressive conduct of the defendant. Generally the amount of such damages is a matter for the jury, which may consider not only the oppressiveness or maliciousness of the conduct, but also the wealth (or lack of wealth) of the defendant, since wealth is a factor in assessing the degree of punishment.

A distinct majority of the states do not allow punitive damages for breach of contract.[2] However, when a breach of contract is accompanied by a separate, independent tort (e.g., fraud), this tort (a tort is a private wrong against a person or his/her property; see Chapter 19) may give rise to punitive damages. (This is the rule formulated in RESTATEMENT (SECOND) OF CONTRACTS § 335 (1981).) Also, actions that breach a contract may be considered tortious (constitute a tort), too, in which case the suit may have both contract and tort counts, the latter seeking punitive damages such as for intentional wrongdoing—e.g., battery, defamation, invasion of privacy, conversion, and intentional infliction of emotional distress.[3] Only a few state courts have conceptualized a willful breach of contract, such as a deliberate, completely unprovoked failure to pay money due, as itself justifying punitive damages. Indeed, most courts remain adamant that for punitive damages to be in play, something else must be present—a tort, a special fiduciary relationship—something besides just a deal "gone bad," no matter how outrageous one side's breach may seem.

Example: A Suit with Both Contract and Tort Counts

Under a contract to deliver goods to the plaintiff's pier by barge, the defendant's barge captain strikes the pier and destroys it. The suit may be both in contract (failure to perform) and tort (reckless destruction of property). If the captain acted maliciously (out of spite) or otherwise intentionally and wrongfully (e.g., becoming intoxicated), punitive damages may also be recovered.

OTHER REMEDIES

SPECIFIC PERFORMANCE

In Chapter 1, the equity courts first established in England by the Norman kings were discussed. Certain extraordinary relief requiring the

---

[2] Canada has been more receptive to punitive damages claims in the contract context. The Canadian courts have awarded punitive damages for contract breaches in commercial (e.g., franchising) or other contexts without even expecting a related tort claim by the plaintiff. Criteria for possibly awarding punitive damages due to a breach tend to be that the breaching defendant:
  1. carried out a planned and deliberate breach
  2. had illegitimate intentions and motives
  3. knew its actions were wrong
  4. concealed or tried to conceal the misconduct
  5. persistently, over a long time period, engaged in the wrongdoing
  6. profited from the misconduct
  7. knew that the misconduct violated and harmed interests of the plaintiff that were irreplaceable or deeply personal (e.g., the plaintiff's professional reputation)
[3] These and other torts are discussed in Chapter 19.

power of the king, such as **specific performance** of contract or injunction, were reserved to the king's equity court; money damages were available in the regular English law courts. This division exists to this day as a matter of technical procedure; however, as in the old law, equity is used only as a matter of last resort. If damages will suffice, the plaintiff must seek them in a regular court of law.

Basic Principle of Law

Specific performance of a contract will not be granted if a money award of damages will make the plaintiff "whole."

Suppose X has agreed to sell a new smartphone, model Z, to A for $350. If X refuses to perform her contract of sale, A cannot obtain specific performance in an equity suit. A must buy model Z for the best obtainable price and sue X for the difference in damages.

Two Kinds of Cases in Which Equity Can Be Counted on for Relief

1. The subject matter of the contract is unique (not available in the marketplace).

2. There is a contract for the conveyance of real estate.

    Since real estate is, in a sense, unique, the two categories can really be considered as one.

Suppose that, in the example of the new automobile, the car, instead of being new model Z, were an irreplaceable antique. Equity would then grant relief in specific performance. The same result would apply to parcels of ground, houses, and other items of realty: either buyer or seller can order specific performance in equity.

There is one kind of contract in which specific performance is *not* available: a personal service contract for the work of either a laborer or a professional. These personal service contracts are not enforceable in equity. Courts cannot supervise work to be done; moreover, they cannot be a party to involuntary servitude—a jail term for contempt of court arising out of breach of contract would be a giant step backward in modern law.

INJUNCTION

Injunction is a second form of relief available in equity in certain situations. An **injunction** is a court order to a person or party to do, or refrain from doing, a specific thing. The equity court order may prohibit a breach of contract that has not yet occurred if the prospective breach threatens "irreparable injury." For example, in an employment contract in which a person agrees not to work for a competitor in a specific area for a specific period of time after termination of employment, injunction may be obtained to block the person from violation of his/her agreement. In such a case, great injury may result if the employee works for a competitor even briefly, since the new employer may have full access to the first employer's business secrets through this breach of contract.

REFORMATION AND RESCISSION

If a judge can determine what the parties truly intended, but a written contract does not reflect the parties' intent, the judge may reform the contract. A *reformation* thus states the actual agreement of the parties. When reformation is impractical or the law of mistake otherwise prevents the "rewriting" of a contract, the judge may order a *rescission*. This equitable remedy means that the contract is canceled (rescinded).

YOU SHOULD REMEMBER

The law does not concern itself with trifles, and litigation for abstract principles that have no financial implication should be avoided. An award of money damages is the general goal of contract litigation.

The courts will award compensation for damages only if (1) damages can be proved with reasonable certainty, (2) they were reasonably foreseeable when the contract was made, and (3) the plaintiff used every reasonable effort to mitigate damages.

To receive consequential damages for injury or lost profits, the principles of foreseeability and certainty must be met.

A liquidated damage clause should be considered as a provision in every contract. This is an attempt to specify the anticipated dollar loss should the contract be breached. If the amount is unreasonable, it is not enforceable.

Punitive damages are not generally available in a suit involving a simple breach of contract, since they represent a tort remedy. If, however, there is a tort aspect (e.g., fraud) to the contract suit, punitive damages may be claimed.

Equity actions—specific performance and injunction—are extraordinary relief and will not be allowed if money damages will make the plaintiff "whole." Specific performance may be obtained when the subject matter of the contract is unique or it is impossible to have satisfaction without the contract actually being performed. Injunction should be considered where "irreparable" damages will occur in the absence of a court order requiring performance.

KNOW THE CONCEPTS
DO YOU KNOW THE BASICS?

1. What is the difference between the words "discharge" and "performance"?
2. State the four broad categories for the ways in which a contract can be discharged.
3. In a contract what words and phrases create express conditions?
4. When does the law consider "satisfaction" to be objective and not a matter of taste? What difference does this distinction make in setting up a "condition"?
5. How can a contract be breached before the date of performance arises?
6. When should one obtain a release?
7. Discuss the legal significance of the word "impracticable."
8. Is an "act of God" the same as a *force majeure*?
9. Is a contract obligation "wiped out" (erased) by the passage of time provided in the statute of limitations?
10. What are the three essential elements to a contract case in court? Which is most difficult to prove?
11. What limits are placed on compensatory damages?
12. When are consequential damages not allowed?
13. What prevents the parties, by mutual agreement, from placing any desired dollar amount of damages in their contract as the definition of liquidated damages if the contract is breached?
14. Why does the court permit a jury to hear about a defendant's wealth in a case involving punitive damages?
15. Name two equity remedies available in some breach of contract cases.

TERMS FOR STUDY

accord and satisfaction
anticipatory breach
breach
compensatory damages
conditions
conditions concurrent
conditions precedent
conditions subsequent
consequential damages
damages
de minimis
discharge
exemplary damages
express conditions
force majeure

foreseeability
grandfather clause
implied conditions
incidental damages
injunction
liquidated damages
mitigation
mutual rescission
Nachfrist notice
punitive damages
reformation
release
rescission
specific performance
waiver

PRACTICAL APPLICATION

1. In a contract dated February 15, Wright agreed to build a drugstore on a lot owned by Peoples, near Washington, D.C. The drugstore was to be completed and ready for occupancy by January 1 of the following year. In September, a hurricane struck the Washington area and flooded the work site, where excavations had just been commenced. No further work was done, and Wright walked off the job. On December 1, Peoples declared Wright to be in breach of contract and employed Turner to complete the job. What damages are available to Wright and Peoples, respectively?

2. Assume that plaintiff P and defendant D had a contract, with P to perform specified services in return for D's payment. P claims that he has performed the required services, but D refuses to pay P anything. P sues D. What damages award can P receive if:

   (a) P substantially, but not fully, performed the services?

   (b) P's performance of the contract had barely begun and D received only a small benefit?

3. Gunther, a German national, was the owner of a valuable patent covering dehydrated food processing filed in the U.S. Patent Office. In July 1936, he made a contract with Samson whereby Samson received exclusive rights to manufacture, market, and sell foodstuffs in the United States in accordance with the patent. Samson agreed

to pay Gunther a royalty of 12% on all foodstuffs made and sold in accordance with the patent. Samson's payments were duly made until late December 1941, at which time Samson ceased these payments for "patriotic reasons" (war between the United States and Germany, commencing December 1941 and ending May 1945). In July 1946, Gunther sued for an "accounting" (statement of sales and amounts due) and for back royalties. What would be the result?

4. Willis, a senior at Charlestown University, rented a room from Thomas by oral lease for a period of 10 months to expire June 1. On January 1, Willis moved from the room without notice to Thomas, but left the room occupied by Goldman, also a student. Thomas accepted Goldman's personal check for the January rent, but Goldman moved out on February 1. Thomas now seeks rent from Willis for the months of February, March, April, and May. Can he collect?

5. Singleton was transferred from employment in Dayton, Ohio, to Atlanta, Georgia. In June, he purchased an old house in Atlanta and made a contract with "We Fix It" to have the house ready for occupancy by September 1, "time being of the essence." The contract contained a "liquidated damage" clause providing for damages to Singleton in the amount of $100 per day for each day, after September 1, required for completion. The house was not ready until October 10. Is this damage clause enforceable if (a) the price of the work was agreed to be $10,000 and (b) Singleton had a family that included two teenage children, and (c) the fair rental value of the house was $400 per month?

ANSWERS
KNOW THE CONCEPTS

1. "Discharge" refers to any of the ways in which a contract may be completed or ended; "performance" is one way to discharge.

2. The four categories for discharge are performance, breach, agreement of the parties, and operation of law.

3. "Condition," "of the essence," "subject to," and equivalent words or phrases.

4. "Satisfaction" is considered to be objective if the contract contains a definition of performance, such as a reference to plans and specifications, or if performance is determined by ascertainable criteria. If satisfaction can be objectively proven, it is not a condition.

5. Anticipatory breach may occur before the date of performance arrives, if one party signifies or implies that he/she cannot or will not perform.

6. A release should always be obtained if there could reasonably be a question of performance of one's contract.

7. Many courts consider that a contract performance is "impossible" if it is commercially "impracticable." However, some unforeseen contingency must occur that was not bargained for and that custom or usage in the trade or business does not require one to assume.

8. *Force majeure* (superior force) is broader than "act of God" (natural forces), although it includes acts of God. *Force majeure* applies to any third force or action beyond the control or power of the contracting parties.

9. The statute of limitations does not "wipe out" (erase) the contractual obligation. This obligation may be revived by renewal of the promise.

10. These three elements are (1) that there was a contract, (2) that defendant breached it, and (3) that as a result of the breach, plaintiff was damaged. Depending on the nature of the case, difficulty of proof varies. An implied-in-fact contract is sometimes hard to prove; where performance is complicated, breach may be difficult to show; damages are difficult to prove when bills were not rendered or accounts not kept.

11. The limits are (1) reasonable certainty, (2) reasonable foreseeability, (3) mitigation of damage.

12. Consequential damages are not allowed if they were not reasonably foreseeable.

13. The parties cannot agree upon an unreasonable, unconscionable amount of damages under the guise of "liquidated" damages. To be enforceable, the agreed-upon damages should be related in some way to the expected or anticipated loss that would occur upon breach.

14. In order to assess an appropriate amount for such damages. A person of great wealth is not punished by a money damage award against him/her to the same extent as is a person of more modest means who is subject to the same award.

15. Specific performance of contract, and injunction to prevent breach of contract.

PRACTICAL APPLICATION

1. Peoples is entitled to a completed drugstore for the same price as agreed upon by Wright. This "make whole" principle governs this case. Wright is entitled to the value of the work performed in quasi contract, but this amount would no doubt be absorbed by People's greater damages. The September storm, an act of God, could be *force majeure*, excusing late performance, but Wright gave no notice—he merely walked off the job. Employment of Turner should have occurred early in order to mitigate damages; leaving the work unattended and uncompleted would conflict with the mitigation requirement. Compensatory damages are probably too uncertain; however, incidental damages caused by getting a new contractor to complete the work may well be allowable.

2. (a) Because the contract has been substantially, but not fully, performed, P is entitled to the contract amount minus the cost of completion.

   (b) Because performance of the contract has barely begun, P cannot recover on the express contract; P may be entitled, however, to the fair value of the work performed based on quasi contract.

3. Gunther is entitled to the "accounting" and to back royalties during the war years. Samson's obligations were only suspended during this time (World War II).

4. Thomas is required to mitigate damages by finding a new tenant comparable to Willis, if possible. He found this tenant when he accepted Goldman and Goldman's rent for January—probably a novation. Willis has no further obligation on the oral lease.

5. Is $100 a day liquidated damages, or is it an unenforceable penalty? This $4,000 penalty for 40 days amounts to nearly half the price of the work. It is also too large when compared with the fair rental value of the house ($400 per month). In all events, there should have been a ceiling (e.g., $1,000) on the $100 per day penalty; moreover, it should have been tied to some other ascertainable dollar cost—rental of two hotel rooms, for example. Conclusion: This damage clause is an unenforceable penalty.

9

SPECIAL PROBLEMS CONCERNING SALES CONTRACTS

KEY TERMS

chattel an item of personal property; a movable piece of property

merchant one who deals in goods or has knowledge or skill with regard to goods

sale transfer of title to goods for a consideration or price

This chapter deals specifically with sales contracts and Article 2 of the Uniform Commercial Code. It serves also as a review of Chapters 4 through 8 on general contract principles. A comparison of the law of sales with the common law of contracts will be helpful in understanding both.

ARTICLE 2 OF THE UNIFORM COMMERCIAL CODE

Article 2 of the UCC deals specifically with contracts for the sale of personal property or movables, that is, **chattels** (goods). Much of Article 2 retains common law principles and restates or expands upon the general law of contracts. Sometimes, the Article fills niches and advances legal positions not found in the common law. Also, just as the common law pervades much of Article 2, so too have courts returned the favor, with interpretations of Article 2 affecting the general law of contracts. Judges and legal commentators have tended to extend the code's principles to contracts generally, not just sales contracts.

PRINCIPAL CHANGES FOR SALES CONTRACTS IN ARTICLE 2

HIGHER STANDARDS FOR MERCHANTS

Article 2 imposes higher standards of conduct on merchants than on nonmerchants. Section 2-104(1) defines a **merchant** as one "who deals in goods of the kind or otherwise by his occupation holds himself out as having knowledge or skill peculiar to the practices or goods involved in the transaction...."

A number of provisions of the code implement the higher standards for merchants. For example:

(a) Section 2-103(1)(b): *Every* contract imposes on the parties an obligation of "good faith." "Good faith" in the case *of a merchant* means *both* "honesty" and the observance of "reasonable commercial standards of fair dealing in the trade."

(b) Section 2-201(2): A written confirmation *from one merchant to the other* of an oral agreement satisfies the Statute of Frauds unless the recipient, within 10 days, objects in writing.

(c) Section 2-205: A written firm offer of a *merchant* to buy or sell goods is irrevocable even without consideration, for up to 3 months. (See page 102.)

(d) Section 2-207(2): *Between merchants*, an acceptance may vary the offer, without being treated as a rejection, unless (i) the offer prohibits such varying, (ii) the proposed terms *materially* alter the offer, or (iii) the offeror objects within a reasonable time. Section 207(1) provides that, as to nonmerchants, an acceptance with new terms is an acceptance of the offer as made, not a rejection. The new terms are treated as proposals for additions to the contract unless the offeree specifies, as a condition, that they must be part of the agreement. This section attempts to solve a "battle of forms" in which each party tries to bind the other to his/her version of the contract by a last communication containing such a version. How can merchants avoid the "battle of the forms"? Merchants should limit acceptance to the terms of the offer or should closely monitor the form of all "acceptances."

(e) Sections 2-312 and 2-314n (or 2A-211 and 2A-212): These provide for implied warranties of title, non-infringement, and merchantability by merchants.

STATUTE OF FRAUDS

Under the UCC, an agreement for the sale of goods for $500 or more is subject to the Statute of Frauds. The requirement that the principal terms of the agreement be stated is satisfied if there is "some writing sufficient to indicate that a contract for sale has been made between the parties," but the contract is not enforceable for any quantity of goods beyond that shown in the writing. A reference to price is not required.

GREATER FLEXIBILITY

In general, *more relaxed, flexible rules* are permitted in the creation of sales contracts to carry out the intent of the parties. For example, the common law requires agreement on price before a contract can be said to have been formed. Under the code, a contract for the sale of goods may be silent about price, permitting the parties to set as a price whatever is "reasonable" at the time of delivery of goods. A clause permitting either party to fix the price is enforceable under the code, requiring the party setting the price to act in good faith.

INTERPRETATION OF THE AGREEMENT

To interpret a contract a jury or court tries to determine the intention of the parties. Article 2 of the code sets out certain criteria for determining the meaning of a sales contract. These principles, while usually developed from concepts in the common law of contracts, sometimes reject common law formalism and require judges and juries to consider a transaction's commercial context. Under the UCC, the parties' intent is shown by (a) "the course of performance accepted or acquiesced in without objection" [Section 2-208(1)] and (b) "a sequence of previous conduct between the parties … as establishing a common basis of understanding for interpreting their expressions and other conduct," and (c) "practice or method of dealing … in a place, vocation or trade.…" These rules of interpretation, although specifically for sales contracts, are widely used by the courts to determine the meaning of any contract.

Caution: As stated previously, Article 2 of the code is limited to *sales of personal property* (movables or chattels). It does not cover sales of real estate, nor does it apply to contracts for services or for employment. If personal property is conveyed along with real estate, or if the contract calls for both services and sales (such as supplying and installing automobile parts, or supplying blood for a blood transfusion), the courts attempt to determine whether the predominant factor, or primary purpose, of the contract is to supply services (not covered by the code) or goods (covered by the code). This primary purpose, of course, is shown by the intent of the parties, the nature of the transaction, the terms of the contract, and the like. Thus the sale of a residence, including furniture and lawn equipment, would *not* be covered by the code; a blood transfusion has been held by some courts to be covered by the code, although other courts disagree. However, a vaccination is generally considered a sale of vaccine and hence a transaction under the code!

YOU SHOULD REMEMBER

The principal ways in which the UCC changes sales contracts are as follows:

1. For merchants the code provides that
   (a) higher standards of conduct must prevail;
   (b) written confirmation of an oral agreement may satisfy the Statute of Frauds;
   (c) a firm offer to buy or sell goods may be irrevocable;
   (d) an acceptance may vary an offer without being considered a rejection;
   (e) implied warranties of merchantability and ownership are established.

2. The code establishes a Statute of Frauds for the sale of goods for $500 or more.

3. The code provides for more flexible rules in determining the existence of a sales contract.

4. The code lays down specific criteria for determining the meaning of a sales contract; these criteria are less technical and rely on performance, past conduct, and custom.

5. The sales contract changes in the UCC have influenced courts with regard to the conduct of sellers (courts have become buyer oriented) and the interpretation of contracts generally.

THE CONVENTION ON CONTRACTS FOR THE INTERNATIONAL SALE OF GOODS

Although international trade has taken place since there were first "nations," the emergence of multinational and global business enterprises is a twentieth-century phenomenon. As early as the 1930s, the political, legal, and business leaders of many nations saw the need for, and began to develop, uniform laws to cover contracts for the international sale of goods. The ultimate result of this important legal development was the 1980 Vienna Convention on Contracts for the International Sale of Goods, or CISG. Nearly ninety countries, including most important trading nations, have ratified the CISG. (Key nonsignatories include India, Indonesia, Saudi Arabia, South Africa, and the United Kingdom.) The CISG, as a compromise between the common law/UCC system and the Civil Law system, has been used by courts and other authorities as evidence of international custom.

The United States ratified the CISG in 1987. It thereby became the governing law for most international sales transactions carried out by U.S. firms.

The CISG applies only to contracts between business entities located in two different countries, both of which have ratified the CISG. The application of CISG provisions is not mandatory, however, because any U.S. company dealing with a firm located in another signatory country can, by agreement, provide that another law, and not the CISG, will apply. The specific language used in such a provision must be as follows:

The provisions of the Uniform Commercial Code as adopted by the state of _____ [e.g., Florida], and not the Convention on Contracts for the International Sale of Goods, apply.

The CISG does not apply to domestic sales (e.g., between parties both from the same country), to noncommercial sales (consumer sales of goods bought for family, household, or personal use), or to the sale of services. In situations in which an international contract calls for both services and goods, if the sale of goods outweighs the sale of services then the CISG applies. In these respects, the CISG is very similar to the Uniform Commercial Code.

Like the UCC for domestic sales, the CISG generally controls only when the parties to an international transaction have failed to specify in writing the precise terms of the contract. That is when the CISG fills in the terms for the parties. Here are some specific contract law resolutions under the CISG that differ from domestic American law.

THE FIRM OFFER RULE

The CISG's firm offer rule does not, as the UCC does, require a signed writing (except in those nations that specifically require written contracting). Further, *the creation of a CISG firm offer is more casually established than under the UCC.* CISG Article 16(2) states, "An offer cannot be revoked: (a) if it indicates, whether by stating a fixed time for acceptance or otherwise, that it is irrevocable; or, (b) if it was reasonable for the offeree to rely on the offer as being irrevocable and the offeree has acted in reliance on the offer." Additionally, the CISG does not limit firm offers to a three-month maximum, as the UCC does.

Note that (1) the CISG does *not* limit firm offers to a three month-maximum, as the UCC does; and (2) under the French Civil Code and the French Code of Commerce rules, anyone can make a firm offer, not just merchants.

THE BATTLE OF THE FORMS

The *mirror image rule* has been followed in many nations (e.g., under both the common law tradition of Great Britain and the Civil Law of France). It is, in effect, the law under CISG Article 19(3), which defines "additional or different terms" (material terms) between an offer and an acceptance in such broad, sweeping language—covering, among other things, anything related to price, payment, quality and quantity of goods, place and time of delivery, liability, and settlement of disputes. Thus, *almost all offer/acceptance differences appear to be material alterations and mean that no contract was formed.*

The offeror could ignore the significance of a contrary response and act as if a contract has been formed. Thus the offeror may have "accepted" the offeree's proposed terms. The offeror's conduct—by not objecting (not even orally) to the reply's discrepancies could lead, under CISG Article 19(2), to a contract, with the terms those of the so-called acceptance rather than the offer. Moreover, trade usage, course of performance, and industry standards are clearly important under the CISG. Article 9 of the CISG says, "(1) The parties are bound by any usage to which they have agreed and by any practices which they have established between themselves; (2) the parties are considered, unless otherwise agreed, to have impliedly made applicable to their contract or its formation a usage of which the parties knew or ought to have known and which in international trade is widely known to, and regularly observed by, parties to contracts of the type involved in the particular trade concerned."

Still, CISG Article 19(1) states that any reply to an offer purporting to be an acceptance but containing "additions, limitations or other modifications" is a rejection and a counteroffer (not an acceptance). Also, CISG Article 19(2) states, "However, a reply to an offer which purports to be an acceptance but contains additional or different terms which do not materially alter the terms of the offer constitutes an acceptance, unless the offeror, without undue delay, objects orally to the discrepancy or dispatches a notice to that effect." If there is no objection, the terms of the contract are "the terms of the offer with the modifications contained in the acceptance."

STATUTE OF FRAUDS

There is no CISG Statute of Frauds. The international practice of oral contracting is lawful under CISG Article 11, which states, "A contract of sale need not be concluded in or evidenced by writing and is not subject to any other requirement as to form. It may be proved by any means, including witnesses." This means that CISG-covered sales contracts need no writing to be enforceable (except for those signatory states that, under CISG Article 96, exempted themselves from the provision). Eight CISG nations (Argentina, Armenia, Belarus, Chile, Hungary, Paraguay, Russia, and Ukraine) specifically reserve the right to demand writing for sales contracts. Therefore, an American business contracting with, for example, a business located in Argentina or Russia (both of which opted to retain a writing requirement) would still be governed by a writing requirement in regard to purely executory contracts.

Three common law nations that still have the Statute of Frauds— Australia, Canada, and the United States—did not opt out of the CISG oral contracting rules when they ratified the CISG. The effect is that the domestic Australian, Canadian, and U.S. sales law (e.g., in the United Sates, it is UCC §2-201) has a Statute of Frauds, whereas these nations' international sales law (the CISG) does not.

PAROL EVIDENCE

The CISG has no parol evidence rule. Parol evidence is admissible. This is in accord with the Civil Law tradition, which while sometimes requiring the introduction of a written agreement for cases involving contracts above a certain monetary amount (in effect, something akin to the U.S. Statute of Frauds), once that written evidence is presented then witnesses' testimony or any other evidence is allowed.

NONSALES TRANSACTIONS

Before sales transactions can be fully understood, it is necessary to understand nonsales transactions. The law sets up three important categories of nonsales: bailments, leases, and gifts.

BAILMENT

A **bailment** is a transfer of *possession, care and/or control* of personal property by the owner or possessor (**bailor**) to another (**bailee**) *for a limited time for a special purpose*. Bailments include temporary conveyance of goods for storage, repair, cleaning, and other such transfers of possession of chattels without transfer of title or ownership. There is a detailed discussion of bailments in Chapter 20.

LEASE

A **lease** is a transfer of rights of *possession* by the owner (**lessor**) of real or personal property to another (**lessee**) *for that person's use during a period of time* for an agreed-upon consideration (rent). First proposed in 1987, UCC Article 2A applies many general UCC principles (course of dealings, trade usages, etc.) to the leasing of goods and has been adopted by every state except Louisiana.

GIFT

A **gift** is a transfer of *title* by the owner of goods (**donor**) to another person (**donee**) without consideration. Whereas an executory (promised) gift is not an enforceable agreement, a fully executed (completed) gift will not be legally disturbed. An executed gift requires (a) delivery, (b) donor's intent to make a gift, and (c) donee's acceptance.

DEFINITION OF A SALE

Both the code (Section 2-106) and the common law agree that a **sale** of goods is the transfer of title from a seller to a buyer for a consideration known as the price.

Sometimes, however, the UCC and the common law of contracts differ. For example, in some states, the statute of limitations for a breach of a sales contract (four years under the UCC) and for other types of breaches of contract may be different time periods; in such a case, whether a transaction involves goods, and is thus a sale, could make the difference in whether a lawsuit can proceed.

Under UCC Section 2–102, "goods" are tangible, moveable, personal property (e.g., motor vehicles, ships, animals, mobile or modular homes, machinery, etc.). Services, real estate, and intellectual property are not goods and therefore are not governed by UCC Article 2. For example, bailments or loans of an item, book publication contracts, commission contracts, construction contracts, security or financing agreements generally, and equipment installation or maintenance agreements are not goods.

Example: The sale of a business ordinarily encompasses transfers of equipment, furniture, and other moveables (perhaps inventory), which are goods. But it also often includes, among other things, customer accounts, goodwill, and real property (*non*goods). For such "*mixed*" *transactions* (involving both goods and nongoods), the courts try to find what the predominant purpose is: does it provide goods or services? In other words, which of the two dominates, while—conversely—which is merely incidental to the main transaction?

GOODS OR SERVICES? (the usual classification)

Goods	Service
carpeting (although installed)	alarm systems
computer software programs or systems (although intellectual property is involved)	architectural work or building construction
concert tickets	caskets (part of funeral services)
film (including processing)	blood (from an individual to a blood bank)
granite blocks (to be put into buildings)	herbicide spraying
jet aircraft (even though there is training of flight and maintenance personnel)	hog confinement (pig pen) drains
prescription drugs	lockers (including installation)
rare coins	steel for a bridge
shrubs, sod, and trees (even if planted as part of a landscaping contract; but once planted they become part of the real estate)	swimming pools (construction)
	tanks and power-washes
	tour tickets or tickets for amusement rides
	waste-disposal systems
	wedding photos (including photographic services)

The Special Case of Utilities

Public utility transmission of natural gas and water is usually held to be goods; likewise for electricity that has passed the home meter and been measured. However, electricity is usually deemed a service when transmitted by high voltage wires before being converted into usable electric currents.

TRANSFER OF TITLE

One of the cornerstone principles of the common law is that a seller can transfer only the title (rights) that he/she has. If the seller has no title (e.g., a thief) or has a defective title (e.g., subject to mortgage or lien) he/she transfers merely these limited rights, even though the parties may call the transaction a "sale."

The code, however, recognizes three exceptions to the common law, three circumstances in which a buyer may obtain a better title than the seller has had:

1. A person with a **voidable title** (i.e., title received by a buyer subject to cancellation by the seller) can pass a good title to a bona fide purchaser (a purchaser who has no knowledge of defect).

2. A person who in good faith buys goods from a retailer in the regular course of the retailer's business will get a good title even though the retailer *has transferred a prior interest to* others.

3. A person who in good faith buys goods from a dealer in such goods obtains a good title even though the goods in question may have been entrusted to the dealer by others.

In the first circumstance the seller's right to cancel under the code generally occurs because of some kind of fraud practiced by the buyer: giving a bad check, for example, or making some false representation. The buyer, thus in possession and with color (appearance) of title, *can* transfer title to a good-faith purchaser. The original seller who trusted the original buyer can sue only the buyer with whom he/she dealt.

The other two code exceptions to the common law rule against a buyer acquiring a good title from a seller having a less than perfect title involve *dealers in goods*. In the first, the dealer may have previously sold or committed the goods to another person, for example, on "layaway"; in the second, the goods were entrusted to the dealer or merchant for a special purpose—e.g., repair or storage (as in a bailment)—and the bona fide purchaser reasonably believes the dealer or merchant to be the rightful owner. In both of these dealer situations, the real owner's only remedy is against the dealer, not against the innocent buyer from the dealer.

RISK OF LOSS

Before the widespread adoption of the Uniform Commercial Code, the risk of loss of goods *in the process of being sold and delivered* hinged on the answer to the question, "Who had title at the time of loss?" Thus, if goods were lost during the process of delivery, that is, on the high seas, or were stolen from a warehouse, or were damaged while in rail cars, legal questions of title at the moment of loss or damage determined the liability for repair or replacement.

Under the code, buyer and seller are expected to deal with the problem of potential loss, before or in the course of delivery, by *contract provisions*. If there are no contract provisions, the code establishes general principles for determining risk of loss, depending on whether the contract of sale and delivery is a "shipment contract" or a "destination contract" (Section 2-509).

SHIPMENT CONTRACTS

A **shipment contract** passes the risk of loss to the buyer when the seller delivers the goods to a carrier. The carrier is deemed the agent (representative; see Chapter 14) of the buyer *in any situation in which the contract does not include a requirement for the seller to deliver the goods to a specified destination.*

Frequently, the use of certain shipping phrases creates a shipment contract:

1. *FOB (free on board)*, sometimes with "point of origin," "seller's plant," or "manufacturing facility," together with the statement of FOB point, imposes the risk and cost of loss on the buyer at the FOB point, including the cost of shipment and loading at that point, the seller's factory. However, FOB car or vessel (statement of a different FOB point) requires the seller to load the goods into the buyer's carriage facilities.

2. *FAS (free alongside ship)* requires the seller to deliver the goods at his/her expense and risk to a specified ship and port. For example, "FAS *White Star*, Baltimore, Maryland" would require the seller to deliver the goods to the dock alongside the *White Star* in Baltimore. Cost of loading onto the ship is for the account of the buyer.

3. *CIF (cost, insurance, and freight)* means that the price of the goods includes the cost of shipping and insuring the goods to the buyer's delivery point. These costs are thus passed to the seller.

4. *C & F (cost and freight)* means the same as CIF *without* the insurance obligation falling on the seller.

DESTINATION CONTRACTS

A **destination contract** passes the risk of loss to the buyer when the goods are delivered to the specified destination. The following terms create destination contracts:

1. *FOB destination*: See item 1.
2. *Ex-ship*: This term does not require that the contract name a specific vessel; risk and expense of loss are borne by the seller until the goods have actually been unloaded from the ship.
3. *No arrival, no sale* (UCC, Sections 2-324; 2-613): If the goods do not arrive, there is no contract; and neither buyer nor seller has an obligation to the other unless the seller has caused the nonarrival. If the goods arrive damaged or in violation of the contract, the seller is responsible.

OTHER PRINCIPLES TO DETERMINE RISK OF LOSS

Sometimes it is difficult or impossible to ascertain whether the contract is a shipment or a destination contract *and* there may be no terms in the contract providing for risk of loss. *Section 2-509(3) provides that, if the seller is a merchant, he/she bears the risk of loss until delivery to the buyer; if the seller is not a merchant, risk of loss passes to the buyer when the goods are tendered for delivery, that is, become available to the buyer.* This is another example of the higher duty imposed by the code on merchants.

Occasionally, contracts call for delivery of goods held by a person other than the seller or buyer. If the agreement does not describe the movement of these goods, then the buyer takes the risk of loss once he has the power to possess the goods (e.g., receives a document of title).

Lastly, for breaches: (1) if goods are nonconforming and unaccepted, the risk of loss stays with or reverts to the seller; and (2) if there are identifiable, conforming goods, a buyer who repudiates the contract is liable for a commercially reasonable time for any uninsured loss or damage.

SALE ON APPROVAL/CONSIGNMENT

On occasion, a seller may deliver goods to a buyer for the buyer's inspection and approval (on trial) or for the buyer's resale (*consignment*), title remaining in the seller (*consignor*) and subject to the terms of a contract between the parties. *Until approval* (approval may be express, implied, or conveyed by silence after the passage of a contractually specified period of time), *risk of loss remains in the seller. However, if the goods are delivered on consignment, risk of loss passes to the consignee (person receiving delivery) and this person may convey title freely to others.*

Consigned goods may be seized or possessed by the consignee's creditors. The consignor may protect his/her interest in the goods by placing the public on notice of the consignor's ownership through proper filing of a notice of a security interest under the code, or placing a sign or other clearly visible statement of ownership where the goods are held for sale.

PERFORMANCE OF THE SALES CONTRACT

Performance of the sales contract is governed by Part 5 of Article 2 of the Uniform Commercial Code. Before the provisions of Part 5 are discussed, it will be helpful to review both the common law of contracts and some other provisions of the code that touch on the question of performance.

As always, the performance obligations of parties to a contract are to be found, if possible, in the contract itself. At the beginning of this chapter we discussed the code requirement of "good faith"—"honesty" and, in the case of a merchant, observance of standards of "fair dealing" applicable to his/her trade. In truth, the code did not create the requirements of "good faith," "honesty," or "fair dealing"; they were, and are, part of the common law.

> Unless specific provisions of the code affect or define the performance obligations of the parties, questions of performance are determined by the contract itself or by the general law of contracts.

TENDER

Section 2-507(1) of the UCC requires that the seller of goods "tender" their delivery as a condition of the buyer's duties to accept them and, unless otherwise agreed, to pay for them. Section 2-511(1) requires that, unless otherwise agreed, the buyer's "tender" of payment is a condition to the seller's duty to "tender and complete delivery of the goods."

The word "tender" is a legal term with specific meaning as defined by the code and the common law. As used here, "tender" means merely "to proffer" or "make available."

• WHO TENDERS FIRST?

Although the code sections may seem to create an impasse as to whether the seller or the buyer makes the first tender, in practice an impasse rarely occurs. In most contracts, whether shipment contracts or delivery contracts, including FOB place of shipment or buyer's plant and FAS seller's or buyer's port, the first move must be made by the seller: he/she must tender (make available) the goods to the buyer unless the contract specifically requires that the buyer tender payment, or part payment, before the seller's tender is made.

• SELLER'S TENDER; THE PERFECT TENDER RULE

Under the common law of contracts, substantial performance of a contract is considered performance. The code changes this rule with regard to the seller's obligation to tender conforming goods; the goods must be made available strictly in conformity with the contract (the **perfect tender rule**). Substantial performance will not suffice. Section 2-601 of the code provides that, if the *tender of delivery or if the goods* "fail in *any respect* to conform to the contract," the buyer may do one of three things: (a) reject all the goods, (b) accept all, or (c) accept conforming goods and reject the rest. The buyer must pay for all accepted goods.

Other aspects of the seller's tender are also governed by the code, but these are generally mere codifications (statutory enactments) of the common law. The seller must hold the goods for the buyer for a reasonable time; the goods must be tendered within a reasonable time; if the contract does not specify or imply an obligation to deliver to a specified place, the place of tender is the seller's place of business. Here, also, such terms as "FOB," "FAS," "CIF," "C & F," and "No arrival, no sale," discussed earlier in this chapter, also apply.

• BUYER'S TENDER

In the absence of contract provisions to the contrary, once the seller has made the goods available to the buyer, the buyer must tender payment before taking possession. Section 2-511 provides that "payment" is sufficient if in accordance with the ordinary course of business. This permits payment by check; if the seller requires cash, the buyer must be given a reasonable period of time within which to procure it. Of course, if the check is dishonored, the buyer's title to the goods is voidable and the goods may be repossessed by the seller.

BUYER'S RIGHT OF INSPECTION

Section 2-513 of the UCC provides that the buyer has the right to inspect the goods before payment or acceptance. Cost of inspection must be borne by the buyer unless the goods do not conform to the contract; then these expenses—and the risk of loss—revert to the seller. *A C.O.D. delivery does not provide the buyer with the right of inspection before payment of the price [Section 2-513(3)(a)].*

YOU SHOULD REMEMBER

The contract itself is the best guide to determine the performance obligations of the parties to a contract.

In the absence of express provisions in the contract, the seller has an obligation to tender (make available) the goods; the buyer is obligated to tender payment. Generally, the first move must be made by the seller. The code requires perfect tender (absolute compliance with the contract) by the seller.

The buyer generally has the right to inspect the goods before accepting or paying for them. Ordinarily the buyer may pay for the goods by check; if cash is required, he/she is entitled to a reasonable period of time to obtain it.

REMEDIES FOR BREACH OF SALES CONTRACTS

GENERAL PROVISIONS; THE "MAKE WHOLE" PRINCIPLE

Section 1-106(1) of the code provides that the remedies provided for shall "be liberally administered to the end that the aggrieved party shall be put in as good a position as if the other party had fully performed…." This code provision is a statutory confirmation of the general contract rule for damages (see Chapter 8). The expression "liberally administered" requires the courts to lean over backward in complying with the "make whole" principle in attempting to assess damages.

The code (Section 2-718) provides for liquidated damage clauses in sales contracts (if not unconscionable, penal, or excessive), as does the general law. Section 2-719 permits the parties to exclude or limit consequential damages (e.g., lost profits). However, such a limitation is considered *prima facie* unconscionable in the sale of consumer goods (where it would protect the merchant), but not so in the sale of commercial goods (sold to a merchant or in the course of trade).

There is one other important general provision in the code concerning remedies: *the statute of limitations for a sales contract (period within which suit must be filed) is 4 years* from date of breach (Section 2-725). The code goes on to state that the contract may provide for a shorter period down to 1 year, but may not extend the period beyond 4 years. Limitations for other kinds of contracts vary from state to state.

SELLER'S REMEDIES FOR BREACH BY BUYER

A buyer may breach a sales contract by (i) wrongfully refusing to accept the goods, (ii) wrongfully returning the goods, (iii) failing to pay for the goods when payment is due or (iv) expressing an unwillingness to go forward with the contract.

The code is quite detailed as to a seller's remedies (right to be made whole) upon the occurrence of a breach. Among other things, the seller may cancel the contract and hold up delivery, resell the goods to another buyer and recover damages for any difference in price (see Section 2-706 for this procedure), or recover damages for nonacceptance or repudiation. These rights are cumulative (the seller does not have to choose one to the exclusion of others). As stated, unless limited by contract, the seller is entitled to consequential and incidental damages. (See page 169.)

BUYER'S REMEDIES FOR BREACH BY SELLER

A seller may breach a sales contract by (i) failing to deliver the goods as agreed, (ii) delivering goods that do not conform to the contract, or (iii) expressing an unwillingness to go forward with the contract.

As in the case of the seller's remedies, the code is detailed as to the buyer's remedies upon breach by the seller. The buyer (Section 2-712) may buy other goods (known as "covering") and recover damages for any difference in price plus additional expenses, recover damages based on the difference between the contract price and the current market price (Section 2-713), recover damages for goods that do not comply with the contract, or obtain specific performance if the goods are unique (see pages 171–172).

The reader should compare the provisions of the code for breach of sales contracts with the general common law provisions already discussed. The code does not attempt to rewrite the law: it attempts to improve where appropriate and possible, and to make uniform.

YOU SHOULD REMEMBER

The UCC applies the "make whole" principle to damages incurred by buyer or seller when a sales contract is breached. The statute of limitations is set at 4 years after date of breach, but may by contract be reduced to a shorter term (no less than 1 year).

KNOW THE CONCEPTS
DO YOU KNOW THE BASICS?

1. Why is there a special article in the Uniform Commercial Code dealing with sales contracts but not an article dealing with contracts in general?

2. Give some examples of the higher standard of dealing imposed on merchants by the code.

3. Name two legal transactions that transfer possession, but not title.

4. How does the UCC permit a possessor of property to convey a *better* title than the possessor himself/herself has?

5. Does the UCC rely entirely on contract terms in determining risk of loss during the process of sale and delivery of goods?

6. How does the perfect tender rule change the common law rule of performance?

7. Ordinarily, which tender much occur first: the seller's tender of the goods, or the buyer's tender of payment?

8. What does the UCC's "make whole" principle confirm?

TERMS FOR STUDY

Article 2	lease
bailee	lessee
bailment	lessor
bailor	merchant
chattel	method of dealing
CISG	perfect tender rule
covering	prima facie case
destination contract	sale
disclaimer	shipment contract
donee	tender
donor	voidable title
gift	

PRACTICAL APPLICATION

1. Anderson, purchasing manager for Fast Kolor Paint Company, mailed a purchase order to AB Can Corporation for 100,000 cans. The order form contained 17 printed conditions on its reverse side. The third condition stated: "Buyer may reject any defective goods within 30 days of delivery." AB Can sent a letter confirming the order, but the letter stated: "Any objection to goods shipped must be made in writing within 5 days of receipt of goods." Anderson sought to object to 10,000 of the cans, as defective, on the seventh day after receipt. What would be the result?

2. AG Gas Wells, Inc. and Trans-American Pipelines Company enter into a contract whereby AG agrees to sell natural gas to Trans-American. The price is to be set by AG based on "the average price then being obtained by gas producers in the state of Oklahoma for sales of gas in interstate commerce." If all essentials other than price are established in the contract, is the contract binding as to price?

3. Smith takes an overcoat to XYZ Dry Cleaners to be dry cleaned. He inadvertently left a $200 gold piece in one of the pockets. XYZ sells this coin to Gould, a coin collector. Can Smith recover the coin from Gould?

ANSWERS
KNOW THE CONCEPTS

1. Sales contracts involve both consumers and merchants, categories with high levels of visibility and concern in the law of business. Also, there is a greater need for uniformity of law in these categories.

2. Merchants must observe not only rules of honesty, but also reasonable standards of fair dealing in their trade; they are subject to an implied warranty of merchantability; their contracts are interpreted in accordance with methods of doing business in their trade; they have a high standard of duty to make disclosures to uneducated and untrained buyers; they may be subject to strict liability in tort; they have limited ability to disclaim liability for consequential damages in their sales contracts.

3. Bailment and lease.

4. A person with a voidable title can pass a good title to a bona fide purchaser; a purchaser from a retailer who had previously sold an

interest in the goods to some other person can acquire a good title; a purchaser may get a good title from a dealer in goods even though the dealer is holding the goods for someone else.

5. If the contract terms are clear about risk of loss, these terms control. If the contract contains no provision, the seller bears the risk until delivery of goods to the buyer.

6. The common law rule of performance considers "substantial" performance as an acceptable performance. The perfect tender rule requires absolute compliance with the contract before the tender is considered to have been performed.

7. Ordinarily, the seller's tender of goods is to occur before the buyer's tender of payment.

8. UCC Section 1-106(1) confirms for sales contracts the common law of contracts principle that, in general, the remedies for breach are to be "liberally administered" to make the aggrieved (non-breaching) party *whole*: "put in as good a position as if the other party [the breaching party] had fully performed."

PRACTICAL APPLICATION

1. This is a "battle of forms" question. If Anderson objected to the 5-day notice-of-defect provision in the seller's letter of confirmation, he should have promptly notified the seller. Failure to object sets up the 5-day requirement as part of the contract, and the buyer cannot object after this period of time since the proposed term did not "materially vary the offer."

2. An agreement permitting one of the parties to set the price is enforceable if that party acts in good faith. The gas producer must make a genuine effort, and document this effort, to determine an average price being charged for interstate gas sales in the state of Oklahoma.

3. Smith cannot recover the coin from Gould, a bona fide purchaser, from a party in possession with a voidable title. Smith can, however, sue XYZ Dry Cleaners for the value of the coin.

COMMERCIAL
RELATIONS

10
NEGOTIABLE INSTRUMENTS: DEFINITIONS, CONCEPTS, AND NEGOTIATION

KEY TERMS

commercial paper in its broadest sense, documents used to facilitate the transfer of money or credit

negotiable instrument a type of commercial paper; a written, signed, unconditional promise or order to pay a fixed amount of money to order or bearer either on demand or at a definite time

negotiation the process by which both possession of, and title to, an instrument are transferred from one party to another, with the transferee becoming a holder

holder a person who possesses a negotiable instrument issued, drawn, or indorsed to that person or his/her order or to bearer

The term **"commercial paper"** encompasses a variety of documents used to facilitate the exchange of money, including extensions of credit. There are two important types of commercial paper: a *promise* to pay money (e.g., the promissory note and the certificate of deposit) and an *order* to pay money (e.g., the draft and the check).

Chapters 10 through 12 will discuss the major forms of commercial paper and the uniform law governing those forms.

THE NEGOTIABLE INSTRUMENT AS A FORM OF COMMERCIAL PAPER

The development and use of commercial paper resulted from, and in turn helped to accelerate, the growth of trade. As the words themselves suggest, only after the development of *commerce* did people need *commercial* paper. Once it became impracticable to pay always in cash or commodities, society needed a money substitute that would have the ready acceptability of cash, but would entail much less risk of loss or theft. Various types of commercial paper, including the check, have met these requirements.

Commercial paper, though, is not merely a substitute for cash. It can also serve as a means of extending credit. The borrower agrees in writing to repay his/her loan, and that document (e.g., a promissory note), like a simple money-substitute document (e.g., a check), is a special type of commercial paper: the **negotiable instrument**.

Negotiable instruments are constantly being used by businesses and consumers. One such instrument, the check, is clearly the most common form of commercial paper (excluding money itself), and millions of checks are written every day.

DEVELOPMENT OF THE LAW GOVERNING NEGOTIABLE INSTRUMENTS

In England, negotiable instruments law was part of a field of law known as the *law merchant*, which was first developed and enforced in special merchant courts. Based on the customs among merchants, this law's major concern was to aid the growth of trade.

The merchant courts were abolished in 1756. By then, the law merchant had been incorporated into the common law but remained incomplete and chaotic. Lord Mansfield, Chief Justice of the King's Bench from 1756 to 1788, extended the commercial law and refined the terms and rights of parties under that law.

Relying on Mansfield's work, the British Parliament formally codified the negotiable instruments law by enacting the Bills of Exchange Act in 1882. Many American lawyers, judges, and bankers realized that the United States needed a similar codification, and by 1924 all of the states had enacted a set of proposed uniform laws termed the "Negotiable Instruments Law."

By the late 1940s, changes in commercial practice, as well as divergent interpretations by state courts, led to the belief that negotiable instruments law had to be reformed and made truly "uniform."

THE UNIFORM COMMERCIAL CODE, ARTICLES 3 AND 4

Negotiable instruments law is part of the Uniform Commercial Code, specifically Article 3 (Negotiable Instruments) and Article 4 (Bank Deposits and Collections). These articles, like the overall code, do not represent a brand-new approach to an old subject; rather they attempt to simplify, clarify, and make uniform the nation's commercial law. The process is ongoing. Indeed, a 1990 revised form of Article 3 has been adopted by 49 states (all but New York).[1] Almost all of the law stated in Chapters 10–12 applies to either the original or revised article, but the discussion and UCC references concern revised Article 3.

Although some negotiable documents, such as documents of title and investment securities, are covered in other articles of the UCC, Articles 3 and 4 concern the two fundamental, omnipresent forms of commercial paper: promises to pay money and orders to pay money. As mentioned earlier, promissory notes and bank certificates of deposit are examples of promises to pay money. An order to pay money is called a draft. By far the most common type of draft is the check, which is an order directed to a bank.

ELEMENTS OF NEGOTIABILITY

Section 3-104(a) of the Uniform Commercial Code states the requirements for negotiability. To be negotiable, an instrument must

(a) be written;
(b) be signed by the maker or drawer;

---

[1] UCC Articles 3 and 4 were updated in 2002 to include rules for new technologies and practices in payment systems, but only eleven states have adopted these 2002 amendments. Of course, that does not mean that there are no answers, but simply that there may not be uniformity. Instead, when commercial disputes arise for which the UCC has no provisions, the courts have fashioned their own, often varying approaches, such as for nonpaper payments not yet governed by a UCC Article 3 or 4 revision.

(c) contain an unconditional promise or order to pay a fixed amount of money, with or without interest or other charges described in the instrument; and no other undertaking or instruction given by the maker or drawer, except as authorized by Article 3;

(d) be payable on demand or at a definite time; and

(e) be payable to order or to bearer.

An instrument that meets all of these requirements except the last one (i.e., it is not payable to order or to bearer) is treated like a negotiable instrument if it is otherwise a check (e.g., payable on demand and drawn on a bank) (UCC 3-104(c)(f)).

The five requirements given above are strictly construed. Ambiguities are resolved in favor of nonnegotiability; and, if an instrument is plainly nonnegotiable, the parties to that instrument cannot agree to make it negotiable.

Section 3-104(a) negotiability is thus restricted to drafts, checks, certificates of deposit, and notes. Section 3-102(a) states that funds transfers (Article 4A) and money are not governed by Article 3. While other forms of commercial paper, including investment securities, may be negotiable instruments under Article 3, any conflicting rule in the Federal Reserve System or in Articles 4 (Bank Deposits and Collections), Revised Article 8 (Investment Securities), or Revised Article 9 (Secured Transactions) prevails over Article 3 for those instruments (UCC 3-102).

SIGNATURE OF MAKER OR DRAWER

A "signature" is any symbol that a party executes or adopts in order to authenticate a writing [UCC 1-201(39)]. It need not be handwritten, but must be on the instrument itself [UCC 3-401].

The law presumes that a signature is authentic and authorized, that is, made with the actual, implied, or apparent consent of the person who is to be bound by the signature [UCC 3-308(a)]. In some cases, even an unauthorized signature is treated as if it were authorized (UCC 3-403); for instance, if the person whose signature is unauthorized knew about it but failed to inform innocent parties who reasonably believed that the signature was authorized. UCC 3-403(a).

UNCONDITIONAL PROMISE OR ORDER TO PAY

The term "unconditional" generally means that the promise or order is not limited or changed by a clause or any other item contained within or incorporated into the instrument. Conditions include tying payment to the occurrence of an event or to the performance of an agreement.

• *INTACT NEGOTIABILITY*

Numerous statements can be placed on an instrument without destroying its negotiability. Such statements, which are not deemed to be conditions on the promise or order to pay, include mentioning

(a) the transactions or agreements that gave rise to the instrument;

(b) the instrument's consideration;

(c) a separate writing;

(d) that the obligor waives the benefit of laws (e.g., on debt collection) intended for his benefit;

(e) that rights concerning collateral, acceleration, or prepayment are in a separate writing;

(f) that the instrument is secured (but inclusion of the security agreement or mortgage in the instrument itself will make it conditional);

(g) that a confession of judgment is authorized upon default.

These statements are covered in UCC 3-104(a) and 3-106.

• *DESTROYED NEGOTIABILITY*

Under UCC 3-106(a), two types of statements make an instrument conditional, and thus nonnegotiable:

1. An express condition on payment.

2. A statement that the instrument is subject to or governed by another agreement.

Any instrument that is not a check can be rendered nonnegotiable by issuing it with a conspicuous statement that it is "Not Negotiable." UCC 3-104.

FIXED AMOUNT OF MONEY

To constitute a fixed amount, the amount must be expressly stated or readily verifiable from the terms of the instrument. An amount is "fixed" even if it includes a specified interest rate, installment payments, particular discounts or additions, collection costs, attorney's fees, or other charges.

The term "money" encompasses all means of exchange authorized by some government as part of its currency. Therefore, an instrument payable in dinars, euros, or some other foreign currency can be negotiable (UCC 3-107).

PAYABLE ON DEMAND OR AT A DEFINITE TIME

To be negotiable, an instrument must be payable either on demand or at a definite time (UCC 3-108).

• *ON DEMAND*

A negotiable instrument that does not state a time for payment, states that it is payable on demand, or at sight, or otherwise indicates that it is payable at the will of the holder is a demand instrument (e.g., a check) (UCC 3-108). It becomes due (is to be paid) simply upon being presented for payment.

• *AT A DEFINITE TIME (UCC 3-108(b))*

A "definite time" instrument may be payable

(a) at a fixed date or dates;

(b) at a fixed period after sight (presentment) or acceptance;

(c) at a time which was readily ascertainable when the instrument was issued;

(d) at a fixed or readily ascertainable time subject to (i) prepayment, (ii) acceleration (advancing the date of payment to a sooner, definite time), (iii) extension (postponing the date of payment) at the holder's option, or (iv) extension to a further definite time if by the maker or acceptor or if automatic (upon or after a specified act or event).

The payment time cannot be based on a special act or event that is uncertain as to time of occurrence, *even though the act is certain to happen some time*. Thus an instrument is nonnegotiable if it is payable on Mr. X's death; although death is a certainty, when Mr. X's death will occur is uncertain.

PAYABLE TO ORDER (UCC 3-109(b)) OR TO BEARER (UCC 3-109(a))

"To order" includes instruments that state:

(i) pay to the order of A (an identified person) and (ii) pay to A or his/her order.

"To bearer" includes instruments that do not state a payee, and instruments that state

(i) pay bearer;

(ii) pay to the order of bearer;

(iii) pay A or bearer; and

(iv) pay cash or to the order of cash.

A person can indorse an instrument in such a way as to convert it from order to bearer paper, or vice versa.

RULES OF CONSTRUCTION

Negotiable instruments may be postdated, antedated, or undated (UCC 3-113), and need not state the place where the instrument is drawn or payable (UCC 3-111). The dates on instruments are presumed correct.

Rules of agency (see Chapter 14) are applicable. Thus authorized agents may complete an instrument (UCC 3-115).

If it is unclear whether a negotiable instrument is a draft or a note, the holder may treat it as either (UCC 3-104(e)).

When there are disputes as to the terms of an instrument, the following rules govern:

1. Handwriting prevails over typewriting and print.
2. Typewriting prevails over print.
3. Words prevail over numbers.
4. An unspecified rate of interest is treated as being the same as the judgment rate (interest rate earned on unpaid judgments) for the place where the instrument is paid. Unless stated differently in the instrument, interest runs from the date of the instrument or, if undated, from the issue date. (UCC 3-112, 3-113, and 3-114).

Two or more persons may sign in the same role (e.g., as comakers or codrawers). Unless otherwise specified, each such person is fully responsible for any liability charged to that "role," be it maker, drawer, or whatever.

That an instrument is nonnegotiable does not mean it is worthless. It still may evince a valid, enforceable contract.

TYPES OF NEGOTIABLE INSTRUMENTS
NOTE

The **note**, often called a promissory note, is a two-party instrument in which one person (the **maker**) makes an unconditional, written promise to pay another person (the **payee**), or a person specified by the payee, a fixed amount of money either on demand or at a particular time in the future.

$ __10.02__	Date __May 30, 2016__
__Ninety days__ after the date above __I__ promise to pay to	
the order of _____ Matthew Klein _____	
----------------------ten dollars and 02/100 --------------------------------------	
No. __8165__ Due: __August 28, 2016__	Jim Jones

Jim Jones is the maker, and Matthew Klein is the payee.

Issued by a *financial institution* (e.g., a bank) as an acknowledgment that the institution has received a particular sum of money, the certificate of deposit is the institution's note to pay the depositor that sum of money, plus a stated rate of interest.

DRAFT

A **draft** is a three-party instrument in which one person (the **drawer**) orders a second person (the **drawee**) to pay a fixed amount of money to a third person (the **payee**), or another person specified by the payee, either on demand or at a particular time in the future.

$ __76.54__	Washington, D.C. April 17, 2016

__60 days after date__ Pay to the order of

Pseudo Manufacturing Company

Seventy-six dollars and 54/100--

Value received and charge the same to account of:

To: Erstwhile Services, Inc.

Anytown, U.S.A.   12345   Tom Thompson
                                                    Drawer

Thompson is the drawer, Erstwhile is the drawee, and Pseudo is the payee.

CHECK

A **check** is a special type of draft in which the *drawee* is always a *bank* and the instrument is *payable on demand*.

Date __September 2, 2016__

Pay to the order of __Mary Merchant__ $ 2.00

Two --- dollars

NAME OF BANK

For: __Memorandum__   Bob Buyer

012345666 70 114679

Mary Merchant is the payee, Bob Buyer is the drawer, and Name of Bank is the drawee.

A check drawn by a bank upon itself is a *cashier's check*. The *traveler's check* is likewise a check in which the financial institution is both drawer and drawee, but with the payee/holder required to sign a specimen signature on the instrument when it is issued and then sign it again when cashing it. *Certified checks* are checks that have been "accepted" by the drawee bank, that is, the bank certifies that there is money in the drawer's account to cover the check.

THE PARTIES TO A NEGOTIABLE INSTRUMENT

A note originates with two parties:

1. The maker, who promises to pay.

2. The payee (depositor), who will be paid by the maker.

All drafts start with three parties:

1. The drawer, roughly comparable to the note's maker.

2. The drawee, the party ordered by the drawer to make payment.

3. The payee, essentially equivalent to the note's payee.

> Whereas the maker of a note simply promises to pay, more or less directly, the payee, the drawer of a draft states that a third-party, the drawee, will actually pay the payee. The drawee pays with funds from an account the drawer maintains with the drawee.

Both notes and drafts may have additional parties known as indorsers. Although indorsements come in different forms, they all have a common feature: the signature of the indorser.

YOU SHOULD REMEMBER

A note has two initial parties: a maker and a payee. A draft has three initial parties: a drawer, a drawee, and a payee. Both notes and drafts may have additional parties who are indorsers.

ADVANTAGES OF NEGOTIABLE INSTRUMENTS OVER ORDINARY CONTRACTS

Negotiable instruments are frequently preferred over nonnegotiable types of commercial paper or ordinary contracts. *The major reason for this preference is that, in exchange for greater formal requirements, the negotiable instrument conveys to its holder rights superior to those of someone trying to enforce an ordinary contract* (e.g., a nonnegotiable instrument). (See page 201 for the definition of "holder.") Also, rights, duties, and liabilities of the parties are generally clearer under Article 3 of the UCC than under the common law of contracts.

In the ordinary contract, consideration must be proved. With a negotiable instrument, consideration is presumed unless evidence to the contrary is introduced. Even if the other party proves that there was no consideration, the holder's case will generally not be affected if he/she is deemed to be a *holder in due course* (HIDC) defined in Chapter 11. Whereas past consideration (e.g., a preexisting debt) is not usually an enforceable basis for ordinary contracts, it is sufficient for negotiable instruments. Most important, the assignee of an ordinary contract is subject to personal defenses (see Chapter 11), but a HIDC generally is not (i.e., many defenses ordinarily available under contract law are not as readily available against some holders).

YOU SHOULD REMEMBER

Negotiable instruments are often easier to enforce than ordinary contracts because (1) consideration is presumed, (2) past consideration is sufficient, (3) a HIDC usually need give no consideration, and (4) a HIDC is generally not subject to personal defenses.

THE ASSIGNEE OF A CONTRACT VERSUS THE HOLDER OF A NEGOTIABLE INSTRUMENT

ASSIGNEE OF CONTRACT

In the "ordinary" contract, one party may be able to assign to someone else his/her rights under the contract (e.g., the right to receive money or goods). The party to the contract is called the **assignor**, and the person to whom the assignor assigns his/her contractual rights is the **assignee**. Although not usually a party to the original contract, the assignee "steps into the shoes of the assignor" and not only gains all of the assignor's contractual rights, but also is subject to all of the contractual defenses to which the assignor was subject.

Example: Rights and Risks of an Assignee

Otto's Outerware Outlet (OOO) contracts with Brenda's Bikini Boutique (BBB); OOO is to supply BBB with 25 specially designed "OOO-La-La outfits" at $40 per outfit. If OOO later assigns to a third party, Inga, its rights under the OOO-BBB contract, then Inga has whatever rights OOO had at the time of the assignment. Inga would be entitled to receive $1,000 from BBB if the 25 outfits were delivered to BBB in proper condition and on time. The money would properly belong to Inga because OOO had performed as promised, was thus entitled to the money from BBB, and had assigned to Inga the right to receive the money from BBB.

But what if OOO failed to conform to the terms of the contract, perhaps by not delivering the outfits or by delivering cheap imitations of the "OOO-La-La" line? Then Inga would be subject to BBB's defense against payment to OOO.

The assignee takes a risk, particularly if he/she cannot verify the rights and defenses that are being assumed. For this reason, the potential assignee may request a "premium" (high or extra payments) for taking assignments, and may instead insist on taking a negotiable instrument whenever possible.

HOLDER OF NEGOTIABLE INSTRUMENT

For commercial paper to be readily accepted as a safe substitute for cash, the potential "acceptor" must be confident that the commercial paper does not entail many of the risks assumed by the assignee of an ordinary contract.

A holder possesses an instrument passing to him/her via an unbroken chain of negotiation, if transferred (see below) and (1) issued, drawn or indorsed to him/her or to his/her order, or (2) payable to bearer. To qualify as a **holder in due course (HIDC)**, the holder must have good title to an instrument for which he/she paid value, against which the holder had no notice of any claims or defenses, and which the holder acquired in good faith. See Chapter 11 for a detailed discussion of the holder in due course.

Example: Advantages of a HIDC

If Hollis is the HIDC of a check issued by Baker Co. to pay for an industrial appliance sold by Smith, then Hollis is not subject to Baker's claim against the seller for breach of warranty or for fraud inducing the sale. These are personal defenses against payment on the instrument, which the buyer, Baker, cannot assert against a HIDC. However, these defenses can be used against Smith and any assignee of Smith.

YOU SHOULD REMEMBER

A holder possesses an instrument passing to him/her via an unbroken chain of negotiation (if transferred) and issued, drawn, or indorsed to the holder or to his/her order, or payable to bearer. If the instrument is negotiable, and the holder is a HIDC, then the HIDC generally can defeat personal defenses that would work against an assignee.

NEGOTIATION

The inherent value of negotiable paper rests largely on the easy, relatively safe manner in which possession of such paper and title to it can be transferred. The transfer process is called **negotiation**. The negotiable instrument is "negotiated" (transferred) to a **holder**.

Bearer paper, such as checks made out to "Cash" or indorsed in blank (the holder's name is signed on the back without any accompanying instruction, such as "Pay to the order of X" or "For deposit only"), can be *negotiated merely by a change in possession*, that is, by "delivery." Holders of such instruments may not be the lawful owners; for instance, a thief may take bearer paper.

Order paper negotiation, on the other hand, requires not only delivery but also the proper indorsement(s).

An instrument payable to the order of Joe Smith is not negotiated to Barbara Brown until delivered to her with Joe Smith's indorsement. Without the indorsement, Barbara (and anyone else who acquires the instrument from her) is a mere transferee.

To have rights under an instrument (e.g., obtain payment), a mere transferee (someone to whom the instrument was transferred, but to whom there was no effective negotiation) must prove that the instrument is valid and that he/she has title to it. There are no presumptions in favor of the transferee's claim.

A holder, though, benefits from negotiation. Opposing parties have the burden of proving that the holder is not entitled to payment.

YOU SHOULD REMEMBER

A holder is not necessarily the "owner" of an instrument. A holder can obtain payment on an instrument, however, unless the opposing party proves a defense to payment. Mere transferees, though, must prove their right to payment.

INDORSEMENTS
DEFINITION

Written on a negotiable instrument by or on behalf of the holder, an **indorsement** is the signature of the holder, with or without additional or qualifying words, so that title to the instrument and the holder's property interest in the instrument are transferred to a new holder. An instrument may be indorsed on its front or back, or on an **allonge** (a paper physically attached to, and made a part of, the instrument). When the role of a signatory is ambiguous, his/her signature is treated as an indorsement. Moreover, if a name is misspelled in the instrument, the indorsement may be made in either the correct name, the name as misspelled, or both. (Dual indorsement can be demanded by the person taking the instrument.)

TYPES OF INDORSEMENTS

There are several different types of indorsements.

Blank (general) **indorsements** specify no particular indorsee; a mere signature constitutes a blank indorsement. The effect is to make the instrument payable to bearer. UCC 3-205(b).

Special indorsements specify the person to whom, or to whose order, the instrument is payable. Such an indorsement makes the instrument order paper. UCC 3-205(a).

Example: Special Indorsement

John Smith, the payee of a check, specifically indorses the check to Mary Jones by writing on the instrument "Pay to the order of Mary Jones [signed] John Smith."

John Smith could simply indorse "Pay Mary Jones," and it would still be a special indorsement. It renders the instrument order paper (to Mary Jones), even though the front of a negotiable instrument should not be made out that way (see page 206 and UCC 3-104(a)(1).

An instrument may have any number and combination of blank and special indorsements. The last (most recent) indorsement determines whether the instrument is bearer or order paper.

A third type of indorsement is the **restrictive indorsement**. There are four main types of restrictive indorsements:

1. Those that are conditional. Indorsements can contain conditions that would destroy negotiability if they were in the instrument itself. However, despite its negotiability, no holder (except a bank handling or paying instruments in the normal course of collection) has any right to enforce the conditionally indorsed instrument until the condition is met. UCC 3-206.

Example: Conditional Indorsement

John James, the payee of a check, indorses it as follows: "Pay Jane Jones when she delivers 250 shares of Blue Chip Stock to me [signed] John James."

John then delivers the check to Jane, who in return promises to transfer the stock to John. Jane could negotiate the check to another holder. However, until she met the condition, most subsequent holders could not enforce payment.

2. Those that attempt to prohibit further transfer of the instrument. Like a conditional indorsement, an indorsement prohibiting further transfer has no effect on the instrument's negotiability. An example is: "Pay to the order of Joe Doe only." In effect, the UCC [Section 3-206(a)] converts such an indorsement to "Pay to the order of Joe Doe."

3. Those that include the words "for collection," "for deposit only," "pay any bank," or similar expressions. Like conditional indorsements, those made to facilitate deposits or collections have no effect on negotiability. However, the holder who first receives such an indorsed instrument must obey that indorsement, although subsequent holders need not. "Pay any bank" also means that only a bank may be a holder of the instrument unless it is specially indorsed by the bank or returned to the indorser. UCC 3-206(c).

4. Those that state that they are for the benefit or use of the indorser or another person. An example of this type of indorsement is: "Pay

X in trust for Y." The instrument's first new holder must take any money transferred to him/her via the instrument and apply the money in accord with the indorsement. Subsequent holders have no such constraints unless they know that the terms of the indorsement were violated. UCC 3-206(d).

Regardless of type, the indorsement can have a **disclaimer**. Such an indorsement places subsequent holders on notice that the indorser disclaims liability on the instrument if it is not paid. The most frequent disclaimer is the phrase "without recourse" (a *qualified indorsement*).

KNOW THE CONCEPTS
DO YOU KNOW THE BASICS?

1. Name two purposes of commercial paper.
2. (a) Name the parties to a note.
   (b) Name the parties to a draft.
3. (a) What article of the UCC covers the law of negotiable instruments?
   (b) What article of the UCC covers the law of bank deposits and collections?
4. How is a check different from other drafts?
5. State the differences in the role of consideration when one attempts to enforce a negotiable instrument rather than an ordinary contract.
6. What advantage does a holder-in-due-course have over the assignee of a contract?
7. Which usually requires greater formality (adherence to specific requirements for proper formation): a negotiable instrument or an ordinary contract?
8. What are the requirements for an instrument to be negotiable?
9. *True* or *false*?
   (a) Ambiguities are to be resolved in favor of negotiability.
   (b) By agreement of the parties, a nonnegotiable instrument can become negotiable.
10. What types of statements may affect the amount due under an instrument, but do not leave the instrument without a fixed amount?
11. What types of statements do not make a promise or order conditional?

12. *True* or *false?*

(a) An instrument "payable upon drawer's death" is negotiable.

(b) Agents may complete an instrument for their principals (e.g., employers).

(c) Dates and signatures on an instrument are presumed correct.

13. In disputes about the terms of an instrument, which usually takes precedence?

(a) Handwriting or typing

(b) Typing or print

(c) Handwriting or print

(d) Words or numerals

14. How are negotiable instruments negotiated?

15. What is the effect of a blank (general) indorsement?

TERMS FOR STUDY

allonge

assignee

assignor

bearer paper

blank (general) indorsement

certificate of deposit

check

commercial paper

disclaimer

draft

drawee

drawer

holder

holder in due course

indorsement

maker

negotiable instrument

negotiation

note

order paper

payee

promissory note

restrictive indorsement

special indorsement

UCC Articles 3 & 4

PRACTICAL APPLICATION

1. Weaver, who had an account at Boris's Bank & Trust, borrowed money from Porter. In an attempt to repay Porter, Weaver sent him to Boris, Sr., President of Boris's, with this writing:

April 21, 2016

To: Boris's Bank & Trust
From: W. Weaver

I would be very appreciative if you would pay to the order of J. B. Porter $100.00 (one hundred dollars).

(signed)
W. Weaver

Is this a negotiable instrument?

2.

January 20, 2016   78-84
                                                     ————
                                                     1397

BANK OF MAYFLOWER

Pay _____ Wallace Wimpy _____ $ 58.70

Fifty eight and 70/100 --Dollars

For ____ Career Counseling ____   ____ /s/ ____
                                              Eddie Eager

:1585::0045::802:5

Is this a negotiable instrument?

3. (a) Miss O'Hara obtains a loan of $300 from Mr. Butler, to whom she dates and signs a written "I owe you" (IOU) for $300.00. Soon thereafter, Butler expresses to O'Hara his resolute apathy as to her future whereabouts and seeks recovery of the $300 from O'Hara. Is the IOU a negotiable instrument? Is the IOU crucial, merely helpful, irrelevant, or in fact harmful to his case?

   (b) Suppose Butler, in order to get some cash quickly, discounts his IOU from O'Hara and transfers it to Mr. Dashing Silkes for the sum of $200, with Butler placing his "indorsement" on the back of the IOU. May Silkes collect from O'Hara on the IOU?

4.

```
┌─────────────────────────────────────────────────────────────────┐
│                  LAST COUNTY BANK OF KINGSVILLE                   │
│                                                                  │
│  $2,500.00                                      August 22, 2016  │
│                                                                  │
│  Arnold Anonymous has deposited in this bank                     │
│                                                                  │
│  Two thousand five hundred and no/100 dollars payable to         │
│  Arnold Anonymous at maturity   6   months from date upon return of this │
│  instrument properly indorsed, with interest at 9¼% per annum from date. │
│                                                                  │
│                                   E. Moneybags                   │
│                                   Cashier                        │
└─────────────────────────────────────────────────────────────────┘
```

Is this a negotiable instrument? If so, what type?

5. A promissory note states that one year from the instrument's date the maker will pay the amount set out in the note "with interest at the current rate." Is this a negotiable instrument? If so, what type?

6. (a) Jerry Joker makes a note payable to Kid Kooke "five days after Nate Nerd's first kiss." Is the note negotiable?
   (b) What if Kid gets tired of waiting and plants one, that is, a kiss, on Nate?

7. An instrument from A to the order of C is handed by C to B.
   (a) What should B request from C?
   (b) What may B do if he is afraid that A may not be good for the money and a subsequent holder may seek the money from B, instead?

ANSWERS
KNOW THE CONCEPTS

1. Extension of credit, money substitute.

2. (a) Maker, payee.—(b) Drawer, drawee, payee.

3. (a) Article 3.—(b) Article 4.

4. The drawee of a check is always a bank, and a check, unlike some drafts, is payable on demand.

5. Ordinary contract: consideration must be proved; past consideration generally insufficient.
   Negotiable instrument: consideration presumed; consideration unnecessary for holder-in-due-course; past consideration sufficient.

6. A holder-in-due-course is usually not subject to personal defenses, as an assignee is.

7. The negotiable instrument. Some special contracts (e.g., land transactions) must meet formal requirements to be enforceable. Generally, though, contracts do not require such formality.

8. It must be (1) in writing, (2) signed by the maker or drawer, (3) an unconditional promise or order to pay a fixed amount of money, (4) without any other undertaking or instruction, except as permitted by UCC Article 3, (5) payable on demand or at a definite time, and (6) payable to order or to bearer.

9. (a) False. (b) False.

10. Specified interest rate, stated installments, collection costs, attorney's fees, particular discounts or additions.

11. Statements that mention: the underlying transaction or agreement; the instrument's consideration; a separate writing; that the obligor waives the benefit of laws intended for his protection; that rights concerning collateral, acceleration, or prepayment are in a separate writing; that the instrument is secured; that upon default a confessed judgment is permitted.

12. (a) False.   (b) True.   (c) True.

13. (a) Handwriting.   (b) Typing.   (c) Handwriting.   (d) Words.

14. Bearer instrument: by delivery

    Order instrument: by delivery and proper indorsement.

15. It makes the instrument bearer paper.

PRACTICAL APPLICATION

1. No. The instrument does not contain a promise to pay or an order to pay. It merely says that Weaver would be very appreciative.

2. Yes. Although it is not to bearer or to order (it should read: Pay *to the order of* Wallace Wimpy), the instrument is otherwise negotiable. Under UCC 3-104(c), it is treated as negotiable because it is otherwise a check (payable on demand and drawn on a bank—the Bank of Mayflower).

3. (a) The IOU should be helpful. Although not a negotiable instrument, it is evidence of a loan to O'Hara from Butler.

   (b) Perhaps. Silkes is, at best, an assignee of Butler's rights and duties under Butler's contract with O'Hara (the IOU). Silkes is subject to personal defenses O'Hara may have had against Butler.

4. Yes. A type of note known as a certificate of deposit.

5. No. A "current" interest rate is unclear. Thus there is no sum certain. (If the interest rate were not specified at all, then the judgment rate could be used, so as to render a fixed amount.)

6. (a) No. It is not payable at a definite time.
   (b) The note is still not a negotiable instrument. The happening of an uncertain event does not convert an indefinite as to time (hence nonnegotiable) instrument into a negotiable instrument. However, such a triggering event could make enforceable the contract that may underlie the nonnegotiable instrument.

7. (a) An indorsement.
   (b) When B cashes the instrument, he should indorse it "without recourse."

11

NEGOTIABLE INSTRUMENTS: THE HOLDER IN DUE COURSE, DEFENSES, LIABILITY, AND DISCHARGE

KEY TERMS

holder in due course (HIDC) a holder who takes an authentic-appearing negotiable instrument (1) for value, (2) in good faith, and (3) without notice that it is overdue, has been dishonored, or has certain defenses or claims against it

"real" ("universal") defenses defenses to the enforcement of an instrument that are good against anyone, including HIDCs

personal (limited) defenses any defenses not "real" defenses; generally, insufficient against HIDCs

dishonor to refuse to pay (or accept for later payment) an instrument

discharge the removal of parties' liability on an instrument, usually by payment

The holder in due course (HIDC) of a negotiable instrument is not generally subject to claims or personal defenses that could be raised by the original parties to the instrument. This protection from claims or defenses is the central tenet of negotiable instruments law.

In Chapter 10 you learned what negotiable instruments are and how their title and possession can be transferred (negotiated). This chapter mainly concerns HIDCs, other holders, defenses, and liability among parties. In essence, it covers what happens when something goes wrong.

HOLDER IN DUE COURSE

A holder, you have learned, possesses a negotiable instrument drawn, issued, or indorsed to the holder or his/her order or to bearer. The **holder in due course (HIDC)** is a special type of holder, one who takes possession and title free of most personal defenses (see pages 211–212) that could be raised against the HIDC's transferor.

Payees can be HIDCs. However, in the vast majority of cases, the payee was directly involved in the transaction that caused the instrument to be issued (e.g., the payee sold goods or services to the maker or drawer). So the payee very likely would have had notice of any claim or defense against his/her being paid by the maker or drawer, and the payee would not be a HIDC (UCC 3-302(a)(2)(v) & (vi)).

REQUIREMENTS FOR A HIDC

For a holder to be a negotiable instrument's HIDC:

(1) the instrument when issued or negotiated to the holder must not bear evidence of forgery or alteration or other irregularities or incompleteness calling into question the instrument's authenticity; and (2) the holder must take the instrument (i) for value, (ii) in good faith, and (iii–vi) without notice that it is overdue, has been dishonored or altered, contains an unauthorized signature, or has certain defenses or claims against it (UCC 3-302(a)).

• *TAKING FOR VALUE*

EXTENT OF CONSIDERATION, SECURITY INTEREST, OR LIEN ON INSTRUMENT

A holder takes an instrument for "value" to the extent that (1) the agreed-upon consideration has been performed, or (2) he/she acquires a security interest or lien on the instrument (UCC 3-303(a)(1-2)). "Value" does not arise, however, from security interests or liens obtained via legal proceedings, such as deficiency judgments. (For more on security interests or liens, see Chapter 13.)

Example: Taking for Value

Carrie is to pay Bart $500 in order to receive a check from Anne to Bart in the same amount. If Carrie pays Bart $500, then Carrie can be a HIDC for the full amount of the check. If Carrie gives less than $500, however, then she can be a HIDC for *only* that amount for which she actually gave value to Bart. It does not matter what consideration, if any, passed between prior parties, such as Anne and Bart.

Although an executory promise (to do something in the future) is generally good consideration for contracts, including those under the UCC, it does *not* constitute the "value" necessary to make a HIDC.

PREEXISTING CLAIMS, RECIPROCAL NEGOTIABLE INSTRUMENTS, AND IRREVOCABLE COMMITMENTS

There is also HIDC "value" when a person takes an instrument as security or payment for a preexisting claim, whether or not that claim is due (UCC 3-303(a)(3)). If Baker claimed that Connor owed him money, an instrument from Connor to pay Baker's claim would be for "value." HIDC "value" also occurs when, in order to take an instrument, a person gives a negotiable instrument or makes an irrevocable commitment to a third party (UCC 3-303(a)(4-5)). For instance, Smith gives "value" by giving Jones a check in return for taking Jones's promissory note.

The following are not HIDC "value": (1) gifts, (2) inheritances, (3) unperformed promises (except binding ones to third parties), (4) purchases pursuant to legal proceedings such as foreclosures, and (5) bulk transfers not made in the ordinary course of business.

• *GOOD FAITH*

A person takes an instrument in **good faith** if he/she acts honestly [UCC 1-201(19)]. The test is *subjective*: Did the holder actually believe that the instrument was regular (genuine, authorized, and conforming with the law)? It is usually irrelevant that a reasonable person (the "objective" test) might have acted differently.

Obvious defenses may, though, lead to a presumption against subjective good faith. In addition to the size of any discount from the instrument's face amount, courts will look at the parties' relationship, the instrument's appearance, the time remaining before the due date, and the time and place of the instrument's transfer.

• *ABSENCE OF NOTICE*

Most disputes about HIDC status concern alleged notice of a claim or defense; whether "value" was given is generally easy to determine, and good faith is usually assumed.

"Notice" includes both what the holder actually knew and what he/she should have known from all of the facts and circumstances [UCC 1-201(25)]. Under this *objective* test, obvious forgeries, alterations, or blanks in material terms are themselves sufficient to suggest potential claims or defenses to the instrument; hence nothing else is necessary to show notice. In most other cases, the court will have to look beyond the instrument itself to determine notice.

UCC 3-302(a)(2) covers the defects about which a holder, in order to be a HIDC, must not have had notice.

1. *The instrument is overdue.* For *time* instruments (those with a specific due date), "overdue" means that some or all of the amount of the instrument remains unpaid after the due date. Unless the holder knows that acceleration has occurred, there is no notice of an overdue instrument merely because an installment note or draft contains an acceleration clause.

   For *demand* instruments, "overdue" means either that a demand for payment has been made, yet money remains due, or that the instrument has been outstanding for an unreasonable period of time (more than 30 days, presumably, for certified checks; longer for other instruments).

2. *The instrument has been dishonored.* To **dishonor** an instrument is to refuse payment on, or acceptance of, the instrument. For drafts the dishonoring is generally by the drawee, while for notes it is usually by the maker.

3. *There are defenses against, or claims to, the instrument.* Aside from obvious forgeries or alterations (UCC 3-302(a)(1)), notice of claims or defenses arises from awareness that the obligations of one or more parties are voidable or that the parties have been discharged.

   Merely filing a document or recording it (e.g., in the land records, with a governmental agency or the like) does not provide notice to a holder (UCC 3-302(b)). Courts look beyond such "constructive" (legally implied) notice to determine whether the holder actually knew or should have known about that defense or claim.

Example: Notice of a Defense

If Gary Gullible pays Skippy Skunk $10,000 in cash to obtain a check payable to Skippy in the amount of $11,000 and with the words "trustee for Molly Minor" written in bold face in the memorandum section of the check, Gary may be deemed to have notice of a defense to payment. The words in the memorandum section seem to indicate that payment is intended to be for the benefit of Molly Minor, but from the $1,000 discount and the fact that payment is in cash a person could reasonably infer that Skippy will keep the money for himself.

Without the discount or the cash payment, Gary probably could argue successfully that he neither knew nor should have known that Skippy was violating his duties as Molly's trustee. See UCC 3-307 (Notice of Breach of Fiduciary Duty).

Notice of a Claim or Defense?
(UCC 3-302(a)(2), 3-305 & 3-306)

Generally Yes	**Generally No**

1. Instrument Itself:

Generally Yes	**Generally No**
a. Incorrect indorsements	a. Antedated or postdated
b. Material omissions	b. Originally incomplete
c. Important alterations	and later completed

2. Knowledge of Facts:

Generally Yes	**Generally No**
a. Party's obligation void or voidable	a. Parties to the instrument
b. Obligor has a claim in recoupment against the payee (e.g., the payee failed to deliver conforming goods to the instrument's obligor)	include accommodation parties or fiduciaries (trustees)
	b. Instrument issued or negotiated for an executory promise
c. Obligor has a contract defense against the person trying to enforce the instrument	c. Instrument accompanied by separate agreement
d. Obligor is discharged (e.g., in bankruptcy)	d. Default in interest payments on this instrument
e. Transferor's title defective because of fraud, illegality, theft, etc.	e. Default on another instrument [except (g) in left column]
f. Unauthorized signature and/or completion of the instrument	
g. Default on any other instrument that is part of a series with this instrument	

Notice is effective only if received early enough to give a potential holder time to respond. UCC 3-302(f)

Example: Inadequate (Untimely) Notice

If Company X's branch manager in one store receives notice 30 seconds before Company X's branch manager in another store accepts the instrument in question, Company X may still be a HIDC. Notice was not timely.

Obviously, later notice cannot serve to undo HIDC status; however, it can limit such status to cover only the amount already given for an instrument. Thus the HIDC is not an HIDC for subsequent, postnotice value provided on that instrument.

Lastly, in most cases no connection need exist between (a) whatever deprives a person of HIDC status, and (b) the defense or claim being asserted against the would-be HIDC.

Example: Personal Defenses Against Holder Need Not Be Related to the Notice That Deprived Holder of HIDC Status

If holder Harry takes a note that Harry knows or should know has been dishonored, maker Mike can assert personal defenses against Harry not necessarily related to the reasons for dishonoring the note. In other words, "A miss is as good as a mile"; if Polly Smith is not a HIDC, it does not matter how close she came to being one—she is subject to the same personal defenses as are other mere holders.

THE SHELTER RULE

• *WHO IS COVERED?*

Non-HIDCs usually take whatever rights their transferors had. Thus a transferee who is not a HIDC (e.g., a donee—there is no "value"; the instrument is a gift), but who takes the instrument from a HIDC, acquires all the rights of a HIDC [UCC 3-203(b)]. This **shelter rule** furthers the transferability of instruments and the benefits of HIDC status; HIDCs and potential transferees know that the latter will acquire HIDC status.

Example: The Shelter Rule

Maker is induced by Payee's fraud to issue Payee a promissory note. Payee negotiates the note to Course, who takes it for value, in good faith and without notice that it is overdue, has been dishonored, or has defenses or claims to it. After the note becomes obviously overdue, Course negotiates it to Safehaven.

Although Safehaven is clearly not a HIDC (he has notice that the note is overdue), Course was. Therefore Safehaven takes all the HIDC rights that Course had, and Safehaven is free of Maker's personal defense (fraudulent inducement).

The shelter rule covers anyone who can trace his/her title back to a HIDC. Thus, in the preceding example, once Course takes the instrument, all subsequent transferees, no matter how far down the line, also have HIDC rights.

• *WHO IS EXCEPTED?*

Transferees cannot use the shelter rule if they participated in fraud or illegality affecting the instrument (UCC 3-203(b)). It would be unseemly to let a party acquire HIDC status by "laundering" an instrument through one or more transferees and then reacquiring it. In the preceding example, the fraudulent Payee cannot become a HIDC no matter how far down the chain of title he reacquires the instrument; Course's and the subsequent transferees' HIDC right will not pass to Payee.

YOU SHOULD REMEMBER

A holder has all of the rights of an assignee. A HIDC is a holder who takes a negotiable instrument for value, in good faith, and without notice that it is overdue, has been dishonored, or has defenses or claims against it. Although a mere holder is subject to all defenses, the HIDC is free of personal defenses raised by a party with whom the HIDC has not dealt.

HIDC "value" includes presently performed or past consideration, most security interests or liens, negotiable instruments, and irrevocable commitments to third persons. Gifts, inheritances, mere promises, purchases pursuant to legal proceedings, and most bulk transfers do not constitute HIDC "value."

HIDC "good faith" is tested subjectively: Did the holder believe that the instrument was regular (genuine, authorized, and conforming with law)? The "without notice" issue is measured objectively: besides the holder's actual knowledge, notice also arises whenever a reasonable person would have known. Notice of specific claims or defenses is outlined in UCC 3-302(a), 3-305, and 3-306.

Once HIDC status has occurred, it is not removed by later notice. Personal defenses raised against a holder need not be the same as the defense or other factor that deprived the holder of HIDC status.

The shelter rule extends HIDC benefits to all transferees in the chain of title after a HIDC. The exceptions are transferees who (1) were parties to fraud or illegality affecting the instrument, or (2) as prior holders, had notice of a claim or defense to the instrument.

DEFENSES

The key to understanding the HIDC's special status is to distinguish between **"real" defenses**, which work against even HIDCs, and **personal defenses**, which do not.

"REAL" DEFENSES

These include:

1. Fraud in the execution (factum). Before signing an instrument, the maker, drawer, or indorser is led to believe (with no reasonable opportunity to discover otherwise) that he/she is signing something else, not an instrument.

2. **Forgery** (writing another person's name as if that person had done so) or an **unauthorized signature** (a signature indicating that the signer has authority to bind another person when such is not the case) wholly inoperative for passing title, unless the person whose name is signed ratifies the signature (consents or acquiesces to it) or is estopped to deny it (conducts him-/herself in such a way that another party reasonably assumes that the signature is authorized, and then relies on this assumption). However, a good-faith, paying transferee always has the right to enforce the instrument against the actual forger.

3. Other defenses sufficient (under other law) to nullify the obligor's duty, namely duress, illegality, or incapacity.

4. The obligor's infancy, to the extent it is a defense to a simple contract.

5. Discharge of the instrument, if the holder became a HIDC with actual notice of the discharge.

6. Discharge of the obligor in an insolvency proceeding (e.g., a bankruptcy discharge).

7. The obligor has a claim for recoupment (compensation in the same matter that the instrument concerned), *if* the claim is against the *holder*.

8. Material (important) alteration of the instrument, giving the instrument a different legal effect (e.g., one or more of its terms changes the liability, duties, and/or rights of one or more parties to the instrument). (Nonmaterial alterations, e.g., crossing an uncrossed "t" or changing the date of a note without any effect on its maturity, are not even personal defenses.) The HIDC can still enforce the instrument's terms as they existed before alteration. Also, as with forgeries or unauthorized signatures, a party can ratify or be estopped to deny an alteration.

Example: Material Alteration as a "Real" Defense

If Cora Careless signs a check for $10 and a transferee erases the period and otherwise changes the amount to $1,000, Cora may have a real defense against a HIDC for all but the original $10. The HIDC's hopes for collecting the additional $990 would depend upon estopping Cora—showing that she carelessly left large gaps in her writing or in some other manner made it easy for someone else to change the amount without being detected.

PERSONAL DEFENSES

These include the following:

1. Lack or failure of consideration.

2. Fraud in the inducement. The maker, drawer, or indorser knows that he/she is signing an instrument for x amount; the fraud concerns misrepresentation about the consideration or other matters. If fraud in the execution (factum) could reasonably have been discovered, it is treated as merely a personal defense, like fraud in the inducement.

3. Ordinary contract defenses, such as another party's breach of contract (nonperformance, failure to pay, or the like).

4. Undue influence, mistake, slight duress, infancy (in some states), illegality, incapacity, or other defenses rendering the contract voidable.

5. Payment violating a restrictive indorsement (e.g., a prior transferee's cashing a check indorsed "for deposit only").

6. Breach of warranty when a draft was accepted (UCC 3-417(b)).

7. Modification of the obligation by a separate agreement.

8. Conditional issuance of an instrument.

9. Nondelivery of unauthorized delivery of an instrument.

10. Failure to countersign a traveler's check.

11. Acquisition of lost or stolen bearer instruments.

Example: Acquisition of a Stolen Instrument

Thad Thief picks the pockets of Abner Obtuse and discovers among his ill-gotten gains a bearer check, which Thad indorses to the order of Harry Holder. The theft operates as a personal defense; Abner's title remains good against all but a HIDC or someone taking possession of the check under the HIDC shelter rule. There can be a holder, and even a HIDC, because the bearer paper does not require Abner's forged signature.

12. Unauthorized completion of an instrument. Because the UCC generally permits authorized persons to complete instruments on behalf of others, the burden of paying for unauthorized completions is placed on *the person who might have been more careful*, rather than the HIDC.

Example: Unauthorized Completion of an Instrument

If Barry Bumbler signs a blank check and then loses it, with the finder filling in x amount, a HIDC could collect x from Barry. Of course, if Barry's signature were forged or the check's material terms were altered, the defense would be "real."

13. An obligor's claim for recoupment against someone other than the holder.

RESTRICTIONS ON THE HIDC CONCEPT

HIDC status encourages the use of negotiable instruments, which are almost as transferable as money, yet safer. To paraphrase words Lord Mansfield used, the negotiable instrument is a "courier" not bogged down with any luggage. This is especially the case for a HIDC.

• *STATE LAWS TO PROTECT CONSUMERS*

UCC 3-302(g) subordinates HIDC status to any laws favoring consumer protection and other public policy concerns. With that in mind, some state legislatures and courts have reduced or eliminated the HIDC's right to collect from consumers who have personal defenses. Another approach is simply to eliminate HIDC status in *certain situations*, such as for finance companies closely tied to sellers of consumer products.

So, if Connie Consumer buys a refrigerator from Manny's Manufacturers, the usual law of commercial paper would allow a HIDC to enforce payment from Connie on her check to Manny; it would not matter that Manny is not entitled to payment from Connie because of numerous problems with the refrigerator. Although Connie would not be protected against the HIDC under the UCCC (the instrument was a check), a state court or agency applying other consumer protection principles may seek to shield Connie from being compelled to pay a HIDC.

• *THE FEDERAL TRADE COMMISSION RULE*

To make consumer protection more uniform, as well as to cover states which had failed to act, the Federal Trade Commission (FTC) in 1976 adopted a rule requiring that a consumer credit agreement include the following statement in very bold type.

NOTICE

ANY HOLDER OF THIS CONSUMER CREDIT CONTRACT IS SUBJECT TO ALL CLAIMS AND DEFENSES WHICH THE DEBTOR COULD ASSERT AGAINST THE SELLER OF GOODS OR SERVICES OBTAINED PURSUANT HERETO OR WITH THE PROCEEDS HEREOF.

The notice is required not just when sellers themselves extend credit. If a party other than the seller lends the money needed for a consumer purchase, the loan documents must contain the same bold-type statement (without the words "pursuant hereto or") *if* the lender is affiliated with the seller by common control, contract, or business arrangement or *if* the seller otherwise referred the consumer to the lender.

The net effect is to bar HIDC status. UCC 3-106(d) expressly provides that statements required by legislation or regulation, such as the above FTC-mandated Notice, do *not* make a promise or order conditional (hence, non-negotiable) but *do* preclude the possibility of a HIDC. Thus, a debtor's/consumer's defenses and claims against the seller can be asserted against all subsequent holders.

Of course, if the bold-type statement is missing, the holder could become a full-fledged HIDC. However, that situation is extremely unlikely; those who violate the FTC rule are subject to such severe fines that compliance is usually assured.

LIABILITIES AMONG PARTIES

Heretofore, we have assumed that a person being sued on an instrument is liable unless he/she can successfully assert a defense. We now directly consider liability.

In the absence of a defense, *liability may be based on the underlying contract, on a breach of warranty, or on the instrument itself*. A third type of liability, warranty liability, is discussed later in this chapter.

UCC 3-401(a) provides that no one is liable on the instrument unless it contains his/her signature or the signature of an authorized agent.

PRIMARY AND SECONDARY LIABILITY ON THE INSTRUMENT

The parties to an instrument are either primarily or secondarily liable. **Primary parties** are drawers (for unaccepted drafts), makers, and acceptors (usually drawees), while **secondary parties** are indorsers.

The primary party must pay on an instrument (1) as it existed when drafted by the drawer or maker or accepted by the drawee, or (2) for an incomplete instrument, as it was ultimately completed (if the completion was authorized). A secondary party usually can assume that the primary party will pay on the instrument.

If the primary party has not paid, the secondary party has an obligation to pay, provided that (1) the person seeking payment first demanded payment from the primary party, and (2) the secondary party received notice that the primary party dishonored (refused to pay) the instrument.

The indorser's secondary liability is for the amount stated at the time of his/her indorsement. This contractual liability can be avoided by signing with the words "without recourse." The indorsement is then "qualified." The indorser is saying, "I make no guarantee that the primary party will pay; if he does not, I will not pay, either." (When multiple, unqualified indorsements are on an instrument, the indorsers are generally liable to one another in the order in which they indorse (i.e., each indorser is liable to the subsequent indorser); that chronological order is presumably the order in which signatures appear on the instrument.)

Aside from these contractual liabilities (which can be qualified), secondary parties also may face liability on warranties (see pages 236–237).

THREE MAIN TYPES OF LIABILITY BASED ON THE INSTRUMENT

Three main types of liability problems involve negligent persons, impostors or fictitious payees, and signers lacking capacity or authority.

• *NEGLIGENT PERSONS*

Under UCC 3-406(a), any person whose negligence substantially contributes to the alteration of an instrument or the making of a forged signature is precluded from asserting such alteration or signature against anyone who pays the instrument in good faith or takes it for value or for collection. UCC 3-406 defines negligence in the same way as is done for the common law tort of negligence: failure to exercise ordinary care. It further provides that if the party asserting a 3-406 preclusion also was negligent, then the loss is apportioned between those negligent persons according to the comparative negligence standards found in tort law.

> Remember: To preclude a claim because of UCC 3-406 negligence, the negligence must be significant ("substantially contributes"), not just remotely responsible.

Examples of UCC 3-406 negligence include the following:

1. Upon receiving notice that forgeries are occurring, failure to act to prevent more forgeries.
2. Negligence in controlling access to, and use of, a signature stamp.
3. Drawer's failure to include a corporate designation (e.g., Co., Corp., Inc.) after a corporate name.
4. Delivery of an instrument to the wrong person.
5. Failure to audit corporate books.

• *IMPOSTERS, FICTITIOUS PAYEES, AND TRUSTED EMPLOYEES*

UCC 3-404 and 3-405 say that indorsements in the payee's name are effective for negotiation purposes under the following circumstances:

1. An imposter induced the drawer or maker to issue the instrument to the imposter or his/her accomplice. (This usually involves bona fide payees, with an imposter obtaining the instrument directly from the drawer or maker.)

2. The payee was never intended to have an interest in the instrument, and an agent of the maker or drawer supplied the latter with the payee's name or simply signed the instrument on the maker's or drawer's behalf. (This generally entails "fictitious payees"—made-up accounts actually controlled by dishonest employees.)

3. An employee of the drawer or maker takes the instrument and forges the payee's indorsement; or the employee takes instruments naming the employer as the payee, indorses those instruments in the employer's name and/or has them deposited (with or without indorsement) in an account under the employer's name, but actually used by the employee personally. The key factor is that the employer entrusted this employee with one or more responsibilities involving the issuing, receiving, indorsing, processing, or otherwise handling of the instrument.

With negotiation effective, there can be holders and even HIDCs down the chain of title. Thus the duped drawer, maker, or employer-payee cannot raise the personal defense of fradulent inducement against someone shielded with HIDC status. (Of course, for what it is worth, the drawer, maker, or employer-payee could proceed against the person(s) who duped him/her.)

UCC 3-404's and 3-405's underlying policy is plain: it encourages the ready transfer of instruments, and it discourages carelessness by makers, drawers, and employer-payees.

• *SIGNERS WITHOUT CAPACITY OR AUTHORITY*

Negotiation is effective even though it may be subject to rescission because of incapacity, illegality, duress, fraud, mistake, or break of duty (UCC 3-202). Furthermore, negotiation cannot be rescinded against a HIDC if the problem amounts to merely a personal defense, not a "real" defense. Like UCC 3-404, the UCC 3-202 provision is to be distinguished from blatantly unauthorized signatures (forgeries), which simply do not constitute negotiation and thus cannot create holders, let alone HIDCs.

EXAMPLES OF LIABILITY PROBLEMS

By way of review and example, let us look at two liability problems involving forgery: (1) the drawer's forged signature, and (2) the indorser's forged signature. Then we will examine a hypothetical case involving rescission.

Example: Drawer's Forged Signature

Ira Innocent loses a check that he has not yet written. Fanny Forger finds the check. She fills it out, making it payable to the order of Paula Payee for $2,000, and signing Ira's name as drawer. Fanny, using her fake identification cards as Paula Payee, obtains payment from Tammy Transferee, who takes it for value, in good faith, and without notice of the forgery.

May Tammy recover from Fanny? Yes. An unauthorized signature still operates as the signature of the unauthorized signer [UCC 3-403(a)]. Fanny is also liable for breach of warranties.

May Tammy recover from Ira? Probably not. Ira's signature would be necessary to make the check negotiable and to make him liable on the instrument. Since Ira did not ratify the signature, it remains unauthorized and, having failed to receive a duly negotiated instrument, Tammy is not a holder, let alone a HIDC. Only if Ira was negligent *and* if this negligence "substantially contributed" to what Fanny did, could Tammy recover from Ira (UCC 3-406). To make such a case, Tammy would need more facts.

Incidentally, Tammy cannot force the drawee bank to pay her on the instrument unless the bank has accepted (certified) it (UCC 3-408).

Example: Forged Indorsement

Mary Maker issues a note to the order of Pam Payee for $3,000. Donald Devious steals the check, forges Pam's blank indorsement, and then himself indorses "without recourse" and to the order of Trudy Transferee. Trudy takes it for value, in good faith, and without notice of the forgery. She in turn gives an unqualified indorsement to Troy Transferee, the note being a gift to Troy.

May Troy recover from Donald Devious? Yes. It does not matter that Donald himself indorsed "without recourse." Donald's forgery of Pam's signature leaves him accountable as if he were Pam (UCC 3-403(a). Furthermore, Donald is liable for breach of warranties.

May Troy recover from Trudy? Yes, if Troy indorses the instrument and the primary party (Mary Maker) refuses to pay. Aside from any breach of warranties, Trudy is secondarily liable on the instrument because she failed to qualify her indorsement.

May Troy recover from Mary or Pam? No. As in the preceding example, Trudy is not a holder, let alone a HIDC. (The note was "order paper" to Pam, not properly negotiated by Pam.) Thus Troy (a non-HIDC for the same reason as Trudy and also because of the fact that he did not "take for value") cannot acquire HIDC rights under the shelter rule. Furthermore, there is no indication that either Mary or Pam acted negligently and thus permitted Donald to steal the check and forge Pam's signature (i.e., no recourse under UCC 3-406).

May Pam require Mary to issue another note? Yes, UCC 3-309 gives her that right, although a court might require security indemnifying Mary from loss by possibly having to pay twice. (Such a possibility is more a concern for drawers than makers; under UCC 4-401, a drawer can require the drawee to recredit the drawer's account for the payment of a forged instrument.)

Example: An Instrument Subject to a Defense: Rescission

Ignatius Insane issues a note to the order of Pat Payee. Pat knows that Ignatius is insane. The note is then indorsed without qualification by Pat and given to Arnie. In turn, Arnie indorses "without recourse" to Sue, who pays value in good faith and without notice of Ignatius's condition or any other defense or claim. By the time that Sue transfers the note to Sam, it has, on its face, become overdue.

Can Sam collect from Ignatius? It depends on whether Ignatius's insanity is a "real" defense (sufficient to nullify obligor Ignatius' duty). If it is merely a personal defense, then Sam wins, for he took possession from a HIDC, Sue, and thus acquired rights under the shelter rule. Sam acquired Sue's rights even though he could not himself become a HIDC. (The note was, by the time he took it, obviously overdue.)

Can Sam collect from Pat? Yes, if the primary party, Ignatius, refuses to pay. Pat is secondarily liable; her indorsement was unqualified.

Can Sam collect from Arnie? No, unless Arnie breached a warranty. On the instrument itself, Arnie qualified his indorsement.

What about rescission (cancellation) in order to discharge the instrument? If Ignatius or his guardian rescinded at any time before the formation of a HIDC, then Ignatius probably would be free from paying (UCC 3-306). But what if, after hearing about the rescission, a holder went ahead and transferred the instrument? The holder's actions appear to be in bad faith, and he would probably have to reimburse Ignatius for any amount Ignatius has to pay to a subsequent HIDC.

WARRANTIES ON PRESENTMENT OR TRANSFER

Negotiable instruments are often issued or transferred as part of an underlying contract (e.g., a sale of goods or services). The law governing such matters is the law of contracts, discussed in preceding chapters.

A second type of contractual liability, which we have just finished examining, is based on the negotiable instrument itself. In this case, a signer to the instrument is either primarily or secondarily liable. By signing, having someone else sign on his/her behalf, or ratifying a signature, the primary or secondary party has, in the absence of a qualified signature, made a type of contract to pay according to the instrument's terms.

There is another basis for liability: *warranties.* Any person who obtains payment or acceptance of an instrument, or who transfers an instrument and receives consideration, makes warranties. Under these, like other warranties (e.g., sales warranties under UCC 2-312, 2-313, 2-314, and 2-315), a party may be liable for damages if they are breached. (Note: HIDCs ordinarily can enforce payment on an instrument despite the presence of alleged warranties.)

Some warranties are *imposed on* both the *person who obtains payment or acceptance* [in negotiable instruments law, acceptance is "the drawee's signed engagement to pay a draft as presented" (UCC 3-409(a)] and all prior transferors. There are three such presentment warranties, which are given only to the person who in good faith pays or accepts the instrument (UCC 3-417):

1. That the person is entitled to enforce the draft (obtain the draft's payment or acceptance) or is authorized to act for someone else so entitled. This warranty is given to makers and to drawees of either unaccepted or accepted (certified) drafts. UCC 2-403(1).

2. That the person has no knowledge that the drawer's signature is unauthorized. The warranty only, in effect, protects drawees of unaccepted drafts. UCC 2-403(2)-(3).

3. That the instrument has not been altered. This warranty only protects drawees of unaccepted drafts. UCC 2-403(2)-(3).

These presentment warranties are given only to the person who in good faith pays or accepts the instrument (usually, the drawee). UCC 3-417.

The other warranties are warranties on transfer. They are made by any person who transfers an instrument and receives consideration. This group includes sales agents or brokers, unless they have disclosed that they are acting solely on behalf of someone else. If they make such a disclosure, then they warrant only their good faith and authority.

The five warranties on transfer are as follows:

1. That the transferor is entitled to enforce the instrument.

2. That all signatures are authentic and authorized.

3. That the instrument has not been altered.

4. That the instrument is not subject to a defense or claim in recoupment which can be asserted against the transferor.

5. That the transferor has no knowledge of any insolvency proceeding commenced with respect to the maker, the acceptor, or (for an unaccepted instrument) the drawer.

These transfer warranties are given to the immediate transferee and, if the transfer is by indorsement, any subsequent holder who takes the instrument in good faith. UCC 3-416. This means, in effect, that a remote holder can sue the indorser-warrantor directly without having to sue intermediate transferors also.

Neither the presentment warranties nor the transfer warranties can be disclaimed with respect to checks. UCC 3-416(c) & 3-417(e). Moreover, within 30 days after having reason to know about a breach, the claimant must notify the warrantor about the alleged breach or else lose its right to damages caused by that delay in notification. UCC 3-416(c) & 3-417(e). Generally, damages are the difference between the instrument's value had the warranty not been breached and the instrument's actual worth because of the breach. That difference usually translates into damages equaling the face amount of the instrument, with both UCC 3-416(b) and UCC 3-417(b)(d) also permitting an award for expenses and loss of interest resulting from a breach.

OTHER AVENUES OF LIABILITY

Article 3, in addition to providing specifically for warranty liability and contractual liability on the instrument, also provides that a person may be sued for the tort of conversion (UCC 3-420). (For further discussion of conversion, see Chapter 4.) Also, as already discussed, negligence may preclude a person from recovering on, or maintaining a defense on, an instrument (UCC 3-406).

Aside from possible remedies or legal theories outside of Article 3 (e.g., recovery on the underlying contract), there is one other major form of liability: that of accommodation parties or guarantors.

• *ACCOMMODATION PARTIES (UCC 3-419)*

An **accommodation party** signs an instrument in some capacity (e.g., maker, drawer, indorser, or acceptor) to lend his/her credit status to another party to the instrument. (Generally, an indorsement not in the instrument's chain of title is an accommodation indorsement.) The accommodation party is essentially a surety for the accommodated party; therefore, without first seeking recourse from the accommodated party, subsequent holders for value can enforce the instrument against the accommodation party, who can assert only the defenses available to the accommodated party as well as general surety defenses. (For more on sureties, see Chapter 13.) Of course, the accommodated party has no right to enforce payment from the accommodation party. That right is held by other parties to the instrument.

• *GUARANTORS*

Indorsement with the words "payment guaranteed" or their equivalent converts an indorser's secondary liability to primary liability. The holder may proceed directly against the indorser **(guarantor)** once the instrument falls due and is unpaid.

Another type of guarantor, though, is not liable until it is clear that proceeding against the primary party (maker or acceptor) is useless. Such a guarantor has indorsed with the words "collection guaranteed" or their equivalent. UCC 3-419(d).

If the words of guarantee do not specify their nature, they are deemed to guarantee payment, not just collection.

Example: Guarantor

If Guarantor Smith does not want to be primarily liable for a note signed by Dead-Beat Dingham, Smith should plainly indicate that the guarantee extends simply to collection.

YOU SHOULD REMEMBER

Secondary parties (indorsers) can avoid potential liabilities on an instrument (except for warranties) by indorsing "without recourse."

If a person's negligence substantially contributes to a material alteration or an unauthorized signature, that person cannot use the alteration or signature as a defense against a HIDC or anyone else who in good faith pays for the instrument. Although a drawer or maker issues an instrument to an impostor or fictitious payee, the negotiation remains effective; usually, the drawer's or maker's only recourse is against the imposter or other persons who got him/her to issue the instrument.

Presentment warranties cover title, signature authorization, and lack of alteration. Transfer warranties cover these areas as well as (1) lack of good defenses and (2) absence of knowledge about the insolvency of the maker, acceptor, or (for an unaccepted instrument) drawer.

DISCHARGE

A party's liability to pay an instrument may be discharged (terminated). Discharge *usually arises by payment or other satisfaction.* See UCC 3-602. However, some or all of the parties may be discharged of their liabilities by any of these other methods:

1. Tender of payment (even if unaccepted). UCC 3-603.
2. Cancellation. UCC 3-604.
3. Impairment of reimbursement rights. UCC 3-605(c-f).
4. Fraudulent alterations. UCC 3-407(b).
5. Check certification or other acceptance of a draft. UCC 3-414(c).
6. Reacquisition of an instrument by a former holder. UCC 3-207.
7. Unexcused delay (e.g., more than 30 days) in presentment. UCC 3-415(e).
8. Unexcused delay (generally, more than 30 days) in notice of dishonor. UCC 3-503.
9. Acceptance varying a draft. UCC 3-410(c).
10. Any agreement or act that discharges a simple contract to pay money. UCC 3-601(a).

Discharge is generally effective against all parties except a HIDC who lacked notice of the discharge when he/she took the instrument. UCC 3-302(b).

KNOW THE CONCEPTS
DO YOU KNOW THE BASICS?

1. Define a HIDC.
2. (a) Name three characteristics of an instrument that usually indicate notice of a claim or defense.
   (b) Name two that do not.
3. (a) Name at least three facts that, if known by the would-be HIDC, usually indicate notice of a claim or defense.
   (b) Name at least three that do not.
4. Name at least five "real" defenses and seven personal defenses.
5. Which type of defense works even against a HIDC?
6. In regard to consumer protection versus the HIDC concept, one approach reduces the HIDC's power to evade personal defenses, while another approach makes it more difficult for someone to become a HIDC. Which approach has been followed by many state legislatures? By the FTC?
7. Name at least three types of negligence that can so substantially contribute to unauthorized alterations or signatures that they preclude recovery against persons paying in good faith.

8. (a) State the three main types of liability between parties to a negotiable instrument.
   (b) What tort is expressly listed as a remedy (e.g., for wrongful payment of an instrument) in UCC 3-420?
9. Name the areas covered by the three presentment warranties.
10. Name the areas covered by the five transfer warranties.

TERMS FOR STUDY

accommodation party

discharge

dishonor

forgery

good faith

guarantor

holder in due course (HIDC)

personal defenses

presentment warranty

primary party

"real" defenses

secondary party

shelter rule

unauthorized signature

warranty on transfer

PRACTICAL APPLICATION

1. Jim pays Joan $50 for a check in the amount of $75. Can Jim be a HIDC? If so, for what amount?

2. Fred Fraud owes Helen Holder $500. Fred fraudulently induces Tom Taken to buy a worthless stereo system for $500. Helen knows nothing about Fred's misdeeds but is told that, if she releases Fred from his debt to her, Fred will have Tom issue a check to her for $500. Two weeks later, Helen takes the check to the bank. By then, however, Tom has discovered Fred's fraud. Tom asserts that payment may be refused because:
   (a) Helen is a payee, not a HIDC.
   (b) Helen did not act in good faith.
   (c) Tom can successfully raise Fred's fraud against Helen.
   (d) The check was overdue.
   Discuss the merits of each reason.

3. Paul Payee indorses a negotiable instrument "to the order of Julia Jumper," who takes the instrument for value, in good faith, and without notice of claims or defenses to it. The instrument is not overdue, nor has it ever been dishonored, when Julia indorses it and gives it to Debbie Dole. Apparently, however, Paul still has not

performed the services for which the instrument was issued. Now the issuer refuses to pay Debbie. Discuss.

4. What is meant by the statement, "A negotiable instrument is a courier without any luggage?"

5. Having performed services for Poe Credit, you are concerned about the check that you received as payment: Is Poe really "good for the money"? You owe Jane an amount somewhat less than the face value of Poe's check. Jane is willing to take the check as complete payment of the debt. She seems to be impressed by the amount of Poe's check, while you are more concerned about whether one can really collect on the check. In indorsing the check to Jane, what can you do to protect yourself if Jane or a subsequent transferee has trouble collecting?

6. M issues a note payable to P's order. C steals the note, forges P's indorsement, and sells the note to X. M pays X. On the assumption that M has to pay P for conversion (UCC 3-420), may M recover from other parties?

7. In Problem 3, what warranties, if any, have been breached?

8. John drafts a check on Bank Y, payable to the order of Pat. For money, Pat negotiates the check to Viola. Pat has been declared insolvent in a federal bankruptcy court. What warranties, if any, have been breached?

ANSWERS
KNOW THE CONCEPTS

1. A holder who has taken a negotiable instrument for value, in good faith, and without notice that it is overdue, has been dishonored, or has defenses or claims against it.

2. (a) Incorrect indorsements, material omissions, important alterations.
(b) Antedated or postdated, originally incomplete and later completed.

3. (a) Party's obligation void or voidable, parties discharged, defective title, unauthorized completion of instrument, default in principal payments or on series instruments.
(b) Parties include fiduciaries or accommodation parties, instrument issued or negotiated for an executory promise, existence of separate agreements, default on interest payments or on different instruments.

4. "Real" defenses: fraud in the execution (factum), forgeries and unauthorized signatures, defenses nullifying the obligor's duty, infancy (sometimes), the obligor's claim in recoupment against the holder, a bankruptcy discharge of the obligor, other discharges of the instrument that the holder had actual notice of when he became a HIDC, and material alterations.

Personal defenses: lack or failure of consideration, fraud in the inducement, ordinary contract defenses, breach of warranty when a draft was accepted, modification of the obligation by a separate agreement, conditional issuance of an instrument, defenses rendering a contract voidable, payment violating a restrictive indorsement, acquisition of lost or stolen bearer paper, nondelivery or unauthorized delivery of an instrument, unauthorized completions, some "real" defenses in which the party asserting the defense was negligent.

5. "Real" defenses. Only in cases of consumer protection does a personal defense have any likelihood of defeating a HIDC.

6. The first approach.   The second approach.

7. Doing nothing to stop known forgeries, negligence as to signature stamps, failure to include a corporate designation when appropriate, delivery of instrument to wrong person, failure to audit.

8. (a) The underlying contract, contractual liability on the instrument, warranty liability.
   (b) Conversion.

9. Title, signature authorization, lack of material alteration.

10. Same as answer 9, plus: lack of good defenses and absence of knowledge about insolvency of makers, acceptors, or (sometimes) drawers.

PRACTICAL APPLICATION

1. Yes, if Jim meets the remaining HIDC requirements. If Jim had agreed to pay Joan more than $50 for the check, he can be a HIDC only to the extent that he has furnished consideration (here, $50). However, if $50 was the agreed-upon consideration, then Jim has fully met the "taking for value" element and—if he meets the other HIDC requirements—is fully a HIDC.

2. (a) Poor reasoning—payees can also be HIDCs.
   (b) Wrong—under the subjective test, it appears that Helen acted in good faith.
   (c) If indeed Helen "dealt" with Tom, then Tom's personal defense (fraudulent inducement) can be raised against Helen even if Helen is a HIDC.
   (d) Wrong—only 2 weeks old, check not overdue.

3. Debbie took the instrument from a HIDC, Julia. Nothing indicates that Debbie is an exception to the shelter rule. Therefore Debbie should be able to enforce the instrument against the issuer, who has raised only a personal defense.

4. Unlike ordinary contracts, negotiable instruments are not necessarily weighed down with the assignee's potential liabilities or other baggage. If properly drafted and negotiated, a negotiable instrument may be free of these personal claims or defenses, because a HIDC will take it. Moreover, the shelter rule will then protect most subsequent transferees.

5. You can seek to have the drawee bank accept the instrument. If it does accept, you then have a bank with primary liability ahead of your secondary liability as an indorser. (But at that point you might as well seek to collect the money from the check, rather than just sell it at a discount to Jane.)

If Poe's instrument were a note, not a check, you could seek to disclaim your transfer warranties. You should still indorse the check with the words "without recourse" to eliminate your potential contractual liability as an indorser, but—unlike former Article 3—such an indorsement no longer disclaims any of the transfer warranties.

6. Yes, M may recover on the presentment warranty (breach as to title) from X and/or C.

7. Payee has breached the transfer warranty that there is no defense of any party good against him.

8. None. Pat is not a maker, acceptor, or drawer; thus the insolvency proceeding against him is not of the type to which a transfer warranty could extend.

12

BANKING PROCEDURES AND THE BANK/ CUSTOMER RELATIONSHIP

KEY TERMS

overdraft a check for more than the amount in the customer's account

stop-payment order an order, oral or written, by a depositor directing his/her bank not to honor a specified check

You have already learned that a check is a special type of draft: one drawn on a bank and payable on demand. For most purposes, it is treated like any other draft under UCC Article 3. However, questions may arise concerning the processing of checks or the bank/customer relationship. These matters are governed by Article 4 of the Uniform Commercial Code.

The purposes of Article 4 are the same as for the rest of the UCC: rendering fair results to individual parties and also assisting the overall goal of efficient commerce. Although conflict between Article 4 and Article 3 is quite unlikely, Article 4 is given priority in such a situation.

THE CONTRACT BETWEEN BANK AND CUSTOMER

When someone deposits money in a checking account, the bank acquires title to the deposited money. In effect, the account-holder is the bank's creditor, and the bank is the account-holder's debtor. If the bank becomes insolvent, the customer is only a general creditor, not a secured party with specific property he/she can seize to pay his/her account. (This usually does not matter, however, because in most cases the account is insured by the Federal Deposit Insurance Corporation.) Chapter 13 discusses the concepts of creditor and secured party in much greater detail.

Because the bank owes money to the customer, it is subject to garnishment by the customer's creditors. (For information on garnishment, see Chapter 13.) Likewise, because the customer does not actually "own" the bank funds, he/she cannot assign the funds. All a customer can do is order the bank to make payment (by writing a check: "Pay to the order of …"). Since the order is not an immediate "assignment," a customer may die, issue a stop-payment order, or otherwise undermine the order before it takes effect; and, unless the check is certified, the holder has no recourse against the nonpaying bank. (The holder would instead sue the drawer and/or indorsers.)

THE BANK'S DUTY TO THE CUSTOMER

The bank's primary duty to its customer is to honor his/her checks when the customer has sufficient funds on deposit. Banks are thus liable to their customers for **wrongful dishonor**. If the wrongful dishonor was a mistake (i.e., not intentional), the customer's recovery is limited to his/her actual damages, which are, however, liberally defined as including harm to credit or reputation, arrest for writing bad checks, or other proved, consequential damages.

Note that dishonor must be *wrongful*. For instance, banks are not liable for refusing to pay on insufficient funds or on improper or missing indorsements.

A second duty of the bank is to maintain customer signature cards and to be familiar with the depositor's authorized signature, so that forgeries can be detected before any payment is made.

Rules under the federal Expedited Funds Availability Act (1988) limit the maximum length of holds a financial institution may place on the funds from local and non-local checks deposited at the institution. The Act also requires disclosure of hold policies and of the specific hold placed on a deposit.

THE CUSTOMER'S DUTY TO THE BANK (SECTION 4-406)

The first duty of the customer is to maintain sufficient funds in an account to cover the checks that he/she expects to write. In addition, under section 4-406, the customer has a second important duty.

As mentioned above, banks are supposed to maintain customer signature cards and thus be able to verify the authenticity of a customer's signature, whether as drawer or indorser. As a practical matter, however, the enormously high volume of checks frequently renders it impossible for a busy bank to examine the authenticity of every check in every account. Therefore, while the drawee bank is charged with knowing its drawer's signature and with otherwise avoiding payment on altered or forged instruments or indorsements, the customer is also expected to do his/her part in preventing or correcting unauthorized transactions.

Section 4-406 of the Uniform Commercial Code requires that the customer promptly review his/her bank statements and any other documents (e.g., canceled checks) sent by the bank. Generally, if failure to do so results in his/her not discovering and reporting an alteration or unauthorized signature, the customer is precluded from asserting a claim against the bank in the following situations:

1. The bank suffered a loss because of the customer's failure to discover and report.
2. The bank paid in good faith and without notice of the type of problem (fraud by the same wrongdoer) that the customer should have discovered by the time payment was made.

Example: Failure of Customer to Review Bank Statement

If Customer Carol had reviewed the bank statements sent to her by Big Bank, she could have told Big Bank about a check forged by Fanny Fraud. Carol is thus precluded from having her account recredited if prompt reporting to Big Bank would have spared the bank a loss (item 1 above).

More important, if Fanny Fraud continues to practice her deceit, Carol is barred from asserting against Big Bank these later forgeries by Fanny; simply put, Carol's diligence could have prevented these later problems because she would have put Big Bank on notice (item 2 above).

Preclusion under 4-406, as well as preclusion under 3-406 (drawer's negligence) and 3-404 (impostor/fictitious payee), is discussed in Chapter 11. However, note that, *as under Sections 3-404 and 3-406, the bank cannot take full advantage of 4-406 unless the bank itself was not negligent.* If the bank, also, failed to exercise ordinary care (here, in paying an item), and that failure substantially contributed to the loss, then the loss is apportioned between the customer and the bank under a comparative negligence approach.

Customers who review their bank statements and are not otherwise negligent are entitled to have their accounts recredited not only for checks bearing their own forged signatures, but also for checks containing other persons' forged indorsements.

Example: Bank Customer Rights

Agnes writes a check for $700 "to the order of Tim." Chris forges Tim's indorsement and cashes the check. So long as Agnes is not precluded by her own failure to inspect or other negligence, she is entitled to have the bank recredit her account for the $700. The bank failed to carry out Agnes's order to pay "to the order of Tim."

Besides going after Chris, Agnes's bank can recover its loss from the bank that cashed the check; The cashing bank breached its warranty that there were no forged indorsements. (Warranties were discussed in Chapter 11.) For a forged drawer's signature, though, the drawee bank can recover only from the forger unless others were negligent or actually knew that the signature was unauthorized. Again, the drawee bank is charged with knowing its drawer's signature.

RULES GOVERNING THE PAYMENT OF CHECKS

The drawer's bank is the primary agent in the collection process, that is, the sequence of events through which a check goes before final settlement. Article 4 of the UCC sets forth specific rules governing the payment of checks:

1. The bank need not (but may) pay **overdrafts** (checks for more than the amount in the customer's account). If the bank has specifically agreed to pay overdrafts, then it must do so.

2. The bank can charge the customer's account for the full amount that it pays on an overdraft.

3. The bank can refuse to pay **stale checks** (uncertified checks drawn more than 6 months before presentation for payment).

4. In the check-collection process, a bank may supply necessary indorsements for a customer, except when the missing indorsement is that of the payee and the check expressly requires the payee to sign.

5. If a customer dies or is adjudged (declared by a court) to be incompetent, the bank may continue to honor his/her checks (pay them from the customer's account) until it receives notice of the death or incompetence and has had a reasonable opportunity to respond. Even with notice, the bank may pay or accept checks during the first 10 days after death (unless it receives a stop-payment order from someone claiming an interest in the decedent's account).

6. The customer can order the bank not to pay a particular check, provided that the bank has enough time to act on the **stop-payment order**. Such orders can be either oral orders effective for 14 days or written orders (including written confirmations of oral orders) that last 6 months. The written order can be renewed for additional 6-month periods if the customer, in writing, so requests. *If the bank fails to comply with a stop-payment order, it is liable to the customer for his/her actual losses.*

These rules, as well as other Article 4 requirements, are not absolute. A bank and its customer may, by their contract, alter these rules. The only unchangeable terms are these: a bank's responsibility for its lack of good faith or ordinary care (dishonesty or negligence), and the measure of damages resulting from such lack of good faith or ordinary care. Indeed, so long as the terms are not plainly unreasonable, the bank and its customer may even state in their agreement the standards by which bank responsibility is to be decided.

CERTIFICATION OF CHECKS

Initially, a check is only as good as the credit of the drawer. To ensure payment, a payee or subsequent holder should have the check certified (accepted). Certification prevents the drawee bank from denying liability; the certified check is the bank's guarantee that sufficient funds (presumably from the drawer's account) have been set aside to cover the check.

The drawee bank is not required to certify a check. Refusal to certify is not dishonor; the bank merely refuses to agree in advance to cover a check.

Once the check is certified, the drawer and all indorsers prior to certification are released from liability on the check. If, when payment is later sought, the drawee bank discovers that there was not in fact a "hold" on sufficient funds in the drawer's account, the drawee must make up the difference. Furthermore, the bank can never revoke certification against someone with HIDC rights or any other good-faith holder who changed position in reliance on the certification. It is thus easy to see why banks are generally very cautious about certifying checks. As is the case for cashier's checks (where the account-holder has the bank issue a check to a particular payee, the bank being both drawer and drawee), the bank tends to subtract the amount of the check from the customer's account immediately.

ALTERATIONS

If the drawer was negligent (e.g., left unreasonably large spaces in writing the check), then Section 3-406 may completely bar bank liability for payment if the check was altered (generally, the amount was increased). If the drawer was *not* negligent, however, then these are the general rules:

1. The bank bears a loss to the extent of the raised amount.
2. The bank may charge the drawer's account for the original amount of the check.
3. The bank may recover from the person who presented the check for payment (warranty liability).

For certified checks, the crucial question on alterations is "when?" Alterations before certification are deemed to have been accepted by the certifying bank, whereas alterations after certification could not, of course, have been accepted by the bank when it certified the check. Therefore, unless the drawee bank negligently goes ahead and pays the altered amount, the drawee bank ordinarily will be liable only for the check as it stood when certified *unless there is a HIDC subsequent to the alteration*. To avoid such a scenario—having to pay the HIDC the altered (i.e., raised) amount—accepting banks can, while certifying a check, state the amount certified; that limits the acceptor's liability to the stated amount, no matter what happens thereafter (UCC 3-413(b).

SUMMARY OF IMPORTANT ARTICLE 4 RULES

UCC 4-401: *Charge Against Account*	Bank may charge customer for every properly payable item even if an overdraft.
UCC 4-402: *Wrongful Dishonor*	Bank is liable to customer for wrongful dishonor. Unless more than just a bank "mistake," damages are limited to damages actually proved, but can include consequential damages (e.g., loss of credit, arrest and prosecution).
UCC 4-403: *Stop-Payment Orders*	Bank is liable for payment over a timely stop-payment order. Oral orders bind for 14 days, but can be confirmed (and extended) by putting the order in writing. Written orders last for 6 months and are renewable.

UCC 4-404: *Stale Checks*	Bank has no duty to pay uncertified checks more than 6 months old, but may in good faith pay them.
UCC 4-405: *Death or Incompetence*	Bank may pay checks as long as it does not know of customer's death or incompetence. Despite knowledge, bank can honor or certify checks in first 10 days after customer's death (unless a stop-payment order is issued by a person claiming an interest in the dead customer's account).
UCC 4-406: *Customer's Duty to Examine* *Bank Statements*	Customer must examine account statements and notify bank of unauthorized signatures or alterations. Bank exercising reasonable care is not liable to customer if (a) customer's failure to examine and report results in banks loss or (b) customer fails to examine and report within a reasonable time period (no more than 30 days) after receiving the bank statement and there were continuing unauthorized signatures or alterations by the same wrongdoer.
UCC 4-406(f): *Statute of Limitations*	More than one year after receiving relevant bank statement, customer is precluded from asserting against bank unauthorized customer signatures or alterations. The statute bars claims against even a negligent bank.

ELECTRONIC FUNDS TRANSFER ACT

Most banks have sought to substitute, when possible, electronic communications for a time- and paper-consuming check-collection process. Electronic funds transfer (EFT) is practically instantaneous. No checks are needed, with payment being by electronic signal. The most common methods of EFT are automated teller machines, paycheck direct deposits/withdrawals, pay-by-phone systems, and point-of-sale terminals (e.g., direct transfers from consumers' accounts to store accounts).

Between 1990 and 1996, every state adopted a new UCC Article, 4A, which governs fund transfers between the bank accounts of large, highly sophisticated businesses. Much more comprehensive in scope (covering *consumer* EFT) and applicable in all states, is the federal *Electronic Funds Transfer Act* of 1978. This act, in combination with its implementing law, Federal Reserve Board Regulation E, details some of the rights and duties of financial institutions (hereinafter, "banks") and their consumer-customers:

1. Limits are placed on customer liability for charges on a lost or stolen bank card (e.g., a "debit card" used to transfer funds directly from the customer's bank account to the account of a merchant from whom the customer makes a purchase). The limits, though, increase or even disappear entirely if the customer fails to tell the bank about the loss or theft.

2. Banks must furnish receipts for computer terminal (e.g., ATM) transactions, but not for telephone transfers. Also, banks cannot distribute unsolicited EFT access devices (e.g., debit cards).

3. Banks must furnish a statement for each month that an electronic funds transfer occurs. Such statements have to show amounts, dates, names of retailers, locations of terminals used, and any fees. An address and telephone number for customer inquiries and error notices must also be included.

4. The customer must discover any errors on the monthly statement and notify his/her bank within 60 days. If the bank takes longer than 10 days to investigate, it must, for the time being, credit the disputed amount to the customer's account. (Obviously, if there was no error, the bank gets this money back.)

5. Information about rights and duties under the act must be given to customers opening an EFT account. Among the many items covered must be error-resolution procedures as well as the conditions under which a customer can revoke authorization for preauthorized electronic funds transfers.

Several federal agencies are empowered to enforce the Electronic Funds Transfer Act. Customers can sue for violations of the act. They may recover their actual damages as well as statutory penalties. There are also criminal provisions.

KNOW THE CONCEPTS
DO YOU KNOW THE BASICS?

1. Are checks assignments?
2. Are banks subject to garnishment by a customer's creditors? Why?
3. Give at least three proper reasons for dishonoring a check.

4. State the two ways of making stop-payment orders and the length of time for which each is effective.

5. What Article 4 legal requirements can a bank and its customers *not* change via the bank/customer contract?

6. When can certification of a check be required?

7. (a) What does Section 4-406 require of bank customers?
   (b) If the customer fails to meet the 4-406 requirements, what can happen to him/her?

8. What is the statute of limitations for a customer's claim against his/her bank on unauthorized customer signatures or alterations?

9. Name at least four areas covered by the Electronic Funds Transfer Act.

TERMS FOR STUDY

alterations
certified check
Electronic Funds Transfer Act
Expedited Funds Availability Act
Federal Reserve Board
  Regulation E

overdraft
stale check
stop-payment order
UCC Articles 4 & 4A
wrongful dishonor

PRACTICAL APPLICATION

1. Horace Holder presents a check to Big Bank. The check was drawn by Big Bank account-holder Cory Careless to the order of Horace for the amount of $900, and it contains all of the proper signatures. Big Bank pays it, although Cory's account contains only $750. Cory says that Big Bank should not have paid Horace.
   (a) Is Cory correct?
   (b) What may the bank do in regard to Cory and to Horace?

2. Assume that Big Bank refused to honor the check, and Cory therefore lost a major business contract. Could Cory win a lawsuit against Big Bank?

3. Sharon Survivor's uncle has just died, leaving Sharon as his next of kin. Sharon believes that her uncle wrote several "crazy" checks in the last few days of his life. She is concerned that her uncle's bank will honor these checks. What should she do?

4. Gary Greedy wants to bring a certified check to his meeting with Robert Reelistate. However, Gary feels that he needs every last cent of interest he can get from his account. Are these conflicting goals?

5. During a 3-month period, Boris Baddie forges Dudley Dewgood's signature on several checks, makes Dudley's supposed checks payable to Boris, and then cashes them. Dudley takes each month's bank statement and simply puts it in a box. Six months later, Dudley discovers Boris's fraud.
   (a) May Dudley recover from the bank?
   (b) What if the checks were themselves inartfully drawn copies, not the ones actually sent by the bank to its customers?

ANSWERS
KNOW THE CONCEPTS

1. No.
2. Yes. In essence, the bank is a debtor of the customer/account-holder.
3. Insufficient funds, improper or missing indorsement, unauthorized drawer's signature, stale check (over 6 months old).
4. Written and oral. Written last 6 months and can be renewed. Oral last 14 days, but can be confirmed in writing (and thus extended to 6 months).
5. The bank's responsibility for its lack of good faith or ordinary care (dishonesty or negligence) and the measure of damages resulting from such dishonesty or negligence.
6. Generally, never. It is the bank's option whether to certify.
7. (a) That the customers promptly examine bank statements and report any unauthorized signatures or alterations.
   (b) The customer can be precluded from recovering for unauthorized signatures and alterations that he/she could have discovered, unless the bank was itself negligent.
8. One year after receiving relevant bank statements.
9. Customer liability limits on lost or stolen bank cards, receipts for transactions, monthly statements, customer examination of monthly statements, bank investigation of alleged errors, information about the act for new customers.

PRACTICAL APPLICATION

1. (a) No. Banks generally have the option to pay overdrafts.

(b) Big Bank may seek reimbursement from Cory for the remaining $150 (plus perhaps a penalty). It may charge Cory's account directly, assuming that more money is deposited.

As for Horace, once Big Bank honored the check, its only recourse against him would be claims arising under Article 3. However, Horace may well be a HIDC.

2. Not ordinarily. However, checking account arrangements can specifically provide for the payment of overdrafts. If Cory had such a contract with Big Bank, then he could hold the bank liable.

3. Sharon should immediately contact the bank to inform it of her uncle's death and her status as next of kin. She should also demand that it stop payment on any checks in her uncle's account and thus give the estate time to determine the propriety of the "crazy" checks.

4. Probably. When a check is certified, the bank usually withdraws the amount from the account *immediately*. Unless Gary's bank has some other arrangement (or somehow continues to credit interest until the certified check is actually cashed), Gary will lose further interest on the amount of the check once he has the check certified. Of course, with ordinary checks, interest earnings are unaffected until the check is collected.

5. (a) Unless the bank was itself negligent, Dudley certainly cannot recover for checks drafted toward the end of the 3-month period; by that time, if Dudley had examined his bank statements, he could have detected the fraud and put the bank on notice in order to prevent further forgeries. Even for the earlier checks, Dudley cannot recover if his prompt review of the bank statements would have left the bank able to prevent a loss (e.g., by getting the money back from Boris or some other party to the instrument).

(b) If the bank was negligent, as in this case, Dudley's failure to examine does not matter. The bank's cashing of inartfully drawn copies constitutes the type of bank negligence that eliminates 4-406 preclusion of Dudley's claim.

13

CREDITORS' RIGHTS AND DEBTORS' PROTECTION; BANKRUPTCY; SECURED TRANSACTIONS

KEY TERMS

surety a person who has expressly or implicitly agreed to be liable for another's debts even if the creditor has not exhausted all remedies for collection

guarantor a person who has expressly or implicitly agreed to be liable for another person's debts if the creditor cannot collect directly from the debtor

bankruptcy a legal procedure for settling the debts of individuals or business entities that are unable to pay debts as they become due. The debtor's business may be reorganized; a set payment may be arranged, or the debtor's nonexempt assets may be liquidated and distributed to creditors. Proper completion of the bankruptcy procedures leaves the debtor free from liability on some or all of the remaining debts.

secured transaction any transaction involving a security interest, which generally is an interest in the debtor's personal property (or fixtures). The security interest is held by the secured party (the creditor) as a means to ensure payment or performance of the debtor's obligation.

History has not been kind to debtors. In various places and at various times, debtors have faced prison, slavery, torture, dismemberment, and/

or death because they were unable to pay in full their creditors. For good measure, a debtor's relatives were often punished.

Under modern law, the creditor is not the only one with rights. In fact, the emphasis on consumer protection and on giving people a "second chance" (or more) has led to creditors' complaints that debtors now receive *too much* protection. However, the law generally reflects society's choices; as long as society cannot definitively decide the relative worths of competing values, neither can the law. In the meantime, both creditors and debtors have many rights or remedies available through statutes, the law of contracts, and the common law.

CREDITORS' RIGHTS: COLLECTION OF DEBTS

There are several major debt-collection mechanisms. A creditor may:

1. *Place a lien upon the debtor's property.* When real estate owner Red receives services or materials intended to repair or improve his premises, a *mechanic's lien* on the real estate may develop if Red does not fully pay his bill. A lien is an encumbrance upon Red's property—if the lien remains unpaid, the security held by the creditor can be sold to satisfy the debt (lien). In Red's case, the real property itself is security; after following the mechanic's lien procedures outlined in the relevant state statutes, including a filing of notice, the lien holder may foreclose (force a sale).

Other liens include *artisan's liens* and *hotelkeeper's liens*, both of which involve personal property. As long as the lien holder retains possession of the debtor's personal property, he/she may have a lien on that property for unpaid services or for unpaid repairs, improvements, or care of the debtor's property.

2. *Obtain a prejudgment attachment.* A **prejudgment attachment** entails a court-ordered seizure of the debtor's property before the creditor's claim and the debtor's defenses have been fully adjudicated. It is designed to prevent the waste or removal of assets pending the completion of a lawsuit. Obviously, this remedy carries the potential for abuse, including deprivation of property based on claims that the "debtor" later successfully refutes; therefore Fourteenth Amendment due process considerations limit the scope and use of prejudgment attachments.

Generally, the creditor must strictly comply with the state statutes governing such attachments. For instance, the creditor must file an affidavit, as well as post a bond covering court costs, loss of use of the property, and the value of the property itself. Seized property is not sold immediately, but remains under the sheriff's control until a judgment is entered.

3. *Take a security interest in the debtor's property*. See the sections on secured transactions later in this chapter.

4. *Recover the debt before or during the course of a bulk transfer*. A **bulk transfer** occurs when (1) a business sells or otherwise disposes of a substantial portion (e.g., more than half) of its materials, supplies, merchandise, or other inventory, (2) this sale or other disposal does not occur "in the ordinary course of business," and (3) the buyer ordinarily knew or should have known that the transferor (e.g., the seller) would not continue to operate the same or a similar business after the transfer. See UCC Revised Article 6, at 6-102(1)(c)(ii). Services and the operations of nonretail manufacturers are usually excluded from coverage under bulk transfer laws, such as UCC Revised Article 6, adopted by about seven states (the original Article 6 has been repealed by every state that adopted it). These laws require the would-be transferor of goods to list both its creditors and the property to be transferred, and that the would-be transferee notify the creditors of the proposed transfer, tell creditors whether debts will be fully paid, and provide other information.

Creditors then have time before the transfer (e.g., 10 days under Revised Article 6) to take the steps necessary to protect their rights (e.g., levying of execution on property, suing for an injunction on the sale). If these procedures have not been followed, the creditors have time after learning about the bulk transfer to file suit and/or to levy against the transferred property (e.g., six months under Revised Article 6).

5. *Proceed against property fraudulently conveyed to a third party*. Just as improper bulk transfers may be set aside, so the law does not permit other transfers by debtors trying to avoid debt payment by selling or giving away their assets. Such a transfer is termed a **fraudulent conveyance**.

6. *Seek payment from a surety or guarantor, who has expressly or implicitly agreed to be liable for another person's debts*. A **surety** is *primarily* liable—the creditor need not exhaust all of his/her remedies against the debtor before holding the surety liable. A **guarantor** is *secondarily* or collaterally liable—the creditor can seek payment from the guarantor only after first trying to obtain relief directly from the debtor. Suretyships need not be in writing, but usually are. All guaranty agreements, though, fall under the Statute of Frauds requirement of a written contract.

Some guaranty agreements are *general* (applying to all creditors who agree). Others are *special*; they apply only to a named creditor and are usually not assignable.

Performance bonds and *fidelity bonds* are examples of suretyship contracts. Performance bonds cover the costs of a party's failure to meet the terms of a contract, such as one for construction of a building. Fidelity bonds protect against losses from the dishonest acts of employees or others. In either instance, payments under the bond cover the costs or losses up to a maximum amount stated in the bond.

Both sureties and guarantors "step into the shoes of the debtor," and may thus raise any claim or defense that the debtor might have advanced, except infancy, bankruptcy, and—in some cases—the statute of limitations. Two other major defenses for sureties or guarantors are that (1) the debtor tendered payment; (2) the debtor's obligations were materially altered without the consent of the surety or guarantor.

Upon paying the creditor, most sureties and guarantors are entitled to reimbursement, if possible, from the debtor. This right is sometimes referred to as **subrogation**. In subrogation (also frequently invoked by insurance companies that have paid a claim), the surety or guarantor is substituted for the original creditor, thus acquiring the latter's right to collect from the debtor.

7. *Foreclose on real property.* If a loan is secured by real property, there is a mortgage agreement between creditor (mortgagee) and debtor (mortgagor). Upon mortgagor's default, mortgagee may initiate foreclosure procedures.

A few states permit the mortgagee to acquire absolute, immediate title to the foreclosed property ("strict foreclosure") or to take immediate possession and then gain title after a waiting period. Most states allow foreclosure and sale to occur pursuant to terms within the mortgage agreement. The *customary method* of foreclosure, though, is a **judicial sale**; after proper notice, the sheriff or other court official takes control of the property and sells it. As with forced sales arising from liens, writs of execution, or otherwise, the sales proceeds are applied first toward the costs of the foreclosure (advertising, court filing fees, etc.) and then toward payment of the debt. Any surplus goes to the debtor. In most states (California is one exception), if the proceeds do not cover the debt, the mortgagee can obtain a "deficiency judgment" against the mortgagor for the remaining amount owed and then collect from other, nonexempt property owned by the mortgagor.

From the time of default until the foreclosure sale, the mortgagor has a right, called **equity of redemption**, to redeem (recover) the property by fully paying the debt, plus the foreclosure costs to date and any interest. Most states also allow mortgagors to redeem within a brief, specified time after the sale ("statutory period of redemption"); this type of redemption serves to cancel the sale, but usually requires the debtor to cover yet another set of costs, namely, the nonrefundable expenses incurred in the sale.

8. *Obtain a writ of execution and/or a garnishment.* After obtaining a judgment in a lawsuit on a debt, an unpaid creditor ("judgment creditor") may request a prompt *accounting* of the judgment debtor's assets. The defendant's failure to provide information can lead to a finding of contempt of court and—ultimately—jail. The creditor may seek a court order that (a) a sheriff or other authorized official seize and sell the debtor's nonexempt property (**writ of execution**); (b) third parties

holding property of (owing money to) the debtor send to the judgment creditor the nonexempt portion of that property (**garnishment**). After costs have been paid, the proceeds go to the creditor until the judgment debt is satisfied. For garnishment, common third parties are employers (who hold wages due) and banks (who hold checking or savings accounts).

9. *When there are two or more creditors, accept a composition and/or extension agreement or an assignment to a trustee.* In the first situation, the debtor and creditors agree that each creditor will receive a certain percentage (less than 100%) of the amount owed (the composition) and/or extend the payment period (the extension). The debtor's full compliance constitutes a **discharge**, that is, a release from obligation, of the entire debt. In the second situation, the debtor transfers to a trustee the title to some or most of the debtor's property. The trustee in turn sells or otherwise disposes of that property for cash and then distributes the proceeds *pro rata* among the creditors. A creditor accepting such payment discharges the entire debt owed to him/her.

In *Grupo Mexicano de Desarrollo SA v. Alliance Bond Fund, Inc.*, 527 U.S. 308 (1999), the U.S. Supreme Court ruled that while a U.S. plaintiff's contract claim for damages was being decided, a U.S. court could not grant a preliminary injunction barring a failing Mexican defendant company from using its only assets to pay its local creditors. The decision could mean that by the time certain investors find out they have prevailed in a legal claim, there may be no assets left with which to pay them. So the message to American investors in foreign businesses is that when a default occurs and the assets are abroad, these investors cannot expect American courts to intervene.

PROTECTION FOR DEBTORS

Both state and federal laws provide certain measures of protection for debtors.

EXEMPTION STATUTES

State law exempts certain types of property from being seized and sold to satisfy debts. Most states provide for a **homestead exemption**. When a home is sold to pay a judgment, a specific amount may be retained by the debtor, free of the judgment debt. Although mortgages are not subject to this exemption, it is generally meant to provide a debtor with sufficient funds to protect his/her family and find another home.

Example: Homestead Exemption

X owns a house with a $150,000 mortgage on it, and Y has a judgment against X for $45,000. If the mortgage agreement antedates the judgment, proceeds from the sale of the house must go first to pay the mortgagee, not Y.

If the state homestead exemption is $25,000, and X's house sells for $195,000, the mortgagee receives $150,000, X then gets $25,000 (the exemption), and Y takes the remaining $20,000. Y can, of course, collect the remainder of the debt from other nonexempt property that X may own.

Exemption statutes also cover personal property. Most states protect up to a *specified dollar value* for household furnishings, clothes, personal possessions, motor vehicles, livestock, pets, and veterans' pensions.

LIMITS ON GARNISHMENT

A provision in the federal Consumer Credit Protection Act (commonly known as the Truth-in-Lending Act) bars employers from terminating an employee because of garnishment for any *single* debt, regardless of the number of levies made or collection proceedings instituted. The law limits garnishments in any week to the *lesser* of either (1) 25% of that week's disposable earnings, or (2) the amount by which that week's disposable earnings exceed 30 times the federal minimum hourly wage. (Disposable earnings are net income after withholding for federal and state income taxes and social security.) Federal garnishment restrictions do not apply to federal or state tax debts, and some bankruptcy orders. Moreover, up to 50% of disposable earnings may be garnished to pay court orders for alimony or child support (up to 60% if the worker is not supporting another spouse or child), with another 5% subject to garnishment for support payments over 12 weeks in arrears. The federal law permits states to substitute, in effect, an even larger exemption of disposable earnings; many states have done so. Some even permit judges to set a higher exemption rate so as to prevent undue hardship. Finally, five states outright prohibit garnishment of wages. Florida bars such garnishment from the head of family (a wage earner providing a spouse or child more than half of his/her support).[1] North Carolina, Pennsylvania, South Carolina, and Texas forbid garnishment except in special circumstances such as for unpaid taxes or child support (not ordinary debt collection).

---

[1] To get a court order barring garnishment, the Florida head-of-family debtor must file an affidavit attesting to his/her earning $750 or less per week or, if he/she makes more than the $750 threshold, that he/she has not agreed in writing to garnishment.

CONSUMER PROTECTION STATUTES

Many regulatory agencies, both federal and state, conduct investigations, promulgate rules, punish violators, and otherwise deal with unfair and deceptive trade practices and consumer fraud. The federal agencies include the Federal Trade Commission, the Federal Communications Commission, the Food and Drug Administration, the Department of Housing and Urban Development, the Securities and Exchange Commission, and the Postal Service. Regulated practices include advertising, labeling and packaging, pricing, sales practices, and warranties. Also, state attorneys general and state departments of consumer affairs seek to protect consumers through enforcement of various state labeling laws, privacy acts, deceptive sales practices statutes, and warranty provisions (e.g., "lemon laws").

The following deceptive practices often violate federal law:

Deceptive comparisons—an inaccurate advertisement in which the defendant makes false statements about either the quality or the price of its own product/service as compared to a competitor's products/services. The federal Lanham Act prohibits such false statements if they are likely to cause damage to businesses or individuals.

Bait and Switch—a low price is advertised to bait the customer into the store. The salesperson then tries to switch the customer to another, more expensive item. It is unlawful bait-and-switch advertising if the store refuses to show the advertised item, fails to have adequate quantities of it available, fails to promise or deliver the advertised item within a reasonable time, or discourages employees from selling the item.

Deceptive Testimonials and Endorsements—when advertisements are intended to make consumers feel that someone other than the seller believes in a product's or service's benefits, FTC guidelines require that the endorser be a user of the product or service. If the advertisement claims that the endorser has superior expertise in making a judgment about the product/service, the endorser must, in fact, have the experience or training that qualifies him/her as an expert.

Five other federal laws are:

1. The *FTC Door-to-Door Sales Rule* (1973). It singles out for special treatment door-to-door sales because of their potential for high pressure tactics placing consumers on the spot. A seller must give consumers a notice of their right to cancel a sale within three days after the sale takes place.

2. *Interstate Land Sales Full Disclosure Act* (1968). This statute regulates the sale of unseen land in order to cut down on the seller's opportunities for fraud by mandating full disclosure of relevant information.

3. *Mail Fraud Statutes*. They specify criminal penalties for using the mail to engage in a fraudulent enterprise. The statutes also provide civil penalties, such as intercepting fraudulent mail, returning all mail, and seizing some types of mail.

4. *Mail-Order House Regulations*. Because consumers have less ability to check out completely what they are getting from a mail-order house (as compared to purchases made in stores), these purchases are regulated. One type of sale is the "negative option plan" (offered, for example, by book and CD clubs). These plans must disclose all their terms, must send members a notice of intent to send the product in enough time for the member to accept it or reject it, and must include a rejection form for use by the club member.

5. The *Telemarketing and Consumer Fraud and Abuse Prevention Act* (1994). This act empowers the FTC and the state attorneys general to enforce this law, and 1995 FTC regulations, against such practices as falsely claiming a government affiliation, or an ability to improve a consumer's credit record or to assist him in obtaining loans, goods, or cash. Fines are potentially as high as $10,000 for each violation. Financial institutions, telecommunications carriers, airlines, insurers, franchisors, on-line services, people regulated by the SEC, and not-for-profit organizations are exempt. The 1995 FTC regulations require several disclosures by telemarketers. The caller must identify himself/herself and the product offered. The recipient must be informed the call is for sales purposes; misrepresentation is prohibited. The product's total cost and special contractual terms must be disclosed. Calls may be made only after 8:00 A.M. and before 9:00 P.M. Many state telemarketing laws are more stringent.

Numerous federal consumer protection statutes apply to the *debtor/ creditor relationship*.

1. The *Truth-in-Lending Act* (1968) states that a lender, or a seller who is extending credit, must comprehensively disclose credit terms, including finance charges. The act covers all transactions in which the creditor, during the ordinary course of business, makes a loan or extends credit in an amount less than $25,000; the loan or credit must go to an individual or individuals and must concern real or personal property used for personal, family, household, or agricultural purposes.

2. The *Fair Credit Billing Act* (1974) (an amendment to the Truth-in-Lending Act) requires the prompt posting of payments and a notice of prospective finance charges on new purchases, prohibits credit card issuers from forbidding merchants to offer cash discounts, and provides procedures for disputes about credit statements, billings, or purchases.

3. The *Fair Debt Collection Practices Act* (1977) prohibits certain abusive practices by debt collectors. It applies mainly to collection agencies, but also to others, such as attorneys who regularly engage in consumer-debt collection activity (*Heintz v. Jenkins*, 514 U.S. 291 (1995)). The Act does not restrict the initial creditor (the one who originally extended the credit to the defaulting debtor), but only future assignees of that creditor.

4. The *Fair Credit Reporting Act* (1970) (part of the Truth-in-Lending Act) provides for debtors' access to credit reports and sets forth procedures for correcting misinformation or otherwise protecting a consumer's credit reputation.

5. The *Fair Credit and Charge Card Disclosure Act* (1988) requires fuller disclosure of terms and conditions in credit-card and charge-card applications and solicitations.

6. The *Equal Credit Opportunity Act* (1976) prohibits discrimination in the extending of credit.

7. Credit card rules in the Truth-in-Lending Act (a) limit the liability of a cardholder to $50 per card upon notifying the creditor about a lost or stolen card, and (b) prohibit outright billing a consumer for unauthorized charges (e.g., on a card never accepted by the consumer).

8. The 2009 *Credit Card Accountability, Responsibility and Disclosure Act* ("Credit CARD Act") applies only to consumer credit cards (not commercial or business credit cards). It does not limit interest rates. The Credit CARD Act requires that credit card agreements be in plain English and at least 12-point font, prohibits companies from giving credit cards to someone under age 21 unless that person proves he/she has the means to pay the debt or a parent or guardian co-signs, declares that on each billing statement credit card companies must notify cardholders how long a series of minimum payments would take to pay off the balance (or how much must be paid each month to pay off the balance, including interest, in three years), and mandates that any payments above the minimum amount be applied to balances with higher interest rates first. The Credit CARD Act further states that if a cardholder cancels a card, he or she can pay off existing balances at the existing payment schedule and interest rate. The law also provides that a customer has to be more than 60 days behind on a payment before the credit card company increases the rate on an existing balance. Even then, the lender must restore the previous, lower rate if the cardholder pays the minimum balance on time for six months. Companies have to give notice and an explanation 45 days before increasing a customer's interest rate on any new extensions of credit (e.g., on purchases or cash advances).

> The Credit CARD Act limits the scope of the *universal default rule*, which makes a consumer's single default (one late payment on any credit card the consumer holds) grounds for all of his/her credit card companies' raising rates on his cards. Before the Act, the universal default rule often applied retroactively to raise the rate on existing credit card balances. With the Credit CARD Act the universal default rule can only reach future balances—a higher interest rate only coming into effect for newer credit.

Violators of the Credit CARD act may face criminal prosecution and civil remedies.

9. The *Home Equity Loan Consumer Protection Act* (1988) prohibits lenders from changing the terms of a loan after the contract has been signed; it requires fuller disclosure in home equity loans of interest rate formulas and repayment terms.

10. The *Dodd-Frank Wall Street Reform and Consumer Protection Act of 2010* (Dodd-Frank) increases the powers and supervisory breadth of the reorganized and streamlined U.S. government agencies regulating banking. Along these lines, a core reform is a new federal agency, the Consumer Financial Protection Bureau (CFPB), which has broad authority to regulate consumer financial products and services, perhaps especially through the heightened use of a mandatory disclosure regime about credit terms and consumer risks. The CFPB has rule-making powers overseeing banks, debt counseling firms, payday lenders, and others. The CFPB could ban financial products it considers unsafe or confusing to consumers. Theoretically, it could block credit card companies from charging rates above a particular rate.

Dodd-Frank has two major provisions affecting consumer financial protection:

a. Title X of Dodd-Frank (called the *Consumer Financial Protection Act of 2010*) is supposed to prevent hidden fees and charges, increase disclosures to consumers, and abolish deceptive or abusive loan practices. Lenders must use plain language so that consumers can understand the risks, benefits, and costs of consumer financial products and services. Among some of the specific laws are—

(1) a minimum credit or debit card transaction amount, such as at a gas station, can be no more than $10; and only the Federal Reserve Board can raise that minimum.

(2) the Federal Reserve Board can limit the fees on debit card transactions charged by large banks (but this does not apply to credit card issuers such as Visa, American Express, or MasterCard).

       (3) any lender that, because of a would-be borrower's credit score, denies a credit application (e.g., for a mortgage, a car loan, or a store credit card) must, for free, tell the applicant his/her score.

  b. Title XIV of Dodd-Frank (called the *Mortgage Reform and Anti-Predatory Lending Act of 2010*) is meant to eliminate many abusive mortgage loan practices while requiring disclosures from mortgage lenders. The act—

       (1) mandates that mortgage originators and lenders verify a prospective borrower's income, assets, credit history, employment status, debt-to-income ratio, and other factors relevant to the lender's decision for or against extending credit.

       (2) makes lenders undertake a reasonable, good faith determination whether a credit applicant can afford to repay the loan for which he/she applied. Among other things, assets and income must be documented. In a foreclosure action that the lender brings against a borrower, the borrower may—as a defense barring any recovery of money from the borrower—assert that the lender did not meet these "due diligence" or other Dodd-Frank standards.

       (3) gives borrowers the right to sue lenders for engaging in predatory and deceptive practices as well as for violating this Act.

       (4) requires banks to hold onto at least 5% of the loans they make (not sell them to investors).

    Auto dealers making car loans and banks with less than $10 billion in assets are exempt from Dodd-Frank oversight. These dealers remain subject to Federal Trade Commission oversight.

  In addition to these federal measures, the states have their own laws and regulations, which may set maximum interest rates (usury laws) or otherwise protect consumers who have been extended credit. For example, eleven states have adopted some form of the *Uniform Consumer Credit Code* (UCCC), which establishes maximum interest rates and requires a full disclosure of facts to buyers on credit in almost any situation. The UCCC is an attempt to systemize the law; it thus serves to replace particular laws on such matters as usury, credit advertising, small loans, retail installment sales, and service, delinquency, or deferral charges. Perhaps most important, the UCCC forbids (1) multiple agreements in order to obtain higher interest rates, (2) "balloon" payments more than twice as large as the average payment, (3) assignments of a debtor's wages, and (4) in most cases, judgments for money beyond that obtained by repossessing goods purchased on credit. Criminal as well as civil penalties are provided.

LENDER LIABILITY

Lenders increasingly have been sued by debtors and others for damages allegedly resulting from lender misconduct in revoking credit, foreclosing on security, administering a loan, refusing to extend credit, or *even for extending credit*. Liability theories include: breach of contract, fraud, excessive control (e.g., interference with the debtor's contractual relations with others), negligence, economic duress (which may make a loan settlement voidable), breach of fiduciary duties or implied duties of good faith and fair dealing, and even statutory bases such as state consumer fraud legislation and federal environmental, bankruptcy, securities, RICO, and tax laws.

YOU SHOULD REMEMBER

State law exempts some property from seizure to satisfy debts. After the proceeds on the sale of a home have paid the mortgage, most states exempt a specific amount of the remaining proceeds. For personal property, state law tends to exempt up to a specified dollar value for household furnishings, clothes, personal possessions, motor vehicles, livestock, pets, and veterans' benefits.

The federal Consumer Credit Protection Act (known as the "Truth-in-Lending-Act") limits garnishment to 25% of disposable earnings or even less in the case of low-income wage earners; state law may further limit garnishment. Numerous federal and state statutes regulate creditor practices, prohibit abuses, provide dispute-resolution mechanisms, or otherwise protect debtors.

BANKRUPTCY AND REORGANIZATION

Bankruptcy is a method for settling the debts of individuals or business entities that are unable to pay debts as they become due. Under court supervision, all or most of the debtor's assets are used to pay his/her creditors, with creditors of equal status (priority) each receiving the same proportion of the amounts owed to them. Once the liquidation, reorganization, or adjustment plan is judicially approved and then properly completed, the bankruptcy serves to relieve the debtor from all or most of his/her debts even though these debts have not been fully paid.

The U.S. Constitution, Article I, Section 8, empowers Congress to make "uniform laws on the subject of bankruptcies throughout the United States." Congress has structured a system of *federal bankruptcy courts*, with judges appointed to 14-year terms and serving the same or similar geographic areas as do federal district court judges. Appeals go either to the U.S. District Court or (as some U.S. circuits provide) to a bankruptcy appellate panel consisting of bankruptcy judges from within the circuit.

Although matters of state law may arise during a bankruptcy proceeding, the essential issues in the bankruptcy itself are governed by *federal* law as stated in the Bankruptcy Code and interpreted in federal court opinions. For instance, while orders about legal fees and costs in conjunction with a divorce case are matters of state law, it is up to the federal bankruptcy court to decide whether, under federal law, these orders are, in effect, part of a debtor's obligation to pay alimony or child support and thus cannot be discharged in bankruptcy.

CHAPTERS 7, 11, AND 13 OF THE BANKRUPTCY CODE

The Bankruptcy Code provides for three main alternatives: proceedings under Chapter 7 (Liquidation), Chapter 11 (Business Reorganization), or Chapter 13 (Adjustment of an Individual's Debts). A fourth type of proceeding, to adjust the debts of a municipal corporation, is available under Chapter 9 when authorized by the state where the municipal corporation is located. (Both family farming and family fishermen business reorganizations are governed by Bankruptcy Code Chapter 12.)

Under any of these four alternatives, the debtor may file a voluntary petition for bankruptcy, although individuals can file for Chapter 7 or 13 only upon completion of a short Credit Counseling course (about 15–90 minutes long).[2] Creditors may initiate only a Chapter 7 or a Chapter 11 proceeding; this is done by filing an involuntary petition, with the goal being to preserve the debtors' assets and to ensure fair treatment for every creditor.

Any creditor, either individually or joined by other creditors, may file an involuntary petition when the debtor has fewer than 12 creditors. However, when the number of creditors is 12 or more, at least 3 of the creditors must sign the petition. In all cases, the involuntary petition must meet these two requirements:

1. The debtor must owe at least $13,475 in unsecured claims to the petitioning creditors (the ones who have signed the petition).

---

[2] Also, these individuals must take a credit education (personal financial management) course before receiving a bankruptcy discharge.

2. The creditors must allege either that a custodian for the debtor's property has been appointed in the prior 120 days or that the debtor has generally not been paying debts that are due.

A *filing* under any of the four chapters *creates an "estate" consisting of all of the debtor's property*, with an *automatic stay* preventing creditors, other than those owed alimony or child support, from collecting debts or foreclosing on collateral. (Secured creditors may petition the bankruptcy court for relief from the stay.)

• *CHAPTER 7*

In a *Chapter 7* case, the bankruptcy court appoints a trustee to take charge of the estate. The trustee sells ("liquidates") the debtor's nonexempt property, and the proceeds are then distributed to the creditors according to their priorities under law—for example, taxes are usually paid before general creditors are paid.

A Chapter 7 discharge covers debts, including judgments, arising before the bankruptcy order granting the discharge. Just as a bankruptcy petition operates temporarily to prevent most creditors from trying to collect their debts pending the bankruptcy proceedings, the discharge makes this prevention permanent.

Because Chapter 7 discharges cover only individuals, business entities such as corporations and partnerships remain technically liable for their debts. However, the lack of discharge does not matter unless the entity later acquires assets. The effect is to prevent the resurrection of that same entity (e.g., as a "shell" business) after a Chapter 7 liquidation. (Under Chapter 11, a type of discharge is granted.)

Some businesses, though, are simply denied the right to file for bankruptcy. Railroads, banks, savings and loan associations, credit unions, insurance companies, and other financial institutions are regulated in all matters, including insolvency, by administrative agencies, not the Bankruptcy Code. However, railroads are permitted to file for a Chapter 11 reorganization.

• *CHAPTER 11*

Chapter 11 is mainly intended to allow ongoing businesses to restructure their debts. Before restructuring occurs, a court-appointed trustee or examiner conducts an investigation, files reports with the court, and may submit a reorganization plan (if the debtor has not) or (instead) recommend conversion to a Chapter 7 liquidation. Also, a "small business"— one with total debts under $2,490,925—can use a simpler, fast-track Chapter 11 process.

Whether for an individual proprietorship, a small firm, or a large corporation, successful reorganization requires a detailed plan covering all aspects of the organization's business operation and its assets and debts. Then the plan must be accepted by the bankruptcy judge and by two-thirds in amount, and more than half in number, of the claims in any particular class of creditors. Each creditor must receive at least as much as the creditor would be entitled to obtain under Chapter 7 liquidation.

• *CHAPTER 13*

Chapter 13 is available only to individuals with regular sources of income, unsecured debts not exceeding $383,175 (to increase in 2016 and every three years thereafter), and secured debts of no more than $1,149,525 (to increase in 2016 and every three years thereafter). Under the Bankruptcy Abuse Prevention and Consumer Protection Act of 2005 (BAPCPA), Chapter 7 (with its more generous discharge of debtors) ordinarily is unavailable to debtors who earn more than the median income in their state;[3] these debtors must instead use Chapter 13 if they can pay their creditors, altogether, at least $7,475 over five years.

The debtor files a payment plan, with payments beginning no more than 30 days after the bankruptcy petition is filed and continuing for up to 5 years. Payments are made to a court-appointed trustee, who begins paying creditors after the court approves the plan. Upon completion of the plan, and even for "hardship" cases in which plan payments are incomplete, a Chapter 13 discharge (comparable to, but in some ways broader than, a Chapter 7 discharge) is granted.

Usually about one fourth of the debtor's disposable earnings goes to his/her creditors, although the specific amount is somewhat dependent on the debtor's level of income and family responsibilities. As in Chapter 11, payments cannot be any less than a creditor would receive under Chapter 7 liquidation. At any time, the debtor or the court may turn the case into a Chapter 7 proceeding.

PROCEDURE AND EXEMPTIONS

A debtor must file a financial statement (including income and expenses) and must list assets, creditors (with addresses and amounts owed), and exempt property. Under BAPCPA, an attorney representing a debtor in bankruptcy must conduct a thorough investigation to determine whether the information provided in the debtor's petition and schedules (statements about the debtor's financial position) is accurate. The attorney provides a certification, under penalty of perjury, for the information in the petition and can be fined and otherwise penalized for any discrepancies.

Exemptions under federal law include the following (*with dollar figures to rise in 2016 and every three years thereafter*):

---

[3] There are some accommodations for active-duty service members and those with serious medical conditions.

1. Equity in a home and burial plot up to $22,975.
2. Interest in one motor vehicle up to $3,675.
3. Trade or business items up to $2,300.
4. Professionally prescribed health aids.
5. Unmatured life insurance contracts (other than credit life insurance).
6. Federal and state benefits such as social security, local public assistance, and veterans', disability and unemployment benefits.
7. An interest in jewelry not to exceed $1,550.
8. Alimony and child support, as reasonably necessary for support of the debtor or his/her dependents.
9. Certain pensions, stock bonuses, profit-sharing plan payments, annuities, and other such plans to the extent needed for support.
10. An interest in household furnishings or goods, clothes, books, appliances, animals, crops, musical instruments, or other items of a personal, family, or household nature (up to $575 for any one item, with the total not exceeding $12,250).
11. Criminal victim restitution payments, lost earnings payments, wrongful death benefits, life insurance payments to a dependent beneficiary, and—up to $22,975—personal injury payment.
12. Retirement funds that are in a fund or account that is exempt from federal taxation, and some individual retirement accounts with the aggregate amount exempted limited to $1,245,475.
13. Accrued interest or dividends of up to $12,250 in life insurance policies.
14. Some contributions to education and college savings accounts made more than one year before bankruptcy.
15. Any other property worth altogether (a) no more than $1,225, plus (b) up to $11,500 of the unused portion, if any, of the homestead exemption (item 1, above).

States are permitted to substitute their own exemptions for these federal exemptions, and most have done so. The rest of the states permit debtors to choose between the relevant state or federal exemptions. Bankruptcy law reforms in 2005 restrict a state's homestead exemption to $155,675 (adjustable for inflation in 2016 and every three years thereafter) if the person in bankruptcy bought his/her residence less than 40 months before filing. Also, that same homestead cap applies if the bankruptcy court finds that the debtor was convicted for a felony demonstrating that the bankruptcy filing was an abuse of the bankruptcy laws *or* if the debtor owes a debt arising from a violation of federal or state securities laws, fiduciary fraud, racketeering, or crimes or intentional torts that caused serious injury or death in the preceding five years. A debtor's discharge may be delayed while the debtor is involved in a proceeding (e.g., a criminal charge) that might lead to this homestead exemption cap.

THE TRUSTEE'S ROLE IN BANKRUPTCY

The **trustee** acquires title to all of the debtor's property ("the estate") and administers the estate by collecting and liquidating assets as well as deciding claims. The trustee may sue, accept or reject executory contracts, revoke unperfected property transfers, and negate preferential or fraudulent transfers.

> Preferential transfers favor one creditor over others (i.e., the favored creditor gets more than he/she would under the Bankruptcy Code). Such transfers are prohibited when they concern preexisting debts and are made during the 90-day period before the bankruptcy petition is filed.

Creditors with liens on or security interests in the debtor's property may sell or otherwise dispose of the property in order to collect the debt secured by that property. If a sale generates more than is owed, the excess goes into the debtor's estate. If, after disposition of the secured property, the debtor still owes money, the creditor becomes an unsecured, general creditor for the remaining amount owed (category 11, immediately below).

The trustee distributes the debtor's estate (pays costs, claims, or other expenses) in this order:

1. Alimony, child support, and property distribution (domestic support) obligations.
2. Costs of administering, collecting, and maintaining the estate, including attorneys' fees and, usually, taxes and even penalties. BABCPA adds as part of this administrative expenses category "the value of any goods received by a debtor within 20 days before the petition date in which the goods have been sold to the debtor in the ordinary course of the debtor's business." (*BAPCPA further protects sellers as follows: Sellers may reclaim goods sold in the ordinary course of business and on credit to a debtor who received the goods while insolvent. To do that, the seller must demand reclamation in writing no later than 45 days after the debtor received the goods or, if a petition for bankruptcy was filed during those 45 days, within 20 days after that filing.*)

3. For involuntary petitions under Chapter 11, credit extended or taxes incurred in the ordinary course of business during the "gap"—the period after the bankruptcy petition was filed but before a trustee was appointed or an order for relief was made.

4. Unsecured claims up to $12,475 per employee for wages (including vacation, severance, and sick pay) earned 180 or fewer days before the bankruptcy petition was filed or the business ceased, whichever was first.

5. Unsecured claims up to $12,475 per employee for contributions to employee benefit plans arising from services rendered 180 or fewer days before the bankruptcy petition was filed. (However, the combined priority of **4** and **5** (wages and pension contributions) is limited, altogether, to $12,475 per person.)

6. Claims up to $6,150 of farmers and fishermen against debtors owning or operating facilities for storing grain or processing fish.

7. Consumer claims up to $2,775 for deposits with or prepayments to the debtor for undelivered property or unperformed services.

8. Some taxes and penalties due—unsecured claims for unpaid income and gross receipts taxes incurred in the three years preceding the bankruptcy petition and for unpaid property taxes incurred within one year of the petition.

9. Unsecured claims based on the debtor's commitment to the Federal Deposit Insurance Corporation (FDIC) or other such regulatory agency (e.g., to maintain the capital of an insured bank).

10. Claims for liability based on death or personal injury resulting from operation of a motor vehicle where the operator was unlawfully intoxicated from alcohol, drugs, or other substances.

11. Claims of general creditors (almost all other unsecured debts). Those parts of claims that exceed the money or time limits in categories 4, 5, 6 or 7 above fall within this category.

(As with other figures in the bankruptcy laws, these amounts (categories 4–7, above), will automatically be adjusted for inflation in 2016 and every three years thereafter.)

NONDISCHARGEABLE DEBTS, DENIAL OF OVERALL DISCHARGE, AND LIMITS OF DISCHARGE

• *NONDISCHARGEABLE DEBTS*

Six types of debts are considered to be too important to be discharged by bankruptcy:

1. Alimony, child support, and debts in the nature of support, ordinarily also including marital settlement agreements or divorce decree property distributions.
2. Certain loans owed to a pension, profit-sharing, stock bonus, or other plan.
3. Some government fines and penalties.
4. Taxes and related fines owed for the 3 years before bankruptcy.
5. Amounts the debtor borrowed to pay federal taxes.
6. Student loans, unless payment imposes an undue hardship on the debtor or his/her dependents.[4]

The main reason for not discharging a debt may be the debtor's misconduct. These other nondischargeable debts are as follows:

1. Intentional tort claims.
2. Judgments and consent decrees based on drunk driving (or flying or operating a boat while intoxicated).
3. Claims to money or property obtained by fraud, false pretense, embezzlement, larceny, or misuse of funds (including compensatory or punitive damages for fraud).
4. Criminal restitution obligations.
5. Claims not listed in the bankruptcy petition.
6. Debts exceeding $650 for luxury goods/services purchased from one creditor within 90 days before the bankruptcy filing.
7. Certain cash advances exceeding $925 within 70 days before the filing.
8. A debt (e.g., marital) whose discharge results in a benefit to the debtor outweighing any detriment to the debtor's child, spouse, or ex-spouse.

Moreover, if in a prior bankruptcy action the debtor was denied a discharge of a particular claim (for reasons other than the 8-year waiting requirement between bankruptcy discharges), he/she cannot later get a discharge on that claim. (Nor, as discussed earlier, can the debtor use a fraudulent or preferential transfer to avoid his/her responsibilities or favor certain creditors.)

---

[4] The BAPCPA eliminated the prior law's provision allowing a student loan to be discharged once seven years have passed from the start of that loan's repayment period. It also eliminated the distinctive treatment of privately financed student loans, which no longer may be easier to discharge than other student loans.

• *DENIAL OF OVERALL DISCHARGE*

Overall bankruptcy discharge may be denied in these cases:

1. The debtor has: (a) in writing waived his/her right to a discharge; (b) destroyed, concealed, or transferred his/her property and/or records in order to hinder or defraud a creditor; (c) unjustifiably failed to maintain records from which his/her financial status could be determined; (d) not adequately explained a supposed loss of assets; (e) committed a bankruptcy "scam" or other such crime (e.g., lied about his/her financial position when obtaining credit); (f) refused to obey a bankruptcy court order to answer the court's questions or to appear at scheduled bankruptcy meetings or hearings; or (g) failed to complete a required Credit Education course.

2. A bankruptcy court granted the debtor a Chapter 7 discharge or Chapter 11 relief within 8 years of the filing of his/her present petition (just six years after Chapter 13 discharges, and no bar applies when the prior proceeding was a good-faith Chapter 13 plan paying at least 70% of unsecured claims).

3. A prior bankruptcy petition was dismissed 180 days before the present petition was filed.

4. A Chapter 7 discharge by a consumer debtor would be a "substantial abuse" of the system.

In most, if not all of these cases, the debtor's nonexempt assets are still distributed to creditors; but, instead of receiving a discharge, the debtor remains liable for the unpaid portion of his/her debts.

• *LIMITS OF DISCHARGE*

A discharge does not affect the liability of a codebtor, a surety, or a guarantor. Moreover, within one year of a discharge the bankruptcy court may revoke its discharge decree because of evidence that the debtor committed fraud or lied during the bankruptcy proceedings.

Debtors may reaffirm a dischargeable debt; such a **reaffirmation agreement**, though, must be in writing and contain a statement to the effect that the debtor knows of his/her right to rescind the reaffirmation before discharge or within 60 days, whichever is later. The reaffirmation agreement must be filed in bankruptcy court, along with an affidavit by the debtor's attorney that the agreement would impose no undue hardship on the debtor or a dependent of the debtor, and that the debtor was fully informed of his/her rights and entered into the agreement voluntarily. If the debtor was not represented by counsel, a reaffirmation agreement usually requires the bankruptcy court's approval; it must find that the reaffirmation does not impose undue hardship on the debtor and is in the debtor's best interest.

Of course, a debtor may simply volunteer to repay a discharged debt. Such payments cannot be compelled, however, in the absence of a binding reaffirmation.

BAPCPA modifies former section 304 of the Bankruptcy Code concerning cross-border insolvency procedures (for cases where the debtor has insolvency proceedings pending in more than one country). The act is based on the Model Law on Cross Border Insolvency, which had been prepared by the United Nations Commission on International Trade Law. For these concurrent procedures, the act is intended to reconcile differences and keep one country from ruling in ways that render the other countries' procedures moot. To take advantage of this act (Chapter 15 of the Bankruptcy Code), the debtor must file "a petition seeking recognition of a foreign proceeding by a foreign representative."

YOU SHOULD REMEMBER

The test for bankruptcy is: Can the debtor pay debts as they become due?

The Constitution empowers Congress to make uniform laws on bankruptcy. Thus bankruptcy is governed by federal law, with a system of U.S. bankruptcy courts.

The Bankruptcy Code has three main alternatives: Chapter 7 (Liquidation), Chapter 11 (Business Reorganization), and Chapter 13 (Adjustment of an Individual's Debts). Petitions for bankruptcy may be voluntary (filed by the debtor) for all three chapters or involuntary (filed by creditors) for Chapters 7 and 11.

The Bankruptcy Code exempts certain property, or amounts of property, from being used to satisfy creditors' claims.

A court-appointed trustee administers the debtor's property ("the estate") and distributes the debtor's nonexempt property according to the priority of claims outlined in the Bankruptcy Code.

The Bankruptcy Code prohibits the discharge of certain debts and also allows the bankruptcy judge to deny discharges because of the debtor's misconduct.

Discharges do not remove the liability of codebtors, sureties, or guarantors; and a debtor may, in writing, reaffirm a discharged debt.

SECURED TRANSACTIONS

A **secured transaction** is any transaction in which a debtor gives a creditor a security interest in personal property or fixtures.

INTRODUCTION

Revised UCC Article 9, promulgated in 1999 and since adopted by all 50 states, governs secured transactions (as did the UCC's original Article 9). In a typical case, the debtor has borrowed money (often a purchase on credit), with the creditor expecting the debtor's performance (e.g., payments) in compliance with the terms of the loan. As additional protection of his/her right to repayment, the creditor requires that the debtor give a security interest in personal property; if the debtor fails to perform, the *secured creditor* can use that personal property (known as **collateral**) as a substitute for, or a means to collect, the debtor's performance.

Security interests are commonly given in the very property for which a business or consumer has borrowed money (received financing) in order to buy. Secured credit thus permits a consumer or business to make large-scale purchases while assuring the sellers and lenders that they can obtain complete, or at least partial, payment from the secured property if necessary.

PLEDGE

The oldest and simplest type of secured transaction is a **pledge**; there the debtor provides the creditor with physical possession of some of the debtor's property. This collateral may consist of tangible items, such as jewelry or machinery, or intangible personal property, such as stocks. If the debtor defaults, the creditor sells or uses the collateral to satisfy the debt.

Example: Pledge

Ellen Extravagant owes a credit card company $500. She borrows the money from Paul Pawnbroker and leaves a diamond ring worth $800 with Paul as collateral.

One obvious problem with a pledge is that the debtor frequently will not or cannot turn over possession of his/her property. In fact, a pledge contradicts the underlying purpose of many credit transactions, that is, to help the debtor acquire *and use* property, not merely buy property (on credit) and then pledge away its possession.

SECURITY INTEREST

Because of problems with the pledge, the law has long permitted the use of security devices that do not require transfer of possession. Such devices include chattel mortgages, trust receipts, and assignments of accounts receivables; the UCC now labels all of these **security interests**.

• COLLATERAL

The following types of property can be collateral (i.e., property subject to a security interest):

- Consigned goods (including equipment and inventory).

- Documents evincing rights (e.g., accounts, payment intangibles, promissory notes, chattel paper, securities created by a government debtor, health insurance receivables, deposit accounts, guarantees, and letters of credit).

- Proceeds from a security interest.

- Most other personal property or fixtures (e.g., items subject to agricultural liens, collection on a commercial tort claim, and property liens that establish a right to payment).

Excluded interests include those involving wages, landlord's liens, most assignments, and papers or notes for the sale of a business.

Even "after-acquired property" (personal property acquired by the debtor after the security agreement was executed) may be collateral, although UCC 9-204(b) bars such collateral for commercial tort claims and sets limits on after-acquired interests in consumer goods (only permitted for accessions or for property acquired within 10 days after the secured party gave value). Collateral may even secure future credit, not just past or present loans (UCC 9-323).

• REQUIREMENTS FOR AN EFFECTIVE SECURITY INTEREST

ATTACHMENT

To make the security interest effective between the debtor and creditor, the interest must "attach" to the secured property (the collateral). The three requirements of an attachment are as follows:

1. A written agreement sets forth a security interest, describes the collateral, and is signed by the debtor.

2. Value is given by the secured party to the debtor.

3. The debtor has rights in the collateral.

"Value" arises from commitments to extend credit, from consideration sufficient for a contract, or from preexisting consideration. When the secured party obtains possession of the collateral (a pledge), no written agreement is necessary.

PERFECTION

To make the security interest effective against third parties, it must be "perfected." **Perfection** gives the secured party priority over other parties seeking to attach or otherwise use the collateral. In short, if C perfects a security interest in D's equipment, most third-party creditors will not be permitted to seize and sell that equipment in order to satisfy D's debts to them.

The method for obtaining a *perfection* depends on the type of collateral. The four methods are possession, control, attachment, and the filing of a **financing statement**.

1. *Possession* constitutes perfection for pledges. It is a method for perfecting an interest in goods, instruments (e.g., promissory notes), certificated securities (e.g., stocks and bonds), tangible chattel paper, money, and negotiable documents of title (e.g., warehouse receipts, bills of lading).

2. *Control* is the only way to perfect a security interest in a letter of credit or in a deposit account (UCC 9-314). Such control exists only if: (a) the secured creditor is the depositary bank where the account is maintained, (b) the debtor, secured creditor, and depositary bank have agreed that the bank will follow the creditor's instructions without the debtor's further consent, or (c) the creditor becomes the depositary bank's customer concerning the account.

3. *Automatic perfection (perfection by attachment) usually involves a purchase-money security interest (PMSI)* in consumer goods other than fixtures or motor vehicles. Section 9-103 of the UCC defines a PMSI as a security interest that is: (a) held by the seller of the collateral in order to secure all or part of the sales price, *or* (b) held by a person lending money or otherwise giving value that the debtor uses to acquire or use the collateral.

Without automatic perfection, filing offices would be swamped with financing statements concerning PMSIs in consumer goods. Most authorities believe that such increased filing would provide little added protection to other creditors, and might only confuse matters.

The other typical instance of automatic perfection involves assignments of accounts or contract rights that do not, alone or with other assignments to the same assignee, amount to a "significant part" of the assignor's outstanding accounts of contract rights.

4. The fourth and *most preferred method of obtaining perfection* is to *file a financing statement*. Such a statement must contain the debtor's signature, the names of both the debtor and the secured party, and a description of the collateral (UCC 9-502 and 9-504). Filing is necessary for perfection if possession is not the required method for perfection: if the secured party does not in fact have possession; and if the transaction does not involve automatic perfection (usually via a consumer PMSI).

The secured party has the duty of filing the financing statement. Section 9-501 of the UCC provides that for fixture filings and other realty-based collateral, the creditor must file in the office where one would record a mortgage on real estate. For every other filing, besides transmitting utilities, the creditor must file centrally in the office that the state designates as official keeper of the state's UCC files (UCC 9-501(a)(2)). Filings can be electronic. ·

A person in doubt as to whether he/she needs to file a financing statement should—to be safe—file one.

Do not confuse the financing statement with the security agreement. The former cannot replace the latter. Indeed, the financing statement simply furnishes the minimal information needed to put other parties on notice of a security interest. (In some cases, the security agreement itself may be filed as the financing statement.) To obtain further information, the debtor or secured party may have to be contacted directly.

A proper filing will be good for 5 years, unless it indicates a shorter maturity date. Continuations may be filed in order to extend the financing statement for another 5 years. The number of such extensions is unlimited, and the secured party need not obtain the debtor's signature.

When a Debtor Moves to Another State, or Is Succeeded Through a Merger

Perfection by filing continues for four months after a debtor changes his/her jurisdiction. Under a 2010 amendment to Article 9 that all states have enacted, this perfection is extended to collateral: (1) in a debtor's post-move after-acquired property; or (2) that a debtor's successor through merger acquired either before or within four months after the merger.

RIGHTS AND DUTIES OF SECURED PARTIES AND DEBTORS

• *WHAT IS A DEFAULT?*

A **default** on a debt is not defined in UCC Article 9. The parties usually state in their security agreement the conditions that will constitute a default. The typical default is failure to make timely payments on the loan. Another type of default may be to breach a warranty that no liens or other security interests cover the same collateral as that relied on in the security agreement.

• *RIGHTS AND DUTIES BEFORE DEFAULT*

Before default, the parties have certain rights or duties, unless specified differently in the security agreement.

The *secured party*:

(a) may release or assign all or part of the collateral;

(b) may file an extension or amendment of a financing statement, although the latter also requires the debtor's signature;

(c) if in possession of the collateral, must use reasonable care to preserve it.

The *debtor*:

(a) may periodically request and receive from the secured party a written statement as to the current amount of the unpaid debt, and perhaps a full listing of the collateral;

(b) bears the risk of loss or damage to the collateral;

(c) must pay for all reasonable expenses incurred in taking care of the collateral.

• RIGHTS AND DUTIES AFTER DEFAULT

Upon default, the secured party may sue on the underlying obligation or enforce the security interest directly. These remedies are not exclusive, and can be cumulative if need be [UCC 9-601(c)].

UCC Section 9-609 states the secured party's right to take possession after default, unless prohibited by the security agreement itself. Although the secured party may take possession without a court order, such conduct must not lead to a breach of the peace (UCC 9-609(b)(2)). As is the case before default, the secured party has to exercise reasonable care over any collateral it now possesses.

As an alternative, a secured party may require the debtor to assemble the collateral at a place designated by the secured party. In fact, the secured party may choose not to remove collateral equipment, but simply to make it unusable and then dispose of it (e.g., sell it) on the debtor's premises.

SPECIAL PROVISIONS IF THE SECURED PARTY CHOOSES TO KEEP THE COLLATERAL

The debtor may, via a recorded signed statement (or the failure to object to a notice from the secured party), agree to the secured party's retention of collateral in partial or full satisfaction of the debtor's obligation (UCC 9-620 and 9-621). However, if the debtor has paid over 60% of the price or the loan for collateral that consists of consumer goods, the secured party must sell the collateral within 90 days unless the secured party and the debtor otherwise agree (UCC 9-620). Also, for consumer transactions, a secured party may not accept collateral in partial satisfaction of the secured debt. It must be a full satisfaction (UCC 9-620(g)).

For collateral other than consumer goods, the secured party must also notify other secured parties who have given written notice of an interest in the collateral (UCC 9-610). If within 20 days a person entitled to notification (e.g., the debtor or another secured party) objects to the secured party's retention of the goods, a sale must take place. Otherwise, the secured party may keep the collateral (UCC 9-620).

SALE OF THE COLLATERAL

Sale of collateral may be by any method so long as it is "commercially reasonable." It is not enough to show that a different type of sale could have produced a better price; for example, the sale is "commercially reasonable" if it was conducted in the usual manner for a recognized market in the goods, or if it obtained the current market price, or if it conformed to the practices of merchants selling the same type of property.

The debtor, of course, has a right to redeem the collateral before the sale by fully paying the debt, plus the additional expenses incurred by the secured party (UCC 9-623). Moreover, another secured party may, in effect, substitute his/her payment for that of the debtor so as to secure the collateral. Once sold, the purchaser takes the collateral free of claims by the debtor or by secured parties.

Upon sale, the proceeds are distributed in this order to pay:

(a) reasonable expenses related to possessing, preserving, and selling the collateral, including attorney's fees;

(b) the debt owed to the secured party;

(c) claims of other secured parties who gave written notice of an interest in the collateral.

The surplus, if any, goes to the debtor.

As with other debt-collection mechanisms, if the sale does not give the secured party all that he/she is owed, then the secured party (unless barred by the security agreement itself) usually retains a right to collect the deficiency by other means. (The exceptions involve accounts or chattel paper, in which a deficiency is nonrecoverable unless the security agreement specifically provides otherwise.)

TERMINATION STATEMENT

Once the debtor's obligations are satisfied, he/she may require that the secured party file a termination statement wherever a financing statement was filed. For financing statements concerning consumer goods (a rarity because of automatic perfection), the termination statement is mandatory even if the former debtor does not demand it. Failure to file (or, for nonconsumer transactions, at least send a termination statement to the debtor) subjects the secured party to fines and also liability to the debtor for any resulting losses (UCC 9-625). Also, the debtor or some other person can then proceed to file the termination statement without the secured party's permission (UCC 9-509(d)(2)).

PRIORITY OF CREDITORS

Obviously, one major purpose of the secured transaction is to ensure that the secured party can use the collateral to collect the debt before other creditors may do so. Thus one creditor has *priority* over another creditor (*who has an interest in the same collateral and/or is owed money by the same debtor*).

For Article 9 priority rules to apply, at least one party must be a secured party. UCC 9-201 states the basic premise, "Except as otherwise provided in the Uniform Commercial Code, a security agreement is effective according to its terms between the parties, against purchasers of the collateral, and against creditors." So, a secured party wins the priority dispute unless a UCC rule (e.g., in Article 9) decides that it loses.

The following table shows the major priority controversies and their usual outcomes.

Opposing Creditors		Priority Creditor
General Rules		
Perfected security holder	Another perfected security holder	The first to perfect [UCC 9-322(a)(1)]
Perfected security holder	Unperfected security holder	The perfected security holder, regardless of whose security interest arose first [UCC 9-322(a)(2)]
Unperfected security holder	Another unperfected security holder	The first party whose security interest attached [UCC 9-322(a)(3)]
Unperfected security holder	Unsecured creditor (including most unlevied judgment creditors*)	The unperfected security holder [UCC 9-317]
PMSI Exceptions to "First to Perfect" Rule		
Perfected PMSI in inventory	Earlier perfected non-PMSI	PMSI (and also as to PMSI cash proceeds if notice was given to non-PMSI on or before debtor takes possession) [UCC 9-324(a)]
Perfected PMSI in noninventory collateral	Earlier perfected non-PMSI in the same collateral	PMSI and ordinarily its identifiable proceeds, if the PMSI is perfected within 20 days after debtor obtains possession [UCC 9-324(a)]

---

* Ordinarily, tort claims and even judgments cannot be collateral, but commercial tort claims and structured settlements (a form of payment intangibles) can be (UCC 9-102(a)).

Opposing Creditors		Priority Creditor
Lien Creditors		
Lien creditor (including a receiver or an assignee for the benefit of creditors)	Unperfected or later perfected security holder	Lien creditor, except if pre-existing PMSI is perfected before orwithin 20 days after debtor possesses the collateral [UCC 9-317]
Lien creditor (including a receiver or an assignee for the benefit of creditors)	Perfected security holder	Lien creditor, but subject to the perfected security interest inasmuch as (1) it secures advances the secured party made before or within 45 days after the lien creditor obtained the lien, or (2) it secures advances made without knowledge of the lien [UCC 9-323(b)]

Other Exceptions to "First to Perfect" Rule:

Purchasers of the Debtor's Collateral and Trustees in Bankruptcy*

Opposing Creditors		Priority Creditor
Purchaser and/or holder of negotiable instruments, documents of title, and/or securities	Earlier perfected security holder	The purchaser [UCC 9-331]
Purchaser of chattel paper	Earlier perfected security holder	The purchaser, if gave new value, acted in good faith, took possession in the ordinary course of business, and had no actual knowledge of the security interest (last requirement unnecessary when chattel paper claimed as proceeds of inventory) [UCC 9-330(a)(b)]
Purchaser of goods (other than farm products bought from a farmer), with the goods purchased from the original consumer in the ordinary course of business	Earlier security holder for a perfected security interest created by the goods' seller	The purchaser, even if the purchaser knows of the security interest [UCC 9-320(a)]

---

* Of course, a purchaser or trustee may not, in fact, be a "creditor." Nonetheless, priority disputes often arise between purchasers (or trustees) and creditors.

Opposing Creditors		Priority Creditor
Purchaser of consumer goods	Earlier PMSI or other security interest even if perfected	The purchaser, if gave value, bought before the filing of a financing statement covering the goods, had no knowledge of the other security interest, and used the goods for personal, family, or household purposes [UCC 9-320(b)]
Trustee in bankruptcy	Unperfected (when the bankruptcy petition was filed) security holder	Trustee in bankruptcy, under Bankruptcy Code § 544(a) and UCC 9-102(a)(52) and 9-317(a)(2) (treating the trustee like a lien creditor*)
Trustee in bankruptcy	Earlier perfected security holder	Perfected security holder, unless the security interest was perfected no more than 90 days before the bankruptcy petition was filed and constituted a preferential transfer under Bankruptcy Code § 547(b)**

Fixtures to Real Estate and Accessions to Personal Property

Perfected security holder in a fixture	Conflicting real estate claimant (e.g., mortgagee)	First to file, except that PMSIs filed within 20 days of affixation always have priority [UCC 9-334(d)]
Unperfected security holder in a fixture	Conflicting real estate claimant	Conflicting real estate claimant [UCC 9-334(c)]
Security holder in an accession—goods physically united with other goods in such a manner that the identity of the original goods still exists (UCC 9-102(a)(1))	Security holder in the chattel to which the accession is added	Generally, the security holder in the accession, if security interest was perfected in the accession before the accession was added to the chattel [UCC 9-335]

---

* Normally, the filing of a bankruptcy petition has a broad and immediate effect by automatically staying the security holder's enforcement of his/her security interest (as it also stays other creditors' rights). The secured creditor ordinarily will have to transfer collateral in his/her possession to the debtor's trustee. However, absent a preferential transfer, the trustee typically releases the collateral back to the perfected security holder, without any charge.

** A perfection within one year before the petition, if concerning a fraudulent conveyance (very rare), could also be voided by the trustee.

YOU SHOULD REMEMBER

UCC Article 9 governs secured transactions. A security interest may be taken in almost any type of personal property.

To make the security interest effective between the debtor and the creditor, it must "attach" to the secured property (collateral). Attachment requires (1) a written agreement stating a security interest, describing the collateral, and signed by the debtor; (2) value from the secured party to the debtor; and (3) rights of the debtor in the collateral.

To make the security interest work against third parties, it must be "perfected," depending on the type of collateral, by possession, control, attachment, or—most commonly—the filing of a financing statement. Upon default, the secured party may sue on the underlying obligation or enforce the security interest directly; these remedies can be cumulative.

In some cases, the secured party may keep the collateral as satisfaction of the defaulting debtor's obligations. In *all* defaults, the secured party may sell the collateral by any "commercially reasonable" method, with the debtor having a right to redeem up to the time of sale. Proceeds are distributed first to cover expenses, then to pay (1) the secured debt, (2) other secured parties, and (3) if any money remains, the debtor.

Satisfaction of the debtor's obligation is evinced by the secured party's filing of a termination statement.

The order in which creditors are paid follows an established system of priorities, in which the first to perfect a security interest usually takes precedence.

KNOW THE CONCEPTS
DO YOU KNOW THE BASICS?

1. Name ten lawful methods for collecting debts.
2. Name five or more types of personal property that may be at least partly exempted from debt-collection enforcement.
3. (a) Name at least five federal statutes that regulate creditor practices, prohibit abuses, provide dispute-resolution mechanisms, or otherwise protect debtors.

   (b) Would you include the UCCC in your list?
4. Which law, federal or state, governs bankruptcy proceedings?
5. Under the Bankruptcy Code, what is the test for insolvency (the "bankruptcy test")?

6. Name the three main chapters of the Bankruptcy Code, the type of relief under each chapter, and the party that may ask for that relief.
7. Name at least four types of assets (property) *totally* exempt from being liquidated or otherwise disposed of to help pay claims against a bankrupt debtor.
8. Name at least four types of nondischargeable debts and state the main other reason a debt might not be dischargeable.
9. Does a bankruptcy discharge affect the liability of a codebtor, surety, or guarantor?
10. What is the simplest type of secured transaction?
11. Name four types of property that can be subject to a security interest.
12. (a) What are the requirements for an attachment?
    (b) What does an attachment accomplish?
13. (a) What are the four methods for making a security interest "perfect"?
    (b) What does perfection accomplish?
14. Upon default, what may a secured party do with the collateral?
15. What is the general rule governing priority between two conflicting security holders?

TERMS FOR STUDY

accession
accounting
attachment
bankruptcy
Bankruptcy Abuse Prevention
   and Consumer Protection Act
   of 2005
bulk transfer
collateral
control
default
discharge
equity of redemption
financing statement
fixture
foreclosure
fraudulent conveyance
garnishment
guarantor

homestead exemption
judicial sale
lender liability
lien
mortgage
perfection
pledge
prejudgment attachment
priority
purchase money security interest
reaffirmation agreement
secured transaction
security interest
subrogation
surety
termination statement
trustee
UCCC
writ of execution

PRACTICAL APPLICATION

1. Sure-Thing Surety has entered into suretyships with the following debtors. Coincidentally, in each case the creditor is Wanda Wealthy.

(1) Dirk Debtor owes $10,000 on a loan. Payments are in default. Dirk is 15 years old.

(2) Daphne Delinquent purchased a number of items on credit. Wanda demands payment. Daphne says a check is in the mail.

(3) Ollie Obligor persuaded Wanda to extend the duration of his loan, in return for Ollie's agreeing to pay a higher interest rate. Ollie now defaults.

(4) Karen Komitted goes bankrupt. She receives a discharge of her debt to Wanda.

    (a) For each case, state whether, on the limited facts given, Wanda can obtain payment directly from Sure-Thing Surety.

    (b) What additional two defenses might be raised if Sure-Thing were a guarantor, not a surety?

2. Harry Homeowner owes $120,000 on a mortgage for a house, owned solely by Harry and lived in by the entire Homeowner family. Harry also owes $5,000 to unsecured creditor A, as well as $3,000 to creditor B, the latter debt being secured by a perfected security interest in Harry's sailboat. Harry is in default on all three debts. The house would sell for $178,000 with costs of sale being $7,000. The state homestead exemption is $25,000.

(a) If the mortgagee conducts a foreclosure sale, what will happen to the sales proceeds?

(b) If Harry files for bankruptcy, what will happen to the boat and the home, and what will be the distribution of proceeds?

3. Betty's Boutique (BB) has filed for a Chapter 7 liquidation. BB's creditors are as follows:

Corporation A: $7,000 claim for business deliveries (similar to previous deliveries) occurring between time of bankruptcy petition and appointment of trustee.

Ms. B and Mr. C: Deposits of $400 and $3,775, respectively, for purchases of consumer goods not yet provided.

State D: Unpaid taxes of $10,000 for the past 2 years.

Workers E, F, and G: $3,800, $5,000, and $13,475, respectively, owed for the last 2 months of work as BB's employees.

Secured creditor H: $5,000 owed on a car loan (perfected security interest in the car).

Unsecured creditors J and K: $8,000 owed to each.

(a) Assume that the proceeds, after costs, from a sale of BB's car are $3,000. Assume that the liquidated value of the estate is $61,450 with costs of administration, collection, and maintenance being $10,000. State the distribution to each creditor.

(b) If BB proposes a Chapter 11 reorganization, name one creditor whose lone objection would not render the plan inoperative. How much must that creditor receive under the plan?

4. Delia Debtor purchased an automobile on credit. May her creditor take priority over a previously perfected security holder who took a security interest in Delia's present and after-acquired motor vehicles?

5. A lends money to B. As collateral, A takes possession of stocks and promissory notes owed to B. B subsequently receives a business loan from C, with a security agreement (and properly filed financing statement) specifying a security interest in (among other things) B's stocks, promissory notes, and other documents. Who has priority as to the stocks and promissory notes, A or C?

6. (a) Don Debtor is lent money by Bob Bucks, who takes an unperfected security interest in a number of items, including the computer Don has owned for 3 years. If Telly's Shop (TS) obtains a lien for repairs on Don's computer, does Bob or TS have priority?

(b) What if Bob now perfects his security interest?

7. Joe, for money lent to Kay, receives a signed agreement stating a security interest and describing the collateral (Kay's accounts receivable). Kay already has a judgment against her in favor of A. She also already owes money to B, although no collateral or security interest is in effect. After Joe lends Kay the money and takes her security agreement, C also lends Kay money and gets her to sign a security agreement almost identical to the one with Joe (it, too, covers Kay's accounts receivable). C follows up by filing, in the correct location(s), a financing statement containing Kay's signature, the full names and addresses of Kay and Joe, and a description of Kay's accounts receivable.

In each of the following, who has priority?
(a) Joe or A   (b) Joe or B   (c) Joe or C

8. (a) Mary has a perfected security interest in Nancy's inventory of 100 widgets. Nancy regularly sells widgets, and soon sells 8 widgets to Opal. Opal knows about Mary's security interest, but knows nothing that would indicate the sale to her violates that security interest. If Nancy defaults, can Mary enforce her security interest against the 8 widgets that Opal bought?

(b) Assume that the widgets are consumer goods. Further assume that Mary has a PMSI perfected by attachment, not filing. If Nancy is not ordinarily in the business of selling widgets, can Walter, a widget purchaser, be free of Mary's security interest?

ANSWERS
KNOW THE CONCEPTS

1. Lien (mechanic's, artisan's, or hotelkeeper's), prejudgment attachment, use of security interests, preventing or setting aside bulk transfers or fraudulent conveyances, payment from sureties or guarantors, mortgage foreclosure, writ of execution, garnishment, composition and/or extension agreement, and assignment to a trustee.

2. Homes, household furnishings, clothes, personal possessions, livestock, pets, and veterans' pensions.

3. (a) The Dodd-Frank Act, the Consumer Credit Protection Act (Truth-in-Lending Act), the Fair Credit Billing Act and Fair Credit Reporting Act (both part of the Truth-in-Lending Act), the Fair Debt Collection Practices Act, and the Equal Credit Opportunity Act.
   (b) The Uniform Consumer Credit Code (UCCC) is not a federal statute, but has been passed by some states.

4. Federal.

5. Inability to pay debts as they become due.

6. Chapter 7, Liquidation (straight bankruptcy), voluntary or involuntary (debtors or creditors); Chapter 11, Reorganization of a Business, voluntary or involuntary (debtors or creditors); Chapter 13, Readjustment of an Individual's Debts, voluntary (debtors).

7. Criminal victim restitution payments, prescribed health aids, unmatured life insurance policies, alimony and child support, pensions and annuities, and federal and state benefits such as social security, disability, and unemployment benefits.

8. Alimony, child support, some government fines and penalties, taxes owed for the 3 years before bankruptcy, student loans received within 7 years of bankruptcy. The other main reason is the debtor's misconduct.

9. No.

10. A pledge.

11. Almost any type of personal property: goods (including equipment and inventory), documents evincing rights (e.g., commercial paper, securities, bills of lading), accounts receivable, after-acquired property.

12. (a) Requirements are that (1) a written agreement sets forth a security interest, describes the collateral, and is signed by the

debtor; (2) value passes from the secured party to the debtor; and (3) the debtor has rights in the collateral.

(b) It makes the security interest effective between the secured party and the debtor.

13. (a) Possession, control, attachment, and the filing of a financing statement.

(b) It makes the security interest effective against most third parties.

14. Either (1) take it in satisfaction of the debtor's obligation (although the debtor or another secured party may prevent such action), or (2) sell the collateral and apply the proceeds toward payment of the debtor's obligation.

15. The first to perfect has priority.

PRACTICAL APPLICATION

1. (a) (1) Yes. Dirk's infancy is not a defense for Sure-Thing.
      (2) Perhaps. It depends on whether Daphne has indeed mailed a check. If Daphne has tendered payment, then Wanda's claim against Sure-Thing would be reduced (by the amount of a partial payment from Daphne) or eliminated (if the payment was complete or otherwise settled the debt).
      (3) No. Ollie's obligations were materially altered (higher interest rate, longer loan) without the consent of Sure-Thing.
      (4) Yes. Karen's bankruptcy is not a defense for Sure-Thing.
   (b) Guaranty agreements must be in writing, and the creditor must first try to obtain relief from the debtor. Neither is necessary for a suretyship.

2. (a) First, $7,000 to pay the foreclosure costs; second, $120,000 to the mortgagee; third, the remainder to Harry. There is no indication that creditor A or B has obtained a judgment or otherwise acquired a right to some of the remaining proceeds. If the creditors had, they would take only after Harry exercised his homestead exemption.
   (b) The boat and home will be liquidated.

   Proceeds from the home sale will be applied first to costs of sale and second to the mortgagee, with Harry then being entitled to the state homestead exemption of up to $25,000. (Unless precluded by state law, Harry could instead choose the federal list of exemptions; although the federal homestead exemption is only $22,975, other exemptions may make the federal list altogether better than the overall state exemptions.)

   Proceeds from the boat sale will go first to sales costs and then to B. If there is a deficiency, B will become an unsecured creditor for the remainder. If there is a surplus, that goes into the estate.

In summation, the mortgagee and house sales costs will be paid in full. Of the remaining $51,000 either $25,000 (state) or $22,975 (federal) will be kept by Harry. The rest goes to the estate, for distribution according to priority of claims. As an unsecured creditor, A is at the bottom of the priority list. B is in the same position as A with respect to any deficiency after the sale of the boat.

3. (a) The easiest way to answer this problem is to proceed in order of priority, from top claims down to the lowly "general creditors." Also, note that H would receive $3,000 from the car sale and become a general creditor for the remaining $2,000 owed.

Payments, in order of priority, would be as follows:

1. Costs of $10,000 for administering the estate.
2. Corporation A: $7,000.
3. Workers E, F, and G: $3,800, $5,000, and $12,475, respectively. (For his/her remaining $1,000, G becomes a general creditor.)
4. Ms. B and Mr. C: $400 and $2,775 respectively. (For his remaining $1,000, C becomes a general creditor.)
5. State D: $10,000.

General creditors and amounts of claim would be as follows: C, $1,000; G, $1,000; H, $2,000; J, $8,000; K, $8,000; (total $20,000).

Liquidated value $61,450 minus total amounts in categories 1–5 ($51,450) equals $10,000. Because the amount left in the estate is $10,000, whereas the general creditors' claims total $20,000, each general creditor will be paid half of his/her claim. Thus C and G each get $500 to add to the $2,775 and $12,475, respectively, already received; H gets $1,000 in addition to the $3,000 received from the sale of his/her collateral (BB's car); and J and K get $4,000 apiece.

(b) Worker E or Worker F, with that worker receiving $3,800 or $5,000, respectively. If both object, than the plan would not have the necessary majority approval and two-thirds in amount approval of the employee creditors. (If either E or F voted with Worker G to approve the plan, then the other worker's objection would not scuttle the plan.)

4. Yes, *if* the creditor perfects before or within 10 days after Delia, the debtor, takes possession of the automobile.

5. A. Here possession generally constitutes perfection. Even if C's actions constituted perfection, A's perfection by possession has occurred before C's attempted perfection by filing; thus A wins under the general "first to perfect" rule.

6. (a) TS. Lien creditors prevail over *unperfected* security holders, except for some PMSIs. Because Don had owned the computer for 3 years, clearly his loan from Bob did not enable Don to purchase the typewriter (so *not* a PMSI).

(b) Bob has priority, at least inasmuch as his security interest concerns a loan made before or within 45 days after Telly's lien.

7. (a) Joe. Unperfected security holders have priority over unlevied judgment creditors.

(b) Joe. Unperfected security holders have priority over unsecured creditors.

(c) C. Unperfected security holders lose to subsequent *perfected* security holders [UCC 9-322(a)].

8. (a) No. UCC 9-320(a) provides that a purchaser of goods in the ordinary course of business prevails over a perfected security holder.

(b) Yes. Walter's ownership would not be subject to Mary's PMSI if Walter gave value to Nancy, he bought before Mary filed a financing statement covering the goods, he did not know about Mary's security interest, and he used the widgets for personal, family, or household purposes [UCC 9-320(b)]. Mary's prior filing of a financing statement, although not needed to perfect a PMSI in consumer goods, would prevent this type of outcome: Walter could not then take the 8 widgets "free and clear" of Mary's security interest.

BUSINESS FORMATIONS

14
AGENCY

NATURE OF AGENCY AND AGENCY LAW

Agency is of fundamental importance to all business. An **agency** is a legal relationship in which one person represents another and is authorized to act for him/her. The person who acts is the **agent**; the person for whom the agent acts is the **principal**.

Agency law consists of all the rules, recognized and enforced by society, whereby one person acts for another. Without the body of agency law, every person would have to act directly for him-/herself and could not send a representative, a salesman, or a messenger. Since corporations can act only vicariously through employees, officers, and agents, corporations could not function at all and would cease to exist.

> Without the ability of a principal to act through an agent, business would be severely crippled.

By and large, agency law is state common law. Neither federal law nor the Uniform Commercial Code deals expressly with the subject of agency.

AGENCY AND OTHER LEGAL CONCEPTS WHEREBY ONE PERSON MAY OR MAY NOT PERFORM SERVICES FOR ANOTHER

1. *Agency may include employment.* An agent may or may not be the principal's employee. It depends on whether the agent meets this definition of "employee": under the control and supervision of his/her employer, who determines not only what is to be done, but also how it is to be done and other details of performance. Conversely, the Restatement (Second) of Agency (1959) holds that employees always are agents. Some courts and commentators have disagreed—stating that certain types of employees have no power to represent the employer and thus are not agents.

2. *Agency includes and may be created by a power of attorney.* In its broadest sense, the word "attorney" denotes a representative or agent. An **attorney-at-law** is a legal representative, employed to represent a client in lawsuits and other legal matters. An **attorney in fact** may represent another person as an agent for general or special purposes other than legal ones. An attorney in fact is named as representative or agent in a **power of attorney**, a written document setting out the appointment of the attorney. The appointment may be general, that is, for broad agency purposes ("to do any act for me"), or special ("to sell my real estate known as "Blackacre") for named and limited purposes.

3. *Agency generally does not include independent contractors.* An **independent contractor** is hired to achieve a purpose, to do a job, to undertake a contractually defined result. How the contractor achieves the end result and what tools and techniques are used are his/her responsibility. (Only if the independent contractor is a representative does he constitute an agent.)

> The tort or contractual responsibility of a principal for the acts of his/her agent moves from very great when the agent is an employee to far less in the case of an independent contractor.

4. *Personal service obligations cannot be performed by an agent.* As discussed in Chapter 7, a number of personal service obligations cannot be delegated to another. These nondelegable obligations require the special skill of a designated person who cannot send a representative (agent) to act in his/her place. Thus, without the approval of the benefitted third party, a doctor or lawyer, for example, cannot name an agent to act in his/her place. Similarly, a member of a corporation's board of

directors, charged with the personal responsibility of a fiduciary (trustee), cannot act through an agent but must discharge his/her board duties in person. *What can be delegated* to an agent or subagent? Administrative, clerical, or mechanical duties—almost anything in which the delegating party's special skills or judgment are not involved.

5. It is very important to distinguish between employees (who often are agents) and independent contractors (who rarely are agents). There are *advantages to using independent contractors* instead of employees: no tort liability under *respondeat superior*, less administrative burdens, as much as 40% less in benefit expenses (e.g., no social security tax, no unemployment tax), avoidance of worker discipline and performance evaluations, reduced exposure to potential discrimination or other wrongful treatment liabilities, and far less regulation as to labor, workers' compensation, OSHA and many other laws. *Disadvantages* include: less control over a worker's performance and over his use of the hirer's proprietary information, potential liability beyond workers' compensation levels, the possibility that misclassification will result in penalties costing far more than simply classifying, initially, someone as an employee.

Is he/she really an independent contractor? Look at the parties' actions and circumstances, not just what the parties say (e.g., their written agreement), but what is actually done. Is the hired person really "independent"? Does the hirer only determine ultimate goals, while the hired person decides how to do the job?

There are many tests for whether someone is an employee or an independent contractor, with different standards found at many different administrative agencies, such as the NLRB, the Labor Department (for FLSA purposes), the Social Security Administration, and the Internal Revenue Service. The common law approach is to look at how much the hirer has a "right to control" the hired person. The *"economic realities" test* uses numerous factors, often focusing on this very important question: does the worker depend on the hirer's business for the opportunity to render service (employee) or does the worker depend on his own business (independent contractor)? Some factors to consider are: (1) degree of skill (employees often receive training from their employer, while independent contractors already have expertise—a specialized or skilled occupation); (2) level of supervision (little or none for independent contractors, who usually exercise some judgment and initiative); (3) who supplies the tools, materials, and equipment (an independent contractor tends to supply his own); (4) is the work part of the hirer's regular business (e.g., waiters and waitresses at a restaurant are employees), or it is part of a distinct enterprise (e.g., caterers for a business that normally does not dispense food very likely are independent contractors); (5) the opportunity for profits/losses (e.g., franchisees are usually not employees); (6) the method of calculating payment for the work (by time worked—a regular salary or an hourly wage—is more for employees, while by the job—e.g., payment upon completion—is more for independent contractors); (7) the setting, time, place, and manner of performing the work (usually determined by the independent contractor or by employers, not employees); (8) the permanency and exclusivity of the work relationship (the more there is, the more likely the relationship is one of employment); (9) the providing of annual or sick leave of medical, retirement benefits, and of employer-paid social security taxes (more such payments indicate employment); and (10) the parties' intent, such as evidenced in a written agreement, concerning employee or independent contractor status. It is a balancing test. Misclassification of an employee as an independent contractor can result in administrative penalties and suits against the employer.

CREATION OF AGENCY

BY EXPRESS CONTRACT OR CONSENSUAL AGREEMENT

The agency relationship is always consensual. It usually is created by contract, oral or written. Sometimes, though, the contract element of consideration is lacking. For example, the power of attorney creates a consensual, but often noncontractual agency. The attorney in fact makes no promise to act, nor does the power granted necessarily provide for his/her payment or compensation. In some states, the power of attorney to sell real estate must be in writing, signed by the principal.

When an agency is not contractual, either party can terminate it at any time without liability to the other for failure to continue performance of the agency. However, there is responsibility for tasks completed, undertaken, or underway. Even if there is no contract, the parties are bound by all of the general duties and responsibilities of principal and agent (described in pages 302–304).

BY THE CONDUCT OF THE PARTIES

Implied contracts of agency may be judicially determined because the words or actions of the parties would lead others to believe that an agency existed, that one party was acting for another. This is the test for implied contracts, generally. *Indeed, because of the way persons act, third parties may depend upon there being an agency relationship even though the parties, as between themselves, may deny the existence of an agency.*

BY RATIFICATION OF AN UNAUTHORIZED ACT

Even though there was no agency when an "agent" performed a valid act ostensibly on behalf of another person, that person may ratify the act by accepting its results after the fact. There is no ratification unless the party that supposedly ratified: (1) was in existence when the "agent" acted, (2) had full knowledge of all material facts before it ratified, and (3) ratified the entire act of a would-be agent, not simply the favorable parts.

Example: Implied Contract by Ratification of an Unauthorized Act

Tara Tenant employs an interior decorator to install draperies and rugs in a residence owned by Larry Landlord. Larry will be responsible on the contract by ratification if he accepts the benefits of the work knowing of the transaction and knowing that the decorator expects to be compensated.

Since the ratification can be express or implied, in order to avoid responsibility Larry should repudiate the action as soon as he learns of it.

BY ESTOPPEL

Estoppel is conduct by one person that causes another person, reasonably relying on this conduct, to act to his/her detriment or to change his/her position. A would-be agent's actions alone do not create *agency by estoppel*. Although most scenarios involve actions or words of the supposed agent that convey to others the false impression he/she is an agent, that apparent agent cannot give himself apparent authority; instead, he/she acquires apparent authority from his/her purported principal if the "principal," by his/her conduct (acts or omissions) leads another to reasonably believe that the "agent" is in fact authorized to act on the purported principal's behalf. The third party's reliance on the appearance of authority binds the purported principal, who is estopped (precluded) from denying the agent's authority.

> *Example:* Connie Customer enters the Tech Store and pays cash for an item that she is told will be in stock later that day. Connie receives a Tech Store receipt and "IOU" from Sally, the apparent salesperson wearing a Tech Store shirt. Sally is not actually a store agent or employee, but rather just took the shirt and invoice book from the back of the store, where they had been lying near an unattended sales register. The Tech Store's careless supervision—allowing Sally to take the shirt and the invoice book and to then operate in the store as a fake salesperson—estops Tech Store from liability to Connie for Sally's actions.

BY NECESSITY

There are a few special situations in which one person, for example, a parent, is responsible for the necessities of another, a child. In such a case, the parent may be responsible as a principal for a contract made by the child for his/her necessities (e.g., for medical treatment when away from home). The contract, of course, must be reasonable, and the provider of the service will be liable to the parent (principal) for failure to perform the contract with proper care.

YOU SHOULD REMEMBER

Agency can be created by contract (express or implied, oral or written), by ratification (assent is given either to an act done by someone who had no previous authority to act or to an act that exceeded the authority granted to an agent), by estoppel (a person allows another to act for him/her to such an extent that a third party reasonably believes that an agency relationship exists), or necessity (a person acts for another in an emergency situation without express authority to do so).

THE AGENT/PRINCIPAL RELATIONSHIP

DUTIES OF THE AGENT TO THE PRINCIPAL

When the agent is appointed by contract, the terms of the contract determine the duties of each party to the other. However, the duties of an agent may be modified by express agreement. In the absence of specific terms or modifications by contract, these duties are as described in this section.

The law considers that an agent acts in a fiduciary capacity to his/her principal. The obligations of a **fiduciary** are very strict; failure of the fiduciary to account for monies collected for his/her principal, **commingling** of such monies with the fiduciary's own, or appropriation of the principal's property to the fiduciary's own use may be not only a breach of the agency contract, but also a criminal act (embezzlement, larceny after trust).

In keeping with this high degree of fidelity, the following duties are required of the agent (unless modified by contract):

1. *Duty to obey instructions.* This duty is self-evident; it involves no more than might be expected from any contract obligation. Bear in mind,

however, that the agent may be undertaking duties of the highest and most complex nature: buying and selling, entering into contracts, and the like, all as an **alter ego** (other self) for the principal. The agent is *personally liable* to the principal if he/she (a) causes the principal to become responsible for unauthorized contracts, (b) improperly delegates his/her duties to another, or (c) commits torts for which his/her principal may be responsible.

2. *Duty to act with skill.* An agent undertakes to act with the degree of skill ordinarily expected from others undertaking such employment. A business agent, a stockbroker, a manufacturer's representative—all undertake their agencies with the understanding that they will perform with skill. Any case for breach of contract requires proof (a) of the proper standard of care or skill and (b) of failure of the agent's performance to rise to that level.

3. *Duty to avoid conflict of interest (duty of loyalty). An agent who is acting for a principal cannot act for him-/herself with respect to the same matter.* An agent buying property for a principal cannot purchase property in which he/she has some personal or private interest; an agent selling the principal's goods cannot sell to him-/herself or to friends or relatives at a special or lower price. An attorney cannot act for conflicting parties in a lawsuit, or represent conflicting interests in any business transaction. On occasion a conflict, or possibility of conflict, can be resolved by full disclosure of all facts to both principals, followed by their fully informed consent to such double representation.

The disclosure of conflict or possible conflict must be complete, and the consent of the principal must be given with realization of all consequences.

---

4. *Duty to protect confidential information.* Obviously, the principal must be free to disclose all necessary information to his/her agent, including trade secrets and proprietary information. The agent must protect this property from the general public, third persons, and the principal's competitors. Also, such proprietary and confidential information must be restored to the principal upon termination of the agency.

5. *Duty to notify.* Since the agent is, in some respects, an extension of the principal, he/she is, by this extension, the eyes and ears of the principal. Consequently, the agent must notify the principal of all information that is or may be useful to the principal in evaluating the matter at hand. In this way, the principal can make further choices with respect to his/her business and continue to give the agent proper guidance.

6. *Duty to account.* The contract of agency will specify times and manner of accounting. In all cases, the agent must maintain "an open book" for the principal so that the principal may assess the progress of the work. At termination of the agency, all property must be accounted for and all income turned over to the principal in accord with the agency agreement. *Commingling of funds is a violation of the agent's duty of fidelity.*

> Failure to account and breach of the relation of trust may be criminal.

DUTIES OF THE PRINCIPAL TO THE AGENT

The duties of the principal to the agent are governed by the contract of agency. The primary duty is to compensate the agent for his/her services. If the contract is implied, the compensation is the agent's fee as understood, or generally understood. If there is no contract, express or implied, the agent is entitled to compensation in quasi contract calculated at the reasonable value (*quantum meruit*) of the services performed. If, however, the agent agreed to perform the agency gratuitously, no compensation is due.

The principal must (1) pay all expenses the agent reasonably incurred in furtherance of the principal's business, and (2) inform the agent of dangerous risks the principal has reason to know exist. If the agent is an employee, he/she is entitled to a place to work and to the equipment, supplies, and accessories necessary to perform the employment.

YOU SHOULD REMEMBER

An agent is a trustee, and this trust relation requires a high degree of loyalty. The law implies a number of duties of performance, but these may be modified by contract.

The primary duty of the principal to the agent is to compensate the agent according to the terms of the agency agreement or, if no agreement exists, at the reasonable value of the services performed.

LIABILITY OF PRINCIPAL AND AGENT TO THIRD PARTIES

LIABILITY OF THE PRINCIPAL FOR CONTRACTS MADE BY THE AGENT

Concerning the principal's business, the agent is an extension of the principal, an alter ego. Thus, when an agent is acting within the authority granted by the principal, he/she can bind the principal to the deal; otherwise, creation of agents (representatives) would serve no purpose, would make no sense. Justinian's code stated it this way: *Qui facet per alium, facet per se*, that is, "Who acts through another, acts himself."

The principal is bound contractually if the agent has either the *actual authority* to make a contract for the principal or has the *apparent authority* to do so.

Actual authority is either *express* (based on oral or written words to the agent) or *implied* (inferred from words or conduct manifested by the principal to the agent).

Implied authority to make contracts for the principal is a common sense fulfillment of the agent's job, a going forward with the purposes of the principal's business. If the agent can buy goods, manage real estate, or set up a branch office, he/she has the implied authority to make contracts to achieve these purposes. Remember that almost every business transaction involves a contract, and the authority to transact the principal's business usually carries with it the authority to make contracts in furtherance of that business.

Apparent authority, unlike implied authority, arises out of actions or conduct of the principal which causes a third party to reasonably believe that the agent has the authority to make contracts for the principal. Lawyers and judges sometimes say that an agent is "clothed" with apparent authority, that is, the principal has "dressed" the agent in such a way as to lead others to rely on his/her authority. If the agent is given an office, a title, and a staff, third parties may reasonably believe the agent can bind his/her employer or principal. Indeed, any trappings or other evidence of agency may create apparent authority. An officer's position within a corporation provides apparent authority (termed *authority by position*) if, although the officer had no *actual* authority in that particular situation, a third person reasonably assumes the officer's authority is consistent with his/her holding that corporate office.

Actually, unknown to the third party, there may be a private order or memo to the agent that he/she is *not* to bind the principal, that the agent has no authority. The third party's reasonable, albeit false, understanding that the presumed agent can bind the principal is sufficient to establish apparent authority (e.g., bind the principal to the agent's contracts with the third party).

If a corporation permits an office manager to exercise general supervision over office employees, the office manager may have apparent authority to discipline these employees or to increase their compensation, even though secret or confidential limitations may have been placed upon this authority.

LIABILITY OF THE PRINCIPAL FOR TORTS OF THE AGENT

• *DIRECT LIABILITY*

A principal is directly responsible for his/her agent's torts under any of the following circumstances:

1. The principal gave the agent improper orders or instructions that caused the tort to occur.
2. The agent was improperly or negligently chosen or employed.
3. The principal failed properly to supervise or oversee the work when he/she had a duty to do so.

This direct liability of the principal for tort does not derive from the agency relation. Rather, it is the very act of the principal that is negligent.

Examples: Direct Liability of the Principal

An agent hired by the principal to drive the principal's bus has a record of drunken and negligent driving.

A company car to be driven by an agent has defective brakes.

An agent is given chemical pesticides with improper instructions for application to the fruit trees of a third person.

• *INDIRECT LIABILITY*

Even though the principal has committed no act of negligence, the agent's negligence is imputed (charged) to the principal if the agent is acting for the principal in the scope of his/her employment. This liability is founded on the common law doctrine of respondeat superior: "Let the superior respond."

The key requirement of indirect liability, *respondeat superior*, is that the agent be acting in the scope of his/her employment. The expression "scope of employment" is a technical legal phrase, and the concept must meet four tests:

Tests for *Respondeat Superior* (set forth at common law and in the Restatement (Second) of Agency, § 229)

1. The conduct must be of the kind the agent was employed to perform.[1]

2. The conduct must occur at the authorized place and time of employment.

3. The conduct must be motivated, at least in part, by service to the principal (rather than the agent's self-interest).

4. The use or means employed by the agent could have been anticipated by the principal.

If a night club bouncer evicts a drunken patron with such force as to cause death, the club owner is indirectly liable under the doctrine of *respondeat superior*. If, however, an elevator operator pulls a knife from his/her jacket and seeks to carve up a passenger, this tort would *not* be imputed to the building owner, the principal, under the doctrine of *respondeat superior* since the first, third, and fourth tests above are not met. (*However, the negligent employment of this operator might give rise to direct tort responsibility.*) Moreover, under the aided-in-the-agency-relation doctrine, an employer can be vicariously liable for a tort that an employee commits outside the scope of employment if the authority of the employer made it possible for the employee to commit the tort. For example, this may be grounds for holding an employer liable for sexual assaults or harassment that an employee committed, although the employer had not known, at the time, about such misconduct.

---

[1] Even when the conduct was unauthorized, the principal can still be held accountable if the conduct would have been authorized had there been time to seek such authorization. Also, even if the conduct was unusual and thus *not commonly performed* by the principal's agents, the principal may be held accountable if the agent's response is seen as a common or at least reasonable response to that unusual situation.

Commuting

Is commuting to or from work something for which an employee's negligence can be the basis of the employer's liability? The employer is not vicariously liable because the employee is not then within the employer's control.

Different facts may lead to a different result: If an employee/agent is already at work (e.g., at a conference, for his/her employer, in another city), then going to or from a worksite (e.g., from the hotel where the employee is staying) may be seen as travel within the employer's control; all 24 hours may be, in effect, "during the workday," with the employer potentially vicariously liable.

The principal is responsible for such torts as fraud and misrepresentation since they clearly meet the *respondeat superior* tests. Note that liability for fraud and misrepresentation is present notwithstanding the fact that the agent has no authority to misrepresent the product he/she is selling.

The vicarious responsibility of the principal arises out of the fact that the agent is an extension of the principal. The agent was chosen by the principal; and it is the action of making the choice, holding the agent out to the public as the transactor of the principal's business, that creates liability for the principal.

• *TORTS OF INDEPENDENT CONTRACTORS*

An independent contractor does not act under the supervision and control of the person who hired him/her. The contractor is chosen to accomplish a result by his/her own means. Consequently, the doctrine of *respondeat superior* does not apply to the torts of an independent contractor.

It is not always possible, however, to avoid liability by delegating work to an independent contractor. Under the law of torts, strict liability is imposed in regard to certain "ultrahazardous activities," such as blasting and the transport of volatile chemicals or wild animals. Responsibility for mishaps arising from such activities cannot be delegated to an independent contractor.

The person hiring the independent contractor may be *directly* responsible, however, if the contractor is negligently chosen, or if other conditions of direct liability are present.

PERSONAL LIABILITY OF THE AGENT FOR THE PRINCIPAL'S CONTRACTS

• *DISCLOSED PRINCIPAL*

If a third party knows, or should know, that the agent is acting for a principal *and* if the third party knows the identity of this principal, the principal is a **disclosed principal**.

> If these conditions are met, the agent has *no* personal responsibility for a contract made on behalf of this principal.

The fact of the agency and the identity of the principal are usually disclosed in any contract with a third party. If the contract is between P, the principal, and T. P., the third party, A, the agent who negotiates the contract and signs P's name, is obviously the agent. Nevertheless, *some word of agency should be used when A signs*; such words as "by" or "for" or "agent for," or, if A signs in her employment capacity, "President," "Sales Manager," or "Secretary"—all of these indicate the representative capacity and bind the principal, not the agent.

> Failure to identify the principal and to use agency words upon signing may create personal liability for the agent. Thus, for corporations, limited liability companies (LLCs), and any other entities with distinct legal status apart from their owners-managers, persons acting on behalf of those entities must make clear the capacity in which they are acting. For example, all stationery used by LLC managers should include the LLC's name and its status as an LLC. As with corporate officers, LLC managers/members should execute contracts as follows: NAME OF ENTITY By: Name and Title of Signatory.

Even if a principal is disclosed, however, the agent may have personal liability *if, in fact, he/she had no authority*. Obviously, if agent A merely claims to act for principal P, but P has not given her authority or clothed her with any appearance of authority, A is on her own and is bound by the contract, not P. Indeed, such a case gives rise to a tort by A (fraud and misrepresentation) and possibly a crime.

On the other hand, if A, the agent, frequently acts for P and has the apparent authority to do so, but in fact P has either not given authority or has withdrawn it, *both* A and P may be liable to the third party. If the third party sues P and recovers, P may in turn recover from A, who had no authority in fact. In all cases where an agent discloses a principal, the agent is deemed to make an implied warranty that he/she has the authority to make a contract for that principal.

• *PARTIALLY DISCLOSED PRINCIPAL*

In this case the third party knows that the agent is acting for a principal but does not know the identity of the principal. This **partially disclosed principal** situation occurs when a principal wishes privacy or seeks for financial reasons to conceal his/her identity. For example, a wealthy developer, seeking to accumulate a large commercial tract of land from a number of small landowners, may send his agent to obtain contracts with these owners. The *fact* of the agency is disclosed but *not the name or identity of the principal*. In such a situation the agent is liable on the contract. If the principal's identity can be determined and the agent cannot satisfy the contract, the principal may be liable on the contract also.

• *UNDISCLOSED PRINCIPAL*

If neither the fact of agency nor the identity of the principal is disclosed (**undisclosed principal**), the agent is liable on the contract since the third party was led to believe that the agent was the real party on the contract.

An agent may recover from the undisclosed or partially disclosed principal for any costs it incurred as an agent, including a third party's breach of contract claims. If the third party learns of the agency, he/she, too, may recover directly from the principal, not just the agent.

TORT LIABILITY OF AGENTS

An agent who commits a tort, whether acting within the scope of his/her employment or not, is personally liable for the tort. If the agent is acting within the scope of employment, both he/she and the principal are simultaneously liable for the tort. In cases of such **joint and several liability**, the injured party may sue either principal or agent, or both. Of course, the victim may not have a double recovery, and any recovery from one party is deducted from the recovery from the other. The agent, the party who actually committed the tort, is liable to indemnify the principal for the latter's loss to third parties because of the agent's tort.

Example: Joint and Several Liability

Charlie Careless, a truck driver for the XYZ Hauling Co., while hauling a load of goods for the company, negligently runs over a child riding her bicycle. Both the principal (XYZ Hauling Co.) and the agent (Charlie Careless) are liable to the child for the tort. Technically, Charlie is liable to XYZ Hauling Co. for any judgment obtained by the child or her parents.

LIABILITY FOR CRIMES

If a principal directs, approves, or participates in a crime of his/her agent, the principal is criminally liable, as is the agent. An employer whose employees are violating criminal statutes in furtherance of their employment may be liable if the employer knows, or *should know*, of the criminal acts. Employees who violate pollution laws or antitrust laws create criminal liability both for themselves and for their employers if the employers fail adequately to supervise their job performance or negligently delegate work that the employees perform in a criminal manner.

Scienter (a Latin word used in law to mean a broadly construed form of knowledge—what one knows *or should know*) is imputed to the employer if the employer fails to learn what he/she has a duty to know.

YOU SHOULD REMEMBER

The agent may have actual authority or apparent authority to make contracts for the principal. *Actual authority* is either express or implied. *Apparent authority* arises from a signal to a third party that the agent is clothed with authority to bind the principal in contract.

The principal has direct or indirect responsibility for the torts of an agent. *Direct responsibility* involves a negligent act of the principal him-/herself, including negligence in the choice of agents. Indirect responsibility arises from torts committed by the agent while acting within the scope of his/her employment.

The agent has no personal responsibility for contracts made for his/her principal if the principal is fully disclosed, provided, of course, the agent has authority to make the contract. If the principal is undisclosed or partially disclosed, the agent is responsible (and, once discovered, the principal is, also).

An employer who knows, or should know, of criminal acts by his/her employees is jointly responsible with the employees for these acts.

TERMINATION OF AGENCY BY ACTS OF THE PARTIES

The parties may terminate the agency by any act that would terminate a simple contract. If the agency was created for a specified time or for a specified purpose, it terminates upon the passage of that time or the accomplishment of that purpose. If no time is specified, the agency is terminated by the passage of a reasonable time.

The agency can also be terminated by mutual rescission, by revocation of authority by the principal, or by renunciation by the agent. Both revocation and renunciation are achieved by a simple communication, oral or written, manifesting withdrawal of consent. (*Remember that agency is consensual; in the absence of a contractual obligation to continue the agency, the consent may be freely withdrawn by either party.*)

To assure that there is no *lingering apparent authority*, the principal generally must give actual notice of termination to third persons who previously dealt with the agent; for other third parties, the former agent's apparent authority may arise only if there was not even **constructive notice** of the termination (e.g., an announcement in a trade publication that the agency had ceased would suffice as notice to these third parties, whether they actually read it or not.)

BY OPERATION OF LAW

The agency relation is terminated by any of the following:

1. The death or permanent incapacity of either the principal or the agent.
2. The bankruptcy of either party.
3. Frustration of the purpose of the agency. This frustration may occur because of the destruction of the subject matter (e.g., fire damage or loss to goods or property being bought or sold), changes in business conditions, or changes in the value of property being bought or sold.
4. Subsequent illegality of the business or of the business venture. This would occur, for example, if the business were prohibited, or if the agent were required to have a license which he/she could not reasonably obtain, or if the property were rezoned so as to prevent the legal operation of the business.
5. Impossibility of performance by either principal or agent. This is an example of termination of a contract by impossibility (see pages 164–165).
6. Material breach of the agency contract by either principal or agent.

YOU SHOULD REMEMBER

An agency may be terminated by acts of the parties (any act that would terminate a simple contract) or by operation of law (e.g., either party's death, permanent incapacity, bankruptcy, or material breach of the agency).

INTERNATIONAL COMPARISON ON AGENCY: EUROPEAN UNION LAW

The European Union (EU) Commercial Agents Directive automatically applies some terms and protections to commercial sales agents in the EU regardless of what the agent's agreement with the manufacturer states. The directive provides for mandatory compensation or indemnity upon the sales agency's termination. When a commercial agent carries out activity in the territory of an EU member state, the directive applies no matter what law the parties may have selected in their agreement's choice-of-law clause. So, American businesses with sales agents in Europe need to understand this directive.

KNOW THE CONCEPTS
DO YOU KNOW THE BASICS?

1. Why would corporations be unable to function without agency law?
2. What is the difference between an employee and an agent?
3. How does an attorney in fact differ from an attorney-at-law?
4. Is the agency relationship always created by contract?
5. Why is an independent contractor usually not an agent?
6. Give examples of obligations that cannot be delegated to an agent.
7. Can a person further his/her own goals and objectives while acting for a principal?
8. How does the term *alter ego* play a part in the agency relation?
9. What is meant by "commingling" of funds?
10. Does insanity of the principal make a power of attorney void?
11. Why do lawyers and judges say that an agent may be "clothed" with apparent authority?

12. Explain the difference between the principal's direct and indirect liability for his/her agent's torts.

13. When can the hirer of an independent contractor be liable for the contractor's tort?

14. What does the expression "partially disclosed principal" mean?

TERMS FOR STUDY

actual authority
agency
agent
alter ego
apparent authority
attorney at law
attorney in fact
commingling
disclosed principal
estoppel
EU Commercial Agents Directive
fiduciary

implied authority
independent contractor
joint and several liability
lingering apparent authority
necessity
partially disclosed principal
power of attorney
principal
ratification
respondeat superior
scienter
undisclosed principal

PRACTICAL APPLICATION

1. XYZ Oil Company, a corporation that owned and operated a number of gasoline filling stations in northern California, hired Tom's Tank Company to dig up and replace underground tanks at one of its stations in San Francisco. While this work was being done, Cora Endicott, a customer, fell into the open and unprotected hole and was severely injured. The hole was left open and unattended by Sam Jones, an employee of Tom's Tank Company, who was drunk at the time. Cora sues both XYZ Oil and Tom's Tank in tort. What will be the result?

2. Jim Mason, a janitor at the Celestial Trade Center in Dallas, Texas, ordered 500 cartons of paper products from MX Toilet Supply Company. Celestial Trade Center duly paid the invoice rendered for this merchandise. A year later, Jim ordered 1000 cartons of goods from the same supplier. Celestial Trade Center refused to pay this bill, citing a memorandum to Jim after the last order forbidding him to order supplies. What would be the result?

3. Seedy Apartments employed Melvin Malefactor as a painter for the interior of its apartments in Kansas City. Unknown to Seedy, Melvin had been convicted of assault 3 years previously and of indecent exposure 17 years ago. Seedy checked Melvin's references and found that he was an excellent painter on his last two jobs. Three weeks after his employment, Melvin raped a tenant while painting her apartment. Is Seedy liable for this tort?

4. Pollutant Company operates a large manufacturing facility in Factory City, Anywhere. Stuart Smedley, its plant manager, has caused sulfuric acid from the manufacturing operations to be dumped into an adjacent river for years. Is Pollutant (a) criminally liable for this violation of the environmental laws, and (b) liable in tort to downstream property owners whose wells have been contaminated by the acid?

ANSWERS
KNOW THE CONCEPTS

1. A corporation has no "arms and legs" of its own. It can act only through agents.

2. "Agent" is a broader term than "employee" and includes representatives of various kinds. An employee is an agent who is under stricter control and supervision than other agents; indeed, some authorities find that certain types of employees are not agents at all.

3. The word "attorney" designates a representative. An attorney in fact represents his/her principal for general or special purposes other than legal purposes; an attorney-at-law represents his/her principal for legal purposes only.

4. No. The agency relationship is consensual. The element of consideration is not present in every case.

5. An independent contractor usually is not a representative, but is employed to achieve a specific purpose or to do a specific job.

6. Obligations that require relationships of personal trust, skill, or confidence cannot be delegated to some other person. These can be performed only by the principal.

7. The principal's purpose must always come first; therefore any person who also helps him-/herself while helping the principal is open to a charge of conflict of interest. If agents believe that they can accomplish their own personal ends as well as the goals of their principals, they should advise the principals in advance and obtain their approval.

8. The term "alter ego," meaning "other person," describes the agency relationship in that the agent serves as an alternate person for a principal and acts in his/her place.

9. "Commingling" of funds refers to mixing of the agent's funds with those of the principal. Agency law prohibits such a mixing since the agent's creditors might attempt to reach this money; moreover, the agent may be spending the principal's money on personal obligations—an action that is a breach of the agent's duties and probably criminal.

10. As a rule, insanity of the principal voids a power of attorney. Under the law in many states, however, the power may contain an express provision permitting it to survive insanity or incompetence of the principal.

11. Apparent authority is a kind of outward appearance causing others to believe that the agent can make a contract for the principal. The word "clothed" is appropriate to express this outward appearance.

12. Direct responsibility of the principal arises out of personal participation in the negligent act, that is, his/her own negligence is involved, instead of or in addition to the agent's negligence. Indirect liability arises from negligence of the agent, which is charged or imputed to the principal.

13. When the hirer of an independent contractor has a direct (but not indirect) responsibility for a negligent action of the contractor. If, for example, a contractor is improperly chosen or erroneously instructed, his/her hirer may be liable.

14. "Partially disclosed principal" refers to the situation where a third party knows that the agent is acting on behalf of some other person, but does not know the identity of that person.

PRACTICAL APPLICATION

1. Tom's Tank Company is an independent contractor, hired to do a job, not to represent XYZ Oil Company. Unless there was some kind of direct negligence by XYZ Oil Company, XYZ has no responsibility for the tort. Sam is an agent for his employer, Tom's Tank Company, and his employer is liable for this tort, which was committed in the scope of Sam's employment. Of course, Sam is personally responsible also, but is probably without funds to pay a judgment.

2. Since Celestial Trade Center has paid at least one previous bill arising out of its employee's contract, MX Toilet Supply Company is entitled to rely on the "apparent authority" of Jim, the employee.

The private memorandum between master and servant does not negate the appearance that has already been created.

3. Seedy is liable for the tort since it is directly responsible for its negligent employment of Melvin. However, a good argument can be made that the reference check of previous employers was the only precaution Seedy should have been required to take in hiring a painter. The counterargument is that an employer should check police records before exposing apartment house tenants to strangers.

4. (a) Pollutant is liable for criminal acts committed by its plant manager in furtherance of his employment if the company knows or should know of these actions. The company has a duty to supervise, and it would appear that failure to do so may have permitted the wrongdoing.

   (b) As to the tort liability, Stuart is clearly acting within the scope of his authority as plant manager, and consequently Pollutant is responsible for this tort, which is inflicted on persons whose existence is known and the harm to whom can be foreseen.

15

TYPES OF BUSINESS ORGANIZATIONS; PARTNERSHIPS; FRANCHISES

KEY TERMS

sole proprietorship the simplest form of business, in which a sole owner and his/her business are not legally distinct entities, the owner being personally liable for business debts

partnership the association of two or more persons who have expressly or implicitly agreed to carry on, as co-owners, a business for profit

general partnership a partnership in which there are no limited partners, and each partner has managerial power and unlimited liability for partnership debts

limited partnership a partnership conforming to statutory requirements and having one or more general partners and one or more limited partners

corporation an artificial being created by operation of law, with an existence distinct from the shareholders who own it

franchise a contractual arrangement in which the owner (franchisor) of a trademark, trade name, copyright, patent, trade secret, or some form of business operation, process, or system permits others (franchisees), for a fee, to use said property, operation, process, or system in furnishing goods or services.

limited liability company a business format that is a hybrid of the corporation and the partnership; it is taxed as a partnership but has the limited liability of a corporation.

TYPES OF BUSINESS ORGANIZATIONS

There are three basic types of business organizations:

1. The **sole proprietorship**, the simplest form. The sole owner and his/her business are not legally distinct entities. The owner has unlimited liability for debts of the business.

2. The **partnership**. Two or more individuals are the owners, having expressly or implicitly agreed to establish and run a business for profit. The two types of partnership, **general** and **limited**, are discussed in this chapter.

3. The **corporation**. A distinct legal entity having an existence separate from its shareholder owners is created, usually, under state law. For tax purposes, a business entity is deemed a corporation rather than a partnership only if the entity has at least three of the following four traits: limited liability, centralized management, continuity of life, and free transferability of interests.

   Corporations are discussed in detail in Chapters 16, 17, and 18.

There are many subtypes: limited partnerships, general partnerships, S corporations, close corporations, professional corporations, nonprofit corporations and general corporations, to name a few. Even organizational forms not strictly classified as either partnerships or corporations—for instance, syndicates, business trusts, associations, limited liability companies, joint ventures, and cooperatives—rely on partnership and/or corporate law for most, if not all, of their governing principles. Because one of the forms, the limited liability company, has risen in prominence, it is included in the comparative chart that follows.

Comparison of Sole Proprietorships, Partnerships, Limited Liability Companies, and Corporations

Item	Sole Proprietorship	Partnership	LLC	Corporation
1. Creation	Few, if any, requirements (easiest to organize)	By agreement of partners (generally should be written, but can be implied; limited partnerships, though, must complete and file a statutory form)	Similar to corporation —must file articles of organization	By statutory authorization (must meet state requirements to receive a state charter)

Item	Sole Proprietorship	Partnership	LLC	Corporation
2. Formality required	Little	Some (more for limited partnerships)	Some	The most
3. Governmental regulation of the business structure	Almost none	Little, except for limited or other special partnerships	Some	The most
4. Governmental regulation based on the type of business (products, markets, etc.)?	Yes	Yes	Yes	Yes
5. Owners	The proprietor	The partners	The members	The stockholders
6. Transfer of an owner's interests	By sale of business, inheritance, or any other lawful means chosen by proprietor	Buyer can receive some but not all rights of a partner unless remaining partners agree; limited partner's interest is freely transferable	Similar to a general partnership; a member's LLC interest is transferable, but membership position cannot pass on without the approval of a majority of the LLC members	In most cases, stock is freely transferable, subject only to limits that might be placed in contracts between stockholders

Item	Sole Proprietorship	Partnership	LLC	Corporation
7. Legal entity separate from owners?	No	Generally no, but most states recognize the partnership as a legal entity for a few purposes, such as owning property in the firm's name	Yes, although company citizenship is that of all members—not just the principal state of business and the state where documents creating it were filed (the corporation standard)	Yes for almost all purposes; e.g., a corporation can acquire and transfer property and sue or defend lawsuits, and it has a domicile, duration, and tax status distinct from owners
8. Agency	If business has employees (agents), proprietor is principal	Except for limited partners, each partner is both a principal and an agent of the other partner(s)	In absence of agreement among the members, it is similar to general partnership; or members can opt for a manager-managed LLC with members more like shareholders	Officers are the corporation's agents; stockholders and directors are not
9. Division of labor	Usually the least conducive to such efficiencies of scale			Usually most conducive
10. Liability of individual owners for business debts or actions	Unlimited	Unlimited except that in a limited partnership the limited partners usually can lose only their investments	Limited; similar to shareholders	Limited; stockholders generally can lose only their actual investments

Item	Sole Proprietorship	Partnership	LLC	Corporation
11. Access to specialists	Usually, the least			Usually, the most
12. Use of business funds to pay personal debts	Generally permitted	Usually barred	Prohibited	Prohibited
13. Profits and losses	Solely the proprietor's	Shared equally by partners, unless partnership agreement states otherwise	Similar to a general partnership, with the members' operating agreement often spelling out the arrangement	Calculated after paying salary to employees, including officers; profits are retained by corporation and/or distributed pro rata to stock holders as dividends
14. Management	The proprietor	General partners— equal votes unless otherwise in expressly stated partnership agreement; limited partnership— limited partners have no management rights	Similar to a general partnership, it may depend on the decisions already made in the operating agreement	Management distinct from owners; officers are appointed by directors, who are elected by stockholders (generally each stockholder's number of votes equals the number of common shares he/she owns)

Item	Sole Proprietorship	Partnership	LLC	Corporation
15. Changes in business formation documents	Need not file	Need not file, unless a limited partnership	Need not file the operating agreement but would file any amended articles of organization	Must file and perhaps must obtain state permission (which is usually a mere formality)
16. Organizational fee, annual licensing fee, and annual reporting requirements?	No	Generally no	Some	Yes
17. Requirements for doing business in other states	Usually none	Usually none, but limited partnerships must file copies of a completed statutory form	Usually none, but concern about the possibility	Generally must qualify to do business and obtain state certificate of authority
18. Ability to raise capital	Although dependent on many factors (size, type of business, profitability), often difficult	May be difficult without adding new partners, to which all general partners must agree	About the same as for partnerships	Relatively easy; may just issue (and sell) additional stock

Item	Sole Proprietorship	Partnership	LLC	Corporation
19. Income taxes*	Profits part of personal income; no separate tax for the proprietorship	Each partner's share of profits (whether distributed or not) is part of his/her personal income; no separate tax for the partnership	Same as partnership	"Double taxation"—corporation pays income tax on net profits (no deductions for dividends); each stockholder's dividends are part of his/her personal income and thus are taxed
20. Termination	By sale, insolvency, or voluntary cessation of business; or by death or incapacity of proprietor	By terms of partnership agreement; by subsequent agreement of partners; by death, incapacity, or withdrawal of one or more partners; or by sale, insolvency, or voluntary cessation of business	Similar to a partnership	Can have perpetual existence, as provided by statute and/or articles of incorporation; can continue despite death, incapacity, or withdrawal of officers, directors, and/or stockholders
21. Size of business	Can be substantial, but tends to be small	Can be substantial, but tends to be small	Can be substantial, but tends to be small	Varies from small to the largest business entities in existence: although most corporations are *not* large, the biggest, most significant businesses are or become corporations

* The IRS "Check the Box" regulation permits many smaller business entities (e.g., one-owner firms) to simply check a box in the "Entity Classification Election" tax form and thereby choose whether to be treated, for federal tax purposes, as a corporation, a partnership, or a single owner choosing to be disregarded as a separate entity. This "check the box" choice is, in effect, disregarding the business entity's status as partnership, corporation, LLC, or another format under laws such as the state's law on business incorporation or partnership formation.

Advantages and Disadvantages of the Two Major Business Forms

General Partnership's Advantages over the Corporation

Formation:	Easier
Organizational costs:	Usually less
Taxes:	(a) No "double taxation"
	(b) No tax on exempt interest (e.g., from municipal bonds) partner receives from partnership
	(c) Share of business operating losses more easily and immediately deducted from partner's personal income
	(d) In many states, no state income tax on the partnership itself
	(e) No social security tax for partners (Disadvantage: may have a self-employment tax)
Owner's voice in management:	A more direct role
Multistate operations:	Few legal formalities
Governmental regulation:	Generally less
Flexibility of decision making:	Generally greater

General Partnership's Disadvantages

Taxes:	(a) Partners required to pay tax on undistributed income
	(b) Missing many of the other tax advantages of a corporation
Control:	Unless changed to a limited partnership, cannot raise capital by increasing number of "owners" without affecting actual or potential control of business
Number of owners:	As a practical matter, there are limits
Ability to raise capital:	Usually more difficult
Duration:	Depends on good relationships of partners; withdrawal or death of a single partner can unhinge the entire partnership
Owners' liability for entity:	Unlimited
Owners' liability for other owners' acts:	Often liable
Ability to transfer ownership interest:	Usually more difficult

Corporation's Advantages over the General Partnership

Taxes:
    (a) No personal tax on undistributed profits (sometimes, though, a corporate tax penalty for accumulations of undistributed income)

    (b) Favorable tax treatment of some expenses or benefits

    (c) Employee stock option purchase plans are available

    (d) For some corporations with a limited number of stockholders, Subchapter S status is available: this permits the favorable tax treatment that a partnership sometimes has (no double taxation, immediate deductibility on personal income for business losses), while allowing corporate form in other respects

Control:
    By use of nonvoting or preferred stock, can raise capital and increase number of "owners" without affecting control of business

Number of owners:
    Unlimited

Ability to raise capital:
    For medium or larger corporations, generally easier and can obtain larger amounts

Duration:
    Can be perpetual; not structurally dependent on individual owners' good relationships or health

Owners' liability for entity:
    Limited (However, lenders or other parties contracting with a small corporation often require that the corporation's stockholders furnish personal guarantees)

Owners' liability for other owners' actions:
    Usually none

Ability to transfer ownership interest:
    Generally easier

Corporation's Disadvantages

Formation:
    More complicated

Organizational costs:
    Usually more

Taxes:
    (a) "Double taxation": corporate tax on the corporation's income (no deduction for dividends) plus a personal tax on the stockholder's income (including dividends)

    (b) Exempt interest distributed by corporation is fully taxed income for stockholders

    (c) Subject to state income tax (deductible on federal income tax)

    (d) Missing some of the tax advantages of a partnership

Owners' voice in management:	May have little or no role even if actively sought
Multistate operations:	Generally must qualify to do business and register in each state as well as make other filings
Governmental regulation:	Generally more
Flexibility of decision making:	Generally less

YOU SHOULD REMEMBER

For businesses owned by more than one person, the major types of organizations are partnerships and corporations. The decision as to which organizational form to use depends on numerous factors, such as costs, relationships among owners, desirability of linking ownership and direct management, need to limit potential individual liability, raising of capital, size of the business, and (often most important) tax consequences.

A general partnership should require fewer legal formalities and afford a more direct tie between ownership and management. However, individual liability is unlimited, and duration is less assured (more dependent on continued good relations among all owners).

A corporation can increase both the number of owners and (usually) its capital without drastically affecting management, the duration is more definite (can be perpetual), and ownership interests are more easily transferred. Disadvantages for corporations include "double taxation," greater formal requirements and costs, and greater potential for separation and estrangement of persons into either owners or management, but not both.

GENERAL PARTNERSHIPS

INTRODUCTION

Partnerships[1] are one of the oldest forms of business. Laws on partnerships can be found in Hammurabi's code as well as in early Hebrew and Roman texts. Although corporations, a more recent phenomenon, are the prevailing form among medium-sized and larger American businesses, and corporate law now involves an extensive body of statutes and case

---

[1] Usually, the word "partnership" without any adjective (e.g., "general" or "limited") refers to a general partnership. That is the typical practice in law and business, and this text follows that practice. To avoid possible confusion, one should, at the outset, make clear the form of business one has, wants, or otherwise is discussing.

law, the law of partnerships remains very important. Without a knowledge of partnership law, a businessperson may be unable to decide intelligently what organizational form to use for a new, expanding, or recently acquired business. Moreover, a businessperson will encounter partnerships in many of his/her personal and business activities and certainly should know something about their creation, structure, operations, and liabilities.

CREATION OF PARTNERSHIPS

Unlike corporations, partnerships usually require no special formalities in order to be created. All that is needed is a partnership agreement.

Like most other contracts, the partnership agreement can be express or implied, and no writing is necessary except for contractual matters generally covered by the statute of frauds. Thus, for example, a partnership agreement that permits partners to transfer real estate, or that has a set term exceeding one year, must be written to be enforceable, at least with respect to these matters.

From a practical point of view, a written document is usually the best way to assure that partners, from the outset, understand the nature of their agreement. The absence of such writing probably increases the chances of disputes between partners; in many cases, it makes disputes harder to settle.

• *BY EXPRESS AGREEMENT*

Some typical provisions in an express partnership agreement include the following:

1. The partnership's name.
2. A description of the partnership's business.
3. A listing of the present partners.
4. A statement of the contributions made and/or to be made by the present partners.
5. A means of determining what constitutes partnership expenses rather than personal expenses.
6. A method for dividing profits and losses (otherwise, the assumption is that partners share profits and losses equally).
7. A statement of the general powers of individual partners and the limitations on their authority.
8. For the partnership itself, required and prohibited acts.
9. A system for quickly managing routine matters while bringing more serious issues before a management committee and/or the full partnership.

10. Allocations of salaries and/or drawing accounts among partners.

11. Treatment of a partner's outside business interests.

12. Conditions on an individual's withdrawal from or addition to the partnership, and rules for such withdrawal or additions, including due to death or disability.

13. Methods of transferring a partnership interest.

14. The procedure for amending the agreement.

15. The partnership's term of duration.

16. The closing out or selling of the business upon the partnership's dissolution.

17. Access to books and records.

18. Management of employees.

19. Accounting methods.

20. Form of management.

21. Arbitration of disputes.

22. The rights of continuing and departing partners.

• *BY IMPLIED AGREEMENT*

Is there an implied agreement? The key issue is: Did the alleged partners intend to be co-owners of a business?

Example: Implied Agreement of Partnership

If Jones, Smith, and Gray *jointly* own property, contribute money to run a business on the property, decide how to conduct the business, and share the profits or losses from the business, a court would probably decide that Jones, Smith, and Gray have formed a partnership. In reaching this decision, the court would look to *three factors*:

1. Joint ownership of a business.

2. Sharing of profits or losses.

3. Equal management rights.

Generally, there must be some evidence of all three factors. That A and B merely own property together and receive rent for it will usually be insufficient. Likewise, the mere fact that C's payments to D are pegged at a percentage of C's business profits does not mean that C and D are partners. In each case, at least one of the three crucial factors is missing. (Note that installment payments on loans, as well as interest payments, wages, rents, annuities, or money from the sale of business goodwill do *not* constitute profits.)

The *Uniform Partnership Act of 1914*, as amended, once was the law in every state but Louisiana. It has been replaced in 37 states by a new *Uniform Partnership Act of 1997* (UPA), which in turn has been amended several times since 1997, including as recently as 2013. These uniform laws furnish guidance on partnership issues (including whether a partnership exists) *when* there is *no partnership agreement* or the *agreement does not cover the issues in question*. Thus, the UPA permits partners to fashion their own rules, bound only by the law of contracts and little else (except for limited partnerships).

• *BY ESTOPPEL*

Although almost all partnerships are based on consent, there is one important exception: the partnership by estoppel. When a person represents, or allows someone else to represent, that that person is a partner when in fact he/she is not, the law estops (prevents) that person from denying that he/she is a partner with respect to third persons who reasonably relied on the misrepresentation and were thereby injured. The partnership to which the "partner" allegedly belonged may be fictitious, or it may be a real partnership, but one in which he/she is not a partner. In either event, the alleged partner is liable to the third persons.

Example: Partnership by Estoppel

Suppose that Sam Slick tells Big Bank that he is a partner with Rick Rich, and Big Bank thus extends credit to Sam because of Rick's good reputation and extreme wealth. If Rick knew about Slick's falsehood but did nothing, then most courts would treat Rick as a partner for purposes of Sam's dealings with Big Bank; therefore Big Bank could come to "partner" Rick for money owed.

Of course, this partnership by estoppel works only for third parties such as Big Bank; between Sam and Rick themselves, no partnership rights exist. Rick may have to pay Big Bank, but—since he owes Sam no duty (as a partner) to contribute toward the loan payments—Rick can seek complete reimbursement from Sam for any money Rick paid to Big Bank.

YOU SHOULD REMEMBER

Partnerships are created by express or implied agreement. Oral agreements are permitted, although written agreements are preferable. For implied partnerships, the court generally must find: (1) joint ownership of a business, (2) sharing of profits or losses, and (3) equal management rights.

The typical partnership agreement usually covers many subjects (e.g., the partnership's name, type of business, individual partner contributions, division of profits and losses, and authority of partners). The Uniform Partnership Act (UPA) provides guidance on partnership issues not covered by the partnership agreement.

Partnership by estoppel occurs when a person misrepresents or allows someone else to misrepresent that he/she is a partner in a fictitious or a real partnership. The alleged partner is liable to third persons who reasonably relied on the misrepresentation. Between the purported partners themselves, though, no partnership rights exist.

RIGHTS AND DUTIES OF PARTNERS

• *MAKING DECISIONS*

Each partner has both a right and a duty to help manage the partnership (UPA Section 18). Unless the agreement provides otherwise, each partner has one vote, with ordinary business decisions being decided by majority vote. (As in most voting arrangements, a proposal does not pass if there is a tie vote; however, especially for small partnerships, for example, two partners, the partnership agreement may make special provisions for resolving a deadlock.) Certain, very important actions usually require unanimous consent:

1. Amending the partnership agreement.
2. Changing the essential nature of the partnership's business.
3. Altering the partnership's capital structure (e.g., partnership contributions).
4. Adding an entirely new line of business.
5. Admitting new partners.
6. Confessing judgment (admitting partnership liability on a debt *and* agreeing to have a court judgment entered against the partnership on that debt).
7. Submitting to arbitration.
8. Transferring the partnership's goodwill.
9. Placing partnership assets in a trust or assignment for the benefit of creditors.
10. Paying or assuming the individual debt of a partner.
11. Conveying or mortgaging property, unless that is the usual business of the partnership.
12. Serving as a surety or guarantor (unless that is the partnership's ordinary business).
13. Any act not apparently for the carrying on of partnership business in the usual way.
14. Any other act that renders impossible the continuation of the partnership's business.

• *OTHER RESPONSIBILITIES AND RIGHTS*

Other important UPA rules are as follows:

1. Each partner must *work* only on behalf of the partnership, except perhaps for noncompetitive activities that do not infringe on the partnership's time.

2. Although partners are entitled to *profits* (and to reimbursement/indemnification for personal expenses or liabilities incurred on behalf of the partnership), they are *not generally paid a salary* for partnership work, except for services in winding up the affairs of a dissolved partnership.

3. Each partner may examine and make copies of some or all of the partnership's *records*, which should be maintained at the partnership's main place of business.

4. Each partner has a duty to produce, and a right to receive, *complete information* on all aspects of the partnership's business.

5. Partners are entitled to an *accounting* of partnership assets (including profits) and liabilities whenever partners are excluded from the business or from the partnership records (perhaps in violation of item 3, above), whenever profits or other benefits have been wrongfully withheld or diverted, or whenever else such accounting would be "just and reasonable."

6. Each partner must tell the entire partnership about notices to the partnership sent to him.

7. Partners generally have a duty to maintain the confidentiality of partnership information.

8. Each partner has a *property interest* in the partnership equal to (a) a proportionate share of the profits and (b) a return of capital contributions upon dissolution (partners can assign or creditors can attach that interest without dissolving the partnership itself).

9. Partners are *tenants in partnership* of all partnership property; this means that each partner has full possessory rights, that the property can be used only for partnership purposes, that none of the partners can assign, have attached, or in any way transfer specific partnership property (such as equipment, real estate, or office supplies), and that a deceased partner's rights in partnership property pass to the surviving partners, not to the deceased partner's heirs (although his/her heirs have a right to both an accounting and compensation for the value of the deceased partner's property interest).

Partners may also have implied authority to: hire personnel; pay partnership debts with partnership funds; buy and sell inventory; borrow money and issue commercial paper; settle claims; receive notices on behalf of the partnership. These and other implied powers depend on the nature of the partnership.

• *PARTNER AS AGENT AND FIDUCIARY*

Each partner is an agent for the other partner(s). As such, he/she owes the other(s) a high, fiduciary duty of care similar to that required in any principal/agent relationship. See Chapter 14.

A partner must act in good faith for the benefit of the partnership.

A partner may not divert a partnership opportunity for personal benefit. A partnership opportunity includes any business transaction (a) necessary or related to partnership business, (b) offered to or learned about through the partnership, and (c) developed with partnership funds or facilities.

Revised UPA § 404(f) states, "A partner may lend money to and transact other business with the partnership." While doing so, however, the partner must disclose all material facts to co-partners concerning his ownership of property, business dealings, plans, and any other actual or potential interest adverse to the partnership. Disclosure is required under any of these circumstances regardless of whether another partner requested the information. A partner who is purchasing another partner's interest in the partnership owes a similar duty of complete disclosure.

Example: Partner as Fiduciary

When the interest of partnership PR conflicts with Polly Partner's personal interest, Polly must remain loyal to PR's interest. Polly must not keep pertinent information from her fellow partners, and she must account to the entire partnership for any personal gains made while using PR property or otherwise acting in her role as a partner.

AUTHORITY OF A PARTNER TO BIND OTHER PARTNERS

• *APPARENT AUTHORITY*

Each partner also has a responsibility to third persons.

Example: Authority of a Partner to Bind Other Partners

Suppose that partner Pam transacts business with a third person, Theo, and Theo reasonably believes that Pam is engaged in ordinary partnership business. Theo is then entitled to treat the transaction as being one with the partnership itself, regardless of whether Pam had actual authority.

From this example we see that the agency concept of *apparent authority* applies to partnerships. (See Chapter 14.) In fact, a partner's implied authority is usually broader than the authority of other agents. Third persons know that the partner is an "owner"/principal, not simply an employee/agent. Therefore, partners must take strong measures to prevent third parties from making reasonable but erroneous assumptions that a partnership employee or some other nonpartner is a partner. Consider these examples:

1. *Employee—Apparent Partner.* Paulina, a partner in the PQR General Partnership, and one of PQR's senior employees, Evan, are at a business convention. Paulina refers to her long friendship and many projects with Evan, who is not a partner, and calls Evan "my partner in crime." If a third person does not know Paulina is joking, reasonably concludes that Evan is a partner, and deals with Evan because of that, then it is an apparent partnership (Evan's actions can bind PQR as if Evan were a partner).

2. *Outsider—Apparent Partner.* Pauvre applies to an investment capital firm for a debt consolidation loan and brings along her friend, Rich, a wealthy, well-known businessman. Rich tells the firm's chief loan officer of his long friendship and past business associations with Pauvre and then says, "Pauvre's my partner in crime." The firm lends Pauvre the money because it assumes Rich is her partner, which he is not. Pauvre soon fails to make payments on the loan. The firm sues Pauvre and Rich as if the two were partners; the firm seeks repayment of the loan based on partnership by estoppel or apparent authority.

Under the revised UPA, apparent authority is called a *purported partnership.* Revised UPA § 303 permits the partnership to limit such liability by a recorded statement about the limitation on partner authority.

• *THREE OTHER MEANS OF BINDING THE PARTNERSHIP*

Aside from apparent authority, a partner's acts may bind the partnership to a contract because he/she has (1) express actual authority stemming from the partnership agreement; (2) implied actual authority based on the partnership's business and/or the law of partnerships; or (3) ratification by the other partners after the fact. In the last case, any unauthorized action, even one that would not bind the partnership under a theory of apparent authority, may be expressly *or* implicitly ratified by the entire partnership.

Note that, whereas any one of these four approaches (including apparent authority) permits a third person to hold the partnership accountable, only three of them allow the acting partner to do so. A partner with apparent, but not actual or ratified, authority not only has no rights against his/her fellow partner(s), but also may have to indemnify the partnership for binding it to an unauthorized transaction.

Express actual authority and ratification are fairly straightforward. Implied actual authority, however, requires an assessment of various criteria, based mainly on the nature of the business and any industry customs. If the partner's activities were reasonably necessary to conduct ordinary partnership business, and if the partnership agreement did not prohibit such actions, the partner's powers are implied. For example, a partner in a sales business generally can buy or sell goods of the type customarily traded in the business, and can make warranties on the goods. In most partnerships, a partner can hire and fire employees, pay and collect debts, and acquire personal property needed to conduct the business. However, as stated earlier, there are restrictions on implied authority—some actions require the express consent of all partners.

LIABILITIES OF PARTNERS TO THIRD PARTIES

Because of their broad powers, partners can bind the entire partnership to admissions or other statements made during the course of ordinary partnership business. Moreover, once a partner learns of facts relevant to running the partnership or its business, these facts are imputed to the partnership as a whole. Finally, because partners are principals for each other and their employees, they are civilly *liable* under *respondeat superior for breaches of trust* and/or *torts* committed by a partner or employee acting within the scope of his/her authority. (*Respondeat superior*, though, does not apply in criminal law. Therefore a partner who has committed no wrongful acts or omissions will not be held *criminally* liable for another partner's crimes.)

Whereas partners are jointly *and* severally liable for torts and breaches of trust (the plaintiff may sue all the partners together or any one or more of them separately), partners are jointly, but *not* severally, *liable for contracts*. Therefore any lawsuits based on a contract (including partnership debts) must be brought simultaneously against all partners.

YOU SHOULD REMEMBER

In most ordinary business matters, a partner's actions may bind the entire partnership. Routine partnership decisions are usually decided by majority vote, with each partner having one vote. Certain fundamental decisions usually require unanimous consent; two examples are (1) to change the essential nature of the business, and (2) to take action that renders impossible the continuation of the business.

Partners are tenants in partnership. They have *duties* to furnish partnership information to other partners, work on behalf of the partnership, and not compete with the partnership. They have the *right* to examine partnership documents, be provided complete information on the partnership's business and finances, and retain a property interest in the partnership itself.

Partners are principals and agents for each other. Each partner must act in good faith for the benefit of the partnership.

Third persons may bind the entire partnership to the actions of a single partner if the partner had (1) express actual authority, (2) implied actual authority, or (3) apparent authority, *or* if the partnership otherwise ratified the partner's actions. Apparent au-thority depends on the reasonableness of a third person's belief in the partner's authority. Because apparent authority in-volves unauthorized actions, the partnership may have a right to proceed against the partner for unjustifiably binding it to a transaction with a third person.

PARTNERSHIP AS EITHER A DISTINCT ENTITY OR A MERE AGGREGATE OF INDIVIDUAL PARTNERS

At common law, the partnership was considered simply a collection (an aggregate) of individual partners, with no separate status for the partnership itself. This aggregate approach to partnerships tended to dominate twentieth-century case law, but it has, for the most part, been displaced by the notion that the partnership is an entity, with a legal existence distinct from its individual owners (the partners). Although the original UPA of 1914 took no position on the matter, Section 201 of the 1997 UPA expressly declares the partnership to be an entity. As a practical matter, this may not be significant in that the partners usually can spell out their rights and duties in their partnership agreement.

Entity	Aggregate
1. In the case of bankruptcy, liquidation proceedings may be brought in the name of the partnership and thus limited to exclusively partnership assets and liabilities, excluding the nonpartnership assets and liabilities of individual partners.	1. Under federal income tax laws, the partnership is not separately taxed (as the corporation is), the partnership is generally considered to be an aggregate of the partners' interests, and the individual partners are taxed on their shares of the profits. (Partnerships, though, must file informational tax forms.)
2. Judgments against the partnership entity usually must be collected from partnership property before collection remedies are instigated against individual partners.	2. Generally, partners cannot disclaim personal liability for the partnership's acts or omissions; the partnership is not a separate entity.
3. The partnership usually can sue or be sued, have accountings performed and property owned in the partnership's name, and enforce judgments; some states, though, will not allow such actions.	3. A partnership is not an employer of the partners (e.g., departing partners are not entitled to unemployment benefits).
	4. In many situations, the partnership itself has no power or distinct status, but must depend on the sum of individual efforts by partners.

TERMINATION OF PARTNERSHIPS

Partnerships are terminated upon their dissolution and liquidation (winding up).

• DISSOLUTION

Dissolution is a change in the partners' relationship caused when one partner ceases, generally because of death or voluntary or involuntary withdrawal, to be associated with the partnership business (UPA Section 29). There are three methods of dissolution: (1) acts of the parties, (2) operation of law, and (3) court decree.

BY ACTS OF THE PARTIES

"Acts of the parties" can dissolve the partnership by several different means:

1. The partners agree to dissolve the partnership.
2. The partnership's term of duration expires, or its purpose for being formed is completed. (Either eventuality is usually covered in the partnership agreement.)
3. A partner is expelled or withdraws voluntarily from the partnership (unless the partnership agreement provides that withdrawal does *not* cause a dissolution). Under the revised UPA that most states now follow, a partner can leave the partnership and not disrupt the partnership. This is called a *dissociation*.

When the partnership is at will (there is no set term of duration), a partner's expulsion or good-faith withdrawal leaves neither the departing partner nor the remaining partners liable for breach of the partnership agreement. When expulsion or withdrawal occurs before the end of a specified term of duration, however, such an action is a breach *if* not done for good cause.

Departing partners remain liable for partnership obligations existing at the time of their departure. (A withdrawing partner who fails to notify the remaining partners of his/her withdrawal may continue to be bound as a partner for *future* partnership obligations.) In fact, no partner can cancel existing partnership obligations by dissolution. Of course, the remaining partners and any partnership creditor may agree not to hold a departing partner accountable for the debts to that creditor; this type of agreement is inferred when there have been past such arrangements and the creditor, knowing that a partner is leaving, has done nothing to alert the partner that he/she remains liable. As for the partnership *liabilities of a new partner*, they extend *only* to *partnership debts incurred after* the incoming *partner joined* the partnership.

Note that, although a partnership interest may be assigned or attached, such assignment or attachment does not dissolve the partnership. The assignee or attaching party may acquire rights to profits or other rights, but not the right to a voice in management (UPA Sections 27–28).

BY OPERATION OF LAW

"Operation of law" arises in one of the following ways:

1. Illegality (it would be unlawful to continue the partnership's business or to conduct such business with one of the partners).
2. Bankruptcy of the partnership or of a partner (*most* cases serve as a dissolution).
3. A partner's death. Note that under the revised UPA (1994 or 1997 version) there is no "new" partnership just because of membership changes, such as via resignation, retirement, disability, or death.

The partnership obligations of a dead partner pass to his estate. This rule follows the general requirement that dissolution not eliminate a partner's partnership liabilities. However, creditors for other debts have claim to the partner's estate before the estate pays claims from partnership creditors.

BY COURT DECREE

A court decree dissolving a partnership can be applied for by a partner or a third person. The partner's grounds for dissolution [UPA Section 32(1)] are as follows:

1. A partner is insane or otherwise incapable of participating in management.
2. A partner has acted improperly, either by a breach of the partnership agreement, another act severely harmful to the partnership's business, or still other conduct rendering it impracticable to continue the business with that person as a partner.
3. The partnership's business can be operated only at a loss.
4. Other circumstances, such as strong personal conflicts between partners, make dissolution equitable.

The third person's grounds are fewer: if he/she is a partner's assignee or is the recipient (creditor) of a judicial charging order (in essence, attachment) upon a partner's interests, then the third person may obtain a dissolution decree for a partnership at will or for a partnership whose set term or purpose of formation has been completed.

GIVING NOTICE OF DISSOLUTION

No matter how dissolution occurs (except for illegality or bankruptcy), notice of the dissolution must be given to third persons to ensure that the entire partnership is not held accountable for future obligations. *Actual notice* (by mail, telephone, or the like) must be extended to all partnership creditors; *public (constructive) notice* (via a statement in the community newspaper) is all that is needed for others who knew about the partnership. Of course, there is no duty to give notice to third persons who did not know about the partnership or (in cases of withdrawal) were unaware of the withdrawing partner's involvement with the partnership.

Example: Importance of Giving Notice

Proper notice serves to eradicate the potential for apparent authority to bind the partnership. Although dissolution removes partner X's actual authority to bind her partners, third person Z, who does not know about the dissolution, might see X as still having authority. Therefore, without proper notice of dissolution, X probably has the apparent authority to bind the dissolved partnership to transactions with Z.

• *LIQUIDATION*

After the partnership is dissolved, it must be liquidated. This **liquidation** process is often called "winding up"; the dissolved partnership retains authority to complete unfinished business and do whatever else is necessary to terminate the partnership. Winding up typically involves: (1) collection, preservation, and sale or other liquidation of partnership assets, including collection of money owed to the partnership; (2) paying or otherwise settling partnership debts; and (3) accounting to each partner for the value of his/her partnership interest.

A partner who wrongfully dissolves the partnership (e.g., by persistently breaching the partnership agreement or his fiduciary duties), cannot require winding up, has no right to participate in the winding up process, and cannot use the partnership's name in any connection to his current business. Wrongfully dissolving partners are entitled to their share of the partnership's values, minus their share of partnership goodwill and of damages they caused the partnership.

• *DISTRIBUTION OF ASSETS*

Once the winding up is completed, distribution of assets takes place. Distribution proceeds in this order:

1. Payment of third-party debts.
2. Return of a partner's advances (loans) to the partnership.
3. Return of each partner's capital contribution.
4. Distribution of remaining assets to partners in accordance with the division of profits stated in the partnership agreement (if there is no such provision, the surplus is divided equally).

Of course, among themselves, partners can always agree to alter the order of payments they are to receive.

Creditors' Priorities in Looking for Payment from the Assets of:

A Dissolving Partnership	An Individual Partner
Higher priority: the partnership's creditors	*Higher priority:* the individual partner's creditors
Lower priority: individual partners' creditors	*Lower priority:* the partnership's creditors

These are the general approaches in nonbankruptcy cases.

Only after individual and partnership creditors are paid may partners seek contribution from another partner (payment of that partner's partnership obligations).

A partner's personal creditors have no claim against the personal property of other partners. Also, a partnership's creditor must exhaust the partnership's assets before enforcing a judgment against the separate assets of a partner.

YOU SHOULD REMEMBER

Termination of partnerships requires dissolution and winding up.

The three methods of *dissolution* are acts of the parties, operation of law, and court decrees. Notice of dissolution is necessary except for cases of illegality or bankruptcy.

Winding up involves collecting the partnership assets, paying partnership debts, and accounting to each partner for his/her interest in the partnership.

Upon completion of winding up, final *distribution* of *assets* takes place. Partnership creditors generally have first priority as to payment from partnership assets, while a partner's individual creditors have first priority as to his/her personal (nonpartnership) assets.

LIMITED PARTNERSHIPS

INTRODUCTION

A **limited partnership (LP)** must conform to state statutory requirements, including the filing of a LP certificate. In this respect, as well as the limited liability of limited partners, the LP is similar to corporations.

Special laws on LPs have existed since the Middle Ages, and the first LP statutes in the United States were enacted during the early nineteenth century. The Uniform Limited Partnership Act of 1916 (ULPA) was replaced in 49 states by the Revised ULPA of 1976 (RULPA). (Louisiana follows neither the ULPA nor the RULPA.) Some states additionally adopted the 1985 amended version of the 1976 act. (Unless stated otherwise, this text's references to the RULPA apply to both versions.) A new ULPA, promulgated in 2001 and so far enacted by about a third of the states (including California, Florida, and Illinois), stands apart from all previous versions. It incorporates all laws while improving flexibility and protection for partners and third parties.

Limited partnerships can conduct almost any business that could be carried on by a general (ordinary) partnership. Exceptions include banking, insurance, and most professional partnerships, such as law firms.

TWO TYPES OF PARTNERS

The key feature of a LP is that there are *two distinct types of partners, general and limited.* A **limited partner** contributes capital and receives a specified share of the LP's profits, but does not participate in management and is not held personally liable for partnership obligations beyond the amount of his/her capital contribution. A **general partner** in a LP has essentially the same rights and duties as do partners (i.e., general partners) in a general partnership (GP).

STATUTORY REQUIREMENTS

The LP certificate must state the following information:

1. The partnership's name.
2. Its location.
3. The name and address of its agents for service of process.
4. The names and addresses of its general partners.
5. The term of duration.

Under the 1976 RULPA or the ULPA, *additional* information is required:

6. A description of the LP's business.
7. The names and addresses of limited partners.
8. The cash amount or description and value of initial and subsequent (if any) contributions by each partner.
9. A description of all partners' rights to receive distributions, including return of contributions.
10. The method (if any) for withdrawing/changing partners and continuing the business.

Other provisions may also be included. The certificate can be amended, and it tends to resemble both a GP agreement and a corporate charter.

Because limited partners are free from any liability beyond what they have contributed to the LP, *statutory requirements must be carefully followed.* If an LP fails to file in the state office(s) required, third persons dealing with the partnership but having no actual notice that it is an LP will usually be permitted to treat the limited partners as if they were general partners. Moreover, an LP properly certified in its home state should register as a foreign LP in every other state where it does business. (Corporations must likewise register in other states where they do business.)

In every LP, there must be at least one general partner. As with the GP, the one or more general partners are personally liable for partnership debts. (However, in states where general partners can be corporations, the ultimate effect could be to have a LP in which no *individual* could be held personally liable for partnership debts in any amount above that paid into the LP. Although the general partner that happens to be a corporation has unlimited liability, if this general partner/corporation becomes insolvent, its "owners" (stockholders) are not personally liable for these corporate obligations.)

A LP likewise needs at least one limited partner. Ordinarily, there is no specified maximum number of limited partners. Since the limited partners do not participate in management, having numerous limited partners should not prove nearly as unwieldy as having large numbers of general partners, whether in a GP or a LP.

THE LIMITED PARTNER'S ROLE

The limited partner's exemption from personal liability depends on his/her abstinence from any role in management. Under the RULPA:

1. The LP's capital contribution—whether by general or limited partners—must be money, property, services, a promissory note, or another obligation (e.g., a promise of services).
2. The limited partner's last name must be excluded from the partnership name, which has to include, without abbreviation, the words "limited partnership."
3. The limited partner must not misrepresent, or allow others to misrepresent, his/her role as being anything other than that of a limited partner.
4. The limited partner will probably have to withdraw from the LP, or at least renounce any future profits, upon learning that the partnership certificate contains false statements or that the LP was formed defectively. Good faith, substantial compliance with LP legal requirements is sufficient; a minor defect does not destroy the LP.

If any of these requirements are violated, the "limited partner" may become just as liable as a general partner. The RULPA, however, protects the limited partner if the partnership creditor seeking to hold him/her liable did not transact business with the LP while reasonably believing, based upon the limited partner's conduct, that the limited partner was, actually, a general partner. Under the RULPA, limited partners who engage in managerial activities retain the limited liability if their participation in the control of the business is unknown to the partnership creditor. Also, the RULPA, especially the 1985 version, lists a number of "safe harbor" activities in which limited partners may engage without opening themselves to general, unlimited liability. These activities include consultation with general partners about the LP's business, being a contractor, agent, employee or surety for the LP, attending partnership meetings, and proposing—and voting on—various fundamental or structural changes to the LP (e.g., dissolution, sale of all the LP's assets, amending the LP agreement, admitting or removing partners).

The *limited partner* obviously has *no right to bind the partnership*, as a general partner can, *but* does have *almost all of a general partner's other rights*. Some of the more important rights of a limited partner include suing (either individually or for the partnership), reviewing all partnership records, obtaining an accounting of partnership assets and liabilities, deciding whether to admit new partners, assigning his/her partnership interest, and participating in the dissolution process for terminations by court decree.

TERMINATION AND DISTRIBUTION OF ASSETS

Dissolution and winding up generally occur for the same reasons and by the same methods for an LP as for a GP. However, the addition of a general or limited partner does not dissolve the LP, and an LP agreement may permit the LP to continue despite a general partner's withdrawal. Also, a limited partner's withdrawal, expulsion, or death does not dissolve the partnership. (A withdrawing partner ordinarily is entitled to receive the fair value of his/her partnership interest, including business goodwill.)

The RULPA treats all partners in a dissolving LP the same. All creditors, including limited and general partners, are paid first. Unless the LP agreement specifies otherwise, the LP next pays to both general and limited partners any accrued profit shares (unpaid distributions), then returns *all* partners' contributions, and lastly, if LP assets still remain, it pays *all* partners in accordance with the LP's profit-distribution scheme (if nothing is stated to the contrary, payments are proportionate to each partner's capital contribution).

REASONS FOR AND AGAINST FORMING LIMITED PARTNERSHIPS

On the negative side, the LP is not as effective as the corporation in shielding "owners" from personal liability. Moreover, LP agreements and certificates tend to require formal amendment more frequently than do articles of incorporation, which can be very broadly drafted.

Two reasons for forming a LP are these:

1. Tax laws sometimes make a LP more profitable than a corporation, which is subject to "double taxation." Tax laws may also favor R&D (Research and Development) LPs. (However, the 1986 federal income tax reforms reflect a continuing effort to prevent the use of LPs that make little or no economic sense except as tax shelters.)

2. A GP is in the works (and is preferred over a corporation), but (a) one or more important, potential partners are unwilling to assume unlimited liability and/or do not wish to participate in management; (b) the general partners seek a large infusion of capital without giving up actual or potential control of management. [In case (b), securing a bank loan might make more sense than forming a LP.]

YOU SHOULD REMEMBER

The LP must meet state statutory requirements, including certificate filing. Forty-nine states have adopted the Revised Uniform Limited Partnership Act (RULPA).

Limited partnerships have at least one of each of the two types of partners: general and limited. General partners have essentially the same role in an LP as in a GP. Limited partners have almost all of the rights held by a general partner, except the right to bind the partnership to their actions. In most cases, limited partners simply contribute money, property, or services and receive a specified share of the profits; by not participating in management, the limited partner's partnership liability is limited to his/her actual contributions to the partnership. Inappropriate management participation or other noncompliance with statutory requirements may render a "limited partner" generally liable if the partnership's creditor reasonably believed, because of the limited partner's conduct, that the limited partner was actually a general partner.

In distributing a dissolved LP's assets under the RULPA, creditors are paid first, then the partners' accrued profit shares are paid, then the partners' contributions, and—lastly—any profits are distributed to the partners. For distribution of assets the limited and general partners are treated the same.

Tax laws or other factors favoring a partnership may make an LP preferable to a corporation.

LIMITED LIABILITY PARTNERSHIPS AND LIMITED LIABILITY LIMITED PARTNERSHIPS

A newer form of partnership is the registered *Limited Liability Partnership* (LLP). Every state authorizes some form of LLP, which is similar to a general partnership except that (1) a corporation cannot be an LLP partner, and (2) an LLP partner's liability for another LLP partner's acts, such as professional malpractice, is limited to the partnership's assets. Therefore, all that the non-negligent partner can lose is his capital contribution to the partnership.

In some states, the LLP must furnish proof that it has adequate liability insurance or other assets to pay potential claims. An LLP must include the name "Registered Limited Liability Partnership" or the initials "LLP" in its name.

Each partner in an LLP has unlimited liability for his own actions, but—in most states—is protected from personal liability for the partnership's or other partners' acts or obligations. However, rules from state to state vary greatly for the LLP. For example, a few states (California, Nevada, New York, and Oregon) permit LLPs only for professional firms (e.g., lawyers, accountants, engineers, medical doctors, etc.). Over a dozen other states permit only LLP liability protections from negligence claims against the partnership or other partners. Thus, in this large minority of states, the LLP partners are jointly liable for breach of contract and unintentional tort claims, but are individually liable only for their own negligence or that of those directly under their control.

One still newer format used mainly for real estate businesses, such as large commercial building projects, is the limited liability limited partnership (LLLP). Permitted in over half the states, an LLLP is a type of limited partnership, with both general and limited partners, but the LLLP status affords even the general partners limited liability for the LLLP's debts and obligations that occurred while the LLLP status was in place. Most states authorizing the LLLP mandate that any such entity identify itself as an LLLP in its name. *Whether an out-of-state LLLP's general partners have limited liability in states without an LLLP statute remains questionable.* However, at least in those states with an LLLP statute, the LLLP designation of a business may protect all its partners better than would be the case even for the limited partners in LPs. The LLLP name informs third parties that there are *no* partners with unlimited personal liability, while for a limited partnership third persons know that general partners have no such liability shield and may reasonably believe that a limited partner is actually a general partner. In effect, the LLLP designation should estop third parties, at least in those states with an LLLP statute, from drawing such assumptions, as no LLLP partner could have unlimited personal liability.

FRANCHISES

A **franchise** is a contractual arrangement whereby, in return for an initial fee and recurring royalties from the franchisee, the owner (**franchisor**) of a trademark, trade name, copyright, patent, trade secret, or some form of business operation, process, or system permits (licenses) its **franchisees** to use that property, operation, process, or system in furnishing goods or services. Usually, the franchisee conducts a business in accordance with conditions and procedures prescribed by the franchisor, who in turn advertises, advises, perhaps lends capital, and/or otherwise assists the franchisees. The franchise network generally consists of a system-wide marketing plan and/or a "community of interest" between the franchisor and its franchisees.

Note that the franchise is a relationship. The parties to that relationship—the franchisor and franchisees—are business entities whose individual structures, like those of other businesses, tend to be in the form of sole proprietorships, partnerships, or corporations.

Although many commentators believe there is a higher survival rate for franchised businesses than for new, independent businesses, there are, compared with completely independent operations, many additional costs associated with franchising, such as initial fees and continuing charges (royalties). Thus, a bottom-line question for a prospective franchisee is this: "What can the franchisor do for me that I cannot do for myself?" Only if the services, trademarks, goods, and other items obtained from the franchisor cannot be lawfully produced on one's own, and only if they are truly of long-term economic worth, should one pay the franchisor to join its network as a franchisee.

BENEFITS OF FRANCHISING

Typical advantages to *franchisors* are as follows:

1. Franchisees together provide much capital, as well as entrepreneurial skills.
2. Franchisees provide a set distribution network and (usually) greater efficiency in limiting costs and expanding sales.
3. Franchisees absorb much of the risk of losses.

These are typical advantages to *franchisees*:

1. They can start a business despite limited capital and experience.
2. They can rely on the goodwill generated by a regionally or nationally known trade name or product.

3. They can rely on the franchisor's business expertise in such areas as marketing, research, and the training of personnel.

4. They are assured access to supplies and to prices based on volume buying.

A franchise may be based on an agency relationship between franchisor (principal) and franchisee (agent). If, however, the franchisee is able to run the business with few outside controls, he/she will probably be viewed as an independent contractor. (See Chapter 14 on Agency.)

TYPES OF FRANCHISES

Franchises fall into three main categories:

1. Distributorships (a manufacturer licenses dealers to sell products). *Example*: many gasoline or automobile dealerships.

2. Business format systems (franchisees conduct a particular type of business under the franchisor's trade name and customarily follow the franchisor's standard method of operation). *Example*: fast-food franchises.

3. Manufacturing or processing arrangements (the franchisor provides its franchisees with the ingredients or formula for making a product and then marketing it in accordance with the franchisor's standards). *Example*: soft drink bottling franchises.

THE FRANCHISE AGREEMENT

The franchise agreement, almost always prepared by the franchisor, is usually a very lengthy document covering many aspects of the prospective franchisor-franchisee relationship. It ordinarily contains these provisions, among others:

1. The franchisee's initial payment to the franchisor for receiving the franchise, as well as the continuing payments (royalties) throughout the term of the franchise. (Royalties are generally based on a percentage of the franchisee's gross sales, not his/her profits; thus, a franchisee will still owe the franchisor money even if his/her business is unprofitable.)

2. The franchisor's control over, or specifications about, (a) the franchisee's business site, territory (or non-exclusivity), and structure, (b) the franchisee's training, qualifications, operational standards, financing, advertising, and purchases, (c) the franchisee's alleged status as an independent contractor, (d) franchisor ownership of

intellectual property, inspections of the franchisee's business premises, and audits of the franchisee's financial records, (e) franchise
transfers (usually giving the franchisor final control), (f) franchisor
mergers or assignments (giving the franchisor discretion to merge
or sell its business and bring in a replacement franchisor), (g) arbitration, controlling law, and venue in the event of a dispute, and
(h) covenants that the franchisee not compete against the franchisor or its franchises after his/her franchise is terminated.

3. The duration of the franchise, any renewal periods, and the franchisor's grounds for termination (usually numerous).

CASE LAW AND STATUTES GOVERNING FRANCHISES

The franchisor usually has much more bargaining power than does
the franchisee, particularly once the franchisee has joined a system and
sunk its money into a franchised business. Therefore the *case law* on
franchises recognizes the occasional need to protect franchisees. Courts
will find obligations of good faith and commercial reasonableness
in any franchise agreement, and they will not enforce grossly unfair
("unconscionable") provisions.

As for *statutory law*, most states have passed statutes specifically
designed to govern franchises. Some statutes, like the UPA for partnership agreements, set forth guidelines in the absence of provisions within
the franchise agreement; and many franchise relationship statutes forbid
certain franchisor practices, such as franchise termination without "good
cause." Even more state statutes do not deal with post-sale matters but
rather govern the initial offer and sale of franchises, requiring franchises
to file a franchise registration statement, with mandatory disclosure of
pertinent facts about the franchisor.

Via a rule promulgated in 1978 and revised in 2007 (16 CFR Part
436), the Federal Trade Commission (FTC) also mandates disclosure
of detailed information about the franchisor and its business. The 23
items that must be disclosed in the FTC-required Franchise Disclosure
Document ("the FDD") to a prospective franchisee include information
on: (1) the franchisor and its parents, predecessors, and affiliates; (2)
business experience; (3) litigation history; (4) bankruptcy; (5) initial fees;
(6) other fees; (7) estimated initial investment; (8) restrictions on sources
of products and services; (9) the franchisee's obligations; (10) financing; (11) the franchisor's assistance, advertising, computer systems, and
training; (12) territories; (13) trademarks; (14) other intellectual property
(namely, patents, copyrights, and proprietary information); (15) the obligation to participate in the actual operations of the franchise business;

(16) restrictions on what franchisees may sell; (17) renewal, termination, transfer, and dispute resolution; (18) public figures; (19) financial performance representations; (20) outlets and franchisee information; (21) financial statements; (22) contracts; and (23) receipts.

Although there is no franchise registration with the FTC, the government can prosecute for failure to comply with the FTC's disclosure requirements.

Federal and state laws also protect franchisees in special industries. Two examples are the Automobile Dealer's Day in Court Act and the Petroleum Marketing Practices Act (PMPA), both federal laws governing franchise terminations and—for the PMPA—also nonrenewals. In addition, federal antitrust laws may prohibit a franchisor's restrictions on franchisees' sales territories, purchases, pricing structure, and dealings with others. Finally, as franchising has grown tremendously throughout the world, about 40 nations have enacted franchise-specific laws, many of which are more likely to protect franchisees in terms of territorial rights, access to franchisor know-how, mandatory contract clauses, or other rights.

YOU SHOULD REMEMBER

Franchises are based on contractual arrangements between franchisors and franchisees. The franchisee may be an agent or an independent contractor.

Franchises involve (1) product distributorships, (2) business format systems, or (3) manufacturing or processing arrangements.

Because franchisors usually have much more bargaining power than franchisees, the courts and legislatures have provided special protections for franchisees (e.g., forbidding franchise termination without "good cause"). Good faith and commercial reasonableness are imputed in any franchise agreement, and the Federal Trade Commission, as well as many states, require the disclosure of rather detailed information about the franchisor.

KNOW THE CONCEPTS
DO YOU KNOW THE BASICS?

1. What are the three basic types of business organization?

2. Compare these types of business organizations with respect to manner of creation, formality, governmental regulation, ownership, transfer of ownership, legal entity, agency, division of labor, owner's liability, access to specialists, payment of personal debts, management, profits, changes in business formation documents, fees, multistate businesses, raising capital, income taxes, termination, and size of businesses.

3. Name at least 16 typical provisions in a partnership agreement.
4. To what three factors do courts look for evidence of an implied partnership?
5. What actions generally require the partners' unanimous consent?
6. List some duties and rights of partners.
7. Name the four bases for binding a partnership to a contract between third persons and a partner.
8. Name three ways in which a partnership is a legal entity.
9. Name the three methods of dissolution of a partnership.
10. Give five reasons why a supposedly limited partner may be held generally liable for partnership obligations.
11. Between general partners, limited partners, and creditors, state the basic order of distribution of assets for a LP and for a GP.
12. State three customary provisions in a franchise agreement.
13. Federal and state statutes, as well as court cases, have sought to furnish additional disclosures from whom (franchisors or franchisees) and protection from unfair creation and termination of franchises for whom (franchisors or franchisees)?

TERMS FOR STUDY

corporation	limited partnership (LP)
dissolution	liquidation (winding up)
distribution of assets	partnership by estoppel
franchise	Revised Uniform Limited
franchisee	Partnership Act (RULPA)
franchisor	sole proprietorship
general partner	tenants in partnership
general partnership (GP)	Uniform Partnership Act (UPA)
limited partner	

PRACTICAL APPLICATION

1. John wants to control a business completely, knows nobody else with whom he wishes to work, is not worried about lawsuits, and

dislikes formalities, paperwork, and lawyers. What type of business organization would he probably prefer?

2. Mary has the time and expertise to put into a new bakery, but little money. Sally has a substantial sum of money to invest, but no interest in the day-to-day operations. What type of business organization would you recommend?

3. There are six partners in a LP: general partners A, B, C, and D, and limited partners E and F. Under the LP agreement, E and F are each entitled to 20% of the profits. E and F each contributed $20,000. A, B, C, and D are each entitled to 15% of the profits, each having contributed $2,500 and also having assumed managerial duties. C assigns his interest in money receivable from the LP to Ms. C on January 1. On February 1, E sells her partnership interest to Bank E. On March 1, G is added as a new general partner; he has made no capital contribution. On April 1, D dies. Assets and liabilities are as follows:

January 1 to February 14	$95,000 in assets, and no liabilities
February 15 and thereafter	$95,000 in assets (minus a new liability—judgment of $20,000 against the LP)

The LP is now dissolved. It made no profits this year, but the previous year's profits were $60,000, which has not been divided among the partners.

Assume that the LP agreement does not alter the RULPA rules. Discuss (a) the changes in the partnership, (b) the judgment liability, and (c) distribution of the remaining $75,000.

ANSWERS
KNOW THE CONCEPTS

1. Sole proprietorships, partnerships, and corporations.

2. See charts on pages 320–328.

3. Twenty-two typical partnership agreement provisions concern name, description of business, list of partners, statement of contributions, delineation of partnership and personal expenses, division of profits/losses, statement of individual partner's powers and limits, the partnership's required and prohibited acts, management decision systems, allocations of salaries/drawing accounts, treatment of outside business, partners' withdrawals and additions, transfers of partnership interests, agreement amendments, term of

duration, closing out access to books and records, management of employees, accounting methods, form of management, dispute arbitration, and rights of continuing and departing partners.

4. Joint ownership, sharing of profits or losses, equal management rights.

5. Amending partnership agreement, changing essential nature of partnership's business, altering capital contributions, adding a new business or new partners, confessing judgment, submitting to arbitration, transferring goodwill, placing assets in trust or assignment for creditors, paying or assuming a partner's individual debt, conveying or mortgaging property (usually), serving as surety or guarantor, and other acts unusual for the business or rendering business impossible.

6. *Duties*: uncompensated work for, and noncompetition with, partnership, producing information on partnership for other partners, accounting for any personal gains while acting as partner or using partnership property, and maintaining the confidentiality of partnership information.
Rights: examination of books, receipt of information on partnership from other partners and accounting of partnership assets and liabilities, property interest in partnership, tenant in partnership, and other implied rights.

7. Express actual authority; implied actual authority; apparent authority; ratification.

8. Bankruptcy can be brought by partnership; judgments against partnership are first enforceable only against the partnership; in most states, it is possible to sue, having accountings, and own property in partnership's name.

9. Acts of parties, operation of law, and court decree.

10. He participated in management; his last name was part of the partnership's name; he misrepresented or allowed others to misrepresent that he was a general partner; the LP certificate contained falsehoods; the LP was defectively formed.

11. *LP*: under the RULPA all creditors are repaid, then the limited and general partners are paid together, according to various priorities (unless the LP agreement states otherwise)—(a) accrued profit shares, then (b) contributions, then (c) remaining assets in accord with the LP's profit-distribution scheme.

GP: third-party creditors are repaid, then general partners (loans, then capital contributions, then remaining assets according to the division of profits in the partnership agreement). There are no limited partners in a GP.

12. Franchisee's payment to franchisor; franchisor's controls over numerous aspects of the business; franchise's duration and ground for termination.

13. Franchisors; franchisees.

PRACTICAL APPLICATION

1. Sole proprietorship.

2. General partnership seems inappropriate because of disparity in wealth and interests of Mary and Sally. Limited partnership might be suitable, especially since Mary's contribution could come in the form of property other than just money (e.g., rent-free use of her house as the business location) or—under the RULPA—it could even be services or a promissory note. Mary would be the general partner, and Sally the limited partner.

However, a corporation is by no means out of the question. There the decision depends more on the tax consequences, Mary's concerns about her unlimited liability in a partnership, and Mary's and/or Sally's desires as to transferability of ownership. Unless Sally's stock was nonvoting, though, Mary would probably face a situation in which ultimate control would rest with Sally.

3. (a) Ms. C can collect the profits due C; she just cannot participate as a general partner. If there is no agreement to the contrary, E may transfer her entire limited partner interest and status to Bank E without dissolving the partnership. G may be added as a new general partner with the other general partners' permission. D's death dissolves the new LP (the one with G in it).

(b) G is not personally responsible for a debt incurred before his admission, except for an amount no greater than his capital contribution, which is nothing. All of the other partners, however, would be responsible, with even the limited partners liable to the amounts of their capital contributions.

(c) After the liability of $20,000 is paid off, $75,000 remains. There appear to be no other creditors, so the next priority under the *RULPA* is to pay the $60,000 in accrued profits. A, B, Ms. C, and D's estate each are entitled to 15% of the profits of $60,000, and F and Bank E are entitled to 20% each. The remaining $15,000 is distributed *pro rata* according to the partners' contributions. Thus F and Bank E get most of the $15,000, but A, B, Ms. C, and D's estate each get 5% (because each is credited for a contribution of $2,500 out of a total capital outlay of $50,000). G, of course, gets nothing because he made no capital contribution.

16
CORPORATIONS: NATURE, FORMATION, TYPES, AND POWERS

KEY TERMS

corporation an artificial being created by operation of law, with an existence distinct from the individuals who own and operate it

charter a formal document that creates a corporation

articles of incorporation a formal document that creates a corporation; a charter

---

NATURE OF A CORPORATION

A corporation is an artificial being created by operation of law. This artificial being, or entity, is entirely separate from its shareholders, directors, officers, and employees. This separation gives the corporation a life of its own and the responsibility and accountability to the law that are attributable to a natural person.

If all the shareholders, directors, officers, and employees of corporation A were to die simultaneously in a common accident, corporation A would continue to exist: stock ownership would pass to heirs of the deceased shareholders; these new shareholders would name new directors and hire new officers and employees.

A corporation has a totally independent existence apart from the persons who own and operate it.

BACKGROUND OF CORPORATIONS

Although the imperial government of Rome suppressed private societies and associations of every kind, it permitted individuals to form *collegia*, that is, nonprofit, membership clubs for such diverse purposes as education, fire control, and burial of members. In the late Middle Ages and early modern period (the twelfth through the sixteenth centuries) the Roman model was expanded in France and Germany to permit merchants to form trading societies and craft guilds for investment and larger business purposes.

In the 1500s the English government, followed by France and other European nations, began to grant monopolies to groups of individuals (joint-stock companies), for trading and for revenue purposes, with the Crown receiving a share of the monopoly profits. Colonization of the New World and other foreign lands was undertaken through charters to develop specified territories and operate as governments under the general supervision of the king. Trading ventures included the *Massachusetts Bay Company* (English), *Hudson's Bay Company* (English), and *East India Company* (three distinct companies of the Dutch, English, and French).

During the colonization period corporate charters were granted to private individuals by special acts of the colonial legislatures. When the United States became a nation, corporations were created by grant of charter by the several states, first by legislative enactment, and later by special state agencies or commissions created for this purpose. *In all of the states, corporations are created by state corporation commissions, although the management of corporations is left to internal controls within the corporate structure.*

Most states now follow, to some degree, the Model Business Corporation Act (MBCA) proposed in 1950 and frequently amended since (including a completely overhauled Revised Model Business Corporation Act—RMBCA—put forth in 1984 and adopted by half the states). Still, each state's corporation commission, by whatever name it may be called, tends to be little more than the issuer of the corporate charter at the beginning of the corporate life; in practice, the state rarely takes any interest in the actual corporate function. Nevertheless, a corporation must be a good citizen. It may be punished for its crimes, sued for its torts, and held accountable for its contracts. *At all times it must be operated for the benefit of its shareholders, who are its owners.*

CORPORATE ATTRIBUTES

A LEGAL PERSON

For most legal purposes a corporation is a person. Like any citizen, it can sue and be sued, make contracts, own property, and perform other personal acts. Moreover, it can be charged with almost any crime except crimes the sole punishment for which is imprisonment.[1] For most purposes, a corporation is entitled to the protections afforded citizens under the Bill of Rights except the right against self-incrimination provided for in the Fifth Amendment.

CREATION BY STATUTE

Under the provisions of applicable statutes, a corporation is created by contract with the state. The evidence of this contract is the corporation's charter. Under modern corporation law, most state statutes provide that, as a condition to the grant of charter, the state may, by regulation or statute, unilaterally modify the terms of charters already granted. [In the case of *Dartmouth College v. Woodward*, 17 U.S. 518 (1819), the Supreme Court held that, without such statutory permission, a state could not modify or revoke a corporate charter without "impairing the obligation of contracts" as forbidden by Article I, Section 10, of the United States Constitution.]

LIMITED LIABILITY OF SHAREHOLDERS

If a shareholder engages in behavior beyond his/her role as an investor and acts as—declared or not—a corporate agent, he/she can be held civilly liable or even criminally responsible for his/her wrongful acts on behalf of the corporation (see Chapter 14 on Agency). This is distinct from liability for a shareholder simply because he/she owns shares of a corporation that owes debts to third parties. That type of indirect, general liability is unusual, but there are some specific exceptions to the presumption against personal liability for corporate debts. In such special circumstances, a shareholder may be liable for a narrow class of corporate debts, such as the corporation's unpaid employment taxes or sales taxes or for unpaid workers' compensation claims not covered by insurance. More broadly, two states—New York and Wisconsin—impose *pro rata* shareholder liability for the unpaid wages of their corporation's employees.

Except for these special cases (e.g., unpaid taxes), the shareholders' liability to a corporate creditor must meet a high standard of proof. This

---

[1] If a corporation is convicted of a crime, the corporation's penalty could be a fine, to be paid from corporate coffers, or the corporation could lose its corporate charter, or a government license, or its right to contract with the government.

piercing of the corporate veil is not to be granted simply because corporate creditors would otherwise not be fully compensated. There must be more proof.

Since a corporation is a legal entity separate from its shareholders, the corporation, not the shareholders, is liable for its debts. However, the courts will disregard the corporate entity, and hold the shareholders personally liable **(pierce the corporate veil)** if the corporate name is used as a false front or "stalking horse" behind which the owners or operators perpetrate fraud upon creditors or others dealing with them.

The "corporate veil" may be pierced if two conditions are present:

1. a fraudulent purpose, and

2. operation of the corporate business as though the corporation does not exist.

Thus the principal creates a corporation and uses a corporate name; however, the principal holds no corporate meetings, keeps few corporate books or records, and disregards the corporation that he/she has created. In addition, the principal fraudulently permits or causes others to believe that he/she is, in fact, responsible for the corporate business. *Usually undercapitalization is not as much an issue in contract cases— where, after all, the creditor voluntarily dealt with the corporation—as it is in tort cases.*

SOME FACTORS COURTS CONSIDER WHEN DECIDING WHETHER TO PIERCE THE CORPORATE VEIL

Inadequate capitalization is *the most usual argument* for piercing the corporate veil, at least in tort cases. Ten additional factors perhaps favoring the piercing of the corporate veil are as follows:

1. An absence of formalities, structures, and actions that are part of corporate existence, such as issuing stock, electing directors, and keeping corporate records.

2. Placing funds in and taking them out of the corporation for personal rather than corporate purposes (*the second most common argument: commingling*).

3. An overlap in ownership involving common officers, directors, and personnel (the subsidiary temptation).

4. Common office space for the corporation and the individual owner(s).

5. A common address, telephone and fax numbers, and Internet site for the corporation and the individual owner(s).

6. Restrictions on the business discretion displayed by the allegedly dominated (subsidiary) corporation.

7. The related entities (e.g., parent and subsidiary corporations, the individual owner and "his/her" corporation) do not deal with each other at arm's length.

8. The related entities are not treated as independent profit centers.

9. Payment or the guarantee of a dominated corporation's debts by the other person.

10. The dominated corporation has property that the other person used as if it were his/her own property.

A Similar Approach to LLC Members' Personal Liability for Entity Debts

Although usually LLCs are not expected to have as much legal formality as corporations do, in other respects—for LLCs—piercing the veil to hold members liable for entity debts tends to track the law of corporations.

PERPETUAL EXISTENCE

As previously indicated, a corporation has a life of its own, independent of its shareholders and managers. Modern corporations are usually granted *perpetual existence* as a routine charter provision, although corporate existence may also be for a stated or limited period of time.

FORMATION OF THE CORPORATION

THE PROMOTER

A **promoter** is the person who conceives of, organizes, and begins the corporation.

Not only is the corporation his/her "brainchild," but also the promoter finds others who are willing to participate in the development and exploitation of the idea.

Although the promoter is not an agent of the corporation to be created, he/she occupies a fiduciary relationship (position of trust) in regard to the proposed corporation and its investors, shareholders, and creditors. Basically, this trust relation requires that the promoter make full disclosure of his/her anticipated personal gain, the nature of the business, its prospects, and the promoter's plans with regard thereto.

In the course of forming the corporation, the promoter may incur costs, make contracts, and do other acts in furtherance of the corporation. Since the promoter is not an agent, the corporation is not automatically responsible or liable for these obligations and contracts; however, *it may ratify, adopt, or accept them, provided that there is full and open disclosure by the promoter to the corporation.* The promoter remains obligated with respect to such obligations or contracts unless released by the obligee or unless the corporation is substituted for him by a novation (see Chapter 7).

OBTAINING THE CHARTER

The persons wishing to form a corporation (the **incorporators**) apply to the state corporation commission with a form of the charter they want to have granted.[2] Although the charter is usually prepared by an attorney, this is not necessary. A detailed discussion of the nature and content of the charter follows later in this chapter.

The **certificate of incorporation** is the state's official authorization for the corporation to start doing business.

FIRST ORGANIZATIONAL MEETING

The incorporators, after receipt of the certificate of incorporation, call a meeting of the interim board of directors named in the charter to be held, at which time bylaws are adopted, officers are elected, and other necessary business is transacted. *Once stock is issued and sold, the shareholders duly meet and name the regular board of directors.*

DE JURE AND *DE FACTO* CORPORATIONS

A **de jure corporation** *is one that has been formed in accordance with all of the requirements of law; a* **de facto corporation** *is one that has not been properly formed, even though the incorporators made a*

---

[2] The commission reviews a requested charter. If it complies with the law, the charter—along with a certificate of incorporation—will be issued by the appropriate state official (usually, the state's secretary of state).

good-faith effort to do so. The defect in the formation of the *de facto* corporation is technical—there is some omission, for example, in the charter—but the certificate of incorporation is nonetheless granted.

The status of the *de facto* corporation can be challenged only by the state; third parties must accept it as a valid, authentic corporate entity.

TYPES OF CORPORATIONS

PUBLIC OR PRIVATE

A **public corporation** is formed to meet a governmental or public purpose. Generally, a public corporation is created for the direct function of government—town, city, or county.

Most corporations fall into the category of **private corporations**—corporations created for private purposes. In the context of commercial law, the word "corporation" generally connotes a private entity. Public utilities have some features of both public and private corporations.

There is an important group of corporations that might be considered "hybrids," that is, they have features of both public and private corporations. These **quasi-public corporations** are *public utilities*—privately owned businesses created for public purposes. Although these monopolies, or partial monopolies, are strictly controlled both as to services and as to prices (rates), they are permitted a reasonable return on investment, established during the course of a regulatory rate case.

FEDERAL OR STATE

Although the federal government has the right and power to create corporations, the United States has shown great restraint in entering the incorporating field. Since the exercise of this power must be solely within the scope of legitimate constitutional authority, most **federal corporations** are created for narrow and specific purposes. The systems of national banks and of federal savings and loan institutions are examples of federally created corporations, all of which are federally chartered and supervised.

In general, this discussion is limited to state-chartered corporations. Note, however, that within the limits of legitimate constitutional purposes, the United States can readily enter this field. The prospect of federal intervention in corporate law may furnish more of a check on the offering of inducements by states to corporate management, such as through tax relief and reduced regulation, than any competition among the states. That seems especially the case for one state, Delaware, which has long dominated state corporate law. Over half of all publicly traded American corporations and about 60% of Fortune 500 companies are incorporated in Delaware.

Some Basic Features of Delaware Corporate Law

1. Delaware places few restrictions on selling or mortgaging assets, merging businesses, or other key corporate decisions. This strong management flexibility usually extends to fighting hostile takeover attempts.

2. Delaware provides *strong indemnification rights* for officers and directors.

3. Delaware affords few (and fairly weak) dissenting shareholders' rights.

4. Delaware provides staggered elections for boards of directors, so that it is more difficult to take over the board in just one election.

5. Other than when corporate officers or directors face criminal charges, Delaware law usually lets persons applying for corporate status to maintain the confidentiality of some key information about their business purpose or personnel (e.g., the names of their corporation's top executives).

6. Delaware has debtor-friendly courts for corporate bankruptcy cases, and a federal tax code that allows companies to file for bankruptcy in the state of their main office *or* in the state where they are incorporated (so, often Delaware).

7. Delaware has an experienced, extremely capable coterie of corporate and bankruptcy law judges and lawyers.

8. Delaware is the only state with a separate business court. The Delaware court system—the Courts of Chancery—has special recognition of corporate law needs.

9. Delaware has relative certainty of the corporate law: a long, well-developed body of statutory, regulatory, and case law, more extensive and knowable than the law of perhaps any other state, even the largest. This confidence in having answers about the corporate law in Delaware, even if the Delaware position is not always the most management friendly, often makes Delaware the choice of risk-averse incorporators who want an answer more than they are willing to face uncertainty.

Many states join Delaware in providing similar approaches to one or more of points 1–5. But the fact that Delaware does all of the above (1–9) gives some assurance to incorporators that the state will maintain its commitment to being "corporate-friendly."

PROFIT OR NONPROFIT; SOCIAL BENEFIT

Business law primarily concerns corporations organized for profit. *However, nonprofit, charitable, or eleemosynary corporations are of great importance*, even in the business world, not only because of the important tax benefits and concessions accruing to such corporations but also because of the importance of permitting these charitable groups to own property, form contracts, and otherwise engage in business without individual members having personal liability for business matters. Such corporations may be stock corporations, or **membership corporations** (owned by their members without issuing stock).

Since 1983, over 40 states have enacted "constituency statutes" (also known as "stakeholder statutes") allowing directors and officers of ordinary, for-profit corporations to consider non-financial interests when making decisions. The corporation's *constituencies* (persons for whom the officers and directors act) extend beyond simply the shareholders. However, there is little judicial interpretation of these statutes, and there are many interpretations of a corporate board's more traditional duties to shareholders, so businesses find it difficult to know whether and how to consider these additional, *constituency* interests. Because constituency statutes do not mandate, but rather simply permit, consideration of non-financial interests, officers and directors may still face civil claims if they do not strictly adhere to the usual concept of a supreme fiduciary duty to shareholders: maximizing business profits.

In contrast with the constituency statutes' broadening of board considerations (potentially far-reaching, but actually just permissive laws) for all corporations, a newer approach provides not for loosening corporate law generally, but rather is limited to a special corporate format. This format, the **benefit corporation** ("B-corp"), provides an expansive notion of corporate *purposes*, *accountability*, and *transparency*, and it thereby offers more possibilities for socially productive business enterprises. Starting with Maryland in 2010, most states have enacted legislation authorizing a type of corporation (the B-corp) whose *purpose* extends to creating a general public benefit—a positive impact on society and the environment—in addition to the earning of profits. B-corps thus can incorporate mission statements as well as community and ecological principles in their business practices.

B-corp shareholders have the power to determine whether the corporation has had a positive, significant public benefit (*accountability*). B-corp directors and officers must consider the effect of their decisions on all stakeholders: shareholders, employees, suppliers, customers, the community, and the environment. Also, most B-corp laws provide that changing the corporation's control, purpose, or structure ordinarily requires a vote of at least a two-thirds majority (an even higher proportion in some states).

The B-corps must publish an annual benefit report about their social and environmental performance using a comprehensive, independent standard (similar to the Generally Accepted Accounting Principles [GAAP] for financial reports); this report is adopted by the board of directors but is not subject to audits or required to be certified. While the states do not regulate the report's content, most state B-corp laws require the report's delivery to all shareholders and to a public website (excluding only proprietary data), and some states call for even more *transparency* by requiring B-corps to submit their reports to the appropriate state department for corporations. Moreover, B-corp shareholders can sue the corporation in a "benefit enforcement proceeding," which is designed to enforce the B-corp's social mission (i.e., to remedy problems in the setting or meeting of socially impactful goals).[3] Only shareholders and directors have a right to sue for (1) violation of or failure to pursue a general or specific public benefit; or (2) violation of a duty or standard of conduct. As with any corporation, directors and officers still have fiduciary duties, such as when deciding what are public benefits and when taking actions that contemplate non-financial interests, such as actions regarding the employees, community, and environment. Even when selling or buying goods, services, licenses, securities, real estate, or other intangibles or items, the social benefits may be embraced.

DOMESTIC OR FOREIGN

A corporation is said to be **domestic** in the state of its incorporation, the state of its "birth." In respect to all other states, it is a **foreign corporation**. Thus, in Delaware, a Delaware corporation is a domestic corporation; in all other states it is foreign. For lawsuit purposes, a corporation's domicile (place where it is a citizen) also includes—in addition to its state of incorporation—the state in which it has its principal place of business (so the corporation is domiciled in one or two states).

Corporations formed in foreign countries are called **alien corporations**.

CLOSE CORPORATIONS

A **close corporation** is a stock corporation whose shares are held by relatively few persons, frequently members of a family. Such a corporation may be operated like a partnership, sometimes with no board of

---

[3] While LLCs generally could commence with or amend their membership agreements to incorporate provisions similar to those of the B-corp, most commentators believe that the corporate structure of the B-corp is more suited than is the LLC to the needs of institutional investors or to company insiders planning to raise outside capital (e.g., through an initial public offering).

directors, or with other informalities not permitted to general stock corporations for profit.

To permit such loose organization, the laws of most states limit the number of stockholders and permit restrictions on stock transfer by agreement among the shareholders or by charter provision.

S CORPORATIONS (FORMERLY "SUBCHAPTER S" OF THE INTERNAL REVENUE CODE)

S corporations are organized to minimize the effect of federal income taxes on small businesses, principally by doing away with corporate "double taxation." This double taxation, as explained in Chapter 15, is taxation applied first to the corporation's income, and second to the individual shareholders' income in the form of earnings and dividends.

The S corporation does not pay a corporate income tax on earnings; the entire income is taxed to the shareholders, whether distributed or not.

An S corporation must be incorporated in the United States and meet a number of ownership requirements. It cannot have more than 100 shareholders, all of whom must own the same class of stock. Whereas preferred stock is not allowed, voting differences within a class of stock are permitted. Individuals, estates, charitable organizations, pension trusts, financial institutions, employee stock ownership plans, single-member LLCs (see below), and certain small business trusts can be S corporation shareholders. To determine the number of shareholders that an S corporation is deemed to have, all members of a family are treated as one shareholder. The "family" is defined very broadly—every lineal descendant (including adopted children), as well as spouses and former spouses of these descendants, tracing back to up to six generations to a common ancestor.

An S corporation can wholly own another S corporation (be the S corporation parent of an S corporation subsidiary, termed a Q-Sub, short for "Qualified Subchapter S Subsidiary"). Ordinarily, corporations, partnerships, or other non-natural persons cannot be S corporation shareholders. S corporation status is obtained by filing with the Internal Revenue Service a form signed by each shareholder. If there is no filing, then the corporation is a *C corporation* (under subchapter "C" of the federal tax code). In the late 1980s, there were about twice as many C corporations as S corporations; by 2015, S corporations outnumbered C corporations nearly three to one.

LIMITED LIABILITY COMPANIES

Because S corporations have restrictions, the **limited liability company** (LLC) is an alternative. A 1988 IRS ruling that, for federal tax purposes, LLCs are to be treated like partnerships has led every state to authorize the LLC. Unlike the S corporation, the LLC has no restrictions on the number or kind of owners (e.g., partnerships, corporations, nonresident aliens, and other LLCs can be LLC "members"), the class of stock, and the owning of subsidiaries; unlike general or limited partnerships, the LLC permits investors to *manage* the business yet not be personally liable for the business debts. The LLC thus is a *partnership-corporation hybrid*, with the corporate shield protecting against personal liability, but with LLC members like partners in that two of these three partnership characteristics must be present: (1) a member's death or a decision to pull out dissolves the LLC (no perpetual existence[4]); (2) transfer of a membership requires the other members' approval; and (3) the LLC is managed by all of the members (member-managed) rather than elected managers or directors (manager-managed). If the LLC does not provide otherwise in the articles of organization it files with the state or in the operating agreement that outlines the LLC's management structure, most states provide that the LLC is member-managed (with governance like that of a general partnership). If the LLC is managed by some designated members, or nonmembers/outsiders, or a combination of members and nonmembers, then the business is manager-managed (somewhat comparable to a corporation's management, with the inactive members being passive investors).

Although LLP (limited liability partnership) ownership is not a security, LLC membership/ownership may be. Still, *LLCs can be run informally*. LLCs do not have to have the corporate mechanisms of control such as boards of directors. (Unless also a close corporation, an S corporation must follow those formal structures.) But, as stated above, an LLC is limited to four corporate-like elements (the other two elements must be partnership-like), or else the alleged LLC will not be given legal status as such an entity. The four elements are: shields or limiting of the owners' personal liability; centralized (corporate-style) management; transferable interests; and continuity of life. If a business entity has more than two of these elements, then it does not have an LLC—a court could remove the corporate protection for the LLC members, who are thereby subject to personal liability for LLC debts.

---

[4] The LLC's operating agreements could provide for the LLC's continuance in the event of a member's death or withdrawal. However, most states require that the operating agreements set a limit to the LLC's existence (usually 30 years). The members later may decide to continue the LLC's existence.

To some degree, the LLC format is replacing the S corporation format. The LLC is similar to an S corporation (e.g., as with partnerships, *no* double taxation; as with corporations, limited liability of members/ shareholders), but, as mentioned above, has advantages over the S corporation because it is more flexible. Every state permits a limited liability company to be formed and operated with one member (*Single-Member Limited Liability Companies* [SMLLCs]). Also, every state permits a judgment creditor of that member to seek a court order charging the SMLLC ownership interest with a lien. A "charging order" requires the SMLLC to pay all future distributions to the judgment creditor until the judgment is fully satisfied. Since the member alone retains discretionary control over when and if such distributions will be made, the charging order is usually ineffective because the member simply accumulates distributions. Compared with partnerships or corporations, there are some potential problems with LLCs. First, although both partnerships and LLCs are not subject to federal income tax, LLCs (as are S corporations) are *sometimes subject to a state income tax* (e.g., in Florida and Texas), whereas partnerships are not. Second, many states, including California and Florida, do *not* permit licensed professionals (lawyers, accountants, physicians, dentists, engineers, architects, etc.) to form, as a business offering those professional services, the LLC. Third, an LLC may not be permitted to merge directly with a non-LLC. Therefore, the only way to effectuate a merger is for the LLC to dissolve, form a corporation, merge with the other entity, and then revert back into a LLC, with each such business format transformation tending to create tax liabilities. (Conversely, corporations generally can merge without undergoing a dissolution.)

Legal analysis, though, must be tentative: LLC law is still new. The legal principles often are uncertain both within a state and across state borders. For instance, some states tax LLCs as if they were corporations (a few states do the same for S corporations), and some states have "Series LLC" laws allowing the LLC (or sometimes other business formats) to create a series of separate assets within the LLC.

In overall structure, the Series LLC may be labeled a master LLC with separate divisions, similar to an S corporation having Q-subs. Each distinct series of assets within the Series LLC can have different managers and members, but the LLC itself may be able to pay a single state fee and one overall income tax. The IRS and some states have, in effect, approved of the tax treatment sought for Series LLC owners. However, it is still new, and whether the internal "shields" of these assets will protect one series' owners from liability for other debts, either those of the LLC itself or of other series within the LLC, has yet to be well-established in court, nor has there been sufficient Series LLC legislation and regulation among the states.

The differences in and relative newness of each state's LLC approach cause uncertainties and inefficiencies for LLC businesses and their advisors. Most problematic may be the continuing uncertainty from state to state as to whether and to what degree LLC members should have fiduciary duties to their fellow members. Should these standards be subject to standards the members themselves lay out, or discard, in operating agreements? What standards should be the default position when the members' position is unclear? And should there be some standards that cannot be altered by contract? These questions are still being addressed by courts, legislators, regulators, and academic commentators. Even when fiduciary standards are present, there are significant differences between the high, sometimes seemingly self-sacrificing fiduciary duty expected of partners and the greater discretion often permitted for corporate-type fiduciaries. For LLCs spread across 50 states in a still relatively new and growing business and legal environment, a member's duties—both type and degree (whether to treat the LLC member as if a partner or a corporate agent)—often remain uncertain. Furthermore, the limited liability extending generally from the LLC to the members may not be as strong in some states and in some situations as for corporations.

Summary of Some Comparisons Between LLCs and S Corporations

- LLC ownership (numbers and types) and operations (little or no mandatory record keeping and boards) are more flexible, with less regulation;
- S Corporation ownership is more readily transferable;
- S Corporation has a tax advantage related to avoiding employment tax. All earnings above fair market salary levels are considered a distribution of profit, not wages, and thus avoid the employment tax. The LLC's owner usually is considered to be self-employed, so any net profits above a fair market salary are considered wages and are liable for employment taxes.

PROFESSIONAL CORPORATIONS

Professional corporations are created by lawyers, doctors, accountants, architects, engineers, and other professionals in order to gain corporate tax advantages for traditional partnership or proprietorship activities. These corporations, organized under state law enacted in conformity with internal revenue code requirements, are generally identified by abbreviations: P.A. (Professional Association), P.C. (Professional Corporation), or S.C. (Service Corporation).

Although it is a corporation for most purposes, the professional corporation may not be able to shield its shareholders and members from individual tort liability for professional negligence. In effect, these shareholders are treated as if partners and are thus bound to this **basic principle of common law partnership:** Each partner is responsible for the torts and contracts of the other partners within the scope of the partnership venture.

Most states, though, do not apply this principle to professional corporations, thereby providing greater liability protection. This majority approach leaves the individual professional within the corporation or other limited liability entities free from personal liability for the professional negligence of another member of the organization, unless the individual was, in fact, supervising that negligent member or otherwise participating in the tortious acts.

NATURE AND CONTENT OF THE CHARTER; BYLAWS

THE CHARTER

The **charter** (also sometimes called the **articles of incorporation**, or **articles**) is the grant of corporate existence, the birth certificate of the corporation. This formal document, executed by the state through its corporation commission, is the source of corporate authority. Also, the charter is a public document.

Although the charter may contain any number of provisions, drawn formally or informally, modern charters tend to cover only the minimum provisions required by law. *The charter is more or less a "form" document; however, the required coverage may vary from state to state.*

The following information is usually required in the charter:

1. Incorporators
2. Corporate name
3. Corporate address and name and address of resident agent
4. Duration
5. Purpose
6. Capital structure
7. Internal organization
8. Other permissible provisions

• *INCORPORATORS*

The incorporators are the persons who make application for the charter. Their only function is to lend their names and signatures to the incorporating documents. By so doing, they acquire no special legal liability. Generally, the only requirement is that an incorporator be old enough to make a contract, that is, at least 18 years of age. Usually, there must be at least three incorporators. Many states do not require that these incorporators be residents of the state.

• *NAME*

Any name may be chosen for the corporation provided that:

(a) the name indicates that the entity is a corporation by inclusion of one of the following words, or by one of these words abbreviated: Company (in most states), Corporation, Incorporated, Limited, and

(b) the name is not the same as, or misleadingly similar to, the name of any other domestic corporation, or corporation doing business in the state.

In addition, many states limit, in corporate names, the use of certain words closely associated with particular types of businesses or industries. For example, a manufacturing concern would not be allowed to include in its name a word such as "insured," "finance," or "fiduciary."

• *CORPORATE ADDRESS AND NAME AND ADDRESS OF REGISTERED AGENT*

The corporate address is the principal address of the corporation in the state of its incorporation.

The registered agent is a person or another corporation authorized to receive service of process and other legal and official papers. The requirement that a legal agent be named is of more than passing importance: the state is concerned that persons having business with a corporation, or interested in bringing suit against it, be able to discover a way of finding the corporation in order to hold it accountable for its actions.

• *DURATION*

As stated above, the duration may be perpetual or limited to a stated period of time.

• *PURPOSE*

Modern statutes permit a corporation to be organized for any legal purpose, and the charter may contain merely a broad statement of purpose. Usually, however, the charter states the specific purpose for which the corporation is being formed—for example, "to operate a restaurant business"—followed by very broad grants of power and usually a statement of purpose to do any legal act.

Charters that fail to contain the "for any legal purpose" provision are nevertheless granted such broad powers as a matter of right, unless the charter contains restrictions or limitations on certain powers or rights.

• *CAPITAL STRUCTURE*

Requirements concerning charter statements about capital vary from state to state. Generally, state incorporation statutes require information about the number of shares of stock of all classes that the corporation has authority to issue, the number of shares of stock of each class, the par value, and other matters concerning both equity and capital.

• *INTERNAL ORGANIZATION*

State statutory requirements about organization are quite minimal: usually the only requirements are a provision as to the number of directors (e.g., "not more than seven") and the names and addresses of those who will serve as an interim board until the shareholders meet and name the first board.

Other organizational and detailed day-to-day matters are usually left for the bylaws. The relationship among officers, directors, and shareholders (the corporation's *internal affairs*) is governed by the state law in which the corporation is incorporated.

• *OTHER PROVISIONS*

The charter may include other provisions, not inconsistent with law, defining, limiting, or regulating the powers of the corporation, its directors and shareholders, or classes of shareholders. Included may be restrictions on the transferability of stock (creating a close or S corporation), requirements of a concurrence of shareholders greater than a majority for certain actions, provisions for minority shareholder representation by cumulative voting, provisions relating to preemptive rights (see Chapter 18), and other provisions that may be included in the bylaws.

BYLAWS

Generally, the charter should be a lean, sparse document and the bylaws should be more detailed. The reason is that charter amendments must be approved by the state as well as the shareholders. Bylaws are generally adopted by the directors and may or may not be approved by the shareholders.

> Bylaws contain specific provisions for the organization and oper-
> ation of the corporation, including such matters as stocks, bonds,
> and dividends; the election, structure, and operation of the board of
> directors; quorum and voting requirements for shareholders' meetings;
> notices, amendments, and places for meetings.

The bylaws may not contain a provision contrary to, or inconsistent with, the charter.

CORPORATE POWERS AND LIMITATIONS ON THEM

POWERS

Modern corporations are granted very broad powers by law; indeed, in most states they can perform any act not inconsistent with law. Thus it should be assumed that for most purposes a corporation has all of the rights and powers of action accruing to a natural person.

The MBCA and RMBCA list a number of general powers for a corpora-tion, including the power—

to sue and be sued;

to have a corporate seal, which may be altered at will;

to make and amend bylaws, not inconsistent with the articles of incorporation or with law;

to purchase, lease, and otherwise acquire real and personal property;

to sell or dispose of its property;

to purchase, own, hold, vote, or pledge stock;

to make contracts and guarantees, incur liabilities, and issue notes and bonds;

to lend money and invest and reinvest its funds;

to be a promoter, partner, member, associate, or manager of a joint venture or partnership;

to conduct its business and exercise the powers granted by law within or outside the state;

to do any act, not inconsistent with law, that furthers the business of the corporation.

LIMITATIONS ON POWERS

Powers are sometimes limited by statute, by the corporation's charter, by the bylaws, or by a resolution or other action of the board of directors.

• *BY STATUTE*

A number of statutory limitations may be placed on the power of corporations. By way of example, one very common statutory limitation, a limit on the power of the corporation to make a gift, will be discussed.

All corporate property is owned by the shareholders. At the common law, no gift of this property could be made without unanimous shareholder approval. Consequently, *any* gift of corporate property not unanimously approved by the shareholders was illegal. This illegality is preserved in the corporate law of some states. Most states now permit corporate gifts, but place statutory limits on their nature and object. Typically, gifts may be permitted without shareholder approval provided that they are (a) reasonable in amount, (b) approved by the directors, (c) made from profits, and (d) made for charitable purposes.

• *BY CHARTER, BYLAWS, OR ACTION OF THE DIRECTORS*

Further limits and restrictions on corporate power can be placed in the charter or bylaws. These may include such restrictions as limits on the borrowing power of officers, on pensions or salaries, on the purchase of real estate, and on the sale of assets.

Other limits may be established from time to time by resolution or other specific action of the board of directors.

• *BY THE ULTRA VIRES DOCTRINE*

*A corporate action beyond the charter powers of the corporation or of the person purporting to act for the corporation is **ultra vires**,* "beyond the powers." If the action is appropriate and lawful, it is ***intra vires***, "within the powers."

Because of the broad-power concepts of modern law, the *ultra vires* doctrine is not a problem of major consequence. However, *ultra vires* acts can be enjoined by shareholders in a suit against the corporation, or by a derivative suit for damages in favor of the corporation against an officer or against the board because of the unauthorized action; or the state itself may seek to block the unauthorized action (see Chapter 17), even seeking to dissolve the corporation. Of course, if a third party dealing with the corporation knew of the *ultra vires* nature of the corporate act, the act may be set aside. Moreover, if a proposed *ultra vires* act is still executory (not yet performed), the corporation may refuse to proceed with the action unless the third party can demonstrate specific injury through his/her reliance on the corporate proposal.

REGULATION OF FOREIGN CORPORATIONS

If a corporation wishes to *"do business" in a state other than the one in which it was incorporated, it must register or qualify in that other state as a foreign corporation.* Although registration or qualification may be a mere formality, the corporation must pay a fee, sometimes post a bond, and always designate a registered agent in that state to receive service of process and other legal papers.

The out-of-state corporation, having subjected itself to the laws of the state in which it seeks to do business, is vulnerable to the expense and difficulty of suit in a more remote or inconvenient location. Penalties for failure to qualify or register can be severe: loss of privilege of using state courts for the purpose of suit; a fine for every day of failure to register while doing business; and personal liability of officers, directors, and agents for actions in the foreign state.

Under the federal constitution, a state cannot restrict or regulate interstate commerce. Therefore a state cannot require registration or qualification for a foreign corporation doing an *interstate* business, that is, coming through on its way to another state. Indeed, cases dealing with the meaning of the phrase "doing business" abound.

It is generally held that a foreign corporation is "doing business" within a state if it:

(a) maintains sufficient contacts or ties within a state,

(b) on a continuous or regular basis,

(c) so as to make it fair and equitable that the corporation be accountable in that state for its actions.

(See the discussion of personal jurisdiction on pages 55–56.)

KNOW THE CONCEPTS

DO YOU KNOW THE BASICS?

1. List some ways in which a corporation is treated as a person and some ways in which it is not treated as a person.

2. Why might a democratic society be more likely to foster the corporate form of business than a totalitarian society would be?

3. Why is it possible for corporations to function with little or no policing and supervision by the state?

4. Discuss the ways in which a public utility is a public corporation and the ways in which it is a private corporation.

5. What is meant by corporate "double taxation"? Explain several ways in which double taxation may be avoided.

6. What is the meaning of the expression "pierce the corporate veil"? Is this a "moral" as well as a legal principle?

7. Why should the charter be a "lean" (relatively simple and short) document?

8. What is meant by the phrase "misleadingly similar to" in establishing a corporate name?

9. What is the underlying philosophy in requiring stockholders to approve a corporate gift? Why have many states found it necessary to relax this philosophy?

10. Why is the common law doctrine of *ultra vires* not as important to the modern corporation as it was in earlier times?

11. Why is it necessary that a foreign corporation "do business" within a state in order to be subject to the registration requirements of that state?

TERMS FOR STUDY

alien corporation
articles of incorporation
bylaws
certificate of incorporation
charter
close corporation
corporation
de facto corporation
de jure corporation
domestic corporation
federal corporation
foreign corporation
incorporators

intra vires
limited liability company
MBCA
membership corporation
pierce the corporate veil
private corporation
professional corporation
promoter
public corporation
quasi-public corporation
RMBCA
S corporation
ultra vires

PRACTICAL APPLICATION

1. Doctors Hacksaw, Smith, and Spurgeon operate a general medical practice as a professional corporation, known as HSS, P.C. While performing a tonsillectomy on one Samuels, Hacksaw is allegedly negligent, as a result of which Samuels is left partly paralyzed. Each of the doctors is quite wealthy, but the corporation is without substantial assets.

   Advise Samuels as to whether he can expect to win a case against each of the doctors as individuals.

2. In 1990, Soper and his two adult sons, Sam and Steve, created a corporation, Soper and Sons Electrical Company. During the first year or so, they maintained corporate bank accounts, had the name printed on trucks and stationery, and held annual stockholders' meetings. After the elder Soper died in 1998, Sam and Steve forgot about the corporation and failed to hold meetings or otherwise follow the corporate formalities. In 2003, Sam's allegedly negligent electrical wiring caused a disastrous fire at a local elementary school, in which several children and school personnel were injured.

   Are there legal theories under which Steve and Sam can be personally liable to the injured parties?

3. Snyder wishes to create a corporation under the name "First National Liquor Stores, Inc." Should this name be permitted as a good corporate name over the objection of First National Food Stores, Inc.?

4. Good Times Candy Company, an Illinois corporation, is a large manufacturer and distributor of confections and candies in the Midwest. It has never qualified or registered in the state of Iowa as a foreign corporation, although it has passed through Iowa in the course of making sales in other states. Most sales of the company and all of the sales that involve passing through Iowa are made in response to orders shipped FOB Chicago. If Good Times sells its products directly in Iowa for the 2015 Christmas season, should it register as a foreign corporation before doing so again for the 2016 Christmas season?

ANSWERS
KNOW THE CONCEPTS

1. A corporation has all of the constitutional rights of a person except protection from self-incrimination, provided for in the Fifth Amendment to the Constitution. This protection against self-incrimination has been construed to be "a human protection," and the courts have refused to extend it to a corporate entity. Other constitutional rights, such as the protection of property rights, extend to the corporation. A corporation cannot commit a crime the only punishment for which is a jail sentence. Bear in mind, however, that the mere fact that a corporation may be guilty of a crime or liable for a tort does not protect the corporate employee, agent, or officer; these individuals may also be concurrently guilty of a crime or liable for a tort, along with their corporate employer.

2. There are several reasons why a democratic society fosters the corporate form. First of all, the shareholders vote for directors, and the voting power is distributed among the stockholders in equal measure to their actual ownership of stock. These are democratic concepts. Also, the protection of stockholders' property rights is in accord with democratic principles.

3. Since corporations exist for the benefit of their shareholders, it is presumed that the shareholders will protect their interests through regular corporate procedures. Shareholder rights are discussed in the next chapter.

4. A public utility is public in the sense that it performs a public function. Its prices are fixed by regulatory authorities. The rate of return allowed to its investors is set by regulation. Its service territories are

determined by regulators. Another public aspect is its right of eminent domain or condemnation.

As a private matter, a public utility is owned by private investors; its stock may be freely traded. Within legal constraints, some of which are discussed in this chapter, the investors may make a profit. The utility's stockholders have the usual legal rights of shareholders generally.

5. "Double taxation" is taxation on the corporation's profits and further taxation on these profits when they are distributed to shareholders.

The S corporation and the limited liability company provide a direct way of dealing with this problem: professional corporations permit professionals such as doctors, lawyers, and accountants to incorporate without double taxation and receive a number of tax benefits through corporate planning. Of course, in a small "mom and pop" corporation, the principals, who are usually the shareholders, may pay themselves reasonable salaries, expense monies that are not taxed to the corporation.

6. "Piercing the corporate veil" has a moral aspect in that the shareholders are not directly responsible for corporate losses unless the corporate form is abused: the corporation is operated as a "front" for a fraudulent purpose, and the corporate business is operated as though the corporation does not exist.

7. The charter is more difficult to amend or change than bylaws or other documents. Approval of the state corporation commission may be required, as well as that of the shareholders and directors. Therefore, most corporate charters should have no more provisions, and no more specificity in those provisions, than is necessary.

8. Members of the public should not be misled by the name into believing that they are dealing with some other corporate entity. Many corporations spend vast sums establishing an identity or a reputation for excellence; it would not be fair to permit a new enterprise to adopt a similar name and thus benefit from the older company's established identity or reputation.

9. The underlying philosophy is that all corporate property belongs to the shareholders; their assets cannot be given to another without their approval.

Corporate giving may be necessary and appropriate in the modern world. There may be tax, advertising, and goodwill advantages to the corporate gift. Moreover, several shareholders, or perhaps a single shareholder, might otherwise thwart a gift giving against the wishes of a vast majority.

10. The modern view of corporate powers is more relaxed and trusting than the earlier common law view. Most modern corporations are permitted to consummate any lawful act.

11. A state cannot interfere with interstate commerce; hence it is necessary that the state have legitimate control over foreign corporate activity in order to prohibit it or police it in some manner. The state has legitimate interests of its own citizens to protect. If a corporation's business is not interstate (and subject to federal control), but is performed on a continuous and regular basis within the state, it becomes accountable to the state.

PRACTICAL APPLICATION

1. The creation of a professional corporation does not protect the individual doctor from professional torts. Hacksaw is personally responsible. Unless Smith or Spurgeon were personally involved with the tonsillectomy, most states would not hold them responsible for Hacksaw's tort (although if the doctors had held themselves out as general partners each would be liable for the torts of the others). A few courts might hold both Smith and Spurgeon responsible for Hacksaw's negligence on the theory that professional corporations do not alter the old partnership obligations of the members to each other.

2. This question has broad implications beyond the subject matter of this chapter. However, one obvious problem, that of piercing the corporate veil, is covered in the current chapter. The veil would not be pierced in the absence of a showing of a fraudulent purpose; hence this theory is not adequate to reach the individual stockholders or principals. However, in Chapter 14 (Agency) we dealt with the personal responsibility of employee agents for their torts while undertaking company business. Under agency law, Sam and Steve may well be liable if they, or others acting under their supervision, personally committed the tort.

3. "First National Liquor Stores, Inc." is probably not confusing or misleadingly similar to "First National Food Stores, Inc." Not only are the product lines different; the name "First National" is not strongly identified with any special or unusual type of business.

4. Good Times may need to qualify in Iowa as a foreign corporation before doing an intrastate business for the second Christmas in a row. It could certainly be argued that twice is not "regular and continuous"; however, it seems that a pattern of doing business is beginning to emerge. Good corporate practice should be conservative, and doubt should be resolved in favor of complying with the registration requirement. Note that going through the state is an interstate activity and does not constitute "doing business." Note also that an "FOB Chicago" sale causes the title to pass in Chicago; consequently, the sale did not take place in Iowa, and the seller has not entered that state on an intrastate basis.

17

MANAGEMENT OF THE CORPORATION; TERMINATION

CORPORATE OVERVIEW

THE CORPORATE STRUCTURE

The owners of the shares of stock issued by the corporation are the owners of the corporation. These **shareholders** elect a board of **directors**, who oversee the management of the corporation. The directors, in turn, name and employ the **officers**, who are responsible for the operation of the business.

CORPORATE OBJECTIVES

Theoretically, the modern corporation has the power to accomplish any lawful purpose. For larger corporations, there usually are a number of "stakeholders" with an interest in the corporation's well-being; employees, suppliers, customers, creditors, licensees, and the overall community are some of the main groups affected by the company's activities. However, the corporation is owned by its shareholders and under law exists for their benefit. Corporate profits should result in shareholder gain, while corporate losses become shareholder losses.

The managers of the corporation (the board of directors) have wide discretion to determine precisely the best way to funnel corporate powers into shareholder gain (or loss), which is not necessarily measured solely in financial terms. A good corporate image created by conformity with environmental laws, charitable acts of kindness, and good neighbor policies within the larger community may foster profits and serve the shareholder. On the negative side, a corporation with uncaring and hardened management, a polluter of air and water, an enterprise that neglects its employees or imposes on their loyalty may inhibit profits and harm its shareholders.

Still, corporate management must not neglect the shareholders. While the community at large or certain charities may benefit from corporate action, such benefit must somehow contribute to the ultimate good of the corporation and therefore of the shareholders.

SHAREHOLDERS

Shareholders may own either preferred or common stock. The classes of stock are discussed in Chapter 18.

SHAREHOLDER FUNCTIONS

• *ELECTION OF DIRECTORS*

Although the shareholders are the owners of the corporation, this ownership does not carry with it the right of management.

> The primary right of the shareholder is to attend meetings of the shareholders and to vote on matters properly brought before such meetings, including the election of directors and other fundamental matters affecting the corporation and required by statute or by the charter.

In most situations, shareholders can add items to the shareholder meeting agenda or bring new issues to a vote.

Except for attending the shareholders' meetings and casting votes in favor of directors, a shareholder cannot directly interfere with the directors or with their management of the corporation, even though he/she may own or control a majority or all of the outstanding shares.

• *AMENDMENT OF THE CHARTER*

At common law, a corporate charter was considered to be a contract between the state and the corporation, on the one hand, and between the corporation and the shareholders, on the other. Change of this contract required unanimous shareholder approval.

Under modern corporate law a change can be accomplished by a less than unanimous shareholder vote. The percentage of shares required for approval of a charter amendment varies among the states in accordance with the nature of the proposed amendment. Generally, minor changes, such as dropping the word "The" from the corporate name or changing the registered agent, do not require *any* shareholder approval but can be done by the directors.

Drastic changes in the nature of the corporate business, however, or changes affecting the value of the stock or voting rights may require approval of

(a) two thirds of the shares outstanding and entitled to vote, or

(b) a majority of the outstanding shares entitled to vote, or

(c) a majority of the shares present and voting,

depending on the applicable state statute.

Procedures for charter changes require that any change be first proposed by a resolution of the board of directors. Certain changes may specifically require that dissenting shareholders be given the right to sell their stock to the corporation at its appraised value.

• *MERGER AND CONSOLIDATION*

Corporations merge when the stock of one is purchased by another; they are consolidated when a third corporation (generally created for that specific purpose) purchases the stock of both. In a **merger**, corporation A buys all of the stock of B; A continues to exist, but B will be dissolved or continued as a subsidiary of A. In a **consolidation**, corporation C buys the stock of A and B; A and/or B will be dissolved or continue as subsidiaries of C.

In a merger, approval is required in all cases by the shareholders of B, the merged corporation; approval is also required by the shareholders of A, the continuing corporation, unless that corporation already owns most of the stock of the merged corporation, or unless the surviving corporation is so much larger than the merged corporation that the acquisition of the smaller corporation will have no effect on the business of the survivor or on the value of its stock.

Example: Merger

If corporation A, with assets in excess of $50 million, merges with corporation B, with assets of $100,000, approval of the shareholders of A would not be required. The shareholders of B, however, must approve.

> In most states, two thirds of the outstanding shares eligible to vote must approve a merger or consolidation.

• *SALE OF ASSETS*

Sale of all or substantially all of the assets of a corporation other than in the regular course of business requires shareholder approval. The meaning of the phrase "substantially all" varies from case to case, but the principal test is whether the sale affects the corporate business to the extent that the nature of the shareholders' investment has changed.

> *Shareholder approval not required*: The corporation owns five fertilizer plants; two are sold and the proceeds are used to repair and remodel the remaining three.
> *Shareholder approval required*: Two of the five fertilizer plants are sold, and the proceeds are used to invest in facilities and technology for the manufacture of ice cream.

Cautious and prudent business practice dictates that the approval of the shareholders be obtained in any doubtful or borderline case.

As with consolidations and mergers, most states require that two thirds of the shares outstanding and eligible to vote approve the sale of all, or substantially all, of the assets of a corporation.

SHAREHOLDER MEETINGS

The functions described in the preceding section are carried out by the shareholders at their meetings.

• *NOTICE OF MEETINGS*

Notice of both the annual meeting and of special meetings must be given to shareholders of record, that is, shareholders whose names appear on the share transfer books of the corporation at the time of notice. The notice must state the purpose of the meeting, such as amendment of the charter, sale of all or substantially all of the assets, or some other extraordinary matter.

Failure to give notice, or giving a defective notice, will *void* any shareholder action unless the shareholder waives his/her objection by attending the meeting without objection, or by signing a written waiver.

• *CONDUCT OF THE MEETING*

A **quorum** (usually defined by state law as a majority of shares outstanding) must be present in person or by proxy. The president or chairman of the board usually presides, and minutes are kept by the secretary of the corporation. Many states, by statute, permit shareholder action without a meeting, provided that all (in some states, a majority) of the shareholders give their consent in writing to the action or actions taken.

• *VOTING*

Most matters are decided by a majority of the votes cast. If there is more than one class of stock (see Chapter 18) and approval of all classes is required, a majority of each class is necessary. In the election of directors, each share has one vote for each director. This mode of director election is usually referred to as straight voting. If, for example, seven directors are to be elected, the holder of 100 shares may select up to seven nominees out of the pool of those nominated and vote up to 100 shares for each of them.

CUMULATIVE VOTING

Cumulative voting is permitted by law, or by special provision in the corporate charter in most states. In the example just given, in cumulative voting the holder of 100 shares has a potential of 700 votes and may distribute them among seven nominees as she chooses. If this shareholder "accumulates" her votes and casts all 700 in favor of a single nominee, this nominee may very well be elected when there are, for example, a total of 100 shares present and voting.

By cumulative voting, a minority shareholder may be assured of some representation on the board of directors and a voice (albeit a minority voice) in management. The percentage of stock ownership needed to elect one director (*x*) under cumulative voting is seen in this formula:

$$x = 1/(\text{number of directors being elected} + 1)$$

So, if five directors are being elected, a shareholder holding 16.7% of the stock $(1/(5 + 1))$ could elect one director.

PROXIES

A **proxy** is a limited power of attorney whereby a shareholder names an agent or a representative (a proxy) to vote his/her shares. Several shareholders may join forces, name a proxy, and control the corporation. A proxy may be revoked at any time, as is the case with powers of attorney in general (see Chapter 14).

VOTING TRUSTS

Most states permit shareholders to transfer their shares to a voting trustee for the limited purpose of electing directors and for voting on other matters as specified in the trust. Alternatively, shareholders may enter into a contract creating a voting agreement or stock-pooling agreement whereby they combine forces in order to gain a voice or exercise control. Such voting trusts, voting agreements, or stock-pooling arrangements are governed by the law of contracts unless state statute imposes a special restriction or limitation.

SHAREHOLDER RIGHTS

• APPRAISAL RIGHTS (SOMETIMES CALLED "DISSENTERS' RIGHTS")

If shareholders object to certain corporate actions that may diminish the value of their stock holdings, most states give these objectors (dissenters) the right to receive the fair value of their stock from the corporation. "Fair value" may have to be determined by appraisal if it is not otherwise ascertainable.

This right of dissenters is usually provided for following two kinds of majority action: (1) consolidation or merger of the corporation, and (2) sale or transfer of all or substantially all of the corporate assets in other than the usual course of business. In addition, appraisal rights may be provided for with regard to any charter amendment that adversely affects the value of the stock or the rights of shareholders.

The appraisal procedure varies from state to state. If the stock is traded on a recognized securities exchange, the fair value is readily ascertainable. Otherwise, statutes provide for a judicial determination, or for the appointment of an appraiser by the corporation and by the dissenter, respectively, and for the two appraisers to name another one if they cannot agree.

The dissenting shareholder must follow a strict procedure in order to avail him-/herself of the appraisal right: the shareholder must file a written objection to the proposed action, must vote against the proposal (or, in some states, abstain from voting), and must make a written demand for appraisal and buy-out within some specified time.

• RIGHT TO SHARE IN DIVIDENDS

The decision to pay dividends is within the business judgment of the board of directors. In the absence of an agreement to the contrary, however, holders of a particular class of stock have the right to share in a dividend on a parity with other holders of the same class.

• *RIGHT TO APPROVE GIFTS; OTHER MATTERS*

> Since the assets of the corporation belong to the shareholders, no substantial portion of these assets can be given away or transferred to others without shareholder approval.

Most states statutes have special procedures for shareholder approval of eleemosynary gifts from profits approved by the board. Furthermore, bonuses, stock option plans, and incentive plans not tied into contract payments for specific work performed may require shareholder approval since such payments may be judicially construed as gifts.

Conflict of interest questions involving members of the board of directors may be resolved by the shareholders. Indemnification of directors and officers, as well as all other matters pertaining to benefits and potential benefits to the corporate managers, may be subject to stockholder approval. Indeed, prudent corporate management favors obtaining shareholder approval for major, fundamental decisions vitally affecting the corporation.

• *RIGHT OF INSPECTION*

Statutes in practically all states permit shareholders to inspect corporate books and records. However, this right of inspection may be limited with respect to the nature of the records sought, depending on the number (or percentage) of shares making the request and, in some states, the purpose of the request.

As a general rule, any shareholder (even one with a single share out of 100,000 shares outstanding) may inspect and copy the annual reports to shareholders, minutes of the shareholders' meetings, the bylaws, the charter, and the list of shareholders, together with their names and addresses. In addition, some percentage, frequently the holders of 5% or 10% of the outstanding stock (along with or through their attorneys and accountants), may inspect and copy all books and records, including books of account.

Whether the broad right of inspection accorded the holders of some specified percentage of stock will be permitted without showing good cause varies from state to state. Some courts, arguing that the corporate property belongs to the shareholders, and that the state does not closely police the corporate business, permit unlimited inspection unless the corporation can demonstrate an improper motive, such as proof that these shareholders are "fronting" for a competitor or seeking to discover trade secrets. *Other states take a contrary view: unless a proper purpose or motive is shown by the shareholders, inspection is not permitted.*

• *PREEMPTIVE RIGHTS*

Existing shareholders may have the **right to preempt**, or come ahead of, other purchasers of stock of the same class in order to protect their percentage interest in, or control of, the corporation (these preemptive rights are *antidilution rights*). Thus, if 100 shares of common stock are outstanding, the owner of 20 of these shares has a one-fifth interest in the corporation. If the corporation were to sell 100 additional shares to a new party or to the other four-fifth owners, the ownership of 20 shares would be diluted to a one-tenth interest. However, with a right to preempt, the owner would have the ability to maintain his one-fifth interest (by purchasing 20 of the additional 100 shares).

In most states, in the absence of a charter provision or shareholders' agreement granting preemptive rights, shareholders do not have these rights. Even when such rights are granted, they do not attach to treasury stock (stock previously issued, but not outstanding) or to shares issued for a merger or consolidation or in noncash transactions.

SHAREHOLDERS' LAWSUITS

• *DERIVATIVE SUITS*

Derivative suits are suits brought by one or more shareholders on behalf of the corporation and for its benefit. Since these suits are not for the benefit of the suing party, any recovery belongs to the corporation, and in such event the corporation must pay the stockholder's reasonable attorney's fees. A shareholder who loses the suit, on the other hand, may be required to reimburse the defendant for his/her expenses, including attorney's fees.

Derivative suits are usually brought against individual officers or directors for waste or conflict of interest. There are certain strict requirements for such a suit. The shareholder must first demand that the directors bring the suit (demand may be excused if the shareholder can show that it would have been futile), and that demand must be refused. Some states and the Federal Rules of Civil Procedure also require that the shareholder notify other shareholders of his/her intent to bring a derivative suit in order to give them an opportunity to ratify or confirm the alleged wrongful action.

• *INDIVIDUAL SUITS*

A shareholder may sue the corporation individually to protect his/her personal rights or property in the corporation. Such a suit may seek to enjoin an *ultra vires* act or to protect the right to inspect the books of the corporation.

SHAREHOLDERS' LIABILITIES

Officers and directors can be successfully sued for all sorts of corporate activities in which they were engaged or for which they otherwise had some responsibility, whereas shareholders, in their role as shareholders, ordinarily have no liability for corporate actions.

Basically, the only loss that a shareholder may sustain is his/her investment in the corporation's stock. This limitation on liability for stock ownership is one of the primary reasons for the existence of the corporate form. As Chapter 16 pointed out, however, if the shareholders themselves disregard the corporate entity, and use the corporate form for fraudulent purposes, the "corporate veil" may be pierced and the shareholders may be personally responsible for corporate obligations.

YOU SHOULD REMEMBER

Although shareholders own the corporation, their ownership does not give them the right of direct management, a function of the board of directors. Shareholders have the right to elect directors, control major charter amendments, and approve mergers, consolidations, and the sale of all or substantially all of the corporate assets.

Shareholder functions are exercised chiefly at meetings of shareholders, either general or specially called pursuant to proper notice. A quorum of shareholders must be present, in person or by proxy. In the election of directors, straight voting is generally required, although state law or the charter may permit cumulative voting.

In addition to the right to attend meetings and to vote on directors and other corporate business, shareholders have other rights: appraisal rights if they dissent from corporate acts that may affect the value of their stock; right to share in dividends, to approve corporate gifts, and to inspect and copy the corporate books; and, if permitted by the charter, preemptive rights.

Shareholders may bring legal action by derivative suits (suits for the corporate benefit and on its behalf) or by direct suits against the corporation.

BOARD OF DIRECTORS

TERM

Directors are elected to hold office until the end of their term, which coincides with the next annual shareholders' meeting at which those directors may be reelected or successors may be elected and qualify as new directors. Terms can also be staggered, so that only a fraction of the board's terms will expire each year. For example, a board may be split into three groups, A, B, and C; the first year, the terms for group A expire and those directors are either reelected to, or replaced for, three-year terms. The following year, group B will be up for the same reelection or replacement process, and the third year it is the C group that is reelected to or replaced for three-year terms. This is done to ensure that the board at all times at least partially comprises experienced people familiar with the company. It also may make it more difficult for shareholders, even when upset over management's performance, to radically redirect the board and thereby replace management.

The MBCA and RMBCA provide that one or more directors can be removed by the shareholders "with or without cause" unless the charter permits removal only for cause. The common law (case law) and some statute law different from the Model Acts permit removal only for cause. "Cause" includes conflicts of interest or other violations of fiduciary functions, violation of the charter or bylaws, or illegal actions.

FIDUCIARY FUNCTION

Directors are neither employees nor agents of the shareholders; rather, they occupy a position of trust to the shareholders. This trust relation is legally described as that of a **fiduciary**—a position of loyalty to the corporate interest and well being, superior to the director's self-interest or desire for personal gain.

In general, this *fiduciary relationship applies to the officers, as well as the directors*, of the corporation.

Four important aspects of the fiduciary relationship are as follows:

1. *Duty of loyalty.* Directors and officers owe an uncompromising duty of loyalty by the directors and officers to the corporation and its shareholders. Above all, the corporate manager must make full disclosure of any personal interest in a matter involving the corporation or its business and in any doubtful case should refrain from voting upon, or taking any action regarding, any such matter. Corporate loans, bonuses, and gifts to directors and officers are *prima facie* colored by a conflict of interest and should have prior shareholder approval.

2. *No usurpation of corporate opportunity.* Directors or officers violate their fiduciary duty if they personally avail themselves of a business opportunity that should have been reserved for the corporation.

Example: Corporate Opportunity

A director or officer of a corporation owning and operating mineral lands cannot purchase other, similar lands for his/her own private purposes without first giving the corporation the opportunity to make the purchase, or without first making a full disclosure of the private objective.

3. *No personal use of corporate assets.* Obviously, a director or officer cannot use corporate property or personnel to conduct personal business or to achieve his/her own ends. Moreover, directors and officers cannot divulge company secrets or technology without breach of their fiduciary obligations.

4. *Restrictions on transactions in shares.* Directors and officers cannot deal in corporate stock if they receive such stock at an unfair price or on advantageous terms. Moreover, federal statutes require certain disclosures of insider transactions affecting stock values or transpiring in interstate commerce.

Germany's Supervisory Boards

German law requires that board members take into account employee interests, not simply represent shareholders. For any corporations with more than 2,000 employees, the workers, through their workers' councils, appoint half the members of a company's "supervisory board" (*Aufsichstrat*) and the shareholders get the other representatives. This board, similar to an American board of directors, decides who the chief executive officer is and signs off on major investment decisions. With inside and outside directors, and with employee and union representatives, the supervisory board is responsible for the appointment and oversight of a lower "management board" (the *Vorstand*). The latter comprises corporate officers who run the corporation. On issues where labor and management is split down the middle, the chairman, who represents management and gets two votes, breaks deadlocks.

German unions can still strike, but only after exhausting all means of peaceful conflict resolution. In exchange for the unions' restraint, the German system grants the workers' councils extensive power in running companies, including a say in hiring, firing, transfers, working conditions, and all major strategic decisions through their representatives on the *Aufsichstrat*. (Besides extensive employee membership, another German check on their board of directors is that "proxies" [voting rights], which in the United States many shareholders normally give to the board, are in Germany usually given not to the board but to the corporation's main creditors, such as banks.)

BUSINESS JUDGMENT RULE

Both directors and officers of the corporation must govern its affairs with reasonably good judgment. Among other duties, they must attend meetings, remain apprised of corporate business, and not engage in self-dealing or conflicts of interest.

The phrase "reasonably good judgment" is somewhat difficult to define, but is intended to describe a standard of care lower than that applicable to a sharp, well-trained, prudent businessperson but higher than that of a casual, disinterested outsider. Three standards are generally applied to director or officer actions to determine compliance with the **business judgment rule ("BJR")**:

1. *Exercise of due care*—An informed decision, in consideration of what the directors or officers reasonably believe to be all the factors relevant to their decision. Therefore, directors have a "duty to monitor": to assure, among other things, that the corporation has an adequate information and reporting system.

2. *Action in good faith*—The BJR protects directors against claims for wrongful acts, but not against claims for failure to act. Inaction by directors is protected by the BJR only if it is a result of a conscious decision to refrain from acting.

3. *Reasonable belief that the action is in the corporate interest*—Usually, a court will not question whether the directors' action was wise or whether they made an error of judgment or a business mistake. Not all decisions of directors will result in benefit to the corporation. As a result, directors will be personally liable for loss to the corporation only if the elements of the BJR defense are not satisfied.

When officers and directors make a poor decision, one must ask: Was it something that, in retrospect, simply turned out to be a mistake ("20/20 hindsight" by itself does not lead to liability), or was it worse? More is needed to establish liability—damages to the corporation caused by the officers' or directors' gross failures.

So a claim generally is that the harm arose because the directors/ officers knew or should have known that they needed help—usually, more information—yet they failed to obtain that help. An example is the important ruling of the Delaware Supreme Court, *Smith v. Van Gorkom*, 488 A.2d 858 (1985). The *Van Gorkom* court found a corporation's directors grossly negligent because the directors rapidly approved the corporation's being bought out and merged into an acquiring company, all without substantial inquiry or any expert advice. By failing to undertake a good faith, thorough review of and

> research into what the corporation was really worth, the board of directors failed to get the information needed to make an informed decision and breached the duty of care that it owed to the shareholders; protection under the business judgment rule was unavailable.

A court is understandably reluctant to substitute its wisdom or judgment for that of a director—after all, directors are chosen by the shareholders, and they are familiar with the business and with the overall corporate objectives. However, a court may be compelled to substitute its judgment for that of a director who, in effect, forfeits responsibility by breach of his/her fiduciary or loyalty duties.

NUMBER AND QUALIFICATIONS OF DIRECTORS

> Generally, the bylaws determine the number and qualifications of directors.

Except when the shareholders unanimously agree to eliminate the board, or when the corporation has fewer than 50 shareholders, a corporation must have at least one director. Otherwise, the number can reasonably be any number, but for obvious reasons should be an odd number. The board should be of such size as to function well as a committee, although many large corporations, banks, and other widely held corporate entities may have boards of 25 members or more.

In most states, any person who can make a simple contract can be a director. A director is generally not required to own stock. (Indeed, for many corporations the board functions best when it includes at least a few active "outside" directors who may bring a broader—and certainly less self-interested—perspective to board meetings than those who work for and own the business.) In the aftermath of scandals, government officials, institutional investors, public watch groups, and others have called for much greater use of outside directors and for directors to limit themselves to serve on no more than two or three boards (so as not to spread thin their task of overseeing corporate management).

COMPENSATION OF DIRECTORS

At the common law, directors did not receive compensation for their services, although they were reimbursed for their expenses. Today most state statutes permit directors to set their own reasonable compensation; extraordinary compensation must be approved by the shareholders.

MEETINGS OF THE BOARD

Since a director is a fiduciary, he/she can act only in person. In other words, a director cannot delegate his/her duties or attend board meetings by proxy.

A director can act only as a member of the board, not individually. Meetings are held at the times and places designated in the bylaws or at special times and places as indicated in the notices of meetings. *It is important that a director attend director meetings, that minutes be kept of such meetings, and that the director's vote be recorded.* Poor attendance and failure to use business judgment are acts of negligence that may create personal liability to shareholders who sustain loss as a result of such negligence. (The bylaws usually establish the quorum: how many directors—typically a majority—are required to transact business.)

Most state statutes permit action without a meeting or upon telephone or other oral approval, provided that all directors consent in writing.

COMMITTEES

Although board members cannot delegate their responsibilities and duties, committees of board members may be designated to perform a number of board-type activities under the general supervision of the whole board. The executive committee, the finance committee, the audit committee, and the like may meet on a daily or weekly basis to attend to management affairs on a more intimate basis. Such committees keep agendas and minutes of business transacted for the information and ratification of the entire board where appropriate or necessary.

DECISIONS REGARDING EARNINGS

The decision to declare dividends, or to invest and reinvest profits, or to expand the plant or otherwise dispose of earnings and profits are matters for the board of directors, acting within the business judgment rule. In the absence of proof of negligence or bad faith, all such decisions are immune from shareholder attack.

> # YOU SHOULD REMEMBER
>
> Directors occupy a fiduciary (trust) relationship to the shareholders. This trust relationship requires an uncompromising duty of loyalty to the corporation, no usurpation of corporate opportunity, no personal use of corporate assets, no unfair dealing in the corporation's stock, and the exercise of reasonably good judgment in managing corporate affairs.
>
> The bylaws generally provide for the number and qualifications of directors. Most state statutes permit the directors to provide reasonable compensation for themselves. Directors must personally attend board meetings; they cannot attend by proxy.
>
> Committees of board members may be appointed to supervise day-by-day functions, but these committees must report to the full board.
>
> Declaration of dividends is subject to the discretion of the board, acting within the business judgment rule.

OFFICERS

The officers are agents of the corporation. They are named and hired by the board of directors. Designation of the various offices and the duties of each office are set forth in the bylaws. As a rule, the officers are the president, one or more vice presidents, the secretary, and the treasurer. (Ordinarily, a person may hold more than one office; many states, though, require that the same person *not* serve as both president and secretary.)

PRESIDENT

The president is the chief executive officer (CEO) of the corporation. He/she may be a member of the board of directors and preside at meetings of the board and of the shareholders. Frequently, all or some of these functions are performed by a chairman of the board, as the bylaws determine.

VICE PRESIDENT

The vice president usually fills the office of president in the absence of the latter. In most corporations, vice presidents are given responsibility for various line activities—manufacturing, sales, administration, and the like. Sometimes executive or senior vice presidents are designated to supervise one or more vice presidents in order to relieve undue burdens that may otherwise fall on the president. Quite often, at least one vice president is a member of the board of directors.

SECRETARY

The secretary is in charge of the corporate books and records. As such, he/she is responsible for keeping the minutes, giving notices, and affixing the corporate seal. (The seal attests to (witnesses) the corporate validity of action and to the authority of the individual signing the document on behalf of the corporation.) Because of the need for knowledge of corporate functions and of director and officer responsibilities, many corporations, especially large ones, require that the secretary be an attorney. Other than responsibility for books and records, the secretary generally exercises no executive functions, such as executing contracts.

TREASURER

The treasurer is responsible for management of the corporation's funds. The treasurer can bind the corporation by his/her checks, indorsements, and disbursements, but performs no other executive functions.

SEC rules require companies to quantify in their proxy filings the potential payments (severance packages—also known as **golden parachutes**) if an executive is terminated, undergoes a change in responsibilities, or is subject to a change of corporate control.

OTHER EMPLOYEES

The corporation's other employees are hired by the officers and given such duties at such compensation as is within the authority of the officers. The bylaws may designate specific duties to one or more employees.

Note: The law of agency governs the authority of these corporate agents. Chapter 14 (Agency) should be reviewed with respect to the corporation's responsibility for contracts, torts, and crimes committed by its employees, either in its name or while acting in a representative capacity. Moreover, the general law of agency governs the personal liability of the agent for acts committed in furtherance of corporate business.

YOU SHOULD REMEMBER

The officers are named and hired by the board of directors. The officers and their duties are prescribed by the bylaws.

Officers usually include the president (chief executive officer), one or more vice presidents (generally with responsibility for line activities), a secretary (with responsibility for maintaining books and records), and a treasurer (with responsibility for management of corporate funds). The secretary and treasurer generally do not have other executive responsibilities.

TERMINATION OF THE CORPORATION

Although most corporations have perpetual existence, the law contemplates both nonjudicial and judicial **dissolution**.

Corporate existence is terminated by dissolution followed by (a) winding up of its affairs, and (b) liquidation of its assets.

NONJUDICIAL DISSOLUTION

Shareholder approval is usually required for nonjudicial dissolution, although an act of the state legislature, as well as expiration of the period of existence stated in the charter (if a period is stated), will result in nonjudicial dissolution without shareholder action. Voluntary dissolution is achieved by (a) passage of a resolution by the board of directors and (b) approval of the directors' resolution by a majority of the shares entitled to be voted at a shareholders' meeting called for that purpose.

JUDICIAL DISSOLUTION

There are three methods of judicial dissolution:

1. The shareholders may petition for judicial dissolution upon their claim that the directors are hopelessly deadlocked, or that the shareholders themselves are deadlocked with regard to election of directors or to some other matter requiring shareholder approval, or that the directors are operating the corporation in an illegal or fraudulent manner.

2. Creditors may implement court action if (a) the corporation cannot pay its debts in the usual course of business *and* a creditor has obtained a judgment against the corporation that the corporation cannot satisfy, or (b) the corporation has stated in writing that it cannot pay the claim of a creditor.

3. The state itself may bring about judicial dissolution if the corporation fails to file its annual report with the secretary of state, fails to pay its annual franchise tax, abuses its corporate authority, or fails to maintain a registered agent in the state.

In the case of failure to file an annual report or pay the annual franchise tax, the secretary of state usually dissolves the corporation by *administrative action*. After giving the corporation notice and after the passage of a specified period of time (and generally publication of proposed dissolution), the secretary dissolves the corporation by signing a certificate of dissolution. *Many, if not most, small and insignificant corporations, and corporations merely created but allowed to languish without conducting any business, are dissolved by administrative action in this manner and without penalty.*

WINDING UP AND LIQUIDATION

After dissolution, the board of directors liquidates the assets of the corporation and distributes the proceeds, first to creditors, second to preferred shareholders (if any), and finally to common shareholders.

KNOW THE CONCEPTS
DO YOU KNOW THE BASICS?

1. Can a majority shareholder, acting alone, dismiss an officer of the corporation?

2. Should a charitable donation be considered, in all cases, a corporate gift subject to the approval of shareholders?

3. Why are the directors of a corporation having assets of over $100 million not required to submit to their shareholders a proposed merger with a corporation having assets of less than $1 million?

4. What advice should be given to someone who strongly objects to the consolidation of a corporation in which he owns a stock interest with another corporation?

5. How can you determine the necessity of attending a special meeting of shareholders?

6. What is cumulative voting?

7. Why can a shareholder attend a shareholders' meeting by proxy, but a director must attend in person?

8. Can the president of a corporation conduct a telephone poll of the members of the board of directors and use the result of that poll as the basis of a board decision?

9. Do shareholders have the right to compel the board to declare a dividend?

10. Why should a vice president of a corporation also be a member of the board of directors?

11. What is one relatively effective and inexpensive way to cause a corporation to be dissolved?

TERMS FOR STUDY

attest	officer
business judgment rule	preemptive right
committee	president
consolidation	proxy
cumulative voting	quorum
derivative suits	secretary
director	shareholder
dissolution	treasurer
fiduciary	vice president
merger	voting trust

PRACTICAL APPLICATION

1. You own about 1% of the outstanding stock of XY corporation. A number of shareholders believe that the management is paying a grossly exorbitant salary to Ms. X, secretary to the president of the company and believed to be his mistress. Ms. X and the president are known to take trips to Europe and other places on "corporate business" and at corporate expense. What course of action should be considered to protect your rights as a shareholder?

2. The vice president of corporation AB, a jewelry company, attends an auction at the direction of the corporation. She is directed to

bid up to $100,000 for the Omega diamond. The bidding reaches $125,000, and the vice president then buys the diamond for her own account for $126,000. Is this action proper?

3. MM Corporation has received an order of the state department of health to cease the discharge of acid into the waters of the state. The board of directors has before it the proposal of a management team to spend over $50 million for capital equipment that will correct the effluent discharge. The company has operated at a loss for the past 2 years. Director Q and a majority of the board vote against the proposal. Later the corporation is fined $1 million for acid discharge, and shareholders ultimately bring a derivative suit against Q, claiming violation of the business judgment rule. What will be the result?

ANSWERS
KNOW THE CONCEPTS

1. A shareholder, even the owner of all of the outstanding stock, cannot directly dismiss an officer or other employee. The shareholder can only elect a board of directors that will consider his/her wishes with regard to corporate management, including the hiring and firing of officers.

2. Charitable gifts are usually subject to state statutes and, if reasonable in amount and approved by the board of directors, do not require shareholder approval (see Chapter 16). A small or reasonable donation for a good cause may also be good business and inure to the benefit of the corporation and the shareholders. As such, it may be a proper business expense and not require submission to shareholders.

3. The purchase of such a disproportionately small business would not affect the nature of the business of the larger corporation or the value of its stock. Shareholder approval is, therefore, not necessary.

4. He must file a written objection to the proposed consolidation, attend the shareholders' meeting in person or by proxy, vote "no," and promptly demand a "buy-out" of his shares. If the stock is traded on a national exchange, the value will have been set by the board of directors as of some previously specified date. If the stock is not traded, the shareholder will proceed to have "fair value" determined by the appraisal routine.

5. You are entitled to a notice of the meeting, which will set out its purpose and any matters to be voted upon.

6. Cumulative voting is the right to concentrate all of your voting rights on fewer than all of the directors being elected. Thus, if you own 10,000 shares and 5 directors are being elected, you have 50,000 votes, all of which may be voted for 1 or 2 directors.

7. A director is in a fiduciary relationship to the shareholders and cannot delegate his/her duties to a proxy or agent. Failure of the director to attend to his/her duties in person may give rise to a charge of neglect. Shareholders are exercising a right when they attend shareholder meetings and vote their shares; rights, unlike fiduciary duties, may be assigned to others by proxy.

8. In most states, telephone action of the board is permissible if all of the directors consent in writing to the action. This consent should be given promptly and affixed to the corporate resolution pursuant to which the action is taken.

9. Declaration of a dividend is usually regarded as a question for the board, not the shareholders. Of course, the decision is subject to the business judgment rule.

10. Generally, a vice president should be a member of the board so that he can preside over board meetings in the absence of the president.

11. If the corporation fails to file an annual report with the state, or fails to pay its annual franchise tax, the state may cause it to forfeit its charter by administrative action.

PRACTICAL APPLICATION

1. So far, you have only hearsay and suspicion as a basis for objection to improper payments and corporate expenditures for Ms. X. Assuming that your state permits shareholders freely to inspect the corporate books but that some minimum percentage of shares is required (e.g., 5%) in order to make demand, you should join with other shareholders in order to develop the requisite percentage.

    If inspection rights are obtained without litigation (filing a petition in court), you should inspect the corporate expense records, probably with an attorney or an accountant. If waste or impropriety is discovered, you may consider a derivative suit. This, of course, will be preceded by a demand on the directors to take action to stop the waste and to cause the president to account for the misappropriation of funds. State law should be checked to determine whether other shareholders must be notified of the wrongdoing and planned lawsuit.

2. The question is one of corporate opportunity. Has the vice president seized for herself an opportunity belonging to the corporation?

Probably not; she had no authority to exceed $100,000. To have purchased the stone for a price in excess of that amount for the corporation would have violated the terms of her employment. She was impliedly authorized, therefore, to act for her own account and for her own opportunity.

3. The shareholders would probably lose their suit against Q. If he acted in the reasonable belief that his negative vote was in the corporate interest, if he acted in good faith, and exercised due care, he acted properly. We are not told of his other options; we do not know what other competent advice he may have received. We do not know the history of the violations or the reasonableness of the corporation's course of action.

18

CORPORATIONS: FINANCIAL STRUCTURE; SECURITIES REGULATION; LIABILITY OF ACCOUNTANTS

KEY TERMS

share (of stock) a proportionate ownership interest in a corporation or in its equity

stock a term used synonymously with "share"; also, the physical evidence of share ownership, the share certificate; also, the aggregate of corporate shares

dividend a distribution of cash or stock to the shareholders

blue sky laws state laws regulating the intrastate issuance and sale of securities

---

Up to this point we have thought of shareholders as the ultimate source of power in the corporate structure. In this chapter we consider their role as investors. Also, we distinguish and define the various sources of corporate financing and investigate the issuance, trading, and regulation of corporate securities.

CORPORATE FINANCIAL STRUCTURE

SOURCES OF CORPORATE FUNDS

> Funds to operate the corporation are derived in three principal ways:
> 1. By the issuance or sale of corporate debt securities (debt).
> 2. By the issuance of equity securities (equity)—e.g., via an IPO (initial public offering).
> 3. Through retained earnings.

• *CORPORATE DEBT SECURITIES*

The corporation may raise money by borrowing. Unless there is a special limitation or other provision in the charter, the decision to borrow is a matter for the board of directors and does not require shareholder approval. When the corporation borrows, it becomes a debtor; the holder of the security that it issues as evidence of this debt is a creditor.

Short-term borrowing is generally accomplished by the issuance of promissory notes or other commercial paper subject to the general principles of negotiable instruments law. **Debt securities** are of two main types: notes and bonds.

NOTES

The corporation's notes are promissory notes subject to the Uniform Commercial Code (see Chapters 10 and 11). These notes may be secured or unsecured.

BONDS

Bonds are written promises to pay a fixed sum of money at a set maturity date, with specified interest paid at stated intervals. Bonds may be secured by real or personal property. Bonds may be **debentures**, which are *unsecured*. If the corporation can redeem (pay off) the bond early, it is a **callable bond**. A **convertible bond** may be converted by its holder (at such time as he/she believes most favorable) into other securities of the corporation, such as preferred or common stock.

An indenture is a contract stating the terms under which debt securities are issued. For secured bonds, the indenture may describe, along with other contract provisions, the collateral and conditions of default. For debentures, the indenture may restrict other corporate borrowing or declaration of dividends, and place various other limitations on management in order to protect the debenture holder.

• *EQUITY SECURITIES*

Funds to operate the corporation may be generated by the sale of shares of stock, that is, **equity securities**. *The equity in the corporate enterprise, that is, the residual value of the assets after the payment of all debts following dissolution, belongs to the shareholders.*

Equity financing may open up participation in corporate ownership (and, indirectly, management) to additional investors. Sound corporate structure attempts to maintain a fair balance between debt and equity.

There are two classes of equity stock: common shares and preferred shares.

COMMON SHARES

In Chapters 16 and 17 all references to "shareholders" were to common shareholders (or stockholders). Holders of **common shares** participate in management control; however, these owners of the corporation are in for the "ride"—losses or gains in the value of their holdings follow the vicissitudes of the corporate enterprise. Common shareholders have a threefold interest in the corporation: (a) to vote for directors and on other fundamental matters, (b) to participate in the distribution of dividends, and (c) to share in the distribution of net assets (equity) after dissolution and liquidation.

PREFERRED SHARES

Preferred stock may be cumulative or noncumulative, and either participating or nonparticipating.

Advantages of Owning Preferred Shares

Preferred shareholders are "preferred" to common shareholders in two respects:

1. *In the distribution of dividends.* If the directors determine that a dividend is to be paid, holders of **preferred shares** may receive a specific percentage share of the dividend before the common stockholders are paid.

If the preferred stock is **noncumulative**, the preferred shareholders lose their dividend rights for years in which no dividend is declared; if the preferred stock is **cumulative**, unpaid dividends accumulate for years of nonpayment, and these accumulated dividends, plus current ones, are paid before common shareholders receive any dividend.

2. *In distribution upon liquidation.* The preferred shareholders may also be owners of part of the equity; upon dissolution and liquidation,

after the payment of debt, they may receive the first distribution of the net assets, before payment to the common stockholders, provided that such precedence is expressed in the articles of incorporation. Otherwise, the preferred shareholders participate pro rata with the holders of common stock upon liquidation. Not only does **participating preferred stock** receive preference when dividends are declared, but also holders of these shares may "double dip," that is, share also in the dividend to common stock on a pro rata basis.

Participating preferred shareholders receive, first, a distribution of net assets, and then a pro rata share of what remains. Holders of **nonparticipating preferred stock** do not share in this secondary distribution of any surplus but only have the initial liquidation preference (the first distribution of net assets).

Other Aspects of Preferred Shares

1. *Redemption*. The corporation may be given the right to purchase (redeem) preferred shares, even over the objection of their owners. The right of redemption by the corporation, as well as the price to be paid (the **call price**), is set out on the share certificate. The articles of incorporation provide for the right of redemption, if such right exists.

2. *Conversion*. If the articles of incorporation so provide, the corporation may, at its option and under the terms stated, convert preferred stock into common stock or convert from one class of preferred stock to another. Shareholders may also have rights (e.g., to acquire more shares) so that their interests are not *diluted*.

3. *Voting rights*. Generally, preferred shareholders have no voting rights. However, the articles of incorporation may give them such rights or may permit them to vote for directors in the event that the corporation fails to pay dividends.

CLASSIFICATION OF SHARES

- Authorized **shares**: the number of shares that the articles of incorporation permit the corporation to issue. Authorized shares may or may not be issued.

- Issued shares: authorized shares that have actually been sold to shareholders.

- Outstanding shares: the same as "issued stock," except that some issued shares may have been repurchased by the corporation after issuance. Such repurchased stock ceases to be "outstanding."

- Treasury shares: shares repurchased by the corporation.

- Canceled shares: shares that have been repurchased by the corporation and canceled. Such shares then cease to exist.

STOCK OPTIONS

Stock options grant their holders the right to purchase stock, at such time and price as are specified in the option. Stock options may be granted to employees, directors, and officers as incentive payments, and to purchasers of other classes of securities as an added inducement to buy.

• *RETAINED EARNINGS*

Retained earnings are earnings and profits not distributed to shareholders as dividends, but held back to be invested or "plowed back" into the corporate enterprise.

YOU SHOULD REMEMBER

There are three sources of corporate funds: debt, equity, and retained earnings. Debt securities consist of notes, bonds, and debentures. Notes are short-term promissory notes. Bonds are *secured* long-term securities; debentures are *unsecured* long-term securities.

Equity securities consist of common and preferred shares. Common shareholders participate in the election of directors and in other fundamental matters; preferred shareholders may be preferred over common shareholders in regard to dividends and to distribution upon liquidation. Preferred stock may be subject to redemption and conversion into other securities.

DIVIDENDS AND DISTRIBUTIONS

The expectation of a dividend or distribution is one basic reason for an investor to purchase the shares of a corporation.

A distribution of *cash* or *stock* is usually referred to as a **dividend**; distribution of *corporate assets*, while also a dividend, is generally referred to as a **distribution**. (Stock or shares of stock are not corporate assets.)

• *DECISION TO DECLARE A DIVIDEND*

The decision to declare a dividend or distribution is within the business judgment of the board of directors. This decision may not be "second guessed" by shareholders in the absence of director abuse or a wrong motive, such as deliberate withholding of accumulated cash without good business reasons. Once a dividend is declared by a proper resolution of the board, it is a legal debt of the corporation and is enforceable in a court of law.

• *FORM OF DIVIDEND*

The dividend may take the form of cash, other property or assets, or shares of stock. Real estate, merchandise, or other tangibles may be distributed to the shareholders.

A **stock split** is not a stock dividend, but merely an across-the-board aggregation of additional shares for shares already held (e.g., for every two shares one owns, an additional share is issued to that owner—someone owning 5 shares would end up with 7.5 shares). A stock split does not alter the total value of an individual stockholder's investment.

However, a common purpose of a stock split is to reduce the per share market price in order to induce more trading and a resulting higher price per share.

• *RESTRICTIONS ON DIVIDENDS*

If a corporation has borrowed large sums of money, creditors may have restricted (by means of "loan agreements") its ability to declare dividends, particularly without the prior approval of the creditors. Moreover, all states prohibit the payment of a dividend or other distribution if such payment would render the corporation insolvent, that is, unable to pay its debts as they become due in the ordinary course of business. Further statutory restrictions vary among the states; most states require that dividends be paid from earned surplus. A few states (including Delaware) permit the payment of **nimble dividends**, that is, payment from current earnings even though there are debts outstanding from prior years.

• *EFFECT OF ILLEGAL DIVIDEND OR DISTRIBUTION*

Directors who vote in favor of an illegal dividend are jointly and severally liable for the illegal portion of the dividend, that is, the amount by which the dividend exceeds the legally permissible limit. ("Joint and several" means that each director can be held fully responsible for any payment, but whoever actually pays is entitled to then collect contributions from whichever other directors were also liable.) Directors who rely in good faith upon the financial data and statements of accountants and financial officers of the company are not liable. Only shareholders who know, or ought to know, that the dividend is illegal can be made to return it.

CONSIDERATION FOR SHARES

• *PRESENT VERSUS FUTURE CONSIDERATION*

Stock may be paid for in cash, by check, with tangible or intangible property, or by services *previously* rendered. The value to be placed on noncash items (property or services) is usually considered to be a matter for the good-faith judgment of the members of the board fixing the value, although some states consider this value to be a question of fact to be determined by a jury in the event of litigation.

In some states, contracts for future services or benefits or for promissory notes (including postdated checks) are not good considerations for shares. The trend, though, has been to permit such "future consideration"; MBCA amendments (1979) and the RMBCA both allow it.

• *PAR AND NO-PAR SHARES*

A *par share has a specific dollar amount indicated on the share certificate.* The par value can be any amount chosen by the board (or by the incorporators), and may or may not reflect the actual value, but the par value must be set out in the articles of incorporation.

> The corporation must receive, as a minimum, the par-value price for each share it sells.

No-par shares are issued for any amount that the board assigns to such shares, arbitrarily or otherwise. Consideration received for shares in excess of the par value is **capital surplus**. With respect to no-par shares, the directors may arbitrarily assign a designated portion of the consideration for such shares to capital surplus, that is, surplus that may be used in the calculation of dividends. The excess of consideration over par value, or the designated portion of the consideration assigned to capital surplus in the case of no-par value, is an important factor in determining the lawfulness of a dividend.

• *TREASURY SHARES*

Treasury shares (shares issued and then repurchased by the corporation) may be reissued for an amount equal to their fair value even though this amount may be less than the par or stated value.

• *DISCOUNT SHARES*

"Discount shares" are shares issued for less than par value or stated value.

> A shareholder who purchases shares at discount from the corporation is liable to the corporation for the amount of the discount.

A shareholder buying discounted shares from another shareholder is liable for the amount of the discount only if he/she knew that the shares had been originally purchased at discount.

SHARE SUBSCRIPTIONS

A **subscription** is a promise to buy shares at a specified price. Although such a promise may be made after the corporation has been formed and is a going concern, most of the legal problems associated with subscriptions involve preincorporation subscriptions.

> Since the promoters require assurance that sufficient equity capital will be raised to support the corporate venture, it is important that subscribers be bound to their promises to purchase stock that the corporation (not yet formed) will issue.

Section 6.20 of the RMBCA deals fully with share subscriptions and should be consulted as authoritative even though its provisions may not have been adopted in a specific state. *This section provides that, if the corporation is yet to be organized, a subscription is irrevocable for a period of 6 months unless the subscription agreement provides otherwise or unless all subscribers consent to revocation.* The section also provides that, unless the subscription agreement specifies otherwise, the price shall be paid in full at the time of the agreement or in installments at times determined by the board of directors.

Under the MBCA, RMBCA, and the other corporate law of most states, preincorporation subscription may result in a binding contract if all conditions for a contract are present. This contract may be enforced by promoters and creditors relying on it. This may be true even though the corporation is not yet formed, since the *promoters and their creditors* may legally enter into agreements looking toward the formation of the corporate enterprise and the creation of its underlying capital. Preincorporation share subscribers should expect that persons extending credit to the venture may seek redress from subscribers if obligations are not paid by the promoters.

ISSUANCE OF SHARES

A **share** in a corporation is a fractional interest in the ownership of the corporate entity.

> The share interest may be physically represented by a share certificate (a stock certificate), or it may be uncertificated under general state corporate law or under the provisions of the MBCA.

In the modern electronic, computerized world documentary transfer is not always practicable. Revised Article 8 of the Uniform Commercial Code (promulgated in 1994 and since enacted in all 50 states) deals with investment securities and specifically recognizes that such securities may be uncertificated but states that the share or participation "may be registered upon books maintained for that purpose by or on behalf of the issuer" (Section 8-102).

The issuer of a certificated security (which, of course, includes stock or share certificates) must maintain, or cause to be maintained, books of registration of share ownership.

UCC 8-207 provides that the issuer may treat the registered owner as the person "exclusively entitled to vote, to receive notifications, and otherwise to exercise all rights and powers of an owner." UCC 8-405 permits the owner of a lost, destroyed, or stolen certificate to obtain a new certificate if (1) the owner notifies the issuer before the issuer learns of a protected purchaser now holding the certificate and (2) the owner has posted a sufficient indemnity bond.

• *TRANSFER OF SECURITIES*

Article 8 of the UCC also governs the transfer and registration of investment securities. Share certificates, bonds, debentures, and corporate notes are covered by its provisions. Article 8 provides that, even though a certified security (certificate) meets the requirements of Article 3 (Negotiable Instruments), a security is nevertheless governed by the provisions of Article 8.

Securities certificates are either in registered form (registered with the issuer, usually the corporation, in a specific name) or in blank (payable to the holder). A registered certificate is transferred by delivery plus indorsement or by delivery plus the execution of a stock power (or assignment).

If a share certificate is transferred without designating a transferee by name, the certificate is a **street certificate** and may be further transferred by delivery only, without indorsement.

The transfer of a certificate may, however, be restricted. Restrictions may be intended to maintain voting controls, to preserve an S corporation or a close corporation, or to maintain exemption from federal or state securities laws requiring registration for *public* offerings. Restrictions on transfer are accomplished by a number of legal devices, such as options, rights of first refusal, and buy-and-sell agreements. UCC 8-204 requires that the restriction be noted conspicuously on the certificate or—for uncertificated securities—in the initial transaction statement, unless the transferee has actual knowledge of the restriction.

YOU SHOULD REMEMBER

The decision to declare a dividend is within the business judgment of the board of directors. The dividend may take the form of cash or of other property or assets.

A dividend cannot be paid if the corporation is insolvent or if the payment would make the corporation insolvent. Most states require that the dividend be paid from earned surplus.

In most states, shares must be paid for in cash or other valuable present consideration, or by services previously rendered. If the shares have a par value, that value establishes a minimum price. No-par shares are issued for an amount established by the board of directors. Shares may not be sold at a discount; otherwise, the purchaser may be liable for the discount.

Share subscriptions obligate the subscriber to purchase the stock at the time of the subscription agreement or in installments as determined by the board. Promoters and creditors who rely on the subscription agreement may enforce its terms.

Share interest may be shown by a share certificate, or the share may be uncertified. Names of both certified and uncertified owners of securities are registered in books maintained by the issuer, and these persons are treated as the owners for all legal purposes.

Free transfer of securities may be restricted, but the restriction must be noted on the share certificates.

SECURITIES REGULATION

Statutory regulation of securities operates within three broad categories (although there are other important but more specifically directed statutes):

1. The Securities Act of 1933.
2. The Securities Exchange Act of 1934.
3. Securities regulation within the various states.

THE SECURITIES ACT OF 1933

The Securities Act of 1933, a federal "consumer protection law" for investors, requires that the public be given complete and full disclosure about *new securities* being offered for sale. This act is administered by the Securities and Exchange Commission (SEC), established in 1934.

Congressional investigation during the early 1930s into the stock market crash led to passage of the Securities Act of 1933. The goal of this act is twofold: (1) to assure the investor of the opportunity to make informed decisions, and (2) to protect honest enterprises seeking capital through public investment.

• *DEFINITION OF "SECURITY"*

The Securities Act defines "security" not only as a note, stock, bond, warrant, right, debenture, stock subscription, voting trust certificate, limited partnership interest, or evidence of indebtedness, but also as an "investment contract," or a "fractional undivided interest in oil, gas, or other mineral rights, or, in general, any interest or instrument commonly known as a 'security'." This broad statutory reach is designed to prevent circumvention of the law by the form of the document; rules of contract and statutory construction such as *ejusdem generis* ("of the same kind or class") or *noscitur a sociss* (words are explained "by their company with other words") require that general words and phrases be construed in their broad generality within the scope of Congressional goals and purposes. Statutes enacted to remedy widespread abuses or alleviate large societal concerns are liberally construed to achieve their legislative objectives.

In the 1946 case of *Securities and Exchange Commission v. W. J. Howey Co.*, 328 U.S. 293, the Supreme Court laid down four requirements to bring an "investment contract" within the definition of "security": (1) an investment of money, (2) a common enterprise, (3) the expectation of profits, and (4) profits solely from the managerial efforts of persons besides the investor (i.e., a promoter or third party). In the *Howey* case, contracts offering investors acreage in orange groves to be cultivated and marketed by others were held to be "investment contracts" and consequently "securities" within reach of the 1933 act.

However, the Securities Act does not apply to pension funds, insurance, stock dividends, bank accounts, warranty deeds to real property, interests in joint ventures for selling real estate, or distributorships or franchises (unless the distributor or supposed franchisee has no obligation and merely reaps profits).

Although the reach of the 1933 act must be fully understood, most of the cases, both at the Securities and Exchange Commission (SEC) level and in the courts, pertain to stocks, bonds, debentures, and traditional securities.

• *SECURITIES EXEMPT BY STATUTE*

Section 3(a) of the Securities Act exempts a number of securities (although administrative agencies other than the SEC impose regulation in some cases):

1. Any security issued or guaranteed by the United States, by any state, by any political subdivision of any state, or by a public instrumentality of any state. Municipal bonds and industrial revenue bonds, as well as "authority" bonds and securities are excluded under this exemption.

2. A note or draft that has a maturity date at time of issue not exceeding nine months.

3. Securities issued by an organization operated exclusively for religious, educational, benevolent, fraternal, charitable, or reformatory purposes, and not for profit.

4. Securities of domestic banks, savings and loan associations, building and loan associations, cooperative banks, and the like.

5. Securities whose issuance is regulated under other federal laws.

6. Securities issued by a receiver or trustee in bankruptcy.

7. Any insurance or endowment policy or annuity contract issued by a regulated insurance company.

8. Securities issued for conversion or exchange with existing shares of a security holder where no commission or other remuneration is paid or given, directly or indirectly.

9. Securities issued for local (intrastate) investment only. This exemption applies to the local financing of an issuer having at least 80% of its gross revenues and 80% of its assets in that state. Not only must at least 80% of the offering proceeds be used in state but the offering must only be to investors in that one state. In-state purchasers cannot buy for the purpose of reselling to persons outside the state. Moreover, regardless of an investor's original intent, SEC Rule 147 bars absolutely any out-of-state resales for at least nine months. While delivery of shares to a resident temporarily out of the state is permitted, just one sale or offer to sell to a nonresident (even a friend or relative) will vitiate the exemption status.

• *REGISTRATION OF SECURITIES*

Registration is the heart of the 1933 act.

THE TWO ASPECTS OF REGISTRATION

Registration Statement

The registration statement, filed with the SEC, *contains all relevant information* about the securities to be offered, the issuer and the business involved, and plans for use of the dollar proceeds of the issuance. The registration statement makes the party executing it (chief executive officer, financial officer, board of directors) liable for errors in the statement, which becomes effective on the 20th day after its filing with the SEC, although this date may be advanced by the SEC. Substantive amendments may require a recommencement of the 20-day period.

Statutory Prospectus

The statutory prospectus for potential investors is derived from the registration statement. It is a comprehensive and detailed booklet concerning the security, its issuers, the use of monies to be generated, the terms of reimbursement to the investors if minimum financing (as defined) is not obtained, the prospects of success of the venture, financial statements, and other matters, including special items that may be required by the SEC and as provided for in SEC Regulation C.

> The prospectus is an informing, not a promoting, document, and is intended to enable the prospective purchaser to evaluate fully the prospects, both good and bad, of the proposed venture.

The booklet must state the following on its outside cover in boldface roman type:

"THESE SECURITIES HAVE NOT BEEN APPROVED OR DISAPPROVED BY THE SECURITIES AND EXCHANGE COMMISSION, NOR HAS THE COMMISSION PASSED UPON THE ACCURACY OR ADEQUACY OF THIS PROSPECTUS. ANY REPRESENTATION TO THE CONTRARY IS A CRIMINAL OFFENSE."

COMMUNICATION WITH INVESTORS

Before the filing date there should be no communication with the public or potential investors concerning the planned offering, although Rule 135 of the SEC permits the publication of a limited informational notice. After the filing date, but before the effective date (i.e., during the waiting period), the securities may be offered, but not yet sold: (1) orally (in person or by telephone); (2) by certain summaries of information from the registration statement; or (3) by a **tombstone advertisement** that identifies the security, its price, and the party by whom orders will be executed.

During the waiting period, a *preliminary prospectus*, tentatively reviewed by the SEC, must accompany any *written* offer. This preliminary prospectus is known as a **red herring prospectus** because of a mandatory red-ink warning on its cover that the registration is incomplete and that the securities are not yet available for sale. Even though the SEC may finally allow the prospectus, such allowance is not a "blessing," and the issuer is responsible for the fullness and accuracy of the document.

> After the effective date, the securities, accompanied by the final pro-
> spectus, may be freely offered to investors.

• *EXEMPTED TRANSACTIONS*

Section 4 of the Securities Act exempts transactions (a) by any person
other than an issuer or underwriter (or persons acting under the control of an issuer or underwriter) and (b) by an issuer that are not public
offerings (private offerings). For example, without having to furnish any
information, an issuer under Securities Act section 4(6) may privately
offer up to $5 million in shares solely to accredited investors (i.e., statu-
torily defined businesses or wealthy investors).

BROKERS AND DEALERS

The Securities Act is intended to cover the issuance and original distribution of securities.

> The act does not cover *trading transactions* or transactions involving
> persons other than issuers and underwriters (persons dealing with the
> issuer as part of the plan of original distribution).

Brokers' and dealers' transactions are exempt to the extent that these
transactions are not part of the plan of distribution.

PRIVATE OFFERINGS

In differentiating a public offering from a private offering, the SEC follows general guidelines permitting, as exemptions, offerings to no more
than 25 persons, *provided that such a small offering is not a scheme to
promote a wide distribution in circumvention of the Securities Act*. Also,
the exemption pertains *to the number of offerees and not to the number
of purchasers*. Thus a meeting with 40 persons to promote a small "private offering," of whom only 3 persons actually consummate a purchase,
would constitute a violation of the 1933 act.

> The burden of proof is upon the issuer that any offering is not a
> public offering, no matter how few the offerees or how small the dollar
> amount of issue.

• *SECURITIES EXEMPTED BY THE SEC*

Section 3(b) of *the Securities Act provides that the Securities and
Exchange Commission may prescribe exemptions applicable to issues*

of limited dollar amounts. Section 4 of the act provides, however, that there can be no advertising or public solicitation in connection with such a dollar-exempt transaction. Furthermore, the issuer must file "such notice with the Commission as the Commission shall prescribe."

The SEC has issued, among others, the following regulations under this section:

REGULATION A (SMALL PUBLIC OFFERINGS)

This regulation permits a simplified and limited registration for an issuer's public offerings of up to $50 million of securities in any 12-month period. The seller must notify the SEC at least 20 days before the initial date of offering, furnishing general information concerning the issuer, the nature of the securities, the purpose of the issue, and a description of the arrangement (if any) to return investors' funds if the financial objectives are not met. The seller must also distribute to potential investors an offering circular, containing essentially the same information as the notification to the SEC. Offers may be solicited, but no sales can occur until the 20-day waiting period is over.

Only privately held U.S. or Canadian corporations can offer and sell Regulation A offerings. Investment companies; businesses issuing oil, gas, or mineral rights; and firms whose owners have violated the securities laws (designated "bad boys" under SEC Rule 262) cannot rely on Regulation A.

Under the Jumpstart Our Business Startups Act (JOBS Act) of 2012, an "Emerging Growth Company" (EGC) is exempt from many securities registration requirements. The JOBS Act's Title I (also known as "the IPO On Ramp") provides that the EGC only needs to provide two years of audited financial statements (not the usual three years) and can follow a streamlined process with far fewer financial disclosures. The EGC can privately communicate with accredited investors to "test the waters" before actually going forward with an initial public offering (an IPO), and it can file with the SEC a *confidential draft registration statement* that—if the proposed IPO is withdrawn—means any confidential business information remains safeguarded from public disclosure. The EGC status expires and it must become a publicly reporting company either five years after its IPO or once the EGC has over 2,000 shareholders of record (or if over 500 of those shareholders are unaccredited). To qualify as an EGC, the company must have *less than* $1 billion in annual revenue (to be adjusted for inflation every five years), $1 billion in debt, and—after the IPO—$700 million in stock outstanding. It also must not have gone public more than five years earlier.

The JOBS Act permits *crowdfunding*, a method to raise capital from many smaller investors in which the EGC uses a website intermediary (a *funding portal*) registered with the SEC. The EGC can raise a maximum of $1 million during any 12-month period, with investors limited to no more than $10,000 in various crowdfunding investments (there are lesser maximum amounts for investors when their annual incomes and net worth are each under $100,000). For a company's crowdfunded revenue under $100,000, no accountant review is required; for EGCs intending to raise between $100,000 and $500,000, a certified public accounting (CPA) firm must independently review its financial statements; and, if the EGC intends to raise over $500,000, it must have an independent audit by a CPA firm. Crowdfunding offerings are subject to the federal securities laws' antifraud provisions.

REGULATIONS B & C

Regulation B covers oil and gas securities. Regulation C deals with general registration requirements, registration by foreign governments, and other rules.

REGULATION D (PRIVATE SALES OFFERINGS)

This regulation is intended to simplify offerings to *informed, sophisticated investors* and to *accredited investors* (Rule 501) such as national banks, insurance companies, private business development companies, investment companies, the issuer's executive officers or directors or partners, registered broker-dealers, business entities or trusts with total assets more than $5 million, and other persons clearly defined in the regulation (e.g., individuals whose net worth exceeds $1 million or whose annual income regularly exceeds $200,000). Under Regulation D, the SEC has promulgated rules simplifying the SEC notification process for certain private offerings; these simplified rules permit filings within 15 days after the first sale.

Rule	Amount	Type of Issuer	Resale	Offering
504	Up to $1 million in any 12-month period (no more than $500,000 of which can be without registration under a state's securities laws)	Private, non-investment company	Permitted, if in compliance with state blue sky law	No limit on number of purchasers, but offering may not be by an investment company, nor may it be publicly promoted unless in compliance with state blue sky law requiring presale delivery of disclosure documents.
505	Up to $5 million in any 12-month period	Non-investment company	Restricted	No limit on number of accredited purchasers; permits up to 35 additional nonaccredited purchasers, provided they receive an offering circular (a private

Rule	Amount	Type of Issuer	Resale	Offering
				placement memorandum giving information such as audited financial statements to all purchasers if there are any unaccredited purchasers) and that all purchasers have the opportunity to ask questions of and receive answers concerning the offering's terms; no public promotion (offers can only be from private non-investment companies)
506	Unlimited	All issuers	Restricted	No limit as to accredited investors, and up to 35 nonaccredited investors; the issuer reasonably believes, immediately before making any sale, that each nonaccredited investor, either alone or with his/her purchaser representative, has sufficient experience to evaluate the risks and merits of that investment (i.e., is a sophisticated investor)

The same private placement memorandum is required as under Rule 505 if there are any unaccredited investors. Again, investors must have the chance to ask questions and receive answers. Because, as with Rule 505, no complex offering documents are required if the sales are only to accredited investors, but—unlike Rule 505—sales are permitted in excess of $5 million, the Rule 506 exemption is the one most commonly relied upon in venture capital financings.

RULE 701 OFFERINGS TO EMPLOYEES

Rule 701 exempts offers and sales of securities by privately held companies (1) pursuant to a written compensatory benefit plan for employees, directors, general partners, trustees (if the issuer is a business trust), officers, consultants, or advisers; or (2) pursuant to a written contract relating to the compensation of such persons. To obtain this offering, consultants or advisers must render bona fide services unrelated to the offer or sale of securities in a capital-raising transaction. Issuers of these exempt Rule 701 plans must provide every plan participant and contractor with a copy of the plan/contract (no other disclosure is necessary). These exempt plans include purchase, savings, stock appreciation, option, bonus, profit-sharing, thrift incentive, and pension plans.

Rule 701 securities offerings cannot exceed, in a twelve-month period, the greater of (a) $1 million, (b) 15% of the issuer's total assets, or (3) 15% of the outstanding securities of the type of class being offered. Once a sale brings the aggregate sales under Rule 701 to an amount above $100,000, the issuer must file a Rule 701 disclosure form with the SEC within 30 days (and annually thereafter).

Issued Rule 701 shares can, 90 or more days after the corporation went public, be sold by these securities holders to the public without any registration (an exception to the one-year holding period that is normally the minimum under Rule 144). This expanded right of resale does not apply to the corporation's officers, directors, or 10% or greater shareholders.

• *RESALE OF RESTRICTED SECURITIES*

SEC Rule 144 allows the purchaser to resell restricted securities only after full beneficial ownership (free from debt) for one year, and provided that information about the issuer is publicly available. The seller may thereafter sell only a limited amount of the securities in any three-month period during the next year. Rule 144A, adopted in 1990, provides further resale rights for sales to qualified institutional buyers (large-scale securities investors such as financial institutions, registered broker-dealers, and major corporations).

• *CIVIL LIABILITY*

Section 11 of the 1933 Securities Act provides for civil liability for the following:

1. Sale of an unregistered security required to have been registered.
2. Sale of a registered security without delivery of a statutory prospectus.
3. Offer of a sale before the filing (or approval) of a registration statement.
4. Inclusion of a false statement in the registration statement.
5. Omission of a material fact from the registration statement.

In the event of an improper offer or sale (item 1, 2, or 3 above), the purchaser's remedy is recission of the transaction or damages. The penalty for inadequate information or a false registration statement is damages: the price the purchaser paid for the securities less the market price of the securities at the time of the lawsuit. Damages may be assessed against the issuer, the chief executive officer, the chief financial officer, the chief accounting officer, the directors, the underwriter, and the experts (auditors or lawyers) who certified the statement or rendered an opinion with regard to its sufficiency. The *issuer* has no defense to a civil suit other than that the purchaser knew about the misstatement or omission when it purchased the security. Other defendants may use both that defense and also a "*due diligence*" *defense*: proof by the defendant (the defendant's burden of proof) that after a reasonable investigation the defendant had reasonable grounds to believe, and did believe, that the registration statement was true and contained no material omission. Defendant experts must not act negligently (e.g., auditors failing to comply with generally accepted auditing standards). Non-experts meet their due diligence defense for parts contributed by experts if non-experts had no reason to believe, and did not believe, that the expertised parts misstated or omitted any material fact. (Ordinarily, non-experts need not investigate the experts' work.)

For non-user defendants, three defenses to Section 11 liability are:

1. the misstatement proved immaterial;
2. the investor knew about the mistake but bought anyway; or
3. the "due diligence" defense—(i) after "reasonable investigation" the defendant reasonably believed that the registration statements were true (what is reasonable depends upon the defendant's financial sophistication and degree of involvement in preparing the registration statement); (ii) non-experts who reasonably believe an expert need not investigate the expert's statements.

• *CRIMINAL LIABILITY*

Willful violation of the Securities Act of 1933 or of rules and regulations promulgated by the SEC pursuant to the act carries a maximum fine of $10,000 and up to 5 years' imprisonment.

• *ANTIFRAUD PROVISIONS*

Section 12 of the Securities Act imposes broad liability *for any person* (1) selling securities without a registration (unless exempt); (2) selling securities before their effective date of registration; or (3) offering or selling any security (whether registered or not) by means of an oral statement or a prospectus that misstates or omits a material fact. Liability also extends to parties that solicit such securities sales and who have a financial interest in those sales. Unlike for Section 11, liability under Section 12 requires privity: the right of private legal action extends only to the immediate purchaser. The defendant may escape liability if it could not reasonably have known of the falsity or omission. Except for exempted securities transactions, purchasers are entitled to recission; as with Section 11, plaintiffs need not prove that they acted in reliance on the wrongful conduct.

YOU SHOULD REMEMBER

The Securities Act of 1933 requires that the public be given full information about new securities being offered for sale. This information is provided by filing a registration statement with the SEC and by preparing and furnishing a statutory prospectus for all persons to whom the securities are offered.

The 1933 act does not cover:

1. Securities exempt by statute.
2. Exempted transactions: (a) trading transactions and (b) private offerings.
3. Securities in issues of limited dollar amounts under SEC-defined exemptions.

The Securities Act provides for both civil and criminal penalties.

THE SECURITIES EXCHANGE ACT OF 1934

The Securities Exchange Act of 1934 is a federal statute concerned with *existing securities* in the marketplace. This statute established the Securities and Exchange Commission to administer federal securities laws, including the 1933 Securities Act.

• *PURPOSES OF THE ACT*

There are four major goals:

1. To regulate the securities market and securities exchanges.
2. To make available to persons who buy and sell securities information relating to the issuers of such securities.
3. To prevent fraud in trading in securities.
4. To prevent the use of insider information for the private gain of a privileged few, to the detriment of outsiders.

• *IMPORTANT PROVISIONS*

REGULATION OF EXCHANGES AND BROKERS

The Securities Exchange Act created the SEC and charged it with responsibility for administering the 1933 Securities Act and other federal securities laws. It requires that all stock exchanges, over-the-counter brokers, and dealers register with the SEC. A 1990 statute, the Market Reform Act, permits the SEC to regulate trading practices and even suspend trading during periods of extreme volatility (e.g., when program trading causes the stock market to rise or fall suddenly). The 1991 Securities Enforcement Remedies and Penney Reform Act further provides the SEC with far greater powers than almost any other administrative agency: authority to impose large fines, issue cease-and-desist orders, and obtain a federal court order barring a securities defrauder from ever serving as an officer or director of a publicly held corporation.

REGISTRATION OF TRADED SECURITIES

Every issuer with a 1933 Act registration or with securities traded on a national stock exchange must be registered with the SEC. If an issuer has gross assets in excess of $10 million and at least 2,000 stockholders (or at least 500 shareholders who are not accredited investors), securities traded in the over-the-counter market must be registered with the SEC.

REGISTRATION REQUIREMENTS

Registration requires disclosure of: financial and organizational information concerning the business; terms governing outstanding securities; names of underwriters and security holders with at least 10 percent of any class of registered security; and balance sheets and profit and loss statements for each of the three preceding fiscal years.

UPDATING REPORTS

1. *Annual report.* The 10-K report to the SEC includes audited financial statements for the year of filing, together with certain required information about the business, its management, and its outstanding securities.

2. *Quarterly report.* The 10-Q report is a quarterly, unaudited operating statement with an updated statement covering capitalization and shareholders' equity.

3. *"Current" report.* The 8-K report is an update covering any change in the amount of securities, any default under the terms of any issue of securities, an acquisition or disposition of assets, a company bankruptcy or receivership, a change in company control or in the business' certifying accountants or in the fiscal year calendar, amendments to or waivers of the company's code of ethics, a

temporary suspension of trading under the company's employee benefit plans, a revaluation of assets, and details concerning any other materially important event relevant to the larger aspects of the business. It must be filed within four business days after a reported material event has occurred. Such events are so frequent that a mandatory 8-K filing is very common.

The 22 reportable 8-K events include a broad range of items affecting gains and losses. Among the major developments requiring immediate disclosure are the departure and hiring of senior executives and directors, any mergers and acquisitions, all changes in the bylaws, and transactions that have contingent liabilities that could unexpectedly affect a company's financial condition, entry into or termination of an important agreement, the creation or increase of an off-balance sheet obligation, unregistered sales of securities, and modifications to the rights of security holders.

The reports must be filed electronically with the SEC and are immediately publicly available. A reporting company's filing obligations are suspended if: (1) it has fewer than 300 shareholders of record (1,200 shareholders for banks or bank holding companies); or (2) it has fewer than 500 shareholders of record and less than $10 million in total assets for each of its last three fiscal years.

Foreign corporations file annual reports with the SEC on Form 20-F or, for larger Canadian companies, Form 40-F. They do not have to file quarterly reports or 8-K reports. Still, some foreign companies voluntarily file Forms 10-K, 10-Q, and 8-K, mainly to compete with domestic companies by providing a body of more detailed, more frequent, disclosure documents comparable to those furnished by their U.S. competitors.

The SEC has held that corporations do not have to disclose merger negotiations if

1. the corporation did not make any prior disclosures about those negotiations;
2. no other SEC rules require disclosure; *and*
3. management determines that disclosure would jeopardize completion of the merger transaction.

STATEMENTS BY 5% SHAREHOLDERS

Pursuant to Section 13(d) of the Securities Exchange Act, the SEC requires the beneficial owner of more than 5% of any class of security registered under the act to file a notification statement with the commission, with the issuer, and with each exchange on which the security is listed. The purpose of this statement is to inform potential investors of a possible attempt to take over corporate management.

• *PROXY SOLICITATIONS*

The SEC has established rules for the solicitation of **proxies** by management, those opposing management, and other persons involved in solicitations, consents, and authorizations, directed toward holders of registered securities or of debt securities. The proxy rules establish disclosure requirements to be met before solicitation, and—before any meeting—mandate full disclosure of material facts to stockholders (including shareholder proposals). SEC Rule 14a-3 requires that the proxy statement be accompanied by the annual report if the election of directors is to come before the meeting.

• *TENDER OFFERS*

A tender offer is a bidder's public offer to buy a company's equity securities directly from its shareholders at a specified price for a fixed time period. Opposing offers are called *hostile tender offers*. The Williams Act (1968) amended the Securities Exchange Act to require bidders and target companies to provide shareholders with the information needed to make an informed decision. Most states have enacted statutes tending to protect the target company from a hostile takeover.

• *INSIDER TRANSACTIONS AND FRAUD*

An **insider** is a director, officer, or owner of 10% or more of the corporate stock of an issuer listed on a national stock exchange. Section 16(b) of the Securities Exchange Act prohibits an insider from engaging in "short-swing" trading based on inside information not available to the public. The Securities Exchange Act provides that any profit realized by the insider because of either a purchase and sale or a sale and purchase of securities within any period of less than 6 months shall be recoverable by the issuer.

For purposes of the regulations, "insider" includes not only "top management" and controlling shareholders, but may include also any employee, broker, dealer, or consultant with access to special information. It may include relatives, friends, or other "tippees" of directors, executives, or other corporate fiduciaries. The tippees' liability arises from trading based on their receiving (and not disclosing) confidential, inside information that they knew or should have known was nonpublic and that materially affects the value of the corporation's securities such as the planned sale of the corporation or its assets, the issuance of dividends, mineral discoveries, or know-how and technological breakthroughs. Tippees are liable for their own inside trades (profits and penalties), and tippers also are liable for their tippees' profits. A tippee can in turn tip other persons (remote tippees), with the original tippee now also a tipper.

Under 1984 and 1988 federal statutes, persons convicted of insider trading now face substantially harsher maximum penalties: up to $1 million in fines ($2.5 million for corporations), prison sentences up to ten years, and civil penalties that, in effect, could require payments of four times the profits gained or losses avoided. *SEC Rule 10b-5* permits the SEC and private parties to sue for rescission and damages those who have *knowingly* (with *scienter*) engaged in fraud and thereby gained an unfair advantage in buying or selling securities. The rule, and Securities Exchange Act Section 10(b), apply to *any* communications with investors. Privity of contract is unnecessary, but 10b-5 claimants must show that they relied on the defendant's wrongful conduct and that they actually purchased or sold securities while so relying.

In *Central Bank of Denver v. First Interstate Bank of Denver*, 511 U.S. 164 (1994), the Supreme Court held that there is no implied private right of action for secondary, aiding and abetting liability under 10b-5. Investors instead can only sue *primary* violators, who directly misstated or omitted material facts. Furthermore, in *Stoneridge Investment Partners, LLC v. Scientific-Atlanta, Inc.*, 552 U.S. 148 (2008), the Supreme Court rejected the concept of "scheme liability"—that secondary defendants, such as banks, accountants, or attorneys, can be liable for taking actions integral to a fraudulent scheme undertaken in conjunction with the primary culprit, the party that communicated directly with investors. Under the *Stoneridge* holding, to win its 10-b case, a plaintiff must show that it actually relied on a defendant's deceptive acts; the alternative, *presumed* reliance, is only sufficient for a winning 10-b or 10b-5 case if (1) the defendant had a duty to disclose information, and it failed to do so, or (2) the defendant's allegedly deceptive statements became public (the *fraud-on-the-market doctrine*). Most defrauded investors cannot show that they meet one of these presumed reliance standards, and thus they cannot successfully sue bankers, lawyers, or other third parties who did not directly mislead investors but instead worked with corporations (e.g., Enron) that did so. Moreover, in *Halliburton Co. v. Erica P. John Fund, Inc.*, 573 U.S. __ (2014), the U.S. Supreme Court held that, before a class of plaintiffs is certified in a 10-b case based on the *fraud-on-the-market doctrine*, the defendant has the right to present evidence about the alleged misinformation's impact on stock prices; "event studies," for example, may play a central role in determining whether there was a statistically significant change in the company's stock price when the misrepresentation was made or disclosed.

Statute 10-b & Rule 10b-5: Anti-Fraud Securities Laws
Very broad in scope, these laws cover almost any type of securities transaction (*anything connected to interstate commerce*). To win, plaintiffs must show that the defendant had *scienter* (knew or should have known that there was a misrepresentation). Under 10-b or 10b-5, only actual buyers or sellers of securities have standing to sue.

• *MARGIN REQUIREMENTS*

Margin requirements are restrictions placed on the percentage of the value of securities that may be borrowed to purchase the securities. The term **margin** refers to the amount that must be paid in cash. These restrictions are created to prevent the excessive, large-scale use of credit for the purchase of, and investment in, securities. The Securities Exchange Act provides that the Board of Governors of the Federal Reserve System shall prescribe rules and regulations with respect to margins and may set lower or higher margins (up to 100%) for securities investment.

• *FOREIGN CORRUPT PRACTICES ACT (FCPA)*

The FCPA, a 1977 amendment to the Securities Exchange Act, is discussed in this book in Chapter 28.

• *THE PRIVATE SECURITIES LITIGATION REFORM ACT*

The Private Securities Litigation Reform Act of 1995 (PSLRA), among other things:

1. requires plaintiffs, for cases involving securities fraud, to present in their complaint details "giving rise to a strong inference" of fraud—scienter (as the Supreme Court held in *Tellabs, Inc. v. Makor Issues & Rights Ltd.*, 127 U.S. 2499 (2007), plaintiffs would have to put forth a "cogent inference" of the intent to deceive "at least as compelling as any opposing inference of nonfraudulent intent");

2. provides that any discovery is frozen pending a judicial ruling on a defendant's motion to dismiss;

3. substitutes proportionate liability for the old law, under which every liable party was responsible for all damages; in most circumstances, under the PSLRA, the amount for which, say, a defendant accounting or law firm could be held liable would be only a fraction of the 100% for which it might previously have been sued; and

4. creates a "safe harbor" zone of immunity for corporate forecasts—companies are not to be liable for inaccurate "forward-looking"

statements that previewed earnings and products and were accompanied by meaningful, cautionary assertions (not merely boilerplate disclaimers) identifying important factors that could cause materially different results.

Responding to an increase in securities fraud cases in state court by plaintiffs seeking to avoid PSLRA standards, Congress in 1998 enacted the Securities Litigation Uniform Standards Act (SLUSA) requiring removal of many such cases to federal court: Only state securities cases that are not class actions and do not involve more than 50 plaintiffs can be tried in state court. However, there are a few exceptions—lawsuits by states or local governments, claims based on a contract between the issues and an indenture trustee, and the *Delaware carve-out*. This last exception lets shareholders otherwise barred by the SLUSA bring: (1) a state law derivative suit against directors or officers, such as for breach of fiduciary duty; or (2) a suit against a corporation and its directors if (a) the suit is based on the law of the state in which the issuer is incorporated; (b) the suit involves the issuer's communication to its shareholders about the sale of the issuer's securities; and (c) the suit concerns specified shareholder decisions, such as a response to a tender offer or the exercise of appraisal rights (dissenters' rights).

• *THE SARBANES-OXLEY ACT*

In 2002, Congress enacted a long and detailed statute, the Sarbanes-Oxley Act (SOX), in response to a rash of corporate scandals. The act is meant to prevent or reduce accounting fraud and thus to bolster the investing public's confidence in the integrity of reported financial data. To accomplish those purposes, SOX requires higher levels of disclosure, better internal controls and audits, and certification of financial documents by corporate officers. Publicly traded corporations must disclose in their annual reports information about their internal controls, the composition of their audit committees (which are to have solely independent directors), and their ethics codes. Violations can lead to corporate and individual penalties, as well as the forfeiture of compensation by corporate officers.[1]

---

[1] For example, if a public company engages in material noncompliance with SOX financial reporting mandates, and the company must restate its financial statements, the company's chief executive officer and chief financial officer must reimburse the company for all bonuses, securities trading profits, incentive pay, or other compensation they made due to the noncompliance.

What Companies Are Covered under SOX?

Both in the statute itself and by mandatory SEC and stock exchange regulations, SOX requires reports and corporate governance processes from a broad class of "Reporting Issuers"—U.S. and foreign companies that:

- list their securities on U.S. stock exchanges; or

- file registration statements to offer securities to the U.S. public (even if the registration statement has not been made effective and no securities have yet been sold); or

- register their shares and thus become subject to continuing SEC reporting requirements because they have more than $10 million in assets, 500 or more shareholders worldwide and, for foreign private issuers, at least 300 shareholders resident in the United States. Note that a foreign corporation may not have listed its shares or made a public offering of those shares in the United States, but it still could meet the reporting threshold of 300 or more shareholders in the United States due to private placements to U.S. residents or U.S. residents purchasing shares in foreign markets.

Besides creating new criminal offenses, the Sarbanes-Oxley Act provides that the many enforcement powers under the Securities Exchange Act of 1934 can be used to punish violations. Most public companies must file annual certifications in which chief executive and financial officers personally vouch for the accuracy of their corporations' financial statements. Each officer is expected to swear, "to the best of my knowledge," that these financial reports are accurate. If the executives will not attest to the report's accuracy, they must file a statement explaining why.

KEY SECTIONS

Section 906(a) mandates that both the chief executive officer and the chief financial officer certify the financial statements included in each periodic report as: (1) fully compliant with the Securities Exchange Act of 1934, and (2) fairly presenting, in all material respects, the corporation's financial condition and operations results. SOX's other key requirements include Section 302 (Corporate Responsibility for Financial Reports) and Section 404 (Management Assessment of Internal Controls).

Under Section 302, a corporation's chief executive officer and chief financial officer must each certify that they have reviewed the annual and quarterly report, that the report contains no untrue statement of material fact nor omits a material fact that would make the report misleading, and that to the certifying officer the report "fairly presents" the corporation's financial condition, results of operations, and cash flows.[2] A corporation must disclose all material off-balance sheet transactions and reconcile even its pro forma filings with the corporation's financial condition under generally accepted accounting principles. Based on the most recent evaluation, the certifying officers need to disclose to the corporation's audit committee and external auditors any significant deficiencies in internal control and any fraud involving management or other employees with a significant role related to internal control.

The certifying officers must establish, maintain, and evaluate the effectiveness of disclosure controls and procedures, which have to be current—evaluated within 90 days of any filing date. Any significant changes in internal controls for financial reporting or in other factors affecting internal controls, or any actions taken to correct significant deficiencies and material weaknesses, need to be disclosed in their reports.

SOX's Section 404 requires companies to include in their annual reports a self-assessment of the effectiveness of their internal control structure and procedures for financial reporting, with each registered public accounting firm that prepares or issues an audit report for the company required to attest to, and report on, that assessment. The SEC—which is charged with enforcing the act—has adopted rules implementing Section 404 and requiring ultimate compliance even by small businesses and foreign-owned companies if they are publicly traded (an EGC is exempt).

DOCUMENT RETENTION AND ETHICS

SOX states that anyone who knowingly destroys, alters, conceals, or concocts documents or files that may relate to a federal investigation or a bankruptcy filing can be imprisoned for up to 20 years. Even without that provision, the legal doctrine concerning "spoliation of evidence" permits tort suits or direct judicial action (e.g., contempt of court, fines, directing a verdict against the offending party) if someone deliberately destroys evidence that a court order or subpoena ordered preserved, or that he/she knew or should have known was going to be sought. A well-written policy that calls for deleting documents (e.g., e-mails) after given periods of time adhering to applicable document-retention laws ordinarily works fine, but businesses must have a warning system in place by which corporate lawyers can advise employees to immediately stop erasing data when a lawsuit is anticipated, a bankruptcy is being considered, or a government agency is investigating the business.

SOX recognizes the value of corporate codes of ethics, which should help businesses handle conflicts of interests, disclosures in periodic reports, regulatory compliance, and internal reporting of violations.

---

[2] Knowing, willful violations are punishable with fines and up to 20 years in prison.

Corporations must disclose whether they have adopted a code of ethics, and they must rapidly disclose via Internet posting or 8-K report any change in or waiver of their code of ethics for senior financial officers (e.g., accounting officers and controllers) or—per SEC rules implementing SOX—for other principal executive officers. The SEC defines the term "waiver" to include "implicit waivers": a company's failure to respond within a reasonable time to an officer's material violation of a code of ethics provision.

ACCOUNTANTS AND LAWYERS

SOX imposes restrictions on accountants, including accounting firms that perform audits and consulting services for the same client. It raises criminal penalties for securities fraud, increases corporate financial disclosure obligations, and prohibits most corporate loans to senior corporate executives or directors. The act provides for a Public Company Accounting Oversight Board (PCAOB), whose five members (including the chairperson) must have exactly two current or former certified public accountants (CPAs), with the chairperson—if a CPA—not having practiced as one for at least the previous five years. The SEC appoints the board's chairperson and other members, and the PCAOB promulgates rules, investigates firms, and otherwise regulates firms that audit publicly traded corporations, with a focus on quality control and standards for auditors' independence from the companies they audit.[3]

All regulated audit firms, both American and foreign, must register with the PCAOB. SEC rules under the Sarbanes-Oxley Act call for the partner in charge of a company's audit, and the partner who concurs in the audit opinion, to rotate off the account after five years of service and not be allowed to return to the audit for another five years. In addition, the PCAOB can review audits in some detail, providing an additional set of eyes to determine if an auditor followed proper procedures.

The act requires lawyers to report up the corporate ladder any discovery of past or impending securities law violations, beginning with the general counsel or chief executive officer, and, if ignored, then to the corporate directors or audit board. Under SEC rules pursuant to the act, lawyers may at some point be required to have a "noisy withdrawal":

---

[3] Auditing companies are prohibited from performing these services for those businesses that they audit: (a) bookkeeping and related services; (b) financial information systems design and implementation; (c) appraisal or valuation services, fairness opinions, or contribution-in-kind reports; (d) actuarial services; (e) internal audit outsourcing services; (f) management or human relations functions; (g) broker, dealer, investment advisor, or investment banking services; and (h) legal services or other expertise unrelated to the audit. While tax services usually are permitted, the audit company cannot help a client by taking an "aggressive interpretation" of applicable tax laws and regulations, by planning or opining on the tax consequences of a listed or confidential transaction (as defined by Treasury Department regulations), or by assisting the immediate relatives of, or the individuals themselves, who in the audited firm perform financial reporting oversight roles.

resigning from service for a client corporation and disavowing improper filings to the SEC if up-the-ladder measures fail.

Most state laws, modeled after American Bar Association recommendations, give lawyers discretion on how to handle evidence of fraud so long as they are acting in the corporation's best interests. Furthermore, as the SEC administers it, "minimum standards of professional conduct" have been established for the thousands of lawyers who practice before the SEC.

Whistleblowing, the False Claims Act, and SOX

The False Claims Act, first enacted in 1863 but later amended, and significantly strengthened, in 1986, is meant to help identify contractors guilty of defrauding the government. The Act encourages whistleblowing because whistleblowers shed light on why something is wrong and their insights can help hold the bad actors responsible, fix problems, and achieve reforms. The Act promises to whistleblowers an award *qui tam* (for "acting on behalf of" the government) of 15% to 30% of the money the government recovers.

SOX also calls for whistleblowing in the context of publicly traded companies, their advisors and officers, and the investing public's need for timely, accurate information. Both SOX and the False Claims Act protect whistleblowers from being fired, but only the False Claims Act has triple damages and gives whistleblowers a reward.

STATE SECURITIES REGULATION (BLUE SKY LAWS)

Many states regulated the *intrastate* sale of securities long before the 1933 Securities Act. Since these statutes were enacted to protect unsophisticated investors from unscrupulous securities salespersons often peddling "the blue sky," these statutes, now found in every state, are sometimes referred to as "blue sky laws."

Unlike the federal securities laws, many of these state securities statutes do more than simply require information disclosures: these states have *merit registration*, which means that state authorities may deny registration as unduly risky, as promising too little in return, or both (finding the issuer's business plan and proposed issuance are not fair, just, and equitable). A Uniform Securities Act, permitting state securities registration via the same statement filed under the *federal* Securities Act, has been enacted in most of the states and by the District of Columbia and

Puerto Rico. The blue sky laws, together with the Securities Act of 1933 and the Securities Exchange Act of 1934, completely cover the intrastate and interstate regulation of securities.

YOU SHOULD REMEMBER

The Federal Securities Exchange Act of 1934 established the Securities and Exchange Commission and is concerned with *existing* securities. It provides for the regulation of stock exchanges, brokers, and dealers; the registration of traded securities; the updating of reports; and the imposition of margin requirements.

The blue sky laws are state statutes and are similar in scope and purpose to the Securities Act of 1933. They require full-disclosure registration and a statutory prospectus.

Generally, private offerings (offerings to no more than 25 persons) are not subject to registration requirements under the state securities laws.

LIABILITY OF ACCOUNTANTS

Lawyers and accountants, acting as employees or consultants (independent contractors), are an integral part of every corporate team having responsibilities for finance and securities. These attorneys and accountants are subject to tort suits for malpractice, as well as ethics inquiries reviewing their performance under the relevant professional code of conduct. These professionals also have extraordinary liability exposure in some instances under statutory law.

LIABILITY UNDER THE SECURITIES LAWS

• *CIVIL LIABILITY*

Section 11 of the *Securities Act of 1933*, imposing civil liability upon issuers of new securities for misstatements or omissions of material fact in registration statements, specifically includes accountants and financial officers within its sweep. A complaint against an accountant or financial officer under Section 11 is sufficient if it alleges (a) that the investor purchased the security pursuant to a registration statement that (b) contained a materially defective financial statement (c) certified by the accountant or financial officer, and (d) that as a result of the material defect the plaintiff suffered damages. Under Section 11, there is no requirement that the plaintiff relied on the materially defective financial statement. *The plaintiff is not required to prove negligence; the accountant has the burden of proving due diligence (lack of negligence).* The 1933 act also contains a statute of limitations: suit must be brought within 1 year after the omission or error was discovered or 3 years after the securities were offered to the public.

The Securities Exchange Act of 1934 imposes civil liability on accountants who furnish false or misleading statements in reports or documents filed with the SEC. Unlike a suit based on the 1933 act, in a Securities Exchange Act suit (based on Section 18) the accountant is faced with a lawsuit from a purchaser *acting in reliance* on the alleged false or misleading statement. As is the case with civil suits under the 1933 act, however, the plaintiff must prove damages proximately caused by the false or misleading statement.

The accountant's usual defense is that he/she acted in good faith and without knowledge that the information was misleading.

• *CRIMINAL LIABILITY*

The 1933 Securities Act provides that any defendant, including a participating accountant, may be criminally liable for a fine of not more than $10,000 or imprisonment of not more than 5 years, or both; the 1934 Securities Exchange Act provides for a fine of up to $1 million ($2.5 million for corporations) and/or imprisonment of up to 10 years. *Violations of state securities laws carry similar criminal sanctions.* The SEC can prohibit anyone who has committed securities fraud from being a public company's officer or director.

COMMON LAW TORT LIABILITY

Malpractice suits against professionals (doctors, lawyers, accountants, etc.) are based on three claims:

1. There is a professional standard of care applicable to the services rendered by the professional.
2. The professional employed by the plaintiff failed to conform to the standard.
3. As a direct and proximate result of this failure to conform, the plaintiff suffered compensable damages.

Proof of the applicable standard of care is generally deduced in court by the testimony of other professionals who state the standard that they consider applicable to the circumstances of the case. The defending professional, although not necessarily disagreeing with plaintiff's experts regarding the applicable standard of care, may disagree as to whether the defendant conformed to the standard. *The applicable standard, as well as defendant's conformity to the standard, is a question of fact to be determined by a jury.*

For accountants, this standard usually is GAAP (generally accepted accounting principles) or GAAS (generally accepted auditing standards). GAAP and GAAS are embodied in the rules, releases, and pronouncements of the SEC, the American Institute of Certified Public Accountants (AICPA), and the Financial Accounting Standards Board (FASB). These principles and standards are especially important because courts and legislatures usually defer to the members of the accounting profession in determining what the ordinarily prudent accountant would do. Therefore, an accountant who fails to adhere to GAAP or GAAS runs a large risk of being held culpable for any resulting harm.

LIABILITY TO THIRD PARTIES

In preceding chapters we discussed the *foreseeability standard* in determining tort and contractual responsibility for damages to secondary and remote persons. In the case of product liability, for example, a manufacturer of defective goods is responsible to all persons in the chain of distribution whom he/she could foresee as a user and hence to any party who could reasonably be expected to suffer damages.

In a leading case (*Ultramares Corp. v. Touche*), 174 N.E. 441 (N.Y. Ct. App. 1931), the New York Court of Appeals refused to apply the foreseeability principle to damages based on an accountant's alleged negligence. The court limited claims for damages to persons receiving the *primary benefit* of the accountant's services (the **Ultramares principle**). These persons would be (1) those in privity to the accountant (clients) and (2) third-party beneficiaries of the accountant's work—persons known to the accountant, with an identified, specific purpose for using the accountant's works and in whom the accountant acted in a way calculated to induce reliance on his/her reports; liability would *not* extend further, to creditors and other third parties who might incidentally rely on statements and documents certified to be correct. *This narrowly construed, primary benefit test is still used by courts in a dozen states, including New York. At the other extreme, only two states, Mississippi and Wisconsin, now hold the accountant responsible to any injured party whose existence and injury he/she might reasonably have foreseen.*

Of the remaining states, about ten still have no case law directly on point, and around 25 states have an approach between the strict *Ultramares* principle and the broad foreseeability approach. It is the standard enunciated in Restatement (Second) of Torts Section 552: if the accountant knows the nature of the transaction for which his/her work will be used, then the accountant's potential liability extends to any class of persons the accountant knows may thus rely upon his/her work. It is unnecessary for the plaintiff to be identifiable or known to the accountant as an individual when the accountant did his/her work. The accountant simply must have known, when delivering his/her work to a client, that the work's recipient intended to transmit the information to a person or group of persons similar to that of the plaintiff. As an official comment to Restatement Section 552 notes, potential liability does not extend to "the much larger class who might reasonably be expected sooner or later to have access to the information and foreseeably to take some action in reliance upon it." As broadly stated in *United States v. Arthur Young & Co.*, 465 U.S. 805 (1984), accountants must serve a broad public interest and have the duty "to preserve the integrity of the securities market."

KNOW THE CONCEPTS
DO YOU KNOW THE BASICS?

1. What are some advantages and disadvantages of raising corporate capital by equity financing vis-à-vis debt financing?
2. What is the principal difference between a bond and a debenture?
3. In what three ways do common shareholders have an interest in the corporation?
4. How may shareholders influence the directors' decision to declare a dividend?
5. What is a nimble dividend? What general dividend requirement does a nimble dividend violate?
6. Under what theory of contract law can creditors sue subscribers to the stock of a corporation not yet formed? Does this violate the privity rule?
7. State how a UCC section can give the corporate issuer access to information about uncertified ownership of the corporation's shares?
8. What are some reasons for restricting the free transfer of share certificates?
9. Which came first, state or federal regulation of the issuance and marketing of securities?
10. Why are the common law rules of fraud and misrepresentation insufficient to protect investors from unscrupulous securities sales-

persons? In any case, does the modern day rule of *caveat venditor* ("let the seller beware") not afford the gullible investor sufficient legal protection?

11. Does allowance by the SEC of a statutory prospectus constitute SEC approval of the securities described or of the prospectus?

12. What is the underlying rationale for various exemptions to the federal securities laws?

13. Is the term "insider" limited to a defined group?

14. Why should accountants receive special attention for civil and criminal liability under the securities laws?

15. Is a professional malpractice case merely a "swearing contest" between two sets of professional "experts," with one set claiming that the defendant's professional work did not conform to the standard of care, the other set claiming that the work did conform?

TERMS FOR STUDY

accountants
authorized shares
blue sky laws
call price
canceled shares
capital surplus
common shares
conversion
convertible bond
cumulative preferred stock
debenture
debt security
discount shares
distribution
dividend
due diligence
equity security
exempted transaction
fraud-on-the-market doctrine
indenture
insider
issued shares
malpractice suit
margin
merit registration

nimble dividend
noncumulative preferred stock
nonparticipating preferred stock
no-par shares
note
par shares
participating preferred stock
preferred shares
proxy
red herring prospectus
redemption
registration statement
retained earnings
share
statutory prospectus
stock option
stock split
street certificate
subscription
tender offers
tombstone advertisement
treasury shares
UCC Article 8
Ultramares principle
voting rights

PRACTICAL APPLICATION

1. ABC Gulf Investment Co. owns 1000 acres of gulf-front property in Manatee County, Florida. It flies 35 persons of "substantial" means from various parts of the country to Tampa to tell them of the "opportunity of a lifetime." The "opportunity" is the offer of a contract with ABC to buy 20-acre tracts of "prime" undeveloped land, designated on a property plat, for a price of $100,000 each, payable over 30 years. Twelve persons, including Shuster, sign contracts. If the only written information concerning the property was a promotional brochure, can Shuster void this contract on ground of illegality?

2. Sawyer is the owner of a large, unincorporated country estate on which is located an established golf course. Approximately 100 persons regularly play golf on the course, paying semiannual dues for the privilege.

   Sawyer needs to raise $1 million to build a club house and put the course in "first-class" condition. He proposes to create a corporation and issue $1 million of $10-par-value capital stock. Each of the 100 present members signs a stock subscription agreement for 1000 shares of stock, and Sawyer enters into contracts with builders and developers for the work. Sawyer defaults on these contracts, and the contractors bring suit on the subscription agreements. What should be the result?

3. In Problem 2, suppose that Sawyer wishes to form a corporation in Kentucky (where the golf course is situated) and sell the capital stock, all as described, to the present members, under Kentucky's blue sky law, which has essentially the same registration and prospectus requirements as the federal Securities Act of 1933. However, the capital to be raised is $2 million of which $1 million (100,000 $10-par-value shares) will be issued to Snead, for which Sawyer will deed the country estate to the corporation.

   Discuss the following:

   (a) The liability of Jones, CPA, for errors in Sawyer's financial statements leading to an overstatement of the value of Sawyer's estate in the amount of $300,000.

   (b) The liability of Sawyer for violation of the Securities Act of 1933 if 12 of his members, residents of Ohio, resell their shares in Ohio within 6 months.

ANSWERS
KNOW THE CONCEPTS

1. Equity financing does not have to be repaid; however, ownership and control of the business enterprise must be shared with equity investors. Although issuance of debt securities may not require sharing ownership or control, the necessity of repayment may limit the scope and freedom of corporate activity.

2. Both are long-term debt securities; however, a bond is secured, whereas a debenture is unsecured. Both bonds and debentures are subject to the terms of indenture agreements.

3. Common shareholders may vote for directors and on other fundamental matters; they may participate in the distribution of dividends; they may share in the distribution of net assets after dissolution and liquidation.

4. Shareholders may influence the directors' decision to declare a dividend only through their power to elect or reject directors. Unless the directors abuse their discretion with respect to dividends, shareholders play no role in the dividend process.

5. A nimble dividend is a dividend payable from current earnings even though *there are debts outstanding from previous years*. Such dividends are not permitted in most states because of the general requirement that dividends be paid only from earned surplus.

6. The privity rule states that only a person who is a party to a contract can sue on that contract. However, there are two classes of third-party beneficiaries who can bring suit without privity: donee beneficiaries and creditor beneficiaries. If it is assumed that the subscriber could reasonably anticipate that creditors of the embryonic enterprise would extend credit in reliance on his/her promise to purchase stock, the subscriber should be legally responsible to such "creditor beneficiaries."

7. Section 8-102 of the Uniform Commercial Code requires that uncertificated shares be "registered upon books maintained for that purpose by or on behalf of the issuer." The corporate issuer can access this registration.

8. To retain voting controls within a defined group, to preserve an S corporation or a close corporation, or to maintain exemption from federal or state security laws requiring registration for *public* offerings.

9. State regulation came first. The state of Kansas was the first regulator of securities, passing its underlying statute in 1911. However, many states did not enter the field of intrastate regulation until many years after the passage of the basic federal laws in 1933 and 1934.

10. Modern law places a great burden on sellers to make full disclosures to buyers, particularly where there is a disparity of education and training between them. However, the 1933 Securities Act not only requires full disclosure of all relevant facts, but also defines the nature and extent of that disclosure. Reliance on general principles of *caveat venditor* would leave the parties uncertain of their rights and duties without resorting to litigation in every case.

11. The SEC explicitly takes no position with respect to the securities or to the accuracy or adequacy of the prospectus. The SEC has no duty or responsibility to investigate the contents of the registration statement or of the prospectus, even though these documents are in complete statutory and regulatory form. Both civil and criminal liability attach to the issuer for omissions and inaccuracies in these documents. The SEC cannot lead the public to believe that such omissions and inaccuracies do not exist.

12. The primary purpose of the federal securities laws is to protect the investing public. To the extent that an investor is sophisticated or informed, he/she requires less protection. The evils that the legislation was designed to prevent involve large-scale promotion of dubious and ill-designed plans or of schemes for the secret profit of their promoters.

13. Although the term "insider" basically means "top management" and controlling shareholders, it extends to any party with inside knowledge or information giving him/her an unfair advantage over ordinary members of the investing public. Included are employees, consultants, and total outsiders who are "tipped off" directly or indirectly by insiders.

14. As the compilers and preparers of financial data, accountants are in a unique position to mislead or deceive (intentionally or carelessly) not only regulators but also issuers and their managers, as well as the investing public.

15. Almost every case in a court of law turns on the credibility of conflicting witnesses. In Chapter 3 we learned that the strengths and weaknesses of both defendant and plaintiff are explored in pretrial discovery. If experts cannot be found to testify truthfully and conscientiously for one side or the other, litigation may not proceed to trial or the case may be settled without trial. In any event, the jury will have full opportunity to evaluate both sides as presented by opposing experts.

PRACTICAL APPLICATION

1. The question presented is whether the contracts to purchase the real estate tracts are "securities" within the meaning of the Securities Act of 1933. Of the four tests laid down in the *Howey* case, the fourth—the expectation of profits solely from the efforts of a promoter or third party—is clearly lacking. As a matter of fact, this contract is an ordinary real estate contract. Such contracts have been treated by the courts as a mere interest in a joint venture to sell real estate. Of course, the offer to sell to 30 persons and the interstate nature of the transaction might bring the matter to the attention of the SEC. However, since the contract is not a "security," there is no violation of law.

2. Persons relying on the subscription agreements would be able to sue subscribers who had not paid the agreed-upon subscription price. On the assumption that the contractors know of the subscription agreements, they should be successful in their litigation.

3. (a) On the assumption that the Kentucky blue sky law and any application of professional liability thereunder would follow the Securities Act of 1933, Jones, CPA, would be liable not only to the Kentucky authorities, but also to Sawyer and other persons with whom he had a direct contract. He may also be liable to investors who may have relied on his erroneous financial statements. Under the broader interpretation of accountant liability, he would be responsible to *all* persons whose injury or loss he could have foreseen. The Kentucky blue sky law would be applicable since the offering is to 100 persons and would be a public sale subject to the Securities Act.

   (b) If the securities were sold to residents of Ohio who came to Kentucky to purchase these securities, the out-of-state residency would not itself cause the transaction to be an "interstate sale" unless there is a "scheme" to violate the federal statute. The facts given do not suggest such a scheme, and there would appear to be no violation of federal law in failing to file a registration statement under the 1933 act. However, the securities cannot be sold by the Ohio residents or by other purchasers outside the state of Kentucky for at least 9 months.

SPECIAL
TOPICS

19

CRIMES AND TORTS

KEY TERMS

crime a public wrong, committed with intent or by negligence, for which the law provides punishment or recompense to society

tort a private wrong against a person or his/her property. Aside from certain limited circumstances, all torts arise from either an intentional, wrongful action or from a negligent action.

burden of proof the degree of proof necessary for a criminal conviction (beyond a reasonable doubt) or for a successful civil suit (preponderance of evidence)

Most court cases fall within one of three major divisions of law: *crimes, torts*, or *contracts*. This chapter focuses on crimes and torts. Although these two broad subjects are not usually as important to business as are contracts, businesspersons often also must deal with torts or crimes. Therefore, any serious student of business law must know about them.

This chapter compares crimes and torts, provides examples, and discusses defenses.

IMPORTANT FACTS ABOUT CRIMES

American criminal law is primarily codified law, based on statutes and regulations rather than merely on past judicial decisions. The same act or omission may be a **crime** *under both federal law and state law*. For instance, murder, a state crime, may also be a federal crime (e.g., a violation of the victim's civil rights) and thus may be prosecuted in separate criminal cases in each of the two court systems. (Certain legal doctrines, as well as basic fairness, however, sometimes limit the use of such dual trials.)

THE U.S. CONSTITUTION AND AMERICAN CRIMINAL LAW

A fundamental premise of our criminal justice system is that it is *far worse to convict one innocent person than to let many guilty people go free*. The procedural guarantees for alleged criminals are thus much greater than for civil defendants. Many, if not most, of these guarantees are found in the state and federal constitutions, particularly the Fourth, Fifth, Sixth, and Eighth Amendments to the U.S. Constitution. Almost all *rights* in those amendments have been incorporated into the Fourteenth Amendment's *due process clause*, as described in Chapter 2. Thus, *criminal procedure* is now generally governed by nationwide standards of constitutional interpretation.

The *Fourth Amendment* protects against unreasonable searches and seizures and requires probable cause before a search warrant or arrest warrant is issued. Some case law exceptions to the search warrant requirement are: "hot pursuit" of a suspect, evidence in plain view or about to be destroyed, searches of arrested persons, and *good faith* police behavior. Also, when an arrest for a serious offense is supported by probable cause, the suspect's being required to furnish a DNA sample is—like being fingerprinted and photographed—constitutional; the evidence can be used for that case or other, different charges against the suspect. *Maryland v. King*, 569 U.S. ___ (2013). On the other hand, police cannot, without a search warrant, search the data on a cell phone seized from the arrested person. *Riley v. California*, 573 U.S. ___ (2014).

The *Fifth Amendment* prohibits compulsory self-incrimination; hence people sometimes "take the fifth" rather than testify. Other provisions include a prohibition against double jeopardy (trying someone again for the same crime once he/she has been acquitted of that crime) and the federal due process clause (comparable to the Fourteenth Amendment's state due process clause; see Chapter 2). The amendment is a constitutional basis for our presumption of a criminal defendant's innocence.

The *Sixth Amendment* outlines the criminal defendant's right (1) to a speedy and public trial by an impartial jury, (2) to know the charge against him, (3) to confront and subpoena witnesses, and (4) to have a lawyer. Under the doctrine announced in *Miranda v. Arizona*, 384 U.S. 436 (1966), any person about to be interrogated who "has been taken into custody or otherwise [significantly] deprived of his freedom" must be warned that (1) he has a right to remain or become silent, meet with an attorney before any questioning, and have a lawyer present during questioning; (2) anything he says can be used as evidence against him; and (3) if he wants a lawyer but cannot afford one, the state will provide one free of charge.

The *Eighth Amendment* prohibits excessive bail, excessive fines, and cruel and unusual punishment.

A Criminal Defendant's Testimony: Comparative Law

There are three basic approaches to a defendant's testifying:

1. Some countries do not let the criminal defendant refuse to take the stand (e.g., in China, the defendant has no right to remain silent). In Germany, the defendant cannot testify as a witness and, therefore, does not enjoy the privilege against self-incrimination. Also, in France, defendants cannot prevent questions from being posed, although they can refuse to answer particular questions.

2. Some nations protect criminal defendants against self-incrimination, but allow the judge or jury to draw an adverse inference from a defendant's decision not to testify. In 1997, Great Britain abandoned the U.S. standard and adopted this approach—no required testimony, but prosecutors can ask the judge/jury to draw adverse inferences. Great Britain thus permits the judge or jury to presume that the nontestifying defendant had something to hide, such as guilty conduct.

3. The U.S. approach—no required testimony and no adverse inference—is a relatively rare protection for the accused (e.g., this approach is also followed in Argentina, Canada, Israel, Italy, Morocco, and Russia).

CLASSIFICATION OF CRIMES

The three classes of common law crimes are **treason, felonies**, and **misdemeanors**.

Treason against the United States, the only crime defined in the U.S. Constitution, is a comparatively rare charge.

The distinction between a felony and a misdemeanor is usually found within each state's criminal code. Felonies are more serious crimes, punishable by imprisonment. Murder (which can carry the death penalty in most states), manslaughter, aggravated assault, arson, bribery, burglary, embezzlement, forgery, grand larceny, kidnapping, price fixing, rape, robbery, and tax evasion are felonies. Misdemeanors are generally punishable only by fines or, at most, a brief stay in the local jail. Simple assault, disorderly conduct, gambling, petty larceny, prostitution, and trespass are usually classified as misdemeanors. Certain minor offenses, such as violations of city ordinances or traffic regulations, may not even be considered misdemeanors in some jurisdictions (i.e., they are too petty to be labeled as crimes, and are often called "infractions" or "violations").

Three other ways of categorizing crimes are these:

1. **White-collar**: nonviolent crimes, perpetrated by people in positions of trust, usually against businesses or governments.
   Examples: embezzlement, mail fraud, bribery.
2. **Organized**: crime by groups in the "business" of crime, such as the Mafia.
3. **Victimless**: crimes that are sometimes considered to have no specific victims (just society as a whole).
   Examples: prostitution, gambling, tax evasion

Crimes can also be classified according to whom or what they are committed against: a person (e.g., assault, battery, kidnapping, manslaughter, murder, rape), the government (e.g., bribery, perjury), the general public (e.g., antitrust or environmental violations, food and drug law violations, disorderly conduct, trafficking of illegal narcotics), the home (e.g., burglary), and other property (e.g., blackmail, embezzlement, forgery, larceny).

CRIMINAL INTENT AND CAUSATION

In most cases, a crime must include both a criminal act (*actus reus*) and a criminal intent (*mens rea*).

Example: No Actus Reus
Dave Deviant thinks about assaulting Veronica Victim, but does nothing about it. *No crime*, not even attempted assault.

Example: No Mens Rea
Ida Innocent, through no intent, negligence, or other fault of her own, collides with Veronica Victim and kills her. *No crime*.

Usually, a person is presumed to intend the natural consequences of what he/she knowingly does. Moreover, in a felonious action, the doer may be deemed responsible for even unwanted results, that is, *mens rea* is transferable from the intended felony to the one that actually occurred.

Example: Unintended Harm
Ed Evildoer, maliciously attempting to throw a brick through Ida Innocent's window, instead hits Ida. Ed is guilty of criminal assault and battery, although he intended a lesser, property crime.

Example: Unintended Victim
Betty Bad puts poison in Ivan Innocent's coffee. However, Todd Toughluck drinks the coffee instead and is injured. Betty is guilty of criminal assault and battery on Todd, although she meant *him* no harm. Her intent to injure Ivan is transferable.

Only certain *specific-intent* crimes (e.g., burglary and arson) require proof of intent to commit that particular crime.

In statutory law, unlike the common law, some crimes either presuppose or do not require criminal intent; the forbidden act is a *crime per se*. Such laws are most commonly found in state or municipal traffic codes, food and drug purity/safety laws, and liquor or narcotics laws (e.g., proof of alcoholic beverage sales to a minor is a crime even if the seller did not intend to sell to a minor).

Note that the law distinguishes between *intent* and *motive*. Intent involves an express or implied desire to perform a particular act; it is a state of mind preceding or accompanying the act. Motive is the overall goal that prompts a person's actions, and good or bad motives may be taken into account in assessing punishment.

CRIMINAL PROCEDURE

• *PRETRIAL STAGES*

A criminal case passes through several phases before trial. First, the crime is reported and investigated. Then, if there is **probable cause**, that is, reasonable grounds—something more than mere suspicion, to believe that a particular person committed the crime, that person can be arrested. A warrant for arrest is necessary unless the pressure of time requires immediate action (e.g., before the suspect flees).

Searches and Seizures

Routine Collection of Data

In *Maryland v. King*, 569 U.S. __ (2013), the Supreme Court held 5–4 that police can collect DNA through swabs of the cheek from people arrested for serious crimes and keep that data for future use (as to other crimes), even against a person who was not convicted of the crime for which the swab was taken.

Random Searches Are Okay

Generally, warrants are needed for both searches and arrests. Random or systematic searches may be okay. For example, in *Illinois v. Caballes*, 543 U.S. 405 (2005), the Supreme Court found it constitutional for police to use drug-sniffing dogs to check stopped cars whose drivers gave police no particular reason to suspect illegal activity.

Different National Rules for Warrants

Whereas the United States, Canada, and some other nations ordinarily require that warrants must be preceded by the approval of judicial authorities, other countries (e.g., China, Italy, South Africa) permit warrants simply to be issued by prosecutors or the police. Not in the United States but in many nations (e.g., Argentina, China, France, Israel, Russia), during the search of a dwelling, witnesses are

> required. Again, not in the United States but in a number of nations (e.g., Argentina, England, France), searches may not—absent special circumstances—occur at night.

Finally, criminal charges must be lodged against the defendant. Depending on the state, the charges, usually called either an **indictment** (by a grand jury) or an **information** (by a magistrate or police officer), must be based on probable cause, preponderance of evidence, or prosecutor's evidence that supports a belief in the defendant's guilt. (For information on *extradition*, see page 58.)

Most cases are resolved without a trial. Prosecutors and defense counsel usually reach a *plea bargain*. The judge must decide whether the guilty plea was freely given and whether there was some factual basis for the plea, but judicial disapproval of an agreed-upon plea is rare.

In *Padilla v. Kentucky*, 559 U.S. 356 (2010), the U.S. Supreme Court held that a defense lawyer's bad advice, which persuaded a defendant to plead guilty, amounted to ineffective assistance of counsel (and entitled the defendant to have his/her conviction overturned, with the prosecutor then deciding whether to proceed against the defendant again). In *Missouri v. Frye*, 566 U.S. ___ (2012), the U.S. Supreme Court held that the constitutional guarantee of a fair trial extends to pre-trial actions such as plea bargains: "defense counsel has the duty to communicate formal offers from the prosecution to accept a plea on the terms and conditions that may be favorable to the accused." In *Lafler v. Cooper*, 566 U.S. 1 (2012), the Court held that defendants are entitled to a remedy when they show (1) a reasonable probability they would have accepted the plea bargain offered had they not received bad advice from their lawyer (in effect, the advice was absurd enough to violate the defendant's Sixth Amendment right to effective assistance of counsel), and (2) the trial court would have accepted the guilty plea. In such cases, the trial court would then have the discretion to replace the stiffer sentence given after a conviction with the plea agreement, or to throw out part of the conviction and resentence accordingly, or to leave the original, stiffer sentence in place.

• BURDEN OF PROOF

At trial, there is a crucial difference between criminal and civil cases in the level of proof required.

> A civil plaintiff merely needs a *preponderance of the evidence*; the judge or jury need only find that the evidence favors the plaintiff over the defendant.
>
> A successful criminal prosecution requires proof of *guilt beyond a reasonable doubt*.

Absolute proof is not mandatory; the prosecution need not eliminate *all* doubts—merely all *reasonable* doubts.

A verdict of "not guilty" does not necessarily mean that the judge or jury believes the defendant to be innocent. It is simply a finding that there was insufficient evidence to prove guilt beyond a reasonable doubt.

Comparative Law: The Presumption of Innocence

While they may not adopt a standard as rigorous as "proof beyond a reasonable doubt," most countries accept the concept that the criminal defendant is presumed innocent and that the state must prove his/her guilt. This presumption is increasingly a fundamental concept not just in common law countries, but worldwide. For example, the European Convention on Human Rights and Fundamental Freedoms (Rome, 1950)—now adopted by almost every nation in Europe—recognizes in its Article 6(2) that "Everyone charged with a criminal offense shall be presumed innocent until proven guilty according to law."

• *EVIDENCE*

Criminal trial courts have numerous, complex rules about what evidence is admissible, and how it may be introduced. The rules are supposed to exclude irrelevant, unreliable, or unfairly prejudicial matters, especially in jury cases. (The system presupposes that a judge is less likely to be swayed by improper evidence.) The judge's or jury's verdict is to be based solely on the evidence properly brought out at trial. Otherwise proper, highly relevant evidence may be excluded because it was obtained in violation of a defendant's constitutional rights. Criminal appeals often are decided on such so-called technical issues.

• *APPEALS*

Appellate courts cannot overturn a verdict simply because they disagree with it—e.g., with how the jury weighed the evidence and decided to believe one witness more than another witness. Appeals tend to focus on problems in the trial judge's legal rulings, the instructions to the jury, and the trial procedures, not simply in the jury's or judge's factual interpretations.

Ironically, the factor that studies indicate is most typically linked to an erroneous conviction—eyewitness error—is not generally something that can be challenged directly on appeal. Factual assessments, such as to witness credibility, are for the trial court judge and jury. Thus, challenges on appeal go more toward procedural defects or other legal problems that may *indirectly* have led to, or at least kept from scrutiny, witness errors or other such mistakes.

YOU SHOULD REMEMBER

In both federal and state criminal cases, the most important aspects of the investigation, arrest, and trial are governed by guarantees contained in the U.S. Constitution, particularly the Fourth, Fifth, Sixth, and Eighth Amendments.

Crimes are generally classified as either *felonies* or *misdemeanors*. Felonies are the more serious crimes, with harsher punishments.

Other labels include white-collar, organized, and victimless crimes.

At common law, *actus reus* (criminal act) and *mens rea* (criminal intent) were the two necessary elements of a crime. These two concepts remain important, although some statutory offenses are crimes *per se*, with the *mens rea* requirement presumed or eliminated.

Arrests and searches must be based on probable cause, not mere suspicion. Criminal charges may have to meet an even higher standard. At trial, guilt must be proved beyond a reasonable doubt.

Rules of evidence, designed to exclude irrelevant, unreliable, or unfairly prejudicial matters, control the version of the facts presented at trial. Constitutional guarantees may necessitate further restriction of evidence.

Since the judge or jury is supposed to consider only the evidence properly introduced at trial, and since the prosecution must meet a high standard of proof, "not guilty" is not a synonym for "innocent."

IMPORTANT FACTS ABOUT TORTS

A **tort** is a private wrong, a trespass against a person or his/her property, for which a damages award or other judicial remedy may be sought. Most torts arise from either an intentional, wrongful action or from a negligent action. Many actions that constitute torts also constitute crimes, and most crimes involve tortious acts. Thus a single action may result in two trials: a criminal trial and a tort (civil) trial.

CLASSIFICATION OF TORTS

• *INTENTIONAL TORTS*

To constitute an **intentional tort**, the defendant's act must be expressly or implicitly intended; the resulting harm need not be intended, but must have been reasonably foreseeable. Examples of intentional torts are assault and battery, false imprisonment, slander, and invasion of privacy.

• *NEGLIGENCE*

In a tort case arising out of **negligence**, the plaintiff must show four things: (a) there was a duty imposed on the defendant in favor of the plaintiff, (b) the defendant breached (violated) that duty, (c) the breach was the proximate (natural and foreseeable) cause of the harm (causation), and (d) plaintiff suffered damages.

Example: Tort of Negligence

Suppose that a building collapses, and X thus wants to sue architect Y for negligence. To win, X must prove that (a) Y designed or was responsible for the design of the building; (b) Y had a duty to design, or review the designs of, the building in accordance with reasonable standards of her profession; (c) this duty, owed to present and future passersby, people in the building, and persons with property in or near the building, covered X; (d) the duty was breached by Y; (e) if Y had exercised due care, the building would not have collapsed; and (f) the collapse damaged X or his property.

DUTY AND "THE REASONABLE PERSON"

The **duty** (standard of care) is that of a reasonable, prudent person acting with ordinary care and skill (the "reasonable man" standard). What would a reasonable person do in the situation faced by the defendant? This hypothetical person is given the defendant's physical attributes, including age, but is treated as having average intelligence and temperament. However, a highly educated or skilled defendant (e.g., a person accused of professional malpractice) may be held to a standard commensurate with his/her actual knowledge and ability.

In some cases, both duty and breach are, in effect, automatically demonstrated because the defendant's conduct constituted **negligence per se**. *Per se* means "in and of itself" or "by itself." In the context of negligence, *per se* means that there has been a violation of a rule (e.g., a statute, regulation, or ordinance), and that violation, by itself, proves duty and breach. The plaintiff, to win, must be a member of the class of persons protected by the rule, and the plaintiff's harm must be of the type that the rule was intended to prevent. Suppose that a statute requires nursing homes to install hand railings along all walkways at the home. An able-bodied young adult visitor to the nursing home is injured in a fall that would have been prevented by a railing. Under this interpretation, since the statute was not meant to protect this visitor (but to protect the elderly or otherwise infirm nursing home residents), most courts would probably not invoke the negligence *per se* doctrine. For example, dumping hazardous waste in violation of environmental statutes or Environmental Protection Agency regulations, or speeding through a red light (violating a traffic ordinance) would be negligence *per se* scenarios. However, in all cases, the plaintiff would still need to show the other two elements of negligence: harm (generally of the type that the rule is intended to prevent—the "protected harm") and causation.

CAUSATION

Breach of duty is not enough. The plaintiff must also prove **causation in fact**: that the damages would not have occurred but for the defendant's wrongful acts. An act need not be the sole or immediate cause of the damages. In fact, when two or more defendants act wrongfully, the defendants may be held *jointly and/or severally liable*; each defendant is liable for plaintiff's entire damages.

The second issue in causation, **proximate cause** (also called **legal causation**), involves foreseeability. Were the plaintiff's damages the *natural and probable consequences* (that is, closely and significantly connected to) of the defendant's unreasonable acts? Although caused by the acts, the harm to the plaintiff may be so remote in time, distance, or chain of events that causation is not proximate. That is, the defendant's legal responsibility does *not* extend to all consequences of his/her actions—just to the harms tied closely enough to the actions for which, as a matter of justice or social policy, the defendant should be liable.

A term referring to causation is "scope of liability," which may encompass (1) "a continuous sequence" substantially contributing to the alleged damages, and (2) the requirement that "but for" the negligence, the injury would not have occurred. Legal or proximate cause thus deals with the presence or lack of intervening or superseding causes (sometimes requiring a **direct** connection between the injury and **foreseeability**).

A NEGLIGENCE *PER SE* FLOWCHART: P sues D

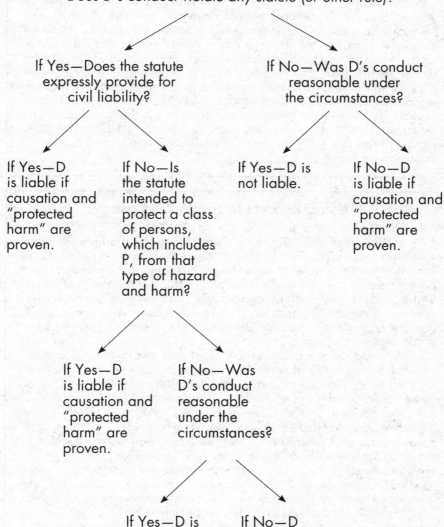

Does D's conduct violate any statute (or other rule)?

If Yes—Does the statute expressly provide for civil liability?

If No—Was D's conduct reasonable under the circumstances?

If Yes—D is liable if causation and "protected harm" are proven.

If No—Is the statute intended to protect a class of persons, which includes P, from that type of hazard and harm?

If Yes—D is not liable.

If No—D is liable if causation and "protected harm" are proven.

If Yes—D is liable if causation and "protected harm" are proven.

If No—Was D's conduct reasonable under the circumstances?

If Yes—D is not liable.

If No—D is liable if causation and "protected harm" are proven.

Classic Case on Foreseeability: *Palsgraf v. Long Island R.R. Company*, **162 N.E. 99** (Court of Appeals of New York, 1928)

A man carrying a package was rushing to board an already moving train. Two railroad guards helped to get him aboard, and the man dropped his package, which contained fireworks. Nothing about the package would have caused someone to discern its contents. The package exploded. The shock waves caused decorative scales to fall from the station's ceiling onto Mrs. Palsgraf, who was standing some distance from the three men and the exploding package. A divided court held that Mrs. Palsgraf was not a foreseeable plaintiff; hence there was no duty. This is the approach taken by most courts, but some courts and the Restatement (Third) of Torts (Scope of Liability, § 29) consider plaintiff-foreseeability to be a matter of proximate cause.

Using Experts to Prove the Case

In *Daubert v. Merrell Dow Pharmaceuticals, Inc.*, 509 U.S. 579 (1993), the U.S. Supreme Court limited the admissibility of scientific testimony. The *Daubert* standard is that "expert" opinions that are not scientifically reliable should be excluded, that is, kept out of the evidence admitted at trial. The court ruled that, under Federal Rule of Evidence 702, the admission or not of scientific testimony depends on (1) whether the theory or technique is generally accepted (supported in the scientific community); (2) whether it has been subjected to peer review and publication; (3) whether it can be tested (done according to proper scientific methods); and (4) whether the known or potential error rate is acceptable. In summation, *Daubert* holds that courts must ensure that "all scientific testimony or evidence admitted is not only relevant, but reliable."

In *Kumho Tire Co. v. Carmichael*, 526 U.S. 137 (1999), the Supreme Court applied *Daubert* to nonscientific expert witnesses, such as engineers and other specialists. The court unanimously concluded that the *Daubert* holding "applies not only to testimony based on scientific knowledge, but also to testimony based on technical and other specialized knowledge," including new technology, databases, and computer simulations. Trial judges must, the *Kumho Tire* court stated, "make certain that an expert, whether basing testimony upon professional studies or personal experiences, employs in the courtroom the same level of intellectual rigor that characterizes the practice of an expert in the relevant field."

• *MALPRACTICE*

Malpractice is discussed on pages 436–437, especially in the context of the securities laws. In essence, malpractice is the failure to adhere to professional standards. It is negligence in a professional context.

Therefore, the breach of duty in a malpractice case is the failing to do what a competent, reasonable doctor, attorney, accountant, engineer (or whatever the profession be) would have done in those circumstances. The failure is measured by the standards for *professionals in that field— e.g., cosmetic surgery, probate law, tax accounting—not what ordinary people (lay-people) would or could have done.* As an example, note that medical malpractice could encompass not just poor diagnosis or treatment of a patient, but also the lack of a patient's informed consent. Patient P gives his/her informed consent to a particular treatment, T, only if (1) P receives a thorough disclosure concerning T; (2) P acts voluntarily; (3) P is competent to give consent; and (4) P in fact consents to T.

ADDITIONAL THEORIES OF TORT LIABILITY

• *RES IPSA LOQUITUR*

When a certain type of accident occurs ordinarily because of negligence, and the defendant had exclusive control of the instrument causing the injury (e.g., an airplane that crashed, a scalpel left in a patient's stomach), a presumption arises that the defendant was negligent. *Res ipsa loquitur* ("the thing speaks for itself") shifts the onus of coming forward and explaining the occurrence to the defendant. The ultimate burden of proof (looking at the *res ipsa loquitur* inference and all other evidence), however, remains with the plaintiff.

• *RESPONDEAT SUPERIOR*

Respondeat superior is the doctrine by which an employer may be liable for the tortious acts of an employee if the employee was acting in the scope of employment. Of course, regardless of *respondeat superior*, the employee is him/herself liable for his/her actions. This concept is discussed further in Chapter 14. Incidentally, parents generally are *not* liable for torts by their children.

Comparative Law: Islamic Law and *Respondeat Superior*

The doctrine of *respondeat superior* is well established in the legal systems of the United States and most Western countries. However, many predominantly Islamic countries only narrowly employ the doctrine. Islamic law, codified in the Sharia, holds to a strict principle that responsibility for human actions lies with the individual and cannot be vicariously extended to others. To find an employer liable for the acts of its employee, the Sharia looks for direct orders from the employer to its employee. Absent the employee obeying a direct order of the employer, the employee's actions—and liability therefrom—do not extend beyond the employee to also include the employer.

• *STRICT LIABILITY*

Under the doctrine of **strict liability**, the defendant is liable for the plaintiff's injuries despite the absence of negligence or intentional, wrongful acts. If the defendant was engaged in abnormally dangerous activities (e.g., blasting with dynamite, crop dusting, keeping wild animals), especially activities unusual for that locale, courts and legislatures have decided that he/she should bear the cost of any harm done. As in other areas of liability without fault (e.g., products liability, workmen's compensation), the strict liability of some manufacturers or employers is a matter of public policy based on the assumption that these defendants are in a better position to shoulder the costs of injury than are potential plaintiffs.

TORT PROCEDURE AND TORT REFORM

Lawsuits involving torts are tried in civil courts and generally follow the procedures outlined in Chapter 3.

Some Congressional bills and Justice Department proposals are: make product liability laws *uniform*, in both federal and state courts (either for all aspects of a case or at least the punitive damages issue); establish a national statute of limitations; bar suits involving long-standing products (ones used in the workplace for many years, e.g., machines 15 years old or older); limit punitive damages; bar punitive damages for defects in a product that the Food and Drug Administration approved (so long as the manufacturers did not deceive the FDA); require arbitration or another alternate dispute resolution early in the process; permit the defenses that the victim's alcohol/drug abuse helped to cause his/her injuries; abolish joint and several (individual) liability (presently, when two or more defendants are found liable, the plaintiff can collect the full damages award from any one of the defendants, such as the corporate defendant with the most assets) or restrict it to economic damages; and the reforms, below, at the state level.

State tort reforms, often proposed, but so far enacted in only a few states, require arbitration; set higher damages thresholds (before one can bring suit); limit or eliminate pain and suffering awards; allow suits only for personal injuries (not property damage); set shorter statute of limitations periods; cap contingency fees; and excuse wholesalers and retailers from liability if they did not cause, or help to cause, the defect.

For product liability cases, several states have taken defenses that previously were allowed only concerning negligence—e.g., comparative or contributory negligence, and assumption of risk—and now allow them for strict liability and/or breach of warranty claims. Some states have changed the causation or "unreasonably dangerous" element from foreseeable misuse to likely misuse. Thus, those states' product liability laws no longer cover misuse of a product unless that misuse either was probable or by someone lacking capacity (e.g., a child with a toy).

(Product liability law is discussed later in this chapter.)

YOU SHOULD REMEMBER

An intentional tort involves intended acts, not necessarily intended harm.

In negligence, *duty of care* is breached if the defendant failed to act as a reasonable, prudent person would have acted in the situation the defendant faced. *Causation in fact* exists if, but for the defendant's wrongful acts, the damages to the plaintiff would not have occurred. However, if the plaintiff and/or his damages were unforeseeable, the defendant may successfully argue that the alleged tort lacks *proximate cause*.

For reasons of public policy, defendants who engage in abnormally dangerous activities are held *strictly liable* for harm resulting from those activities.

COMPARISON OF CRIMES AND TORTS

The following table compares these two divisions of law.

Crime	Tort
1. A public wrong against society	1. A private wrong against individuals or businesses
2. "Plaintiff" (prosecutor) is the state (offended person is usually a witness)	2. Plaintiff is an individual or a business
3. Mostly statutory law	3. Mostly common law
4. Prosecutor's burden of proof: guilty beyond a reasonable doubt	4. Plaintiff's burden of proof: preponderance of the evidence
5. Consent rarely a defense	5. Consent usually a defense
6. No damages are necessary.	6. Damages must be shown.
7. Basis for criminal guilt: an intentional act, and sometimes gross negligence or recklessness	7. Basis for tort liability: an intentional act, negligence, or strict liability

EXAMPLES OF TORTS

· Most torts are defined by common law precedent. Courts may (and occasionally do) define a new tort, such as infliction of emotional distress, invasion of privacy, or abusive discharge from employment—three twentieth century tort refinements. Courts and legislatures also abolish torts that no longer reflect concerns that society deems worthy of protection (e.g., alienation of affections).

NEGLIGENCE

Most common law torts arise out of negligence, that is, unintentional breaches of duty. *Examples*: poorly manufactured products, professional malpractice, traffic accidents.

In the United States, over a million tort cases are filed annually. The largest number, over 40%, involve auto accidents.

INTENTIONAL TORTS

• *INTERFERENCE WITH THE PERSON*

Assault: arousing in another individual the apprehension of an *immediate* harmful or offensive contact with his/her body. Words alone are insufficient; they must be accompanied by some act. *Examples*: threats while raising fists, reaching toward what seems to be a concealed weapon.

Battery: unjustified contact with someone else's body or anything connected to it (purse, chair, cane, etc.). The contact may be direct (e.g., a slap) or due to a force put into motion by the defendant (e.g., shooting a bullet that strikes the plaintiff). It includes actions exceeding one's authority for physical contact. *Example*: a masseuse suddenly shaves a customer's head.

False arrest: detention of the plaintiff, without his/her permission, under the falsely asserted authority of the defendant. No physical barrier, force, or threat of force is necessary. *Example*: An insurance investigator posing as a police officer searches a person and detains him for questioning.

False imprisonment: wrongful use of force, physical barriers, or threats of force to restrain the plaintiff's freedom of movement. *Example*: A merchant forcibly detains a suspected shoplifter without reasonable cause for suspicion. Most states have "merchant protection" laws against suspected shoplifters, but the merchant must have reasonable grounds for suspicion, and the confinement must also be reasonable (accomplished without excessive force, and for no longer than necessary).

Intentional infliction of mental (emotional) distress: disturbance of the plaintiff's peace of mind by the defendant's outrageous conduct. Although damages are not limited to bodily injury, usually some physical harm must be shown. *Examples*: extreme actions by bill collectors, extensive cursing and threats of future violence, continued abuse about a sensitive person's stuttering or physical appearance, slipping a dead mouse into someone's lunch.

Invasion of privacy: interference with a person's right to be left alone. The right to solitude can be invaded in four different ways: (1) public disclosure of private facts (e.g., revelation of a private person's debts or drug use; publishing information obtained from the psychiatric files of a business competitor); (2) publication of information placing a person in a false light (e.g., a large headline states, "Rape Suspect Arrested" with a photograph underneath of a man actually the subject of an article elsewhere in the newspaper); (3) intrusion upon a person's private life (e.g., illegal searches of a home, harassment by unwanted and continual telephoning, unlawful wiretapping); or (4) unauthorized appropriation of name or likeness (e.g., picture) for commercial purposes (infringement on a person's exclusive right of publicity—to exploit one's own name or likeness—such as by making and selling for profit baseball cards without the permission of the ballplayers pictured). The first three must be disclosures or intrusions highly offensive to a reasonable person. For each of the four, *truth is no defense*.

Employers' spying on employees: with blood, urine, and psychological tests, and with computers, telephone taps, and video cameras, employers today are probably much more likely to "invade" workers' privacy than the government is. Employer spying is intended to maintain or improve productivity, to stem rising health-care costs, to fight pilferage and employee lying or cheating, and otherwise to reduce expenses or bolster a moral view. Tests or surveillance can show that people are smoking, drinking alcohol, taking drugs, gambling, eating fatty foods, romancing coworkers, or otherwise behaving in a manner counter to employer goals. Also, the employer's duty to prevent harassment (notably, sexual harassment) and its obligation to protect confidential information (e.g., of shareholders' financial interests) may necessitate the monitoring of employees' Internet and e-mail use while on the job. "Spying" via social media (Facebook, Twitter, etc.) has become common; employers often monitor employee usage (e.g., catching them on "sick days" posting pictures of themselves at the beach) and check job applicants' electronic footprint prior to hiring them.

The Drug-Free Workplace Act (1998) requires the federal government and private contractors supplying the federal government to establish and enforce drug-free policies. It also permits (but does not mandate) drug testing and rehabilitation services. Most states have similar statutes permitting drug testing. Urinalysis or other testing for prospective new hires is much more likely than for existing employees, who—unless in a field affecting public safety—tend to face such testing, if at all, only when there is "reasonable suspicion" or "probable cause" that substance abuse has impaired an employee's performance. Random testing is less common but can be permitted if public safety is involved. Employers with written drug-testing policies can generally avoid invasion of privacy claims.

Federal law prohibits most use of lie-detectors (polygraph tests); and most states protect lawful behavior off of the job, such as smoking and drinking. (Exceptions involve public safety issues, such as alcohol abuse by airline pilots or truck drivers.) Other state laws, such as those protecting human rights, have been invoked by employees claiming that the employer violated their privacy rights. Also, collective bargaining agreements between a business and its workers' labor union tend to protect employees from corporate surveillance and testing except insofar as it directly relates to job performance. But most workers are not unionized (therefore, not protected by labor contracts), and *the Constitutional "right of privacy" protection extends only to governmental intrusions, not those of private business.*

• *INTERFERENCE WITH BUSINESS RELATIONS*

Abusive discharge: modification of the common law doctrine that "at will" employees (ones without a set term of employment) may be terminated for any reason. This tort occurs if a firing violates a clear mandate of public policy. *Also see* page 573. *Example*: a firing that stems from the worker's notifying authorities about criminal activities being carried on in the workplace.

Disparagement (trade libel): a business defamation that involves injurious falsehoods about a product or a competitor's reputation. *Example*: stating falsely to customers that a competitor's products contain carcinogens.

Infringement of copyrights, patents, trademarks, or trade names: these will be considered in the intellectual property section of Chapter 19.

Interference with contract: a tort requiring that (1) a valid contract exists between A and B; (2) C knows about the contract; (3) C intentionally causes A or B to breach the contract, or C otherwise prevents performance. *Example*: Interfering, Inc., persuades an employee who has another 6 months to run on her year-long employment contract with Contract Company to breach that contract and work for Interfering. Contract Company may sue Interfering for the tort (interference with contract) and sue the employee for breach of contract.

Interference with prospective economic advantage: a tort with roughly the same three requirements as interference with contract (simply substitute "prospective economic advantage" for "contract"). *Example*: Gary Greedy has his employees stand outside a competitor's store to divert customers to Greedy's shop.

Unfair competition: a tort that, in its broad sense, overlaps other torts such as infringement of intellectual property or interference with contracts or prospective economic advantage. In its more narrow application, this tort concerns trying to "pass off" goods or services upon the public as if they were the goods or services of another, more reputable business or product. *Other examples*: deceitful advertising injures a competitor, secret rebates or concessions, bribery of a competitor's employees, use of a former employer's trade secrets.

Note: Lanham Act Section 43(a) essentially creates a federal law of unfair competition, giving business competitors the right to sue a business defendant for a wide range of false, misleading, confusing, or deceptive statements or practices involving goods or services (e.g., deceptive advertising; imitating or infringing of the plaintiff's trademarks, trade names, packages, labels, employee uniforms, and overall appearance and sales image).

In *POM Wonderful LLC v. Coca-Cola Co.*, 573 U.S. ___ (2014), defendant Coca-Cola asserted that the Federal Food, Drug and Cosmetics Act (FDCA), an act designed to ensure the safety of food products, did not require different labeling of a fruit drink Coca-Cola marketed in competition with POM Wonderful. However, the Supreme Court held that the FDCA did not bar a private party such as POM Wonderful from suing a competitor for its allegedly inaccurate food descriptions in violation of the Lanham Act. Such suits for unfair competition due to misleading advertising and labeling serves "a distinct compensatory function"—one not in conflict with the FDCA; and, by motivating injured persons to bring claims, Lanham Act suits also "provide incentives for manufacturers to behave well."

• INTERFERENCE WITH PROPERTY

Conversion: unauthorized, unjustified exercise of control over another's personal property. There are two requirements: defendant must (1) appropriate the property to his/her own use, and (2) indefinitely withhold its possession from the plaintiff and/or destroy it. A mistaken belief that one owns the property or is entitled to keep or use it is no defense. *Examples*: acts of arson, robbery, or embezzlement, taking someone else's umbrella, coat, or other personal property and keeping it after discovering that fact.

Nuisance (Liability for nuisances can be based not only on intentional acts but also on negligence or strict liability): substantial interference with the individual plaintiff's right to use and enjoy his/her property (private nuisance) or with rights common to all (public nuisance). Nuisance usually refers to wrongs arising out of the defendant's unreasonable or unlawful use of his own property. *Examples*: excessive noise, fumes or smoke; storing dangerous chemicals. *Private nuisance*—the defendant's watering his lawn so much that the plaintiff's land is flooded. *Public nuisance*—interfering with the general right to health, safety, peace, comfort, or morals, and including, for example, pollution, brothels, and drag strips. There are "mixed" nuisances (both private and public).

Nuisances in Cyberspace and by Telephone

The CAN-SPAM ("Controlling the Assault of Non-Solicited Pornography and Marketing") Act of 2003 prohibits false headers and deceptive subject lines in unsolicited commercial e-mail messages, which must have some form of label as well as include opt-out instructions and the sender's physical address. The Federal Trade Commission is authorized (but not required) to establish a "do-not-e-mail" registry.[1]

Similarly, the Telephone Consumer Protection Act of 1991 (TCPA) outlaws autodialing to fax machines (for other provisions, see page 619). The Junk Fax Prevention Act (2005) directs the Federal Communications Commission (FCC) to amend its TCPA rules about fax advertising. The FCC's revised rules (1) clarify that unsolicited fax advertisements are permitted when there is an "established business relationship," which the rules define; (2) specify the circumstances under which a person may "opt out" of any future faxes; and (3) require the senders of fax advertisements to put on the fax the specific notice and contact information needed by recipients who do want to "opt out."

---

[1]Unlike the National "Do Not Call" registry for telemarketing, the FTC determined in June 2004 that an e-mail version of such a registry is, at least for now, unworkable.

Trespass to personal property: unjustified interference with the plaintiff's possessory interest (e.g., use) in personal property. *Example*: without permission, a person takes someone else's lawnmower, cuts her own lawn with it, and then returns the machine.

Trespass to real property: unauthorized entry onto the plaintiff's land, either by a person or by something the person caused to enter the land. This tort can also occur when presence on the plaintiff's property becomes unauthorized, but continues. *Examples*: building a dam so that water backs up onto someone's land, throwing rocks or trash onto another's land.

• *OTHER INTENTIONAL TORTS*

Abuse of process: the use of a court process (e.g., attachment, injunction) for a purpose for which it was not intended. *Example*: attachment on excessive amounts of X's property in one case so as to force X to dismiss an unrelated lawsuit.

Defamation: a false communication by the defendant to a third person (a "publication") that harms the plaintiff's reputation. *Slander* is oral; *libel* involves writing, broadcasting, or any other recorded medium. It is no defense that one was merely repeating what someone else wrote or stated. The media may claim in defense that the statement concerned a public official or a public figure[2] and was made without malice. A plaintiff seeking to show malice must prove actual knowledge of falsity or a reckless disregard of the truth. *Example*: an employee tells his boss that another employee, whom he names, is a harlot, has repeatedly cheated on her income tax returns, and makes a practice of taking 3-hour lunches; the employee telling these tales knows or should know that they are false. (There tends to be immunity for a defendant Internet service provider (ISP) or others (e.g., telephone companies) who do not have, nor could they have reasonably be expected to assume, any editorial responsibilities for what is, for example, a defamatory e-mail message from an ISP customer.)

Under the doctrine of *self-publication*, an employer's derogatory statement to an employee may constitute publication if the employer could foresee that the employee would be required to repeat the statement to, for example, a prospective employer. Most state courts or legislatures considering the doctrine have decided that public policy concerns favor the rejection of the doctrine.

Fraud (deceit, misrepresentation): a very important intentional tort; depends on a false, material representation of fact that the defendant either knows to be false or recklessly makes knowing that the information is incomplete. The defendant must intend that the plaintiff rely on the representation, and the plaintiff must in fact justifiably rely upon the representation and thereby be damaged. Representations are usually by words, but can be by conduct (e.g., setting back an odometer). "Material" means any representation that would influence a reasonable person in the plaintiff's situation.

Opinions generally are not considered representations of fact, unless given by experts in their area of expertise. "Puffing" or other sales talk about the value of goods or services is usually treated as mere opinion unless a special, confidential relationship exists between buyer and seller.

---

[2] Public figures are persons in the public eye because of their celebrity status or their having voluntarily involved themselves in matters of public controversy

> **Three Factors to Help Distinguish Between Actionable Lies (for which a claim of fraud may succeed) and Mere Puffing (which does not rise to the level of a fraudulent misrepresentation)**
>
> CLASSIFYING STATEMENTS AS LIKELY
>
> <u>A representation of fact (possible fraud)</u>   OR   <u>Mere puffing (not fraudulent)</u>
>
> A statement that is
>
> | | |
> |---|---|
> | Specific | General |
> | Capable of measurement | Nonmeasurable |
> | Couched in terms of fact | Phrased as an opinion |

Silence generally does not constitute fraud. A major exception involves silence when a defendant had a duty to speak (e.g., when the defendant knew that the plaintiff had misconstrued the silence, or when a statute or regulation required the defendant to furnish information).

Infringement of intellectual property rights (copyrights, patents, trademarks): see Chapter 26.

Malicious prosecution: the instigation of criminal proceedings against someone for an improper purpose and without probable cause, with those proceedings terminating decisively in the criminal defendant's favor (e.g., by acquittal or dismissal for lack of evidence). When the improper proceedings are civil, the tort is called **malicious institution of civil proceedings**.

Negligent misrepresentation: Incorrect statements of opinion or fact made by persons who breached a duty to exercise reasonable care in ascertaining the truth; such persons may include accountants, lawyers, title examiners, or others supplying the plaintiff with business guidance. This tort generally has the same requirements as does fraud, except that negligence replaces fraud's *scienter* (knowledge of falsity or reckless disregard of truth or falsity).

Of the foregoing torts, *assault, battery, false arrest, false imprisonment, unfair competition, conversion, infringement of intellectual property, nuisance, trespass to personal or real property, libel, and fraud are also crimes or are directly related to particular crimes.*

YOU SHOULD REMEMBER

Duty, breach, causation, and damages are the crux of any tort case concerning negligence.

For intentional torts there are specific definitional requirements. For all tort cases, even those involving the same type of tort, the particular facts in the case remain crucial.

EXAMPLES OF BUSINESS CRIMES, WITH TORT EQUIVALENTS

The following are typical business crimes:

Arson: willfully setting fire to and burning a building. It is criminal fraud to burn a building in order to collect insurance. *Tort equivalent: trespass to real and personal property, conversion.*

Attempt: specific intent to do a criminal act, and—in furtherance of that intent—some action beyond mere preparation. *No tort equivalent.*

In the example on page 450, Dave Deviant could not be found guilty for merely thinking of, or even preparing a plan for, assaulting Veronica Victim. However, since Dave has the requisite intent to commit an assault, once he pours "knockout" drops into Veronica's glass of wine, once he drives her to a remote spot, or once he has taken some other affirmative action beyond "mere preparation," Dave can be criminally liable for attempted assault, if the assault itself does not occur.

Bankruptcy frauds: filing false claims by creditors or debtors, fraudulent transfer or concealment of assets, or obtaining credit with the specific intent to avoid paying debts. *Tort equivalent: fraud.*

Bribery: illegal payments or offers to pay, whether of money, property, or services, to a political campaign, to governmental officials, or to other persons such as the employees of a competing firm, for the purpose of receiving favorable treatment, proprietary information, or other assistance that the briber either is not entitled to receive or—at the very least—cannot lawfully receive by the method chosen (kickbacks or payoffs). *No direct tort equivalent: depending on the facts, a business competitor may have a claim for unfair competition, conversion, infringement of intellectual property, fraud, or tortious interference with a contractual or business relationship.*

Burglary: at common law, breaking and entering a dwelling at night with the intent to commit a felony, such as larceny. Modern statutes have tended to widen the definition by eliminating the requirements that the crime be at night, that there be an actual breaking, and that the building be a dwelling. *Tort equivalent: conversion, trespass to real and personal property.*

Compounding a crime: accepting money or anything else of value in return for not reporting or prosecuting a crime. *No tort equivalent.*

Computer crimes: see Chapter 26.

Corporate crime: a crime by a corporation and/or its personnel. For a corporation to be guilty, intent either is no element or can be implied. Although a corporation cannot specifically intend a crime, its officers and employees can. Thus corporate personnel can be convicted of certain crimes (e.g., perjury) for which the corporation may not be liable. *Tort equivalent: depending on the facts, fraud, conversion, or trespass to personal property.*

Embezzlement: unlawful use of money or property for one's own purposes by a person with lawful possession or access to that money or property. Embezzlement may involve bank employees, company bookkeepers, or other money managers who decide to "borrow" the funds entrusted to them. In most jurisdictions, it is no defense to claim that the money or property would have been returned. *Tort equivalent: conversion.*

Forgery: falsely making or materially altering a legal document (e.g., a check or credit card) in order to defraud another person and/or otherwise affect rights. *Tort equivalent: fraud, conversion.*

Fraud against consumers: activities such as fraudulent solicitation in the mail, false advertising about products, and false labeling. *Tort equivalent: fraud.*

Larceny (theft): unlawfully taking personal property with the intent to deprive the owner of it. Two examples are shoplifting and theft of company property by employees. *Tort equivalent: conversion, trespass to personal property.*

Mail and wire fraud: use of mails, telephones, radio, or television to further or execute a scheme to defraud (the fraudulent scheme need not itself be a crime). These federal criminal statutes are used against a wide variety of crimes, including kickbacks to private employees and bribery of public officials. *Tort equivalent: fraud, conversion.*

Misappropriation of trade secrets: use of an employer's, a competitor's, or some other person's trade secrets (see Chapter 26) for personal advantage and without the owner's permission. *Tort equivalent: unfair competition, perhaps infringement of intellectual property.*

RICO (Racketeer Influenced and Corrupt Organizations Act) violations: use of income from two or more racketeering actions (within ten years of each other) to create, acquire, operate, or have an interest in any type of "enterprise" (broadly construed to include not just any business, but also almost any other organization), or to conspire to do so. "Racketeering activity" is defined expansively to include any one or more of numerous types of "predicate acts"— federal crimes such as interstate transportation of stolen property, interference with interstate commerce via violence or threats of violence, various statutory frauds (e.g., as to securities, mail, currency reporting, and bankruptcy), and embezzling from pension, welfare or union funds; also, state felonies such as arson, bribery, drug dealing, extortion, gambling, insurance fraud, kidnapping, loan sharking, murder, and robbery. While intended to combat organized crime's "infiltration" into legitimate businesses, RICO reaches most white-collar crimes, whether by criminal organizations or by otherwise lawful enterprises. *Tort equivalent: fraud, conversion, RICO civil liability (treble damages and attorneys' fees), perhaps tortious interference with contract.*[3]

Robbery: larceny accomplished by using force or threats of force. *Tort equivalent: assault, battery, conversion, trespass to personal property.*

THE BUSINESSPERSON AS CRIMINAL DEFENDANT

Business crimes include certain activities once thought to be simply "good business." For instance, price restraints, the division of markets, and reciprocal trade arrangements may be criminal, as well as civil, violations of antitrust laws. Failure to monitor industrial discharges can subject a company and its officers to fines and imprisonment under federal water pollution legislation. It may mitigate punishment, but does not alter criminality, that the offending monopolist or polluter did not intend to violate the law.

Most white-collar culprits, however, know full well that their actions are illegal. Using stealth rather than force, the white-collar criminal frequently makes money, or avoids paying debts, by violating the trust reposed in him/her.

White-collar crimes include tax evasion, bribes, extortion, embezzlement, kickbacks, pilferage, forgery, computer crimes, antitrust violations such as bid rigging and price fixing, RICO offenses, and all types of fraud concerning consumers, credit cards, securities, insurance, bankruptcy, bank loans, and countless other areas.

Fraud is the essence of many, if not most, white-collar crimes. A criminally fraudulent act is any deceitful action or omission that (1) is intended to deprive another of his/her property or other rights, and (2) achieves this purpose.

The definition of **criminal fraud** is thus no more limited than the criminal mind itself; it stands ready to include the latest "scams" and the newest abuses of technology.

---

[3] Here is one exception to RICO's normally broad interpretation: The Private Securities Litigation Reform Act (1995) provides that conduct deemed to be fraud under the securities laws cannot be the basis of a RICO claim unless the defendant first has been criminally convicted for that fraud.

GENERAL DEFENSES TO CRIMES AND TORTS

Even if a person has committed the act for which he/she is charged or is being sued, defenses may serve either to negate the crime or tort or—at the very least—to prevent a successful prosecution or lawsuit.

Good **defenses** result from a failure to meet the definitional requirements of a specific crime or tort and/or, more generally, from falling short of the level of proof required in *any* criminal or civil case. Furthermore, while all defendants have "due process" and other constitutional rights, the seriousness of criminal charges has led to additional procedural protections for criminal defendants, as outlined earlier in the section "The U.S. Constitution and American Criminal Law."

The following are some general defenses to crimes and/or torts:

Act of God is a defense to negligence when natural forces such as lightning, earthquakes, or hurricanes are the proximate cause of injury. However, when a person negligently created a situation whereby a foreseeable act of God could cause damage, no defense is available to foreseeable damages.

Assumption of risk, another defense to unintentional torts, means that a plaintiff who knowingly and voluntarily faced a dangerous situation may not recover for an injury arising out of the known risks inherent to that situation. An exception to this defense is a rescuer acting in an emergency situation.

Unless there is a family relationship or special circumstances exist (e.g., one put someone in danger or worsened his/her situation), one usually has no legal duty to take affirmative steps to try to rescue another person. This *"no duty to rescue"* rule is found in common law countries, but generally is NOT the law elsewhere in the world. Also, eight states—Florida, Massachusetts, Minnesota, Ohio, Rhode Island, Vermont, Washington, and Wisconsin—now have laws modifying the common law and requiring some form of a duty to rescue.

Comparative fault has replaced contributory negligence in almost all states. When the negligence of the plaintiff and the negligence of the defendant are concurrent causes of the plaintiff's damages, any damages awarded to the plaintiff are reduced by an amount proportionate to the degree of the plaintiff's fault. However, only 13 states (Alaska, Arizona, California, Florida, Kentucky, Louisiana, Michigan[4], Mississippi, Missouri, New Mexico, New York, Rhode Island, and Washington) as well as many nations have "pure" comparative negligence, and thereby permit a

---

[4] But Michigan follows only this approach for "economic" damages—e.g., hospital bills and lost wages. The rest of these 13 states follow the standard of the 21 states described later in this paragraph.

plaintiff to recover any damages at all when his/her negligence exceeds the defendant's negligence. Eleven states follow the comparative fault standard so long as the plaintiff's fault is less than the defendant's fault. These "less than" states are Arkansas, Colorado, Georgia, Idaho, Kansas, Maine, Nebraska, North Dakota, Tennessee, Utah, and West Virginia. The remaining 21 states (not counting South Dakota and the four states still applying the contributory negligence standard) have an approach just slightly more lenient toward plaintiffs: comparative negligence so long as the plaintiff's fault is *no greater than* (i.e., less than or equal to) the defendant's negligence.

Example: Comparative Negligence

If the plaintiff's damages are $100,000 and a jury finds that she was 30% at fault, while it assesses the defendant with 70% of the blame, then the plaintiff recovers $70,000. (Under the doctrine of contributory negligence, the plaintiff gets nothing.)

Consent is a defense to *all torts* and *few crimes.* When the criminal law forbids an act against the victim's will, consent makes the act no crime at all. If Ms. Able is a mentally competent adult who consented to sexual intercourse with Mr. Baker, no crime of forcible rape has occurred.

Most crimes are not negated by the individual victim's consent because the real plaintiff is society, which did not consent. Moreover, forgiveness after the crime occurs is not to be confused with consent: although it may affect the likelihood of prosecution and the severity of punishment, forgiveness is no defense. The same applies when stolen property is returned or a defendant pays for damages caused.

Contributory negligence is an absolute defense to negligence in just the District of Columbia and four states: Alabama, Maryland, North Carolina, and Virginia.[5] If the plaintiff was negligent and that negligence contributed to his/her injuries, the defendant is absolved from liability even if the defendant's negligence was much greater than the plaintiff's.

Duress may excuse the commission of a crime while under an immediate and inescapable threat of serious bodily harm or death. The threatened harm must be more serious than the harm to be caused by the crime. Obviously, duress would negate the intent necessary for an intentional tort.

Entrapment is a criminal defense if the criminal act was induced by the government, with criminal intent originating from the police. If, however, the accused was predisposed to commit the crime, then entrapment is not a defense.

---

[5] A fifth state, South Dakota, follows a comparative negligence standard but permits a plaintiff to recover damages only if the defendant's fault is "gross" and the plaintiff's fault, if any, is only "slight."

Immunity from prosecution is sometimes extended to actual or potential criminal defendants, usually to induce testimony and information from them. So long as the person receiving immunity cannot be prosecuted for his/her statements, that person cannot assert the Fifth Amendment privilege against self-incrimination.

Immunity is also a tort defense that may limit or outright bar recovery against governments, public officers, or other defendants specifically protected by statutes (e.g., charities).

Infancy bars criminal liability for children who are under a certain age and/or do not understand that a particular act is wrong. Children have no such immunity for torts: the law is more concerned with compensating the injured than with determining moral guilt. In negligence cases a child's standard of care (duty) is based on his/her intelligence and experience rather than the usual objective standard.

Insanity is a defense if the alleged crime occurred while the defendant lacked the mental capacity for the requisite criminal intent. As with duress or infancy, insanity may negate intent for some intentional torts. However, the mentally incompetent are generally held accountable for their tortious acts (including negligence) on the grounds that to deny compensation would be unfair to their victims.

Intoxication (use of alcohol or other drugs) is a complete criminal defense only when *involuntary*: a person, by force, by mistake, or by some situation beyond his/her control, ingests or has injected an intoxicating substance. *Voluntary* intoxication does not preclude the *mens rea* necessary for intentional crimes, nor does it excuse lesser crimes involving reckless behavior. For torts, intoxicated persons will generally be held to the same standard of care (duty) as if they were sober: intoxication is no defense.

Example: Drew gets drunk, hits Sara, and puts her in a coma. Drew claims he could not have had the *mens rea* needed to be convicted of a crime, because he was drunk. He cannot even remember what he did. However, Drew can be prosecuted for his battering of Sara; voluntary intoxication is generally NOT a criminal defense. Also, Sara (or others acting on her behalf) can successfully sue Drew for the intentional tort of battery.

Mistake of fact depends on whether the mistake negates *mens rea*.

Example: Mistake of Fact

If Nora Nearsighted walks off with Tammy True's child (who bears some resemblance to Nora's own tot), and Nora returns the child as soon as she discovers her mistake, Nora is not guilty of kidnapping.

Mistake of law is a criminal defense when a person honestly did not know that he/she was breaking the law, *and*: (1) the law was not published or otherwise made known to the public, or (2) the person relied on an erroneous but official statement of the law, such as a statute, court decision, or administrative order. Usually, ignorance of the law is no excuse.

Privilege is an immunity existing under law and sometimes constituting a defense in, for example, cases involving interference with contract, interference with prospective economic advantage, or defamation. Privilege involving the two interference torts frequently involves the concept of free competition (within bounds); for instance, strikes are usually privileged. For defamation, defenses include not only truth and the immunity for ISPs or the like, but also the absolute privilege extended to statements of attorneys and judges at trials and legislators during floor debate.

Self-defense (or defense of others) permits people to use the degree of nondeadly force that seems necessary to protect themselves (or others) from criminal force. Deadly force (likely to result in death or serious injury) is also permitted if (1) an attacker is using unlawful force, (2) the victim did not initiate or provoke the attack, and (3) the victim reasonably believes that he/she will otherwise suffer death or serious bodily injury. Some jurisdictions allow deadly force whenever it appears necessary to prevent a felony within a dwelling.

In tort cases, self-defense is judged by the "reasonable man" standard: if the defendant reasonably believes him-/herself to be in danger and responds reasonably, there is a defense. Defense of others is a similar tort defense, although some courts are more likely to find no defense for the actions of an "intermeddler" than for such actions taken in self-defense.

Statutes of limitations are statutorily defined periods of time within which a legal action must be brought. In civil actions, the stated time varies from state to state and depends on the subject matter—as little as 6 months or 1 or 2 years for certain defined torts, as much as 20 or more years for real estate actions. Generally, there is no period of limitation for crimes unless the statute creating the crime sets forth such a period.

The rationale for statutes of limitations is as follows:

1. People should not have to worry indefinitely about potential claims against them.

2. The law should encourage prompt prosecutions and lawsuits, which reduce the period during which memories fade, evidence is lost or destroyed, and witnesses die, disappear, or otherwise become unavailable.

Superseding (intervening) causes break the causal connection in torts between the defendant's act and the plaintiff's damages. As a general rule, they offer a defense based on lack of either causation in fact or proximate cause.

Comparative Law on Multiple Causes of Harm

France, Sweden, and some other European countries are more likely to accept multiple alleged causes and to reject the defense of superseding causation than is the case for American courts.

Example: Superseding (Intervening) Cause

Annie Absentminded leaves her grocery cart in a crowded, badly lit parking lot. Tom Thief places it in the back of his car and drives off. A half-mile later, the cart falls out and strikes Peter Pedestrian. Annie's negligence as to the cart would not render her liable to Peter; Tom's actions are a superseding cause of the accident.

PRODUCT LIABILITY

American product liability law has been criticized for its expansive theories of liability, heightened damage recoveries, and higher insurance costs. The system's defenders maintain that its problems have been exaggerated and that its benefits—especially safer products—outweigh the costs.

At both the state and federal level, numerous proposals have been advanced. Some of the following suggested changes perhaps represent a middle ground between business and insurance groups on one side and plaintiffs' lawyers and some consumer and safety advocates on the other. (1) Provide juries with a scale setting dollar amounts as at least guidelines for determining damages per type of injury (much as is often done for workers' compensation cases). (2) Give the defendant's compliance with government standards a very strong presumption that the defendant should not be liable for compensatory damages and make it an outright bar to punitive damages.[6] (3) Preserve the plaintiff's right to noneconomic, pain and suffering awards but restrict such awards to

---

[6] However, in a 7-2 ruling, *Bates v. Dow AgroSciences*, 544 U.S. 431 (2005), the Supreme Court held that pesticide makers may be sued for damages in state court if their products cause harm; the suits were *not* preempted because the pesticides carry a federally approved warning label. Likewise, in *Wyeth v. Levine*, 555 U.S. 555 (2009), the Supreme Court held that drug makers cannot rely on federal regulation to shield them from lawsuits brought under state consumer protection laws; and in *Altria Group, Inc. v. Good*, 555 U.S. 70 (2008), the high court ruled that the Federal Cigarette Labeling and Advertising Act does not preempt state law deceptive practice claims about the advertising of cigarettes as "light" or containing "lower tar and nicotine." In effect, the only assurance of federal preemption is when a U.S. law expressly preempts the type of case brought under state law. That was the holding in *Riegel v. Medtronic, Inc.*, 552 U.S. 312 (2008), with the Supreme Court finding that the Medical Device Amendments to the Food, Drug, and Cosmetic Act contained such a statute pre-empting common-law suits against manufacturers of FDA-approved medical devices.

only severe injuries. (4) Make defendants pay the legal fees of successful plaintiffs.

No broad, national product-liability reforms have been enacted. In recent years, many state legislatures have enacted reforms, such as restrictions on strict (no-fault) liability (e.g., no strict liability for a defendant that just passed a product along without changing it) and the capping of noneconomic and punitive damages. These constraints on liability findings and caps on damages awards have raised due process concerns for plaintiffs just as—from the opposite perspective—high punitive damages awards relative to low compensatory damages has led the Supreme Court to acknowledge due process rights in the defendant (see the Court's *Campbell* decision, discussed in Chapter 2). Some state courts have struck down the tort reform legislation as unconstitutional, but other state courts have upheld these laws.

• *PUNITIVE DAMAGES AND MORAL DAMAGES: A COMPARATIVE PERSPECTIVE*

Almost all common law nations, such as Australia, Canada (including Quebec), England, India, New Zealand, and South Africa join the United States in permitting punitive damages. However, how such damages may be calculated varies tremendously.

A few Civil Law nations also permit their courts to grant punitive damages to civil plaintiffs; these nations include Israel, Malaysia, Norway, the Philippines, Poland, and Taiwan (China's law is unclear). The vast majority of nations, though, do not allow punitive damages. Instead, some Civil Law countries let plaintiffs collect "moral damages," something not found in American jurisprudence. These damages are available in nations such as Argentina, Armenia, Belgium, Bolivia, Brazil, Ecuador, Egypt, France, Georgia, Iran, Iraq, Libya, Malta, Mexico, Peru, Russia, Ukraine, and Venezuela, and they appear to be a form of exemplary relief, since a judge may grant moral (or perhaps "emotional") damages independent of compensatory damages and losses. Whereas some countries see these damages as just another form of compensation for the victim, many Civil Law nations (e.g., Brazil) explicitly find a moral component to the award: that it also serves as a penalty to a wrongdoer for contract breaches involving a wide range of cases, including personal matters such as breach of a promise to marry, the mishandling of corpses, botched cosmetic surgery, errors in taking or developing photographs, and faulty transportation as well as misplaced baggage.[7]

---

[7] Only these special cases (mishandling a funeral, etc.) may permit consequential damages in the United States for a nonmonetary, contractual-based injury—mental anguish (see page 169)—while the Civil Law tradition allows for a broader array of claims for such damages.

An Example of a Type of Moral Breach

If Boris, simply out of spite, breaches his contract with Natasha, such obnoxious behavior is something Russian and many other Civil Law courts will not tolerate. They will give Natasha a damages award for her pain and suffering. These are "moral damages"—in Russia, perhaps also justified as an award because of *bespokoistvo* (the "annoyance" that the defendant inflicted upon the plaintiff): Boris's behavior was plain wrong and distressed Natasha mentally. However, that such behavior may be highly annoying does not matter for American courts, which, except in rare, special types of cases involving outrageous and foreseeable damages, do not award breach-of-contract damages beyond actual, verifiable compensatory amounts.

Finally, note that just because most nations do not let their courts award punitive damages does not mean that foreign awards of punitive damages will be denied. Many such nations will enforce foreign awards of punitive damages.

Broad Class (and Long Chain) of Potential Plaintiffs and Defendants in a Case Involving a Defective Product

Plaintiffs	Defendants
Purchaser	Producer of component part
End-user	Manufacturer of a product
Borrower (for free)	Wholesaler or other distributor
Second-hand buyer	Retailer
Donee	Other sellers, if any
Lessee	
Injured Bystander	

PRODUCT LIABILITY ARISING OUT OF CONTRACT

The general discussion in Chapter 5 of the law of contracts mentioned the movement of the law away from the old *caveat emptor* ("let the buyer beware") basis to a more balanced principle protecting the buyer from the seller's deceit, failure to correct misunderstandings, and the like. It was suggested that some courts may even go so far, in protecting buyers from unscrupulous or craftily silent sellers, as to lean toward imposing a rule of *caveat venditor* ("let the seller beware"). Much of this movement in favor of the buyer and against the seller is the result of "buyer-friendly" provisions of Articles 2 and 2A of the code. Although these articles relate specifically to the sale or lease of goods, they have tended to color the common law of all contracts.

Code provisions concerning warranty are at the heart of product liability imposed on sellers by contract.

• WARRANTIES

The word warranty is synonymous with "guarantee" (sometimes written as "guaranty"). Warranties are of two kinds: express and implied.

EXPRESS WARRANTIES

Like express contracts, express warranties arise out of words or actions that establish a promise.

Under the code [UCC 2-313(1) and UCC 2A-210(1)], three kinds of representations *express* a promise of warranty (even though the word "warranty" or "guarantee" may not be used):

1. *An affirmation of the fact of conformance.* This affirmation may be simply a statement that the goods will do a specified thing or serve a specified purpose.

2. *A description of the goods.* Such a description is a warranty that the goods are as described or specified.

3. *Reference to a sample or model.* This reference may be by picture, diagram, drawing, standard, or prototype. It expresses a warranty that the goods are as shown in the sample or model.

   Note: Under general contract law, statements about value, statements of opinion, "huffing and puffing," sales talk, advertisements, and the like are not grounds for misrepresentation or fraud. *Moreover, they do not give rise to warranties or guarantees under the code.*

IMPLIED WARRANTIES

An *implied warranty* is implied by law and arises out of the buyer-seller or lessor-lessee relationship. *The implied warranty is the common-sense implication arising from the fact that the seller is selling goods to a buyer who has certain reasonable expectations.* This warranty can be disclaimed (denied) by a specific denial (see below). However, in the absence of a disclaimer, implied warranties arise under the code as a matter of law in two respects:

1. *Warranty of merchantability.* This warranty is imposed upon the *merchant* with respect to the goods that it is his/her business to sell or lease. The code defines merchantability [UCC 2-314(2) and UCC 2A-212(2)] by a number of stated rules, but the primary assurance is that the goods "are fit for the ordinary purposes for which such goods are used," and would thus pass without objection in the

trade. The implied warranty of merchantability, however, does not form the basis of lawsuit without proof that: (i) the goods were not merchantable at the time of sale, and (ii) the plaintiff was injured because the goods failed to meet the merchantability standard.

2. *Warranty of fitness for a particular purpose.* The warranty of **fitness** (UCC 2-315 and UCC 2A-213) differs from the warranty of merchantability in two major ways: first, it applies not only to merchants but also to any other sellers of goods, and second, it implicitly warrants that the goods will be fit for the buyer's *particular* purpose, which may or may not be the general purpose for which the goods were intended. For this warranty to apply, the seller or lessor must, when the contract was made, have "reason to know of any particular purpose for which the goods are required and that the buyer [or lessee] is relying on the seller's [or lessor's] skill or judgment to select or furnish suitable goods." UCC 2-315 (sales); UCC 2A-313 (leases). Thus, if the seller knows that the buyer is purchasing a mower for a 10-acre field of weeds and undergrowth, the fitness warranty applies and is more severe than the merchantability warranty.

> Warranties are about *character, quality, and time* (how long).
> A purchaser's reliance on a UCC Article 2 (sales) warranty is not a prerequisite to his/her claim for a breach. This is different from warranties for other contracts, where reliance is necessary.

• DISCLAIMERS

The code and the common law permit a seller to avoid both express and implied warranties through general contract principles, that is, *through mutual agreement the parties may eliminate or modify the warranty obligation.* This avoidance of warranty is a **disclaimer**.

The best and simplest way for sellers to protect themselves from all warranty obligations is by use of the words "as is," "with all faults," or "without warranty of any kind, whether express or implied." "As is" is particularly recommended as a simple, direct, and unambiguous statement of contractual understanding with regard to used or second-hand merchandise or even new merchandise "on sale."

In addition to the "as is" disclaimer, UCC 2-316 provides that there is no warranty if the buyer, before entering into the contract, examined the goods, or refused to examine the goods when such examination would have revealed the defect. (This is the common law principle of unilateral mistake referred to in Chapter 5.) Moreover, an implied warranty may be found not to have occurred because of some previous performance between the parties or because of usages of their trade [UCC 2-316(3)(c)].

Caution: Disclaimers are most effective in contractual dealings between parties of approximately equal bargaining ability and equal skill and background. Merchants dealing with the entire public on a serve-one-serve-all basis *must lean over backward to make their nonexpressions of warranty just that: statements of value or opinion, with abundant exclusion and qualification. In addition, their written disclaimers should be in bold type or type of a different color, difficult for even the most uneducated or careless reader to miss or claim not to have seen.*

> For a contract to exist, minds must meet and language must be clear and discernible. Whether the buyer saw the disclaimer or should have seen the disclaimer may be a question for a jury to decide.

A careful seller, in short, takes pains to call attention to the disclaimer. Disclaimers in fine print, on tickets, and on the reverse sides of invoices are weak and may be ineffective to establish intent.

Even with all of the safeguards mentioned above, the disclaimer may be unenforceable if it is unconscionable because of the uneven bargaining powers of the parties or some other fundamental inequality in their respective circumstances. Many states, for example, have statutes prohibiting or otherwise restricting the use of limitations on implied warranties or on remedies for their breach. These laws are especially intended to protect consumers.

• *THE MAGNUSON-MOSS WARRANTY ACT*

This federal statute, enacted in 1975, was intended to provide consumers with greater protection from merchants than was thought available under the code warranties. The act is mainly enforced by the Federal Trade Commission and does not *require* that a merchant give warranties, nor does it alter the nature of implied warranties. It does provide that, for items purchased for amounts in excess of $10, any warranty by the merchant shall (1) phrase warranties/disclaimers in simple, understandable, *conspicuous* language, (2) make warranties available for inspection before sale, and (3) be conspicuously designated as either a "full" (statement of time, for example, 24 months) warranty: or "limited" warranty.

The "full warranty" is just that: it prohibits the merchant-seller from disclaiming, modifying, or limiting the duration of an implied warranty and requires the warrantor to remedy defects within a reasonable time and without charge. The "limited warranty" may clearly state any limitations on consequential damages or on the duration of implied warranties. However, the act provides that the substance of an implied warranty may *not* be disclaimed or modified if *in addition* the seller makes a written warranty or provides a service contract within 90 days of the time of sale.

• *IS PRIVITY OF CONTRACT REQUIRED TO RECOVER FOR BREACH OF WARRANTY?*

Privity, it will be recalled, is the requirement that a person be a party to a contract to bring a suit on that contract. From two entirely different points of view, privity of contract poses a problem with respect to breach of warranty.

From the point of view of the seller, does his/her responsibility for damages extend only to the buyer of the seller's goods, the party with whom he/she has privity? Or can other injured parties—a member of the buyer's family, a guest in the buyer's house, a customer in the buyer's place of business—bring suit against the seller of defective goods, even though there is no privity? Today most courts hold that persons on the same level of consumption as the buyer—guests, bystanders, family members—can sue the seller or manufacturer of the goods, even though there is no **horizontal privity** from the buyer or seller to these other persons, so long as the seller could reasonably anticipate that such persons would be exposed to, and might be injured by, the defective product. For example, exploding canned goods, defective cosmetics, contaminated foods—all subject their seller to claims for damages by *foreseeably* exposed persons (see UCC 2-318).

From the point of view of the buyer, can he/she seek redress not only from the person selling the goods but also from the manufacturer, the wholesaler, the distributor, and other persons in the chain of distribution with whom he/she had no contract, no privity? This question of **vertical privity** is answered in much the same way as that of horizontal privity. If these more remote persons could have foreseen the chain of sales placing the goods into the hands of the ultimate buyer, and could have reasonably foreseen that the persons subsequently injured by defects in the product would be exposed to the item, liability is established notwithstanding the absence of privity. This disregarding of privity, whether in contract/warranty or tort/negligence cases, began with the classic negligence case, *MacPherson v. Buick Motor Co.*, 111 N.E. 1050 (Court of Appeals of New York, 1916). Manufacturer Buick sold a car with defective wheels to a dealer who, in turn, sold the car to MacPherson. Buick was held directly liable to MacPherson for his injuries from a crash caused by the defective wheels; the court found this sequence of events foreseeable, and thus it extended Buick's duty of care to the remote, plaintiff consumer, despite a lack of privity between Buick and that consumer.

Note: Privity requirements tend to remain strong in many countries, such as Germany, South Africa, and the United Kingdom. Even in those countries where the privity concept has been weakened, it can still be a serious obstacle for plaintiffs, because exceptions to privity: (1) may apply only to particular kinds of defects, as in France (hidden defects only), (2) may be limited to the consumer context, as in Australia, Canada, and the Philippines, and (3) rarely extend rights to mere bystanders, as in Australia, Belgium, and some American states.

YOU SHOULD REMEMBER

The law has moved from *caveat emptor* toward *caveat venditor*. Part of this movement has been achieved by warranties.

Express warranties arise because the seller represents that the goods will do a specified thing, meet a certain description or specification, or be like a picture, drawing, or standard. An *implied warranty* arises from the implications of the fact that the seller is selling goods. If he/she is a merchant, the goods should be merchantable; if the seller (merchant or not) knows of some special use by the buyer, he/she implies that the goods will suit that purpose.

Warranty can be avoided by means of a *disclaimer*, such as the words "as is" or "without warranty of any kind, either express or implied." A disclaimer should be clearly evident by large, bold type and/or prominent position. Disclaimers are most effective between parties of approximately equal bargaining ability. They may be unenforceable if fundamental unfairness in circumstances exists.

The Magnuson-Moss Act sets certain requirements for warranties by merchants for goods costing over $10. The merchant-seller who gives a full warranty or a limited warranty is held to certain strict standards and must clearly identify the extent of the warranty.

Privity of contract is no longer required for suit based on warranty. In both horizontal and vertical privity, the usual test is *foreseeability*, that is, whether manufacturers, sellers, and distributors could reasonably foresee the kinds and groups of persons who would be exposed to the goods to be sold and thus possibly injured by them.

PRODUCT LIABILITY ARISING OUT OF TORT

So far the discussion of sales has dealt with product liability arising out of contract. We now turn to the tort liability of a seller of goods, that is, responsibility arising out of one of the following:

1. *Intentional* harmful action.

2. *Negligent* harmful action.

3. *Strict liability*, a relatively modern category.

Since intentional harmful action is rarely a factor in product liability cases, this discussion will deal with the *negligence* of a seller or manufacturer and with *strict liability*. Acts and defects resulting in liability (whether from negligence or strict liability) may arise from improper manufacture or inspection, a failure to warn, or problems in design.

As discussed on pages 455–458, negligence is failure to follow some generally accepted standard of care. Thus, if manufactured goods explode, if cosmetics cause injury to the face or eyes, if plaintiff becomes ill upon consuming defendant's canned soup, a negligence case must demonstrate, first, some standard of care generally applicable in the manufacture of such goods, and, second, failure by the defendant to rise to the level of such standard of care.

Obviously, these requirements for proving negligence can be difficult if not impossible for a plaintiff to meet, and modern common law has devised principles to assist the plaintiff in certain carefully delineated kinds of situations.

One of these principles is *res ipsa loquitur* ("the thing speaks for itself"). Under this principle, negligence need not be proved by plaintiff if (a) the product was under the exclusive control of defendant at the time of its manufacture, and (b) injuries such as those suffered by plaintiff do not ordinarily happen in the absence of negligence. Thus, in the exploding bottle case—(a soft drink bottle exploding as it is being placed in a grocery cart), *res ipsa loquitur* may be used as a substitute for the requirement of proving negligence by the manufacturer when the drink was bottled. (*Res ipsa loquitur* is discussed on page 459.)

Strict liability is another exception to the negligence requirement. This theory, a modern common law (not statutory) development, imposes liability on manufacturers and sellers *as a matter of public policy*. As set forth in the Second Restatement of Torts §402A (used by most courts), there are three requirements: (1) that the product was sold in a defective condition and as such was unreasonably dangerous to the user; (2) that the seller is in the business of selling such a product (a merchant); (3) that the product reached the user without substantial change. Cases abound dealing with the liability of automobile manufacturers and others making or dealing a vast array of consumer products.

The word "defective" does not have the literal meaning usually ascribed to it; rather, it means merely that the goods were not in such condition or of such manufacture as an ordinary consumer might reasonably expect (the "consumer expectations test"). Thus, electric saws or drills without proper guards or protective devices, nightgowns that are readily combustible when exposed to the flame of a stove or oven, a child's toy that might easily cut or otherwise injure the child—all may be "defective" even though carefully manufactured. So, the defect can stem from poor design, unknown hazards, or insufficient warnings, not simply manufacturing problems. (For defective design cases, some states have adopted the standard proposed in the Restatement (Third) of Torts: Product Liability § 2—requiring the plaintiff to prove the existence of a *reasonable alternative design*.)

It is a balancing test, also often called a *risk-utility test*, because the product is considered defective if its risk outweighs its utility (it is more dangerous than absolutely necessary in light of the product's purpose); thus, the possibility of a better—at least as useful, but less dangerous—alternative product is a crucial consideration.

The European Union (EU) Directive Article 6(2) follows the "consumer expectations" test, which is also the standard in the vast majority of countries throughout the world. Ironically, the national legal system responsible for creating that test, the United States, now leads the way in promoting the other approach, the risk-utility analysis. Still, the consumer expectations paradigm is also used in the United States, often in combination with the risk-utility analysis. And the risk-utility analysis is occasionally used in other countries (e.g., Canada, the Netherlands), although mainly to define negligence in general tort law cases, not just product liability matters.

WHO IS LIABLE FOR A DEFECTIVE PRODUCT?

Each party in the chain of distribution may be liable.

Manufacturers, particularly of end products (not just component parts), may be liable even if a subsequent party (e.g., a distributor) is responsible for final inspections of, and possible corrections of, the product.

Component part manufacturers are liable if it is their defective manufacturing or design of the part that is the basis for the suit. However, unless they had reason to believe the manufacturer was in error, component part makers are not ordinarily liable for design defects in a part that they simply made per the manufacturer's erroneous specifications.

Wholesalers are usually liable for defective products they sell, except that some states relieve them of liability for latent or hidden defects when the wholesaler merely sold the product in the same condition that it received them.

Retailers often are liable, but some jurisdictions excuse from responsibility a retailer who did not in any way help cause the product's defective condition.

Because they usually extend no warranties and buyers generally have no great expectations when dealing with them, *sellers of used goods* are rarely liable except for (1) some states' special laws requiring warranties from used-car sellers and (2) their own conduct in poorly making, replacing, or repairing a part.

Successor corporations tend to be liable for the acquired company's debts, including product liability judgments or claims stemming from the acquired business's actions before it was acquired.

Comparative Law: Who Can Sue,
and for What Type of Damages?

The most "liberal": The United States, Japan, and most Canadian provinces are among the few places where anyone—an individual or a business—can sue whether the damage occurred to consumer property or to commercial property.

The most restrictive: In many Latin American countries (e.g., Argentina, Brazil, and Peru), in the Pacific Rim (e.g., China, Malaysia, the Philippines, and Taiwan), and in Russia and India as well as a few Canadian provinces, only consumers have rights under special product liability laws, such as suing in strict liability.

A middle approach: In the European Union (Article 9 of the EU Directive on Product Liability (1985)) and countries such as Australia, Israel, Norway, and Switzerland, anyone can sue for personal injuries, but claims for property damage can proceed only if to consumer property.

The seller's remedy for possible strict liability may be in full and adequately placed warnings. Even with such warnings, however, plaintiffs may have little or no difficulty framing a *prima facie* case—a case strong enough to reach a jury.

In reaction to the seeming ease in which strict product liability cases have proceeded, some courts have adopted rules that better enable defendants to fight such suits. The following five defenses are among those that may bar or reduce a product liability plaintiff's recovery in a number of states. (1) *Product misuse* is the plaintiff's using the product in a patently improper and unforeseen manner, combining the product with another product to make it dangerous, or failing to maintain the product in good working order. (2) *Assumption of risk* is the plaintiff's using a product with known risks, such as tobacco or a medicine with well-publicized side effects. (3) *Sophisticated purchaser* is when the plaintiff's experience or training renders him/her far more knowledgeable than is common about a particular product's dangers—e.g., a chemist working with certain volatile substances. (4) *Preemption* is when federal statutes or regulations concerning a product may expressly or implicitly remove from state courts the power to decide state claims in that same field. (5) *State of the art* is when the defendant has complied with the best available technology—similar to the "no reasonable alternative design" standard mentioned above—or everything the defendant did met a high standard of care *and* the dangerous nature of the product was not known nor could it reasonably have been discovered in the time period when the product was made.

KNOW THE CONCEPTS
DO YOU KNOW THE BASICS?

1. What are the key guarantees for criminal defendants under the U.S. Constitution?

2. Discuss the levels of evidence necessary at each of the four phases of criminal procedure: investigation, arrest, lodging of charges, and trial.

3. (a) What are the rules of evidence intended to do?

    (b) What effect may U.S. Constitutional guarantees have on the introduction of evidence?

4. Name two methods by which crimes can be classified.

5. How is intent transferable?

6. Name the basic elements needed to prove negligence.

7. Distinguish between intent and motive.

8. Name (a) six intentional torts involving interference with the person, and (b) four concerning interference with property.

9. List some white-collar crimes.

10. Compare the law of crimes and torts with respect to burdens of proof, damages, consent, sources of the law, and types of acts required for guilt or liability.

11. *True* or *false*: If A does not disclose every problem he has had with a machine that he is selling to B, then B will probably win a suit against A for fraud. Explain your answer.

12. Name two crimes where the defendant's alleged behavior does not constitute a tort.

13. Name nine crimes for which the culprit may also be subject to tort liability for conversion.

14. Name four defenses to negligence that are not defenses to crimes.

15. What is the basis of a seller's contractual liability for defective goods? How can sellers protect themselves from this liability?

16. What is the basis of a seller's tort liability for defective goods? How can sellers protect themselves?

17. How does the Magnuson-Moss Act affect warranty law?

18. Is privity of contract required for a person to win a claim for breach of warranty?

TERMS FOR STUDY

actus reus
"as is"
burden of proof
causation in fact
consumer expectations test
crime
  arson
  attempt
  bankruptcy fraud
  bribery
  burglary
  compounding a crime
  computer crime
  corporate crime
  criminal fraud
  embezzlement
  forgery
  fraud against consumers
  larceny
  mail and wire fraud
  misappropriation
  RICO
  robbery
defense
  act of God
  assumption of risk
  comparative negligence
  consent
  contributory negligence
  duress
  entrapment
  immunity
  infancy
  insanity
  intoxication
  mistake of fact
  mistake of law
  preemption
  privilege
  product misuse
  self-defense
  sophisticated purchaser
  state of the art

statute of limitations
superseding (intervening)
  causes
disclaimers
duty (of care)
express warranties
felony
fitness warranty
implied warranties
indictment
information
Magnuson-Moss Act
mens rea
merchant
merchantability warranty
misdemeanor
negligence *per se*
organized crime
privity
probable cause
proximate cause
reasonable alternative design
self-publication
tort
  intentional tort
    abuse of process
    abusive discharge
    assault
    battery
    conversion
    defamation (libel, slander)
    disparagement
    false arrest
    false imprisonment
    fraud
    intentional infliction of
      mental (emotional) distress
    interference with contract
    interference with prospec-
      tive economic advantage
    invasion of privacy
    malicious institution of civil
      proceedings

malicious prosecution
negligent misrepresentation
nuisance
trespass to personal
  property
trespass to real property
unfair competition
negligence
  res ipsa loquitur

respondeat superior
strict liability
treason
victimless crimes
warranty
white-collar crime

PRACTICAL APPLICATION

1. You believe that wealthy Sam Sick has been molesting your 10-year-old child. However, a jury has acquitted Sam of all criminal charges. (a) Can he be sued? (b) How would a civil trial be different from the criminal case?

2. For several months Derek Dirt has allowed his garbage to accumulate in his backyard, next to a school playground. Little Wendy Wanderer, age five, sees what to her promises to be a nice toy among the trash. Upon coming closer, she is bitten by a rat.
   Wendy screams and then faints. Her nearby mother calls an ambulance, which, on the way to the scene, jumps a curb and strikes Paul Pedestrian, seriously injuring him.
   Wendy requires a series of rabies shots. Except for some bad dreams, she apparently recovers.
   (a) Discuss the lawsuits based on negligence that Wendy and her parents may bring against Derek.
   (b) Discuss who might be liable to Paul.
   (c) Discuss possible negligence by persons other than Derek.

3. Workers from a moving company are delivering furniture to an apartment. While Holly Hapless is walking by, a chair crashes through a window of the apartment and lands on her foot, causing injury. What two Latin terms may play key parts in Holly's case against the moving company?

4. Larry Loaded drove his 18-wheeler into the side of a schoolhouse. He destroyed the school cafeteria, frightened but left physically uninjured a number of children, and did serious harm to his own body. When the school principal pulled Larry out of the wreckage, she found a nearly empty bottle of bourbon under the front passenger seat. The school nurse treated Larry for shock and, for good measure, took a blood sample, which showed a high alcohol

percentage. In a hearing before his criminal trial, Larry claims that evidence of the bottle and the samples should be excluded.
   (a) On what grounds does Larry base this claim?
   (b) What arguments would you make in response if you were the prosecutor?
   (c) What would the judge decide?
   (d) With what crimes should Larry be charged?
   (e) For what torts may he be held liable?

5. One of your employees may have embezzled thousands of dollars from your company. What may you do to stop her, to investigate her, to convict her?

6. In a negligence case, a jury decides that plaintiff C suffered $250,000 damages and assesses the blame for C's injuries at 60% for C and 40% for defendant. How much would the plaintiff's damages award be (a) under contributory negligence; (b) under comparative negligence?

7. Sally Silly is or was your embezzling employee. Alas, she may not be "quite right in the head."
   (a) In a criminal prosecution, what defense may her attorney raise?
   (b) What if Sally's problems stemmed from alcoholism?
   (c) What if Sally claims she stole from the company out of love for a man she thought was Albert Schweitzer, a man who gladly took most of her gifts of money and encouraged her to steal more?
   (d) As a prosecutor, would you give her immunity to testify against "Albert"?
   (e) What problems might you face?
   (f) What torts have been committed?

8. (a) Should the finding "not guilty, by reason of insanity" be replaced by the verdict "guilty, but insane"?
   (b) If so, how should such "guilty" defendants be punished?

9. Early one evening, Lucy Luscious stops Sidney Susceptible on a city sidewalk in the "red light" district. Hitching up her tight skirt a notch as she sits on a bench, Lucy asks for the time. Sidney gives it. Lucy asks Sidney to light her cigarette. He does. Lucy asks Sidney to sit down and join her for a smoke. He sits. While talking to Sidney, Lucy puts on rouge and more bright red lipstick. Sidney offers her money for sexual services. Lucy flashes her badge and arrests Sidney for solicitation.
   (a) What defense might Sidney raise? Will he succeed?
   (b) What tort has been committed?

10. Cory Criminal takes a bicycle left unattended on Vera Victim's front porch. Cory rides the bicycle all over town and fastens to the frame his own flashing neon bicycle license plate, emblazoned "CORY'S."
   (a) What crime has Cory committed?

(b) What crime would it be if Cory broke through a window of Vera's house, entered, and then took the bicycle?

(c) What if Cory put a knife to Vera's throat, made her get off her two-wheeler, and rode away with it?

(d) In each case, name the torts, also.

11. Wally Worker suspects that his employer, Crass Conglomerates, Inc., may have rigged prices with its main supposed competitor. He raises questions with his superior, Brenda Boss, who fires him. Wally's union goes on strike in protest. The strike prevents Crass from meeting its existing contracts or making new ones. Furthermore, a shotgun, albeit unloaded, has been pointed at strikebreakers by union member Vera Vigilante.

Crass management orders an investigation of the union leaders. Thus Crass manages to photograph and distribute pictures of the union's treasurer, Leo Leader, leaving a video club with several X-rated films, the titles plainly visible, in hand. Leo has countered by falsely telling Crass customers that certain Crass "super-balsam" products are actually made of papier-mâché. What torts have been committed, and by whom?

12. Free State Fireworks Company, Colesville, Maryland, purchased a shipment of fireworks from Hercules Powder Company, FOB seller's plant, Apopka, Florida. While the shipment was in transit from Apopka to Colesville, the fireworks exploded, killing three persons and causing a vast amount of property damage. There is some evidence of negligent manufacture of the fireworks. Discuss the possible liability of Free State and Hercules.

13. Sunshine Pharmaceutical Company manufactures drugs and medicines. It produced a vaccine for a national swine flu immunization program. Speck, a vaccinee, was partially paralyzed after being vaccinated, and medical experts believe that the vaccine caused the paralysis. Does Speck have a valid claim against Sunshine? On what basis?

ANSWERS
KNOW THE CONCEPTS

1. Fourth, Fifth, Sixth, Eighth, and Fourteenth Amendments. Fourth: protection from unreasonable searches and seizures; Fifth: due process of law (federal) and prohibition of compulsory self-incrimination and double jeopardy; Sixth: speedy and public trial, impartial jury, information as to charges, calling and confronting witnesses, having a lawyer; Eighth: proscribes excessive bail, excessive fines, and cruel and unusual punishment; Fourteenth: due process of law (state).

2. Investigation: no level; arrest: probable cause; charges: probable cause, preponderance of evidence, or prosecutor's evidence supports belief in guilt; trial: guilt proved beyond a reasonable doubt.

3. (a) To streamline the trial, among other things. To exclude irrelevant, unreliable, or unfairly prejudicial matters. (b) Constitutional guarantees, especially their violation, may necessitate the restriction or outright barring of otherwise admissible evidence.

4. (1) Classification as either felony or misdemeanor; (2) classification according to the type of harm caused.

5. If one knowingly commits a criminal or tortious act, one is presumed to intend the natural consequences of that act. Moreover, if the consequences occur to someone not intended as the victim, or if the consequences are different from those intended, the law may transfer the *mens rea*, or tortious intent, from what was intended to what actually occurred.

6. Duty, breach of duty, causation, and damages.

7. Intent is the *mens rea* preceding or accompanying the act. Motive is the overall purpose, good or bad, for which the act is done.

8. (a) Assault, battery, false arrest, false imprisonment, intentional infliction of mental (emotional) distress, and invasion of privacy; (b) conversion, nuisance, trespass to personal property, and trespass to real property.

9. Tax evasion, bribes, extortion, embezzlement, kickbacks, pilferage, forgery, computer crimes, antitrust violations, RICO offenses, and fraud concerning consumers, credit cards, securities, insurance, bankruptcy, and bank loans.

10. Crimes: proof of guilt beyond a reasonable doubt, damages not necessary, consent usually no defense, mainly statutory law, and guilt requires intentional or grossly negligent acts.
Torts: preponderance of evidence, damages needed, consent a defense, mainly common law, and liability based on intentional acts, negligence, or no-fault (e.g., strict liability).

11. False. In most cases, there is no duty to volunteer information. Even if, in this case, there were a duty to speak, it is not at all clear from the facts that (1) the nondisclosure was of a material fact; (2) A intended that B would rely on the nondisclosure; (3) B justifiably relied on the nondisclosure; and (4) B was damaged. All of those points would have to be proved, in addition to demonstrating that A had a duty to speak (e.g., because A knew that B had misconstrued A's silence).

12. Attempt and compounding a crime. In some cases, other crimes (e.g., bribery) may also have no tort equivalents.

13. Arson, bribery, burglary, computer crimes, corporate crimes, embezzlement, forgery, larceny (theft), and robbery.

14. Act of God, assumption of risk, contributory or comparative negligence, and superseding (intervening) causes.

15. Express and/or implied warranties. By a disclaimer.

16. Negligence or strict liability. Provide a conspicuous, comprehensive warning about possible injuries and the need of the buyer and other users to be very careful.

17. The Magnuson-Moss Act sets certain requirements for warranties. They must be either full warranties (without limitations) or limited warranties (with clearly stated limitations).

18. No. Parties usually are liable for a breach of warranty if they could have foreseen the existence of, and potential injury to, the purchaser of a defective good, as well as others exposed to that defective good.

PRACTICAL APPLICATION

1. (a) Yes. Double jeopardy applies only to the filing of the same *criminal charges*.

   (b) The burden of proof for you, the plaintiff, would be only a preponderance of evidence, not—as it was for the prosecutor in the criminal case—proof of guilt beyond a reasonable doubt. There are, of course, other differences; for instance, some evidence may be more easily admitted in a civil trial.

2. (a) Certainly, Derek has acted negligently: he had a duty not to allow his garbage to accumulate over several months, and he breached that duty. The key issue is proximate cause.
   Wendy should be able to obtain a damages award against Derek for the physical and emotional harm suffered. It is foreseeable that rodents might gather in a festering pile of garbage, and that a rat might bite someone nearby. If Wendy were an adult or older child, she might be deemed contributorily negligent or to have assumed the risk, but for a five-year-old her actions appear to be reasonable. Moreover, the foreseeability of injury to a child is heightened by the close presence of a playground.
   Wendy's parents should be able to recover from Derek for their expenses in having Wendy transported, examined, and treated. Damages would include any of their costs that directly and proximately follow from the injury. Wendy's mother may also sue for trauma suffered, particularly if she actually saw her child being bitten; however, questions of duty, proximate cause, and actual damages may undermine such an action.

(b) Although ambulances often have to travel rapidly, Paul may show that, in these circumstances, climbing the curb amounted to negligent driving. If, however, the ambulance company is part of a governmental or charitable agency, immunity may serve as a partial or absolute defense.

Paul's claim against Derek appears to be too attenuated. Few, if any, courts would find proximate cause between Derek's negligence (accumulation of the garbage) and the force causing Paul's injuries (the moving ambulance). There is no foreseeability. Also, superseding cause may be a defense.

(c) Derek may claim that Wendy's mother was herself negligent in supervising Wendy. That is a question of fact for the jury. Even if her mother was contributorily negligent, that defense would not bar Wendy's suit. [However, Derek might file a third-party claim (see page 64) against the mother to receive a contribution from her for damages he must pay to Wendy.]

As for Paul, Wendy's conduct (assuming she was negligent) and the mother's supposed negligent supervision of Wendy were no more the proximate cause of his harm than was Derek's negligent accumulation of garbage; the calling of an ambulance also did not foreseeably lead to Paul's injuries, nor was it breaching a duty of care in the first place.

3. *Res ipsa loquitur* and *respondeat superior.*

4. (a) Fourth Amendment protection against unreasonable search and seizure, Fifth Amendment protection against self-incrimination.

(b) Actions taken were not by government (or, at very least, school officials are not police toward whom the amendments are really geared); search was reasonable; blood sample is not the sort of compulsory "testimony" that Fifth Amendment concerns.

(c) Probably admit both the blood sample (more likely) and the bottle. May exclude bottle as unreasonable search (argument that bottle is unfairly prejudicial would probably fail; the fact that evidence is harmful does not make it inadmissible).

(d) Among others, with drunken driving, reckless endangerment, destruction of public property.

(e) Negligence, trespass to real and personal property.

5. Contact the authorities. Watch out not to be overzealous; this may lead to charges of malicious prosecution, abusive discharge, defamation, and so on. However, to countenance embezzlement by sending the embezzler on to another employer may amount to compounding a crime and may subject you to a civil suit from a subsequent employer.

6. (a) Nothing. (b) Under "pure" comparative negligence, 40% of $250,000 ($100,000); otherwise, nothing.

7. (a) Insanity.

(b) Does alcoholism constitute an involuntary or voluntary intoxication defense? Although intoxication may be a cause of personal anguish leading to embezzlement, it is hard to see how it can result in intentional acts of fraud, as opposed to mere recklessness. Even if it could, assuming that Sally has any moments of lucidity in which she realizes what she has done, she will probably be held accountable for failing to take corrective measures.

(c) Sally's infatuation for "Albert" may be evidence of insanity, but it would not be duress.

(d) If you, the prosecutor, consider Sally to be relatively innocent compared to Albert, you may decide that Sally's assistance is necessary to apprehend and convict Albert. Immunity may be deemed a necessary means to obtain Sally's full assistance.

(e) Some problems: (1) before trial, how guilt should be apportioned between Sally and Albert; (2) how much leeway should a prosecutor have; (3) if immunity is given, how may Sally's credibility be ensured.

(f) Sally: conversion; Albert: conversion (using Sally as his agent), perhaps fraud upon Sally.

8. (a) This question should induce much discussion, since there are many possible answers. One is that, since the insane person lacks *mens rea*, a finding of guilt would mean that the act is a crime *per se*.

(b) The punishment, if any, is generally a question of community standards: the range of choices deemed to be neither too lax nor too severe.

9. (a) Entrapment. The question is whether Sidney initially had the necessary predisposition or whether his *mens rea* was induced by Lucy. Was Lucy's conduct the sort that would have caused an "innocent" man, one without predisposition toward solicitation, to do what Sidney did?

(b) There is no tort equivalent to solicitation. Even if Sidney's act were tortious, could Lucy or any other individual prove damages?

10. (a) Larceny.

(b) Burglary (and larceny).

(c) Armed robbery (larceny is part of the crime).

(d) The first two crimes involve the torts of trespass to real property and conversion. The third crime's tort equivalents are assault, battery (assuming Cory or the knife touched Vera), and conversion; intentional infliction of mental (emotional) distress may also be raised, although assault, battery, and conversion should be easier to prove and each is a basis for complete recovery of compensatory as well as punitive damages.

11. If Crass has rigged prices, then it and the other price-riggers have engaged in antitrust violations and unfair competition. Depending on other facts, this activity may constitute interference with contracts or prospective economic advantages.

Wally may have an action for abusive discharge against Brenda and Crass (the latter under *respondeat superior*).

Strikes are privileged conduct; hence, they do not constitute tortious interference with contracts or prospective economic advantages. However, Vera's act is probably an assault upon the strikebreakers who saw it and—with reason—believed that the shotgun was loaded.

Concerning the distribution of photographs showing Leo with several X-rated films, Crass is probably liable for invasion of privacy (public disclosure of private facts, intrusion upon a person's private life), and perhaps also liable for intentional infliction of mental distress. Of course, so long as the photographs truly show the movies in Leo's hand, defamation is negated on the grounds of truth.

Lastly, Leo's statements to the customers appear to be disparagement (trade libel). That Crass has provoked Leo's ire is no defense; his remedy is to sue Crass, not counter its torts with his own.
Note that the individuals at Crass who authorize or carry out a tort are liable for that tort just as the company is.

12. Free State is responsible for risk of loss in transit because of the term "FOB seller's plant," which designates the buyer's assumption of the risk. (This subject was explained in Chapter 9.)

However, the *real* cause of the explosion and the resultant loss of lives and property damage may be negligent manufacture by Hercules. In a claim or cross-claim for negligence, Free State could probably use *res ipsa loquitur* to place on Hercules the burden of putting forth evidence. Depending on the circumstances of the sale, Free State may also proceed against Hercules for strict liability and/or breach of warranty.

Against others, both parties suffer from the obvious fact that fireworks can be extremely dangerous and that both the manufacturer and the purchaser need to take that into account when making the shipping arrangements.

13. Speck may have a *prima facie* case against Sunshine. Vaccines, properly tested and manufactured, should not cause paralysis. Thus, the doctrine of *res ipsa loquitur* may be used, in a negligence case, to place on Sunshine the burden of putting forth evidence. Speck may also sue Sunshine in strict liability and in warranty (e.g., breach of warranty of merchantability).

20
PROPERTY

KEY TERMS

real property land, whatever is growing or built on land, and the rights associated with ownership and use thereof

personal property all property, tangible and intangible, except real property; generally property without a permanent location

bailment delivery of personal property into the care, control, and possession of another, without passing ownership interests

intellectual property protected expressions of scientific, artistic, or other creative and/or commercial endeavors. The main types are evinced by patents, copyrights, and trademarks.

In law, property is a collection of rights and interests, generally associated with the idea of ownership. There are two main types of property: (1) real property, which is land, the buildings, trees, or other items attached to the land, and the rights of land ownership and use; and (2) **personal property**, which is all other property, tangible or intangible, except real property.

PROPERTY AS A LEGAL CONCEPT

The law of contracts has an enormous influence on property. Unless a contract involves solely services, it probably has property (goods, land, etc.) as its subject matter. Indeed, a contract itself may be a form of property; the contractual rights and interests are owned by the parties to the contract, and generally are both transferable and enforceable in court.

Using this broad perspective, one sees that, for example, a negotiable instrument is a form of both a contract and property. Under the broad definition of property as a "bundle of rights," property is anything capable of ownership, whether individually, collectively, or for the benefit of others.

PERSONAL PROPERTY

TANGIBLE AND INTANGIBLE

Personal property (also called "personalty") can be tangible or intangible. **Tangible personal property** is subject to physical possession. It can include almost anything that takes up space and is movable (nonmovables would be real estate or fixtures).

Intangible personal property consists of rights in something that lacks physical substance. Examples include contracts, stocks, bonds, computer software (programs), employment, utility services (telephone, electricity, etc.), and intellectual property (copyrights, patents, and trademarks). Documents or other materials related to such property are really just evidence of the property; they are *not* the property with which we are concerned.

For instance, a written agreement evinces a contract, but the rights under the contract are the important property interest. Likewise, it is not the stock certificate, the computer disk, the employment card, or the certificate of copyright registration that is the key property interest; these are evidence of property, but the property itself is not capable of physical possession. One cannot control a portion of IBM equal to a 10-share interest in that company; nor can one simply pick up job tenure and put it in one's pocket; nor can one physically possess the exclusive right to publish the latest "great American novel." All such rights (stock ownership, employment, copyright) are real, but intangible.

FIXTURES

Another class of property is called a **fixture**. Consisting of what was personal property that has become attached to real property, the fixture is generally treated as part of the real property. Once personal property has become so incorporated into real property that it is difficult, costly, and/or impossible to remove, the personal property is considered a fixture. The main question is often whether an item's value is intrinsically related to the surrounding real property; the more closely the two are connected, the more likely the item (be it a backyard swing, a clothes dryer, a chandelier, or the like) is a fixture.

In the absence of agreement by the parties, courts often look to the parties' apparent intent to have, or not have, a fixture. This "intent test" considers:

(1) the item's purpose;

(2) the way in which it was attached; and

(3) the usual practice and custom with respect to such an item.

An exception is the **trade fixture,** placed on leased premises by a tenant for use in his/her business, not simply to benefit the entire property, but solely to meet the tenant's specific business needs. Unlike the situation for other would-be fixtures, the tenant can continue to treat a trade fixture as personal property. However, if removal causes damages, the tenant must reimburse the landlord. (If removal would cause severe damage, the trade fixture may have to stay, with the tenant compensated by the landlord, such as [a] the amount the fixture enhances the value of the leased premises overall [the unit rule"], or [b] the cost of reproducing the trade fixture less depreciation.)

Determining the amount of payments to the other party from whichever party retains the trade fixture often involves weighing the difference in value and costs of the trade fixture remaining in place or as severed (as "salvage value"). Legal principles from the law of accession (see page 500) may apply. A commercial lease may help parties avoid later disputes by specifying in the written document whether something is a trade fixture and even detailing the procedures—including any payments to be made—concerning the removal (or not) of that property from the premises.

ACQUIRING TITLE TO PERSONAL PROPERTY

• *CONTRACTS, SALES OF GOODS, AND TRANSFERS OF COMMERCIAL PAPER*

Contracts in general, as well as UCC Article 2 (sale of goods), have already been discussed in Chapters 4–9.

The transfer of negotiable instruments under UCC Articles 3 and 4 was covered in Chapters 10–12.

• *GIFTS*

A **gift** is a voluntary transfer of property from its owner (**donor**) to another person (**donee**) without any compensation for the donor. When the donee is a minor and the property is held in trust, the Uniform Gifts to Minors Act often outlines the custodian's (trustee's) duties and the minor's rights.

ELEMENTS OF A GIFT

The three elements of a gift are as follows:

1. Donative intent (language or circumstances indicate that the owner intended to give away the property).

2. Delivery [the property was actually or symbolically (e.g., keys to an automobile) placed in the donee's hands, with the owner giving up control].

3. Acceptance by the donee (usually presumed).

Because delivery is essential, there are no "executory" gifts; in the absence of consideration, a mere promise to give something is unenforceable.

TYPES OF GIFTS

The three categories of gifts are *inter vivos, causa mortis,* and *testamentary.*

Gifts inter vivos are made during the donor's lifetime, when he/she is *not* facing imminent death. The three elements are those listed above.

Gifts causa mortis are a type of conditional gift, which places a precondition on permanent retention of the item. When the donor, believing that his/her death is imminent, conveys property with the intent that the donee keep it after the donor's death, that is a gift *causa mortis.* The property must be returned to the donor if (1) the donor recovers, or dies from a cause quite different from that contemplated by the parties; (2) the donee predeceases (dies before) the donor; or (3) the donor revokes the gift.

A **testamentary gift** is stated in a will. It serves to transfer property when the maker of the will dies. Because wills are freely revocable until death, the effect is to make testamentary gifts likewise revocable. There is no actual gift until after death.

• *ACCESSION*

Accession is an addition to the value of personal property, by labor, materials, and/or natural process (e.g., growing fruit).

Examples: Accession

1. Adding an air conditioner to an automobile.
2. Turning an uncut diamond into a finished gem.

The property owner has a right to the increased value. Typically, he/she has paid for or performed the accession.

If ownership is at issue, these principles control:

1. Accessions performed by a thief or otherwise done in bad faith and without the owner's consent: The original property's rightful owner is entitled to the accession.

2. Accessions performed in good faith: The more the accession increases the value of the property, the more appropriate it becomes to place title with the person responsible for the accession. If the original owner keeps the property, he/she must (unlike the situation above) compensate the improver for the accession. If the improver gets the property, he/she must pay the original owner for its preaccession value.

Example: Accession Performed in Good Faith

Bobby Booby, thinking that a beat-up chair in his late Aunt Esmeralda's house was left to him, does extensive work to refinish it. A formerly $20 chair is now worth about $100. Actually, the chair was left to cousin Kate.

Bobby probably will be allowed to keep the chair, after giving Kate $20 for what it was originally worth. If, instead, Kate takes the chair, Bobby should be compensated for the accession.

• *CONFUSION*

When the personal property of different owners is commingled, there is **confusion** of goods: the various owners' properties can no longer be distinguished. For collective warehouses, silos, storage tanks and the like, confusion is avoided by maintaining thorough records showing how much of a fungible good (e.g., a particular grade of oil or grain) is held by each owner.

If the confusion was the intentional or otherwise wrongful act of one of the owners, then title rests exclusively with the innocent owner(s). On the other hand, all owners share equally if the confusion occurred by the owners' consent or agreement, through an accident or honest mistake, or by an act of God or a third party. The only way for one owner to obtain more than an equal share (or, perhaps for insurance purposes, to show a disproportionate share of loss) is to produce records that adequately support such a claim.

• *POSSESSION*

> When personal property is lost, mislaid, or abandoned, or clearly had no prior owner, a person may obtain title simply by taking possession of it.

Property is **lost** when it is accidentally left somewhere by its owner, who cannot find it but does not intend to give up ownership. The finder of lost property is a gratuitous bailee for the true owner, with title against all other persons but the true owner. (A "gratuitous bailee" has a right of possession, but the owner retains superior title interests. This bailee usually must take measures, but only those reasonable under the circumstances, to protect the property and locate the owner. Bailments are discussed later in this chapter.)

There are, however, two exceptions: if the property is found by a *trespasser* or by an *employee at work*, then the owner of the premises on which the item was found, not the finder, acts as bailee and has the title interest.

Property is **mislaid** when it is intentionally put somewhere, but then forgotten. In most states, the owner of the premises, not the finder, becomes the gratuitous bailee with good title against everyone but the true owner.

Property is **abandoned** when the owner discards it without intending to reclaim it. Title passes to the first person who takes possession of the property and intends to keep it. Valuable items, however, presumably are mislaid, not abandoned.

According to the **treasure trove rule** followed in most states, a nontrespassing finder has title to money or other treasure buried for so long a time that it is unlikely a prior owner will return. (Otherwise, the landowner usually has the rightful claim.) More important are the **estray statutes** found in most states: they provide the procedures (including publication of notice) whereby the finder/holder of lost or mislaid property may claim full title to it if it is not reclaimed by the true owner within the statutory period.

• *OPERATION OF LAW*

Federal, state, and local laws provide for transfer of property title via intestate succession or escheat (see the discussion of wills, pages 526–527), via bankruptcy or execution on judgments (see Chapter 13), or via lawsuits for conversion (see torts, Chapter 19). Except in certain limited instances (e.g., a UCC "bona fide purchaser" of goods; see Chapter 9), even innocent third persons cannot obtain title to stolen property; the thief never obtained title, which remains with the true owner.

• *CREATION*

The final method of gaining title—by invention, art, or other intellectual endeavor (e.g., creating a painting, writing a book, knitting a sweater, developing a computer program) involves a topic, intellectual property, considered in Chapter 26.

BAILMENTS

A **bailment** involves a transfer of personal property possession, but not title. The **bailor** (owner) transfers possession to the **bailee**.

The requirements for a bailment are as follows:

1. Bailor retains title.
2. Bailee obtains possession:
   (a) delivery by bailor,
   (b) acceptance by bailee.
3. Possession is for a specific purpose.
4. Possession is temporary; property ultimately reverts to bailor or bailor's designee.

• *TYPES OF BAILMENTS*

There are three general categories of bailments: (1) bailments solely benefitting the bailor; (2) bailments solely benefitting the bailee; and (3) bailments beneficial to both parties.

Bailments are generally express or implied agreements, but they can be imposed by operation of law (**constructive bailments**).

BAILMENT TO BENEFIT SOLELY THE BAILOR

Example: Only the Bailor Benefits

Barbara Bailor leaves her cat with Boris Bailee while Barbara is on vacation; Boris is to take care of the cat, with no compensation expected or received.

Also known as a **gratuitous bailment**, this bailment is really a favor performed by the bailee. Thus the bailee usually *owes just a slight degree of care*; only gross negligence will leave him/her responsible for damages to, or loss of, the bailed property.

Constructive bailments usually fall into this category. The constructive bailee has found lost or stolen property, has received a misdelivery, or has otherwise had the property "thrust upon him/her." Once the constructive bailee takes control of the property, he/she is held to the standard of care (that is, slight care) associated with a gratuitous bailment.

BAILMENT TO BENEFIT SOLELY THE BAILEE

Example: Only the Bailee Benefits

Bob Bailor lends his car to Barry Bailee, with Bob neither expecting nor receiving compensation for the "loan."

Because here the bailor is doing the bailee a favor, with the bailee passing nothing in return to the bailor, it seems only fair to hold the bailee to a *duty of great (extraordinary) care*. Unless he/she was exceedingly careful, the bailee may be held accountable for damages to, or loss of, the bailed property.

BAILMENT OF MUTUAL BENEFIT

Example: Both the Bailor and the Bailee Benefit

Goods are left with a firm entrusted to packing and storing them. The bailors pay for the bailee firm's services.

Here the bailee owes a *duty of ordinary care*. In effect, he/she is held to the "reasonable person" standard found in the tort law of negligence.

Note that parking lot bailments involve transfer of the keys of the vehicle and physical control of it. If a person parks the car and retains the keys, he/she has merely rented parking space. There is no bailment because delivery and acceptance of possession are lacking.

• *MODERN TREND IN DETERMINING THE BAILEE'S DUTY OF CARE*

As just discussed, most courts decide the bailee's duty of care according to whom the bailment benefits. An increasing number of courts, however, treat the issues of whether the bailment benefits only one of the parties, and whether the bailee is compensated, as being two important, but not necessarily decisive, factors in determining the duty of care. The question is simply: What was reasonable care, given all the circumstances present in a particular case? Obviously, the overall effect may not be different from the older three-tiered standard; for instance, most judges and juries will hold that the degree of care reasonable when the bailee is simply doing a favor for someone is lower than when the bailee is compensated for his/her services.

• *THE BAILOR'S DUTIES*

Just as the bailee has a duty of one of three levels of care, so the bailor also has duties. He/she must deliver to the bailee property safe and fit for the bailment's purpose, must defend against any third party's wrongful claim to title in the property, and must tell the bailee about property defects of which the bailor has or should have knowledge.

• *LIMITS ON THE BAILEE'S LIABILITY*

Express, written bailments can expand or (more typically) limit the bailee's potential liability. For bailees bearing a special, public interest (e.g., parking garages, hotels), liability limits may be forbidden by state statute or municipal ordinance; even if not prohibited, limits must be reasonable. For purely "private" bailments, liability limits are usually permitted unless they defeat the bailment's purpose. The modern law's emphasis on consumer protection has led to most states' requiring that liability limitations be clearly expressed, via a method that would be noticed by a reasonable bailor before, or at the outset of, a bailment.

• *BAILMENT TERMINATION AND THE RETURN OF PROPERTY*

Bailments are terminated by performance, time, destruction of bailed property, acts of the parties, or operation of law.

Performance arises when the bailment's purpose has been fulfilled or when the agreed-upon duties of bailor and bailee have otherwise been completed.

Time terminates the bailment when the period expressly provided or implicitly agreed to by the parties has lapsed.

Destruction of bailed property can occur through a third party or by an act of God (e.g., a hurricane). It also arises when the bailed property is no longer appropriate for the bailment's purpose.

Acts of the parties include (a) the parties' subsequent agreement to terminate; (b) *either* party's decision to terminate a bailment that is for the sole benefit of one party and/or has an indefinite duration; (c) the "innocent" party's choice to terminate and, if applicable, to seek damages, because the other party has materially breached the bailment agreement (e.g., the bailee used the property in a way not agreed to by the bailor).

Operation of law concerns the bailee's death, incompetence, insolvency, or other such event that renders performance impossible.

Upon termination, the bailee must return the bailed property to the bailor *unless:*

    (a) it was lost, stolen, or destroyed through no fault of the bailee;

    (b) it was delivered to someone with a better claim to it than the bailor has;

    (c) it was taken by legal process (e.g., attachment); or

    (d) the bailee has an unpaid lien on it.

Most states have statutes permitting a *bailee's lien* on the bailed property if the bailee has not been paid for services performed on the property. After notice, the property is sold to pay off the lien (see discussion of liens in Chapter 13). Usually the lien is solely possessory (if the bailee gives up possession, the lien ends) and cannot be used for work done on credit.

• *THE COMMON CARRIER AS A SPECIAL TYPE OF BAILEE*

A **common carrier** holds itself out to the public as available for transporting goods or passengers.

A common carrier may be regulated by state agencies or, if an interstate carrier, by federal agencies such as the Interstate Commerce Commission. Although this discussion will focus on carriers of goods, note that carriers of passengers are also subject to extensive state and federal regulation. *Passenger carriers* are *not insurers* of their passenger's safety (hence not strictly liable), but they are usually *held to a high duty of care*—more than just avoiding ordinary negligence.

When *transporting goods*, the *common carrier is a special type of bailee*, strictly liable for property damaged, lost, or taken while in its possession unless the damage, loss, or taking resulted from one of the following:

1. The shipper's actions, such as improper packing, if the resulting problem was not obvious to the carrier. (The "shipper" is the party sending the goods via the carrier; e.g., the owner or seller of the goods.)

2. Governmental acts, such as attachment or confiscation pursuant to legal processes.

3. An act of God, such as a severe flood, tornado, earthquake, or other unforeseeable natural catastrophe.

4. An act of a "public enemy," a term that includes nations, groups, and individuals seeking the violent overthrow of the government.

5. The inherent nature of the property, such that the shipper should have made special carrying arrangements. The nonnegligent carrier is thus not responsible if, for example, perishable goods spoil.

It is usually the common carrier's burden to prove that the damages arose from one of these exceptions.

Once transportation is completed, the common carrier is considered a "warehouse" for goods still in its possession. Thus strict liability (with just the five exceptions listed above) ends when (a) the goods are unloaded from the common carrier and placed in a storehouse; or (b) the consignee (the person to whom the shipment was sent) has had reasonable time to inspect and take possession of the goods (with some states also requiring that the consignee receive notice of the goods' arrival).

The common carrier as warehouse owes a duty of ordinary care. Like warehouses generally, the carrier is then held just to a negligence standard, not one of strict liability.

Common Carrier's Liability Limitations

Intrastate commerce: most states permit limits except for gross negligence.

Interstate commerce: federal law [and UCC 7-309(2)] allows limits if the shipper can obtain a higher amount of liability by paying increased rates.

• *INTELLECTUAL PROPERTY*

A special type of intangible property, arising from the creative endeavors of the human mind and known as **intellectual property**, is evinced by patents, copyrights, and trademarks and trade names. It is discussed in Chapter 26.

JOINT OWNERSHIP OF PROPERTY

Both personal and real property may have more than one owner. The four main categories of co-ownership are joint tenancy, tenancy by the entirety, tenancy in common, and community property.

A **joint tenancy** is established when equal interests in property are conveyed by an instrument expressly stating that the parties acquire the property as joint tenants. Four "unities" are preconditions to the joint tenancy: the owners must all have received their interests in the property (a) at the same time (unity of time), (b) from the same source (unity of title), (c) in equal interests (unity of interest), and (d) with each owner having a right to possess the whole (unity of possession).

Perhaps the most important aspect of joint tenancies is that the owners have a **right of survivorship**: when one of the joint tenants dies, his/her interest passes equally to the surviving joint tenants. Moreover, just as a joint tenancy interest cannot pass by inheritance (it goes to the surviving joint tenants, not the deceased joint tenant's heirs), so it cannot be transferred by one of the joint tenants; such a transfer destroys the unity of time and converts the new tenants' ownership to that of a tenancy in common (see below); the new owner, as well as the remaining old owners, hold the property as "tenants in common."

A **tenancy by the entirety**, which only a married couple can create, is similar to a joint tenancy in that there are four unities and a right to survivorship. Unlike the situation in a joint tenancy, though, a unilateral action of one tenant (e.g., an attempt to transfer his/her interest to a third party) cannot turn a tenancy by the entirety into a tenancy in common. Only death, divorce, or agreement by both spouses terminates this tenancy. Many states, including all community property states no longer recognize this tenancy.

A **tenancy in common** requires only one of the four unities: unity of possession. There is no right of survivorship; a deceased common tenant's heirs receive his/her interest in the tenancy. If the type of co-ownership is unspecified or otherwise unclear, a conveyance to two or more persons is treated as creating a tenancy in common.

Lastly, some states (Arizona, California, Idaho, Louisiana, Nevada, New Mexico, Texas, Washington, and to a certain extent Wisconsin) follow a system known as **community property**. Almost all property acquired by the husband or wife during the marriage, except for gifts or inheritances, is owned equally by both spouses. Property acquired before marriage is not included, unless it becomes so "commingled" with community property that it can no longer be traced.

A special form of real property, the **condominium**, features sole ownership of individual office or apartment units, with joint ownership (by all the sole owners) of the land and common areas. The owners' management participation and their shares of expenses are governed by state law and the terms of the condominium agreement. Condominium owners typically have the right to enjoy free and equal use of the common areas, and to transfer their units subject only to lawful restrictions in the condominium agreement.

YOU SHOULD REMEMBER

The major forms of joint ownership are joint tenancy (with survivorship rights and the four "unities"—time, title, interest, and possession) and tenancy in common (with no survivorship rights and only one "unity," possession).

Many noncommunity property states still permit tenancy by the entirety, which is similar to joint tenancy, but harder to terminate and available solely to married couples.

Two other forms of joint ownership are community property and condominiums.

All of the above forms of ownership can apply to both personal and real property, except for condominiums, which are real property.

REAL PROPERTY

Real property interests center around ownership, use, and possession.

ACQUISITION OF TITLE

Ownership (title) may be acquired in many ways.

• *VOLUNTARY TITLE TRANSFER BY DEED*

The transfer, by sale or gift, is formally accomplished by delivering to the grantee a **deed**, which customarily includes the following:

1. Names of the grantor and grantee.
2. Consideration paid, if applicable.
3. "Words of conveyance," stating the parties' intent to convey.
4. A precise, formal description (metes, i.e., measures, and bounds, i.e., directions) of the property.
5. Exceptions or reservations, such as easements or profits (both described shortly).

6. Quantity (acreage).

7. Covenants or other warranties.

8. The grantor's signature.

General warranty deeds include all of the usual covenants (title, no encumbrance, quiet enjoyment, i.e., possession without disturbance). The grantor warrants title against defects or encumbrances arising *before* or *during* his/her ownership.

Special warranty deeds include the general warranty's covenants, but warrant only against defects or encumbrances arising *after* the grantor acquired the property.

Deeds (whether general warranty or special warranty) usually warrant the grantor's "good and merchantable title." If disputes over title arise later, the grantor may be subject to a breach of title lawsuit.

A **quitclaim deed**, however, contains no warranty of title; it simply grants all of the grantor's rights in the property, whatever these rights may be. Unless the quitclaim and the grantor's actions were fraudulent, he/she is not liable to the grantee even if it turns out that the grantor had no title at all and hence conveyed none to the grantee.

Recording the deed in the local records office is not needed to transfer title. However, recording provides notice to others, and in many states establishes priority over unrecorded deeds involving the same property.

FACTORS INVOLVED IN REAL PROPERTY SALES

The sale of real property generally involves the following:

1. Contract of sale, which must be in writing to be enforceable (Statute of Frauds).

2. Title search, generally performed to determine if the grantor has a marketable title.

3. Mortgage(s), when money is borrowed to purchase the property.

4. At closing, delivery of the deed to the buyer, who pays the purchase price. The money may then be disbursed to, among others, the broker or agent (if any), the title company (if applicable), the seller's mortgagee (if money is still owed), and the seller.

MORTGAGES

Mortgages are a type of security transaction involving real property. (See Chapter 13.) The mortgage is a document, and a conveyance, from the mortgagor (debtor) to the mortgagee (creditor), with real property described and given as security for the loan made by the mortgagee to the mortgagor. The loan itself is usually evinced by a promissory note.

Most states consider the mortgagor to have title, even if in default, until court action has resulted in a foreclosure; in essence, the mortgagee simply has a lien on the property. Some states, though, treat title as resting with the mortgagee, whose interest is subject to a condition subsequent (payment of the debt), which would place title with the mortgagor; in effect, this "title theory" makes little difference, as the mortgagor retains possession and other property interests, as well as such duties as paying taxes. (For a discussion of foreclosures, see Chapter 13.)

ALTERNATIVES TO THE MORTGAGE

Two alternatives to the mortgage are as follows:

1. **Deed of trust.** The property is conveyed to a third person (the trustee), who holds it in trust as security for the debt. The debtor retains possessory and other property rights (see pages 512–513). Foreclosure is generally along the same lines as for mortgages, but the trustee, not the sheriff, may conduct the public sale.

2. **Installment land contract.** The seller retains a security interest until the total purchase price is paid. The buyer possesses the property, with forfeiture conditions (such as for default in payments) stated in the contract.

• *INVOLUNTARY TITLE TRANSFER BY OPERATION OF LAW*

1. **Foreclosure sale.** Title may pass because of an unpaid mortgage or a mechanic's lien. For more, see Chapter 13.

2. **Judgment sale.** Title may pass because of an unpaid judgment, leading to a writ of execution for the judgment creditor. For more, see Chapter 13.

3. **Eminent domain.** The right of the federal and state governments, as well as some other entities with governmental powers, to take privately owned real property for the public benefit is called **eminent domain**. The Fifth Amendment to the U.S. Constitution requires that the owner be compensated for the property taken; the amount awarded is generally the property's fair market value before the taking occurred.

4. **Adverse possession.** If a trespasser actually occupies property continuously, exclusively, openly, and in a manner hostile to the owner's rights (without permission), and if this state of affairs lasts for the period of time required by state statute (it varies from about 5 to 20 years), then the owner's title passes to the trespasser by **adverse possession**. Some states require that the trespasser have had at least some claim of title beforehand, and most states look to whether the would-be adverse possessor paid taxes on

the property. Neither government land nor land occupied by permission of the owner can be acquired by adverse possession.

• *TRANSFER BY INHERITANCE*

Title to real property may be transferred either through a will or intestate succession.

RIGHTS ASSOCIATED WITH LAND OWNERSHIP

The law has long held that certain rights naturally accompany land ownership.

1. *Surface rights*. A landowner holds the exclusive right to occupy the surface of a piece of land.

2. *Subterranean rights*. A landowner has the exclusive right to oil, minerals, and other substances found beneath the land's surface. He/she is also entitled to a reasonable use of percolating (subsurface) waters; this last right is often treated as a riparian right (see 8).

3. *Air rights*. A landowner has the exclusive right to the air above his/her land, to that height over which control is reasonable. (Obviously, absent zoning restrictions, a landowner cannot prevent airplanes from flying over his/her property at a safe altitude.)

4. *Right to trees, crops*, or *other vegetation* on the land.

5. *Right to fixtures* on the land (e.g., a shed or a patio).

6. *Right to lateral and subjacent support*. A landowner's neighbors may not excavate or otherwise change their own land to such an extent that the owner's lands or buildings are damaged.

7. *Right to be free of public or private nuisances*. A landowner may request a court order to abate pollution, noxious odors, excessive noise, or other interference with his/her enjoyment of the land. (If governmental actions make the land uninhabitable, the owner may seek "inverse condemnation"—an order that the government take the property by eminent domain and compensate the owner.)

8. *Riparian rights*. A landowner may use a natural waterway within his/her property. (Title to navigable streams extends only to their low water mark, with the federal government owning the rest.)

In conjunction with these rights comes the obvious duty not to interfere with other landowners' rights. For example, an owner's riparian rights do not permit the owner to pollute or divert a waterway passing through his/her property. Most states also do not allow the owner to diminish unreasonably a waterway's flow.

The law of real property is very much tied to important, basic principles that go back to English common law or, depending on a state's history, to other legal traditions. For example, in the southwestern United States, statutes on water rights and property ownership take many of their precepts from *Las Siete Partidas* (The Seven Books of Law) created in the thirteenth century in the courts of Alfonso X of Castile and Leon in Spain.

RESTRICTIONS ON LAND-USE RIGHTS

• *GOVERNMENTAL CONTROLS*

The owner's right to use his/her land is now usually subject to many governmental controls, including zoning and building codes.

Zoning is legislative action, usually at the municipal level. It regulates the use of property, including the types of construction permitted within different zoning districts.

Like other administrative rulings, zoning decisions are subject to judicial review but are presumptively valid. Courts are extremely reluctant to overturn decisions unless they were *clearly* arbitrary or otherwise violated due process.

Unlike eminent domain, zoning changes generally do not afford landowners an opportunity to receive compensation from the government. Typically, to qualify for compensation, some or part of the land must actually be taken, not merely adversely affected by land-use regulation.

• *PRIVATE RESTRICTIONS*

So long as they are not unlawful or otherwise contrary to public policy, private restrictions may also be placed in deeds, subdivision plans, or the like; such restrictions are usually upheld if they benefit the landowners as a whole. Examples of use restrictions include limits on the size and design of houses or other buildings, and prohibitions of commercial establishments or certain other buildings.

POSSESSORY AND NONPOSSESSORY (USE) INTERESTS

• *POSSESSORY INTERESTS*

There are three main types of possessory interests in real property:

1. **Fee simple estate**. The highest form of ownership and possession, fee simple estate includes all rights in the land. Owners in fee simple may pass to others rights in the land without giving up absolute ownership.

Besides fee simple absolute (FSA), there are **fee simple determinable** (FSD; ownership automatically ends if a specified action occurs) and **fee simple subject to a condition subsequent** (FSSCS; ownership is subject to a grantor's right of repossession if a specified action occurs). In either case, ownership and possession are absolute until and unless the specified action occurs.

Example: FSA

Land is granted to X. There are no conditions and no possibility of reversion.

Example: FSD

Land is granted to a university "so long as the land is used for educational purposes." If the educational purpose ceases, the land automatically reverts back to the grantor or his/her heirs.

Example: FSSCS

Land is granted to a museum, but "if a painting by Pablo Picasso is ever exhibited on the premises, the grantor or his/her heirs may re-enter." If a Picasso is shown, it is up to the grantor or his/her heirs whether to have the land revert.

2. **Life estate**. Here the term of a person's possessory interest in land is the duration of one or more human lives as specified in the granting instrument. Usually the estate is for the life of the grantee (the person receiving the life estate). Upon the death of the life tenant, the land either reverts to the grantor or his/her heirs (a reversionary interest) or passes to another party designated in the granting instrument. In the latter case, the remaining estate is called a "remainder," with the ultimate recipient being the "remainderman."

Life tenants may generally do anything with their property, including leasing or transferring it, that will not cause permanent damage to it. Of course, if A has a life estate for the life of B, she cannot give to C a fee simple estate or any other estate that exceeds the lifetime of B, that is, A cannot transfer more than she herself has.

---

3. **Leasehold**. Both fee simple estates and life estates are labeled "freeholds"; in both cases, the estates are of uncertain duration. A leasehold, however, generally has a set term. Unlike the freehold situation, the property's owner is distinct from its occupant, because a leasehold grants only possession, not title. (See the discussion of leases later in this chapter.)

• *NONPOSSESSORY INTERESTS*

Three nonpossessory interests are easements, profits, and licenses.

1. **Easements**. Created either by agreement (express) or by operation of law (implied), the easement gives to its holder a limited right to use, or forbid the use of, another person's land for a specific purpose. Although most easements are *affirmative*, that is, they grant the use of another person's property (e.g., a farmer's driving on his neighbor's private road to get to a second parcel of land that he owns), they can also be *negative*, that is, they restrict a property owner's use of his/her property, the servient estate, because such a use would affect an adjoining, dominant estate (e.g., servient estate S cannot build in such a way as to deprive dominant estate D of access to sunlight). (The effect of negative easements is similar to that of **restrictive covenants**. The latter are express provisions, usually placed in deeds, that attempt to restrict the transfer or use of property.)

Deeds transferring title, or documents accompanying deeds, are the usual means of creating express easements. One main type of express easement is the **appurtenant easement**, which concerns adjoining land: the dominant estate holds a negative or affirmative easement over the neighboring, servient estate. Appurtenant easements, intended for holders of particular property, "run with the land." Thus, when the dominant estate is transferred, the appurtenant easement also passes to the new owner.

The other main type of express easement, an **easement in gross**, is given for a specific purpose. There is no adjoining, dominant estate. At common law, this "personal" easement could not be transferred. However, most states now allow such transfers, especially for easements necessary for commerce or other public purposes.

Example: Easement in Gross

A utility company's right to run lines on private property.

Implied easements, like implied contracts, are based on the parties' presumed intent. Other nonexpress easements include **easements by prescription** and **easements by necessity**. The former is similar to title by adverse possession; it results from actual, open, continual, and nonpermissive easement use of another's land for the statutory period of time needed to establish adverse possession. (Like adverse possession, prescriptive rights typically cannot be acquired in public lands.) An easement by necessity arises if a land conveyance makes such an easement necessary for the use and enjoyment of granted or retained land.

Example: Easement by Necessity

Olive Owner transfers some land to Bill Buyer. Bill's tract has no access to a public road except through Olive's retained land. Thus there is an easement by necessity through Olive's land.

2. **Profits**. A profit is the right to obtain a possessory interest in some aspect of another's land, such as crops, timber, or minerals. An easement usually accompanies the profit, so that the profit holder can enter the land to remove the particular crop, mineral, or whatever.

3. **Licenses**. The owner permits someone to use his/her land, generally for a limited, specific purpose (e.g., to camp, hunt, hike, or fish). The license is subject to revocation at any time.

TENANT/LANDLORD RELATIONSHIP

The owner of real property may be a **landlord**, having put possession in the hands of a **tenant**.

• *THE LEASE*

The rental agreement, a **lease**, is between the lessor (owner) and lessee (tenant). Although most leases should be express and stated in writing, most states permit short-term leases (one year or less) to be oral or simply implied. The Statute of Frauds, however, bars enforcement of an unacknowledged, unwritten lease covering more than one year. Also, federal, state, and local fair housing laws bar discrimination in sales, rentals, advertising, and financing based upon race, color, religion, national origin, sex, disability, or familial status. State or local laws may also cover discrimination based on age, gender identity or expression, lawful source of income (e.g., receiving public assistance), marital status, or sexual orientation.

TYPES OF LEASEHOLDS

There are four main types of *leaseholds* (nonownership, possessory interests in realty):

1. **Estate for years**. Tenancy is for a definite period of time, and usually ends on or by a date stated in the lease, although termination may instead occur because of the parties' mutual agreement, a condition stated in the lease, operation of law (e.g., bankruptcy), or merger (lessee acquires fee simple title to the property).

2. **Periodic tenancy**. Tenancy is for a definite period of time, often month to month, which automatically renews until a contrary notice is given by the lessor or lessee (usually one rental period, e.g., a month, in advance).

3. **Tenancy at will**. Either party may end the tenancy at any time, although most states require a termination notice.

4. **Tenancy at sufferance**. Tenancy continues after the lease has expired, with most jurisdictions holding that this leasehold implicitly becomes a periodic tenancy.

COVENANTS

Most written lease agreements contain covenants, that is, statements about the parties' rights and duties. Covenants customarily cover security deposits, rent (e.g., requiring payment in advance), lease assignments or subleases (e.g., whether, and in what circumstances, they are permitted), and restrictions on use of the premises (e.g., as solely a retail store—no manufacturing allowed). Even if not in writing, there generally are implied covenants that (1) the landlord has the right to transfer possession to the tenant; (2) the tenant will not cause "waste," that is, damage the property beyond normal wear and tear; (3) the landlord grants "quiet enjoyment," that is, will not disturb a lawful tenant's use and enjoyment of the premises; and (4) the property is livable—in good repair (warranty of habitability).

TERMINATION OF THE LEASE

Before its term has run, a lease may be terminated for the following reasons:

1. Frustration of the lease's purpose due to zoning changes, eminent domain, or the like. Also, if a mortgage predates a lease, its foreclosure ends the lease.

2. Tenant's breach of covenants. The landlord must generally serve notice and follow other statutory provisions before evicting a breaching tenant.

3. Constructive eviction. When a landlord materially impairs the tenant's ability to enjoy the premises, the tenant may terminate the lease. (The law considers the landlord's conduct to be, in effect, an eviction.) Other breaches of covenant by the landlord usually permit the tenant just to collect damages, not terminate the lease.

A tenant's unilateral abandonment of the premises does not terminate the lease. He/she remains liable for the remaining rent, with the landlord usually subject to a statutory duty to mitigate damages (attempt to get a new tenant).

• MAINTENANCE OF RENTED PROPERTY

The common law left maintenance completely up to the tenant. Now, though, statutes, case law, and leases themselves may place maintenance responsibility on the landlord, tenant, or both. Obviously, landlords are in charge of common areas (facilities used by all tenants, such as parking lots, halls, and shared electric and plumbing systems).

TORT LIABILITY FOR REAL PROPERTY CONDITIONS CAUSING INJURY (PREMISES LIABILITY)

A landowner may be liable in tort for a visitor's personal injuries resulting from property conditions.

The traditional approach is to label the visitor an *invitee* (e.g., someone entering the premises to engage in business, such as shop or make repairs), a *licensee* (e.g., a social guest or household member), or a *trespasser*. The property owner's duty to invitees extends beyond the issuance of warnings to the exercise of reasonable care in protecting invitees against all dangerous conditions they are unlikely to discover; his/her duty to licensees is to warn them of known, dangerous conditions they are unlikely to discover; his/her duty to trespassers is merely not to injure them intentionally, simply for trespassing. When the landowner knows or should know that children, attracted by a swimming pool or some other feature or artificial condition, are likely to trespass, he/she generally has a higher duty of care (the "attractive nuisance" doctrine).

Most states no longer look only at the status of the injured party. Instead, the test of due care is the overall reasonableness of the landowner's acts or omissions, considering all facts and circumstances. Therefore, status as an invitee, a licensee, or a trespasser is only one consideration out of many.

Some other general principles in establishing liability are as follows:

1. Tenants, as occupants of the premises, have the primary potential liability to injured persons.

2. Most states have **recreational use** statutes: when real property is used for recreation, and without charge, then these statutes remove from the landowner any duty to make property safe or to post warnings.

3. Case law and statutes have increasingly held landlords responsible under fitness warranties customarily involved in land sales. Thus a landlord may be responsible to third parties injured because of the landlord's failure to (a) repair defects as required by the lease; (b) reveal known defects to the tenant; and (c) keep the premises in accord with the local building code. Indeed, landlords and tenants may both be held accountable for injury-causing failure to maintain the premises.

4. A lease may provide that the landlord is not liable for injury to anyone on the premises. However, such **exculpatory clauses** often are not upheld, particularly if the circumstances indicate that it would

be inequitable to do so (e.g., the landlord knew or should have known about an extremely dangerous defect in a stairway, while the injured person had no such actual or constructive knowledge).

Crimes can lead to lawsuits against real property owners and managers. Victims of crime have successfully sued the owners and operators of hotels, shopping centers, schools, bars, gas stations, stores, parking lots, banks, ATMs, office buildings, and hospitals for neglecting to secure the premises from crimes and to warn tenants or guests of the risks. Alleged negligence has concerned, among other things, the lighting, use of guards, perimeter security, access control, cameras, and alarms. Damages in violent assaults (e.g., rape) may even include compensation for post-traumatic stress disorder.

COMPARISON OF MAJOR PROPERTY ARRANGEMENTS

The table on the next page shows the comparative characteristics of the major arrangements governing property.

KNOW THE CONCEPTS
DO YOU KNOW THE BASICS?

1. Name at least five forms of intangible personal property.
2. What are the three basic elements of a gift?
3. What are the four requirements for a bailment?
4. Name four types of bailments and the bailee's duty of care for each.
5. If your state follows the community property system, in what region of the United States do you most likely live?
6. Is it necessary to record a deed? If not, why do it?
7. (a) Name two examples of voluntary transfer of real property, and name the document that must be delivered in order to make such transfers.

   (b) Name three types of deeds.

   (c) Name four methods of involuntary transfer of real property.

Property Arrangement	Characteristic					
	Transfers Title	Transfers Possession	Right to Use*	Right to Assign Possession or Use*	Consideration Necessary to Be Enforceable	Right to Sell/Keep Property to Pay Owner's Debts*
Bailment	No	Yes	Rarely	No (although may create a subbailment)	No (can be gratuitous)	If permitted by statute
Lease	No	Generally, yes	Yes	Generally, yes unless lease specifically prohibits	Yes	No**
Sale (see Chapter 9)	Yes	Yes	Yes	Yes	Yes	Already completely has the property Yes
Security interest (see Chapter 13)	No	Generally no (except for pledges)	Generally no	Generally no	"Value" given—cannot be gratuitous	Yes

*Such right would be by the person that acquired this property interest (i.e., the bailee, lessee, buyer, or secured creditor).

**Tenant cannot "convert" a leasehold to fee simple even if landlord owes tenant money.

8. Name eight rights associated with land ownership.

9. Name three possessory and three nonpossessory interests in real property.

10. (a) What are the four main types of leaseholds?

    (b) Name four implied covenants.

11. In most states, what is the test of the landowner's due care toward visitors?

TERMS FOR STUDY

abandoned property
accession
adverse possession
air rights
appurtenant easement
bailee
bailment
bailor
common carriers
community property
condominium
confusion
constructive bailment
covenants
deed
donative intent
donee
donor
easement (affirmative or
  negative)
easement by necessity
easement by prescription
easement in gross
eminent domain
estate
estate for years
estray statutes
exculpatory clause
fee simple determinable
fee simple estate
fee simple subject to a condition
  subsequent
fixture

general warranty deed
gift
gift *causa mortis*
gift *inter vivos*
gratuitous bailment
intangible personal property
joint tenancy
landlord
lease
leasehold
license
life estate
lost property
mislaid property
mortgage
periodic tenancy
personal property
premises liability
probate
profit
quitclaim deed
real property
recreational use statutes
restrictive covenant
right of survivorship
right to lateral and subjacent
  support
riparian rights
special warranty deed
subterranean rights
surface rights
tangible personal property
tenancy at sufferance

tenancy at will
tenancy by the entirety
tenancy in common
tenant
testamentary gift

title
trade fixture
treasure trove rule
zoning

PRACTICAL APPLICATION

1. Daryl Dentist leases an office from Laura Landlady. He has hung several abstract paintings on the walls, and has strongly bolted and attached his dental equipment to the walls and to plumbing and electric outlets. Now that his lease is expiring, Daryl wants to take all of this property to a new location. Laura claims that he cannot do that; the paintings and equipment are now hers. Discuss.

2. Joe suffers a heart attack. Believing he hears the "flapping wings of the Angel of Death," he gives his prized sports trophies to Herb. Joe recovers. When he asks for the trophies back, Herb says, "Sorry, Joe; they're mine now."

(a) Can Joe get the trophies back?

(b) What if Joe recovers, thinks about asking for the return of the trophies, and then dies in a car accident?

3. While you are in a restaurant, you find a diamond-studded hat under your chair. Is it now yours? Discuss.

4. Shipper's goods are damaged during transit by a common carrier. No one can show why. Who will probably be liable?

5. (a) Husband Harry and wife Wilma own property P as tenants by the entirety. Without telling Wilma, Harry transfers his interest in P to Otherwoman Olive. Harry dies. Wilma then dies, with her will leaving each of her heirs an equal interest in P. How much of P do the heirs own, and how much does Olive own? What type of tenancy now exists?

(b) Same questions as (a), but assume that husband and wife held P as joint tenants.

6. A fee simple owner conveys a life estate to L, with the remainder to R. L wants to lease his interest. May he do so?

7. Carrie Kiddie passes through Nellie Neighbor's yard every school day in order to catch the bus, and to return home after getting off the bus. This use continues for several years, during the school year. When Carrie's parents sell their house, the new owners start to use Carrie's former pathway to walk to and from a local store. Nellie asks them to stop. If she goes to court, who will win?

ANSWERS
KNOW THE CONCEPTS

1. Contracts, stock, bonds, computer software (programs), employment, utility service, and intellectual property.

2. Donative intent, delivery, and acceptance.

3. Bailor keeps title, bailee obtains possession (delivery and acceptance), possession is for a specific purpose, possession is to be temporary.

4. (1) Bailment solely for bailor's benefit (gratuitous bailment)—slight
   (2) Bailment solely for bailee's benefit—great
   (3) Mutual benefit bailment—ordinary
   (4) Constructive bailment—usually slight

5. Probably in the Southwest or the West.

6. No. To provide notice to others and to establish priority over unrecorded deeds to the same property.

7. (a) Gift and sale; deed.
   (b) General warranty, special warranty, and quitclaim.
   (c) Foreclosure sale, judgment sale, eminent domain, and adverse possession.

8. Subterranean, surface, air, riparian, and lateral support rights; the right to fixtures; the right to trees, crops, or other vegetation; the right to be free of nuisances.

9. Possessory: fee simple estate, life estate, and leasehold. Nonpossessory: easement, profit, and license.

10. (a) Estate for years, periodic tenancy, tenancy at will, tenancy at sufferance.
    (b) Landlord has right to transfer possession, tenant will not cause "waste," landlord warrants habitability, and landlord grants quiet enjoyment.

11. Reasonable care given all facts and circumstances, including but not limited to the visitor's status as invitee, licensee, or trespasser.

PRACTICAL APPLICATION

1. Laura evidently claims that the various properties are fixtures. However, if the dental equipment is a fixture, it is obviously a trade fixture. Thus Daryl can take it, although he will have to reimburse Laura for any costs or damages associated with detaching the equipment.

The paintings probably are not fixtures. Only if they were attached in such a way as to make removal difficult and costly, or only if other circumstances indicate they were intended to remain on the premises, will Daryl be barred from taking them. Laura then likely will have to pay Daryl compensation for the dental equipment, such as an amount equal to how much the equipment enhances the leased premises' value or the cost of reproducing the equipment minus depreciation.

If the paintings are fixtures, Daryl may claim that they are subject to the trade fixture exception. However, unless the paintings are actually pictures of bicuspids or otherwise oriented toward dentistry, a court may hold that they are not crucial to Daryl's business. Even if they are trade fixtures, removing them might be, on balance, too costly to be permitted. As with any retained dental equipment, Laura likely then would have to pay Daryl compensation for keeping the paintings (retaining the trade fixtures).

2. (a) Yes. First, a gift *causa mortis* is freely revocable. Second, Joe recovered, so the trophies revert to him anyway.

   (b) It does not matter. Even though merely thinking about asking for return would not constitute revocation, Joe's recovery automatically rescinds the gift. To be effective, the death must be of the type contemplated; the car accident certainly is not.

3. It appears unlikely that the hat was abandoned; valuable items are presumably mislaid. In most states, the restaurant owner would become a gratuitous bailee. After following the mandates of the estray statute (found in most states) and otherwise reasonably attempting to locate the owner, the hat would become the restaurant's. However, if the property were deemed to have been lost rather than mislaid, or if there were a specific statutory provision on this point, you, the finder, might get the hat (after attempts to locate the owner have failed).

4. The common carrier. Usually a strict liability standard is applied, with the carrier having the burden of proving an exception to liability.

5. (a) Heirs—all; Olive—none. The present tenancy could be joint or in common, depending on how the will sets it up.

   (b) Heirs—half; Olive—half. Unlike situation (a), the transfer to Olive is effective, although it does convert the tenancy to one in common (no longer joint).

6. Yes. However, because L can rent out the land only for as long as he is alive, prospective tenants should be informed of that fact, including the possibility that R may suddenly become their new landlord. Depending on landlord/tenant law, the rental agreement may have to make the lease subject to early termination upon a condition subsequent: L's demise.

7. Probably Nellie. The question appears to be whether the new owners have an appurtenant easement. Carrie's use, if it constituted an easement, was probably an easement in gross—to Carrie personally, for purposes of catching and leaving a school bus. As such, it would not pass on to the new owners. There are no facts that show that the owners have to use the pathway (easement by necessity), or that the previous use was long or frequent enough (note that the pathway was used only when school was in session) to constitute an easement by prescription. Actually, the judge may decide that Carrie's use was merely a license, not transferable, and, in any case, freely revocable by Nellie.

21
INSURANCE, TRUSTS, AND WILLS

TRUSTS AND WILLS

A person's real and personal property is his/her **estate**. When the person dies, the estate passes to others by trust, will, or state statute.

TRUSTS

To establish a **trust**, one party (the settlor—also sometimes called the donor, creator, or trustor) transfers property to another party (the trustee), who administers it for the benefit of a third party (the beneficiary). People can create a trust while still alive, or provide for one through a will.

Requirements for Creation of an Express Trust (the usual type)

1. Capacity of settlor to make a contract or will
2. Intention to create a trust
3. Adherence to any formal, statutory requirements
4. Conveyance to trustee of specific property that settlor has the right to convey
5. Clearly identified beneficiary
6. Trust not violative of law or other public policy

Two types of **implied trusts** are imposed by law to remedy unjust situations: (1) *constructive trusts,* used to require the return of wrongly obtained property (a trust meant to correct fraud or other misconduct); and (2) *resulting trusts,* making a person who received property he/she was not intended to receive a trustee for the intended beneficiary (a trust meant to correct mistakes).

WILLS

A will is an instrument, executed by a **testator** (male) or **testatrix** (female) with the formalities required by statute, stating how that person's estate is to be distributed after death. It may also specify guardians of the person and/or property of minors or others for whom the testator/testatrix acts as guardian.

Most states require that a will be (1) in writing; (2) made by someone who is an adult and of sound mind; (3) signed by the testator/testatrix in the presence of two or three witnesses, who also sign in the presence of each other and the testator/testatrix.

To amend a will, the testator/testatrix completes a **codicil**, which must meet the same formalities of procedure as a will itself. Although a will can be revoked by the testator's or testatrix's simply destroying it, the clearest expression of revocation—rather than worrying about possible "unrevoked" copies—is to execute a new will, which specifically revokes all previous wills.

Wills are submitted and approved by a court according to the process known as **probate**. An **executor** (sometimes referred to as a personal representative) is usually named in the will itself; if not, the probate court names an administrator, usually a close relative or friend of the decedent. The executor or administrator takes inventory of the estate, settles debts and taxes, oversees sales or other liquidation of assets, and (if there is a will) distributes the estate in accordance with the decedent's intentions as expressed in the will.

INTESTATE SUCCESSION BY STATE STATUTE

To die **intestate** is to die without leaving a valid will. Distribution of the estate is then governed by intestate succession laws. Each state has its own such law, specifying the order in which the estate is divided among surviving relatives. Only if there are no surviving relatives does the estate pass over (**escheat**) to the state.

INSURANCE

Insurance is a special contract intended to transfer and allocate risks from the insured (person taking out the policy) to an insurance company (insurer). The insurer issues an insurance policy covering a possible loss. The policy is a special kind of agreement between the insurer and the insured. For the insurance agreement to be enforced, it must meet the usual requirements of a contract and the insured person must have an insurable interest in the subject matter (e.g., property, health, life) that is being insured.

An **insurable interest** is a legal or equitable interest in the subject matter such that the insured benefits from its preservation and/or incurs a loss if it is destroyed or damaged.

For property (real or personal) insurance, the insurable interest is usually ownership. However, many states also permit any lawful economic interest (e.g., the insurer is a creditor whose money helped the insured buy some property, and thus the insured has an insurable interest in that property even though it does not own the property). For property insurance, the interest must exist when the loss insured against actually occurs.

For life insurance, the insurable interest may be the insured's own life, or that of his/her spouse, children, parents, business partners, debtors, fellow shareholders (in close corporations) and key personnel (for business entities). The interest must exist when the policy is issued. Also, an insured policyholder can update his/her beneficiaries at almost any time; the policyholder should keep them current. A number of states, such as Florida, have enacted laws providing that—even without a beneficiary change by the policyholder—the dissolution of a policyholder's marriage means that the policyholder's death benefits designated as going to a now former spouse are instead deemed payable to the current spouse.

Insurable losses are accidents that occur by chance. If the loss is an intentional act or results from normal wear and tear (or other occurrences certain to take place), then the loss is uninsurable.

There are many types of insurance, such as term life, whole life, variable life, variable universal life, health and disability. Property insurance covers automobiles (personal or business), homes, fire, and theft. *Liability insurance* covers damages that are the insured's legal responsibility to pay to a third party. Liability insurance is often found in property insurance policies. Workers' compensation is a special type of liability insurance where the injured employee is paid by the employer's (insured) insurance policy.

Federal Law: GINA and the Affordable Care Act

Insurance generally is a highly regulated field. States often have rules governing who and what can be insured, for what amounts, and how any claims should be evaluated.

While insurance is predominantly a matter of state law, occasionally the federal government intervenes. An example of a national law targeted at a specific problem of insurance and employment is the *Genetic Information Nondiscrimination Act* of 2008 (GINA). This law prohibits discrimination by health insurers (e.g., in coverage or premiums) or by employers (for any employment decision—hiring, firing, promotion, pay, and so forth) due to genetic tests of an individual or that individual's family or due to information about the manifestation of a disease or disorder in the individual's family. Subject to limited exceptions such as court orders, GINA also requires insurers and employers to keep genetic information confidential. States may provide greater protection than GINA does, but very few states do. GINA does not cover the military, nor does it reach life insurance, disability insurance, or long-term care insurance.

An extremely comprehensive federal law is the *Patient Protection and Affordable Care Act* (2010), commonly called the *Affordable Care Act* (ACA) or "Obamacare." This law requires that employers with 50 or more employees working an average of 30 or more hours a week must offer health insurance to at least 95% of their workers (and the workers' dependents) or pay an excise tax; the policies offered must meet certain standards in terms of coverage and premiums (e.g., the employee contribution can be no higher than 9.5% of the employee's rate of pay). Also, individuals without health insurance coverage (such as from an employer's or family member's policy) may have to buy coverage or pay a tax. Nearly all health insurance companies offer coverage to individuals as well as employers and are required to sell and to renew health insurance policies for all consumers, including those who have or had an illness ("preexisting conditions").*

Coverage for individuals and small employers (employer groups with fewer than 50 full-time employees) can only have variable premiums based on age, tobacco use, family size, and geography—generally, just a single state-wide risk pool for individuals or groups—and premiums

---

* This ban on preexisting conditions applies regardless of age, gender, or policy type, and even extends to "grandfathered plans" (i.e., policies in effect since before the ACA was enacted).

cannot be based on other factors such as health status, gender, occupation, or, for other than large group coverage, claims experience. The ACA requires that any insurance plan offered by employers provide essential health benefits. Such benefits include emergency services, hospitalization, laboratory services, maternity and newborn care, pediatrics, mental health and substance use disorders, prescription drugs, rehabilitative services and devices, and preventive and wellness services.

Businesses generally have commercial liability policies. They also may have fidelity insurance, which covers an employer to protect against losses caused by dishonest employees (e.g., a bank may purchase fidelity insurance to cover losses for embezzlement by its employees). Another type of coverage is business interruption insurance, which covers losses due to equipment malfunctions or other covered risks that stop a business' normal operations. Many large corporations carry directors' and officers' liability insurance (D&O insurance) to protect directors and officers from liability for the actions they take on behalf of the corporation. (Few small corporations purchase this coverage because it is usually quite expensive.)

Insurance policies may include an incontestability clause, which provides that after a policy has been in force for a specified length of time, usually two or three years, the insurer cannot contest statements made in the insured's insurance application. Especially common in many commercial lines of insurance is the coinsurance provision: the insured business agrees to carry, from another insurer, additional insurance on a portion of the insured property's value. If the second policy is not in force, there would be a pro rata reduction in the amount paid for a loss.

Insurers usually must give permission before a property or liability insurance policy can be assigned to a third party. As for policy interpretation, ambiguities are interpreted most strongly against the contract's preparer (almost always the insurer). *Insurers must act in good faith. Failure to do so (e.g., denying a legitimate claim) is an act of "bad faith" that may lead to liability for compensatory and punitive damages.*

Via subrogation, an insurer "stands in the shoes" of the insured. Having paid for an insured's loss, the insurer may seek reimbursement from a third party whose intentional or negligent act caused the loss. There is, however, no subrogation right against a third party who causes the death of someone covered by life insurance.

Like most written contracts, insurance policies may be canceled by either party upon giving required notice (normally in writing). Most policies contain a grace period that allows for delinquent payments or otherwise prevents a lapse in coverage. Other than failure to pay premiums, a policy also loses enforceability if: (1) important contractual sections, such as those on notice of loss (promptly informing the insurer about a loss) and on proof of loss (demonstrating the insured's damages), are ignored; (2) the policy was procured by fraud; (3) there is no insurable interest; or (4) certain acts are illegal or otherwise violate public policy.

KNOW THE CONCEPTS

DO YOU KNOW THE BASICS?

1. State the two most basic categories of trusts.
2. Name three general requirements for a will to be effective.
3. What insurable interest can a person have in (a) life insurance; (b) property insurance?
4. Name several types of insurance.

TERMS FOR STUDY

bad faith
business interruption insurance
codicil
D&O insurance
escheat
estate
executor
express trust
fidelity insurance
good faith
implied trust
incontestability clause
insurable interest
insurable losses

insurance
intestate
liability insurance
life insurance
personal representative
probate
property insurance
settlor
subrogation
testator
testatrix
trust
will

PRACTICAL APPLICATION

1. Ollie Oldman dies intestate. He had no wife and no children or other descendants. Ollie's parents have long been dead. His only sister and only brother predeceased Ollie, but those two siblings each had three children, all of whom are alive. What happens to Ollie's estate?

2. (a) Ichabod Insured has a liability insurance policy covering all negligent acts by employees. One of his employees behaves negligently, and Ichabod is sued. The insurer refuses to provide Ichabod with a defense because it believes that the employee was not meant to be covered by the policy. Ichabod wants to file a claim against the insurer for bad faith. Discuss.

(b) Assume that the insurer pays on the policy. Is subrogation possible? If so, against whom?

ANSWERS

KNOW THE CONCEPTS

1. Express trusts and implied trusts.

2. In writing, by a competent adult, and signed by the testator or testatrix in the presence of two or three witnesses (who also sign, as witnesses).

3. (a) The insured's own life or that of his/her spouse, parent, child, debtor, partner, or other shareholder in a close corporation, and (for business entities) lives of key personnel. (b) Usually ownership, but can be any legal, economic interest existing when the loss occurs.

4. Term life, whole life, health, disability, automobile, home (property), fire, theft, liability, workers' compensation, business interruption, D&O insurance, and fidelity insurance.

PRACTICAL APPLICATION

1. Ollie's estate passes in six equal parts to Ollie's closest relatives, his six nephews/nieces. That Ollie had no direct descendants (children or grandchildren) only means that more distant relatives will take from his estate under the intestate succession laws. Escheat occurs only when there are no surviving relatives at all.

2. (a) Presumably the insured prepared the policy. Unless it can point to language in the policy supporting its interpretation, the insurer will be bound by these facts: (1) the policy appears to cover all employees, and (2) any ambiguities should be resolved in favor of the insured (the non-preparer of the policy). A claim for bad faith could succeed if Ichabod shows the usual elements necessary to receive punitive damages, including willful or incredibly reckless acts by the defendant and resulting harm to the plaintiff.

(b) The only person we know about is the employee. Unless barred by the policy itself, or by a separate policy between that particular employee and the insurer, or by virtue of public policy, the insurer might proceed against the employee. Note, however, that if the employee had a right to indemnity from his/her employer (Ichabod), the insurer's claim would be self-defeating.

22

ANTITRUST LAW

KEY TERMS

antitrust law statutory, regulatory, and case law, the most important being federal, designed to prevent and correct unreasonable restraints on trade

per se **violations** actions that are automatic violations of antitrust laws

rule of reason the antitrust doctrine whereby most unintentional, reasonable restraints of trade are lawful if economically efficient and connected to a valid business purpose considering all facts and circumstances

Because the U.S. economic system is generally based on capitalism and free enterprise, the common law traditionally has tried to maintain open competition in the marketplace. Sometimes, however, economic changes outpace the law. Thus America's industrial revolution led to the pyramiding of economic interests in large business aggregates, such as "trusts," and monopolies emerged. Because state legislatures and the courts were unable to control this vast new concentration of powers, a body of **federal antitrust law** was designed to advance free competition while at the same time regulating the activities of businesses engaged in interstate commerce.

The four main antitrust statutes are the Sherman Antitrust Act, the Clayton Act, the Robinson-Patman Act, and the Federal Trade Commission Act.

SHERMAN ACT

The Sherman Act (1890) outlaws contracts, combinations, or conspiracies "in restraint of trade," as well as monopolization or attempted monopolization. Taking into account all circumstances, the courts (since a 1911 Supreme Court ruling, *Standard Oil Co. of New Jersey v. United States*, 221 U.S. 1) have applied a "**rule of reason**" test. Therefore, in practice the Sherman Act is subjective and relatively lenient, requiring *actual* adverse impact on competition before finding a violation and subjecting the violator to criminal penalties and civil suits.

"Reasonableness" depends on all of the surrounding circumstances: the actual anticompetitive effects of an alleged antitrust violation. Under the rule of reason, most restraints of trade are lawful if (1) they are connected to a legitimate business purpose, and, (2) as interpreted by courts, they are deemed economically efficient. There are many instances in which trade is restrained, but to prohibit that restraint would be detrimental. Indeed, whenever Seller A sells a good to Buyer B, trade is restrained because that good cannot be sold to someone else, also.

Some types of agreements among supposed competitors, though, are **automatic ("per se") violations**—proof of the wrongful act automatically proves an antitrust violation. (In essence, the harmful market effects are assumed.) The *per se* rule is credited with improving judicial efficiency and providing clear guidance for business managers in their decision-making. It remains controversial, however, as economists and other analysts continue to debate whether certain business behaviors truly harm competition and deserve to be classified as *per se* violations.

Actions deemed illegal under the per se *rule are horizontal price-fixing, group boycotts, production quotas, certain horizontal territorial limitations or market divisions, and some "tying arrangements."*

1. *Horizontal price-fixing:* businesses at the same level of competition (e.g., retailers) setting prices (e.g., a mandatory rate schedule) for products and/or services. Arranging to set arbitrarily a common price among competitors is the most direct way to reduce competition. It is no excuse that competitors sought to set "reasonable" prices or eliminate "ruinous" competition.[1]

   Courts broadly define the term "price-fixing." Credit terms and discounts cannot be fixed, since they are inextricably related to price. That also holds true for agreements to set freight prices. (Such arrangements eliminate competition based on a purchaser's distance from a supply source.) Even agreements among competitors to buy any excess amounts of their commodities may constitute price-fixing.

---

[1] On rare occasions, the courts have used a rule of reason approach to review restraints of trade involving incidental price-fixing peculiar to an industry. For example, the Supreme Court upheld the blanket-fee arrangements used for copyright licensing and royalties in the music industry because (1) it is highly impractical for copyright owners to separately negotiate licensing fees for every performance of their work; and (2) the blanket-fee arrangements made by umbrella organizations such as BMI (Broadcast Music, Inc.) and ASCAP (American Society of Composers, Authors, and Publishers) actually encourage licensing and enforcement of music copyrights. *Broadcast Music, Inc. v. CBS,* 441 U.S. 1 (1979).

Three Important Concepts Related to Price-Fixing, but Judged by a "Reasonableness" Standard

Competitors need not meet and explicitly fix prices or related terms to be engaged in price-fixing. If only a few firms control a market (an oligopoly), these firms—if they follow the pricing policies of the leading firm in that industry (or otherwise mimic one another's pricing behavior)—may effectively restrict competition. This **conscious parallelism** is legal, though, as long as there is no other evidence of collusion. What gets firms in trouble are arrangements, understandings, practices, etc., however informal, that take from the individual firm its capacity to set prices independent of what other firms have done or may do.

Resale price maintenance (RPM) is a vertical restraint of trade. In order to manage and exert control over profits, suppliers state implicitly or explicitly that retailers are to sell the goods at a minimum price, i.e., no discounts below the minimum price level. (Some retailers secretly seek RPM as a way to fix prices horizontally.) Courts are to apply a rule of reason analysis to RPM issues, per the Supreme Court's decision in *Leegin Creative Leather Products, Inc. v. PSKS, Inc.*, 551 U.S. 877 (2007) (involving Brighton belts, handbags, and other accessories).

The law may allow **vertical "maximum price agreements,"** in which a manufacturer or wholesaler requires that businesses down the chain of distribution (e.g., retailers) charge no more than a maximum price for a good or service. Although fixing a relatively low, maximum price may drive competitors out of business and reduce nonprice competition for product services or optional benefits, it may foster market efficiencies and benefit consumers with lower prices. Thus, vertically imposed price ceilings are judged by the "rule of reason" test, as held by the Supreme Court in *State Oil Co. v. Khan*, 522 U.S. 3 (1997).

2. *Group boycotts:* excluding other businesses from dealing in their product(s) (e.g., a group of distributors pressure a manufacturer to terminate its sales to a "rebel" distributor). However, "refusals to deal," often a manufacturer's decision not to sell to a particular wholesaler or retailer, are usually allowed. A refusal to deal usually only becomes illegal if coupled with harassing monitoring of retail pricing behaviors or otherwise used as a "disciplinary tool" to influence the buyer's adoption of a resale price maintenance plan. (Boycotts organized for noneconomic political expression are protected under the Constitution's First Amendment.)

3. *Production quotas:* arbitrarily restricting the supply of certain goods in order to increase prices.

4. *Horizontal territorial limitations or market divisions:* competitors dividing up and keeping exclusive geographic areas for the sale of their products (thereby restricting the number of competitors dealing in a particular region or with specific customers). This territorial allocation or **division of markets** is illegal *per se* because it gives a producer, for each market segment, an effective monopoly.

5. *Tying arrangements:* requiring the purchase of a "tied" product in return for a contract involving another, more highly desired, "tying" product. A tying arrangement is illegal if it affects a substantial portion of commerce in the tied product and if the seller has strong economic power in the tying product's market (i.e., it can force a tie-in due to a patent or to a large market share in the tying product).

   Sometimes the allegedly tied and tying items are part of the same product (e.g., for a television set, the electronic circuits and the screen really are part of the same overall product); these items together constitute what is viewed as one piece of merchandise, with *inseparable* elements (at least in the eyes of the law). Since a single commodity cannot be "tied" to itself and therefore must be deemed legal, is the sale of an automobile with a built-in radio a tying arrangement? It is very unlikely.

   Finally, sellers may allege that the tied product is the only product suitable for use with the tying product. Courts rarely accept that defense because for most tied products suitable substitutes exist.

The Sherman Act sets forth civil sanctions and *criminal penalties* (up to 3 years' imprisonment and fines of up to $350,000 for individuals and $10 million for corporations). Plaintiffs who prove direct damages because of antitrust violations recover three times the actual damages (treble damages). Other civil remedies, including injunctions, attorneys' fees, costs of suit, and interest, are also available in antitrust actions under the Clayton and Robinson-Patman Acts.[2]

A plaintiff has standing to sue only if he/she can prove a *direct injury*. Fixed prices or other illegal costs, while perhaps passed on to purchasers down the stream of distribution, do not confer standing on these *indirectly* harmed persons. (Many states, though, permit indirect purchasers to sue under state antitrust laws.)

In *Bell Atlantic Corp. v. Twombly,* 550 U.S. 544 (2007), the Supreme Court further toughened the standards for plaintiffs to get into court. An

---

[2] However, in *F. Hoffman-La Roche v. Empagran,* 542 U.S. 155 (2004), the U.S. Supreme Court held that foreign customers cannot sue international companies in U.S. courts over alleged antitrust violations (in this case, price fixing by an international cartel) that do not harm American consumers. A ruling the other way would have opened U.S. courthouses to lawsuits from around the world.

allegation of two companies seeming to act together ("parallel conduct"), even if there was diminished competition, must be accompanied by specific examples of collusion. The court required "plausible grounds to infer an agreement" in violation of Sherman Act §1: "enough fact to raise a reasonable expectation that discovery will reveal evidence of illegal agreement." In other words, some factual context—not mere conjecture—must "nudge" the plaintiff's claims "across the line from conceivable to plausible."

OTHER RESTRAINTS OF TRADE

Monopolies resulting from business skills, patented or otherwise protected products, or sheer luck do not violate antitrust laws. If, though, the monopoly or an attempted monopoly is the result of intentional restraints on trade (i.e., a conspiracy to acquire monopolistic powers), then it probably violates the Sherman Act.

• *VERTICAL NONPRICE RESTRAINTS OF TRADE*

Often manufacturers that are unable to take advantage of resale price maintenance use other methods (exclusive distributorships, exclusive dealings, or tying arrangements) to exert similar control over retailers.

An **exclusive distributorship** occurs when a firm acquires the sole right to sell a manufacturer's product within a given geographical region. Although some recent cases find these distributorships to be illegal *per se*, most court decisions have held exclusive distributorships to a rule of reason test (finding illegality only when there are few substitutes for the product and thus there exists very little competition).

Exclusive dealing involves requiring the buyer to resell only the products of a single manufacturer. Exclusive dealing is illegal under Section 3 of the Clayton Act if it tends to create a monopoly or substantially lessens competition. Regulation of the manufacturer extends also to termination of the dealer contract. (Both federal and state laws protect against some types of arbitrary franchise termination. As a rule, a manufacturer is allowed to terminate a dealer when the dealer is unsuccessful, when he/she breaches key provisions in the distributorship agreement, or when the manufacturer changes its marketing strategy.)

With **tying** (previously defined), a seller may charge near-monopoly prices for the tied product. Tying arrangements in almost any area (e.g., goods, land, services, intellectual property) are potentially unlawful under the Sherman Act. They are also prohibited by the Clayton Act when the tying exclusively concerns commodities.

Regulation of vertical trade restraints (e.g., agreements between a supplier and retailer) leads inexorably to this question: Which competition is preferable, **intrabrand** (between the same brand) or **interbrand** (between different brands)? Many economists, judges, and legal scholars argue that when all vertical restraints are deemed illegal, there exists a **"free rider"** problem. When a manufacturer cannot set a minimum resale price or minimal amount of required service work, for example, consumers seeking complex goods may learn about the products from skilled technicians at high-priced stores, and then buy the products from discount stores (which "free ride" off of the better services provided by other stores). This intrabrand competition may force higher-priced retailers that offer good customer service to cut back their service and/or get out of the business (thereby lessening customer satisfaction). Proponents of vertical restraints say that it is better to promote interbrand competition, which results in more innovation and efficiency in the market.

Vertical restraints are judged by a rule of reason. If there are legitimate economic and business objectives in restraining intrabrand competition (such as furthering interbrand competition), then the courts will approve such restraints. In deciding these cases, the courts examine the degree of competition, the shares of market power, and the barriers to entry for new competitors.

CLAYTON ACT

The "rule of reason" and apparent loopholes in the Sherman Act led in 1914 to the enactment of the Clayton Act. This law is much stricter on allegedly monopolistic activities than is the Sherman Act because *Clayton Act* violations require only a *probable adverse impact* on competition (i.e., anticompetitive tendencies) rather than proof of completed anticompetitive effects (the *Sherman Act* standard, which is *actual adverse impact*).

The government or private parties can obtain federal court injunctions for the following practices that the Clayton Act forbids:

1. *Exclusive dealing and tying arrangements* for the sale of commodities when such contracts may substantially reduce competition or tend to create monopolies.

2. Two or more *significantly competing* companies having the same individual serve as a director or a high-level officer (one chosen by the board of directors). Such an **interlocking directorship** is unlawful if each company has capital, surplus and undivided

profits altogether exceeding $10 million. "Significant competition" means that competing activities account for at least 4% of one company's total sales and—for each company—the directly affected sales amount to more than $1 million and at least 2% of total sales.[3]

3. *Monopolistic mergers,* that is, mergers that substantially lessen competition or tend to create monopolies in either a product market or a geographic market. The three types are:

(a) *Horizontal:* the merged entities operated the same type of business at the same level (e.g., both were car manufacturers). This is often illegal, particularly if it results in a significant increase in market concentration or otherwise has a probable anticompetitive effect.

Besides a rising market share, courts searching for "substantially lessened competition" may consider industry trends toward consolidation. Those trends could be a basis for enjoining mergers with short-term pro-competitive effects, but which would result in a concentration permitting future collusion.

(b) *Vertical:* the merged entities operated the same type of business, but at different levels (e.g., an automobile manufacturer merged with a car dealership or, at the other end of the vertical chain, with a supplier of steel or other materials used to build cars). This is generally permitted. Courts may outlaw a vertical merger if it would likely foreclose to competition a large share of the relevant market.

Vertically integrated firms tend to exclude competitors from sources of supply or from customers (and thereby impose barriers to market entry by new firms). Often, vertically integrated firms also are accused of discriminating in price and favoring captive consumers over nonintegrated competitors. However, unlike horizontal mergers, vertical mergers do not immediately result in more concentrated markets and can even make an industry more efficient; so antitrust challenges are fewer and less likely to succeed than for horizontal mergers.

(c) *Conglomerate:* the merged entities are in unrelated businesses (e.g., a restaurant chain and an airline), geographic areas, or both. This is very likely permitted. Grounds for disallowing such a merger arise when the merger eliminates potential competition or gives an unfair advantage to the merged entity.

---

[3] A 1990 Clayton Act amendment to §8 requires that each year, starting in 1991, these figures ($10 million and $1 million, respectively) are to increase by a percentage amount equal to the percentage increase in gross national product. Therefore, as of 2009, the figures had risen to more than $26,161,000 and $2,616,100, respectively.

It is sometimes argued that "conglomerate" mergers eliminate the "potential entrant effect." The potential for a new entrant (a new market competitor) should cause competitors to remain efficient in order to discourage these possible entrants from actually entering the market. If a potential entrant merges with an existing company, this competitive discipline is weakened.

A plaintiff challenging conglomerate mergers must first prove that existing competitors were influenced by the potential entrant. Second, the acquiring firm must have had reasonable means to enter the given market without merging. Third, the number of potential entrants cannot be large; otherwise, the elimination of only one would have an insignificant effect on competitive discipline.

One common merger justification is the "failing firm defense." Claiming that the merger would increase market efficiency by saving an insolvent firm, the acquiring firm may avoid antitrust sanctions. The alleged insolvency must be proven with evidence that: (1) the "failing" firm was and is unable to reorganize successfully under Chapter 11 of the bankruptcy laws, and (2) the "failing" firm genuinely tried, but failed, to find other suitable merger partners that might have led to less market concentration.

Whereas the Clayton Act looks at market share, anti-competitive behavior, and the degree of competition in an industry, not mere "bigness," the Hart-Scott-Rodino Antitrust Improvements Act of 1976 amended the Clayton Act on mergers, with further amendments in 2000 to §7A requiring that pre-merger notification be filed with the U.S. Justice Department if (1) one party's assets or annual sales exceed $10 million, and (2) the other entity has assets or sales in excess of $200 million, and (3) the merger involves an acquisition "cost" of more than $50 million or more than 15% of the voting shares of the acquired company.[4]

MONOPOLY POWER: SOME IMPORTANT CONCEPTS

When determining whether illegal monopoly power is present, a number of factors need to be considered.

Elasticity of Demand. The number of competitive firms in an industry affect the elasticity of demand for goods or services. When the number of competitors is large, each firm's demand elasticity (percentage

---

[4] Those figures are adjusted for changes in gross national product. In 2009, the figures, above, are $13.0 million, $260.7 million, and $65.2 million.

change in quantity, divided by percentage change in price) should be high. The opposite is true when there is a monopoly. When a monopolistic firm raises the price of a good or service, the demand drops off very little (giving the firm much control over consumers).

Market Power. To be unlawful, the monopolist's use of market power must exist over (1) a specific product and (2) a particular geographic area. After defining the relevant geographic and product markets, a monopolist's market power is found by determining the cross-elasticity of demand between the monopolized product and possible substitute products. That cross-elasticity is the consumers' willingness to substitute physically different products for the same purpose or use. Plaintiffs in an antitrust suit (e.g., one concerning alleged motor oil monopolization) usually claim low cross-elasticities (very few substitutes—e.g., no similar motor oil), while the defendants allege that there are many substitutes for the product (high cross-elasticities—e.g., many other comparable motor oils). In determining cross-elasticity, courts look to a number of factors, such as price, quality, use, and industry custom.

Market Share. This figure is a percentage: the dollar amount of the monopolist's sales as a percentage of the total sales amount for all firms in that market. Anywhere from perhaps 70% of the market or greater is usually considered a monopoly. Even if a company has only 20% (or less) of the market, a merger initiated by that company could be prohibited as anticompetitive. Thus, there is no litmus test for determining whether a particular market share constitutes a monopoly.

Illegal Use of Monopoly Power. The mere existence of monopoly power does not violate the antitrust laws. Some industries (e.g., utilities) actually may be more efficient when operated as a monopoly. Antitrust plaintiffs need to show that the defendant unlawfully *used* its market power. True monopolies only exist when the firm's market power abuses customers or competitors, whether intentional or not. (Mere skill, foresight, and diligence are not abusive.)

Examples of using monopoly power, perhaps unlawfully: (1) a company with 75% market share will only lease its product, never sell it (that was an antitrust problem for IBM); (2) a company with extreme market power in one area (computer operating systems) allegedly uses that as leverage to force businesses/consumers to buy less desirable software. (Microsoft has faced such charges.)

ROBINSON-PATMAN ACT

Price discrimination occurs when a seller charges different prices to different buyers for commodities of like grade and quality. The Robinson-

Patman Act (1936) forbids such price discrimination by sellers in interstate commerce if the sales occur fairly close in time and if their effect may be to substantially lessen competition, to tend to create a monopoly, or otherwise to harm or prevent competition. The FTC or individual plaintiffs can bring actions against the alleged violator.

Price discrimination is not illegal without proving some form of "injury" to the seller's competitors, the buyer, or the competitors' or buyer's customers. Usually, the level of business at which the injury occurs must be identified. A **primary line injury** occurs when the discriminating seller hurts one of its direct competitors. When a buyer suffers because the seller sold the same commodity for a lower price to the buyer's competitors, a **secondary line injury** occurs.

A controversial theory of price discrimination involves injury to a buyer's customers. This **tertiary line injury** is said to occur when customers of retailer X do not obtain the cost savings retailer Y's customers receive because Y was sold a commodity at a discriminatory, lower price than was X. (Therefore, in selling, leasing, or otherwise furnishing that commodity to its customers, Y can pass on its savings from the price discrimination; without such a special, low price as was bestowed upon Y, X has no cost savings to pass on to its customers.)

As a practical matter, price discrimination usually only succeeds when buyers lack information about the prices other buyers are paying or do not know about the other buyers' secret discounts in the form of kickbacks or rebates.[5] As a legal matter, price differences are allowed only if they result from disparities in costs (e.g., shipping expenses), from a good-faith reduction in price to meet competition in a particular region, or from changing market conditions (e.g., imminent deterioration of perishable goods, distress sales, end-of-season sales of obsolete goods). Buyers may also be liable for requesting or knowingly receiving an illegal price differential.

FEDERAL TRADE COMMISSION ACT

The Federal Trade Commission Act (1914) outlaws "unfair or deceptive [business] practices" and "unfair methods of competition." What those terms mean has been left for the courts to decide. The act grants the Federal Trade Commission (FTC) sole authority to investigate possible violations and to enforce the law.

---

[5] The law of price discrimination shows how antitrust law sometimes has conflicting goals. Although trade association activities, such as price list sharing, are frowned upon as anticompetitive (possible price-fixing), the absence of price lists may cause buyers to be ignorant of what their competitors are paying and thus become prey to unlawful price discrimination.

The FTC considers the following factors when deciding whether a business activity violates the act: (1) Is it against public policy? (2) Is it immoral, oppressive, unscrupulous, or otherwise unethical? (3) Does it cause substantial harm to consumers?

The FTC exercises its powers via

Advisory opinions—counseling businesses on the legality of a proposed activity.

Consent decrees—in return for the business' agreement to stop doing something, the FTC agrees not to impose severe penalties.[6]

Cease and desist orders—telling businesses to stop breaking certain laws. Violations can subject the offending business to fines of up to $10,000 per day.

Extreme measures—e.g., requiring divestiture (selling off) of a business' assets or subsidiaries; ordering that the business be dissolved.

ANTITRUST LAW ENFORCEMENT

State attorneys general may sue Sherman Act violators on behalf of injured state residents, whether consumers or competitors. Moreover, private parties injured by Sherman or Clayton Act violations may bring civil damage suits. For concerted, nationwide efforts at creating a uniform antitrust policy, though, one usually must turn to the FTC or the U.S. Justice Department (Justice). Each has issued guidelines setting forth enforcement policies: Justice discusses when it will oppose mergers, and the FTC covers certain industries. In addition to both agencies having Clayton Act powers to bring civil actions, Justice can seek judicial enforcement of the Sherman Act. The FTC and Justice also enforce other, lesser known laws, such as the section of the Lanham Act that prohibits deceptive trademarks.[7] Only the Justice Department has the power to bring criminal as well as civil actions (e.g., under the Sherman Act).

The FTC's function continues to be controversial. Businesses often resent FTC trade regulation rules and enforcement, but consumer organizations often criticize the FTC as being too lenient on business. (Both groups' criticisms are common for other agencies as well, such as the Occupational Safety and Health Administration, Food and Drug Administration, and Federal Communications Commission.)

---

[6] Subsequent damage suits by private plaintiffs may not use a consent decree as proof of a violation, but must prove their cases independently.

[7] The FTC has the power to cancel deceptive trademarks.

Clearly, the extent of antitrust regulation is related to the political climate. When the public is upset with a particular industry or problem, heightened regulation and enforcement tend to follow, whereas regulation—or, at least, enforcement—sometimes decreases when the predominant concerns are governmental interference and the stifling of would-be entrepreneurs. (Of course, FTC actions may be reviewed and, in effect, overturned by Congress or the federal courts.)

The FTC has proven reluctant to pursue antitrust cases against certain professions, thus giving them a limited, *de facto* exemption. Certainly, doctors, lawyers, and other professionals can no longer maintain minimum fee schedules or otherwise forbid competitive pricing. However, traditions of self-policing, federalism, and professional independence have been advanced as reasons to leave regulation to the profession itself and to the individual states.

EXEMPTIONS FROM ANTITRUST LAWS

The actions of government officials (foreign or domestic), fishing and agricultural cooperatives, Major League Baseball (but no other professional sport), export associations, labor unions, and persons associating together in order to petition the government usually are exempt from antitrust laws. Also generally exempt are business activities required or exclusively regulated by state, federal, or foreign laws or administrative regulations. Moreover, the insurance industry has an antitrust exemption to the extent it is already regulated by the states.

The scope of these exemptions tends to be narrow. Only activities specifically designated as exemptions are allowed, with little variation from a literal reading of the law. For example: (1) the insurance industry's exemption is restricted to activities related to the sale of policies; (2) labor union activities that provide aid to nonlabor groups or that tend to control marketing are not exempt; and (3) only "persons engaged in agricultural production" are entitled to an antitrust exemption, not those involved in packing, or both production and distribution.

KNOW THE CONCEPTS

DO YOU KNOW THE BASICS?

1. Name the four major statutes comprising the body of federal antitrust law.

2. What is the name of the antitrust law doctrine that holds that most accidental and reasonable restraints of trade are not prohibited if connected to a legitimate business goal?

3. Name two advantages of judging antitrust cases according to the *per se* rule.

4. Name five *per se* antitrust violations.

5. What three elements must be established to prove an illegal tying arrangement?

6. Name three activities declared unlawful by the Clayton Act.

7. What sanctions are available under (a) the Sherman Act; (b) the Clayton Act?

8. Explain the potential entrant effect.

9. What two facts must be proved for a "failing firm defense" to be successful?

10. What is the relationship between elasticity and market power?

11. What are the two relevant markets to consider when alleging the illegal use of market power?

12. Under what circumstances are different prices permitted under the Robinson-Patman Act?

13. What are six items necessary to prove price discrimination illegal?

14. (a) What are three factors that the FTC considers in determining whether business practices are unfair or deceptive?

    (b) What may the FTC do to enforce the antitrust laws?

15. (a) List at least five activities exempted from the antitrust laws.

    (b) How much "leeway" is allowed in interpreting antitrust exemptions?

TERMS FOR STUDY

advisory opinion
antitrust law
cease and desist order
Clayton Act
conglomerate merger
conscious parallelism
consent decree
division of markets
elasticity of demand
exclusive dealership
exclusive dealing
exemption
failing firm defense
Federal Trade Commission Act
free rider
group boycott
horizontal merger
horizontal territorial limitations
interbrand competition
interlocking directorship

intrabrand competition
market power
market share
monopolies
monopolistic mergers
per se violations
potential entrant effect
price discrimination
price-fixing
primary line injury
production quotas
resale price maintenance
Robinson-Patman Act
rule of reason
secondary line injury
Sherman Act
tertiary line injury
tying arrangement
vertical merger
vertical restraint

PRACTICAL APPLICATION

1. Bambi's Bikes is the major wholesale distributor of bicycles and bike parts in North and South Carolina. Its closest competitor is Wilma's Wheels, another bike and bike parts business. Bambi's Bikes and Wilma's Wheels agree that Bambi will distribute bikes throughout all of the Carolinas except the Charlotte metropolitan area, where Wilma will from now on do all of her business. Choose the correct answer (a, b, c, or d). The Bambi-Wilma agreement is an example of:
   (a) vertical territorial restrictions, and the rule of reason applies;
   (b) horizontal territorial restrictions, and the rule of reason applies;
   (c) vertical territorial restrictions, and is *per se* illegal; or
   (d) horizontal territorial restrictions, and is *per se* illegal.

2. Ivy League universities signed a consent decree with the U.S. Department of Justice agreeing to stop meeting and exchanging among themselves information regarding their costs of operation

and the financial needs of their students. The tuition charged by each of these private universities is close to the same amount charged by the others. For (a) and (b), below, choose the best answer (1, 2, 3, 4, or 5).

(a) Most likely, the charges against these universities were that they had engaged in: (1) vertical price fixing, (2) horizontal price fixing, (3) a Robinson-Patman Act violation, (4) illegal monopolization, or (5) exclusive dealing.

(b) The universities' conduct was: (1) *per se* illegal, (2) only illegal if it unreasonably restrained competition, (3) only illegal if a substantial amount of interstate commerce was negatively affected, (4) conscious parallelism, or (5) illegal under the Clayton Act.

3. Tinytown is served by only a single convenience store, Pop's Place. There is adequate space for like stores to be built, but none have been constructed in years. Visitors to Tinytown notice that the prices at the store are much higher than those at stores from their hometown. Under what circumstances could Pop's be considered a monopoly?

4. Irvin Inventor has recently developed a unique hat cleaner. To reap a "fair" profit (Irvin earns royalties on each cleaner sold), and to protect his product from intrabrand competition, Irvin has allowed only one retailer per state to sell his product.

(a) What kind of arrangement has Irvin set up, and what antitrust law determines whether it is legal?

(b) Assuming that Irvin holds a patent for his hat cleaner, can he require that businesses desiring to purchase the hat cleaner must also buy another, unrelated product?

5. Amalgamated Bigshot Buckshot Company (ABBC) controls 80% of the market in retail sales of buckshot. ABBC wants to take over (1) Diddly Squat Sales (DSS), which controls 7% of buckshot retail sales; (2) Mid-Sized Manufacturers (MSM), which has no retail sales but manufactures approximately 30% of all buckshot; and (3) Little-of-Both Operations (LOBO), which has about 1% each of retail buckshot sales and buckshot manufacturing, and runs a hamburger joint so customers can eat while they mull over their buckshot purchases. Which merger is most likely to be permitted? Which is least likely?

6. You are the chief executive for a nationwide, Fortune 500 Company. A little firm in the Midwest keeps underselling your company's product, P. Can you lower P's price in response, doing so only in the Midwest?

ANSWERS

KNOW THE CONCEPTS

1. The Sherman Antitrust Act, the Clayton Act, the Robinson-Patman Act, and the Federal Trade Commission Act.

2. The "rule of reason."

3. The *per se* rule is credited with improving judicial efficiency and providing clear guidance for business managers in their decision-making.

4. Horizontal price fixing, group boycotts, production quotas, tying arrangements, and territorial limitations.

5. First, there must be evidence of the seller's sale of one product conditioned on the purchase of another, distinct product. Second, the seller must have sufficient economic or market power to force the tie-in. Third, the level of competition restricted in the tied (less desirable) product must be substantial.

6. Exclusive dealing and tying arrangements for the sale of commodities; interlocking directorships; and monopolistic mergers.

7. (a) Criminal penalties (up to 3 years' imprisonment and fines of $10 million) and civil sanctions (treble damages, injunctions, and costs of suit, including attorney's fees);
   (b) same civil sanctions as for the Sherman Act.

8. The potential entrant effect causes competitors to remain efficient so as to discourage the potential entrant from entering the market. Once potential entrants begin to merge with existing companies, competitive discipline is reduced.

9. In order for the "healthier" firm to exempt itself from antitrust enforcement, 1) the "failing" firm must have been unable to reorganize successfully under Chapter 11 of the bankruptcy laws, and 2) the "failing" firm must have made unsuccessful attempts to find other suitable merger partners that might reduce market concentration.

10. When the number of competitors is large, the demand elasticity (percent change in quantity/percent change in price) for each firm is high. Thus, each firm has very little power to raise its income by raising its price. The opposite is true for a monopoly. A monopolistic firm has great control over its consumers, so when it raises a good's price the demand for that good drops off very little or none at all, and its income rises correspondingly.

11. The product market and geographical markets must be considered.

12. When the seller can show that price differentials result from disparities in costs, from a good-faith attempt to meet competition, or from changing market conditions.

13. To establish illegal price discrimination, a plaintiff or the FTC must prove 6 elements: (1) discrimination in price (within roughly the same time period), (2) between two different purchasers, (3) affecting interstate commerce, (4) concerning commodities of like grade and quality, (5) causing a substantial lessening of competition or tending to create a monopoly, and (6) causing injury to competitors of the seller or the buyer or to their customers.

14. (a) Whether the practice is (1) against public policy; (2) immoral, oppressive, unscrupulous, or otherwise unethical; and (3) substantially harmful to customers.

   (b) Advisory opinions, consent decrees, cease and desist orders, and extreme measures such as ordering divestiture or dissolution.

15. (a) Actions of government officials, fishing and agricultural cooperatives, Major League Baseball, export associations, labor unions, insurance companies, persons associating together to petition the government, and business activities required or exclusively regulated by state, federal, or foreign laws or administrative regulations.

   (b) Little leeway is allowed. For example, the insurer's exemption concerns only the sale of policies, and the labor union exemption is restricted to the union's role as its members' bargaining agent with the employer.

PRACTICAL APPLICATION

1. The answer is (d). Both Bambi's Bikes and Wilma's Wheels are at the same level (so horizontal, not vertical); they are engaged in a market division, which is a *per se* violation of the antitrust laws.

2. (a) There is nothing in the facts suggesting a merger (i.e., monopolization of the market), an exclusive dealing, or price discrimination (a violation of the Robinson-Patman Act). Instead, it is price-fixing, by supposed competitors, at the same level of the market; therefore, the price-fixing is horizontal, not vertical—answer (2).

   (b) Answer (1). It is a *per se* antitrust violation outlawed under the Sherman Act. The rule of reason still does not apply to horizontal price-fixing. Conscious parallelism was not present because the parties actually met and colluded (rather than simply followed the pricing structure set by the leading firm). The Clayton Act does not directly govern price-fixing, but instead concerns exclusive dealing, tying arrangements, interlocking directorships, and monopolistic mergers. So that act is not at issue here.

3. Simply being the only store in town does not constitute an illegal monopoly. Perhaps the town only has enough demand for one store. Although the visitors could be from places with very low standards of living, the high prices could be cause for alarm. Is Pop using his "sole supplier" power to his advantage? One has to presume that these prices are fair, and not illegal, because other stores could always open in competition and undercut Pop's prices (unless Pop owned all other land on which stores could be built, or had used a threat of predatory pricing to keep competitors from entering the market).

4. (a) Irvin has granted exclusive distributorships to the retailers. Irvin has a right to choose who he would like to sell his products, but if there are no real substitutes for his product in the areas, these agreements could be found illegal under Section 3 of the Clayton Act.

   (b) No. That would be an unlawful tying arrangement. The patent does not give Irvin a right to mandate tie-ins, but actually provides the type of market power that bolsters claims against a tying arrangement.

5. The DSS acquisition would be a horizontal merger since they are both in the same business; the MSM merger would be a vertical merger because they operate at different levels in the same business; and LOBO is a mixture of both a horizontal and vertical merger, as well as, in part, a conglomerate since LOBO operates a completely different business (the hamburger joint) from what ABBC does. DSS is the least likely merger to be permitted (since it would remove 35% of the remaining competition in a field already dominated by ABBC).

   The MSM merger most likely will be permitted. An argument also can be made to approve the LOBO merger because, although involving some horizontal elements, the acquisition likely would have the smallest probable adverse effect on competition.

6. The resulting price differential probably will not violate the Robinson-Patman Act if it is simply a good-faith effort to meet the competition's price on product P. (Query: Is selling at a loss "in good faith"?) Robinson-Patman is not designed for this type of case, but for preventing firms from dropping their prices on goods in order to eliminate competition and create a market monopoly for themselves. When the number of competitors is large, the demand elasticity (percent change in quantity/percent change in price) for each firm is high. Thus, each firm has very little power to raise its income by raising its price. The opposite is true for a monopoly. When a monopolistic firm has great market power over its usual customers, it can raise the price of a good without suffering much, if any, drop in demand. Thus an anticompetitive, monopolistic firm's income rises correspondingly.

23 ENVIRONMENTAL LAW

Historically, the only recourse against polluters was through trespass and zoning laws or through the doctrines of private or public nuisance. At common law, an individual or a government could seek a court-ordered abatement of pollution. Major efforts to control the effects of industry on the environment have only been in place since the late 1960s, when sweeping federal regulation began. Many statutes have expanded both the types of lawsuits, as well as potential plaintiffs, for private actions against businesses allegedly in violation of federal or state environmental laws. Typical civil or criminal penalties include injunctions, damage awards, fines, and—sometimes—jail sentences.

NATIONAL ENVIRONMENTAL POLICY

The 1969 **National Environmental Policy Act** (NEPA) is the cornerstone of all federal environmental law. It establishes the nation's environmental policy, sets goals, and provides means for carrying out the policy. The overall goal of NEPA is to ensure that environmental information is made available to government officials and the public before decisions are reached or action taken. NEPA tries to accomplish this goal by: (1) creating the Council of Environmental Quality, to review conservation plans or other programs (e.g., construction) affecting the environment, to propose legislation, and to monitor and report yearly on the state of the nation's natural resources; (2) requiring that federal agencies undertaking or proposing "major federal actions significantly affecting the quality of the human environment" prepare environmental impact statements (EIS), which are documents detailing the environmental effects of those actions and their alternatives. (Anything involving federal funds, approval, licensing, or supervision is within NEPA's reach.)

The EIS requirement has a particularly strong impact on power plant activities (construction, maintenance, or abandonment), transportation facilities (railroads, highways, harbors, etc.), and leases of federal land. When preparing an EIS, the federal agency must contact concerned businesses and other agencies in order to report adequately (1) the proposed action's environmental impact, including unavoidable adverse effects on, and commitments of, resources; (2) the tie between local short-term effects on, and commitments of, resources; and (3) alternatives to the proposed action.

POLLUTION CONTROL MEASURES

Federal anti-pollution measures are designed to eliminate or control the diffusion of waste particles through the air, water, and land.

ENVIRONMENTAL PROTECTION AGENCY (EPA)

The EPA, created in 1970, oversees many of the federal pollution control programs. It is the largest regulatory agency of the U.S. government. Its primary function is to establish and enforce standards, conduct research on pollution effects, monitor and analyze the environment, advise Congress of new policies to protect the environment from pollution, and assist state and local pollution control programs.

WATER POLLUTION

The earliest attempt by the federal government to reduce water pollution was the **River and Harbors Act of 1886**, which required permits for dumping into navigable waters. In 1948, the **Water Pollution Control Act** was an attempt to eliminate all pollutant discharge into the nation's waterways. In 1965, the **Federal Water Pollution Control Act** strengthened the previous federal statutes and expanded the national government's powers over dumping. (The **Safe Drinking Water Act**—Public Health Service Act, enacted in 1974, is also important.) A 1996 amendment to that law requires the EPA to set standards for the following pollutants in drinking water: arsenic, chlorine, cryptosporidium, and radon. The EPA must now also screen chemicals in drinking water to see if they mimic the effects of estrogen in the body (a possible cause of breast cancer). The law, though, which most comprehensively governs water pollution is the 1972 **Clean Water Act**, an amendment to the Federal Water Pollution Control Act.

THE CLEAN WATER ACT (CWA)

The CWA has two stated goals: (1) to make the nation's water safe for swimming and fishing, and (2) to eliminate the discharge of all pollutants into navigable waters. To accomplish these goals, the EPA is authorized to establish water quality criteria regulating the concentration of pollutants that are permissible in a body of water and effluent limitations regulating the amount of pollutants discharged from a particular source.

• *NATIONAL PERMIT SYSTEM (THE "NATIONAL POLLUTANT DISCHARGE ELIMINATION SYSTEM")*

Companies must obtain permits from the EPA to discharge pollutants into the navigable waters of the United States. The permit specifies each pollutant that can be discharged and sets average and maximum daily limits, called effluent limitations, on each. Permit holders must monitor their discharges and furnish reports to the authorities.

• *PUBLICLY OWNED TREATMENT WORKS*

Discharges into publicly owned sewage treatment works require no permit. However, industrial users must still meet certain pretreatment criteria standards before they make their discharges. They must treat wastes to remove pollutants before discharging them into the system.

• *HAZARDOUS SUBSTANCES*

The CWA forbids the discharge of hazardous substances in harmful quantities. Dischargers must report any leaking, spilling, pumping, or dumping, and are liable for clean up costs.

• *ENFORCEMENT*

The CWA authorizes the EPA to use administrative, adjudicatory procedures in order to impose civil penalties for permit violations. The EPA administrator may also bring a civil action (a lawsuit in court) to obtain an injunction or a civil penalty against a violator. The administrator may also bring criminal proceedings. However, in some states, the EPA has delegated enforcement to the state government, which has agreed to meet EPA specifications.

The statute also provides for citizen suits. Any citizen having standing may bring a civil action on his or her own behalf against a violator.

THE OIL POLLUTION CONTROL ACT OF 1990

Congress passed the Oil Pollution Control Act in response to the Exxon *Valdez* oil spill off the Alaskan shore in March 1989. The statute provides that a party responsible for a vessel or a facility that has discharged oil upon the navigable waters or adjoining shoreline is liable for the removal costs and damages that result from the incident. Defenses exist for acts of God, acts of war, and acts or omissions of third parties. The act increases defendants' maximum liability, and it mandates thick, double hulls for all newly built oil tankers; after the year 2015, every tanker in use must have these hulls. Perhaps most important, the act establishes a fund, paid for by a tax on oil, to provide the money for federal cleanup efforts. (This is particularly important when the liable person is unknown or the maximum amount of private liability will be inadequate to pay for cleanup costs).

AIR POLLUTION

In 1955, Congress passed the first federal law to deal with air pollution. The most important modern statute is the Clean Air Act.

THE CLEAN AIR ACT

The Clean Air Act (CAA) was originally passed in 1963 and has been amended on several occasions since, including a major revision in 1990. It encourages states to control local sources of harmful airborne particles (carbon monoxide, particulates, sulfur oxides, hydrocarbons, and nitrogen oxides). The CAA authorizes the EPA to determine concentrations of various particles that would be consistent with human health. The EPA thus can regulate the emission of air pollutants from stationary sources, such as power plants and refineries, but must first consider costs, including industry's compliance costs, before deciding whether a regulation is "appropriate and necessary." *Michigan v. EPA*, 576 U.S. ____ (2015). The CAA further requires the EPA to set standards for common pollutants such as dust, carbon monoxide, and ozone. The standards are called the National Ambient Air Quality Standards (NAAQS). As part of ongoing congressional oversight, Title VI of the Transportation Equity Act for the 21st century (1998) codified the implementation dates for new ozone and particulate air quality standards (which may still be adjusted). For example, in 2008 the EPA strengthened the NAAQS for ground-level ozone, the primary component of smog.

• *STATE IMPLEMENTATION PLANS (SIP)*

Once the EPA sets the NAAQS, states are responsible for controlling and cleaning up areas that do not comply with them. States have to detail the measures they would use to achieve the standards, and then submit their plans to the EPA. If a state's implementation plan is inadequate, the EPA can withhold federal funds, prohibit the construction of new air pollution sources, or intercede with its own measures. All SIPs must include emission limitations and measures that will be taken to uphold air standards. Emission limitations are specific rules that operators of pollutant sources must follow to reduce emission from mobile sources of pollution.

• *ENFORCEMENT*

Enforcement of the CAA is accomplished through administrative penalties, injunctions, criminal prosecution, and citizen suits. It permits states to issue permits for noncomplying pollutant emissions, provided that certain conditions (e.g., the polluter's reaching the lowest achievable emission rate) are met. A 1990 amendment mandates stricter automobile emission limits and "cleaner" gasoline blends, requires increasing use of alternative fuel vehicles for companies with car fleets, provides for phasing out the use of ozone-depleting chemicals, calls for tougher emission standards at coal-burning plants and other producers of "acid rain," imposes additional requirements for cities to reduce their carbon monoxide levels, dramatically expands both the list of toxic air pollutants and the EPA's role in curtailing them, and creates a Chemical Safety Board to determine why chemical accidents occur.

LAND POLLUTION

Several federal statutes relate to dumping of materials on land and hazardous waste.

THE RESOURCE CONSERVATION AND RECOVERY ACT OF 1976 (RCRA)

The RCRA addresses the special problems of hazardous waste sites and solid/hazardous waste management (ambient air standards, groundwater quality, waste collection, open dumps, resource recovery, and markets for recovered materials). Under the RCRA, handlers of hazardous wastes must conform to specified standards. Handlers are those who generate, transport, treat, or store hazardous wastes. Hazardous wastes are those wastes that contribute significantly to serious, irreversible illness or pose hazards to human health when improperly managed. These wastes are characterized by toxicity, corrosiveness, reactability, and ignitibility.

• *GENERATORS AND TRANSPORTERS*

Generators and transporters of hazardous waste must notify the EPA of the location and general description of their activities. The EPA issues identification numbers to each handler.

Generators of waste must keep records concerning their hazardous wastes. If waste generators transport the wastes off the site of their manufacture, they must package and label the wastes and ship the packages with a manifest. The manifest identifies the persons originating, carrying, and receiving the wastes and states the nature and quantity of the wastes.

Transporters must comply with the terms of the manifests they receive from generators and must keep a copy of each manifest. If waste discharge occurs during carriage, transporters must take appropriate, immediate action to protect human health and the environment. Rules and guidelines determine whether they are to clean up the discharge or to immediately notify authorities.

• *OWNERS OR OPERATORS*

Owners or operators of a hazardous waste treatment, storage, or disposal facility (TSDF) have to apply for permits allowing them to dispose of their hazardous wastes. Owners and operators of hazardous waste landfills are required to submit, with their permit applications, information about their facility's potential for exposing the public to hazardous substances. Permits are not issued unless certain performance standards are met. In running their facilities, owners and operators must analyze representative samples of waste before transporting, storing, or treating them. They also must provide training for personnel and must inspect facilities to discover malfunctions. Where discharges occur, they must take necessary remedial action.

• *ENFORCEMENT*

EPA employees are authorized to enter facilities at reasonable times. They may inspect samples, and they may copy records. If violations of the hazardous waste provisions are not corrected, violators ultimately are liable for civil penalties. Knowingly making a false statement in required documents is a crime punishable by fine. The RCRA's ban on open dumping of hazardous wastes is enforceable by citizen suits.

THE SUPERFUND LAW

The Superfund Law (1980), formally known as the Comprehensive Environmental Response, Compensation, and Liability Act (CERCLA), deals with the uncontrolled releases of hazardous wastes. CERCLA creates a fund that can be tapped by the EPA and state and local governments to clean up hazardous waste sites in accordance with the EPA's National Contingency Plan. Fund priorities are based on a ranking of the risk per site. This EPA Hazardous Ranking System thus has led to a National Priorities List of sites to be cleaned.

• *NOTICE REQUIREMENT*

Persons in charge of a vessel or a facility that has released a hazardous substance must immediately notify the EPA's National Response Center. Notice must also be provided to potentially injured parties by publication in a local newspaper. Failure to comply with these notice requirements subjects the person in charge to a fine and imprisonment.

• *OBLIGATIONS OF INDUSTRY*

Generators and transporters of hazardous substances, as well as past and present owners and operators of hazardous waste sites, are strictly liable for the costs of cleaning that waste. However, there are limitations on this strict liability statute. Liability is not imposed when a release of hazardous substances results from an act of God, an act of war, or the act or omission of a third party.

Innocent landowners who acquire property without knowledge of contamination, and who had no reason to know of it, are not liable for costs under Superfund. The *responsible persons* from whom the EPA can recover the costs of remedial work include (1) the present owner or operator of the facility; (2) the owner or operator at the time of disposal of the hazardous substance; (3) any person who arranged for treatment or disposal of hazardous substances at the facility; and (4) any person who transported hazardous substances to and selected the facility. The Supreme Court decided in *U.S. v. Bestfoods*, 524 U.S. 51 (1998) that only if a parent corporation was doing more than generally supervising a subsidiary (e.g., the parent's own employees managed or directed some of the activities that caused pollution) may the parent, not just the subsidiary, be held liable for the cleanup of pollution caused by the subsidiary.

• *PUBLIC RIGHT TO KNOW PROVISIONS UNDER SUPERFUND*

Superfund's right to know provision requires owners and occupiers of facilities that produce, use, and store hazardous chemicals to file with local and state officials a material safety data sheet (MSDS) for each hazardous chemical. The MSDS provides government officials with information regarding the use of hazardous chemicals in their communities.

• *ENFORCEMENT*

In addition to EPA enforcement of Superfund, states can also sue private parties (e.g., transporters, generators) for removal costs if such efforts are consistent with the National Contingency Plan. The statute authorizes citizen suits. Although the Superfund fails to impose liability for injuries to private individuals, it does not supersede any state or common law remedies available to private individuals.

THE TOXIC SUBSTANCES CONTROL ACT (TSCA)

TSCA, enacted in 1976, regulates hazardous chemical substances and mixtures. The EPA maintains an inventory of all chemical substances and mixtures handled in the United States. All persons seeking to manufacture any new substance or mixture for a significant new use have to notify the EPA.

The EPA administrator is empowered to make rules necessary to protect both health and the environment against unreasonable risks posed by all substances and mixtures. The administrator must apply the least burdensome rule that will be effective, but the possible rules range from requiring notice of the unreasonable risk of injury to prohibiting entirely the manufacture of a substance or mixture.

THE FEDERAL ENVIRONMENTAL PESTICIDE CONTROL ACT (FEPCA)

FEPCA, enacted in 1972, requires that pesticides in interstate shipments be adequately labeled and unadulterated. The statute also covers interstate manufacturing operations, as well as actual misuse of pesticides.

Pesticides are classified for general and restricted use. Restricted pesticides may be applied only by persons certified to use them. States certify pesticide applicators subject to EPA approval.

The use of a registered pesticide in any way inconsistent with its labeling instructions is prohibited. A farmer or other pesticide applicator's conviction for knowingly violating FEPCA's provisions may result in fine or imprisonment.

Pesticide manufacturers must register with the EPA and must report annually on types and amounts of pesticides produced and sold. EPA agents may inspect manufacturing plants and take samples. When a pesticide violates FEPCA, the EPA administrator may issue an order to stop its sale or use. Pesticides violating the law may also be seized.

THE FOOD QUALITY PROTECTION ACT (FQPA)

The FQPA, enacted in 1996, prohibits the use on crops or processed food of a pesticide that would cause more than one person in a million to develop cancer from eating typical amounts of that food over a lifetime. The statute also allows the EPA, when evaluating pesticides, to consider the impact on children and the likelihood that the chemicals will cause birth defects or reproductive problems. Over time, at least 30 chemicals once commonly in use may have to be withdrawn from the market because they fail to meet the FQPA's standards.

NUCLEAR POWER REGULATION

Nuclear power is handled separately from other hazardous-waste producing processes. Much of the regulation falls under the jurisdiction of the Nuclear Regulatory Commission (NRC).

NUCLEAR POWER DEVELOPMENT

The NRC oversees the private construction, ownership, and operation of commercial nuclear power reactors.

• *NUCLEAR POWER LICENSING*

Persons seeking to build nuclear power plants must apply to the NRC for a construction permit. If a construction permit is issued, the initial application to build is carried over to the operational licensing stage.

• *NRC CRITERIA FOR PLANT LOCATION*

The suitability of an applicant's site is determined by comparing the design and operating characteristics of the proposed reactor with the physical characteristics of the site. The human environment near the site is also considered, with particular regard for the population density in the surrounding area. Otherwise unacceptable sites can become acceptable if compensating engineering safeguards are included in reactor designs.

THE PRICE-ANDERSON ACT

The Price-Anderson Act protects nuclear licensees from the risk of excessive liability resulting from a nuclear incident. A nuclear licensee is required to carry, for potential liability claims, the maximum amount of insurance coverage available at a reasonable cost on the private market (presently about $200 million in coverage). If an incident occurs and liability exceeds the mandatory private insurance coverage, each nuclear licensee (approximately 105 throughout the United States) must contribute a pro rata share up to $63 million per reactor per incident.

The federal government will indemnify (reimburse and hold harmless) licensees and other persons up to $560 million for incidents at non-commercial nuclear reactors. In effect, Price-Anderson makes the nuclear industry strictly liable for many harms arising from nuclear accidents, and—in return—the industry receives some federal indemnification for amounts exceeding a licensee's insurance coverage. Liability is capped at the required private insurance, federal indemnification, and pro rata contribution amounts. That means that, per reactor incident, the absolute liability limit (including possible federal government payments) is about $7.4 billion.

THE NUCLEAR WASTE POLICY ACT (1982)

This act establishes a national plan for the disposal of highly radioactive nuclear waste. The statute puts in motion a process for locating and constructing two temporary repositories (storage facilities) for high-level nuclear fuel until permanent repositories are built.

PROTECTION OF WILDLIFE

Energy demands in the highly industrialized United States have prompted mining, wetlands filling, and other activities that damage lands and displace wildlife. State and federal laws allow development to continue in critical areas, such as virgin lands and scenic places, while minimizing environmental damage. Critical areas include parks, forests, tidelands, wetlands, and the continental shelf. Some important federal statutes are the Marine Protection, Research, and Sanctuaries Act of 1972 (the Ocean Dumping Act), the Coastal Zone Management Act (1972), the Noise Control Acts of 1970 and 1972 (requiring the EPA and the Federal Aviation Administration to set standards and to regulate aircraft noise), the Forest and Rangeland Renewable Resources Planning Act (1974), and the Surface Mining Control and Reclamation Act (1977).

Probably the most significant law in this area, and certainly the most controversial, is the **Endangered Species Act (1973)**. This act protects many species (both plants and animals) from activities that would harm them or their habitats. The act makes it a federal offense to buy, sell, possess, export, or import any species listed by the Interior Department as endangered or threatened, or any product made from such a species. Federal agencies must ensure that their projects do not jeopardize a listed species or adversely affect its habitat. Agencies must obtain a permit by consulting with the Interior Department for land-based species or the Commerce Department for marine species. There are fines for persons who violate the act, and a cabinet-level review committee ultimately determines whether federal projects may be exempted from the act.

THE COST OF ENVIRONMENTAL REGULATION

Pollution control has a price, and trade-offs usually have to be made. Weighing costs and benefits, however, involves controversial fact determinations and value judgments. Ultimately, every member of society contributes to environmental problems and everyone also benefits from correcting these problems. (Of course, the contributions and benefits, while shared by all, certainly are not equal per member; some people pollute, or benefit from pollution abatement, much more than others do.) To deal fairly and effectively with pollution prevention and cleanup, cost allocation systems generally should include a combination of incentives, regulations, and charges or permits for polluting. Because the costs of environmental regulation have proven to be so immense, the government has begun to allow for alternative methods in protecting the environment.

ADR AND ENVIRONMENTAL DISPUTES

The use of **alternative dispute resolution** (ADR) techniques in the environmental field is relatively new and likely to rise rapidly. Environmentalists, businesses, and enforcement agencies increasingly realize that litigation often is not cost-effective.

The Superfund Law incorporates the concept of ADR by requiring the EPA and private parties to try to negotiate settlements. The EPA also promotes ADR for other environmental disputes. An EPA policy guideline defines various methods of ADR and how to select a neutral third party. An enforcement dispute with the EPA may be submitted to ADR only with EPA approval.

ADR organizations exist that will help parties solve their hazardous waste problems. These organizations usually include specialists from business, environmental groups, and universities. Use of ADR in these cases usually focuses on the allocation of cleanup costs.

THE BUBBLE CONCEPT

An innovative approach to reducing the costs of environmental regulation is the **bubble concept**. Previously, each process or industrial pollution-causing unit within a plant or area was treated separately and had to conform to some emission standard. Under the bubble concept, trade-offs can be made within the plant and some processes can be left alone while those that are less expensive to modify are drastically cut. In effect a "bubble" is drawn around the entire plant and an overall emission standard is set, rather than focusing on each process. The concept can further be expanded into the selling of pollution rights (or "credits") where companies with capabilities to more inexpensively lower emissions can sell their rights to those who cannot. The overall pollution standard is still met, but at a cost that is cheaper to society.

INTERNATIONAL ENVIRONMENTAL LAW

Since pollution does not remain confined within national borders, there are numerous environmental concerns that must be addressed by the international community: issues such as air pollution (the "greenhouse effect," acid rain, and radioactive fallout); water pollution (ocean dumping, oil spills, and contaminant runoffs, such as pesticides); soil erosion (often caused by overgrazing or the clear-cutting of all trees and most vegetation); and the degradation or extinction of plant and animal species.

In June 1992, delegates from 172 nations met in Rio de Janeiro, Brazil for the United Nations Conference on Environment and Development. This Earth Summit generated among other things: (1) the Rio

Declaration, a short statement that outlines 27 principles linking environmental protection and economic development, and that recognizes developing nations' "right" to develop responsibly; (2) an agreement by industrialized countries to reduce the emission of gases thought to cause global warming (the "greenhouse effect") to 1990 levels by the year 2000, with these countries' adoption of emission-control policies; (3) a document calling for the prudent harvesting of forests, i.e., conservation practices meant to maintain the viability of forests despite continued logging and other operations; and (4) a statement that signatory nations will establish policies to uphold biodiversity, i.e., to slow the extinction of plants and animals. The statements produced little action, however.

In December 1997, the United Nations Framework Convention for Climate Change (UNFCCC) met in Kyoto, Japan, and adopted the Kyoto Protocol, intended to combat global warming by reducing six greenhouse gases (mostly carbon dioxide) in the United States and 37 other industrialized nations. Just as the Earth Summit aimed to reduce the emitted gases to 1990 levels by the year 2000, so the Kyoto Protocol sought similar reductions to at or below the 1990 benchmark, but with the timetable pushed back (e.g., to 2012 for the United States). Contending that the protocol unfairly exempts over 140 developing countries (including Brazil, China, India, and Mexico) from any obligation to limit their rapidly growing emissions and that the preferable method to fight pollution is through flexible, free-market mechanisms (see "The Bubble Concept," on page 562), not governmental dictates, the U.S. government has strongly opposed the protocol. Without American ratification, the Kyoto Protocol—as presently constituted—will not be implemented.

Rich and poor countries often have different concerns about the environment.[1] It may be unfair for developed nations to insist on environmental protection standards that could slow the economic development and growth needed to lift Third World nations out of poverty (standards which, incidentally, most developed nations did not try to meet when they were at a less developed stage). While economic growth is the cure for poverty, economists and others disagree about how developing nations should approach environmental issues. Some say that only after these nations have risen to a higher level of education, agricultural and industrial production, income, and other standards for economic advancement can they turn aggressively toward environmental matters.

---

[1] In rich nations, environmentalists tend to worry about saving the ozone, preventing severe and permanent climate changes, as well as protecting endangered species or otherwise preserving biological diversity. In less affluent nations the focus usually is on the basic problems of polluted air and water, deforestation, and soil erosion.

Others believe that a strong, highly protective environmental policy is a prerequisite to sustainable economic growth.[2] A middle view seems to be that while economic growth and environmental protection are separate issues, a developing nation may simultaneously pursue both, with advancement in one not necessarily harming the other.

KNOW THE CONCEPTS

DO YOU KNOW THE BASICS?

1. Other than statutes, the main bases for legal relief from pollution have been what type of claims?
2. Name at least ten federal environmental statutes.
3. Name four or more actions that RCRA requires of various hazardous waste handlers.
4. Name the three principal areas covered by the Federal Environmental Pesticide Control Act.
5. Instead of litigation, governments, businesses, and environmental groups have increasingly used alternative dispute resolution techniques to try to resolve environmental disputes. *True* or *False?*
6. Which should developing nations emphasize first, economic advancement or environmental cleanup and protection?

TERMS FOR STUDY

Agenda 21
bubble concept
Clean Air Act
Clean Water Act
Council of Environmental Quality
Earth Summit
Endangered Species Act
environmental impact statement

Environmental Protection Agency
Federal Environmental Pesticide
  Control Act
Food Quality Protection Act
generators of waste
handlers of waste
Hazardous Ranking System
hazardous waste

---

[2] Environmental damage can undermine economic productivity. For example, soil erosion caused by slash-and-burn land clearing or poorly planned strip mining rapidly can diminish land fertility and reduce agricultural production; water pollution can drastically lower fishing "harvests"; air, water, and land pollution, as well as poorly planned development, may mean that fewer tourists visit to enjoy a Third World country's natural beauty, go on safaris, and otherwise spend money.

Kyoto Protocol
manifests
material safety data sheet
National Ambient Air Quality
  Standards
National Environmental Policy Act
National Permit System
National Priorities List
Nuclear Regulatory Commission
Nuclear Waste Policy Act
Oil Pollution Control Act
pollution rights (or credits)

Price-Anderson Act
Resource Conservation and
  Recovery Act
responsible persons
Rio Declaration
state implementation plans
Superfund
Toxic Substances Control Act
transporters of waste
TSDF (treatment, storage, or
  disposal facility)

PRACTICAL APPLICATION

1. You are in charge of a construction project that uses federal funds and will necessitate discharges into waterways and the atmosphere. (a) What three types of documents should you develop or obtain? (b) If you fail to do so, what are the possible consequences?

2. It will be extremely expensive to remove hazardous waste from a section of land that has both a public owner (the state) and a number of private owners. What legal remedies are available?

3. A new, federally funded project will destroy a 30-square-mile section of grasses commonly found throughout the southern United States. It will not directly harm an endangered rodent species that lives almost exclusively in that 30-square-mile area and uses the grasses to hide from its predators. Will the project violate the Endangered Species Act?

ANSWERS

KNOW THE CONCEPTS

1. Common law claims for trespass or for private or public nuisance; alleged zoning ordinance violations.

2. Eighteen federal environmental statues are: Clean Air Act; Clean Water Act; Coastal Zone Management Act; Endangered Species Act; Federal Environmental Pesticide Control Act; Federal Water

Pollution Control Act; Food Quality Protection Act; Forest and Rangeland Renewable Resources Planning Act; Marine Protection, Research and Sanctuaries Act; National Environmental Policy Act; Noise Control Acts; Nuclear Waste Policy Act; Oil Pollution Control Act; Resource Conservation and Recovery Act; Safe Drinking Water Act; Superfund; Surface Mining Control and Reclamation Act; and Toxic Substances Control Act.

3. Keep records; properly pack and label waste; ship waste with a manifest; comply with statutes, regulations, and manifests; clean up waste discharge or notify the EPA; if an owner/operator of a TSDF, apply for a permit, train personnel, and inspect their facilities.

4. Pesticide manufacturing, labeling, and use.

5. True.

6. The answer is unclear. Some analysts contend that developing nations lack the economic resources to protect their natural environment and can only do that after sufficient economic development has occurred. Others say environmental degradation deprives a developing nation of any sustainable economic growth. A third, middle ground argues for simultaneous efforts on both fronts: the economy and the natural environment.

PRACTICAL APPLICATION

1. (a) An environmental impact statement, a Clean Water Act permit (under the National Pollutant Discharge Elimination System), and a Clean Air Act state permit.
   (b) Failure to obtain these documents may bring the project to a halt and/or lead to fines, injunctions, imprisonment, and/or citizen suits.

2. Under the Superfund Law, the EPA, states, and private citizens can sue to be reimbursed for removal costs. Open dumping can be remedied by an RCRA citizen suit. All private and public parties also may sue under common law claims such as trespass and nuisance (e.g., private citizens may try that approach to recover not merely for removal costs, but also for the actual damage to their property and to business and personal uses of that property).

3. Probably. The act covers harms not just to the species themselves, but to their habitats. While the grasses certainly are not endangered, the rodent species is. The destruction of the rodent's grass habitat indirectly harms that rodent by leaving it much more vulnerable to its predators. This habitat destruction thus seems to violate the act.

24
EMPLOYMENT LAW

KEY TERMS

Title VII statute in the federal Civil Rights Act of 1964 that prohibits discrimination in the hiring, firing, promotion, compensation, or any other aspect of employment because of a person's race, color, religion, sex, or national origin

workers' compensation a law, found in all states, requiring employees to relinquish their right to sue their employers for accidental death, injury, or disease arising from or during the course of their employment; in exchange, the employees gain the right to receive financial benefits (according to a statutory schedule of benefits) regardless of fault

The states and the federal government have many statutes concerning employment (employment law). For example, all states have workers' compensation statutes, and many states have minimum wage and maximum hour laws that mirror or approximate federal statutes (e.g., the Fair Labor Standards Act) and cover employees not protected by federal laws. In addition, sometimes state laws cause analogous federal laws to be developed: e.g., following much state legislation prohibiting the use of lie-detector tests (polygraphs), Congress enacted the Employee Polygraph Protection Act of 1998 (EPPA) prohibiting most private employers from using polygraphs, but not proscribing paper and pencil honesty questionnaires—civil penalties, injunctions, and private lawsuits are all authorized remedies for EPPA violations. Employers are exempt from EPPA if engaged in security services, the handling of controlled substances, or the ongoing investigation of an economic loss to the business (e.g., from theft, industrial espionage, or sabotage).

The purpose of employment legislation is to protect workers' health and safety, provide workers with a minimum level of economic support, and—overall—foster a workplace free from both discrimination and disruptive labor/management "wars."

HEALTH AND SAFETY LEGISLATION

WORKERS' COMPENSATION

Historically, the common law tort system imposed huge barriers on employees seeking redress against their employers for work-related injuries. A torts approach required the employee to prove that his employer's negligence caused the injury. Employers typically used three defenses to absolve themselves of responsibility. The first, the fellow-servant doctrine, absolved the employer's responsibility when a fellow employee negligently contributed to the injury. A second defense, assumption of risk, released the employer when an injured employee had voluntarily accepted the job's risks. Finally, the third defense, contributory negligence, barred an employee's suit if the employee had, in any way, contributed to the cause of his own injury.

In the early decades of the 20th century, workers' compensation statutes were enacted to overturn a system that had provided workers with little effective remedy. Thus, each state has a *workers' compensation statute* mandating that employees relinquish the right to sue their employers for accidental death, injury, disease, or illness arising out of or during the course of their employment. In return, the employer must pay an employee financial benefits when such incidents occur, regardless of who—if anyone—was at fault. Common law tort defenses are eliminated, and the employer is strictly liable to the employee. The amount of compensation is defined in, and limited by, a statutory schedule of benefits.

Workers' compensation statutes do not cover actions by or against parties other than the employer and employee. (Such actions are brought in tort law.) Also, employers must assume financial responsibility for potential claims by obtaining insurance, paying into a state fund, or having sufficient assets to qualify as self-insured. Administrative agencies and appellate courts increasingly have allowed workers' compensation for illnesses if they truly are "occupational diseases": related to specific job hazards, with a scientifically supported causal link between hazard and injury. Agencies and courts also are recognizing the need to provide benefits for mental injuries caused by job-related stress. However, most such awards only are granted when some physical impact accompanies the mental injury.

OSHA

Many states also have legislation on health and safety in the workplace. The primary statute in this area, however, is the federal

Occupational Safety and Health Act (1970). This act, which applies to all employers engaged in businesses affecting interstate commerce, states that workplaces are to be "free from recognized hazards" which could cause death or serious injury. The act establishes a federal agency, the Occupational Safety and Health Administration (OSHA), to ensure that both employers and employees comply with health and safety standards. OSHA conducts inspections and investigations: employers must keep comprehensive records on their research, job hazards generally, OSHA enforcement, and—most important—employees' illnesses and accidental deaths or injuries. OSHA rules further maintain that all affected employers must document and report to OSHA not just fatal and harmful occurrences, but any unsafe incidents, accidents, lost workdays, job transfers and terminations, medical treatments, and restrictions on work.

Besides OSHA, the act created the National Institute for Occupational Safety and Health (NIOSH), and the Occupational Safety and Health Review Commission (OSHRC). The NIOSH is charged with conducting research into health and safety standards and recommending new rules or regulations to OSHA. It also conducts training seminars that educate employers and employees on new ways to make the workplace safer. The OSHRC is an independent organization that reviews appeals from OSHA's decisions.

Three trends are apparent: (1) as with most other federal administrative agencies, OSHA cannot make new rules or policies until it has studied and verified that these new regulatory proposals, if enacted, would provide societal benefits exceeding their costs; (2) OSHA has been promulgating regulations, which set forth performance standards focusing on a level of protection rather than a particular device to achieve that protection; (3) OSHA has gone beyond just concentrating on immediate, overt dangers to life and limb, and it instead increasingly emphasizes the "hidden" hazards from relatively low-level exposure to toxic workplace chemicals sometimes linked to "delayed manifestation diseases," such as cancer and asbestosis.

THE FAMILY AND MEDICAL LEAVE ACT OF 1993 (FMLA)

The FMLA requires governmental employers and the private employers of 50 or more workers to provide their employees up to 12 weeks of unpaid leave for their own serious illness, the birth or adoption of a child, or the care of a seriously ill child, spouse, or parent. Eligible employees are those who give reasonable notice and have worked for the employer at least one year—a minimum of 1250 hours annually. The leave can be taken all at once or in increments of as little as an hour at a time. Workers who take such leaves must be allowed to return to the same or equivalent jobs, with the same pay and benefits. (Employers can exempt the highest-paid 10% of their work force, who thus are not guaranteed to get their jobs back.) When state laws or employment contracts are more generous than the federal act, employers must abide by the state law or the contract.

FAIR LABOR STANDARDS ACT

Congress enacted the Fair Labor Standards Act (FLSA) in 1938. The FLSA:

1. Establishes a minimum wage. The minimum wage may be reduced by equivalent rewards in the form of food or lodging. An employer of a tipped employee is required to pay only $2.13 an hour in direct wages if that amount plus the tips received equals at least the federal minimum wage, the employee retains all tips, and the employee customarily and regularly receives more than $30 a month in tips. If the tips and wages together are less than the minimum wage, the employer must make up the difference. State wage laws may also concern tip income and, more generally, minimum wages, with employees entitled to whichever provisions—federal or state—provide greater benefits.

2. Mandates payment of "time and a half" (150% of the normal wage rate) for overtime work, with a regular work week being 40 hours. Travel time to and from work generally is not compensable time unless it is part of preliminary or postliminary activities (e.g., employer transportation of workers to or from the work site). Compensable activities include preparatory actions, such as readying tools and equipment at the beginning of the work day, and post-work actions, such as winding down operations and cleaning up the work site.

3. Exempts from coverage professionals, executives, and administrative or outside sales personnel, as well as workers at very small and/or seasonal businesses, such as agriculture and fishing. Many states, though, have their own state version of the FLSA that applies to some employees not protected under the federal laws.

4. Generally forbids any employment of children under 14 years old.

5. Prohibits employment of persons under age 18 in hazardous occupations (e.g., logging or mining), and further restricts the employment of 14- and 15-year-olds to nonschool hours in nonhazardous, nonmanufacturing jobs, such as at retail stores, food service establishments, and gas stations.

The Secretary of Labor can sue for back wages, an equal amount as a civil penalty, and injunctions. Private parties also can seek back pay, the civil penalty, and attorney's fees. Willful FLSA violations can lead to fines and imprisonment.

INCOME PROTECTION

FOR WORKERS DISCHARGED WITHOUT CAUSE

Unemployment compensation is a state insurance system intended to supplement unemployed workers' incomes. An unemployed worker's total payable benefits are a percentage of his average earnings when he was employed. All private, for-profit employers that have at least one employee working one or more days a week for 20 or more weeks per year, or that have a payroll of at least $1,500 per quarter, are required to participate.

Under a joint federal-state program (both governments making contributions, along with employers), a tax on the participating employers is paid into unemployment insurance plans. The tax is based on the employer's number of employees, the wages they are paid, and the employer's record in laying off or retaining workers. Workers in the covered (taxed) businesses, if discharged "without cause" (through no fault of their own), can collect unemployment compensation. The amount of and time period for this compensation varies from state to state, but there are federally prescribed minimums and the federal government often furnishes supplemental unemployment compensation.

To qualify for unemployment compensation, discharged workers must have worked for at least a minimum time period or have earned at least a minimum amount of wages, with eligibility varying from state to state. At all times the unemployed worker must be seeking a job for which he is qualified. The discharged worker may be disqualified from receiving benefits if he rejects a job offer, or is not ready and available for work, or fails to follow proper procedures in filing claims for compensation.

Another protection is the federal WARN (Worker Adjustment and Retraining Notification) Act that took effect in 1989. This act requires large businesses (those with over 4,000 total work hours per week) to give workers at least 60 days' notice before a plant closing or mass layoff. A shorter notice period is allowed only if due to *unforeseeable* business circumstances. Employees and unions may obtain monetary damages if an employer violates WARN.

FOR DISABLED OR RETIRED WORKERS

The two most important federal statutes on retirement benefits are the Social Security Act of 1935 (SSA) and the Employment Retirement Income Security Act of 1974 (ERISA). Both have been frequently amended.

• *SOCIAL SECURITY*

SSA provides money when incomes from employment are reduced or cease because of death, disability, or retirement. The Federal Insurance Contributions Act (FICA) mandates that, for all of an employee's earnings up to a statutory maximum amount (approaching $100,000 per annum, as annual cost-of-living increases take effect), the employer must withhold a specified percentage of the employee's wages and also contribute a matching amount. This pool of money derived from employee contributions and matching employer contributions goes directly into the Social Security Trust Fund. This fund provides compensation when job incomes decline or cease because of death, disability, or retirement.

Employers must keep detailed records, file quarterly reports, and (usually) make monthly payments of the amounts withheld and matched. Violations can lead to severe civil and criminal penalties.

• *ERISA*

When private pension plans were originally introduced, they were usually gratuitous rewards that could be revoked or reduced at the employer's will. The unpredictability and arbitrariness of these early plans helped lead Congress to pass ERISA. The act was designed to regulate private retirement plans. It does not require that employers establish a pension, but ERISA does contain complex vesting requirements that determine when an employee's right to receive pension benefits is irrevocable.

ERISA sets standards for the funding of private pensions. It governs eligibility for and the taxation of pension plan earnings and benefit payments. In order to be an ERISA qualified pension plan, a plan must be administered by an individual who is charged with the responsibility to handle the pension funds. This administrator has a fiduciary duty to the plan's beneficiaries. He must carefully invest the funds and protect the beneficiaries. In addition, the administrator must disclose to the Labor Department the terms of the plan, annual financial reports, and annual summaries of each beneficiary's interest.

ERISA establishes a Pension Benefit Guaranty Corporation, and both the Department of Labor and the Internal Revenue Service promulgate ERISA regulations. Statutory or regulatory violations are a basis for criminal prosecutions and also for governmental or private civil actions (lawsuits by or for pension holders) alleging pension mismanagement or fraud.

PROTECTION AGAINST DISCRIMINATION

THE DOCTRINE OF ABUSIVE (WRONGFUL) DISCHARGE

At common law, a worker without an employment contract was called an "at-will" employee: the employee could quit at any time, for any reason, and the employer could fire him at any time for any reason. However, federal and state statutes have now limited the scope of the at-will doctrine. For example, under antidiscrimination laws, most at-will employees cannot lawfully be fired because of their race, sex, or religion. Also, most state courts have ruled that certain reasons for firing any person are so pernicious as to be disallowed (i.e., the fired worker can sue for damages).

Examples: Unacceptable Reasons for Firing (thus constituting an Abusive Discharge)

1. A worker asks his superiors to obey securities or environmental laws.
2. An employee is about to become entitled to a bonus.
3. A worker exercises a statutory right (e.g., files a workers' compensation claim).
4. An employee refuses to participate in antitrust violations.
5. A worker seeks to have his/her employer comply with consumer protection laws.
6. An employee reports criminal activity by his/her employer (the whistleblower exception to at-will employment).

Thus, while many employment relationships remain at-will, with the employee always free to quit and the employer usually free to fire, there are now some exceptions to the employer's freedom: broad statutory schemes and case-law requirements that employers obey the law and common notions of public policy. (Apart from this tort doctrine, at-will employment has also been restricted by finding implied contracts of good faith and fair dealing—e.g., implied or even express contracts based on statements in a company's Employee Handbook.)

FEDERAL STATUTES

Although cases on abusive (wrongful) discharge have risen in importance, federal statutes still dominate the law concerning employment disputes. The most important statute on discriminatory employment practices is Title VII of the Civil Rights Act of 1964. Under the Equal Employment Opportunity Act (1972) and subsequent amendments, the Equal Employment Opportunity Commission (EEOC) enforces Title VII and other federal statutes such as the Equal Pay Act, the Age Discrimination in Employment Act, and the Americans with Disabilities Act. The EEOC may investigate, conciliate, and litigate grievances filed by existing and prospective employees. It is also authorized to issue rules implementing the antidiscrimination laws.

Complaints may be filed by individuals, state human rights (fair employment) commissions, or the EEOC itself. Of course, as with other administrative proceedings, appeals may be taken to the courts. (Also, under federal statutes predating Title VII, if a claim includes constitutional rights allegedly deprived "under color of a state law or custom," i.e., with the state's explicit or implicit approval or condonement, a plaintiff can bypass the EEOC and proceed directly to federal court.) Before the EEOC sues an employer, Title VII requires an informal, confidential "conference, conciliation, and persuasion" process. In *Mach Mining, LLC v. EEOC*, 575 U.S. ___ (2015), the Supreme Court unanimously concluded this means the EEOC must: (1) specify for the employer the allegedly discriminatory acts and the employees that were harmed; and (2) try to discuss, and let the employer correct, any wrongful practices. Under *Mach Mining*, if a sued employer presents concrete evidence contradicting the EEOC's affidavit that it did (1) and (2), above, then the judge may order the EEOC to undertake the concilation efforts; throwing out the EEOC's complaint against the employer would not be an appropriate remedy.

Title VII applies to any employment agency (including unions that operate hiring halls) and any business or labor organization that affects interstate commerce and has at least 15 workers/members. Court remedies for winning plaintiffs include back pay, attorney's fees, reinstatement orders, retroactive seniority and pension benefits, injunctions, and consent decrees.

Title VII outlaws discrimination in hiring, firing, promotion, compensation, or any other aspect of employment, because of an individual's race, color, religion, sex, or national origin. Title VII also prohibits any employment discrimination against someone because he/she opposed a Title VII violation or participated in a Title VII investigation or proceeding (e.g., making a charge, testifying or otherwise assisting at a proceeding).* Thus, discriminatory employment practices are illegal if

---

*Many federal statutes, such as Title VII, the Age Discrimination in Employment Act, and the Americans with Disabilities Acts (both discussed later), provide for lawsuit claims if an employer retaliates against someone exercising statutory rights or pursuing statutory remedies. And what is unlawful retaliation is broadly construed. In *Burlington Northern & Santa Fe Railway Co. v. White*, 548 U.S. 53 (2006), the Supreme Court found that illegal retaliation can take place on or off the job and that it applies to situations in which the employer's actions are "harmful to the point that they could well dissuade a reasonable worker from making or supporting a charge of discrimination."

based on a person's membership in a protected class (by race, sex, color, national origin, or religion); the discrimination involves treating other employees or job applicants better than members of the protected class. Employment practices also are unlawful if they help perpetuate previous discrimination.

Certain exemptions or defenses are permitted. Courts recognize a lawful reason to discriminate (a *bona fide occupational qualification/BFOQ*) when religion, sex, or national origin is, in effect, a job requirement.

To establish a BFOQ defense, the employer must do the following:

1. Show that the BFOQ is necessary to the business;
2. Demonstrate that its necessity is established by a verifiable, rational basis;
3. Prove that the rational basis is rooted in a substantial belief that all, or nearly all, employees who are not members of the suspect class do not have the qualifications for the position, and;
4. Demonstrate that this belief can either be proven, through appropriate tests if necessary, or that it would be impossible or impracticable to "deal with all of the excluded class," as validated by expert testimony or generally accepted research and data.

BFOQ defenses are generally construed very narrowly and unfavorably.

Examples: A Baptist church may interview only Baptist ministers for the job of parish pastor; a seminary may consider the religion of its teaching applicants; a theater company may interview only women to play the role of a woman. A BFOQ cannot lawfully be based on assumptions about the comparative employment characteristics of a group (e.g., that women have a higher turnover rate). A BFOQ also cannot be based on stereotyped characterizations of groups (e.g., that men are less capable of assembling intricate equipment than are women). Finally, it cannot be based on the supposed preferences of customers, employers, or coworkers for one group (e.g., women) over another. Gender *may be* a BFOQ if physical attributes are needed for a position (e.g., a wet nurse) or to protect others' right to privacy (e.g., sauna room attendants). Although employers are required to try to accommodate an employee's religious beliefs, that accommodation need only be reasonable; the employer can fire an employee rather than significantly disrupt workplace productivity. (Title VII says that no accommodation is required if it would impose "undue hardship on the conduct of the employer's business.") Furthermore, in *Hosanna-Tabor Evangelical Lutheran Church and School v. EEOC*, 565 U.S. ___ (2012), the Supreme Court unanimously endorsed a "ministerial exception" to discrimination protections: the First Amendment requires civil courts "to defer to a religious organization's good-faith understanding of who qualifies as its minister" regardless of the employee's actual work duties. For such ministers (with religious duties), the employer can terminate them without being subjected to the ADA (or presumably, other anti-discrimination laws).

An employer can lawfully apply different compensation standards or terms or condition of employment pursuant to a bona fide *seniority* or *merit system*. However, there must be no intentional discrimination in establishing or continuing that system. Also, perpetuation of past discrimination is not protected simply because it is the result of an arrangement with a labor union.

Since required procedures before the EEOC or comparable state agencies often are very complicated, it is important that all covered employers, unions, and employment agencies—even those not currently involved in a dispute—maintain accurate records, file any mandated reports, and keep abreast of all employment law requirements. Although the Supreme Court, in *Circuit City Stores, Inc. v. Adams*, 532 U.S. 105 (2001), ruled that mandatory arbitration of employment claims, including claims for discrimination violative of federal statutes, is permissible, the employer may still face tough legal challenges for trying to circumvent the administrative and court processes. The leading challenges are typically that the arbitration clause was invalid under contract law principles, such as adhesion or, more generally, unconscionability. (Indeed, on remand, 279 F.3d 889 (9th Circuit 2002), the lower federal appeals court in the *Circuit City* case applied California contract to throw out the arbitration clause and permit the employee to litigate his claim in court.)

Laws prohibiting discrimination in employment do not prohibit all employment decisions that an applicant or employee may deem unfair. For example, Title VII does not prohibit an employer from "discriminating" against (treating differently) an individual on the basis of merit, initiative, or performance.

To demonstrate unlawful discrimination, an individual must establish a connection between the employment condition or decision, and the prohibited basis, e.g., race, sex, or religion. These connections may be established in the following manner:

- Individual instances of different or disparate treatment based on prohibited criteria, or
- Neutral policies or practices that have a much harsher or adverse impact upon a protected class to which an employee or applicant belongs, such as females or African-Americans.

Either direct evidence or indirect circumstantial evidence can prove such discrimination. Therefore, Title VII not only bans expressly discriminatory practices and actions (cases where discriminatory motives are clear), but also prohibits discrimination under the judicially created doctrines of **disparate treatment** or **adverse (disparate) impact**.

• *DISPARATE TREATMENT*

To win under disparate treatment, the plaintiff must demonstrate what appears to be discrimination on purpose (e.g., she interviewed for a job, she was qualified for that job, she was not hired, and the employer continued to search for a new employee). To make such a prima facie case of intentional discrimination, the employee must prove that (1) he/she is a member of a class of persons that title VII protects and (2) he/she was denied a position or benefit that he/she sought and was qualified for and that was available (e.g. the plaintiff interviewed for and so on). The burden then shifts to the defendant employer to present evidence (but need not prove) that there were genuine, legitimate, nondiscriminatory reasons for its challenged employment decision (e.g. that the employee was fired for excessive tardiness and poor work performance). Finally, if the defendant puts forth such reasons, the plaintiff has the burden to prove that he/she was unlawfully discriminated against and that the grounds the employer offered for its actions were only a pretext or pretense (that the defendant, in fact, practiced discrimination). Such pretext would be shown, for example, if the defendant's alleged hiring criteria were only applied to women, not similarly situated men. As the U.S. Supreme Court noted in *Reeves v. Sanderson Plumbing Prods., Inc.*, 530 U.S. 133 (2000), proof that the employer's explanation for its practices was false may by itself suffice as proof of intentional discrimination.

• *ADVERSE (DISPARATE) IMPACT*

Under this theory, intentional discrimination need not be proven. Plaintiffs must show that the allegedly discriminatory employment practice (tests, educational degree requirements, height and weight limits, etc.), while neutral on its face, has an unequal (disproportionate), negative (adverse) impact on one or more classes of individuals covered by Title VII. The defendant employer must then establish that the practice is a "business necessity," and therefore legitimate (e.g., a test is job-related because it predicts how well a potential employee would perform tasks essential to the job that he seeks). Then, the plaintiff may still succeed if he/she demonstrates that other criteria or methods would achieve the employer's purposes with less impact on (less harm to) the protected group(s). Although the adverse impact doctrine originally arose from cases involving objective criteria (e.g., test and degree requirements), it may also apply to subjective bases for decisions (e.g., interviews and supervisor evaluations).

Reverse Discrimination Versus Adverse Impact

Employers sometimes face the dilemma of trying not to engage in practices which either have an impermissible adverse impact on minority or female employees or job applicants, or constitute "reverse discrimination" against others.

In *Ricci v. DeStefano*, 557 U.S. 557 (2009), the results of a written firefighters' examination meant that 17 whites and two Latinos, but no African-Americans, were slated for promotion to lieutenant or captain at the New Haven, Connecticut fire department. However, New Haven decided to scrap the test results and not promote anyone. In a 5–4 decision, the U.S. Supreme Court held that an employer could not choose to refrain from promoting white employees for fear of an adverse impact lawsuit by minority employees unless there was a "strong basis in evidence" to establish either that the promotion standards were not job-related or that there was a less discriminatory alternative. In effect, when employees meet the established criteria and are thereby due a promotion, they can win a claim for Title VII discrimination if the employer, without a strong basis to believe it would lose an adverse impact case, fails to promote the employees on account of the resulting numbers (e.g., of promoted white and minority employees).

• *PATTERN OR PRACTICE*

If there is a much greater percentage of protected group members in the local labor market as compared to that group's representation in the defendant employer's work force, that fact may indicate a Title VII violation through a **pervasive pattern or practice of discrimination**. However, a defendant employer is permitted to rebut any inference of discrimination by introducing its own evidence that the challenged practice or policy is job related and justified by business necessity. Inconvenience, annoyance, or expense to the employer does not suffice as a defense. As with disparate treatment cases, the ultimate burden of proof rests with the plaintiff.

The two theories, adverse impact and pattern or practice, are also available as methods for proving housing discrimination. In *Texas Dept. of Housing and Community Affairs v. Inclusive Communities Project, Inc.*, 576 U.S. __ (2015), the Supreme Court held that Federal Fair Housing Act violations can be proven via adverse-impact analysis.

SEXUAL HARASSMENT

There are two types of sexual harassment, both of which violate Title VII: (1) **quid pro quo**—requiring an employee to engage in sexual activity in order to keep his/her job, get an increase in salary, obtain a promotion, or the like (e.g., sex with the boss in return for retaining one's job); (2) **hostile work environment**—unwelcome sexual behavior (e.g., sexual advances) and/or an atmosphere so severe or pervasive as to alter the victim's employment conditions and create an abusive (intimidating, hostile, offensive) work environment, such as a barrage of unwelcome sex-related jokes, comments and/or touchings from co-workers. Even if the employee-victim does not lose a tangible job benefit, a hostile work environment can exist. The EEOC has issued guidelines on sexual harassment, which include not only unwelcome sexual advances, but also requests for sexual favors and other unwelcome verbal or physical conduct of a sexual nature.

Employers tend to be strictly liable for quid pro quo harassment by supervisors and also liable for work environment harassment if higher-level managers knew or should have known about the harassment and did not take appropriate corrective action. (Also, employees unfairly treated in comparison to an employee who received a promotion or other benefits because of a sexual relationship (e.g., with a supervisor) have a claim for sexual harassment.)

If no adverse action was taken against an alleged sexual harassment victim (e.g., discharge, demotion, or undesirable reassignment), the employer has an affirmative defense against liability for a supervisor's hostile work environment harassment when the following two conditions are met. (1) The employer used reasonable care to prevent and promptly correct any sexually harassing behavior. (2) The employee unreasonably failed to take advantage of any preventive or corrective opportunities that the employer had provided. Employers, therefore, should inform all employees about the employer's antiharassment policy, which should have an effective complaint procedure specifying persons other than the employee's direct supervisor to whom complaints can be made.

Employers need not immediately discipline the accused harasser. But employers must thoroughly investigate complaints. Employers can be liable for inaction either way: insufficiently investigating, and thus retaining, what proves to have been a harassing worker; or inadequately investigating, and thus firing, a worker who turns out not to have been harassing others. In either case, the employer may be held liable for damages—to the Title VII harassment victim, or to the innocent fired employee for his/her wrongful dismissal (grounds might be abusive discharge, breach of contract, reverse discrimination, or perhaps even defamation).

Both men and women can sue for sexual harassment. Also, Title VII applies to same-sex harassment regardless of whether the conduct is motivated by sexual desire. (See *Oncale v. Sundowner Offshore Serv., Inc.*, 523 U.S. 75 (1998).) Still, Title VII is not meant to be "a general civility code for the American workplace." The court held:

"Title VII does not prohibit all verbal or physical harassment in the workplace; it is directed only at discrimination because of sex. The critical issue . . . is whether members of one sex are exposed to disadvantageous terms or conditions of employment to which members of the other sex are not exposed."

So *Oncale* extends the law to cover not just cases of alleged harassment involving homosexuals, but also, perhaps, sexually tinged jokes and horseplay among heterosexuals of the same sex. Nonetheless, it is often difficult for employees to prove the same-sex harassment covered under *Oncale*. Suing for battery, filing a union grievance, or other actions may be more suitable.

In *Harris v. Forklift Systems, Inc.*, 510 U.S. 17 (1993), the U.S. Supreme Court unanimously decided that sexual harassment plaintiffs need not show a workplace environment so hostile as to cause "severe psychological injury" (e.g., a nervous breakdown). The proper standard is that, for any variety of reasons, "the environment would reasonably be perceived, and is perceived, as hostile or abusive" (a "reasonableness" standard). No single factor is required to show sexual harassment; besides psychological harm, possible circumstances include "the frequency of the discriminating conduct; its severity; whether it is physically threatening or humiliating, or a mere offensive utterance; and whether it unreasonably interferes with an employee's work performance." As two concurring opinions noted, the test is not whether job performance was impaired but whether the harassment altered the working conditions in a discriminatory way. (Several Supreme Court decisions since *Harris* have affirmed and refined the law of sexual harassment, and the number of claims has risen rapidly.)

The employer can be held liable for an employee's harassment by customers or other people who are not supervisors or coworkers. For example, the U.S. Circuit Court of Appeals for the Tenth Circuit held in *Lockard v. Pizza Hut, Inc.*, 162 F.3d 1062 (1998), that a Pizza Hut franchisee was *vicariously liable* under Title VII for the hostile work environment that one of its waitresses had experienced. Male customers, about whom the waitress had previously complained, were again directing crude, sexual remarks at her and even grabbing her. But the restaurant manager ignored the waitress's complaint and insisted she keep waiting on them. The harassment escalated, the waitress quit, and she sued. The employer ended up liable for its manager's failure to protect the employee.

QUOTAS AND AFFIRMATIVE ACTION

Quotas are policies mandating that certain numbers or percentages of minorities or women be hired or promoted, even if that means better qualified persons are turned away. By only hiring or promoting from within certain groups regardless of the qualifications of others, employers subject themselves to "reverse discrimination" liability: Passed over persons (e.g., white males) successfully argue that a quota is illegal race or sex discrimination that violates Title VII.

Affirmative action programs are concerted efforts—plans—designed by the employer to hire and promote larger numbers of women and minorities that have been under-represented in its work force. The law has been that government contractors or others receiving federal funds or licenses must have affirmative action programs. However, Supreme Court holdings and numerous lower court opinions have subjected state (*City of Richmond v. J.A. Croson Co.*, 488 U.S. 469 (1989)) and federal (*Adarand Constructors, Inc. v. Pena*, 515 U.S. 200 (1995)) affirmative action programs to strict scrutiny tests, thereby dramatically increasing the probability of success for reverse discrimination claims. A growing body of case law has started to overturn much of the last 30 years of affirmative action law.

Affirmative action is more likely to survive in the purely private sector, where employers opting to have such programs are not generally subject to constitutional challenge (no "state action"), but only statutory interpretation. So a private, voluntary plan intended to correct a manifest imbalance between one class (e.g., African-Americans, women) and other classes (e.g., whites, men) may still be permitted if it is only temporary and does not "unnecessarily trammel" the rights of individuals in the (nonpreferred) class (e.g., whites, males) or create an absolute bar to their advancement. *Case law*, though, indicates profound skepticism about the public policy arguments underlying many affirmative action programs, whether public or private.

Affirmative Action and Higher Education: In *Gratz v. Bollinger*, 539 U.S. 244 (2003), the U.S. Supreme Court ruled that automatically granting points to every "underrepresented minority" university applicant solely because of the applicant's race is not "narrowly tailored" to achieve the goal of educational diversity and fails to provide the necessary individualized consideration of applicants. Thus, University of Michigan's undergraduate admissions point-system (with 150 maximum points, 100 points guaranteeing admission, and 20 points given for being African-American, Native American, or Latino) violated the 14th Amendment's Equal Protection clause. Moreover, in *Parents Involved in Community Schools v. Seattle School District No. 1*,

551 U.S. 701 (2007), the Supreme Court ruled that using a student's race to govern the availability of a place at a desired public school, even to prevent resegregation, is likewise unconstitutional.

However, in *Grutter v. Bollinger*, 539 U.S. 306 (2003), the U.S. Supreme Court held that campus diversity is a compelling purpose for which the use of race as only a "plus factor" in evaluating applicants is permitted. Therefore, the high court upheld University of Michigan's law school affirmative action admissions program because it was a narrowly tailored approach, with a race-based "plus" just part of an individualized review of each applicant no matter his/her race (including consideration of every applicant's potential contribution to a diverse educational environment). *Grutter's* emphasis on campus diversity distinguishes it from other cases (e.g., on employment or contracting) barring any racial preferences meant to correct societal injustice, foster diversity, or further some other goal besides countering actual discrimination in that specific industry or by that particular employer or contractor. In *Fisher v. University of Texas at Austin*, 570 U.S. __ (2013), the Supreme Court held that courts must closely scrutinize university affirmative action plans to ensure that they are narrowly tailored and there are no workable race-neutral alternatives to achieve racial diversity.

Besides Title VII, several other statutes prohibit discrimination in specific areas of employment:

1. *The Equal Pay Act* (1963), an amendment to FLSA, outlaws differences in pay between the sexes for employees performing essentially the same ("equal") work. The "equal" jobs must involve substantially the same skill, effort, responsibility, and working conditions. Pay differentials are permitted if based on seniority, merit, quality or quantity of production, training bonuses, shift differentials (e.g., paying more to the night shift), or any factor other than sex. Violations can lead to fines of up to $10,000, imprisonment for as long as six months, or both. In private lawsuits, plaintiffs can seek double damages for up to three years of wages, reinstatement, promotion, and liquidated damages.

   What if the jobs are different but, arguably, worth essentially the same? The wage differential between two employees working for the same employer, one performing a predominantly male job (e.g., construction work) and the other performing a predominantly female job (e.g., doing secretarial work), does not violate the Equal Pay Act (or Title VII) since the jobs are not substantially "equal" (same abilities, effort, responsibility, and working conditions). The jobs involve, at the very least, distinct skills and working conditions. Thus a proposed "comparable worth" standard has been rejected in federal law, but continues to be considered by state or local governments. Comparable worth now is most notably a discretionary, policy matter for large corporate or government employers worried about their own pay-scale fairness.

2. *The Age Discrimination in Employment Act of 1967* (ADEA) prohibits job discrimination against people age 40 and older. The business entities covered by the ADEA are somewhat fewer than for Title VII: here the employers must have at least 20 employees, and the labor organizations without hiring halls must have at least 25 members. Sometimes, age can be a bona fide occupational qualification, just as there are such exemptions under Title VII. (For example, safety officers, such as police, firefighters, and airline pilots, are not protected under the ADEA.) Furthermore, in some instances an employer may provide a lower level of fringe benefits (e.g., life insurance) for its older workers if such treatment is justified by the costs involved (i.e., older workers' benefits cost much more to provide). ADEA, though, outlaws almost all mandatory retirement. It can be proven via the same adverse impact theory as for Title VII, and provides for EEOC enforcement, awards *double unpaid wages* for willful violations, and grants a broad set of private lawsuit remedies comparable to those for Title VII violations. In *Meacham v. Knolls Atomic Power Lab,* 554 U.S. 84 (2008), the Supreme Court ruled that the employer, not the employee, must bear the burden of proof (both in producing evidence and in persuading the judge or jury) concerning its supposedly using "reasonable factors other than age" in the decision to terminate employment.[1] Lastly, employers seeking the waiver of potential ADEA claims by a terminated worker age 40 or older must meet an elaborate set of criteria.

3. *The Americans with Disabilities Act* (ADA) was passed in 1990, and applies to virtually the same number of employers as does Title VII, with the minimal number of employees for a covered employer being 15. The ADA forbids employment discrimination[2] against *qualified* individuals (1) with mental or physical impairments (e.g., blindness, cancer, AIDS, HIV positivity, peanut allergies, learning disabilities, or any number of other illnesses or conditions) substantially limiting a major life activity; or (2) with a record of such an impairment; or (3) being regarded as having such an impairment. As amended in 2008, the ADA includes a nonexhaustive, illustrative list of *major life activities*, which include, but are not limited to, caring for oneself, performing manual tasks, seeing, hearing, eating,

---

[1] Unlike Title VII discrimination cases, though, the employer need not show business necessity, and burdens of proof remain comparatively high for the plaintiff. The Supreme Court's decision in *Smith v. City of Jackson,* 544 U.S. 228 (2005), holds that ADEA plaintiffs alleging an adverse impact on workers age 40 or older must identify the specific test, requirement, or practice responsible for the disparity.

[2] And also discrimination by the operators of public facilities (e.g., buses, trains, hotels, restaurants, stores, and theaters).

sleeping, walking, standing, lifting, bending, speaking, breathing, learning, reading, concentrating, thinking, communicating, and working. These major life activities also include the operation of significant bodily functions, including, but not limited to, functions of the immune system, normal cell growth, digestive, bowel, bladder, neurological, brain, respiratory, circulatory, endocrine, and reproductive functions. Even an impairment that is episodic or in remission is a disability if it would, when active, substantially limit a major life activity. The EEOC, U.S. Attorney General, and U.S. Secretary of Transportation all have authority to issue regulations implementing the definition of "disability" and, in doing so, further delineating what a disability is.[3]

A court's decision about whether an impairment substantially limits a major life activity must, under the amended ADA, not consider "the ameliorative effects of mitigating measures" such as medication, artificial aids (e.g., prostheses or hearing aids), assisting technology, reasonable accommodations, and learned behavioral or adaptive neurological modifications. The amended ADA accepts a limited part of the Supreme Court's reasoning in *Sutton v. United Air Lines, Inc.*, 527 U.S. 471 (1999)—that the ameliorative effects of ordinary eyeglasses or contact lenses must be considered in determining whether an impairment substantially limits a major life activity. However, the amended ADA removes an approach, sanctioned in court holdings, that put an employee in an untenable position: his/her corrected vision leaving the employee no longer "disabled" for purposes of the ADA, yet the employer still using the employee's uncorrected vision as the standard when deciding whether he/she was qualified for the job for which he/she had applied. With the 2008 amendments, that approach may still exist in some jobs (including the commercial airline pilot position at stake in *Sutton*), but the ADA now places the burden on the employer to justify its "uncorrected vision" policy as being job related and consistent with business necessity. For example, an employer would have to demonstrate that it is reasonable and necessary for it to judge a job applicant who takes medication to prevent epileptic seizures as if that applicant were leaving his/her epilepsy untreated. In most situations, presumably, the employer could not justify that approach.

As for the "regarded as" basis for an ADA-defined disability, the amended ADA is meant to combat, as the EEOC has put it, the "myths, fears, and stereotypes" about a disability. The 2008 amended

---

[3] Many situations or conditions are not covered disabilities, such as illegal drug use, workplace alcohol use, various sexual behaviors (including homosexuality and bisexuality), compulsive gambling, kleptomania, and pyromania. Also, most testing for psychoactive substance abuse disorders or alcohol abuse has been upheld in court as lawful under the ADA.

law thus adopts a definition nearly identical to an earlier law, the Vocational Rehabilitation Act of 1973, in which Congress recognized that misconceptions may be as handicapping as any physical or mental limitations that flow from the actual impairment. The amended ADA, therefore, looks at one or more actual or perceived impairments and considers the plaintiff to have a disability when

(1) a plaintiff *actually has* a physical or mental impairment that motivated the defendant's adverse action against the plaintiff (e.g., terminating the plaintiff), regardless of how limiting the impairment in fact is [the impairment may not have risen to the level of an ADA disability, but the defendant's reaction to that impairment makes it so]; or

(2) the defendant is motivated to act adversely against the plaintiff because the defendant, rightly or wrongly, *perceives* the plaintiff as having an impairment, regardless of how limiting the defendant believes the impairment to be [the defendant's acts based on its belief that there is an impairment brings the plaintiff under the ADA's protection, regardless of whether or not the impairment is solely in the defendant's imagination].

However, an actual or perceived impairment is not covered under the "regarded as" benchmark if the impairment is transitory and minor. "Transitory" is defined as "an actual or expected duration of six months or less." The ADA, though, fails to explain what qualifies as a "minor" impairment.

Employers may not discriminate against a qualified, disabled person if he/she could perform the job with "reasonable accommodation" by the employer (e.g., modified work schedules; wheelchair-accessible facilities; acquiring better equipment; changing examinations, manuals, or policies; providing readers/interpreters; job restructuring; or worker retraining). Employers, though, are *not* required to accommodate—and thus hire—disabled individuals when that would result in an **undue hardship** for the employer (e.g., significant difficulty or expense).[4] Furthermore, as with Title VII, if an employer can show that its hiring practice is justified as a "business necessity," then its refusal to hire disabled individuals will not constitute a violation of ADA. That is so even if, for example, certain job-related tests or standards reduce or eliminate opportunities for some groups of persons ordinarily protected under ADA. A permissible exclusion from ADA protection is that the employee cannot perform essen-

---

[4]The amended ADA provides that employers and others bound by the act need not provide a reasonable accommodation or a reasonable modification to policies, practices, or procedures if an individual simply meets the "regarded as" definition of a disability.

tial functions of the job or the employment poses a significant risk to the health or safety of others.

4. *The Pregnancy Discrimination Act* (1978) amended Title VII to command that employers treat pregnancy and childbirth just as they treat any other medical condition similarly affecting an employee's ability to work. If a pregnant woman can still perform her job's duties, her employer cannot lawfully fire her or force her to take a leave of absence. Pregnancy leaves may not be treated differently from other leaves for temporary disability. Employers have also been prohibited from firing or refusing to hire women of childbearing age because of fear of exposure to workplace hazards or toxins. *International Union v. Johnson Controls,* 499 U.S. 187 (U.S. Supreme Court, 1991). Employers must monitor the workplace for toxins and dangers and then take measures to protect their employees.

5. *Section 1981 of the Civil Rights Act of 1866* prohibits discrimination on the basis of race, color, and sometimes national origin in the creation and execution of employment contracts, as well as in all other private contract areas. As such, Section 1981 can cover areas of discrimination *beyond simply employment contracts.* Unlike Title VII, there are no small employer exemptions. Compared to Title VII, the Section 1981 time periods to sue generally are longer, the procedures simpler, a jury trial always available, and types of possible damages sometimes more expansive.

6. *Civil Rights Law amendments,* enacted in 1991, provide that Title VII or ADA plaintiffs claiming discrimination based on disability, religion, or sex (including sexual harassment) can receive punitive damages if the employer acted "with malice or with reckless indifference." Such damages in combination with non-pay compensatory damages (e.g., emotional distress or damage to reputation), are capped (between $50,000 and $300,000), depending on the employer's size; under 15 employees—no Title VII; 15–100 employees—$50,000; 101–200 employees—$100,000; 201–500 employees—$200,000; over 500 employees—$300,000). Back pay, front pay, reinstatement, and attorney's fees always have been available under Title VII and are *not* capped, but the amendments provide for other compensation (e.g., for medical treatment) if the discrimination was intentional. While still not as broad as Section 1981, the amendments reduce some of the discrepancies between the treatment of racial discrimination under Section 1981 and the treatment of other forms of discrimination under Title VII.

7. Almost all states have laws similar to Title VII and ADEA, and many have ADA-like statutes. Some states and cities impose higher standards on employers than do the federal laws, such as prohibiting employment discrimination based on marital status,

sexual orientation,[5] political affiliation, and—with a specificity not found in the ADA—having or testing positive for the AIDS virus or HIV. Also, state and local laws apply to governmental bodies and small businesses often exempted by federal employment laws.

KNOW THE CONCEPTS

DO YOU KNOW THE BASICS?

1. Workers' compensation programs are applicable to injuries in the scope of employment, are no-fault programs, generally eliminate the employee's right to sue his employer for negligence, and provide for compensation according to a general schedule of benefits. *True* or *False?*

2. Each state has its own workers' compensation program, with the pertinent law, administration, and funding at the state, not the federal, level of government. *True* or *False?*

3. Name four functions of the Occupational Safety and Health Administration.

4. No one under age 16 is permitted to work, except either for a business owned and operated by relatives or as an unpaid volunteer. *True* or *False?*

5. Name two statutes intended to protect or assist people who are, or likely will be, unemployed.

6. Name two statutes intended to furnish financial protection for people's retirement.

7. Does Title VII apply to all businesses?

8. Name the federal commission that oversees the enforcement of several antidiscrimination statutes.

9. An "adverse impact" case requires proof of intent to discriminate. *True* or *False?*

10. The "pattern or practice of discrimination" case often involves statistical comparisons of the relevant labor market population and the employer's work force. *True* or *False?*

---

[5] Many states and more than 150 municipalities (cities and counties) in the remaining states have laws barring public or private employment discrimination based on sexual orientation or gender identity. Also, some other states simply bar such discrimination for government employment. Finally, regardless of whether their state or local governments have such laws, many employers (particularly most large employers) have voluntarily adopted policies prohibiting discrimination based on sexual orientation.

11. Name an important Supreme Court decision concerning: (a) sexual harassment; (b) mandatory arbitration of employment discrimination claims.

12. What is the difference between *quid pro quo* and hostile work environment sexual harassment?

13. FICA contributions are used to pay for a fund maintained under the Americans with Disabilities Act. *True* or *False?*

14. The Equal Pay Act provides "comparable worth" rights. *True* or *False?*

TERMS FOR STUDY

abusive (wrongful) discharge
adverse impact
affirmative action
Age Discrimination in
  Employment Act
Americans with Disabilities Act
at-will employment doctrine
bona fide occupational
  qualification
comparable worth doctrine
discharged "without cause"
disparate treatment (impact)
Employee Polygraph
  Protection Act
Employment Retirement Income
  Security Act (ERISA)
Equal Employment Opportunity
  Commission (EEOC)
Equal Pay Act
Fair Labor Standards Act
Family and Medical Leave Act
Federal Insurance Contributions
  Act (FICA)

National Institute for Occupational
  Safety and Health
Occupational Safety and
  Health Act
Occupational Safety and Health
  Administration
Occupational Safety and Health
  Review Commission
pattern or practice
Pension Benefit Guaranty
  Corporation
Pregnancy Discrimination Act
quid pro quo harassment
quotas
Section 1981
sexual harassment
Social Security Act
Title VII
unemployment compensation
work environment harassment
Worker Adjustment and Retraining
  Notification Act (WARN)
workers' compensation

PRACTICAL APPLICATION

1. Werner is at work when he is injured by a tool operated by his colleague, Monica. Name three parties against whom Werner might have an action; and for each one state the type of claim.

2. You are very concerned about a series of unreported near-mishaps where you work. Safety procedures failed, and poorly trained

employees almost suffered serious harm. You have told your supervisor that the government needs to be informed. She refuses to do so, nor will she bring the matter to the attention of her boss.
(a) If you report the incidents, to whom should you speak?
(b) If you are fired after speaking with the government, what legal claim may you bring against your employer?

3. An assembly-line worker must leave home at 6:00 A.M. to arrive at work at 6:45 A.M. Once there, he must undertake various readings of instruments and also some maintenance tasks for several pieces of equipment used on the assembly-line. By the time he completes these tasks it is 7:00 A.M. and his work producing goods on the assembly-line commences. The worker has a half-hour break for lunch, works until 5:00, and then cleans up, secures the equipment, and otherwise winds down the daily operations. He ordinarily leaves by 5:15 P.M.

In a typical work week, if the worker makes $15 per hour, how much should his pay (before taxes) be?

4. Corky Creep fires Fanny Fritz, age 50, because he "just doesn't like that dame." What legal actions may Fanny bring (a) without any specific employment statute to rely upon; (b) with respect to federal statutes?

ANSWERS

KNOW THE CONCEPTS

1. True.
2. True.
3. To conduct inspections and investigations, to promulgate rules and set standards, to oversee and review employers' reports, and to work with the NIOSH concerning its research and also its training programs for employers and employees.
4. False. The Fair Labor Standards Act restricts employment for persons under age 18 and limits it further for those under age 16, but it does not prohibit 14- and 15-year-olds working (and getting paid for that work) at various nonhazardous, nonmanufacturing jobs. The employer need not be related to that young worker.
5. Unemployment compensation and WARN.
6. SSA and ERISA.
7. No. It applies just to businesses affecting interstate commerce and having at least 15 workers.

8. The Equal Employment Opportunity Commission.

9. False.

10. True.

11. (a) *Harris v. Forklift Systems, Inc.* (1993); (b) *Circuit City Stores, Inc. v. Adams* (2001).

12. *Quid pro quo* sexual harassment entails the requiring of an employee to engage in sexual activity, such as with a supervisor, in order for the employee to keep his/her job, get an increase in salary, obtain a promotion, or the like. Hostile work environment sexual harassment is unwelcome sexual behavior and/or an atmosphere so severe or pervasive as to alter the victim's employment conditions and create an abusive work environment.

13. False. FICA collects money for social security funds; the Americans with Disabilities Act has no overall fund whatsoever.

14. False. Neither the Equal Pay Act nor Title VII provide "comparable worth" rights.

PRACTICAL APPLICATION

1. Three parties are: (1) the tool manufacturer/wholesaler/retailer—a tort claim; (2) Monica—a tort claim, e.g., negligence; and (3) Werner's employer—a workers' compensation claim.

2. (a) OSHA; (b) Abusive (wrongful) discharge, assuming that: (1) the reason you were fired was to retaliate for your seeking compliance with OSHA and/or your being a whistleblower; and (2) the firing thus violates public policy. (More facts might also bolster other claims, such as breach of contract or a Title VII violation.)

3. Under the Fair Labor Standards Act, the worker's preliminary and postliminary work should constitute work time. Total compensable time is thus 10 hours per day (ten and a half hours minus the half-hour for lunch). Regular pay for a four-day workweek should be $600 (forty hours, at $15 per hour). Once the worker exceeds a forty-hour workweek and is otherwise entitled to overtime pay, those hours will be paid at a rate of time-and-a-half, which translates into $22.50 per hour of overtime.

4. (a) In many states, Fanny must still point to a specific breach of contract. Otherwise, as an at-will employee, she can be fired without cause. Some states, though, might consider this to be an abusive discharge, wrongly based on her age, sex, or appearance, or on other illegitimate reasons.

   (b) Fanny could sue for damages and, if she chooses, reinstatement. The statutes that she might invoke include Title VII and ADEA.

25
LABOR-MANAGEMENT RELATIONS LAW

KEY TERMS

labor relations law statutory, administrative, and case law, almost exclusively federal, dealing with labor/management relations

unfair labor practice any activity by an employer or a labor union that is prohibited by the National Labor Relations Act or an amendment to that Act

Before the 20th century, the employment relationship was governed largely by private contracts between employers and prospective employees. As businesses grew larger, standard and impersonal labor relationships began to develop. In order to ensure the balance of negotiating power between employer and employee, unions were created. The Clayton Act provided the first piece of federal labor law by exempting most union activities from antitrust liability. This was necessary because union collective action arguably acts like a cartel of employees who fix the prices of their wages.

Contemporary labor law seeks to balance two goals. First, it encourages industrial peace and stability through collective bargaining and reasonable dispute settlement. Second, it more nearly equalizes the balance of bargaining power between workers and management. Until 1932, American unions had few recognized rights. Invoking common law notions of conspiracy and restraint of trade, courts often enjoined organizing activities, strikes, or other union actions.

In 1926, Congress passed the **Railway Labor Act,** which requires good-faith bargaining between railroad management and their employees' elected representatives (it now also covers airline workers). A comprehensive federal labor statute, the **Norris-LaGuardia Act** (1932), withdrew from federal courts the power to issue injunctions in nonviolent labor disputes and declared a federal policy that employees are free to form unions. Norris-LaGuardia also outlawed *yellow-dog contracts,* which, as a condition of employment, prohibited employees from joining or supporting a union.

THE NATIONAL LABOR RELATIONS ACT: FRAMEWORK FOR ALMOST ALL LABOR LAW

Until the **National Labor Relations Act (NLRA)** (1935), employers were not required to collectively bargain with unions. Three of the most important provisions in the NLRA, also known as the **Wagner Act,** are: (1) employees have the right to form, join, or assist labor organizations, the freedom to bargain collectively with the employer, and the right to engage in concerted (group) activity; (2) employers must bargain collectively with the employees' certified bargaining representative (union); and (3) the National Labor Relations Board (NLRB) was created as the regulatory body responsible for administering the NLRA.

Section 8 of the NLRA prohibits certain specific acts by employers known as **unfair labor practices:**

1. **Interference with rights to unionize and to bargain collectively.** Undue interference with union solicitation of, and communication with, employees, as well as campaign statements deemed to be misrepresentations, coercive offers of rewards, and/or threats, are unlawful. Employers may legitimately ask employees about a union's progress in organizing the workforce, but intimidating interrogation is considered an unfair labor practice. An employer may not poll employees unless it simply seeks to verify that a majority of employees support the union. Employers cannot completely prohibit any union activities on company property; they must tolerate some inconvenience during union organizing. However, reasonable non-discriminatory restrictions may be imposed. For example, management can prevent the congregation of too many non-employees in work areas if such crowding interferes with productivity or safety.

   Employers commit an unfair labor practice if they withhold customary periodic wage increases from employees who are attempting to unionize. Also, employers confronting a union organizing campaign cannot offer increased benefits, to take place if and when the union loses the election. A promise of benefits is only allowed if it was planned before the election campaign began.

   Employers are not free to relocate, or threaten to relocate, a business simply to discourage or "bust" a union. Economic reasons for relocating are lawful, though, even if the effect is to destroy a union. (Employers are free to mention these economic reasons when discussing a proposed unionization.)

2. **Domination of, or contributing to, unions.** In the decades before the NLRA was enacted, employers created or supported

company unions which usually favored management. The NLRA made this practice illegal.

The test of unlawful employer domination is whether the union is truly independent in representing employees in disputes with the employer. Throughout the process of self-organization, the employer must maintain neutrality. An employer, for instance, cannot solicit employees to join a particular union or to oppose a competing union.

3. **Discrimination against employees because of their union activities or because they filed charges or testified under the NLRA.** Employers cannot lawfully hire, fire, or otherwise mistreat or favor workers because of their union affiliation. The employer typically defends its actions as having an economic purpose, but this defense must be supported by strong independent evidence proving no anti-union motive.

4. **Refusal to bargain in good faith with the employees' elected representatives.**

An NLRA amendment, the **Taft-Hartley Act** (1947) (also known as the **Labor-Management Relations Act)**, sets forth unfair labor practices by unions. These include:

1. **Refusing to bargain in good-faith with the employer.**

2. **Having employees paid for work not actually performed** (feather-bedding).

3. **Charging excessive or discriminatory fees or dues.** Nonunion members who are nonetheless represented by a union can be required to pay agency fees for the collective bargaining activities carried out by the union. But these agency fees (unlike union dues) are not supposed to be used in furtherance of the union's political agenda (e.g., for lobbying expenses). A 1986 Supreme Court decision (*Chicago Teachers Union v. Hudson*, 475 U.S. 292) requires that unions furnish adequate, prompt explanations of the basis for an agency fee, give nonmembers a reasonable opportunity to challenge the amount of the fee before an impartial decision maker, and have all reasonably disputed amounts placed in escrow while agency fee challenges are pending. In *Beck v. Communications Workers*, 487 U.S. 735 (1988), the Supreme Court found that 79% of the agency fees paid to the defendant union went for inappropriate purposes, mainly political activities; it ordered the union to cut its agency fees, refund the excess amounts collected, and keep clear records about union expenditures by category. In practice, though, the *Beck* decision has been difficult to enforce. Employees often are unaware of where their fees are going, and—if they dispute the fees' amount—must resort to litigation to force a return of the excess fees.

4. **Interfering with employees' choice of a labor union.**

5. **Discriminating against certain employees and/or seeking the employer's discrimination against certain employees or potential employees** (e.g., to encourage or discourage membership in a particular union).

6. **Most picketing, striking, and carrying out boycotts against businesses other than the employer involved in the primary labor dispute.** These secondary boycotts and the like are forbidden except for (a) businesses joined with the employer in a common business purpose ("the ally doctrine"), or (b) truthfully advising the public, via limited actions, that the secondary business has ties with the employer.

7. **Strikes or boycotts designed to make an employer assign work to a particular craft group to recognize a union without NLRB certification.**

Taft-Hartley established the concept of "employer free speech." In essence, for an employer's actions to constitute an unfair labor practice he/she must do more than simply state an opinion or present an argument. Speech, to be unprotected, must be accompanied by a threat of reprisal.

The **Landrum-Griffin Act** (1959) (also known as the **Labor-Management Reporting and Disclosure Act**) created for union members a "Bill of Rights" to prevent abuses by union officials. The act prohibits unions from restricting a member's right of free speech, assembly, or participation in union elections and union meetings.

Landrum-Griffin requires that union officers be bonded and accountable for union property and funds. It ensures that increases in union dues only occur after members are afforded an opportunity to vote by secret ballot. Procedures are established for both the employee and the union concerning member grievances.

The Landrum-Griffin Act provides for federal regulation of union internal operations, including NLRB supervision of union officer elections. The act attempts to guarantee fair union elections by creating minimum standards of voting and candidacy:

1. All union members in good standing must be permitted to vote.

2. Elections for local officers must be held at least every three years.

3. Secret balloting procedures must be followed in local elections, though delegates attending a national or international union convention may cast open votes.

4. A reasonable opportunity to nominate candidates must be given to all eligible voting members.

5. The qualifications for candidate eligibility must be reasonable. For example, in *United Steelworkers of America v. Usery*, 429 U.S. 305

(1977), the Supreme Court invalidated a union eligibility rule that required candidates for union office to attend at least half of all union meetings during the last three years. This rule was considered unreasonable because it barred from candidacy 97% of the union's members.

Landrum-Griffin also prohibits "hot cargo" contracts, in which the employer agrees not to use, handle, or purchase products from a specified business. Besides required bonding of union officers, Landrum-Griffin addresses union corruption by requiring certain disclosures by unions, employers, and union officials. Unions must report to their members the names of officers, the union's financial condition, and certain election procedures. Financial transactions between a union officer (or union employee) and the employer must be disclosed by the officer (or employee) and the employer.

THE ROLE OF THE NATIONAL LABOR RELATIONS BOARD

The **National Labor Relations Board (NLRB)** is organized into two major divisions: the board itself and the Division of General Counsel. Both are appointed by the President and approved by the Senate. The board consists of five members, which hear labor matters first heard by NLRB administrative law judges. The Division of General Counsel is headed by counsel independent of the NLRB. This office has "final authority, on behalf of the board, in respect to the investigation of the charges and issuance of complaints and with respect to the prosecution of complaints before the board."

The NLRB resolves disputes about what constitutes an appropriate employee bargaining unit, one in which the employees all have a community of interests—similar workplace conditions and concerns (e.g., supervisors and managerial employees, as well as government workers and independent contractors, are not covered by the NLRA). Besides union officer elections, the NLRB supervises (1) representative elections, whereby employees choose the union that will represent them, and (2) certification or decertification elections, in which employees decide, respectively, whether to have a union or whether to decertify (remove) their union. A union seeking to organize the workers must present signature cards from at least 35 of the worker group requesting an election on union representation. Often, the employer challenges the validity of the signature cards. If the union prevails at this preliminary point, the National Mediation Board sets an election. A majority of workers must support union representation for the union to be certified. Abstentions count as votes against the union.

A certified union has the exclusive right to bargain on behalf of the employees it represents. Thus, individual employees *within the represented group* are not permitted to enter into separate agreements with the employer.

NLRB charges may be settled either in an informal settlement proceeding or at an administrative law hearing. Appeals can be made from the administrative hearing to the entire, five-person board. In unfair labor practice cases, appeals beyond the NLRB may be taken to the federal court of appeals. In representation and election cases, however, the NLRB has primary jurisdiction, and an appeal to the courts is prohibited.

THE LABOR NEGOTIATION PROCESS

In general, the NLRA and subsequent amendments are intended to *promote good-faith bargaining* between employer and union. (E.g., the **Labor Management and Cooperation Act of 1978** expresses the need for more labor/management cooperation and encourages arbitration and mediation of labor disputes.) Although both sides must bargain, the NLRB cannot force an agreement. (The Federal Mediation and Conciliation Service, a U.S. agency, has a panel of recommended arbitrators for labor disputes.) Rather, the NLRB investigates and attempts to remedy unfair labor practices.

After an appropriate bargaining unit selects a particular union as its bargaining representative, both the employer and the union must bargain in good faith. *Good-faith bargaining* is an interactive process in which each side makes offers and counteroffers in an effort to reach an agreement. This negotiation process allows labor markets to reach an equilibrium while performing five basic functions for society: (1) establishes work rules, (2) selects the form and mix of employee compensation, (3) provides uniformity among competitors, (4) sets priorities for both labor and management, (5) permits economic pressures to shape labor-management relations.

There are three basic categories of bargaining subjects. First, mandatory collective bargaining subjects include wages, hours, and other terms and conditions of employment, or the negotiation of an agreement. The second category, *permissive subjects,* are only bargained if both parties voluntarily agree; for example, a permissive subject would be the employer's donations to charitable organizations. Neither party may refuse to bargain on mandatory subjects in an attempt to force bargaining on permissive subjects.

Managerial business decisions are only considered mandatory subjects if they directly affect the employment relationship. In *Fibreboard Paper Products Corp. v. NLRB,* 379 U.S. 203 (1964), management intended to contract out jobs previously performed by union members. This was labeled a mandatory bargaining issue because management gave the union no opportunity to help reduce the maintenance labor costs before unilaterally contracting them out. By contrast, in *First National Maintenance Corp. v. NLRB* (1981), management decided to discontinue operations altogether, but the courts did not give the union a right to bargain. The decision was economic and management did not intend to replace the employees with contracted labor.

The third category of bargaining subjects includes *illegal and prohibited subjects.* For example, the employer may not insist that the union bargain away its status as bargaining representative.

It is an unfair labor practice for either party to refuse to bargain *collectively.* The NLRA requires the union and employer to meet at reasonable times, put their agreement in writing, and bargain on mandatory subjects. Bad faith is difficult to prove but can be inferred from bargaining conduct, such as failing to offer meaningful counterproposals, refusing to discuss economic terms until noneconomic issues are resolved, and attempting to delay meetings or to move the meetings to a burdensome location. There is a thin line dividing permissible "hard bargaining" and impermissible "surface bargaining."

The NLRB cannot force an agreement between two parties. If either party refuses to bargain, however, the board can order it to bargain or may issue a cease and desist order to refrain from bad faith bargaining. Only in unusual situations has the NLRB awarded compensatory damages to the innocent party for the other side's bad faith bargaining.

An *impasse* is when neither party can make an offer on terms any more favorable to the opposing party. Until this time, the employer and union are required to bargain and attempt reconciliation.

Corporate structure is often changed because of mergers, takeovers, or bankruptcy. A firm in bankruptcy reorganization must secure the bankruptcy judge's approval before an existing labor contract may be nullified (*NLRB v. Bildisco*, 465 U.S. 513 [U.S. Supreme Court, 1984]). In response to *Bildisco*, Congress later in 1984 revised the bankruptcy laws with the Packwood-Rodino Act. This act made reorganization somewhat less attractive as a "union busting device" because the bankruptcy judge must find that the labor contract modifications are "necessary" to the bankrupt firm's survival. Furthermore, the act provides that labor contracts may not be rejected unless (1) all creditors are treated fairly and equitably, (2) the union refused the bankrupt's proposed contract modification "without good cause," and (3) the equities favor rejecting the existing union contract.

When a corporation is merged with another corporation or its assets are purchased by another corporation, the Supreme Court has held that the surviving corporation must generally bargain with a duly certified union if there is substantial continuity of operations from the predecessor to the successor. But the successor is not bound by the terms of a preexisting contract unless it expressly or impliedly assumes the predecessor's collective bargaining agreement.

LABOR DISPUTE RESOLUTION: CONCERTED ACTIVITIES

ORGANIZING

Taft-Hartley bans the **closed shop,** which forces all employees to belong to the union before being hired and to remain members throughout their employment. It also prohibits preferential hiring schemes, whereby employers agree to hire only union members so long as the union can supply them.

Taft-Hartley does not ban union shops. The **union shop,** instead of requiring union membership before a worker obtains employment (the closed shop concept), simply mandates that membership must come within a specified time after employment begins.

Taft-Hartley, though, permits states to outlaw union shops. In states with **right-to-work laws,** union membership cannot be required for continued employment. Right-to-work states are the 11 states of the Old Confederacy, plus sixteen more: Arizona, Idaho, Indiana, Iowa, Kansas, Kentucky, Michigan, Nebraska, Nevada, North Dakota, Oklahoma, South Dakota, Utah, West Virginia, Wisconsin, and Wyoming, as well as the territory of Guam.

PICKETING

Picketing, if conducted in a peaceful manner and for a lawful objective, is another concerted activity protected by the Constitution. Picketing generally involves a gathering and patrolling of persons who intend to inform or disrupt others. It is typically found near an employer's place of business. *Primary picketing* (employees) receives the greatest degree of Constitutional protection. *Stranger picketing* (nonemployees) is only protected if it is for a lawful purpose and conducted in a peaceful manner.

Picketing is considered unlawful if it (1) violates federal law, (2) represents an unfair labor practice, (3) violates state law (i.e., is not peaceful), (4) imposes implicit coercion on employees who are attempting to enter the work site, or (5) is by an uncertified rival union picketing an employer who currently recognizes another certified union in a valid union certification election held less than 12 months earlier.

STRIKES AND LOCKOUTS

United States labor law recognizes a right to strike. If the strike concerns an employer's unfair labor practices, upon the strike's settlement the employer must rehire the striking employees. If the strike is over economic issues (e.g., wages, hours), however, upon its conclusion the employer does not have to rehire the strikers or to discharge substitute employees hired during the strike.

Strikes generally are allowed except when they (1) are violent; (2) violate a collective bargaining agreement; (3) are not called by the designated union ("wildcat strikes"); (4) involve physical occupation of the employer's property ("sitdown strikes"); (5) concern government employees (e.g., police, firefighters, air traffic controllers) and are outlawed because of their harm to the public; or (6) violate a court-ordered "cooling off" period of further negotiation. (The President may find that a labor disruption in a particular industry would "imperil the nation's health or safety," and thereby require that workers stay on the job, while negotiations continue; this mandatory "cooling off" period can be no more than 80 days.)

Employers may use lockouts to combat strikes. Thus, when a single union bargains throughout an industry by striking against one or more plants and employers, but not all, the employers not struck may employ a *defensive lockout* mechanism to preclude members of the striking union from coming on to the firm's property. Sometimes, in anticipation of a strike, *offensive lockouts* are permitted.

KNOW THE CONCEPTS

DO YOU KNOW THE BASICS?

1. Under the common law, labor unions were exempt from criminal conspiracy and restraint of trade charges. *True* or *False?*
2. What did the Norris-LaGuardia Act of 1932 do?
3. Federal courts have broad powers to curb or enjoin any strikes found to be economically "counter-productive." *True* or *False?*
4. What is *least likely* to be protected under the NLRA?

   (a) an employee signs a union authorization card
   (b) an employee selected by a committee of ten employees presents the employer with a list of employee grievances
   (c) an employee protests when the employer chooses someone else for a promotion to a supervisory position
   (d) ten employees walk off the job to protest unsafe working conditions
   (e) a state "right-to-work" statute

5. For each action by an employer, state whether it is likely to be an unfair labor practice.

   (a) refusal to bargain collectively with the certified employee representative;

   (b) discharging or discriminating against an employee because he/she filed charges or gave testimony under the NLRA;

   (c) telling a gathering of factory employees that unionization could increase costs and thereby force factory operations to be moved out-of-state or abroad;

   (d) firing employees thought to be union sympathizers;

   (e) restricting access of nonemployee unionizers to work areas that would not interfere with safety or productivity;

   (f) establishing, at the request of workers, a union for those workers;

   (g) refusing to accept workers' demands arrived at unanimously by all union members;

   (h) promising an increase in health insurance benefits if a proposed union loses its certification election.

6. For each action by a union, state whether it is likely to be an unfair labor practice:

   (a) refusing to accept a "reasonable" offer by the employer

   (b) charging the same amount in agency fees as in union dues

   (c) holding local union officer elections every six years

   (d) requiring that the employer not use, handle or buy products from a specified business.

7. Name (a) at least three unfair labor practices by employers, and (b) at least four by unions.

8. While they cannot force workers either to join or leave a union, employers are free to form unions on behalf of their employees. *True* or *False?*

9. State the main goals or functions of the National Labor Relations Board.

10. What is the difference between closed shops and union shops?

TERMS FOR STUDY

agency fees
certification elections
closed shop
collective bargaining
company unions
"cooling off" period
decertification elections
employer free speech
Federal Mediation and Conciliation
    Service
good faith bargaining
"hot cargo" contracts
impasse
Labor Management and
    Cooperation Act
Landrum-Griffin Act (Labor-
    Management Reporting and
    Disclosure Act)
lockout

mandatory collective bargaining
    subjects
National Labor Relations Act
    (Wagner Act)
National Labor Relations Board
Norris-LaGuardia Act
primary picketing
Railway Labor Act
right-to-work laws
secondary boycotts
sitdown strikes
stranger picketing
strike
Taft-Hartley Act (Labor-
    Management Relations Act)
unfair labor practices
union shop
wildcat strikes

PRACTICAL APPLICATION

1. An executive at Heavy-Handed, Inc. tells employees that unionization may lead to higher costs and force the shutdown of factories, resulting in unemployment for many workers. Is that statement a violation of labor laws?

2. Big Business has two groups of unionized workers on strike. Union A's workers are protesting the discharge of their union president from her job with Big Business. Union A claims, and an NLRB administrative law judge ultimately agrees, that the discharge stemmed from the president's union activities. Union B's workers simply want better wages. Big Business has replaced the striking workers. When the strikes are settled, must it rehire the strikers from Union A and/or Union B?

3. A union represents workers at "Boogieboard Industries Group—Cahuna Headphones Extraordinaire & Elaborate Surfboards & Emblems" (BIG-CHEESE). Which of the following union activities is *permitted* under federal labor relations laws?

    (a) Requiring that BIG-CHEESE only hire union members.

(b) Boycotting and picketing BIG-CHEESE until it acts to stop "union busting" behavior by another, unrelated employer.

(c) Fighting a competing union's attempt to have the union representing BIG-CHEESE workers decertified.

(d) Holding *open-ballot* (non-secret) elections of union officers.

(e) Demanding that BIG-CHEESE ignore state "right-to-work" laws because federal law preempts them.

4. Employer Ernst files for bankruptcy and requests that the bankruptcy judge nullify its collective bargaining agreement with the Factory Workers of America (FWA). Ernst also asks FWA to give up its status as the employees' bargaining representative in return for some concessions by Ernst. Finally, Ernst is discussing being merged into, or having its assets purchased by, the New Corporation. New seeks assurance that it will not be bound by the Ernst-FWA agreement, nor will it even have to bargain with FWA. Briefly discuss these matters.

ANSWERS

KNOW THE CONCEPTS

1. False. That was not changed until the 1930s with the passage of the Norris-LaGuardia Act and the NLRA.

2. The Norris-LaGuardia Act withdrew from federal courts the power to issue injunctions in nonviolent labor disputes, declared a federal policy that employees are free to form unions, and outlawed yellow-dog contracts that prohibited employees from joining or supporting a union as a condition of employment.

3. False. The Norris-LaGuardia Act withdrew from federal courts the power to issue an injunction in nonviolent labor disputes.

4. Only answer (c) seems to involve no aspect of labor law and no concerted (collective) actions by employees.

5. (a), (b), (d), (f), and (h) each violate the NLRA; (c), (e), and (g) are permitted.

6. (a) is permitted; (b) violates the Taft-Hartley Act; (c) and (d) violate the Landrum-Griffin Act.

7. (a) Employers—(1) preventing unionization and collective bargaining; (2) control of, or contribution to, unions; (3) discrimination against employees because of their union activities or because they pursued an action under the NLRA; (4) unwillingness to

negotiate in good faith with the elected representatives of the union.

(b) Unions—(1) refusing to bargain collectively with an employer; (2) mandating that an employer pay for work not done (feather-bedding); (3) charging extreme or discriminatory fees or dues; (4) impeding employees' choice of a union; (5) discriminating against particular employees (or requesting that the employer discriminate); (6) conducting secondary boycotts or picketing against businesses besides the primary one in the labor dispute (except against a business that has allied itself with the primary one for a common purpose, or to inform the public through narrow methods that the secondary business has connections with the main employer); (7) striking or boycotting to force an employer to recognize a union without NLRB precertification.

8. False.

9. To oversee enforcement and refinement of the NLRA; to investigate and decide complaints; to determine what is an appropriate employee bargaining unit; to supervise union officer elections, representative elections, and certification or decertification elections; to advance good-faith bargaining between employers and unions.

10. Closed shops are illegal. They require that all employees, before being hired, become and remain union members throughout the course of their employment. Union shops are only illegal in states with "right-to-work" laws. They do not force an employee to join a union before being hired, but do require that the employee become a member within a certain time after employment begins.

PRACTICAL APPLICATION

1. Probably not. Under Taft-Hartley, employers have a right to free speech. Unless the statement was accompanied by something else (and the tone could be important, too), the executive's statement usually would be seen as simply an opinion regarding the potential problems of unionization, not threat of retaliation.

2. Yes as to union A, whose strike was about an unfair labor practice. No as to union B, whose strike was over economic issues.

3. (a) That is a closed shop, which violates the Taft-Hartley Act.
   (b) That is an illegal secondary boycott (and picketing) under Taft-Hartley.
   (c) Permissible activity.
   (d) That violates the Landrum-Griffin requirement that officer elections be by secret ballot.

(e) There is no such preemption. Taft-Hartley expressly grants to the states the power to enact "right-to-work" laws, and thus unions and employers cannot ignore such laws.

4. The bankruptcy judge could nullify or modify the collective bargaining agreement if the judge finds that to be necessary for Ernst's survival. The judge must evaluate the fairness of nullification or modification (e.g., how is FWA being treated compared to Ernst's creditors?).

Ernst's request that FWA give up its position as the workers' bargaining representative is an illegal subject for bargaining. To make such a proposal violates the NLRA.

New will have to bargain with the FWA if it substantially continues Ernst's operations. New will not be bound by the Ernst-FWA agreement unless New expressly or implicitly agrees to do so.

26
LEGAL TOPICS CONCERNING INFORMATION TECHNOLOGY: INTELLECTUAL PROPERTY, COMPUTER LAW, AND PRIVACY

KEY TERMS

intellectual property intangible property arising from the creative endeavors of the human mind, such as literary works and computer software; the major forms of intellectual property are patents, copyrights, and trademarks

computer virus a program that can replicate itself and is specifically designed to cause harm to a system; viruses carry potential tort and criminal liability

INTELLECTUAL PROPERTY

Intellectual property is a special type of intangible property, arising from the creative endeavors of the human mind. The concept of intellectual property came about as it became necessary to protect inventors, authors of literary works, and composers from having their works pirated. Today the law allows for protection of intellectual property through three main forms of registration: patents, copyrights, and trademarks. (There also are unregistered rights, such as trade secrets, and, on occasion, common law copyrights.)

PATENTS

Patent law concerns inventions: designs, manufacturing processes, machinery, electronics, chemical compounds, computer programs, genetically modified life forms (generally, plants and seeds), and other devices. A "utility" or "functional" patent is an exclusive right to make, use, and sell a new and useful process (e.g., for making computer chips), machine (e.g., one that makes airplane parts), article of manufacture (e.g., a new type of light bulb), composition of matter (e.g., a mouthwash formula), human-made microorganisms, or any new and useful improvement on it. This patent, when granted, lasts for 20 years from the date when a U.S. patent application first was filed. Design patents, concerning the appearance of a manufactured article, not its use or operation, last 14 years after they are granted.

Case law since 1950 states that a process or product essentially "equivalent" but not identical to a patented invention may be found to have infringed the patent. *Equivalents* perform essentially the same task, using essentially the same method, to achieve essentially the same result as a product under patent. The idea is that competitors cannot simply make minor changes to a patented device in order to avoid infringement claims from the patent holder. Thus, the doctrine of equivalents allows a patent holder to claim those insubstantial alterations that were left out when drafting the original patent application but that could be created through trivial changes.

To be patented, something must be novel, useful, and nonobvious. Although the range of patentable subjects is broad, some things cannot be patented: natural phenomena (e.g., photosynthesis, or a newly discovered plant or mineral), abstract ideas, perpetual motion devices, or simple "mental steps," and so-called laws of nature (e.g., $E = mc^2$). Discovery itself is insufficient; there must be *applied science*.

In *Association for Molecular Pathology v. Myriad Genetics, Inc.*, 569 U.S. __ (2013), the U.S. Supreme Court held, unanimously, that a naturally occurring human DNA segment cannot be patented merely because it has been isolated; on the other hand, manipulating a gene to create synthetic DNA (complimentary DNA, or cDNA) is patentable. For example, in *Bowman v. Monsanto*, 569 U.S. __ (2013), the Supreme Court unanimously upheld a patent on genetically modified soybeans.

Patent law is exclusively federal. The U.S. Patent Office searches prior patents to determine whether a proposed patent conflicts with a previously issued or pending patent. Also, if—more than one year before the patent application was filed—the invention was sold, publicly used, or the subject of an accepted purchase order in the United States or was described in a written publication, then a *statutory bar* prevents the grant of a patent; it does not matter that the invention may not yet have been fully tested or perfected. (So, for example, trade secrets, once they help to form a design or invention that has been put into public use or sales, cannot be the basis for a patent after this one-year period has lapsed. At that point, the owner's only viable option for retaining intellectual property interests is to maintain the trade secret. There is more on trade secrets later in this chapter.)

No other major country has even this one-year grace period that the United States has. So, to preserve foreign patentability, a U.S. patent application should be filed before any public disclosure or sale is made anywhere in the world.

Patents cannot be renewed. Once a patent lapses, the invention enters the public domain; this means that anyone can make, use, or sell it without obtaining a license from the inventor.[1] However, a person can combine or add to unpatented or lapsed works in such a way as to create a new, patented invention.

Under the *America Invents Act* (2012), if two persons independently invent essentially the same thing, the patent is to be awarded to the first person who applied for the patent regardless of who may have actually first invented it. All major industrial nations follow this first-to-file rule instead of the first-to-invent principle; the United States was the last to still employ the first-to-invent approach (until abandoning it, prospectively—it still applies to pre-2012 patents—with passage of the 2012 law). Whether in Europe, the United States, or elsewhere, the process typically permits third parties to challenge any newly issued patents. **Prior art**, both patented and nonpatented technology now in the public domain (and whether put in existing products or described in written materials), may undermine a patent applicant's claim that his/her invention is novel and nonobvious.

---

[1] Indeed, in *FTC v. Actavis, Inc.*, 570 U.S. __ (2013), the Supreme Court held that profit-sharing deals between brand-name and generic drug companies that have the effect of preserving an expired patent can be struck down as violations of the antitrust laws. More broadly, a long-standing rule, announced in *Brulotte v. Thys Co.*, 379 U.S. 29 (1964), and reaffirmed in *Kimble v. Marvel Entertainment, LLC*, 576 U.S. __ (Supreme Court, 2015), prevents any parties from establishing licenses in which payments must continue even after the patent expires; these post-expiration royalties are *per se* antitrust violations.

COPYRIGHTS

A **copyright** is the exclusive right to print, reproduce, sell, and exhibit written material, musical compositions, art works, photographs, movies and television programs, data systems, and other creations placed in a tangible, preserved medium of expression. This exclusive right also extends to the public distribution, display, or performance of that copyrighted work and to the preparation of derivative works (e.g., a movie version of a copyrighted novel); and 1990 copyright law amendments specifically prohibit the unauthorized lease of sound recordings and computer programs.

To qualify as copyrightable, a creator's (author's) work must be
(1) The author's original work (not someone else's), (2) in a tangible medium of expression (e.g., written, saved on computer disk or drive, recorded on tape), and (3) of some minimal level of creativity. The work need *not* be unique or of high quality; almost any original work, such as something developed for a business, can qualify for copyright protection.

Copyright law is almost exclusively governed by federal statutes. A copyright lasts for the life of the creator, plus 70 years (corporate copyrights last for 95 years from when the work was first published or 120 years from when it was created, whichever occurs first). Copyrights predating the revised federal copyright law (effective January 1, 1978) do not have that time frame but may last for as long as 95 years. Neither publication nor registration with the U.S. Copyright Office is required to secure a copyright. The protection of copyright automatically arises when an original work is first placed in a tangible medium of expression. Although copyright notice ("©, Name, Date, All Rights Reserved") is *not* required, its prominent display does put others on notice that the work is copyrighted and can keep third parties from trying to avoid liability by asserting innocent infringement. Without registration, a person claiming copyright infringement can only win actual damages (including lost profits). Plaintiffs who registered a work within three months of the date it was first published may also win attorneys' fees and statutory damages awards ($30,000 for ordinary infringement of each work; $150,000 for each willful infringement).

Examples of copyrightable works: books, periodicals, lectures, musical compositions, works of art, maps, photographs, dramatic works, movies, illustrations, pictorial, graphic, and sculptural works, sound recordings or other audiovisual works, pantomimes and choreography, and architectural works.

Examples of non-copyrightable works: names, familiar phrases, government publications, standardized information (e.g., dates in calendars), and defamatory, obscene, or fraudulent works. A compilation of facts (e.g., a database) is *not* protected unless the author used some originality and creativity in choosing and presenting the information. However, even without copyright protection, a compiler may require that purchasers of his/her product, in return for their acquiring personal rights to it (e.g., a licensing contract), agree not to reproduce the database for others.

Like other forms of intellectual property, copyrights protect, not ideas, but only the tangible expression of ideas. If an idea and the way it is expressed are inseparable, then no copyright protection is available. For example, the creator of a video game featuring baseball bat swings or ballet dance steps may not copyright the game's swings or steps inasmuch as they are inseparable from the actual standard swings in baseball or set positions in ballet. An important consideration is how many ways an idea can be expressed (e.g., not just a mathematical formula but taking a basic literary plot—a hero succumbing to hubris—and transforming it into a multitude of possible stories). The more ways (e.g., many stories rather than just a few equivalent math equations), the more it is likely to be separable from the underlying idea and thus be copyrightable.

Unlike the situation for patents, the exclusivity of copyrights (as to use, etc.) is subject to a number of exceptions. The two most important are these:

1. **Fair use.** This exception includes, among other things, limited reproduction for classroom purposes. To determine whether the use is fair, these four factors are considered: (a) purpose and nature of the use (e.g., nonprofit or educational vs. commercial); (b) proportion and importance of the part used in comparison to the work as a whole; (c) the nature of the work; (d) the use's effect on the value of the work, including its potential market. Parody can be a fair use. For example, in *Campbell v. Acuff-Rose Music, Inc.,* 510 U.S. 564 (1994), the U.S. Supreme Court unanimously held that 2 Live Crew rap singer Luther Campbell's rendition of the Roy Orbison song, "Oh, Pretty Woman," was a commentary on the original song and thus a noninfringing parody.[2]

2. Limited copying by libraries and archives. They usually can reproduce single copies for noncommercial purposes. Wholesale copying of large works or periodicals, though, is not allowed.

Unlike other forms of intellectual property, U.S. copyrights are usually valid abroad through a treaty (the Berne Convention), although enforcement may be impractical in some countries. To counter that, the World

---

[2] To support its status as noninfringing, the parody should use no more of the original work (e.g., its music and lyrics) than is needed to make it recognizable.

Intellectual Property Organization (WIPO) Copyright Treaty of 1996 not only extends the Berne Convention copyright protections to computer programs and electronic databases, but also imposes on ratifying nations the duty to provide effective legal protection/deterrence (e.g., against technologies used to "steal" intellectual property) and to enforce strong remedies for infringement.

The shop rights doctrine: Employees hired to invent or write for the employer hold no patent or copyright interest in the resulting product. The key thing is that the invention/creation was developed during work time or was derived directly from ideas generated at work. In deciding whether an employee created a work for hire, courts consider several factors: (1) Did the employer have the *right to control*—to direct the manner in which the work was conducted? (2) Who initiated the work's creation? (3) At whose expense was the work created? (4) Who owned the facilities (office, equipment, and so on) where the work was created? (5) What was the nature and amount of compensation the employee received for the work? (6) How much time did the employee spend on the work? Unless the work falls under one of nine statutory categories of commissioned works for hire or there is an express written agreement declaring the work made for hire or assigning over the copyright, an independent contractor, instead of the party who hired him/her, obtains the copyright to the commissioned work he/she produces. One of the nine categories covers, for example, computer software.

Employers whose business substantially involves research and development customarily require that employees sign agreements granting the employer all rights over any inventions directly or indirectly related to the employee's work.

Invention assignment agreements: Such agreement may extend employer ownership over employee inventions to works developed within a specified reasonable time, typically one year, after employment ended. (This assumes the invention relates to the confidential information of and prior work for the employer.)

Is *reverse engineering* of a computer program fair use? It generally has been, although the Digital Millenium Copyright Act of 1998 (DMCA) now prohibits the circumvention of access-control mechanisms, such as encryption and password protection, intended to prevent digital piracy or unauthorized use. The DMCA exempts from this ban the reverse engineering needed to achieve interoperability (i.e., to let programs work on supposedly incompatible systems), but it is unclear how broadly courts interpret this exemption. Moreover, many software licenses expressly forbid reverse engineering, effectively rendering the practice a breach of contract if not a copyright infringement.

COPYRIGHT PROTECTION FOR COMPUTER PROGRAMS

In the 1970s, computer programs did not fit neatly into any category of then-protected works. They were in many ways like literary works, containing the creative expression of the programmer and needing copyright protection. On the other hand, programs were a necessary component to operate a computer, performing as a part of a machine.

The main reason for protecting programs is that almost all the expense for programmers comes with developing, not duplicating, the product. Without protection against unauthorized duplication, the creation of programs would not become profitable and the market for programs would never develop. In 1980, Congress passed the **Computer Software Act**, an amendment to the Copyright Act that granted copyright protection to the expression of computer programs, but left to the courts the details as to what exactly constituted expression. The debate over what parts of the programs constitute expression and what parts are simply ideas or processes is ongoing. Note, however, that the copyright only prohibits copying; there is no infringement if another person independently develops the same or similar programs. Also, certain limited uses of copyrighted materials are permitted, particularly for those who have purchased software. That is why software producers usually market their programs through licenses, not outright sales.

A patent, on the other hand, grants, in effect, a monopoly. The Federal Circuit and some district courts have invalidated several software patents. In *Alice Corp. v. CLS Bank International*, 573 U.S. __ (2014), the Supreme Court set out a two-prong validity test. First, whether the subject matter is eligible for a patent; and second, if so, whether the recitation of generic computer components adds something that is not already present when the steps are considered separately. For software patent applicants, *Alice Corp.* now requires that the method or system (1) improves the functioning of the computer itself, and does more than instruct one to apply the abstract idea on an unspecified generic computer; or (2) effects an improvement in another technology or field. In *Alice Corp.*, the Supreme Court unanimously declared that an invention consisting in significant part of a patent-ineligible concept—for example, a law of nature, natural phenomenon, or abstract idea—cannot be patented unless the remaining parts of the invention have an "inventive concept"—one or more elements that ensure a patent on the invention amounts in practice "to significantly more than a patent upon the ineligible concept itself." A mere instruction to implement an abstract idea on a computer (e.g., store, organize, and retrieve memory in a logical table or organize data in a tabular format) "cannot impart patent eligibility."

Patent claims that are directed to "a method of organizing human activity" are presumptively patent-ineligible. One cannot take a commonplace human activity, do it with a computer, and call that a patentable invention.

An important example of intellectual property piracy concerning computer technology involves semiconductor chips, whose design and manufacture may involve large sums of labor and money. In 1984, Congress enacted the **Semiconductor Chip Protection Act** (SCPA), which provides a 10-year copyright protection for the masks used in producing semiconductor chips. SCPA treatment of infringements includes injunctions, disgorging of the wrongdoer's profits (taking them), and statutory damages up to $250,000.

Although U.S. copyrights are usually valid in other countries due to the Berne Convention (signed by almost every nation, including *all* major trading countries), trade secrets, patents, and trademarks protected via American law usually have no such protection elsewhere unless *also* in compliance with the local country's laws (e.g., European Union via a patent filing in the European Union Offices or via an application for the Community Trademark covering all EU members).

TRADEMARKS AND OTHER TRADE SYMBOLS

A **trademark** is a distinctive symbol, word, letter, number, picture, or combination thereof adopted and used by a merchant or manufacturer to identify his/her goods. Examples include Big Mac (McDonald's Corporation), Mac (Apple Computers), the Nike "Swoosh" logo, and the company slogan, "Built Ford Tough." Even the color of a product can be trademarked when it acts as a symbol to distinguish one brand from others.

The law of trademarks and other trade symbols includes both federal and state statutes and cases. It is meant to keep businesses from "cashing in" on the goodwill and reputation of a competitor's products or services. It helps to prevent or punish the fraudulent marketing of goods or services as being those of another, presumably more reputable, business. Obviously, if unchecked, such unfair competition deceives the public and steals trade from honest businesspersons.

Although not required to do so, the owner or user of a trademark may seek to register it in the U.S. Patent and Trademark Office. A trademark not yet in use may still be registered if it is to be put in use within six months. (This pre-use protection can be extended for up to 30 more months.)

If approved, a registration lasts 10 years from the first use and can be renewed for any number of additional 10-year periods. Infringement of the registered trademark may be enjoined (ordered stopped by a court) and damages awarded.

Immoral, deceptive, confusing, or merely descriptive "marks" are not protected. Also, as the U.S. Supreme Court decided unanimously in *Dastar Corp. v. Twentieth Century Fox Film Corp.*, 539 U.S. 23 (2003), once the copyright on a creative work has expired, others may copy it and pass it off as their own without violating federal trademark laws.

To be protected, a trade symbol (1) must not lapse from disuse; and (2) must remain associated with the business or its products and services (not becoming a generic term). Some former trade names now in common public use (becoming generic, and thus no longer protected) are aspirin,[3] brassiere, cellophane, thermos, trampoline, margarine, raisin bran, dry ice, lanolin, heroin, linoleum, nylon, kerosene, cornflakes, laundromat, Murphy bed, shredded wheat, and escalator. On the other hand, looking at which trademarks deserve the most protection, we see the following: (1) The best phrasing for a trademarked term is an inherently distinctive mark, particularly a fanciful, or made-up, word (e.g., Kodak, Acura, Xerox, Exxon), an arbitrary mark—with real words but ones with nothing to do with the product category (e.g., Apple Computers), or a suggestive mark (that suggests something about a product, but does not merely describe it (e.g., Gleem toothpaste); and (2) much worse are merely descriptive terms, which cannot be inherently distinctive and are thus deserving of little protection, be they self-laudatory (e.g., Great Steaks, Premier Motors), indicative of a product's characteristics (e.g., Rapid Roadkill), or stating geographic origins (e.g., Gainesville Grill, Louisiana Ladders). The latter, if there is a court contest, often requires much time and money to prove that these descriptive marks have acquired a secondary meaning, with a significant number of people associating the mark with a particular company or product.

Besides trademarks, other types of trade symbols include *service marks* (similar to trademarks, but concerning services rather than goods—e.g., Holiday Inn, Jiffy Lube) and *trade names* (may act as trademarks or service marks, but serve mainly to designate the business entity itself). Although trade names cannot be federally registered, infringement is still subject to injunction and damages.

---

[3] Some marks declared generic in one country (e.g., aspirin, in the United States) may remain protected in other countries (e.g., the German company, Bayer, still holds rights to the term "aspirin" for its acetylsalicylic acid product in about 80 nations).

Like the law of trade symbols generally, this area of law permits extensive state statutory, regulatory, and case law development, a far cry from the federal preemption of almost all patent and copyright law.

THREE TRADEMARK CONCEPTS

• *CYBERSQUATTING: TRADEMARK INFRINGEMENT ON THE INTERNET*

The Anticybersquatting Consumer Protection Act of 1999 makes it illegal for a person to register or use an Internet domain name with a bad-faith intent to profit from the name if the domain name is (1) identical or confusingly similar to a distinctive trademark or (2) identical or confusingly similar to or dilutive of a famous trademark. Also, the Internet Corporation for Assigned Names (ICANN) has established an arbitration procedure for all domain name registries to follow; that helps aggrieved mark holders to pursue cybersquatters.

• *DILUTION*

Under the Trademark Dilution Revision Act of 2006, a trademark owner can obtain an injunction against a defendant using a name or term that blurs, tarnishes, erodes, or in some other way dilutes (lessens) the true owner's capacity to identify and distinguish its goods and services. The plaintiff must prove that its mark is famous and that the defendant's use is commercial as well as *likely to dilute* the distinctive quality of the plaintiff's mark. Actual harm need not be shown. To win more than an injunction—disgorgement of the defendant's profits, damages, attorney's fees, and destruction of the infringing goods—the plaintiff must show that the defendant's diluting actions were willful.

• *TRADE DRESS*

Courts have extended Lanham Act protection to trade dress: the packaging or dressing of a product as it relates to a business' overall marketplace image. Unregistered trade dress is protected only if it is distinctive, has acquired a secondary meaning, and is an ornamental feature rather than a functional feature. The design features found in a utility patent are presumed to be functional and thus *not* entitled to trade dress protection once the patent expires.

TRADE SECRETS

Employees owe their employers a duty not to disclose trade secrets. The duty remains even after the job is gone. People can change jobs and join a competitor (unless that is barred in a written employment contract with the prior employer), but they cannot lawfully turn over (misappropriate) **trade secrets**: information, including any formula, process, compilation, customer list, method (e.g., of operation), pattern, program, device, or technique that (i) derives actual or potential economic value because it is not generally known to, nor readily and properly ascertainable by, other people who could obtain economic value from its disclosure or use; and (ii) is the subject of reasonable efforts to maintain its secrecy.[4] So, a trade secret is neither generally known nor readily available in the industry; it is typically used in the production of goods or services, providing the business owner a competitive advantage over competitors, meant to be held in the employee's confidence, and needed by the employee to perform his/her job.

The more valuable an alleged trade secret is to a business owner and the more likely the owner therefore is to try to keep it a secret, the more likely a court is to deem that information a *trade secret*. This duty of nondisclosure implicitly arises out of, and continues beyond, almost any employment relationship (under state statutes such as the Uniform Trade Secrets Act (UTSA) for judge-developed common law principles). However, the duty can be made more extensive and detailed via express provisions placed in a written employment agreement or, more generally (say, covering not just employees but anyone with whom a business deals), via specialized contracts called *nondisclosure agreements*. Besides civil liability, theft of trade secrets also subjects the culprit to potential criminal charges such as mail fraud, interstate transportation of stolen property, various state common law charges, and violation of the federal Economic Espionage Act. A third party also can be held liable for misappropriation of trade secrets (or even be held guilty of that crime—see Chapter 19, if this firm knew or had reason to know that the one transferring to it the trade secret obtained the trade secret through improper means).

Because copyrights can only be used to protect the expression of ideas in computer software, trade secrets have become important in protecting the ideas themselves. Companies who create and sell software often use trade secret licensing practices, such as the agreements now commonly found on sealed packages of new software that restrict the user to only consumer uses for the programs. Such agreements, supposedly agreed to by the consumer upon opening the package, may or may not be enforceable in court. However, the general trend among software companies has been to protect the expression of ideas in the software under the federal copyright law, and to attempt to protect the ideas themselves under state trade secret policies. The trade secret

---

[4] That is the Uniform Trade Secrets Act (UTSA) definition. The UTSA, completed by the Uniform Law Commissioners in 1979 and amended in 1985, has been effectively adopted by 48 states, all but Massachusetts and New York.

remains protected for as long as the information remains valuable and is kept confidential. There is no protection from accidental disclosure, independent creation by a competitor, or disclosure by someone with no duty to maintain confidentiality. Moreover, discovery by *reverse engineering* (starting with the known product and working backward to find the method by which it was developed) is okay, *if* that product was acquired fairly, such as by purchase on the open market.

Trade Secrets or Publishing as an Alternative to Patent Applications

Sometimes a business decides that it is not cost-effective to patent a product. The business may try to retain the intellectual property as a trade secret. At the very least, to prevent a competitor from patenting the business's invention, the business may disclose certain aspects of its invention in specialty journals or on websites. This "defensive publishing" strategy demonstrates "prior art" before others can patent the work.

THE INTERSECTION OF INTELLECTUAL PROPERTY LAWS

Although each category of intellectual property law is aimed at a particular type of intellectual property, the patent, copyright, trademark, and trade secrets laws occasionally intersect with each other for particular intellectual property items. Common examples of this phenomenon are:

Patents and Trade Secrets—some pending patent applications

Copyrights and Trademarks—artwork in a package design (e.g., AA with an eagle between the letters for American Airlines); different aspects of an advertisement

Copyrights and Trade Secrets—computer source code

Patents, Copyrights, and Trademarks—product design, such as jewelry or a distinctively shaped musical instrument. A trademark with a sufficiently original design element could qualify for copyright protection, and—if the design were novel and nonobvious—could also merit design patent protection. The Rolls-Royce "Spirit of Ecstasy" (also called the "Flying Lady") hood ornament, the contoured Coca-Cola bottle, the Rubik's Cube, and the Google Search homepage are examples of products that have been or could be protected under all three types of intellectual property laws.

COMPUTER CRIMES AND TORTS

As businesses increasingly rely upon electronic means to carry out everyday transactions, the potential for criminal activity and tort liability in computer systems is growing at a remarkable pace. Common examples of computer crimes include using computers to embezzle, to defraud, or to steal information. These crimes also may involve damage to or destruction of computer systems. Computer torts may include negligence, infringement of intellectual property, fraud, conversion, or trespass to personal property.

A sophisticated form of harm that can be introduced into a computer system is a **computer virus.** A computer virus is a unique type of program that is specifically designed to create problems within a system and to replicate itself. Viruses can be spread from computer to computer on disk or across telephone wire, hidden as part of an application or file. The deliberate introduction of a computer virus is subject to tort liability similar to that of a battery or trespassing. If the virus is introduced into a system used substantially for U.S. government or financial institution purposes, it may be a crime under the Federal Counterfeit Access Device and Computer Fraud and Abuse Act of 1984 (FCADCFA Act).

Another potential crime and tort is the deliberate sabotage of a system by a computer consultant or programmer. Secret "drop dead" or "time bomb" devices can be set up when a program is installed or modified that disable the system at the programmer's command or after a certain period of time has elapsed. Such devices have been used in the past as extortion tools by programmers involved in contract disputes, as well as in cases of fraud (e.g., a consultant guarantees that his/her services will be needed again by "planting" future problems into a system). The FCADCFA Act (amended in 1986) permits criminal prosecution of those who intentionally access and damage computer systems used substantially for U.S. government or financial institution purposes.

A recent topic for debate in computer law is the tort liability of persons operating bulletin board systems and computer networks: are they liable for defamatory statements posted on their systems? Since the policing of communications on such systems would be so costly in both terms of money and loss of privacy, the courts have generally held that operators of computer networks are more like carriers than publishers of information. The phone companies, after all, are not liable for the conversations they transmit. Whether carriers can be held liable for information that is screened by their operators before posting is still open for debate.

Another issue gaining importance in computer law involves potential antitrust violations. Competitors have accused software giant Microsoft of using practices that limit free competition, such as using codes in its operating systems that make it difficult for companies other than Microsoft to create programs for the system.

A final set of issues that must be addressed are the potential problems associated with the **Internet,** the rapidly growing and largest computer network in the world. Because of the volatile nature of the Internet and the fact that it spreads across international borders, it provides many opportunities for criminals and is extremely difficult for governmental agencies to police or regulate.

PRIVACY ISSUES
COMPUTERS AND PRIVACY

Perhaps the most serious legal problem posed by computers, the Internet, and advances in information technology generally, is the resulting encroachment upon the individual's right to privacy. With their incredible power to search, retrieve, store, and transmit data, computers, networks, and other technology have furnished businesses and governments with the means to access, amass, use, and share a vast amount of information about businesses and individuals. Information kept by government, financial, medical, marketing, and other institutions accumulates, perhaps exponentially. Errors in information can cause numerous, severe problems. For instance, a common practice in finance is to maintain extensive credit records about individuals, with this information (or, sometimes, misinformation) thus being crucial when people seek loans. Moreover, using only absolutely accurate information does not always prevent legal problems (e.g., due to inappropriate disclosures to third parties). By increasingly recording and cataloging postings on the Internet, business soon may make it possible to access the entire history of a person's communications on a bulletin board system. Despite this technology, privacy rights may rest with these "recorded" and "catalogued" citizens even if the disclosed information is correct.

It has long been recognized that, as computers make it easier to probe into people's personal affairs, special precautions may prove necessary to protect individuals from invasions of their privacy. In 1974, Congress passed a Privacy Act restricting the types of computerized records that the government may maintain and its uses of those records. This act also gives the individual access to the data on themselves, as well as the right to copy, challenge, and correct what they find in these records. In many cases, data may not be released unless the individual concerned is notified.

The Computer Security Act of 1987 and the Computer Matching and Privacy Protection Act of 1988 also protect the public against the release of U.S. government computer data. Seven other significant federal laws are: (1) the **FCADCFA Act** (previously discussed in this chapter) prohibits the unauthorized use of computers to obtain certain restricted information and also bans dealing in U.S. government computer passwords; (2) the **Right to Financial Privacy Act** (1978) restricts the federal government's right to review bank account records; (3) **Title III of the 1968 Omnibus Crime Control and Safe Streets Act,** as amended by the **Electronic Communications Privacy Act** (1986) and other laws, makes unauthorized interceptions of wire and electronic communications (including all telephone conversations, even via cordless phones) a criminal offense, subject to fines and imprisonment, and also providing an aggrieved party the right to sue for damages; (4) the **Telephone Consumer Protection Act** (1991) outlaws autodialing to fax machines, pagers, and cellular phones, as well as prohibits prerecorded calls to a residence without the resident's consent, with the Federal Communications Commission enforcing this act (for more on fax and e-mail advertisements, see page 466); (5) the **Cable Communications Policy Act** (1984) restricts cable operators' collection or disclosure of information on individual customers without the customers' consent; (6) the **Video Privacy Protection Act** (1988) provides for civil actions against video rental businesses for disseminating a customer's renting history; and (7) the **Children's Online Privacy Protection Act of 1998** (**COPPA**), concerning online collection of personal information from children below age 13, details what website operators must include in their privacy policies, how verifiable consents are to be obtained from a parent or guardian, and when the operator must protect children's online privacy and safety, including restrictions on marketing to the under-13 set.

In the continuing battle to enact effective but constitutional statutes to combat child pornography, Congress in 2003 passed the Prosecutorial Remedies and Other Tools to End the Exploitation of Children Today Act (called the PROTECT Act). It bans the pandering (advertising, promotion, presentation, distribution, or solicitation) of "any material or purported material in a manner that reflects the belief, or that is intended to cause another to believe" that the material is illegal child pornography. The PROTECT Act broadly construes illegal "kiddie porn" as sexually explicit images of children, both images of real children and computer-generated images of realistic "virtual" children. In a 7–2 decision in *United States v. Williams* (2008), the Supreme Court concluded that PROTECT was not overly broad—an individual soliciting or claiming to possess child pornography is engaged in an offer to engage in illegal transactions, a type of speech categorically excluded from First Amendment protection.

Many states have enacted similar privacy laws affecting their governmental agencies. Other than a few specific areas (e.g., wiretapping of telephone calls), state regulation has lagged in regard to record-keeping and data dissemination by private businesses.

Two additional federal acts involving electronic data systems were discussed in prior chapters. The **Electronic Funds Transfer Act** (1978), which governs bank transactions, is discussed in Chapter 12.

The Fair Credit Reporting Act (1970) (part of the Truth-in-Lending Act, discussed in Chapter 13) provides for debtors' access to credit reports and sets forth procedures for correcting misinformation or otherwise protecting a consumer's credit reputation. The FCRA has the following provisions:

1. Credit information may be shared only in these permitted cases:
   (a) credit, insurance, and employment applications;
   (b) relevant business transactions (those involving the person whose credit now matters);
   (c) governmental license applications;
   (d) sharing consented to by the person concerned or ordered by a court.

2. The use of out-of-date negative information is prohibited. Generally, this includes data older than 7 years, bankruptcies older than 14 years, and specially prepared investigative reports from more than three months ago. There is no time limit on information used in deciding applications for life insurance policies worth at least $50,000 or jobs paying at least $20,000.

3. Governmental use of information is limited.

4. Credit-reporting agencies are required to:
   (a) follow reasonable procedures for assuring maximum accuracy;
   (b) disclose to a requesting consumer the information in his/her file (except for medical information or for the sources of information) and the identities of those who have received credit information.

5. Those who order an investigative report must inform the consumer and, if rejection stems from a credit report, tell the consumer the reasons and the name of the reporting agency.

6. Consumers may dispute the information on file, force a reinvestigation, and even include a statement (no more than 100 words) in the file, with copies going to businesses that received the disputed information.

7. Violations of the act are punishable by fines or even jail, with civil actions open to persons who can prove financial damages.

Another privacy issue gaining attention is the use of technological means by supervisors to monitor employees at work. The widespread use of rather intrusive safety and health measures, such as drug testing of certain employees (e.g., transportation workers), has become accepted as reasonably related to a compelling need—protecting the public. But the use of polygraph testing, video surveillance, cellular telephone eavesdropping, genetic testing, computer monitoring of employees (e.g., their job performance), and other technologies is highly controversial, and the conflicting rights of employees, employers, and the public will continue to be addressed in the legislatures and the courts.

INTERNATIONAL LAW TOPIC

While the U.S. government grapples with privacy issues, the European Union (EU) has already taken the initiative in protecting privacy interests. A directive was issued in 1992 and amended in 1994. It directs member nations to take steps to protect the privacy of all "personal data" that can be linked to an individual. The directive states that all such data should be processed fairly and lawfully, and it also addresses concerns not only of accuracy but of information transfers that should be prohibited. The directive governs both governmentally controlled or generated data *and* the data processed or held by private organizations; it also reaches "networks," such as for telephone communications. The directive emphasizes the need to obtain an individual's informed consent before engaging in many uses of his/her "personal data." The individual has the right to access the information about himself, and the directive's "Data Subjects' Bill of Rights" places on public and private processers and controllers of data some large burdens that do not exist in the United States.

KNOW THE CONCEPTS

DO YOU KNOW THE BASICS?

1. For each of the three main types of intellectual property that can be registered, state its duration, two examples (or a definition), and the degree to which the law is federal not state law.
2. What three characteristics must an invention have in order to be patentable?

3. Can computer programs be (a) copyrighted; (b) patented?
4. Name two elements needed to show the existence of a trade secret.
5. Name several types of crimes and torts that can be committed via computer.
6. Credit information about a particular debtor may not be shared among different creditors without the written approval of the debtor. *True* or *False?*

TERMS FOR STUDY

Berne Convention
Cable Communications Policy Act
computer crimes
Computer Matching and Privacy Protection Act
Computer Security Act
Computer Software Act
computer torts
computer virus
copyrights
cybersquatting
design patents
Electronic Communications Privacy Act
equivalents
Fair Credit Reporting Act
fair use
Federal Counterfeit Access Device and Computer Fraud and Abuse Act
intellectual property
Internet

invention assignment agreements
nondisclosure agreements
patents
prior art
Privacy Act
Right to Financial Privacy Act
service marks
shop rights doctrine
statutory damage awards
Telephone Consumer Protection Act
Title III of the 1968 Omnibus Crime Control and Safe Streets Act
trade dress
trademarks
trade names
trade secrets
utility (or functional) patents
Video Privacy Protection Act
Work for hire

PRACTICAL APPLICATION

1. Irma Inventor invents something she calls "portavision." It works on exactly the same principles as does broadcast television. To make it "doubly portable," Irma attaches wheels to her portavision set so that it is easily moved. Will Irma receive a patent on her portavision process and/or her movable portavision set?

2. For each activity undertaken without the permission of any copyright holder, state whether it is likely to be a "fair use":

(a) An impromptu, unpaid speech quoting two lines from a recent movie.

(b) Photocopying for a profitable resale to others ten pages out of a 1,500-page textbook.

(c) Selling T-shirts of the Mona Lisa painting with a big milk mustache on Mona Lisa's upper lip.

ANSWERS

KNOW THE CONCEPTS

1. Patents—20 years from when the patent application was first filed (for design patents, 14 years from when the patent was granted); examples: a new type of mechanical process, a new industrial cleaning formula; exclusively federal law.

Copyrights—creator's life plus 70 years (corporate copyrights last for 95 years); examples: a song, a novel; almost exclusively federal law.

Trademarks—no set term, ten-year registrations can be renewed any number of times; definition: any distinctive mark used by a business to identify its goods; state law plays an important role, with federal law rarely preempting the state law.

2. To receive a utility patent for an invention, the applicant must demonstrate that the invention is novel, useful, and nonobvious.

3. (a) Yes; (b) Generally not.

4. A formula, process, or method to produce goods or services that is (1) meant to be held in employees' confidence, and (2) needed by employees to perform their jobs.

5. Crimes—embezzlement, extortion, fraud, infringement of intellectual property, theft, vandalism, and statutory crimes under the FCADCFA Act and various federal privacy laws.

Torts—conversion, fraud, infringement of intellectual property, invasion of privacy, negligence, trespass to personal property, and civil actions for violations of various privacy protection statutes.

6. False. Under the Fair Credit Reporting Act, there are many instances in which creditors, employers, government agencies, and others are free to exchange information (and often can be expected to do so) without having to first obtain a debtor's permission. Except for when investigative reports are prepared or a consumer/debtor requests information, the very fact that information is being disclosed ordinarily need not be disclosed to a consumer/debtor.

PRACTICAL APPLICATION

1. No. To be patented, something must be novel, useful, and nonobvious. Irma's portavision process fails because it is nothing new; it is just another term for the broadcasting of pictures and sound via television. Irma's portavision set also fails because it is obvious. There is nothing original and nonobvious about attaching wheels to an item.

2. (a) Yes. The use has these characteristics: no profit; small proportion; speech not duplicating the work itself, which was a movie; and no impact on the work's market value.

(b) No. The work has these characteristics: for profit; duplicating the same sort of material as in the work itself (written pages); and possible impact on work's market value, as customers obtain the same pages in lieu of buying the textbook.

(c) Fair use is not an issue. Since Leonardo da Vinci's painting is in the public domain, there is no copyright and thus no need to prove a fair use. If the painting were a modern, copyrighted work, the question would be one of parody, as in the case of *Campbell v. Acuff-Rose Music, Inc.* More facts then would be helpful in deciding the case. Also, note that trademark issues could arise if this shirt were produced to look confusingly similar to a preexisting, trademarked advertising campaign involving present or historic celebrities shown with milk mustaches.

27
TAXATION

KEY TERMS

deductions taxpayer expenditures or other amounts that can be subtracted from the taxpayer's income and thereby lower the taxpayer's taxable income

marginal tax rate the rate applied on the taxpayer's income made "at the margin," that is, on the taxpayer's last dollars earned

tax credit taxpayer expenditures or other amounts that can be subtracted directly from the amount of tax that taxpayer owes

HISTORICAL PERSPECTIVE

In Ancient Rome and other societies, taxes often were assigned (farmed out) to a group of collectors, each of whom was responsible for delivering a certain amount to the state. Typically, the tax collector could keep as a profit any amount collected above the required tribute. In medieval times, taxes usually were paid in the form of services, with taxpayers, for example, laboring on local roads or helping supply the state with farm products. Usually the government would tell a nobleman how many laborers would be needed to cover the taxes appropriate to that nobleman's respective rank or property.

Today, taxes are paid in the form of money, and tax collection is much more systematized (without any for-profit, subcontracted tax "farming").

The most prominent tax in the United States is the federal income tax. Income taxation is fairly new compared to many other types of taxing. France levied one of the first recorded income taxes in 1793. The United States briefly had income taxes during the Civil War and again in 1894. Although the individual and business income tax rate was low, only 2%, the Supreme Court in 1895 declared the tax unconstitutional. Not until 1913, when the Constitution's Sixteenth Amendment was ratified, was the U.S. government specifically granted power to levy an income tax on the national population. Initially, the rate was only 1%, but it has since increased to far above that rate.

THE INTERNAL REVENUE SERVICE

The U.S. Internal Revenue Service (IRS) was started in 1862 to enforce the internal revenue laws. The IRS, an agency of the U.S. Treasury Department, has as its main purpose to ensure compliance with federal tax laws. It performs this task by: (1) providing citizens and taxpayers with information and help; and (2) taking civil enforcement actions and/or preparing cases for criminal charges against people who disobey or ignore the tax laws.

Government revenue is collected through a variety of means, such as income taxes, corporation taxes, estate taxes, and social security taxes. While the main IRS office is located in Washington, D.C., most IRS personnel work for an IRS field office (regional and district offices are located throughout the United States). These offices collect taxes, administer additional tax liabilities, investigate possible tax violations, and help people prepare their annual tax returns.

TYPES OF TAXES

Governments levy many kinds of taxes. State and local governments tax property and base the tax on the assessed value of a residence, commercial real estate, or, sometimes, personal property. Another type of tax is on transactions, such as federal tariffs on imported goods and general state or local retail sales taxes. The latter is an especially important source of revenue for many states.

Governments also tax licenses and may impose excise taxes on the sale of particular products (e.g., tobacco, alcoholic beverages, and gasoline). It is usually only people with high incomes or substantial levels of wealth who may be subject to inheritance taxes, estate taxes, or gift taxes. An estate tax is assessed against a dead person's property before it is passed on to the heirs, while an inheritance tax is levied against the heirs based upon the value of what they have received as an inheritance. The gift tax, paid by the donor, is often intended to keep people from avoiding any estate taxes by giving property away while still alive—gift amounts above a certain yearly limit may be taxed.

Failure to pay taxes, or paying less than is owed, can lead to substantial penalties (besides just paying the taxes owed). If the failure to pay or the payment of an incorrectly low amount is deemed intentional, not merely a mistake, it is a crime subject to more severe penalties, including large fines and imprisonment.

THE INCOME TAX

Income taxes are levied by the federal government, most states, and some local governments. (Only Alaska, Florida, Nevada, New Hampshire, South Dakota, Tennessee, Texas, Washington, and Wyoming do not have a broad-based income tax on wages, although Tennessee and New Hampshire do tax interest and dividends income.) This tax is on personal income, businesses' income, and sometimes the income of estates and trusts. *Personal income taxes* reach the incomes of individuals and families, while *corporate income taxes* apply to corporate earnings. Special taxes, based on income, include the social security contributions made by both employees and employers, as well as the other *payroll* taxes employers may have to pay to fund unemployment compensation, workers' compensation, and other programs.

A proportional income tax applies the same tax rate for all amounts of taxable income. The federal government, and most states, have a *progressive income tax,* instead. There, the tax rate increases as taxable income increases. Thus, for example, a person with $10,000 in taxable income may pay a tax of 15% on that income ($1,500), while a person with a taxable income of $50,000 may pay at a rate of 15% on the first $25,000, but at a higher rate (e.g., 28%) on the income above that level. Under a progressive system, the taxpayer has a *marginal tax rate* that is the rate applied on his/her income made "at the margin"—his/her last dollars earned. This rate can be referred to as one's "tax bracket." (If Ted Taxpayer is taxed on $100,000 of income, and the first $20,000 is taxed at 15%, the next $30,000 is taxed at 20%, the next $40,000 is taxed at 25%, and above that is taxed at 30%, then his marginal tax rate is 30%; someone with taxable income of $70,000 would have a marginal tax rate of 25%, and someone at $25,000 a marginal rate of 20%.)

To determine one's income tax, a person starts with his/her total annual income (salary, wages, dividends, interest, rent, royalties, or almost any other earnings received, not including most gifts, loans, alimony, or government benefits). Certain business expenses, moving costs, and other expenses may be subtracted from this "gross income" to produce an "adjusted gross income." Then, one may exempt a certain amount of income based on the number of dependents (e.g., minor children) one has; also, deductions from the adjusted gross income may be taken for certain expenditures, such as home mortgage interest, charitable contributions, medical or other expenses above a certain percentage (about 7.5%) of one's adjusted gross income, and state and local property or income taxes. The result is one's taxable income. The tax rate, proportional or progressive, is levied against only the taxable income. Some taxpayers are eligible for tax credits—subtracted from the amount of tax due—for such expenses as child care. (A credit is worth more than a deduction because a $500 credit means that the taxpayer pays $500 less in taxes, while a $500 deduction means simply that the taxable income is reduced by $500—at a 28% tax rate (tax bracket), that simply means $140 less in taxes (28% × $500).

EMPLOYER RESPONSIBILITIES: TAXES

Employers have many tax duties. They are responsible for filing all paperwork dealing with the business and with employee taxation. For tax purposes, sole proprietorships, partnerships, and professional service corporations (e.g., in law, accounting, medicine, architecture, performing arts, or consulting) must use a calendar year—one ending December 31. Other, "regular" corporations may choose to turn in tax returns using a fiscal year, which can end at any set point in the calendar year. In order for an S corporation to report taxes on a fiscal year basis, it must show the IRS a substantial business reason to do so, such as that the business is seasonal in nature.

Besides paying their own individual and business taxes, employers must assume the role of Uncle Sam: they must also be a tax collector for their employees. The government mandates that an employer withhold a certain amount of an employee's paycheck to pay the IRS for income taxes, Social Security, and Medicare taxes.[1] The employer must know when to forward to (pay) the federal government these payroll taxes, and often it also must pay comparable payroll taxes and business income taxes to state or local governments. Employers must pay a matching amount for each employee paying Social Security and Medicare taxes. Lastly, employees whose tax payments have been withheld from their paychecks must be informed of the amount withheld for each type of tax.

The amount an employer must withhold from the employee's paycheck is based on the employee's income and what the employee states on a W-4 form. This form establishes the employee's number of dependents and his or her filing status (single, married, or married and withholding at a higher single rate). To find the appropriate withholding amount based on the employee's salary and W-4 factors, business owners can use the tables in an IRS booklet, *Circular E, Employer's Tax Guide*. Amounts that are to be withheld (and then matched by an

---

[1] Another tax that an employer must pay is the federal unemployment tax. It is not paid, in part or in whole, from paycheck withholdings, but from direct payments owed by employers based on the number of employees, average salaries, and past layoff patterns. Employers are given a credit for participating in state unemployment programs. Sole proprietors and partners are not required to pay the tax on the owner's compensation from the business.

employer contribution) for Social Security (FICA) and Medicare taxes are also listed in *Circular E.*

Anyone paid wages or a salary, even a business owner, is an employee for tax purposes. The business owner/employee must complete a W-4 form and have income, Social Security, and Medicare taxes withheld from his paycheck, even if that employee, through partial or total ownership of the business, also constitutes the employer.

Another requirement is that employers deposit, for payment, all withheld amounts with a financial institution. The IRS instructs employers on the IRS coupons that must accompany the deposits and on how often the employers are to deposit these withholdings. An average small business will make deposits into a financial institution once a month. (For larger businesses, ones with more than $50,000 in annual employment taxes, the deposits must occur more frequently: every two weeks.)

Failure to make required deposits subjects a business to severe penalties. If an employer lacks the funds to cover overdue taxes, the IRS can legally hold the business owner personally liable for not just the taxes, but also past due fees and additional penalties. This holds true even when a business is incorporated if the owner was personally involved in managing the business. Also, while many business debts can be discharged (wiped out) through bankruptcy, withheld taxes due to the government cannot be discharged.

Employers can hire a bank or a payroll service to calculate, withhold, deposit, and pay their payroll taxes. A payroll service will issue checks to pay the employees and to pay the taxes, and it will notify the employer when taxes are due. Typically, this service provider also will prepare for the business its quarterly tax returns, and its annual W-2 forms. A bank provides the same services as does a payroll service, except that a bank withholds taxes from the employer's bank account when the payroll is paid. This means that the bank has use of this money once it is removed from the account, even though the taxes are not yet due. Use of a payroll service eliminates this problem. The employer gains extra time to use the withheld amount until the tax deposits actually are due.

BACK TAXES

Employers may even be responsible for back taxes that an employee owes. The IRS initiates this process by notifying an employer that one of its employees owes the government money for past due taxes. The employer is then required to withhold a certain amount of the employee's wages to pay for the taxes. The IRS cannot legally force the employer to retain all of the employee's salary, because the employee is permitted to keep a certain amount of wages based on his/her income and how many dependents he/she has. Employers that do not respond to a "past due taxes" notice will be liable to the IRS for the amount which the employer failed to withhold and thus wrongly gave to the employee. Some states and municipalities have similar powers to require the withholding of owed back taxes from an employee's salary.

INDEPENDENT CONTRACTORS

As an employer, one must realize the difference between independent contractors and employees. For an employee, the employer must contribute to Social Security and Medicare, pay a federal unemployment tax, give to the state's unemployment insurance fund, withhold the employee's income, Social Security and Medicare taxes, and keep records on and eventually report all of these transactions to the state and federal governments. A W-2 form also must be sent annually to each employee stating the amount he/she earned, as well as the total amount withheld for the year for tax purposes. For an independent contractor, an employer is not required to meet any of these requirements. The employer must only complete a Form 1099-MISC if the contractor was paid $600 or more for the job performed. Then, the employer sends a copy of this form to the contractor and the IRS.

It usually saves an employer much time and money to label the people it hires as independent contractors rather than employees. Therefore, the IRS has created strict standards to establish who is classified as a contractor. If an employer misclassifies an employee as an independent contractor, the employer can be severely fined and—for violations constituting willful tax evasion—imprisoned.

Independent contractors are required to fill out a W-9 form and give it to the business that hires them. If a contractor fails to provide the hiring business with a correct Social Security number or employer identification number, the employer may have to keep 31% of the contractor's salary to ensure that the contractor's taxes are paid.

STATUTORY EMPLOYEES

For tax purposes, *statutory employees* are a hybrid between employees and independent contractors. As with independent contractors, for statutory employees the business does not withhold any income tax from their paychecks, nor does it pay a federal unemployment tax except on delivery people or traveling salespersons. As with "regular" employees, for statutory employees the employer still must withhold the worker's Social Security and Medicare taxes and must also match the employee's contribution. Some examples of people who may be classified as statutory employees are delivery people, insurance salespeople, traveling salespersons, and home workers (people doing "piecework," per the employer's instructions, on materials supplied by and returned to the employer). A person in one of those job categories still is not a statutory employee unless: (1) there is a service contract stating or implying that the person personally must perform almost all of the services; (2) other than for transportation (e.g., a motor vehicle), the worker has invested little or nothing in the equipment or other property used to perform the services; and (3) the worker must perform the services on a continuing basis. The strict requirements to qualify as a statutory employee mean that such workers are rare.

SELF-EMPLOYMENT TAXES

The self-employment tax is not actually an employment tax, but is very closely related. It is applied to the income that a business owner receives from working for his business even though he is not an actual employee of the business.[2] The tax is paid in addition to the income tax, and it is equivalent to the employer's and employee's Social Security and Medicare taxes that would be paid on an employee's wages. The tax is computed on an IRS Schedule SE form, which is filed with a personal 1040 Tax Form. But, if a person is working a second job, the income from that job reduces the tax base for the self-employment tax.

The self-employment tax is 15.3% on earnings up to the FICA statutory limit (discussed in Chapter 24), and 2.9% on earnings over that amount. For example, Hardworking Harry has one primary form of employment at a computer company where he earns $80,000 annually, but Harry also consults in his free time. In that venture, Harry receives $35,000 annually. The $80,000 salary is included in the income cap subject to the 15.3% self-employment tax. Assuming that the annual statutory limit is $100,000 that year, then Harry would be taxed for $20,000 of his consulting income at 15.3% ($100,000 − $80,000 = $20,000). The remaining

---

[2] Ordinarily, general partners, but not limited partners, are subject to self-employment taxes. The limited partner's profits from the partnership are not considered "earned income," while the general partner's profits are, for purposes of the self-employment tax.

$15,000 ($35,000 − $20,000 = $15,000) of the consulting income is then only taxed at 2.9%. (Of course, all of Harry's $115,000 is income for purposes of calculating the income tax.)

CASH AND ACCRUAL METHODS FOR INCOME AND EXPENSES

Most small businesses and many larger businesses use the cash method of accounting. The cash method includes in gross income all the payments received during the tax year. Likewise, expenses are deducted from income for the tax year in which the expenses were paid. The two major exceptions are: (1) long-term expenses (e.g., the purchase of an office building) that must be spread over a number of years (capitalization); (2) prepaid expenses meant to cover costs in more than one tax year (deductions are apportioned among the various tax years).

The other major accounting method, the accrual method, treats income and expenses as occurring when one earned the income or became liable for the expense. This method is followed by most large businesses, but it is more complicated than the cash method and must meet IRS guidelines.

Examples of the cash and accrual methods:

A business operating on a calendar tax year provides a service in December 2015, but does not bill for it until January 2016 and is not paid until February 2016. The business also enters into a contract to buy new office stationery in November 2015, but does not take delivery or pay for it until January 2016.

Under the cash method of accounting, the service income and the stationery expense are both 2016 tax items (when payment actually occurred).

Under the accrual method, the service income was earned in 2015 (at the point the business became entitled to be paid); and the office stationery liability also arose in 2015. So 2015 is the appropriate accrual method year for counting the service income and deducting the office stationery expense.

TAX DEDUCTIONS

When an employer computes his/her federal income tax, he/she may deduct from taxable income: employee salaries, vacation pay, many bonuses and gifts, some meals and lodging, and various fringe benefits. There are strict guidelines about what falls into the listed criteria for deduction allowances.

Employee salaries—Most salaries, wages, or similar compensation can be subtracted from gross income as long as these payments are reasonable and the employees receive these payments in exchange for their services. The IRS is extremely strict if a business owner is attempting to pull a scam and pay himself, a friend, or a relative a large sum of unearned money in exchange for a tax deduction.

Vacation pay—This is a deductible expense because it is a type of salary. Businesses using the accrual method of accounting cannot deduct this expense in the tax year before it was actually paid unless this vacation pay liability was incurred in one tax year and paid no later than two and a half months into the next tax year.

Fines and penalties—These generally are not tax-deductible because these payments are meant to serve as punishment and as a deterrent for wrongdoing. Settlement costs, on the other hand, are routinely written off as a normal cost of doing business unless tax-deductibility is directly prohibited (e.g., occasionally a Department of Justice or federal agency settlement with a business expressly forbids writing off on taxes the cost of the settlement).

Bonuses and gifts—Bonuses may be deducted by employers if they are given as additional payment for employee services and not as employee gifts. When cash or similar payments (e.g., gift certificates) are presented to employees, they are considered additions to an employee's salary and the employer must withhold taxes. For noncash items given to an employee and of a nominal value (e.g., a cake, an inexpensive watch, company pens and pencils), the gift may be excluded from the employee's income and thus is not taxable.

Meals—An employer may deduct some employee meals that it provides if these expenses are a reasonable part of doing business. Usually, the employer can deduct from its income only 50% of the meals' cost. As for the employees, the meals' value is excluded from their taxable income if the meals are furnished at the employer's premises and for the employer's own convenience.

Lodging—The cost of lodging employees on the business premises can be deducted from the employer's income if that cost is a reasonable part of doing business. Moreover, if the employee must live at the place of employment as a condition of employment and for the employer's convenience, then the lodging can be excluded from employee income.

(If employees may choose between receiving more pay or having employer-paid meals and/or lodging, the employer must treat meals and lodging as an economic value to be included in the employee's taxable income.)

Fringe benefits—Various fringe benefits may be excluded from taxes, but many deductions depend upon the type of business being run. Some examples of possible benefit deductions are health/dental insurance, group term life insurance, educational assistance programs, moving expenses, and qualified employee benefit plans, such as profit-sharing plans, stock bonus plans and money purchase pension plans. These benefits are tax deductible to the company, yet not taxed to the employee. Some problems with these benefits are that new small companies probably cannot afford to furnish these plans, and the IRS is strict with plans that disproportionately favor the business owners and other top-paid employees. If the IRS finds that a company fringe-benefit plan is thus inequitable, then the favored employees may have to treat those benefits as taxable income and the company will be unable to deduct from its income the cost of these benefits; there may also be fines or other penalties.

KNOW THE CONCEPTS

DO YOU KNOW THE BASICS?

1. Name two functions of the IRS.
2. What are two important taxes for purposes of raising state and local government revenues?
3. Until the end of a full tax year (e.g., for a calendar year, from January 1, 2010 through December 31, 2010), businesses can keep for their own use the tax money withheld from their employees' paychecks. *True* or *False?*
4. What penalty may the employer incur for failing to respond to a past due notice about taxes owed by an employee?
5. Which method of accounting for income and expenses is more complicated, the cash method or the accrual method?

TERMS FOR STUDY

accrual method of accounting
adjusted gross income
calendar year
cash method of accounting
Circular E
deductions
estate tax
fiscal year
Form 1099-MISC
gift tax
income taxes
independent contractor
inheritance taxes
Internal Revenue Service
marginal tax rate

payroll service
payroll taxes
progressive income tax
proportional income tax
Schedule SE form
self-employment taxes
Sixteenth Amendment
statutory employees
taxable income
tax bracket
tax credits
W-2 form
W-4 form
W-9 form

PRACTICAL APPLICATION

1. Tamiko Taxpayer has a total annual income of $102,000 and an adjusted gross income of $90,000. Assume that her exempted income, based on four dependents, is $15,000. Her home mortgage interest, charitable contributions, local property taxes, and other deductible expenses total $17,000. Her tax credits add up to $1,400.

   Assume that there is a progressive income tax of 15% on the first $30,000 and 30% on amounts above that.

   (a) What is Taxpayer's taxable income?
   (b) What is her marginal tax rate?
   (c) What is Taxpayer's tax bracket?
   (d) How much income tax must she pay?

2. Emmet Employer hires a number of young people to be summer camp counselors and to live and eat at Emmet's camp. Name at least five items related to these counselors that Emmet may deduct as business expenses.

ANSWERS

KNOW THE CONCEPTS

1. Providing tax information and other assistance; enforcing federal tax laws against persons who disobey or ignore those laws.

2. Property taxes and retail sales taxes. Also, most states and some local governments collect income taxes.

3. False. Businesses must periodically deposit in a financial institution the employees' withheld taxes. Generally, these deposits must be made on a monthly or bi-weekly basis. By using a payroll service or handling the withholding on their own (instead of using a bank), employers possibly gain up to about a month in which they are withholding employees' taxes but do not yet have to deposit that money. Thus, for a short period, the employer has use of the tax money (e.g., earning interest on it), but that is a far cry from being able to use it for a full year.

4. Liability to the IRS for the amount that the employer failed to withhold as payment of the employee's back taxes.

5. The accrual method is more complicated. Rather than the cash method's focus, in most instances, on simply when actual payments were made or received, the accrual method calls for the often more nuanced assessment of when income was earned or liabilities incurred.

PRACTICAL APPLICATION

1. (a) $58,000 ($90,000 – $15,000 – $17,000).
   (b) 30%.
   (c) same as (b)—30%.
   (d) ($30,000 × 15%) + ($28,000 × 30%) – tax credits = $4,500 + $8,400 – $1,400 = $11,500.

2. Each counselor's salary or wages or other cash payments, any non-cash bonuses or gifts of more than a nominal value, 50% of the cost of meals provided to counselors, the value of free lodging provided to every counselor, and any of a number of fringe benefits if furnished to counselors (e.g., health/dental insurance, education assistance programs, moving expenses, vacation pay, and stock bonus plans).

28
INTERNATIONAL LAW

KEY TERMS

UN Convention on Contracts for the International Sale of Goods (CISG)
law governing sales contracts for goods (not services or warranty
work) between businesses from two different signatory nations, unless
the parties' contract excludes CISG provisions

international law law governing relations between nations, as well as all
business or other activities—public or private—conducted beyond the
boundaries of a single nation; derived from treaties, texts, past court
cases, statutes, customs, and all other sources used in national law

INTERNATIONAL LAW AND U.S. LAW

To understand international law concepts, it is helpful to consider the
world's different types of legal systems. The oldest and most influential is the Roman-Germanic legal system, commonly called **Civil Law**.
Civil Law is only the law contained in codes and accompanying statutes
(i.e., the law of persons, family law, property law, succession law, the
law of obligations, commercial law, labor law, and criminal law). The
Anglo-American legal system of **common law** (discussed in Chapter
1) is based on court decisions, or precedent, rather than on formal
codes. There are other approaches, such as the Islamic legal system (the
Shari'a). It comes from these sources, in order of importance: (1) the
Koran, (2) the decisions and sayings of the Prophet Mohammed, (3) the
writings of Islamic scholars who developed rules by analogy from the
principles established in the *Koran,* and (4) the consensus of the legal
community.

International law is derived from treaties, texts, court cases, statutes,
custom, and all other sources used in national law. It is recognized in
U.S. courts as a part of the common law or as an outside body of legal
doctrines that common law courts will enforce.

Cultural differences play a large role, then, in understanding international law. For example, in the United States, a business contract is likely to include language for every contingency that the parties or their lawyers consider remotely possible. The written agreement is intended to be the expression of everything to which the parties agreed, and anything the parties left out the law usually assumes was intentionally omitted. In Germany or France, by contrast, contracts do not need to include all of the terms about which the parties agree. If there are standard practices in an industry, the parties are expected to know and obey those practices; referring to them in the written agreement is usually viewed as unnecessary, and in fact, redundant, since these practices are already implicit to the contract. In Japan it is less likely that a written agreement even exists. Those contracts that are put in writing often are less extensively delineated than in France, Germany, or the United States. Instead, the focal point—rather than detailed descriptions (U.S.), well-known business custom (Germany), or very flexible proof of oral commercial agreements (France)—is the relationship between the contracting parties. Each side may tend to expect that the other party will accommodate needed alterations to their contract as conditions change. The parties' ongoing relationship—both sides' profiting—is often a fundamental, albeit unwritten concern in reaching and then continuing to carry out the terms of a contract. So, although the formal law may not be dramatically different in these three nations, the way it is implemented in the field of contract law (both by businesses and ultimately the courts) may be quite distinct.

Courts usually recognize another nation's sovereign immunity; this recognition leads to courtesy and judicial restraint (comity) toward another nation's sovereign immunity. However, with the Foreign Sovereign Immunities Act (1976), Congress provided that another country is not protected from suits in the United States that are based on the other country's: (1) commercial activities pursued in the United States; (2) actions in the United States related to a commercial activity pursued elsewhere; or (3) commercial activities performed outside the United States but directly affecting the United States and/or its residents. Some examples of foreign nations' commercial (unprotected) activities are contracts to buy equipment or construct a building, selling or leasing of services, borrowing of money, and investing in the securities of a U.S. corporation.

As a basic principle of law, and certainly as a practical matter, international law controls nations only with the consent of those nations. The **"general consent"** of the international community can be found in the decisions of the International Court of Justice, in resolutions passed

> by the General Assembly of the United Nations, in "law-making" multilateral treaties, in the conclusions of international conferences, and in the conduct and practices of states in their dealings between themselves. **"Particular consent"** between two nations can be found in bilateral treaties (where only two countries are parties). Sometimes, when a provision is repeated over and over in bilateral treaties, courts and law writers will regard the provision as having the general consent of the international community.

Federal courts have exclusive jurisdiction over cases involving foreign officials or admiralty (maritime) law. Also, most other "international" cases can go to U.S. District Court under diversity jurisdiction. (For more on diversity jurisdiction, see Chapter 3.) Lastly, note that treaties are fundamental federal law, superior to all state laws and antecedent federal statutes.

TREATIES AND BUSINESS

The dominant forms of national law regulating international business are treaties. **Bilateral treaties,** which are agreements between two countries, govern how other countries do business in the host countries. They also determine how income derived in one country and remitted to an affiliate in the other country is taxed. Sometimes a national law, although not a treaty, can govern activities outside that nation. One example would be U.S. antitrust statutes, which have been invoked by American governing authorities and private corporations against the practices of foreign businesses, *operating in their own countries,* because these businesses' allegedly anticompetitive behavior has a strong (indeed, intended) impact on American markets.

NATIONAL LAW AND FOREIGN GOVERNMENTS

Both the **sovereign immunity doctrine** and the **act of state doctrine** are extremely important concepts.

The doctrine of **sovereign** or **state immunity** says that domestic courts (i.e., courts operating at a national, provincial, or local level, but not internationally based) must decline to hear cases against a foreign nation (sovereign) out of deference to the foreign nation's role as sovereign. Today, the more commonly accepted rule is one of restrictive sovereign immunity, whereby a state is immune from suits involving injuries that are the result of its governmental ("public") actions, but it is not immune when the injuries result from a purely commercial or nongovernmental activity. Public, thus protected, action includes: determining limitations on the use of the nation's natural resources; granting licenses to export a natural resource; and acts concerning diplomacy, governmental administration, and the armed forces.

The **act of state doctrine** also limits the jurisdiction of domestic courts exercising jurisdiction over foreign states. The rule holds that a domestic court will decline to exercise jurisdiction over a foreign state when (1) that state performed an act that was an expression of its sovereign powers, and (2) the act was done in its own territory.

TRADE

All countries regulate trade. A key U.S. statute mandating export licenses and placing controls on the outflow of valuable goods and technical data is the Export Administration Act (1979). Violations of the Bureau of Export Administration's regulations are subject to both civil and criminal penalties. As for facilitating exports, the Export Trading Company Act (1982) created a Department of Commerce "Office of Export Trade" to promote exports, and the act enables applicants to seek antitrust immunity for their export activities. Two later Acts, in 1984 and 1988, let American *foreign sales corporations* and *shared foreign sales corporations* take tax exemptions or other benefits related to their export income. Another law, the Foreign Corrupt Practices Act (FCPA) (1977) prohibits U.S. companies (the same ones covered by the Securities Exchange Act of 1934) from, in effect, bribing or trying to bribe foreign officials in order to obtain special contracts or other favors—e.g., influencing the awarding of new businesses or contracts or the retention of continuing business activity. (The FCPA does *not* prohibit "grease" payments to low-level clerks or other governmental workers that result in no special favors and are customary in that nation.) The FCPA also requires strict accounting standards and internal control procedures to avoid the hiding of improper payments. There are steep fines and imprisonment for violators.

There are numerous economic "unions" of nations, such as the European Union (EU), that encourage trade by providing a common geographical area, much larger than a single country, where the same or quite similar trade rules cover outside tariffs, trade within the union, and other economic matters (e.g., international movement of capital and labor). Also, there are many international organizations directly or indirectly involved in promoting and regulating trade, often focusing principally on the growth of national or regional economies. Two such entities are the World Bank and the International Monetary Fund.

Accounting for over 95% of world trade, the World Trade Organization (WTO) has over 160 nations (including the United States) as members and another 30 observer nations applying for membership. The WTO originated with the General Agreement on Tariffs and Trade (GATT). Via a series of regular meetings ("rounds") in the past several decades, GATT reduced tariffs and attempted to eliminate unfair trade practices, such as product dumping (a form of price discrimination) and subsidies. GATT also set forth methods for resolving, or at least containing, trade wars. The last GATT round, the Uruguay Round, led to GATT's replacement in 1995 by the WTO, which goes far beyond GATT's exclusive focus on goods to also concern itself with services, finances, intellectual property, and other matters. As GATT had lowered tariffs, nations increasingly were resorting to non-tariff barriers not covered by GATT. These barriers, which the WTO regime opposes, have included export/import quotas; strict, lengthy, confusing, and expensive import license requirements; and, once a product actually crosses borders, government practices that give domestic industries an advantage (e.g., tax regulations and rebates, favorable financing terms, governmental procurement policies).[1]

Perhaps the most fundamental principle of the WTO is that international trade should be conducted without discrimination. This principle is given concrete form in the **"national treatment"** rule (requiring a country to treat foreign products the same as its own domestic products once the foreign products are inside that border) and the **"most favored nation"** rule (MFN) (which requires nondiscrimination at a country's border). MFN basically requires each contracting party to apply its tariff rules equally to all other parties. This rule, however, contains several exceptions, including the use of measures to counter **dumping** and **subsidization,** and restrictions to protect public health, safety, welfare, and national security. Although duties, taxes, and other charges are not disallowed, GATT Article XI forbids the use of other "prohibitions or restrictions" on imports from member states, specifically "quotas, import or export licenses or other measures" intended to restrict imports.

There are also significant bilateral or regional trade pacts, such as the North American Free Trade Agreement that took effect in 1994. These pacts promote dispute resolution, trade barrier reduction, and uniform policies on imports. At the world level, the Organization for Economic Cooperation and Development (OECD) is a 30-nation organization

---

[1] Countervailing duties can be assessed if a foreign subsidy materially injures domestic industry, and if the countervailing duties do not exceed the amount of the challenged subsidy.

intended to coordinate the key economic policies of the major industrialized countries (Australia, Canada, Japan, Mexico, New Zealand, South Korea, Turkey, the United States, and 22 European nations). Also, note that trade occurs not just through direct exports or foreign agents/distributors; joint ventures, franchises, corporate subsidiaries, and licensing arrangements are among the other methods.

Two other key components in bolstering trade are (1) standardization in terms of quality control; and (2) the development of a common legal system for treating international commercial transactions.

The former is aided by ISO 9000, 9001, 9002, and 9003, a series of rules drawn up by the International Organization for Standardization, based in Geneva, Switzerland. That body is composed of industrial-standard-setting groups from about 130 countries. It sets, but does not enforce, international norms on internal procedures, controls, and documentation meant to ensure that a business obtaining ISO approval has high quality control and thus, presumably, high quality products. ISO certification is often a prerequisite to doing business in Europe, where it has become, in many industries, a recognized framework for showing customers how one tests products, trains employees, corrects defects, and keeps records. The certification is now increasingly sought by American and other non-European businesses and is increasingly found in American bidding processes and contract forms.

A large step in the direction of uniform sales law is the United Nations Convention on Contracts for the International Sale of Goods (CISG). Nearly ninety nations, accounting for most of the world's trade, are signatories to CISG, which adapts many principles from UCC Article 2. CISG governs sales contracts for goods (not services or warranty work) between businesses from two different signatory nations, unless the parties' contract excludes CISG provisions. The CISG, therefore, supersedes conflicting national law, including the UCC, concerning sales of goods (but not product liability laws). A number of CISG provisions are discussed in earlier chapters on contract law.

IMMIGRATION

The **Immigration Reform and Control Act of 1986** (IRCA), as amended, is meant to discourage aliens from illegally entering the United States by, among other things, eliminating job opportunities. Employers with actual knowledge that an employee is unauthorized to work in the United States may be fined and, in the case of repeated offenses, even imprisoned. Even if illegal aliens work for a particular business, that employer is shielded from IRCA penalties if it complied with IRCA requirements to verify each new employee's status as either a U.S. citizen or a legal alien authorized to work in this country.

IRCA has no effect on **business visas,** which may be obtained by aliens investing in the United States, working at multinational businesses, performing seasonal work, or qualifying professionals of "distinguished merit and ability."

REGULATION AND NATIONALIZATION

Host nations almost always apply their own unfair competition rules, product liability laws, sharp practices principles,[2] securities regulation,[3] labor and employment laws, and tax and accounting standards to foreign multinational enterprises operating within their territory. The focus of host nation regulation is on making the foreign parent responsible for the conduct of the local subsidiary. This generally leads a host nation's administrative regulators or courts to investigate three issues: (1) has a foreign company consented to the host nation's jurisdiction, (2) is a local firm part of a common enterprise with a foreign firm, and (3) can the independent corporate status of a subsidiary be ignored in order to impose liability on its parent (piercing the corporate veil, discussed on pages 360–361).

Besides the regulation of foreign-based businesses under the same laws as for domestic companies, there are national laws specifically focused on, and restricting, foreign business. For example, international investors seeking to set up a foreign operation may be limited in the kinds of business forms they are allowed to use. Most nations generally prefer that foreigners limit themselves to businesses which (1) have local participation, and (2) fully disclose their activities to the public. Foreign investment laws frequently forbid or limit the percentage of equity that foreigners may own in local businesses. Exceptions sometimes are granted to try to attract capital for selected industries.

Foreign investment is also commonly restricted to only some economic sectors. Regulations typically (1) reserve certain sectors of the economy exclusively to the national government or its citizens, (2) permit a limited percentage of foreign capital participation in some sectors, and/or (3) define certain sectors in which full or majority foreign ownership is allowed or encouraged. Examples of industries often closed to for-

---

[2] Unconscionable contract formation and performance practices (e.g., fraud).

[3] The International Securities Enforcement Cooperation Act of 1990 encourages the SEC to cooperate with other nations' securities regulators. The SEC and many foreign regulators have reached Memoranda of Understanding to facilitate investigation and enforcement of cross-border securities violations.

eign investors are: public utilities and vital or "strategic" industries (e.g., industries related to defense production, agriculture, communications, and domestic transportation).

Occasionally, a firm with operations overseas faces nationalization, which involves changing a private (typically foreign) business into a government-owned business. The nationalizing country, almost always a developing nation, considers this action to be legal. However, if the nation does not have a proper purpose or does not pay just compensation, then nationalization is termed "confiscation" (illegal), not "expropriation" (legal). Of course, the nationalized firm's only real hope for redress may be from insurance (e.g., if it used the Overseas Private Investment Corporation to make the now-nationalized investment).

INTERNATIONAL DISPUTE RESOLUTION

There is no guaranteed technique for resolving international disputes peacefully. For instance, the effectiveness of a U.N. agency, the International Court of Justice, depends on the consent and cooperation of the countries involved. (Since only nations may appear before this court, an aggrieved private business must get its government to espouse its claim.) Also, nations may refuse to enforce a foreign judgment (e.g., one by a U.S. federal or state court). Therefore, businesses often prefer arbitration to appearing before an international tribunal or a national court.

The United States and many other countries provide procedures whereby courts can enforce arbitration decisions. International business contracts increasingly include clauses that require arbitration and state where it will occur, as well as what substantive law will apply. The U.N. and many nations' courts almost routinely enforce contracts' arbitration clauses and arbitrators' decisions. Almost all major trading countries, 156 nations in all, have signed the United Nations Convention on the Recognition and Enforcement of Foreign Arbitral Awards.

KNOW THE CONCEPTS

DO YOU KNOW THE BASICS?

1. Name the major sources of international business law.
2. State two legal doctrines courts may invoke in declining to review the actions of a foreign government.
3. What is the exception to the sovereign immunity doctrine?
4. Name two purposes of the Export Trading Company Act.
5. Name three types of non-tariff barriers.
6. State at least three organizational formats for doing business abroad.
7. What did GATT accomplish?
8. Will an employer be punished under the Immigration Reform and Control Act of 1986 (IRCA), even if he honestly does not know that his employee is an illegal alien?

TERMS FOR STUDY

act of state doctrine
bilateral treaties
business visas
CISG
Civil Law
comity
common law
confiscation
European Union
Export Trading Company Act
expropriation
Foreign Corrupt Practices Act
Foreign Sovereign Immunities Act
GATT
"general consent"
Immigration Reform and
 Control Act

International Court of Justice
ISO 9000
"most favored nation" rule
nationalization
"national treatment" rule
non-tariff barriers
Organization for Economic
 Cooperation and Development
"particular consent"
Shari'a
sovereign immunity doctrine
tariff
UN Convention on the Recognition
 and Enforcement of Foreign
 Arbitral Awards
World Trade Organization

PRACTICAL APPLICATION

1. Rob Resident and Mark Mower enter into a written contract in which Mark is to mow Rob's lawn. There is no written mention of the time of day the lawn is to be mowed, or the type of lawn mower to be used. In case of a dispute, how might the contract be interpreted in (1) a U.S. court, (2) a Japanese court, and a (3) German court? How much do customary practices and standards influence court interpretation in these countries?

2. The Juarez Company of Mexico and Vargas Industries of Brazil, sell each other their respective products. What aspect of these sales is most typically governed by a bilateral treaty between their countries?

3. Harry's Hats currently competes with Charlie's Caps in the American straw hat market. Sahara Straw, an Egypt-based company, currently exports straw to both companies for use in production. If Sahara sells straw to Harry's at one-half the price of what it sells to Charlie's (to help Harry's dominate the market), can U.S. antitrust law be applied to Sahara?

4. Suppose that American companies buy all of their rhubarb from companies in Guyana. The government of Guyana, in response to U.S.-imposed trade restrictions, is attempting to buy out all of the rhubarb-farming companies in Guyana in order to monopolize the rhubarb market and charge high prices to the U.S. companies. How would the sovereign immunity and act of state doctrines be applied in this situation? Would U.S. courts exercise jurisdiction over this action? What other options are there besides a lawsuit in the United States?

ANSWERS

KNOW THE CONCEPTS

1. Treaties, texts, court cases, statutes, custom, and all other sources used in national law.

2. The sovereign immunity doctrine (or restrictive sovereign immunity doctrine) and the act of state doctrine.

3. Purely commercial or nongovernmental activities.

4. Promoting trade; permitting applicants to obtain an antitrust exemption for their export activities.

5. Export/import quotas; strict, lengthy, confusing, and expensive import license requirements; and, once a product actually crosses borders, government practices that give domestic industries an advantage (e.g., tax regulations and rebates, favorable financing terms, governmental procurement policies).

6. Foreign agents/distributors, joint ventures, franchises, corporate subsidiaries, and licensing arrangements.

7. GATT reduced tariffs, provided methods for reducing trade wars, and led to the establishment of the World Trade Organization.

8. No, if he complied with IRCA requirements that he seek to verify each new employee's status as either a U.S. citizen or a legal alien authorized to work in this country.

PRACTICAL APPLICATION

1. U.S. court—According to the precise terms in the agreement. The written instrument is the supreme source of information about the parties' contract.

   Japanese court—Emphasizing the relationship between the contracting parties. Each side may expect that the other party will accommodate needed alterations to their contract, as conditions change.

   German court—Referring to the standard practices in that industry.

2. How income derived in one country and remitted to an affiliate in the other country is taxed.

3. Yes. This is a violation of the Robinson-Patman Act (and other antitrust laws); it is purposely engaged in anticompetitive behavior intended to impact American markets.

4. The Foreign Sovereign Immunities Act permits U.S. courts to review the commercial activities of foreign nations. Unless somehow Guyana's actions are "public" because they concern a natural resource (rhubarb), these actions should be subject to U.S. court jurisdiction because, although not occurring in the United States, the actions directly affect U.S. markets.

   Under the act of state doctrine, the U.S. courts should decline jurisdiction if they find that the Guyana government's land-buying program was an expression of its sovereign powers. (The other element, that the act was done in the sovereign's own territory, has been met.)

The U.S. government could challenge Guyana's actions before the World Trade Organization. Moreover, the U.S. government and/or affected American businesses might proceed to litigate or arbitrate the matter outside of the United States (e.g., in Guyana's courts). Under the restrictive sovereign immunity approach followed now in most countries, Guyana would not be able to avoid having the case heard.

GLOSSARY

abandoned property personal property that the owner has voluntarily relinquished, as to both possession and any claim of title

abandonment surrendering control of property with the intention to relinquish all claims to it. This is a voluntary act; losing property is involuntary. When used in regard to duty, "abandonment" means repudiation.

abandonment (of a trademark) the failure to use a mark after acquiring legal protection may result in the loss of rights, and such loss is known as abandonment

abatement of nuisance removal or cessation of that which is causing a nuisance. Also, a suit seeking to terminate a nuisance.

ab initio (Latin) "from the beginning"

absolute privilege protection from liability for slander or libel; this privilege is given under certain circumstances regardless of the fact that the statements are false or maliciously made; it applies to judicial and legislative proceedings where defamatory statements were allegedly made

absorb to acquire or take in, as a merger

absque injuria without violation of a legal right

abstention to abstain from voting (not vote)

abstract in patent law, a concise paragraph found on the front page of an issued patent certificate that briefly describes the workings and features of the invention

abstract of title summary of the transactions by which property (generally, real estate) has changed hands over the years

abus de droit a doctrine, developed in French courts, modifying employment at will and protecting workers exercising their rights from wrongful discharge or other employer abuses

abuse of discretion failure to exercise reasonable, legal discretion. Referring to errors of law and plainly erroneous conclusions of fact, this is a standard that usually must be met in order to overturn decisions of administrative agencies and trial courts.

abuse of process the use of a court process (e.g., attachment, injunction) for a purpose for which it was not intended

abusive (wrongful) discharge a modification of the common law doctrine that "at-will" employees (those without a set term of employment) may be terminated for any reason. This tort occurs if a firing violates a clear mandate of public policy. Examples include firing an employee for refusing to break the law, for refusing to give up a statutory right, or for whistleblowing.

acceleration clause in a mortgage or a promissory note payable in installments, a provision that default in payment of a single installment makes the entire debt immediately payable

acceptance 1. for contracts: an assent to an offer in accordance with its terms 2. for commercial paper: the drawee's signed agreement to pay a draft upon presentment

acceptance of goods UCC §2-606 states that there are three ways a buyer can accept goods: 1. by signifying to the seller that the goods are conforming or that he/she will accept them in spite of their nonconformity; 2. by failing to make an effective rejection; and 3. by doing an act inconsistent with the seller's ownership

acceptor the person accepting a draft and thus agreeing to be primarily responsible for its payment. *See also* **drawee.**

accession an addition to personal property by labor and/or materials. The property owner generally has the right to increased value, although compensation may be required for an accession added in good faith by another person.

accessory one who assists in or conceals the commission of a crime although not directly participating in the crime

accommodation an arrangement made as a favor to another (and without seeking to accomplish one's own purposes), usually involving a loan of money or commercial paper

accommodation indorser an instrument's signer who is not in the chain of title

accommodation paper a negotiable instrument in which an accommodation party has, in effect, agreed, usually without consideration, to share liability or potential liability on the instrument with another, accommodated party. *See also* **accommodation party.**

accommodation party a person who signs a negotiable instrument in some capacity (maker, drawer, indorser, acceptor) to lend his/her credit status to another party to the instrument, which then becomes accommodation paper

accord agreement to accept performance different from that in the original contract

accord and satisfaction an agreement by the parties to a contract to substitute a new performance in place of, and in satisfaction of, an existing obligation

account 1. for goods sold or leased or services rendered, a right to payment not evinced by an instrument or chattel paper 2. the concept of the individualized funds maintained by banks for each particular customer

account debtor a person obligated to pay on an account, contract right, chattel paper, or other intangible property right

accountant/client privilege law in about 20 states forbidding, in state court, testimony of an accountant against his/her client's wishes when the testimony concerns confidential communications; federal courts do not recognize this privilege

accounting equitable proceeding/remedy, e.g., in partnership law, whereby the court directs an investigation of all potentially relevant transactions and all records to ascertain the rights and responsibilities (e.g., amounts owed and owing) of the parties

account receivable a debt, owed to a business, that is not supported by negotiable paper (e.g., store charge accounts)

account stated an agreement on the final amount due between parties

accredited investors banks, insurance companies, and knowledgeable persons who may receive private sales offerings of securities under Regulation D of the Securities and Exchange Commission

accretion the gradual, natural accumulation of land (sediment) by, and next to, a river or other body of water; method by which a party on whose, or next to whose, real property this sediment (alluvium) accumulates, obtains title over the accumulation

acknowledgment an oath by one who executed a document that he or she executed and that is valid; also, a formal witnessing of an instrument, such as a deed, by a public officer (e.g., notary public or justice of the peace), with the signer declaring that the instrument's execution was voluntary

acquittal verdict or judgment that a criminal defendant has not been proven guilty beyond a reasonable doubt

act of God a natural event (e.g., hurricane, tidal wave) operating beyond the control of a party to a contract and excusing his/her performance; also, a tort defense, a type of superseding (intervening) cause

act of state doctrine the judicial doctrine that courts should refrain from inquiring into the validity of a foreign nation's actions within its own territory

action 1. a lawsuit 2. a legal proceeding commenced by the service of a summons or petition

action *ex contractu* a lawsuit arising out of the breach of a contract

action *ex delicto* a tort lawsuit; a lawsuit arising out of the violation of a duty created by positive law independent of contract

actionable behavior that could be or is the basis for a lawsuit or other legal claim

actions at law civil cases in which the plaintiff seeks money damages

acts laws passed by Congress or a state legislature

actual authority the express or implied authority of an agent to act for a principal

actual cause *see* **causation in fact**

actual malice 1. a statement made with the knowledge that it is false or with a reckless disregard for the truth 2. real and demonstrable evil intent

actus reus (Latin) "a wrongful act"; if it is combined with *mens rea* ("guilty mind"), the actor is deemed to be criminally liable

adeemed bequest bequest cancelled (*ademption*) because the specific item was sold, destroyed, or given away prior to the testator's death

adequate assurance of due performance in contract and sales law (UCC 2-609), when "reasonable grounds for insecurity" arise with respect to either party's performance, the other party may demand adequate assurance of due performance and, until he/she receives such assurance, may suspend any performance for which he/she has not already received the agreed return

adhesion contract a form of contract, usually unconscionable, between a merchant and consumer in which the stronger party (the merchant) dictates the terms, which are in a standard, printed-form contract that the consumer cannot alter

adjudication hearing or otherwise reviewing the claims of litigants and then rendering a judgment; an exercise of judicial power, just as legislation is an exercise of legislative power

adjuster one who settles claims for an insurer; also called a *claims adjuster*

ad litem during the pendency of a lawsuit or other proceeding

administrative agency a governmental body (e.g., a board, a commission) created by the federal, state, or local government in order to implement and administer particular legislation

administrative dissolution involuntary dissolution of a corporation that is ordered by the appropriate state official or board (e.g., the state secretary of state) because the corporation did not comply with state procedures or other corporate law requirements

administrative employee an employee whose primary duty consists of nonmanual work directly related either to management policies or to the general business operations of the employer or the employer's customers

administrative hearing a trial-like judicial proceeding, without a jury, in which an administrative agency rules on matters of the law that the agency is charged with enforcing

administrative law rules, regulations, orders, and decisions issued by administrative agencies. Generally, the term encompasses that body of law created and enforced by the agencies and, on occasion, reviewed by courts of law.

administrative law judge (ALJ) a government official who hears and decides administrative cases. Ordinarily, the ALJ's findings of fact and recommendations are presumed correct by higher administrative bodies and courts.

administrative process procedures governing an agency's exercise of administrative power, as well as a private party's right to advance rule-making proposals, present quasi-judicial claims or defenses, and otherwise take part in administrative proceedings

administrative regulation rules adopted by administrative agencies to implement and administer statutes. They have the force of law, absent successful challenge in the courts.

administrative search usually a governmental civil inspection of a residential or commercial building to determine compliance with fire, health, and other safety codes

administrator the person named by a probate court to administer the decedent's estate. (Generally, either there was no will or the will did not designate an executor.)

admiralty jurisdiction the U.S. Constitution assigns to the federal courts this jurisdiction over matters involving things done upon or relating to the sea, such as navigation, commerce and injuries, also called *maritime jurisdiction*

admissions, requests for *see* **requests for admissions**

ADR *see* **alternative dispute resolution**

ad valorem (according to value) tariff an importer must pay a percentage of the value of the imported merchandise

adversarial system legal system, found in the United States and some other countries, in which the parties initiate, develop, and present their cases. *Compare* **inquisitorial system.**

adverse impact a discriminatory employment practice that, while neutral on its face, unfavorably affects members of a protected group

adverse possession ownership of real property acquired by openly, continuously, and exclusively occupying the property without the owner's permission and over a period of time established by state statute (varies from about 5 to 30 years). Some states require that the adverse possessor have had some claim of title beforehand. Governmental property cannot be acquired by adverse possession.

advisory opinion a judicial ruling on the legality of a governmental action, whether already accomplished or merely contemplated, when there is no case or controversy for the court to decide. Some state courts may issue these opinions, but the federal courts have no such authority.

affectation doctrine doctrine whereby courts refuse to probe Congressional motives and uphold regulatory legislation enacted under the commerce clause, *if* the regulated activity affects, even in a minor way, interstate commerce

affiant the person who makes an affidavit

affidavit a voluntary, written statement of facts sworn to under penalty of perjury, usually before a notary public or another person authorized to administer oaths

affirm to uphold a lower court's judgment

affirmative action a policy that certain preferences will be given to minority or other protected class applicants seeking employment, school admissions, or other benefits or opportunities

affirmative covenant the borrower's promise to do certain things under the loan agreement (e.g., to do something on his/her land, such as building or maintaining a dam, bridge, wall, or irrigation or drainage ditch)

affirmative defense a defense based not merely on denying the facts asserted by the plaintiff, but also on asserting additional facts or legal theories on the defendant's behalf. Generally the defendant has the burden of proving his/her affirmative defenses.

affirmative disclosure administrative requirement, such as by the Federal Trade Commission, that an advertiser include certain information in its advertisement so that the ad is not deceptive (e.g., as a remedy for past deceptive ads or as a disclaimer that the product will not benefit all members of the public and specifying which members will not be helped)

after-acquired evidence evidence submitted in support of an affirmative defense in employment discrimination cases; it is evidence that, before the employer's allegedly discriminatory act, the employee engaged in misconduct sufficient to warrant dismissal had the employer known of that misconduct earlier

after-acquired property property that a debtor obtains after the security agreement is executed

after-acquired title if, when a grant deed is executed, the grantor does not have title to the real property referred to in the grant deed but subsequently acquires it, such after-acquired title is deemed automatically transferred to the grantee

agency a legal relationship whereby one person acts for another

agency by estoppel agency created when a person intentionally or negligently causes or allows a third person to believe that another is his/her agent

agency by ratification an agency formed when a principal approves or accepts the benefits of the actions of an otherwise unauthorized agent

agency coupled with an interest a special type of agency relationship that is created for the agent's benefit; the principal cannot revoke this type of agency

agency fees payments covering the cost of union activities on behalf of non-members whose work unit is represented by a union; the fees are supposed to support only collective bargaining expenses, not other costs such as political activities

agency shop a work place where the employee need not join the union but must pay agency fees

agent a person authorized to act for another person (the principal)

aggrieved one whose legal rights have been obstructed by the act of another is said to be aggrieved; also, one whose pecuniary interest is directly affected by a judgment, or whose property rights may be divested thereby, is considered an aggrieved party

agreement a meeting of the minds; the bargain reached by the parties

agreement not to compete *see* **restrictive covenant** (second definition)

aid and abet to help another commit a crime; the secondary violation in which the aider and abettor knows or is reckless about the other person's crime (the primary violation) and provides substantial assistance to the carrying out of that crime

aided-in-the-agency-relation doctrine an agency doctrine whereby the principal may be held vicariously liable for the wrongful acts of an agent acting outside his/her scope of authority; the liability is because the principal provided the instrumentality or created the circumstances that made it possible for the agent to commit the wrongful act

air bill a document of title serving for air transportation as a bill of lading does for marine or rail transportation

air rights the exclusive rights of a landowner to the air above his/her land, to that height over which control is reasonable

aleatory promise a contractual promise made conditional upon the occurrence or nonoccurrence of an uncertain or fortuitous event

alibi excuse of being somewhere else when a crime was committed

alienation voluntary, absolute transfer of title to, and possession of, real property from one person to another; owners in fee simple have a right to alienate

alien corporation a corporation formed under the laws of a foreign country

allegation an assertion of a claimed fact, particularly in a pleading

allonge a paper physically attached to, and made a part of, a negotiable instrument; this paper generally contains one or more additional indorsements

alter ego (Latin) "other self"; a person (e.g., an agent) who is legally the same as, and interchangeable with, another person (e.g., the principal)

alteration *see* **material alteration**

alternative dispute resolution (ADR) methods of dispute resolution, such as arbitration and mediation, that are different from the traditional judicial process (litigation)

ambient air under the Clean Air Act, the air outside (not in buildings)

amended and restated articles/certificate a document compiling all previous amendments to the articles/certificate of incorporation into one set of articles or certificate, perhaps with further amendments included in the restated articles/certificate

amended pleading a changed pleading, with added, altered, or removed allegations or legal arguments, that replaces a previous pleading of the same type (e.g., an amended complaint takes the place of the original complaint)

American Arbitration Association established in 1926, a private, nonprofit organization whose purpose is to foster improved techniques of arbitration law and to advance the study and use of arbitration for prompt, efficient settlement of disputes

amici (plural of **amicus**) persons or organizations that have no right to appear in a suit but are allowed to file briefs, ordinarily in appeals cases, as a friend of the court (Latin—*amicus curiae*)

amicus curiae **brief** (Latin) "friend of the court" brief, filed by a nonparty interested in the law that an appellate court may decide and develop in a particular case

amortize to liquidate a debt by means of installment provisions

anchor tenant a key tenant of a shopping center, such as a supermarket or department store

ancillary restraint a promise in restraint of trade made as part of an otherwise valid transaction, such as a sale of a business

annotation a critical or explanatory note, such as a brief description of a court opinion interpreting a statute

annual meeting meeting of shareholders or directors, to be held each year at a time that may be stated in the bylaws; ordinarily the meeting is required by statute, although the directors or shareholders are usually permitted to sign written consents for corporate undertakings (including the annual meeting) without actually holding a meeting

annul to deprive a judgment or judicial proceeding of all force and operation

annulment the voiding of a marriage

answer the defendant's response to the complaint; the answer usually admits or denies each of the various allegations in the complaint, and may include affirmative defenses

antecedent debt preexisting obligation

anticipatory breach (also called anticipatory repudiation) a contract breach occurring, even though the time for performance has not yet lapsed, if one party clearly states or implies that he/she cannot or will not perform the contract

Anti-Cybersquatting Consumer Protection Act a federal statute, enacted in 1999, imposing civil liability upon persons who "with bad faith intent to profit from the mark," register, traffic in, or use a domain name that, at the time of registration, is confusingly similar to a trademark or service mark or that dilutes a famous mark

antideficiency statute a statute prohibiting deficiency judgments for certain types of mortgages, such as those on residential property

antitrust law statutory, regulatory, and case law, the most important being federal, designed to prevent and correct unreasonable restraints on trade

apostille a simplified certification of notarized documents allowed by countries that belong to the Hague Convention. With nothing else required, the apostille entitles the document to recognition in the country of intended use.

apparent authority authority created by estoppel, that is, through conduct of a principal that causes a third party to believe that the agent has the authority to make contracts for the principal

appeal a request that a higher court review the decision of a lower court

appearance coming into court, whether in person or via a pleading; performed by the appearing party or the attorney

appellant the party that appeals a court decision

appellate jurisdiction the power of a court to hear appeals from other courts' decisions

appellee the party against whom an appeal is filed

appraisal rights the rights of shareholders (who object to certain corporate actions that may diminish the value of their stock) to compel the corporation to purchase their stock for its appraised value; sometimes called "dissenters' rights"

appropriation taking an item of tangible, personal property for one's own and/or using it for one's own interests. If wrongful, appropriation is a tort (e.g., conversion).

appropriation of a person's name or likeness unauthorized use of a person's name or likeness for financial gain

appurtenances passing as incident to the main thing. For example, an easement consisting of a right of way over one piece of land will pass another piece of land as being appurtenant to it.

appurtenant easement an easement that is attached (appurtenant) to a parcel of real estate (the dominant estate) and "runs with the land" (passes to successive owners of the dominant estate). The dominant estate holds a negative or affirmative easement in the adjoining servient estate. *See also* **easement.**

APR annual percentage rate

arbiter an arbitrator

arbitrary without rational basis, given the facts and/or law; such arbitrariness often must be proven to overturn decisions by juries, trial courts, or administrative bodies

arbitrary and capricious standard if an administrative agency has a choice between several courses of action, a reviewing court will ordinarily presume that the chosen course is valid unless the person challenging it shows that it lacks any rational basis

arbitrary marks real word(s) used in connection with a product or service whose ordinary meaning has nothing to do with the trademarked product (e.g., Apple for computers, Camel for cigarettes, and Shell for gasoline)

arbitration an out-of-court procedure in which a dispute is presented to one or more persons (arbitrators), whose decision is binding on the parties

arbitration clause the section in a contract that provides for arbitration if a dispute develops between the contracting parties. Such a clause either makes arbitration mandatory or permits either party to choose arbitration in lieu of a lawsuit.

arbitrator 1. a person selected by the parties to a dispute to make a decision based on evidence the parties submit 2. the neutral third party who conducts an arbitration to resolve a dispute

arguments statements (written and/or oral) to the court setting forth the opposing parties' positions on the facts and law. The oral arguments by the attorneys at the conclusion of a trial are called the "summation."

arraignment a hearing during which the accused is brought before a court, informed of the charges against him/her, and asked to enter a plea

arrears overdue payments

arrest to take into police custody

arson the act of willfully setting fire to and burning a building

articles/certificate of conversion document filed to convert an entity from one form of doing business to another

articles/certificate of correction document filed to make a nonsubstantive change, such as correcting a typographical error

articles/certificate of dissolution a resolution to cease a corporation's operation that is adopted by the corporation's board of directors and majority of shareholders

articles/certificate of merger or exchange required to be filed with a state's secretary of state or another state official in order to effect a merger or the exchange of shares of stock, this document primarily contains information about the merger/exchange plan and the shareholder approval of that plan

articles/certificate of revocation document requesting the revocation of the certificate of dissolution that the state issued

articles of incorporation a formal document that creates a corporation; a charter

articles of organization a formal document that creates a limited liability company

articles of partnership the written agreement by which a partnership is formed and its terms of operation stated; often called simply the "partnership agreement"

artificial person an entity, such as a corporation, that is treated in law as a person

artisan a skilled worker (e.g., a tailor, carpenter, or auto mechanic) in a trade requiring manual dexterity

artisan's lien a possessory lien held by persons who have added value to (repaired or improved) another person's personal property. The lienholder retains as security the repaired or improved property to ensure payment for his/her service.

artistic work a visual representation, such as an architectural plan, drawing, engraving, map, painting, photograph, or sculpture

"as is" a disclaimer of warranty by asserting that goods are sold "as is," without warranty

assault the intentional tort (or crime) of unjustifiably arousing in another individual the apprehension of immediate harmful or offensive contact with his/her body

assault and battery the compound crime or tort of (a) assault (e.g., threat), and (b) carrying out the threatened harmful or offensive contact (battery)

assessment statute a statute requiring state and local governments to consider, before imposing conditions on development, whether the restriction will constitute a taking (requiring compensation as a form of eminent domain) under federal or state constitutional law

assets all property—real, personal, tangible, intangible, legal, or equitable—that can be used to pay debts

assign to transfer legal rights from one person to another

assigned risk pool insurance plan for those who cannot get insurance from traditional sources

assignee the party to whom an assignment is made

assignment the transfer of legal rights from one party to another

assignment for the benefit of creditors *see* **assignment to a trustee**

assignment to a trustee an arrangement whereby (a) the debtor transfers to a trustee the title to some or most of the debtor's property, (b) the trustee sells or otherwise disposes of the property for cash and distributes the proceeds *pro rata* among the debtor's creditors, and (c) any creditor accepting such payment discharges the entire debt owed to him/her

assignor the party making an **assignment**

associate a lawyer who is a salaried member of the firm but not, at least yet, a partner

association a form of unincorporated entity that can be used for the transaction of business as well as for other, nonbusiness purposes

assumed business name statute a state law requiring that a certificate listing the names and addresses of persons conducting business under an assumed name or trade name be filed in the public records

assumpsit (Latin for "he undertook") a legal action to enforce or recover damages for a breach of contract; a term for a contract or, more particularly, an agreement or promise not under seal

assumption of risk the tort defense that a plaintiff who knowingly and voluntarily faces a dangerous situation may not recover for an injury arising out of the known risks inherent to that situation

attach if the three basic prerequisites of a security interest exist (agreement, value, collateral), the security interest becomes enforceable between the parties and is said to attach (i.e., become an attachment)

attachment 1. court ordered seizure of a debtor's property for payment of money owed to a creditor; may be accomplished before judgment (with property under the sheriff's control until a judgment is entered), in order to prevent depletion of assets pending the completion of a lawsuit 2. a method to make a security interest effective between the debtor and creditor

attempt the crime of intending to do a specific criminal act, and, in furtherance of that intent, taking action beyond mere preparation

attestation the act of witnessing the execution of a written instrument, at the request of the person executing the instrument, and subscribing to (signing) the instrument as a witness

attestation clause a clause in a will stating that the witnesses observed the signing of the will

attorney a representative or agent

attorney-at-law a legal representative; a person, trained in law, employed to represent others in lawsuits and other legal matters

attorney/client privilege privilege whereby disclosure of *confidential* communications solely between the attorney and the client cannot be compelled; the privilege can be waived by the client

attorney in fact a person named as a representative or agent in a power of attorney

attorney work-product doctrine a doctrine protecting from nonconsensual disclosure the information (e.g., notes on litigation strategy, observations about witnesses) that an attorney prepares in the course of his/her work

attractive nuisance an unreasonably dangerous condition that might result in injury to children who cannot learn or appreciate the danger. A landowner may thus be liable for physical injuries to child trespassers caused by artificial conditions on his/her land that 1. attracted those child trespassers and 2. were not adequately barred from the children's use (e.g., via a fence keeping children out of a swimming pool)

"at-will" employee an employee without a set term for employment (i.e., he/she can quit at any time, for any reason)

"at-will" employment doctrine the common law principle that an "at-will" employee can be fired at any time, for any reason; now qualified by modern anti-discrimination statutes, the doctrine of abusive (wrongful) discharge, and the like

auction with reserve unless expressly stated otherwise, an auction is this type, in which the seller retains the right to refuse the highest bid and withdraw the goods from sale

auction without reserve an auction in which the seller expressly waives his/her right to withdraw the goods from sale and must accept the highest bid

audit verification of a business entity's books and records, performed by an independent certified public accountant pursuant to federal securities laws, state laws, and stock exchange rules

authenticate 1. to sign 2. to execute or otherwise adopt a symbol, or encrypt or similarly process a record, with the present intent of the authenticating person to identify the persona and adopt or accept a record

author the creator of an artistic, dramatic, literary, or musical work

authoritative decision a court decision that must be followed regardless of its persuasive power by virtue of the relationship between the court that made the decision (e.g., a state supreme court) and the court to which the decision is cited (e.g., a lower court in the same state)

authority an agent's power to change the principal's legal status, duties, or rights

authorization card in a union organizing campaign, a card signed by the employee indicating that he/she has joined the union and wants it to be his/her collective bargaining representative

authorized stock the number of shares (common or preferred) that the charter permits the corporation to issue

automatic perfection security interest perfection by attachment

automatic stay in bankruptcy law, an order that stops or suspends all civil litigation against a debtor

avoidance in bankruptcy law, power invested in a trustee to rescind a debtor's obligations

avulsion sudden changing of course of a stream or river. Landowners retain the property lines as existed before the change; thus, distinct from property changes caused by accretion

award the decision of an arbitrator

back pay salary and employee benefits required to be paid to an employee upon finding the employee's discharge or layoff in violation of a contractual or statutory right (e.g., due to unlawful discrimination)

back-to-back letter of credit a buyer provides this letter of credit to his/her seller, who uses the letter in his/her favor to finance the seller's purchase of products or materials from his/her supplier

bad faith purposely misleading another person or otherwise acting dishonestly and/ or with ill will; willfully failing to act in accordance with statutory or contractual obligations. *Compare* **good faith.**

bail money or other security given to insure the appearance of a criminal defendant at all proceedings in his/her case; in return, the arrested person is freed ("out on bail") pending trial

bailee the party receiving a chattel for purposes of a bailment

bailee's lien bailee's right to hold bailed property until paid for work or services

bailment the transfer of possession, care, and/or control of a chattel to another person for a limited time for a special purpose

bailor the party transferring a chattel to another for purposes of a bailment

bait and switch a type of deceptive advertising in which the seller advertises the availability of a low-cost discounted item, but then pressures the buyer to purchase more expensive goods

balloon payment a large payment due at the end of the contract term

bank draft a check drawn by a bank either on its own funds within the bank or on funds it has on deposit at another bank

bankrupt the state or condition of one who is unable to pay his/her debts as they are, or become, due

bankruptcy a federal right guaranteed under Article I, Section 8, of the U.S. Constitution allowing the bankrupt person to reorganize or discharge debts

bankruptcy court a unit of the federal district court created to hear bankruptcy cases

bankruptcy estate virtually all of a debtor's existing assets, less exempt property

bankruptcy fraud a business crime and tort (fraud) involving the filing of false claims by creditors or debtors, fraudulent transfer or concealment of assets, or obtaining credit with the specific intent to avoid paying debts

bankruptcy proceeding a legal procedure for settling the debts of individuals or business entities unable to pay debts as they become due

bargain negotiated exchange

bargaining unit a group of employees that, as a unit, the labor union represents

barratry the habitual stirring up of quarrels and lawsuits; a single act does not constitute the offense

battery the intentional tort (or crime) of unjustifiable contact with someone else's body or anything connected to the body

bearer the person in possession of bearer paper

bearer instrument any instrument that is not payable to a specific person, including instruments payable to the bearer or to cash

bearer paper a negotiable instrument payable to "cash," indorsed in blank, or otherwise payable to "bearer," so that it can be negotiated merely by delivery (change in possession)

bench trial trial without a jury in which a judge decides the case

bench warrant a paper issued by the court from the bench to secure the arrest of a person who does not appear in court for a legal proceeding when previously ordered (e.g., by subpoena) to do so

beneficiary one who benefits from the actions of another; a person for whose benefit a trust, a will, a contractual promise, or an insurance policy is made. *See also* **creditor, donee, "incidental,"** and **third-party beneficiary.**

benefit corporation a special recent corporate format providing an expansive notion of corporate purposes, accountability, and transparency and thereby offering more possibilities for socially productive business enterprises; the B-corp is meant to earn profits but have mission statements as well, and it often includes community and ecological principles in its business practices

benefit of the bargain in contract law, after breach, the injured promisee receives the benefit of the bargain if the judicial relief awarded places him/her in as good a position as he/she would have gained if the contract had been performed as agreed

bequest via a will, a gift of personal property (verb form: bequeath). *See also* **devise.**

best interests of creditors test in a Chapter 11 bankruptcy case, dissenting creditors must be given a bundle of rights the current value of which is at least as great as the distribution they would receive through a Chapter 7 liquidation

bicameralism the state of being composed of two legislative chambers; in the United States, Congress consists of the House of Representatives and the Senate, and every state legislature other than Nebraska's (which is unicameral) likewise has two chambers

bilateral contract a contract created by an exchange of promises

bill of attainder legislation intended to single out an individual and/or punish him/her without benefit of trial; forbidden by the U.S. Constitution, Article I, Sections 9 and 10

bill of exchange a form of negotiable instrument, commonly called a "draft." *See also* **draft.**

bill of lading document evincing receipt of goods for shipment, issued by a person engaged in the business of transporting goods

Bill of Rights the first ten amendments to the U.S. Constitution, all ratified in 1791

bill of sale a written document by which one person assigns or transfers his/her right or interest in goods and chattels to another

binder written, temporary insurance policy until a formal policy is issued or the insurer decides not to issue insurance and notifies the insured that the binder is terminated

binding authority any source of law governing the issue to be decided and that a court must follow when deciding a case; binding authorities include constitutions, statutes, and regulations as well as court decisions that are controlling precedents within the jurisdiction

***Bivens* action** a lawsuit brought to redress a federal official's violation of a constitutional right; named for the U.S. Supreme Court case of *Bivens v. Six Unknown Named Agents of the Federal Bureau of Narcotics*, 403 U.S. 386 (1971), allowing federal officials to be sued in a manner similar to that set forth in federal civil rights statutes (42 U.S.C. §1983) for state officials who violate a person's constitutional rights under color of state law

blackmail crime in which a person illegally obtains money or other property by making threats; also called extortion

blanket policy insurance covering (1) property at more than one location and/or (2) two or more types of property

blank (general) indorsement indorsement of a negotiable instrument by a holder whose indorsement lacks any accompanying instruction and does not indicate (e.g., by indorsing "Pay to the order of X") that any other indorser is necessary; thus the instrument is bearer paper, freely negotiable merely through delivery (change in possession)

blue laws laws that prohibit the making of certain contracts or the operation of certain businesses on Sundays

blue sky laws state laws regulating the intrastate issuance and sale of securities

board of directors the managers/trustees of a corporation, elected by the shareholders

boilerplate standardized text that fits in a variety of documents and that, for proposed contracts, the drafting party usually views as relatively nonnegotiable

bona fide (Latin) "in good faith"; genuine

Bona Fide Occupational Qualification (BFOQ) concerning a Title VII employment discrimination complaint, a defense based on the qualifications that the employer requires in order for the employee to perform a job

bona fide purchaser someone who purchases for value without notice of any defects (e.g., in title)

bona fide seniority or merit system a system allowing differences in the terms, conditions, or privileges of employment based on a seniority or merit system, but the difference cannot result from an intent to discriminate; commonly, this system is the result of a union contract

bond a secured, long-term corporate debt security

bondholder the person or company that holds a certificate of debt issued by a company or government and payable on a specified date

booking in criminal law, an administrative procedure carried out after the suspect is arrested—the suspect's name, time of arrest, and alleged crime are registered (booked) in police records

book value the value of capital stock as calculated by the excess of assets over liabilities

bound tariffs the World Trade Organization principle holding that each time tariffs are reduced, they may not be lawfully raised again

bounty payment a reward (payment) given to a person or persons who perform a particular service, such as informing legal authorities of illegal actions

boycott a refusal to deal with, purchase goods from, or work for an employer; a conspiracy to inhibit the carrying on of business and to exert pressure on a party to a labor dispute; sometimes an antitrust or labor law violation

breach nonperformance of contractual obligations

breach of duty failure to perform a legal duty owed to another person

breach of trust a trustee's violation of his/her duty of loyalty or any other duty owed to the beneficiary; the breach renders the trustee liable to the beneficiary for any loss or depreciation in value of the trust property and for any profit resulting from the breach

break-up fee an amount agreed to in a merger agreement to be paid to a friendly suitor company if, through no fault of the friendly suitor company, the agreement with the target company is not consummated

bribery illegal payments to governmental officials or other persons for the purpose of receiving information, favorable treatment, or other assistance that the briber either is not entitled to receive or cannot lawfully receive by this method (e.g., kickbacks, payoffs)

brief a written argument supported by citations of court decisions, statutes, and/or other authorities

broker in securities law, a person who buys and sells stock as the agent for a customer but who does not retain for that purpose a supply of stock. *Compare* **dealer.**

bubble policy an Environmental Protection Agency rule permitting a business entity to expand and emit more pollution from one source of the plant if it reduces pollution from another source; the plant is said to be under an imaginary, overall bubble

bulk transfer a transfer made outside the ordinary course of the transferor's business and involving a substantial part (e.g., over half) of his/her equipment, supplies, and/or inventory.

burden of proof 1. the degree of proof necessary for a criminal conviction or for a successful civil suit. In a civil case, the plaintiff has a "preponderance of the evidence" burden of proof; his/her version of the facts must be considered, by the judge or jury, to be, at the very least, slightly more credible than the defendant's. In a criminal case, the prosecution must prove its case "beyond a reasonable doubt." 2. a party's obligation, when asserting a fact, to *come forward* with evidence supporting that fact

burglary breakage and entering (unlawful entry) into a building with the intent to commit a felony (e.g., larceny)

business agent in labor matters, a local union officer who is paid to administer the union's affairs, enroll new members, handle grievances, and negotiate with the employer

business entity a vehicle used to conduct business, such as a corporation, partnership, or joint venture

business judgment rule a principle of corporate law protecting directors and officers from liability for informed business decisions made in good faith and with due care, even though the decisions turned out to have been mistakes

business necessity justification for an otherwise prohibited employment practice based on proof that the practice is essential for safety and/or efficiency and that there is no reasonable alternative with lesser impact on legally protected interests (e.g., non-discrimination)

business tort the civil wrong of interference with the conduct of the plaintiff's business; it may be created by statute or regulation (e.g., federal securities fraud rules)

"but for" test *see* **causation in fact**

buy and sell agreement a contract, particularly appropriate for partnerships or closely held corporations, whereby the remaining owners or the entity are to buy the interest of a withdrawing or deceased owner

buyer a person who buys or contracts to buy goods

buyer in ordinary course of business a person who buys goods in good faith and without knowledge that the sale violates a third person's ownership rights or security interest in the goods; to qualify as such a sale, the seller, under UCC 1-201(9), must be regularly engaged in the business of selling goods of that kind (and pawnbrokers are excluded from this coverage)

bylaws a comprehensive set of rules providing for the organization and operation of a corporation. *Compare* **charter.**

C & F "cost and freight"—the lump sum price of the goods includes the cost of shipping and freight, but not insurance

call an option to buy a set number of shares at a set price within an agreed period of time; it is the opposite of a put

call a loan to terminate a loan

callable preferred preferred stock that a corporation may buy at its option

canceled stock stock that was issued but has been repurchased by the corporation and canceled

cancellation having the same effect as **termination**, except here a party puts an end to the contract because of the other party's breach; the canceling party retains any remedy for breach of the whole contract or for any unperformed duties (e.g., unpaid balances owed)

cancellation clause an insurance policy clause relevant to the insurer's right to cancel the policy

canon law church law; a body of law developed within a particular religious tradition

capacity a legally defined level of mental ability sufficient to reach an agreement. *See also* **insanity.**

capital; capital assets the total assets of a business; the owners' equity in a business; accumulated goods, possessions, and assets used for the production of profits and wealth

capital stock the class of shares that represent the owners' equity in the corporate business

capital surplus *see* **surplus**

capitalization investment in the corporation by shareholders

captive-audience speech during working hours, an employer's hosting of a speech or meeting that employees must attend; as with mass union rallies, these employer-sponsored gatherings are unfair labor practices if engaged in during the twenty-four-hour period before a union representation election

Carriage of Goods by Sea Act (COGSA) federal statute, enacted in 1936, governing the liability of ocean carriers for loss or damage to goods they carry

carrier person or business entity receiving consideration (e.g., money) for transporting passengers or goods. *See also* **common carrier.**

carrier's lien a carrier's legal right to hold a shipment until payment is made

carte blanche a signed blank instrument intended by the signer to be filled in and used by another person without restriction

cartel a combination of independent producers within an industry attempting to limit competition by acting together to fix prices, divide markets, or restrict entry into the market

case law decisions of the courts, together with their rationale; the whole law as declared by the courts through cases decided before them

case on point a previous case involving facts and issues similar to the case presently before the court

cashier's check a check drawn by a bank upon itself

casualty insurance coverage for property loss from causes other than fire or other elements

categorical imperative a concept developed by the philosopher Immanuel Kant as an ethical guideline for behavior. In deciding whether an action is right or wrong, or desirable or undesirable, a person should evaluate the action in terms of what would happen if everybody else in the same situation, or category, acted the same way.

causation in fact the relationship between an act or omission and an event (including alleged damages to the plaintiff) which would not have otherwise happened; that is, harm would not have occurred but for the defendant's wrongful conduct. *Compare* **proximate cause.**

cause of action grounds for bringing a lawsuit; the right to seek a remedy in a judicial proceeding. Prerequisites are the existence of a right and a violation of that right; facts that establish the two prerequisites constitute the cause of action.

caveat emptor (Latin) "Let the buyer beware"

caveat venditor (Latin) "Let the seller beware"

cease and desist order an administrative agency order or court order prohibiting a business from conducting activities that the agency or court has deemed illegal; an injunction

cert. denied an indication that a writ of certiorari was sought from, but denied by, a higher court (e.g., the Supreme Court)

certificate of deposit a type of negotiable instrument, issued by a financial institution as an acknowledgment that the institution has received the deposit of a specified sum of money; the institution promises to pay the depositor the sum of money deposited, plus interest at a stated rate, at a specified time in the future

certificate of authority certificate that a state official issues to a foreign corporation, limited partnership, limited liability company, or other entity granting it authority to do business in the state

certificate of formation the charter document for a limited liability company; also called articles of organization

certificate of good standing certificate issued by a state's secretary of state, commissioner of corporations, or taxing authority certifying that an entity has paid taxes assessed it through a certain date

certificate of incorporation the state's official authorization for a corporation to commence to do business

certificate of reinstatement certificate issued by a state's secretary of state or other state official that reinstates the existence of a dissolved corporation where it has been shown that dissolution was not called for or that the situation that did call for dissolution has been corrected

certificate of revocation certificate issued by a state's secretary of state or other state official revoking a certificate of dissolution. The existence of the corporation is deemed to have continued without interruption.

certificate of stock physical evidence of share ownership in a corporation

certificate of title official representation of ownership

certificated security a security for which a certificate has been issued

certification a check's acceptance by the drawee bank

certification mark a distinctive symbol, word, or design used with goods or services to certify specific characteristics

certified check a check marked as "accepted" by the drawee, thus certifying that there is money in the drawer's account to cover the check. Certification acts as a guarantee of payment and thus enhances the check's negotiability.

certified (certificated) stock a security (stock) for which a certificate has been issued

certiorari, **writ of** an appellate court's order that a lower court transmit to it for review the records of a case. The writ is requested by the appellant, and a grant or denial of the request is within the discretion of the higher court, as it is for the U.S. Supreme Court. (If the writ is denied, the appeal is denied.) The U.S. Supreme Court usually only grants the writ for cases involving novel federal issues or conflicting decisions among the federal circuit courts of appeal.

cestui que **trust** Latin term for the beneficiary under a trust

chain of title the succession of deeds, wills, and other instruments by which the ownership of real property can be traced back to the original patent or deed from a governmental authority to the first private owner

challenge for cause a party's request that a prospective juror not be one of the jurors because of his/her bias or for some other reason

champerty 1. purchase of an interest in a matter in dispute so as to take part in the litigation 2. an agreement to encourage a lawsuit in which one or more of the parties have no legitimate interest; specifically, an agreement to divide litigation proceeds between the owner of the litigated claim and a party unrelated to the lawsuit who supports or helps enforce the claim; sometimes deemed unlawful or at least unethical—in American jurisprudence the lawyer's contingency fee tends to be acceptable, whereas in other countries it may be deemed illegally champertous

chancellor the judge in a court of equity

chancery an equity court

changing-market-conditions defense in an antitrust price discrimination case, this defense is used by a business to show that a business is selling a product at a lower price because it was discontinuing a product or product line or was offering the item at fire or bankruptcy sale prices

changing order a court order that a creditor is entitled to receive, as satisfaction of a partner's debt owed to the creditor, the partner's interest in the partnership

charge to the jury at a trial, the judge's instructions to the jury concerning the law that applies to the facts of that case

charging order a judicial lien against a partner's interest in the partnership

charter a formal document that creates a corporation; articles of incorporation

chattel an item of personal property; a movable piece of property

chattel paper a document evincing both a monetary obligation and a security interest in, or lease of, specific goods [UCC 9-105(1) (b)]

check a special type of draft in which the drawee is always a bank and the instrument is payable on demand. *See also* **cashier's, certified, stale,** and **traveler's check.**

checkoff a system by which an employer deducts union dues from the employees' paychecks and transfers the funds to the union

checks and balances the governmental arrangement whereby powers of each governmental branch (executive, legislative, judiciary) check and/or balance powers of the other branches

choice-of-forum clause a contract clause that designates the location in which the case will be heard if there is a dispute

choice-of-language clause a contract clause designating the official language by which the contract will be interpreted if there is disagreement over the contract's terms

choice of law clause clause in a contract that states what nation's or state's laws will be applied in deciding a dispute involving that contract

chose in action right to sue on a debt or to get damages; an intangible personal property right for intangible things that can be claimed or enforced by court action, not by taking physical possession

chose in possession a property right in tangible things (i.e., physical objects, such as goods)

churning 1. a practice whereby insurance agents write new policies for customers and pay for the new policies with the cash value of existing policies 2. in securities law, an illegal practice in which the stockbroker excessively trades a customer's account to earn more commissions rather than to further the customer's interests

C.I.F. "cost, insurance, freight"—the lump sum price of the goods includes the cost of insuring and shipping the goods

circumstantial evidence indirect evidence, circumstances, or other secondary facts by which connected, principal facts may be rationally inferred; proof of a chain of facts and circumstances indicating the existence of a fact

citation 1. a reference indicating where a relied-upon legal authority (e.g., statute, court decision) can be found; the heading of a court case—contains the parties' names, the volume and page of the set of books (or electronic database/web site) where it can be found, the court, and the year of the decision 2. an order for a criminal defendant to appear in court and/or answer charges; often used in minor cases (e.g., alleged traffic offenses); analogous to a summons in a civil case

citizen-suit provision a right, specified in some statutes, for private citizens to sue in court to force statutory compliance; winning plaintiffs often are entitled to have the government reimburse their costs

civil action legal proceeding instituted to enforce a private, civil right or remedy, as distinguished from a criminal prosecution

Civil Law 1. codified law based on the Roman Code of Justinian; the basis of the legal system of most European countries and of nations that were once their colonies 2. (spelled without capital letters) noncriminal law

civil procedure the methods, procedures, and practices that govern the processing of a lawsuit from start to finish

civil rights freedoms and rights guaranteed by federal and state constitutions and the court decisions and statutes thereunder

claim 1. generally, an alleged right to payment 2. in bankruptcy and other debtor-creditor law, any right to payment or to receive any equitable remedy, such as specific performance of a contract 3. in negotiable instruments law, a right of payment asserted against a holder either by a prior holder or by a third party nonholder

class action a lawsuit in which a group of similarly situated persons, perhaps large in number, are represented by a few persons; the class is usually a plaintiff, but a defendant class is possible

classified board a board on which directors serve for specified terms, usually three years, with only a fraction of them up for reelection at any one time; also called a staggered board

clean bill of lading bill of lading that has no notations indicating defects or damage to the goods when they were received for transport

clearinghouse an association of banks or other payors that exchanges drafts (e.g., checks) drawn on association members, determines balances, and otherwise "clears" (settles) these drafts

clickwrap agreement a contract (software license) supposedly agreed to when a software purchaser scrolls through the license agreement on the computer screen or otherwise clicks on the "I Accept" (or "Okay") button on the screen. *Compare* **shrinkwrap license.**

cliff vesting a common vesting schedule that provides that if a person granted stock options leaves in the first year of employment, then he/she forfeits all rights to any stock

close corporation a stock corporation the shares of which are held by a relatively few persons, frequently members of a single family

closed shop an employment arrangement, outlawed by the Taft-Hartley Act (1947), requiring employees to belong to a union before being hired and to remain members throughout their employment

closely held corporation a corporation the stock of which is not freely circulated

closing the finalization of a sales transaction (e.g., real estate) in which title to the property passes from seller to buyer

closing argument a trial lawyer's final address to the jury or judge in which he/she summarizes the case, interprets the evidence, and attempts to persuade the jury or judge to reach a desired verdict

cloud on title an outstanding claim or other evidence on record that, if true, would adversely affect the title or other interests of the presumed owner of real property. A quiet title action may be brought by the presumed owner against the claimant(s) who have thus "clouded" the owner's title.

C.O.D. "collect on delivery," usually on a shipping contract

code 1. in Civil Law: a collection of laws into a single, organic whole 2. at common law: a collection of currently effective statutes enacted by legislative bodies, including Congress and state legislatures

codicil a change in, or addition to, a will, executed in the same formal manner as the will itself

collateral an interest in property given by a debtor to his/her creditor in order for the latter to secure payment of the debt. If the debt is paid, the creditor's interest in the property (collateral) generally ceases; if the debt is not paid, the creditor usually may sell or use the collateral to collect all or part of the debt.

collateral contract an express written contract made by a third person who guarantees to pay a debt or perform a duty to one party (the creditor) of an original contract if the original debtor is unable to do so

collateral estoppel doctrine that issues decided in one lawsuit are conclusively resolved for other lawsuits between the same parties

collateral installment note a negotiable instrument that is payable in installments, during which time the negotiable instrument's owner has a lien against the maker's personal property

collateral note a written promise to pay secured by the payee-creditor, with the maker-debtor creating a lien against his/her personal property

collateral promise undertaking to be secondarily liable (i.e., liable if the principal debtor does not perform)

collective bargaining negotiation between the employer's and employees' representatives

collective bargaining agreement a formal agreement between an employer and a labor union covering wages, hours, and conditions of employment secured by collective bargaining

collective bargaining unit a collective unit appropriate for bargaining with an employer on behalf of employees (i.e., a unit in which the employees share a community of interest—they have similar compensation, working conditions, and supervision, and they work under the same general policies)

collective entity doctrine under this doctrine, the custodian of records for a collective entity (e.g., a corporation) may not resist a subpoena for such records on the ground that the act or production will incriminate him or her

collective mark a distinctive mark used to indicate membership in an organization

collegia in Roman law, nonprofit membership clubs, ancestors of modern corporations

color of law action by someone or some entity, generally a government employee or agency, that purports to be authorized by law but which, in fact, is illegal (e.g., police brutality)

color of title, under to possess land under an instrument that purports to pass title but that is ineffective to operate as a conveyance

comaker a person who joins one or more other persons, also called comakers, in the making of a negotiable instrument; the person thus becomes primarily liable (jointly and severally) with the other comakers for the instrument's payment

coming and going rule legal doctrine that a principal usually is not liable for damages caused by its agents and employees while they are on their way to or from work

comity the recognition (deference, judicial restraint) that one nation gives to another nation's laws and judicial decrees

comment period after an administrative agency has published the notice of a proposed rule, the period of time during which private parties may comment in writing on the agency proposal in an effort to influence the policy; the agency is to take any comments received into consideration when drafting the final version of the regulation

commerce clause the authority granted to Congress by Article I, Section 8, of the U.S. Constitution to regulate foreign and interstate commerce

commercial impracticability an excuse for contractual nonperformance because of dramatic changes in circumstances or in the relative benefits and burdens of the contract to each party

commercial law the entire body of substantive law applicable to the rights and duties of persons engaged in commerce or mercantile pursuits

commercial paper in its broadest sense, documents used to facilitate the exchange of money or credit

commercial reasonableness a standard for judging a party's behavior (e.g., under a contract) according to the objective evaluation of reasonable persons familiar with the particular industry and the transaction at issue

commercial speech expressions, such as advertising, made by business; while protected under the Constitution's First Amendment, this type of speech can be restricted as to time, place, and manner in ways that political speech cannot

commercial unit by commercial custom or use, goods constituting a single item for sales purposes (e.g., a machine, a set of matching clothing, a defined quantity of, say, one bushel); to divide such a unit would harm its character or otherwise reduce its usefulness and marketplace value

commingling mixing the money or goods of another with one's own

commodities animals, animal products, foods, grains, metals, oil, and other articles of trade

common carrier a carrier that presents itself to the public as available (for hire) for transporting goods or passengers; it is subject to regulation as a public utility

common law law as developed and pronounced by the courts in deciding cases ("case law"), based on the common law of England and judicial precedent

common law liens liens created by judicial decision that allow creditors such as landlords, bailees, and innkeepers to retain possession of a debtor's property until the debt is paid

common stock the class of shares that participate in the management of a corporation and also own the corporate equity

community property a system of joint ownership in some western and southwestern states whereby almost all property acquired by the husband or wife during the marriage, except for gifts or inheritances, is owned equally by both spouses

company (Co.) one of the words that indicate a business is incorporated; this word usually cannot refer to a partnership or sole proprietorship

comparable worth doctrine a legal principle (not generally applied under existing federal law) that, if two different jobs (one held mainly by men; the other, by women) are essentially worth the same, there should not be a wage disparity or other difference in treatment between such comparably worthwhile jobs

comparative negligence a legal principle applied when the negligence of the plaintiff and the negligence of the defendant are concurrent causes of the plaintiff's damages; any damages awarded to the plaintiff are reduced by an amount proportionate to the degree of his/her fault. This rule for negligence cases has replaced the rule of contributory negligence in almost all states. *See also* **contributory negligence.**

compensatory damages the sum of money needed to compensate an injured party by making him/her "whole"

comp (compensatory) time extra paid vacation time granted, instead of extra pay, for overtime work

compensation statute a state statute that requires the government agency adopting a land use regulation to pay the landowner for the loss in property value if that regulation causes the property's value to decline beyond a certain percentage

complainant 1. a plaintiff; a person who files a complaint 2. in criminal cases, a person who instigates a prosecution by making charges of criminal conduct

complaint the initial pleading in a lawsuit, sometimes called a "declaration," "petition," or "bill of complaint"; it includes a statement of facts, the legal basis of the suit (cause of action), and a request for one or more remedies

complete integration in contract law, a writing intended by the parties to be a complete and exclusive statement of the terms of the agreement

composition and/or extension agreement an arrangement whereby a debtor and his/her creditors agree that each creditor will receive a certain percentage (less than 100%) of the amount owed (the composition) and/or extend the payment period (the extension); the debtor's full compliance discharges the entire debt

composition plan an agreement between an insolvent debtor and his/her creditors whereby the creditors agree to accept a sooner payment of less than the whole amount in satisfaction of the whole amount owed

composition of creditors *see* **composition and/or extension agreement**

compounding a crime the crime of accepting money or something else of value in return for not reporting or prosecuting another crime

compromise an agreement to settle a dispute without resort to litigation or to settle litigation in progress

compulsory counterclaim defendant's counterclaim arising out of the same transaction or occurrence that is the subject matter of the plaintiff's action. It is compulsory in that the defendant's failure to file it generally waives his/her right to bring the action at a later time.

compulsory license a grant to use some form of intellectual property through a means set up by the government in order to meet a public interest

computer crime a crime committed by using a computer (e.g., to steal information, embezzle, or defraud)

computer fraud the unauthorized access of a computer used by the federal government, by various types of financial institutions, or in interstate commerce with the intent to alter, damage, or destroy information or to prevent the authorized use of such computers

computer crime a crime committed by using a computer; e.g., to steal information, embezzle, or defraud

concealment fraudulent failure to disclose a material fact

concentration in antitrust law, a measure of the level of competition in a market—the percentage of market share (usually sales volume) that a firm controls in a product or geographic market

concerted activity the joint actions of employees working together for mutual aid and protection; the National Labor Relations Act protects workers (e.g., from dismissal) for engaging in certain such actions

conciliation mediation in which the parties select an *interested* third party to be the mediator

concurrent jurisdiction the simultaneous authority of two or more different courts (e.g., federal and state) to hear and decide a case

concurrent powers power of either Congress or the state legislature to make laws on the same subject matter

condition in the law of contracts, a fundamental requirement that must be met by one party before the other party has an obligation under a contract. *See also* **express and implied condition.**

condition concurrent a condition to be performed by both contracting parties simultaneously

condition precedent a condition that must be complied with, or occur, before the other contracting party becomes obligated

condition subsequent a condition the occurrence of which removes the obligation of one or both of the parties to the contract

conditional acceptance an offer's acceptance contingent upon the acceptance of an additional or different term

conditional contract obligations contingent upon a stated event

conditional indorsement an indorsement in which the indorser places a present or subsequent condition (other than failure of prior parties to pay) that must be met before the indorser is liable on the instrument

conditional payment the effect of a check or other instrument on the obligation for which it is given. This means the payee, by taking the instrument, surrenders the right to sue on the underlying debt until the instrument is due. If the instrument is not paid when due, the holder may sue on either the debt or the instrument.

conditional sale a contract for the sale of personal property by which the buyer gets possession but not title until the purchase price has been paid in full

conditional use permit a method of relief from the strict terms of a zoning ordinance, this permit provides for other uses of real property that are not permitted as a matter of right but for which a use permit must be obtained

condominium a form of real property featuring sole ownership of individual office or apartment units, with joint ownership (by all the sole owners) of the land and common areas

confession of judgment an admission of liability made by a creditor in the name of his/ her debtor without the formality of the usual adversarial court hearing; instruments frequently contain such admissions, which are to take effect if the debtor fails to pay in accordance with the terms of the instrument

confidentiality the expectation that disclosed information will not be divulged to third parties

confidentiality agreement an employment agreement with a clause barring the employee from disclosing certain information to third parties

confirmation in bankruptcy law, the court's approval of a reorganization

confirming bank a bank located in the seller's jurisdiction that makes a legal commitment to the seller that it will honor the terms of the letter of credit issued by the issuing bank in the buyer's jurisdiction

confiscation governmental seizure of private property and/or business without a proper purpose or just compensation; in international law, nationalization may be confiscation. *Compare* **expropriation.**

conflict of interest in agency law, an act of divided loyalty whereby the agent acts for him/herself rather than for the principal

conflict of laws a body of law concerning the determination of which law should be applied to the facts of a particular case when the laws of more than one state or nation may be applicable

confusion commingling of two or more owners' personal property so that each owner's property (or property interest, e.g., a precise amount of fungible goods) can no longer be determined or distinguished from the property as a whole

conglomerate merger a merger between two or more business entities that are in different industries; not a horizontal or a vertical merger

consanguinity kinship; blood relationship

conscious parallelism doctrine that two or more firms acting the same do not violate the Sherman Act (antitrust laws) if their actions are not concerted

consent the defense, to all torts and a few crimes, that the plaintiff agreed voluntarily to submit to the defendant's actions or proposals

consent order an order issued by an administrative law judge in which a party, without admitting guilt, agrees to stop an allegedly illegal practice

consent decree a judgment in which the parties, having agreed on the disposition of a case, have their agreement approved and recorded by the court

consequential damages damages that include lost profits and other indirect injury caused by a faulty performance or other breach of a contract if the principles of foreseeability and certainty are met

conservator *see* **trustee**

consideration any lawful alteration of responsibilities (any action, nonaction, or promise); one of the requirements for a valid contract

consignee the party receiving goods on consignment

consignment a delivery of goods, title remaining in the seller, for the buyer to sell. Risk of loss passes to the buyer

consignment intended as security a type of consignment creating a debtor-creditor relationship in which the bailee-consignee assumes initial responsibility for the purchase price of goods, whether or not he/she sells or otherwise disposes of them. The consignor retains title to the goods to secure payment for the goods in the consignee's possession.

consignor the party delivering goods on consignment

consolidation 1. combining two corporations by a procedure under which a third corporation purchases the stock of both corporations 2. a court action combining two or more lawsuits into a single lawsuit

consortium 1. the benefits that one person, especially a spouse, is entitled to receive from another, including companionship, cooperation, affection, aid, financial support, and—between spouses—sexual relations; a lawsuit for a loss of consortium may be brought by a spouse, child, parent, or other party to a close relationship against a defendant who has deprived the plaintiff of those relational benefits from the spouse, child, or whomever 2. a group of companies that associate together in an enterprise

conspicuous contract term or clause so written that a reasonable person against whom it is to operate ought to have noticed it

conspiracy an agreement between, or any combination of, two or more persons to commit an unlawful act

constatation (constat) in the inquisitorial approach found in many Civil Law nations such as France, an official report concerning factual situations, excluding opinions, produced by *huissiers* or other investigative magistrates acting per court orders or at the behest of private parties; such reports often effectively substitute for the discovery or testimony that might take place in U.S. litigation

constitution a nation's or state's supreme set of laws, outlining the basic organization, powers, and responsibilities of the government and guaranteeing certain specified rights to the people

construct validity a method of demonstrating that an employment selection device selects employees based on the characteristics required for the job in question

constructive the legal character or nature of a thing regardless of its actual character or nature; implied, inferred, or made out by legal interpretation

constructive abandonment the loss of a trademark's distinctiveness as the result of an owner's acts or inaction (e.g., by allowing a mark to lapse into genericness or by not adequately controlling persons licensed to use that mark)

constructive bailment a bailment imposed by law rather than agreement; for example, a person who finds lost property or receives misdelivered property may be a constructive bailee

constructive condition contractual condition that is neither express nor implied, but is imposed by law to meet the ends of justice

constructive discharge an employer-created work environment so difficult or distressing that a reasonable employee would quit

constructive eviction such material impairment by a landlord of the tenant's ability to enjoy the leased premises as to give the tenant a right to terminate the lease

constructive knowledge knowledge that is imputed, such as via these notions: 1. that what an agent knows, his/her principal knows; and 2. that all persons know whatever is publicly recorded

constructive notice knowledge of a fact, with the knowledge presumed or imputed by law, such as by recording an instrument, filing a document in court, or placing a legal advertisement in a newspaper or trade journal. Such "knowledge" is regardless of actual knowledge, which may never have been present or may have become forgotten.

constructive termination a situation in real estate tenancies, franchise relationships, or other commercial dealings where the "dominant" party (e.g., landlord or franchisor) creates an environment so difficult or distressing that the "subordinate" party (e.g., tenant or franchisee) chose to end that contract

constructive trust a trust imposed by law against a person who wrongfully obtained and/or retains property; this trust is intended to correct fraud or other misconduct

consumer credit credit that is extended to persons for personal, family, or household purposes

consumer expectation test in product liability law, the level of safe performance an ordinary consumer would expect from a product; in food cases, most courts apply this test rather than the foreign-natural test (a foreign substance test)

consumer goods goods bought or used for personal, family, or household use

consumer product tangible personal property normally used for family, household, or personal purposes

contempt of court showing disrespect toward the court; disobeying a court order

content validity a method of demonstrating that an employment selection device reflects the content of the job for which employees are being chosen

contingencies conditions in a contract that may void the contract if not met

contingency clause a clause stating that a contract is discharged and performance excused for circumstances beyond the parties' control

contingency fee a charge permitted in some civil cases (e.g., negligence lawsuits) whereby the attorney's fee is dependent on successful outcome of the case; generally, the fee is a percentage of the client's recovery

continuance adjournment of a lawsuit from one day to another

continuation agreement in partnership law, an agreement through which partners may restrict or deny the liquidation right generally arising upon a partner's dissociation

contra bonos mores "contrary to good morals"—such contracts are voidable; offensive to the conscience and to a sense of justice

contract a legally enforceable agreement, express or implied. *See also* **adhesion, bilateral, destination, executed, executory, express, implied, investment, option, output, quasi, requirements, shipment, unconscionable, unenforceable, unilateral, void,** and **voidable contract.**

contract bar rule a written labor contract bars a union representation election for up to three years or the life of the collective bargaining agreement, whichever is shorter (subject to the "open season" window, the third month remaining on the agreement, in which a rival union can offer a challenge to represent the employees)

contract carrier a carrier that transports goods or people under individual contracts for a limited number of customers

contracts clause constitutional provision (Article I, Section 10) that states cannot retroactively modify public and private contracts

contract remedies judicial relief available to an injured promisee when a contractual promise is not performed or is improperly performed

contribution the right of a defendant liable for a loss to obtain a sharing of expenses (e.g., payments to the plaintiff) by other persons also responsible for that loss

contributory copyright infringement inducing, causing, or materially contributing to the infringing conduct of another with knowledge of the infringing activity

contributory negligence an absolute defense to negligence by the defendant because the plaintiff's own negligence contributed to his/her injuries; replaced by the doctrine of comparative negligence in almost all states

contributory patent infringement knowingly selling an item that has one specific use that will result in the infringement of another's patent

controlling shareholder a shareholder who owns sufficient shares to outvote the other shareholders and thus to control the corporation

convention law adopted by an international organization that was created by a treaty

conversion an intentional tort involving unauthorized, unjustified exercise of control over another's personal property

convertible bond a bond that may be converted by its holder into other securities of a corporation, such as preferred or common stock

convertible stock stock that the corporation may convert from one class (preferred) into another class (common)

conveyance 1. an instrument (e.g., a deed or a long-term lease) by which title or other interests in real property are transferred from one person to another 2. any transfer of property or interests in property

cooling-off laws those laws that allow consumers a period of time, such as three days, in which to cancel door-to-door sales contracts or other agreements initiated by the other party, a business

cooperative 1. an association of individuals formed to carry out a common productive enterprise, the profits being shared in accordance with the capital or labor contributed by each individual or otherwise going to the members without gain to the cooperative itself; cooperatives may be for consumers, workers, labor unions, marketing or business purchasing, financial institutions, farmers, insurers, or others 2. a corporation that owns real estate, with each shareholder entitled to lease a portion of the real estate (usually an apartment)

copyright the exclusive right to print, sell, and exhibit written material, musical compositions, art works, photographs, movies, television programs, data systems, and other creations placed in a tangible, preserved medium of expression

core proceedings bankruptcy proceedings in which creditor claims, allegations of preferences, reorganization plans, and other matters are decided

corporate crime a crime committed by and thus chargeable to a corporation because of activities of its officers or other employees

corporate opportunity a business opportunity available to a corporation; an officer or director who takes personal advantage of a corporate opportunity violates his/her duty to the corporation

corporate social responsibility the concept that corporations can and should act ethically and be accountable to society for their actions

corporation 1. an artificial being created by operation of law, with an existence distinct from the individuals (shareholders) who are its "owners." *See also* **alien, benefit, close, closely held,** *de facto, de jure,* **domestic, dummy, federal, foreign, membership, parent, private, professional, public, quasi-public, shell,** and **S corporation** 2. a word that indicates a business is incorporated

corporation by estoppel when a third party, in all its transactions with an enterprise, acts as if it were doing business with a corporation, the third party may be prevented from claiming that the enterprise is not a corporation

correspondent bank a bank in which another bank has an account (and vice versa) for the purpose of facilitating fund transfers

cosigner a person who signs a document along with another person and (depending on state law) who may be equally liable for any debt associated with the document

cost-benefit analysis computing the costs of a certain activity and comparing them with the estimated value of the benefits from that activity

cost justification in antitrust law (Robinson-Patman Act) cases, a defense that one buyer was offered goods at a lower price than another buyer because of differences in the costs of selling and delivering to those two buyers

costs in litigation, an award to the winning party for expenses incurred (but usually excluding attorney's fees), to be paid by the losing party

counterclaim a reverse complaint—one by the defendant against the plaintiff; sometimes called a *cross complaint* or *countersuit*

counteroffer a cross offer by the offeree that has the effect of rejecting the original offer and proposing a new one

course of dealing the customary method of doing business between two parties; it is a requirement of the Uniform Commercial Code that the course of dealing of the parties be a factor in determining their contractual intent

course of performance the conduct between the parties in the implementation of a contract. This conduct is useful in determining the meaning of the contract and the intent of the parties.

court a unit of the judiciary; a governmental body intended to apply the law to controversies brought before it and to administer justice

covenant an agreement or promise to do or not to do something; an express or implied promise incidental to a deed or contract

covenant for further assurance a real estate seller's undertaking to do any further acts needed to perfect the buyer's title as the buyer may reasonably require

covenant not to compete *see* **restrictive covenant** (second definition)

covenant of (for) quiet enjoyment a grantor's, landlord's, or other landowner's express or implied promise that the grantee or tenant will neither be evicted nor be disturbed in his/her use and enjoyment of real property (e.g., by hostile claimants of title)

covenant running with the land a covenant that concerns the land itself and binds (or benefits) all subsequent owners of that land

covenantor a person who makes a covenant

cover to seek a substitute performance of a contract; when seller S breaches, "covering" permits buyer B to purchase goods which conform to the S-B agreement and charge S for any portion of the substituted goods' price exceeding the S-B agreement price

cramdown confirmation of a bankruptcy reorganization plan over the objections of one or more class of creditors. The plan must not discriminate unfairly against any creditors and must be fair and equitable.

crashworthiness doctrine legal principle that automobile makers must design cars not just to operate safely (and avoid crashes) but to minimize harm, when reasonably possible, if there is a crash

creator *see* **trustor**

creditor the party to whom a debtor owes money or another obligation

creditor beneficiary a person, not a party to a contract, who claims that he/she is owed the performance of the contract

creditors' committee a group of the larger unsecured creditors, with the group's representatives appearing at Bankruptcy Court hearings, participating in negotiation over the reorganization plan, and otherwise supporting or objecting to proposals

crime a public wrong, committed with intent or (in a few cases) by negligence, for which the law provides punishment or recompense to society

crimes *per se* certain crimes that either presuppose or do not require criminal intent so that the act alone constitutes a crime

criminal fraud fraudulent conduct that is a crime (e.g., larceny by fraud, filing false tax returns)

criminal intent *mens rea*; desired or virtually certain consequences of one's conduct

criminal law a body of substantive law governing and defining crimes and punishments for crimes

criterion-related validity a method of demonstrating that an employment selection device correlates with the knowledge and skills needed for successful job performance

cross-claim a claim filed against one or more parties on the same side of a lawsuit as is the claimant (e.g., by one defendant against another defendant)

cross collateralization the collateral for a loan is used to secure obligations under another loan

cross-complaint *see* **counterclaim**

crown jewel a valuable asset of the target corporation that the tender offeror especially wants to acquire in the tender offer

cumulative-to-the-extent-earned preference a dividend preference entitling preferred shareholders to carry forward and accumulate unpaid dividends to the extent that the corporation had earnings available to pay the dividends in the year or years in which the dividends were omitted

cumulative preferred stock preferred stock that receives dividends accumulated for years in which no dividends were declared or paid, to be paid before any dividend may be paid on the common shares; also called a *cumulative dividend preference*

cumulative voting in the election of directors, a voting procedure whereby a shareholder may accumulate his/her votes and distribute them among the candidates as he/she wishes. *Compare* **straight voting.**

cure seller's right, under UCC 2-508, to correct a defective performance rather than be liable for breach of contract

curtesy *see* **dowry**

currency transaction report (CTR) a report that federal law requires financial institutions to file 1. if they suspect criminal activity by a customer who is involved in a financial transaction of $1,000 or more or 2. when a single transaction of currency amounts to more than $10,000

custody concerning personal property, immediate charge and control of the property. Custody is not synonymous with possession or ownership; a person can have custody without owning or possessing.

custom a source of international law, it is a practice involving a consistent course of conduct over a considerable period, a recognition that the practice is consistent with or required by international law and general acquiescence in the practice by other countries

customer Under UCC Article 4, any person or entity (including another bank) having an account with a bank or for whom a bank has agreed to collect on instruments

cyber crime a crime that occurs online, in the virtual community of the Internet, as opposed to the physical world

cyber squatting Internet domain registration confusingly similar or identical to a protected trademark, with the person registering the domain name having no legitimate interest in that particular domain name and presumably registering it in bad faith

cyber tort a tort committed in cyberspace

cyberlaw an informal term used to refer to all laws governing electronic communications and transactions, particularly those conducted via the Internet

cy pres as near as (possible); equity rule for construing instruments, by which the party's intention is carried out *as near as* may be, when it would be impossible or illegal to give it literal effect

damages in general, compensation designed to make an injured party "whole"; in the law of contracts, the compensation due to the nonbreaching party to recover any financial loss or injury caused by a breach of contract. *See also* **compensatory, consequential, direct, exemplary, incidental, indirect, liquidated, nominal, punitive,** and **special damages.**

"danger invites rescue" doctrine legal principle that if attempted rescues are foreseeable, that rescuers injured while going to someone's rescue can recover their damages from the person(s) who caused the dangerous situation

d/b/a "doing business as"

dealer in securities law, a person engaged in the business of buying and selling securities for his/her account as a principal. *Compare* **broker.**

debenture an unsecured, long-term corporate debt security

debit card card that immediately transfers funds from user's bank account upon use

debt a sum of money due, or obligation owed

debt security a security issued as evidence of a corporate debt

debt subordination an agreement whereby one or more creditors of a common debtor agree to defer payment of their claims until another creditor of the same debtor is fully paid

debtor a person who owes someone (a creditor) money or another obligation

debtor in possession in Chapter 11 bankruptcy proceedings, a debtor who is allowed to continue in possession of the estate in bankruptcy (the business) and to continue business operations

debtor rehabilitation bankruptcy code provisions (Chapters 11 and 13) call for the debtor's rehabilitation and reorganization, rather than liquidation, with creditors looking to partial or complete satisfaction of their claims from the debtor's future earnings rather than the debtor's property

deceit *see* **fraud**

deceptive advertising advertising that misleads consumers, either by unjustified claims concerning a product's performance or by the omission of a material fact concerning the product's composition or performance

decertification removal of a union's certification as exclusive bargaining representative upon ascertainment of a loss of a majority favoring the union pursuant to an election requested by a petitioner

declaration *see* **complaint**

declaration by the inventor part of a patent application, it states that the inventor has reviewed the patent application and believes that he/she is the first inventor of the invention

declaratory judgment a court judgment that declares for the parties their rights and duties concerning a specific controversy

decree a judgment, particularly in an equity court

deed a publicly-recorded document by which title to property (usually real property) is transferred. *See also* **general warranty, quitclaim,** and **special warranty deed.**

deed of trust a document similar to a mortgage; when a debtor's purchase of real property is financed (i.e., he/she obtains a loan), a deed of trust conveys title to, but not possession of, the real property to a trustee (someone other than the debtor or creditor), who holds title as security for the debt

de facto in fact, as distinguished from "de jure"

de facto **corporation** a corporation that has not been properly formed, even though the incorporators may have made a good-faith effort to do so. *Compare* *de jure* **corporation.**

defalcation a broad concept for fraudulent and nonfraudulent defaults, including embezzlement, misappropriation, or the failure to meet an obligation

defamation a tort; a false communication, oral (slander) or written or otherwise recorded (libel), by the defendant to a third person that harms the plaintiff's reputation

default 1. failure to perform a duty as promised in a contract, negotiable instrument, deed, loan, or other transaction 2. for loans, an event triggering the lender's right to terminate the loan, accelerate the repayment obligations, and, if the loan is secured, take possession of the property securing the loan

default judgment judgment for the plaintiff because the defendant failed to respond to a summons or appear at trial. (Plaintiff's failure to appear may result in dismissal of the case.) *See also* **nonsuit.**

defect something wrong, inadequate, or improper in the manufacture, design, packaging, warning, or safety measures of a product

defendant the person against whom a criminal prosecution or civil action is filed

defense that which a defendant offers as a reason why the plaintiff should not recover what he/she seeks

deficiency judgment a judgment against the debtor (mortgagor) for the remaining amount if a creditor (mortgagee) is still owed money on a secured debt (mortgage) after the collateral (mortgaged property) has been sold and the proceeds applied toward payment of the debt

defined-benefit plan a pension plan ensuring eligible employees and their beneficiaries a specified regular (e.g., monthly) income for life

defined-contribution plan pension plan under which the employer contributes a fixed amount into a retirement account each year

definiteness in contract law, a requirement that an offer be sufficiently definite and explicit so that, if the offer is accepted, a court in a subsequent dispute has a reasonably certain basis upon which to determine the existence of a breach and to award an appropriate remedy

defraud to deprive a person of his/her rights or property by use of deceit (fraud, misrepresentation)

dehors outside of; disconnected with; unrelated to; beyond the scope of, such that, for example, a trial court could not consider a document because it was outside (dehors) the record

de jure by right, as distinguished from "de facto"; complying with the law in all respects

de jure corporation a corporation formed in accordance with all the requirements of the law. *Compare* **de facto corporation.**

Delaware corporation a corporation chartered in Delaware and subject to the laws of that state

Delaware Court of Chancery the trial court in Delaware that hears corporate law cases

del credere agency an agency in which the agent holds harmless the principal against the default of those with whom contracts are made

delegated authority in administrative law, powers delegated by the legislature to administrative agencies

delegatee the party to whom the duty has been transferred

delegation transfer of duties under a contract from one person to another

delegator the obligor who transferred his/her duty to another party (the delegatee)

delivery the actual or constructive (implied or inferred) transfer of goods or of an instrument from one person to another

demand a request by one person that another person perform an act (e.g., pay an instrument) the performance of which the first person is entitled to receive

demand paper an instrument payable on demand; a negotiable instrument that either (a) expressly states it is payable on demand, presentation, and/or sight, or (b) does not state a time for payment

de minimis part of the Latin phrase *de minimis non curat lex,* "the law does not concern itself with trifles"; thus, trifling, of no legal consequence; this equitable maxim is sometimes applied to exclude the recovery of nominal damages, such as for a breach of contract, when there was neither a disturbance of possessory rights nor any unlawful intent, and where all possible damage was expressly disproved

demurrage compensation for the delay of a ship or train, usually because of a failure to load or unload by the agreed time

demurrer a motion to dismiss; an initial pleading by the defendant alleging that the complaint fails to state a cause of action

de novo (Latin) "new"; a new proceeding without regard to prior legal actions

denial a defense claiming the plaintiff's claim is untrue

depeçage a choice-of-law doctrine under which the court is permitted to apply the laws of different states to different issues when more than one state has an interest in the outcome of a case

dependent covenants covenants made by two parties to a deed or agreement such that the thing promised to be done on each part enters into the whole consideration for the promise on the part of the other, or such covenants as are concurrent and to be performed simultaneously; neither party to this covenant can maintain an action against the other without proving performance on his part

deposition pretrial discovery involving sworn testimony by a party or any other witness, usually recorded and transcribed by a court reporter or notary public; testimony; ordinarily taken in response to oral questions from the parties' attorneys

depository bank the bank where the holder or payee has an account

depreciation a decline in an asset's value because of use, wear, or obsolescence

derivative suit a suit brought by one or more shareholders on behalf of the corporation and for its benefit, claiming waste of corporate assets by directors or corporate principals

descent succession to ownership of an estate by inheritance or any act of law, *not* by purchase

design patent a patent that protects any novel, original, and ornamental design for an article of manufacture

destination bill of lading a bill of lading that is issued at the destination (rather than at the place of shipment) or at any other designated place to ensure that the bill of lading will be available at the destination in advance of the actual arrival of the goods

destination contract a contract that passes the risk of loss to the buyer when the goods are delivered to the specified destination

detinue a common law action, now seldom used, to recover specific personal property unlawfully taken by another person

detriment in the law of contracts, forbearance serving as consideration or value

detrimental reliance the concept that an offeree has rights against the offeror because the offeree changed his/her position due to justifiable reliance on an offer

devise to bequeath property, usually real property, by a will

devisee person who receives devised property

dicta short for the Latin words *obiter dicta*, "statements in passing"; statements in a judicial opinion that are unnecessary for the decision of the case; dicta are not binding, nor do they carry the force of precedent, as do arguments intrinsic to a judicial holding (singular form: *dictum*)

direct damages damages immediately and directly caused by breach of contract

direct effects doctrine the European Court of Justice doctrine that provides that when a European Union (EU) law or treaty provision is very clear, it becomes immediately effective as law in all EU nations

direct evidence testimony from a witness, typically an eyewitness, asserting that he/she has actual knowledge of a fact

direct liability direct responsibility of a principal for torts committed by his/her agent under certain circumstances

directed verdict a judge's decision that one side has not presented evidence sufficient to support a verdict in its favor; thus the court renders a judgment in favor of the other party immediately before jury deliberations begin

directive a European Union (EU) law that establishes an EU standard but allows each member to enact a law in its own nation to implement that law

director a person elected by the shareholders to serve on a board that oversees the management of a corporation

directorates general the cabinet subdivisions of the EU Commission, each one having a particular area of responsibility

disability a physical or mental impairment that limits a major life function

disaffirmance cancellation or rejection of a contract made by a person during his/her minority upon reaching the age of majority or within a reasonable time thereafter

discharge 1. the termination or completion of a contract 2. in commercial paper, the removal of parties' liability on an instrument, usually by payment 3. the release of an employee from his/her employment 4. in bankruptcy law, the release of a debtor from his/her debts

discharge permit a government authorization for an industrial polluter to release limited amounts of certain pollutants into navigable waters

disclaimer 1. a denial of warranty 2. in negotiable instruments law, an indorsement phrase (most frequently, "without recourse") that places subsequent holders on notice that the indorser will not be liable if the instrument is not paid

disclosed principal a principal/agency relationship in which a third party knows, or should know, that the agent is acting for a principal, and the third party knows the identity of the principal. The agent thus has no personal responsibility.

discount a loan on an evidence of debt (e.g., a note), with the compensation for use of the money until the debt's maturity deducted from the principal and retained by the lender from the time the loan was made

discount shares shares issued for less than par or stated value; a shareholder who purchases shares at discount is liable to the corporation for the amount of the discount

discovery pretrial procedures by which the parties to a lawsuit obtain information from other parties and from potential witnesses

disgorge to give up illegally gained profits by court order to prevent unjust enrichment

dishonor to refuse to pay (or accept for later payment) an instrument

disinterested director a director who, for purposes of voting on a specific transaction or arrangement with the corporation, does not have a personal or economic interest in that transaction or arrangement

disparagement trade libel; a business defamation that involves injurious falsehoods about a product or a competitor's reputation

disparagement of property an economically injurious falsehood made about another's product or property. A general term for torts that are more specifically referred to as *slander of quality* or *slander of title*.

disparate impact *see* **adverse impact**

disparate treatment differences in how an employer or other defendant treats potential or present employees, with this type of discrimination—unlike other doctrines (e.g., adverse impact)—required to be intentional in order to be unlawful

dispute negotiation backward looking negotiation that addresses past events that have caused disagreement

dissenting shareholder one who opposes a fundamental change and has the right to receive the fair value of his/her shares

dissenters' rights *see* **appraisal rights**

dissociation the end of a relationship with a partnership

dissolution 1. the termination of a corporation's existence 2. a change in partners' relationship caused when one partner ceases, generally because of death or voluntary or involuntary withdrawal, to be associated with the partnership business

distress for rent the landlord's (or his/her agent's) taking of the tenant's personal property in payment of rent

distribution a distribution of a corporate asset to the shareholders

distribution of assets in the dissolution of a partnership, after winding up is completed, the distribution of partnership assets to creditors and partners

distributive negotiations negotiations in which the only issue is the distribution of the fixed pie; also called zero sum negotiations.

distributorship a business arrangement (e.g., franchise) in which a manufacturer licenses dealers to sell products

diversity jurisdiction the authority of federal courts to hear a civil case based on state law if the case involves parties from different states and the amount in controversy is more than $75,000

divestiture compulsory sale or other removal, by a business entity, of assets acquired in violation of antitrust laws

divided ownership type of fixture dispute that arises when the owner of a chattel (for example, a tenant) annexes it to the land of another (e.g., a landlord) requiring a determination of whether the attached article now belongs to the landowner

divisibility a contract doctrine used to determine when a party who has partially performed, but has failed to render complete performance, is entitled to recover for the part performance. If a contract is divisible, performance of a divisible part entitles the party to the agreed exchange for that part, despite nonperformance of other parts of the contract. Generally, a contract is divisible if full performance can be divided into corresponding pairs of part performances so that the exchange of part performances can be regarded as agreed equivalents.

dividend a distribution of cash or stock to the shareholders of a corporation

division of powers the arrangement in which constitutions (e.g., the U.S. Constitution) give to each branch of government a different, major area of responsibility: legislative (law making), executive (law enforcement), or judicial (law interpretation)

docket in the court records of a case, a book or case jacket briefly stating all pleadings, hearings, and other actions in the case

doctrine of equivalents the doctrine that there is a patent infringement when a patent is not literally copied but is replicated to the extent that the infringer has created a product or process working substantially the same way and accomplishing substantially the same result as the original patent

documentary letter of credit a letter of credit issued by a bank that provides for payment by the bank to the beneficiary upon tender by the beneficiary (or its agent or assignee) of specified documents; frequently used to secure payment for goods and repayment of loans in international transactions

doing business for a corporation, the maintenance of sufficient contacts in a foreign state, on a continuous and regular basis, to make it accountable to that state for its actions

domestic corporation a corporation carrying on business in the state of its creation; in that state, it is "domestic"

domicile an individual's permanent legal residence; for corporations, the central office, where its primary functions are discharged, according to law

dominant estate land whose owner has rights in other land

dominion ownership rights in property, including the right to possess and control the property

donative intent language or circumstances indicating that the owner intended to give away a particular property; a necessary element of a gift

donee the recipient of a gift

donee beneficiary a person, not a party to a contract, who claims that the performance of the contract was a gift to him/her

donor the person who makes a gift

dormant partner one who is both a silent and a secret partner

double indemnity clause life insurance clause doubling proceeds if insured dies accidentally

double jeopardy prohibition in the U.S. Constitution, Fifth Amendment, against trying a person twice for the same crime

draft a three-party instrument in which the drawer orders the drawee to pay a fixed amount of money to the payee, or another person specified by the payee, either on demand or at a particular time in the future

dragnet clause in a security agreement, a provision giving the secured party a security interest in all the debtor's property and in the proceeds from the sale of such property

dram shop acts state statutes imposing liability on businesses that serve alcoholic drinks to the public (e.g., bars, taverns) for injuries resulting from accidents caused by the businesses' intoxicated customers

drawee the person upon whom a draft is drawn by the drawer. The drawee, usually (always, when the draft is a check) a bank, is directed to pay the sum of money stated on the draft.

drawer the person who draws (writes) a draft. The drawer directs the drawee to pay the sum of money stated on the draft.

due care the standard of care a person owes to others in the law of torts; usually that degree of care that a reasonable person would exercise in the same situation. Also referred to as "duty of care."

due diligence for accountants or financial officers, a defense to Section 11 violations of the 1933 Securities Act (material omissions or false statements related to a registration statement)—essentially, the defense is that the accountant/financial officer acted reasonably (was *not* negligent)

due process protection granted by the U.S. Constitution, Fifth and Fourteenth Amendments, against the government's depriving a person of "life, liberty, or property" without according that person fundamental procedural rights. (In some cases of "substantive due process," the deprivation is not permitted, no matter what procedure is followed.)

dummy corporation a subsidiary corporation so completely dominated by its parent corporation as to have no legally recognizable separate existence

dumping selling of imported (often subsidized) goods at unfairly low prices to gain market share

durable power of attorney a document that authorizes an attorney in fact to act for a principal (e.g., write checks, collect insurance proceeds, manage health care issues); the durable power is effective until the principal revokes it or dies and remains in effect even if the principal becomes incapacitated

duress coercion, either physical or mental, that deprives a person of free will to make a contract

duty a legal obligation that the law imposes or that a contracting party creates or voluntarily imposes on himself/herself by making a binding promise

duty of care *see* **due care**

We want to hear your feedback!

Complete our survey at

www.barnesandnoblefeedback.com

or

Text BN to 345345

Your survey code is 0200603-423134

Enter for a chance to win one of twenty
$25 B&N gift cards drawn monthly.

No purchase necessary. Ends 4/30/2020.
Must be legal resident of the 50 US,
including DC and 21+.
Void where prohibited.
Visit www.barnesandnoblefeedback.com for
complete details and official rules.

at Barnes & Noble College bookstores that are listed for sale in the Barnes & Noble Booksellers inventory management system.

Opened music CDs, DVDs, vinyl records, audio books may not be returned, and can be exchanged only for the same title and only if defective. NOOKs purchased from other retailers or sellers are returnable only to the retailer or seller from which they are purchased, pursuant to such retailer's or seller's return policy. Magazines, newspapers, eBooks, digital downloads, and used books are not returnable or exchangeable. Defective NOOKs may be exchanged at the store in accordance with the applicable warranty.

Returns or exchanges will not be permitted (i) after 14 days or without receipt or (ii) for product not carried by Barnes & Noble or Barnes & Noble.com.

Policy on receipt may appear in two sections.

Return Policy

With a sales receipt or Barnes & Noble.com packing slip, a full refund in the original form of payment will be issued from any Barnes & Noble Booksellers store for returns of undamaged NOOKs, new and unread books, and unopened and undamaged music CDs, DVDs, vinyl records, toys/games and audio books made within 14 days of purchase from a Barnes & Noble Booksellers store or Barnes & Noble.com with the below exceptions:

A store credit for the purchase price will be issued (i) for purchases made by check less than 7 days prior to the date of return, (ii) when a gift receipt is presented

for purchases made by check less than 7 days prior to the date of return, (ii) when a gift receipt is presented within 60 days of purchase, (iii) for textbooks, (iv) when the original tender is PayPal, or (v) for products purchased at Barnes & Noble College bookstores that are listed for sale in the Barnes & Noble Booksellers inventory management system.

Opened music CDs, DVDs, vinyl records, audio books may not be returned, and can be exchanged only for the same title and only if defective. NOOKs purchased from other retailers or sellers are returnable only to the retailer or seller from which they are purchased, pursuant to such retailer's or seller's return policy. Magazines, newspapers, eBooks, digital downloads, and used books are not returnable or exchangeable. Defective NOOKs may be exchanged at the store in accordance with the applicable warranty.

Returns or exchanges will not be permitted (i) after 14 days with or without receipt or (ii) for product not carried by Barnes & Noble or Barnes & Noble.com.

Policy on receipt may appear in two sections.

Return Policy

With a sales receipt or Barnes & Noble.com packing slip, a full refund in the original form of payment will be issued from any Barnes & Noble Booksellers store for returns of undamaged NOOKs, new and unread books, and unopened and undamaged music CDs, DVDs, vinyl records, toys/games and audio books made within 14 days of purchase from a Barnes & Noble Booksellers store or Barnes & Noble.com with the below exceptions:

A store credit for the purchase price will be issued (i) for purchases made by check less than 7 days prior to the date of return, (ii) when a gift receipt is presented within 60 days of purchase, (iii) for textbooks, (iv) when

duty of diligence a director or officer must act with reasonable care and skill and make decisions only after properly obtaining all information necessary for an informed decision

duty of fair representation the union's legal duty to represent fairly all members of the bargaining unit

duty to read rule of contract law that a person who signs his/her name to a contract manifests his/her assent to its terms and may not later assert that that he/she had not read it or did not understand its contents

early neutral case evaluation a form of alternative dispute resolution in which a neutral third party evaluates the strengths and weaknesses of the disputing parties' positions; the evaluator is often an attorney or other expert in that area of practice, and his/her opinion forms the basis for negotiating a settlement

earmarking doctrine a bankruptcy doctrine whereby a payment to a preexisting creditor may not be recoverable as a preference if the funds for the repayment were provided by some other creditor and not by the debtor

earned surplus undistributed net profits or income of a corporation

earnest (money) the payment of some part of the price of goods sold, or the delivery of some part of such goods, in order to bind the contract

earwitness one who testifies about something he/she heard but did not see

easement a limited right to use (**affirmative easement**), or a prohibition of use of (**negative easement**), another person's land for a specific purpose

easement by necessity an implied easement that occurs when a land transfer makes an easement necessary to gain access to granted or retained land

easement by prescription an easement acquired in essentially the same manner as title to land is gained through adverse possession: here, actual, open, continual, and nonpermissive easement use of another's land for the required statutory period of time

easement in gross an express easement given for a specific purpose (e.g., for commerce or other public purposes such as placing utility lines). There is no adjoining dominant estate for this "personal easement" (i.e., not running with the land).

e-agent a computer program or some other electronic or automated method for performing specific tasks without review by an individual

ecclesiastical courts early English courts of the Catholic church or other religious orders established to try matters pertaining to religion or offenses against religion; during the time of Henry VIII these courts were merged into the equity courts

e-commerce business transacted in cyberspace

economic strike a strike over economic issues such as a new contract or a grievance; *compare* **unfair labor practices strike**

e-contract a contract that is entered into in cyberspace and is evidenced only by electronic impulses (e.g., those that make up a computer's memory) rather than, for example, a typewritten form

e-court (electronic court) a court that permits or requires the electronic filing of pleadings and other documents related to a lawsuit; also called a **virtual courthouse**

EDGAR acronym for the Securities and Exchange Commission's Electronic Data Gathering, Analysis, and Retrieval System

e-filing (electronic filing) the filing electronically (online) of pleadings and other documents related to a lawsuit; *see* **e-court**

effects test a test for personal jurisdiction that asks whether conduct outside the United States has had a substantial adverse effect on American businesses, consumers, or investors or on securities markets

effluent charge a fee, fine, or tax on a business for its polluting activity, usually on a per unit basis

eiusdem generis (Latin) "of the same class or kind"; a rule of contract or statutory construction indicating that in a series of words or phrases each word or phrase lends meaning to other words and phrases in the series. *Compare* **noscitur a sociis.**

ejectment 1. a civil action to recover possession of real property 2. a civil action to determine whether plaintiff or defendant has title to certain land

election an agency and contract law doctrine that, when the principal is undisclosed but the principal's existence and identity is later discovered, the third party must choose between holding either the principal or the agent liable on the contract

election of remedies choice by a party of one contract remedy to the exclusion of others. Contract law generally does not require that an injured promisee make an election of remedies.

Electronic Data Gathering, Analysis, and Retrieval (EDGAR) system that performs automated collection, validation, indexing, acceptance, and forwarding of submissions by companies that are required by law to file forms with the SEC

electronic signature an electronic sound, symbol, or process attached to or logically associated with a record and executed or adopted by a person with the intent to sign the record

electronic funds transfer a transaction with a financial institution by means of computer, electronic instrument, or telephone

eleemosynary corporation a corporation created for charitable purposes

emancipation the act by which a minor is freed from the control of parent or guardian

embezzlement crime whereby a person lawfully possessing or having access to money or property belonging to another, unlawfully uses that money or property for his/her own purposes

emergency sudden, unexpected event calling for immediate action

emergency authority type of implied authority that arises when the principal cannot be reached and immediate action by the agent is required to protect the principal's interests

e-money prepaid funds recorded on a computer or a car (such as a smart card)

eminent domain the power of, and its exercise by, the government to buy, at fair market value, privately owned real property for the public benefit

emission offset Clean Air Act requirement that existing pollution be reduced as much or more than the new pollution created by a business firm's new or expanded facilities

emotional distress *see* **intentional infliction of mental (emotional) distress**

employee one who agrees to perform work under the control and supervision of another

employee handbook employer-generated document concerning employment policies and procedures disseminated to employees, also called an employee manual

employment a contractual relationship whereby one person agrees to perform work under the control and supervision of another; a master/servant relationship

employment at will the doctrine that an employer may terminate an employee's employment at any time for a good reason, a bad reason, or no reason at all; this doctrine has been modified by statute and by the concept of abusive discharge

employment discrimination hiring, firing, compensating, promoting, or training of employees based on race, color, sex, religion, national origin, or other unlawful classifications

employment law law pertaining to the individual rights of employees and employers (e.g., as to hiring, firing, promotion)

enabling act legislation by which an administrative agency is created and powers are delegated to it

en banc legal proceeding before, or decisions by, the court as a whole (all of its judges) rather than a single judge

encroachment 1. unlawful use or possession of another's property 2. a franchisor's sale of an outlet to a franchisee and then later (a) selling another outlet nearby to another franchisee or (b) establishing nearby his/her own franchisor-owned outlet

encryption the process by which a message (plaintext) is transformed into something (ciphertext) that the sender and receiver intend third parties not to understand

encumbrance a burden on either title to property or on the property itself (e.g., a mortgage, a lien). Also spelled as "incumbrance."

endorsement *see* **indorsement**

enforceable contract a contract in which the promisee is entitled to a contract remedy if the promisor fails to perform

enjoin to issue an injunction

enterprise any individual, partnership, corporation, association, or other legal entity and also any union or group of individuals associated in fact although not a legal entity

entire contract a contract that is not divisible (i.e., a contract in which corresponding part performances are not agreed-upon equivalents)

entirety term for something the law considers as one whole, unable to be divided into parts

entity a being, thing, or organization having a legal existence

entrapment the defense that a criminal act was induced by a governmental agency, with criminal intent originating from that agency (e.g., police)

entrustment rule the rule that when the owner of goods entrusts the possession of those goods (such as for repair or consignment) to a merchant who deals in goods of that kind, the merchant has the power to transfer all rights, including title, in those goods to a buyer in the ordinary course of business; in effect, the owner's only recourse tends to be monetary compensation from the merchant, not return of the goods from that buyer

environmental impact statement a comprehensive statement on the ecological effects, possible alternatives, etc., required by the National Environmental Policy Act (1969) for any action that may significantly affect environmental quality and that involves federal funds, approval, licensing, or supervision

environmental law statutory, regulatory, and case law, the most significant being federal, designed to protect and clean the environment

equal dignity rule the rule that an agent's contracts to sell property covered by the Statute of Frauds must be in writing to be enforceable

equal pay equivalent pay for the same work

equal protection a provision in the U.S. Constitution, Fourteenth Amendment, that no person may be denied "the equal protection of the laws"; generally requires that any differences in treatment be reasonable and related to a permissible, governmental purpose (the "rational basis" test), but for cases involving "suspect" classifications (e.g., by race or religion) or fundamental rights (e.g., voting, marriage) differential treatment must be as narrow as possible and also necessary to achieve a compelling governmental interest (the "strict scrutiny" test)

equitable just, fair, and right; available under the rules of equity

equitable ownership ownership, but with another person having the right of possession and of voting, as in a voting trust

equitable principles and maxims general propositions or principles of law that have to do with fairness (equity)

equitable remedies in contract law, remedies that a court may award when there has been a breach and when the legal remedy (a damages award) would be inadequate; such remedies include injunction, reformation, rescission, and specific performance

equitable servitude a restriction on the use of land that is enforceable by a court

equitable subordination the doctrine that corporate debts to shareholders of insolvent corporations can only be paid out of assets remaining after outside (non-affiliated) creditors are paid

equitable tolling the doctrine that the statute of limitations will not bar a claim if the plaintiff, despite diligent efforts, did not discover the injury until after the limitations period had expired

equity historically, in England and the United States, a parallel and independent legal system based on principles of "fair play" or equity; now merged into the general court system, with responsibility for (among other matters) family law, injunctions, and specific performance of contracts

equity capital capital earned by a corporation through its sale of stock interests; the cash or property contributed to an enterprise in exchange for an ownership interest

equity of redemption the mortgagor's right, from the time of default until the foreclosure sale, to redeem (recover) the property by fully paying the debt, plus the foreclosure costs to date and any interest

equity remedy an appropriate remedy, based on fairness, awarded by court to the harmed party in order to correct the situation

equity securities securities issued to generate funds to operate the corporate enterprise; shares of common and preferred stock

error a mistake of law, or false or inappropriate application of law; *harmless errors* at the trial level (ones that do not prejudice the appellant's rights) are not grounds for reversing or vacating a judgment, while *reversible errors* are

escheat the passage of property to the state when a person dies intestate (without a will) and without any surviving relatives (heirs)

escrow placing a document, instrument, or funds in the hands of a third person, who holds the item or funds as a fiduciary, until the contract is performed or some other event occurs such that the escrow holder should then deliver the item or funds to the proper party (e.g., the grantee)

essence (of the) an expression stating that a certain thing (generally time of performance) is a condition of the contract

Establishment Clause provision in the U.S. Constitution's First Amendment that prohibits the government from either establishing a state religion or promoting one religion over another

estate 1. the sum total of a person's real and personal property; also, the nature, quantity and extent of interest that a person has in real or personal property (his/her right to possess, use, and enjoy the property) 2. in bankruptcy proceedings, all of the debtor's legal and equitable interests in property presently held, wherever located, together with certain jointly owned property, property transferred in transactions voidable by the trustee, proceeds and profits from the property of the estate, and certain property interests to which the debtor becomes entitled within 180 days after filing for bankruptcy

estate for years a tenancy (leasehold) for a definite period of time

estate pur autre vie estate in land granted to an individual with reference to the life span of a second individual

estate tax federal tax imposed on all property remaining in an estate after debts have been paid, together with other property such as certain trust funds and property held in joint tenancy with right of survivorship, less a deduction allowed for property transferred to the decedent's spouse or to charity

estop to be blocked by one's previous actions from asserting certain legal claims or defenses

estoppel a legal circumstance in which a person, by reason of his/her actions, cannot assert certain legal defenses or rights that are contrary to these actions. *See also* **waiver.**

estray statutes state statutory procedures (including publication of notice) whereby the finder/holder of lost or mislaid property may claim title to it if it is not reclaimed by the owner within the statutory period

et al. Latin abbreviation meaning "and another" or "and others"

ethics moral values and principles applied to social behavior

eviction action by the landlord to expel a tenant from the leased premises; eviction may be actual or constructive. *See also* **constructive eviction.**

evidence testimony, documents, and other relevant information presented at a trial, in accordance with the rules of evidence, so that the trier of fact (judge or jury) can determine the truth of facts at issue

Excelsior list named for a 1966 National Labor Relations Board decision, *Excelsior Underwear, Inc.* (156 NLRB 111), the names and addresses of the employees eligible to vote in a representation election are put in a list the employer files with the NLRB and thus makes available to the union, which can contact the employees outside their work environment and beyond the employer's observation and control

exception a formal objection to the court's action at trial, be it findings of fact or—more commonly—an evidentiary ruling; the excepting party is formally noting that it will seek to reverse the court's action, and preserve the benefit of his/her request or objection in some future proceeding

exchange any organization, association, or group of persons that constitutes, maintains, or provides a marketplace or facilities for bringing together purchasers and sellers of securities

excise tax a tax on the sale of a particular commodity, whether *specific* (per unit) or *ad valorem* (a percentage of the total value)

exclusion part of an insurance policy that states what the policy will not cover

exclusionary rule constitutional law doctrine that evidence obtained from an unreasonable search and seizure can generally be barred from introduction at a trial or an administrative proceeding

exclusive-agency listing a real estate listing contract in which the property owner agrees that one agent is the only person—besides the owner—with the right to sell the property during a specified period

exclusive dealing sole right to sell goods in a defined market

exclusive dealing arrangement a requirements contract or an output contract

exclusive jurisdiction the authority of only one type of court (e.g., state or federal) to decide a case

exculpatory clause a provision in a contract excusing one or both parties from the legal consequences of his/her or their actions or negligence

ex contractu (Latin) from or out of a contract.

ex delicto (Latin) from or out of a wrongful act; tortious; tortiously

executed contract a contract fully performed by both parties

execution 1. the legal process of enforcing a judgment, usually by seizing and selling the judgment debtor's property 2. performance of all acts needed to carry out completely a contract

execution sale a sale carried out to execute a judgment under authority of a judicial power

executive an employee whose primary duty is to manage the enterprise (or a department, division, or subdivision of the enterprise) where he/she is employed

executive agreement an agreement that the U.S. president makes with foreign countries without needing the U.S. Senate's consent, as treaties require

executive order a presidential order to establish or to enforce a legal requirement

executive privilege the U.S. president's immunity against forced disclosure of presidential communications made in the exercise of executive power

executor the person named in a will to administer the decedent's estate. Sometimes referred to as a "personal representative."

executory contract a contract that has not been fully performed by one or both parties

exemplary damages damages designed to make an example of the defendant. *See also* **punitive damages.**

exempt property debtor's property protected by state or federal statute from seizure by a debtor's creditor or a trustee in bankruptcy; such property cannot be sold or otherwise taken to satisfy a debt

exempt security a security not subject to the registration requirement of the Securities Act of 1933

exempted transaction a transaction in which the issuance of securities is not subject to the registration requirements of the Securities Act of 1933

exemption legal excuse from a duty imposed by law or from the operation of a law (e.g., property exempt from a bankruptcy proceeding)

exhaustion of remedies a doctrine whereby court appeals are not permitted until administrative remedies are exhausted; the appellants must use all available agency procedures before complaining to a court of law

exit vehicle a method for investors to get their money back without liquidating a company, such as through acquisition by a larger company or through an initial public offering of the company's securities

Exon-Florio provision statutory law allowing the U.S. president to prevent a foreign business' purchase of any U.S. firms, such as airline or defense companies, if such purchase would threaten national security

ex parte (Latin) "on or from one side"; judicial proceeding requested by one party without notice to or attendance by an opposing party (e.g., a hearing to decide whether to impose a temporary restraining order)

expectation theory contract law concept that damages should place the injured party in the position he/she would have occupied if the contract had been fully performed

ex post facto **law** (Latin) "from a thing done afterward"; a law making criminal a past action that was not defined as criminal when it occurred; forbidden by the U.S. Constitution, Article I, Sections 9 and 10

express authority an agent's authority that the principal voluntarily and specifically sets forth as oral or written instructions in an agency agreement

express condition a condition deliberately created by the parties at the time when the contract was made

express contract a conscious, specific contract; it must be written or oral, or partly written and partly oral

express warranty an explicitly made contractual promise about transferred property or contract rights; for sales of goods, an affirmation of fact that the goods meet certain standards of quality, performance, description, or condition

expropriation governmental seizure of private property and/or business for a proper, public purpose and with the payment of just compensation; the governmental taking of a business's assets, such as a manufacturing facility, usually without just compensation. *Compare* **confiscation.**

extension plan a plan by which creditors are repaid the entire indebtedness, but the period for payment is extended beyond the original due date

extortion making threats to obtain property

extraction process by which a debtor uses proceeds from the sale of inventory to pay his/her salary, overhead, and other fixed expenses

extradite to return an alleged criminal to the state in which his/her crime supposedly occurred, and where a trial should take place

extrinsic fraud fraud in which the party is aware of the bargain he/she is making but has been induced to make the agreement by a deliberately false representation; also known as *fraud in the inducement*

eyewitness one who personally observes an event

face value amount of coverage on an insurance policy

fact finding process in which a court, administrative agency, or some other governmental unit or a third party acting on behalf of a court, agency or other unit, investigates the issues and make determinations of fact

factor an agent (a) employed to sell goods for a principal, usually in the agent's own name, and (b) given possession of the goods for that purpose

failing firm defense an antitrust principle that a normally unlawful merger may be permitted because one of the firms is in danger of going out of business

failure to warn failure of a product to carry adequate warnings of the risks involved in the normal use of the product

fair market in real property law, the amount of money that a willing purchaser would pay to a willing property owner considering all uses for which the land is suited or might be applied

fair trade law a federal law providing for temporary relief to domestic industries seriously injured by increasing imports, regardless of whether unfair practices are involved

fair use an exception to the exclusivity of use generally given to copyrights; an example is limited reproduction, for classroom or other nonprofit purposes, of a small portion of a work in such a way as to have little effect on the market for the work. (Literary criticism, social commentary, news reporting, educational activities, scholarship, and research are among the numerous traditional fair uses.)

false arrest the intentional tort (or crime) involving detention of the plaintiff, without his/her permission, under the falsely asserted authority of the defendant

false imprisonment the intentional tort (or crime) involving wrongful use of force, physical barriers, or threats of force to restrain the plaintiff's freedom of movement

family law the law of divorce, adoption, and other family matters, transferred from the ecclesiastical courts of England to the equity court in the time of King Henry VIII

fanciful marks words that have no prior meaning until used as a trademark in connection with a particular product (e.g., Kodak for camera products or Exxon for gasoline)

F.A.S. "free alongside ship"—seller's risk and cost of transport until delivered next to the ship

featherbedding an unfair labor practice, prohibited by the Taft-Hartley Act (1947), whereby employers pay for work not actually performed

federal corporation a corporation organized under the laws of the United States for a federal purpose

federal preemption the federal government's right to regulate matters within its powers to the possible exclusion of state regulation

"federal questions" jurisdiction a type of subject-matter jurisdiction; the authority of federal courts to hear and decide cases involving the U.S. Constitution, federal statutes, or treaties

federalism a form of government in which power is divided between a national government and state (provincial) governments; *compare with* **unitary system**

fee simple absolute the highest form of ownership and possession; a fee simple estate includes all rights in real property

fee simple defeasible ownership of an estate that may last forever, but which may cease (be defeated) upon the happening of an event

fee simple determinable ownership of an estate that automatically ends if a specified action occurs

fee simple subject to a condition subsequent ownership of an estate that is subject to a grantor's right of repossession if a specified action occurs

fee simple subject to an executory limitation a defeasible (qualified) fee simple interest in land that passes to a third party (other than the grantor or his/her heirs) upon the occurrence or nonoccurrence of an event stated in the instrument creating the interest

fee tail an estate of inheritance, descending only to a certain class or classes of heirs (e.g., an estate is conveyed or devised "to B and the heirs of his body," or "to B and the heirs male of his body," or "to B and the heirs female of his body")

fellow servant rule common law defense relieving the employer from liability to an employee for injuries caused by negligence of a fellow employee

felony a serious crime punishable by imprisonment; a crime placed by a state's criminal code in a class more serious than the other main class of crimes, misdemeanors

feminist jurisprudence the theory that law has been dominated by males and needs to adjust to more accurately include female views and experiences

fictitious business name statement an official document that must be filed with the appropriate governmental agency in order for a sole proprietorship to be allowed to use a particular name

fictitious payee a made-up payee whose account is actually controlled by a dishonest employee or other person, with the drawer/maker duped into drafting or making negotiable instruments payable to this fictitious person; under negotiable instruments law, negotiation is effective, and thus the drawer/maker may not have an effective defense against paying the instrument (except to those who actually duped him/her)

fidelity insurance insurance that an employer buys to protect itself from the dishonesty (e.g., theft) of employees

fiduciary a person occupying a position of trust in relationship to another

fiduciary duty duty of upmost loyalty and good faith owed by a fiduciary, such as an agent owes to his/her principal

fiduciary out the allowance in a merger agreement for the target company's directors to remain faithful to their fiduciary duties to shareholders (e.g., by recommending other unsolicited offers) even after signing an agreement with a suitor company

fiduciary relationship a relationship in which one party acts on behalf of another and thus has a duty of loyalty and care to that other party

fieri facias (Latin) "that you cause to be made (done)"; an ordinary writ of execution whereby the court officer, ordinarily a marshal or sheriff, is commanded to levy and sell the judgment debtor's property and to satisfy a money judgment—that is, to "make," if possible, the amount that the judgment creditors demand

final credit the payor bank's payment of the instrument

final-offer arbitration a form of arbitration used most notably in baseball salary disputes; each side submits its best and final offer to the arbitrator, who must choose one of the two proposals

financing statement a document filed to perfect a security interest

firm commitment underwriting the underwriters agree to purchase the entire offering, thus effectively shifting the risk of the offering from the issuer to the underwriters

firm offer an irrevocable, signed, written offer by a merchant to sell or buy goods, stating that the offer will not be withdrawn for a specified period (not to exceed 3 months)

firm offer rule a rule of sales law that a merchant's written, signed offer to buy or sell goods stating that it will be held open is binding without consideration for the period stated, not exceeding three months

"first time is first in right" principle of pure race recording statutes that recording a deed is a race—the first to record has the superior title

fitness (warranty of) an implied warranty that the specified goods are fit for the buyer's use or purpose

fixture what was personal property and has become attached to real property (i.e., so incorporated into real property that it is difficult, costly and/or impossible to remove); generally treated as part of the real property

flame an online message in which one party attacks another in harsh, often personal terms

floater policy an all-risk insurance for loss or damage to personal property from almost any cause

floating lien a security interest in property that the debtor did not possess when the security agreement was executed; a security interest retained in collateral despite the collateral's change in character, classification, or location; examples are liens on after-acquired property, future advances, and sales proceeds

F.O.B. "free on board"—risk and cost of loss pass to buyer at the designated point

force majeure an occurrence that is beyond the control of a party to a contract and therefore excuses his/her performance (e.g., an act of God)

forbearance refraining from acting when one has the right to act. In this sense, forbearance may be consideration

foreclosure the proceeding whereby a mortgagee takes title to, or forces the sale of, mortgaged property in order to satisfy the mortgagor's debt

foreign corporation a corporation carrying on business in any state other than the state of its creation; in all such states, it is "foreign"

foreign-natural test the test some courts impose to determine if foods and beverages are merchantable; if the cause of a plaintiff's injury naturally occurs in the food or beverage (e.g., perhaps bones in a fish dinner), the product is considered merchantable and the merchant is not liable; compare **consumer expectation test**

foreseeable risk in negligence law, the risk of injury to another that a person of ordinary intelligence and prudence should have anticipated (foreseen) when undertaking an action or refraining from undertaking an action

forgery 1. falsely making or materially altering a legal document (e.g., a negotiable instrument) in order to defraud another person and/or otherwise affect rights 2. without authority, writing another person's name (signature) on a legal document as if that person had done so

forum section clause a provision in the contract designating the court, jurisdiction, or tribunal that will decide any disputes arising under the contract

forum shopping a party to a lawsuit attempts to have a case tried in a particular court or jurisdiction where the party feels the most favorable judgment or verdict will be received

forward vertical integration merger in which a business has proceeded forward in the supply chain to acquire a business to whom it sells goods or services (e.g., an automobile manufacturer buys a car dealership)

forward-looking statement a statement issued by a business that projects earnings and losses

four unities time, title (source), interest, and possession. *See* **joint tenancy.**

franchise a contractual arrangement in which the owner (franchisor) of a trademark, trade name, copyright, patent, trade secret, or some form of business operation, process, or system permits others (franchisees) to use that property, operation, process, or system in furnishing goods or services

franchisee a person who is granted a franchise

franchisor a person who grants a franchise

fraud an intentional tort (or crime) consisting of intentional misrepresentation of a material fact, made knowingly with intent to defraud, that is justifiably relied upon by the other party and causes injury to him/her. Also called "deceit" or "misrepresentation."

fraud against consumers a crime (or tort: fraud) involving such activities as fraudulent solicitation in the mail, false advertising about products, and false labeling

fraud in the execution a fraud pertaining to the execution or signing of an instrument or a contract

fraud in the inducement a fraud, pertaining to the value of goods to be sold or services to be obtained, thus inducing the execution of an instrument or a contract

fraud on the market the theory that if the information about a company available to the market is incorrect, then the market price will not reflect the true value of the stock

fraudulent conveyance (transfer) a transfer of property or property rights made to defraud creditors. For example, such a transfer could be the unlawful shifting of assets from an insolvent corporation to shareholders or others rather than to the corporate creditors. Such transfers may be challenged, and the creditor can reach (e.g., attach) the property by following the appropriate legal procedures.

freedom of speech the right to engage in oral, written, and symbolic speech protected by the U.S. Constitution's First Amendment

free exercise clause a provision in the U.S. Constitution's First Amendment that bars the government from interfering with the exercise of religion

freehold 1. real property held for life or in fee (e.g., fee simple) 2. an estate of uncertain duration, as opposed to a leasehold

freeze-outs a majority shareholder prevents a minority shareholder from participating in the decision-making process

frolic and detour when an employee or agent does something outside the scope of his/her employment or agency; actions to further the agent's or employee's own interests (not the employer's or principal's interests), and thus actions for which the employer or principal is not liable under *respondeat superior*

front pay an amount of money awarded a victim of discrimination to make the victim whole for the loss of future work opportunities with an employer due to the employer's wrongful discrimination; any monetary award for loss of anticipated future earnings; money damages for a plaintiff instead of reinstatement or hiring

fruit of the poisonous tree evidence acquired directly or indirectly as a result of an illegal search or arrest, hence generally inadmissible

frustration of purpose doctrine excusing a promisor when the contract's objectives have been completely defeated by circumstances arising after the contract was formed; performance is excused even though there is no impediment to actual performance

"full faith and credit" clause a provision in the U.S. Constitution, Article IV, Section 1, requiring that, once a court with jurisdiction has rendered a judgment, other states honor that decision insofar as it affects the rights and duties arising between the parties to the judgment

full warranty in general, a warranty that guarantees complete repair, replacement, or refund of money for a defective product

functional discount the difference between the price a manufacturer charges for goods to its wholesalers and to its retailers. The discount is a lower price for wholesalers; its legality is governed by the Robinson-Patman Act, which generally permits discounts reflecting compensation to wholesalers for their distribution services (e.g., assuming the risk of loss, warehousing, transportation, and administration).

fungible goods goods that, when mixed, cannot be separately identified, since each unit is basically like any other unit (e.g., grain, minerals, fruit)

future estate an estate, such as a remainder or a reversion, which is not yet vested in the grantee, but is to commence at some specified future time

future goods goods not yet in existence and not yet identified

future interest a legal right in real property, which will or may become full ownership in the future

gambling agreement that a party will win or lose money (or property) depending on the outcome of an event in which the party's only interest is the gain or loss

gap fillers UCC Article 2 provisions that supply missing terms in the parties' agreement

garnishee (as a noun) the person on whom a garnishment is served, usually a debtor of the defendant; (as a verb) to institute garnishment proceedings or cause a garnishment to be levied on the garnishee

garnishment a procedure whereby a court orders a third party holding property of a debtor (e.g., an employer holding wages due, a bank holding a customer's account) to transfer some or all of that property to a judgment creditor (person with an unpaid judgment against the debtor)

general agent 1. one authorized to act for one's principal in all matters concerning a particular business 2. agent authorized to conduct a series of transactions involving a continuity of service

general creditor *see* **unsecured creditor**

general devise a transfer by will payable out of the general assets of a testator's estate. *See* **estate, will, devise.**

general jurisdiction trial court also called a "court of record;" a court that hears cases of a general nature beyond that of the "limited-jurisdiction courts;" the evidence and testimony is recorded and stored for possible appeals and public access

general legacy gift under a will from the estate in general, as opposed to some specific fund or source

general partner a partner who has power to manage partnership business and has unlimited liability for partnership debts

general partnership a partnership in which there are no limited partners, and each partner has managerial power and unlimited liability for partnership debts

general personal jurisdiction when a corporation's activities within a state are so substantial as to justify personal jurisdiction over the corporation as a civil defendant sued for entirely different actions. In other words, the out-of-state corporation's affiliations with the state are so "continuous and systematic" as to render the corporation "essentially at home in the foreign state" (and thus it is fair to subject it to a lawsuit having nothing specifically to do with the corporation's in-state conduct). *Compare* **specific personal jurisdiction.**

general release an agreement by a person engaging in a dangerous activity to assume all risks and hold the party offering access to such dangerous activity free of all liability

general verdict a jury's finding in favor of the plaintiff or defendant. *Contrast with* **special verdict.**

general warranty deed a deed wherein the grantor warrants title against defects or encumbrances arising before or during his/her ownership, and also makes any other covenants typically included in conveyances

generic name a term for a mark that has become a common term for a product line or type of service and therefore has lost its trademark or service mark protection

genericide a trademark's or service mark's transformation into a generic term

gift a transfer of title to goods without consideration; the three elements of an effective gift are donative intent by the donor, delivery (actual or constructive) to the donee, and acceptance by the donee

gift *causa mortis* a conditional gift in which the donor, believing that his/her death is imminent, conveys property with the intent that the donee keep it after the donor's death; the gift is automatically revoked if the donor recovers

gift *inter vivos* a gift made during the donor's lifetime, when he/she is not facing imminent death

golden parachute employment severance arrangements (pay) for the management of a corporation acquired by another person or firm (the acquisition usually being through a successful tender offer)

good cause a fair, reasonable motive for an action; in employment and labor law, a basis for employee discipline that is not arbitrary or capricious nor based on anti-contractual, discriminatory, or other illegal motivation

good faith 1. acting honestly, without knowledge of a legal defect; sincerely endeavoring to behave in accord with one's own agreements, ethical standards in the industry, and the law itself. Generally, the term denotes an honest intention to abstain from taking unfair advantage of another person. *Compare* **bad faith.** 2. in sales contracts, a UCC requirement that a merchant act with honesty and in accordance with reasonable commercial standards of fair dealing in the trade

good faith bargaining sincere efforts to reach a labor agreement; a duty to make such efforts is imposed under labor laws on both unions and employers

good faith purchaser for value a person to whom good title can be transferred from a person with voidable title; persons with good claims against the transferor cannot succeed in getting the purchased item from the good faith purchaser

goods broadly, all tangible items (personal property) movable when identified to (designated part of) a contract; in sales, all things movable and identified to a contract except the purchase money, investment securities, and any rights to recover money or property via a lawsuit

Good Samaritan Law statute relieving medical professionals from liability for ordinary negligence when they render aid to victims in emergency situations

goodwill the special favor or advantage enjoyed by a particular business because of its reputation for skill or judgment; hence, the capitalized value of the excess of estimated future profits over the rate of return on capital considered normal for that kind of business or industry

government contractor defense when a contractor follows specifications provided by the government, the defense that the contractor is not liable for any product defect resulting from those specifications

grand jury a body of jurors (larger in number than a petit jury) that, under the guidance of a prosecutor, decides whether a person or persons should be charged with a crime (indicted)

grandfather clause an exemption from a statute that, but for the exemption, would make certain acts or conditions illegal, provided that those acts or conditions took place before the statute was enacted (e.g., the acts were performed by one's grandfather)

grant to bestow upon another person property, rights in property, an instrument, or some other right or privilege

grant deed a deed containing implied warranties that the grantor has not previously conveyed the same property or any interest in it to another person and that the title is marketable; title, if not present at execution, is automatically transferred to the grantee

grantee the person that receives a grant

grantor the person who makes a grant

gratuitous bailment a bailment to benefit solely the bailor, with no benefit passing to the bailee

gratuitous promise a promise made without consideration

gravamen gist, essence, substance; the grievance complained of; the substantial cause of the lawsuit

gray market goods goods lawfully bearing trademarks or using patents or copyrighted material but entering the American market without authorization; this may breach the contract between an American firm and its foreign licensee, but whether it violates intellectual property law is unclear

greenmail a target corporation's purchase of its own stock at a premium (higher than the ordinary price) from an actual or perceived tender offeror

grievance in labor law, a complaint by the union, employer, or employees usually alleging a violation of the collective bargaining agreement

grievance procedure a procedure for settling disputes set forth in the collective bargaining agreement. It usually involves several steps with the aggrieved worker and representative meeting with the supervisor involved, followed by an appeal system with strict time limits and ultimately ending in binding arbitration.

gross negligence lack of even slight care; recklessness; extreme failure to comply with one's duty of care; conduct appreciably worse than ordinary negligence

gross-up clause a clause in foreign investment contracts by which the local partner/licensee must pay all taxes other than those specifically allocated to the foreign partner/licensor

group boycott a group of competitors' agreement to refuse to deal with a particular person or firm (another competitor); prohibited by the Sherman Act

guarantee(y) in contracts, a promise by one person to pay the debts of another

guarantor generally, a person who has expressly or implicitly agreed to be liable for another person's debts if the creditor cannot collect directly from the debtor, one who makes a guaranty; in negotiable instruments law, an indorser who guarantees payment or collection on the instrument

guaranty of collection the guarantor's obligation to pay only after the lender has unsuccessfully attempted to collect the amount due from the primary debtor

guaranty of payment the guarantor's obligation to pay the lender is triggered, immediately and automatically, if the primary debtor fails to make a payment when due

guaranty of performance a guaranty that specified nonpayment obligations will be performed

guardian an individual appointed to act on behalf of another person (e.g., a child or mentally incapacitated adult) who lacks the ability to perform legally valid acts, acquire legal rights, or incur legal liabilities

guest statute law that a vehicle's driver is not liable to his/her passengers for injuries caused by the driver's ordinary negligence if the passengers took the ride voluntarily and without compensating the driver

guilt beyond a reasonable doubt the burden of proof necessary for conviction of a crime; this standard requires the prosecutor to prove each essential element to the point where the fact finder (judge or jury) has no reasonable doubt as to its existence; also referred to as proof that is entirely convincing to a moral certainty

gun jumping a violation of the securities laws that occurs when an issuer or underwriter conditions the market with a news article, press release, or speech about a company engaged in the registration of its securities

habeas corpus, writ of judicial order that a government official produce a detained or imprisoned person in an action testing the legality of that detention or imprisonment

habitability 1. leased premises fit for ordinary residential purposes; the landlord's implied warranty that the premises are safe and suitable for people to live in 2. a warranty by commercial sellers of houses that the house is in reasonable working order and of reasonably sound construction

hardship discharge a Chapter 13 bankruptcy discharge granted if (a) the debtor fails to complete the payments because of unforeseeable circumstances, (b) the unsecured creditors have been paid as much as they would have been paid in a Chapter 7 liquidation, and (c) it is impractical to modify the debtor's plan of payment

harmonization the process of making the laws of all European Union (EU) nations more similar to one another

hazardous substance superfund a fund that finances federal activity to investigate and take remedial action (e.g., cleanups) in response to a release or threatened release of hazardous substances into the environment

hazardous waste solid substance(s) that may cause or significantly contribute to an increase in mortality or serious illness, or that pose(s) a hazard to human health or the environment if improperly treated, stored, transported, disposed of, or otherwise managed

headnotes paragraphs written by editors summarizing important legal points contained in a decision

health care proxy a power of attorney giving a designated person the authority to make health care decisions

hearsay evidence (an out-of-court statement) heard or otherwise learned (e.g., read) from someone other than the person testifying in court; the truth of the matter rests on the credibility of someone not a witness (hence, not subject to cross-examination)

hedge to use two offsetting transactions to ensure that one breaks even; to make arrangements in advance to safeguard against loss on an investment because of market fluctuations; as an example, a commodities purchaser may contract for a certain quantity at the price then current, yet also sell an equal quantity for future delivery

heir closest surviving descendant; a person who succeeds, by the rules of law, to an estate upon the death of his/her ancestor, by descent and right of relationship

hereditaments a more comprehensive term than either "land" or "tenements" and meaning anything capable of being inherited, whether it is real, personal, or mixed property

Herfindahl-Hirschman Index an index of market power used by the Justice Department to calculate whether a merger of two businesses will result in sufficient monopoly power (too much market concentration) so as to violate antitrust laws; it is computed by summing the squares of the individual market shares of all firms in the market

high-low agreements a party-negotiated settlement range, with the low figure setting the minimum that the plaintiff is assured of receiving, and the high figure the maximum amount that the plaintiff stands to gain, regardless of what the judge or jury awards; these deals are usually struck mid-trial, often during jury deliberations, and are also called *jury-directed settlements*

hinweispflicht a German phrase meaning "hints and feedback;" when combined with the German word for "judicial" (*richterliche*) forms the concept *Richterliche Hinweispflicht*, which refers to the German judge's duty to instruct lawyers and litigants to help them understand all matters (fact and law) that could affect a case's outcome; the judge may ask questions of parties or lawyers in order to clarify and sharpen the key facts and issues and give these persons a chance to make corrections

hiring halls places that refer workers to employment opportunities; often used in casual and seasonal industries; sometimes an arrangement in which a union refers employees to an employer

historical jurisprudence the theory that law is produced and shaped by important historical facts and developments, that one looks to the past to discover what the principles of contemporary law should be

holder a person who possesses a negotiable instrument issued, drawn, or indorsed to that person or his/her order or to bearer

holder in due course a holder who takes an authentic-appearing negotiable instrument for value, in good faith, and without notice that it is overdue, has been dishonored, or has certain defenses or claims against it

holder in due course doctrine a doctrine of negotiable instruments law stating that if a negotiable instrument is negotiated to a holder in due course, the holder in due course takes free of all claims and most defenses to the instrument

holding the rule of law used to resolve the issues in a court case

holding company a corporation that holds or owns the stock of another corporation or corporations

holographic deed or will an unwitnessed deed or will handwritten entirely by the grantor or testator, respectively; its validity depends upon state law

homestead exemption a provision in the law of most states that, when a home (debtor's residence, not rental property) is sold to pay a judgment, a specific amount may be retained by the debtor, free of the judgment debt; mortgages are not subject to this exemption

homicide the unlawful taking of another's life

honor to pay (or to accept for payment) an instrument

honorary trust a transfer of property in trust for the erection or maintenance of monuments, the care of graves, or the care of specific animals. Such an arrangement is not an actual trust under the ordinary definition of trust because it lacks a beneficiary.

horizontal agreement a conspiracy agreement between firms that compete with each other on the same level of production or distribution

horizontal market division per se violation of the Sherman Act that involves dividing a market for the sale of a specific product among competitors

horizontal merger a merger in which the merged business entities operated the same type of business at the same level (e.g., both were manufacturers); if monopolistic, usually illegal under antitrust law

horizontal privity privity among persons at the same level of the chain of distribution or consumption

horizontal restraint of trade a restraint of trade involving an agreement among competitors—persons at the same functional level; often unlawful under antitrust laws; *see* **restraint of trade**

hostile environment harassment unlawful sexual harassment that causes an uncomfortable work atmosphere; harassment subjecting the victim to unwelcome comments or conduct and that may interfere with the employee's work performance

hostile takeover a takeover in which an outside investor attempts to purchase all or a majority of stock in a company against the wishes of corporate management

hostile witness witness called to testify whose position or bias predisposes him/her to favor the side that did *not* call him/her; this witness can thus be asked leading questions, as if on cross-examination, by the side that called him/her

hostile work environment in sexual harassment claims, this term refers to a workplace where the employer permits a sexually offensive environment to exist

hot-cargo contract an unfair labor practice, prohibited by the Taft-Hartley Act (1947), whereby an employer agrees with employees not to purchase, use, or handle products from a specified business; it is thus a type of secondary boycott, usually against nonunionized businesses

hotelkeeper's lien a lien placed on a guest's baggage to ensure payment of hotel charges

hot-news exception a state law doctrine giving the plaintiff the right to preclude others from using information in cases where 1. the plaintiff generated or gathered the information at a cost; 2. the information is time sensitive; 3. the defendant's use of the information amounts to a free ride on the plaintiff's efforts; 4. the defendant is in direct competition with the plaintiff; and 5. the availability of other parties to a free ride on the plaintiff's efforts would so reduce the plaintiff's incentive to provide the product or service that its existence or quality would be threatened

huissiers in the French legal tradition, judicial officers who serve as bailiffs, as people responsible for executing judgments and serving summons, and as investigators who file, under oath, reports to the court about their examination of documents, viewing of premises, questioning of witnesses, or other factual inquiries

hung jury a jury that is deadlocked and cannot agree on a verdict

hushmail a repurchase of shares at a premium over market to ensure silence from a shareholder who has been critical of management

hypothecate to pledge something (e.g., securities) without delivering title of it to the pledge (e.g., a bank lender)

identification in a sale of goods, the express designation of those goods, i.e., setting aside or otherwise designating the particular goods for sale under a contract; also called *identification to the contract*

identified goods in a sales contract, goods that have been designated as part of the contract, either in the original agreement, or when the seller ships, marks or otherwise indicates that certain existing goods are those to which the contract refers; this identification process affects title, transfer, risk of loss, and other matters

identity theft fraudulently using someone else's information (e.g., social security number and mother's maiden name) to obtain credit or commit other financial crimes

illegal bargain a contract that is unenforceable because it violates an applicable criminal or civil statute, constitutes the commission of or inducement to commit a tort, or is otherwise contrary to public policy

illegal contract a contract is illegal if its formation or performance is expressly forbidden by a civil or criminal statute or if a penalty is imposed for doing the agreed-upon act

illusory promise a promise that appears to be real but in fact imposes no legal obligation upon the promisor

immunity an exemption from prosecution granted to an actual or a potential criminal defendant, usually to induce information and/or testimony from him/her

impaired claim a claim that a bankruptcy relief plan fails to provide full cash payment when due and alters the creditors' legal, equitable, or contractual rights in any way (except by curing defaults and reinstating the claim's maturity)

impanel to go through the process of selecting a jury; to list the names of those people chosen for jury duty

impasse a deadlock in negotiations, such as between an employer and a union

impeachment 1. removal from office of an official, such as a judge, for serious misconduct, such as conviction for a crime 2. challenging/undermining a witness's testimony

implementation after impasse doctrine the duty to bargain collectively in good faith prohibits an employer from unilaterally changing a term or condition of employment unless, after bargaining with the union to an impasse, the employer's unilateral changes are consistent with the employer's preimpasse proposal

implied agency an agency implied from the conduct of two parties, the principal and the agent

implied authority 1. the actual authority possessed by an agent, consisting of powers incidental to those expressly given and necessary to effectuate the purposes of the express powers 2. in agency law, a type of actual authority that is perhaps based on custom and usage but usually is inferred from words or conduct manifested by the principal to the agent; it is what an agent reasonably believes is necessary to carry out the agent's express duties

implied condition a condition implied from the nature of the transaction but not expressly specified by the parties; a contingency understood but not expressed by the parties

implied contract a contract implied from the conduct of the parties; sometimes referred to as an "implied-in-fact contract"

implied covenant of good faith and fair dealing obligation, implied by law, that—among other things—the employer/franchisor cannot in bad faith terminate an employee/franchisee

implied-in-fact contract a contract formed in whole or in part from the conduct of the parties (as opposed to an express contract); a promise or agreement inferred from conduct other than language

implied intent if a person does not intend a particular consequence of an act but knew that the consequence of the act was certain, or substantially certain, and does the act anyway, intent to cause the consequence is implied

implied partnership a partnership implied from the conduct of the co-owners of a business

implied powers laws and actions taken by the federal government that are necessary and proper to carry out enumerated powers

implied promise a promise implied from conduct

implied ratification the principal's silence or failure to repudiate an agent's act, thus acquiescing to that act

implied trust trust that arises by operation of law, not by the express language of the settlor. Implied trusts include resulting trusts and constructive trusts.

implied warranty a warranty implied by law, arising out of the buyer/seller relationship

implied warranty of authority agency law doctrine that a person who purports to make a contract for a principal impliedly represents that he/she has the power to bind the principal

implied warranty of fitness for a particular purpose UCC warranty that the goods being sold are fit for the particular purpose for which the buyer is acquiring the goods and of which the seller is aware, also called simply *implied warranty of fitness*

implied warranty of habitability *see* **habitability**

implied warranty of merchantability UCC warranty that the goods being sold are of average quality, are fit for ordinary purposes, and are adequately contained, packaged, and labeled

implied warranty of title UCC warranty that the goods being sold belong to the seller

import-export clause clause of the U.S. Constitution that prohibits a state from imposing a direct tax on imports or exports solely because the goods have been received from or are bound for a foreign country

impossibility such absolute factual impossibility as will discharge a contract; alternatively, commercial impracticability

impossibility defense a defense to strict liability in which a corporate officer might not be held strictly (and vicariously) liable if he or she did everything possible to ensure legal compliance to applicable standards even though the company was still unable to comply

impracticability commercial impracticability created by an unforeseen occurrence sufficient to discharge a contract (treated by some courts as impossibility)

imputed knowledge in agency law, information that a principal is deemed to possess because the agent has such knowledge, whether or not the principal actually does; also known as *constructive knowledge*

imputed liability the imposition of civil or criminal liability on one party for the wrongful acts of another; also called *vicarious liability*

imputed negligence negligence by another party for which one is held liable although he/she did not directly commit negligence. The negligence is imputed because of the relationship, privity or other ties between the negligent party and the "imputed" one. A related term is **vicarious liability.**

inadequate-resources defense the defense for a merger that could create a monopoly but that courts may allow because the acquired firm had inadequate financial resources to compete

inalienable incapable of being alienated, transferred, or conveyed; nontransferable

in camera Latin for "in a chamber," meaning, in the legal context, "in the judge's chambers"; in private

incapacity lack of mental capacity to make a contract

inchoate imperfect; incipient; not completely formed

inchoate crimes crimes that are designed to culminate in the commission of another crime but fail to do so; related terms are *attempt, conspiracy,* and *solicitation*

"incidental" beneficiary a person, not a party to a contract, who receives some slight or indirect benefit from the contractual promise

incidental damages the damages paid to a person to reimburse the cost of his/her minimizing the damages to which the person is entitled (e.g., reimbursement for advertising or other expenses incurred by a landlord to replace a breaching tenant)

income bond 1. bond that conditions payment of interest on corporate earnings 2. the interest rate on the bond would be stated, and that percentage would be paid on the income earned by a named asset in the bond

incompetent evidence that cannot be used in court; lack of ability to discharge a required duty

incomplete instrument an instrument lacking information because all blanks have not been filled in by the maker or drawer

incontestable clause an insurance policy clause preventing the insurer from canceling the policy, after a set time has lapsed, for any reason except nonpayment of premiums

incorporated (Inc.) one of the words that indicate a business is incorporated (i.e., is a corporation)

incorporation the process by which a corporation is formed

incorporation by reference a legal doctrine under which the terms on one identifiable writing are made part of another writing by referring to, identifying, and adopting the former as part of the latter

incorporation doctrine judicial doctrine that the fundamental guarantees in the Bill of Rights are incorporated into the U.S. Constitution's Fourteenth Amendment due process clause and thus applied to state and local governmental action

incorporator a person who meets the statutory requirements to form a corporation and does form a corporation

indemnification a principal's duty to pay the agent for losses the agent incurred while acting as the principal directed

indemnify to hold harmless from, to guarantee against, loss or liability

indemnity contract contract in which the promisor (indemnitor) agrees to save the promisee (indemnitee) harmless from (indemnify or reimburse him/her for) the legal consequences of the promisee's or some other person's conduct

indenture a contract stating the terms under which long-term debt securities (both bonds and debentures) are issued

independent administrator executor who takes charge of a testator's estate without court supervision

independent agency an administrative agency that is not under the control of the president or Congress but is freestanding; such an agency typically has a commission created by Congress, with commissioners appointed by the president, subject to Senate confirmation, and serving for a set term (not subject to removal without cause)

independent contractor 1. a person hired to undertake a contractually defined result without direct supervision (not an employee and usually not an agent) 2. person hired to complete a specific task or project and who, generally, is subject to the hirer's control only as to the end product and not as to the method of performance

independent director a director who does not have employment, family, or other significant personal or economic connections to the corporation other than serving as a director

independent promises a term traditionally used to describe promises in leases and other conveyances of land, meaning that nonperformance of one promise by one party does not excuse further performance of another promise by the other party

indicia signs; indications; circumstances pointing to the existence of a given fact as probable but not certain

indictment a criminal charge (or charges) issued by a grand jury

indirect damages damages not proximately caused by a breach of contract; remote damages

indirect patent infringement one party's active inducement of another party to infringe a patent

indorsee the person to whom a negotiable instrument is transferred by indorsement

indorsement the signature, other than of a maker, drawer, or acceptor, that—alone or accompanied by other words—is made on an instrument for the purpose of negotiating the instrument, restricting the instrument's payment, or incurring the indorser's liability on the instrument; ordinarily, an indorsement operates to transfer the holder's title to and property interest in the instrument to a new holder. *See also* **blank, conditional, qualified, restrictive,** and **special indorsement.**

indorser a person who makes an indorsement

inevitable disclosure doctrine a doctrine that permits a former employer to prevent its ex-employee from working for a competitor when the new position will require the ex-employee to disclose or use the former employer's trade secrets

inevitable discovery exception an exception to the exclusionary rule that permits illegally obtained evidence to be introduced at trial if that evidence would inevitably have been found by other, legal means

infancy the state of minority: in most states, under the age of 18

informal contract any oral or written contract other than a formal contract; most contracts are informal contracts

informal rulemaking the process for creating administrative agency regulations that does not involve a formal hearing

information 1. a criminal charge (or charges) issued by a magistrate, prosecutor, or police officer 2. usually, the prosecutor submits to a judge an affidavit (the information), and the judge then issues the *bill of information* charging a person with crime; this process is used in many states instead of a grand jury indictment

informational picketing picketing (which must conform with the Taft-Hartley Act) designed to apprise the public that an employer either is selling nonunion goods or is operating without a contract with the union

infringement an intentional tort (or crime) involving violation of another person's intellectual property rights (e.g., patents, copyrights, trademarks)

inherent authority an agent's authority, though neither actual nor apparent, to bind the principal over certain unauthorized actions with unsuspecting third parties, because the principal gave the agent the power to perform other actions

inheritance receiving property through a deceased person's will or through the laws of descent and distribution upon the death of an intestate person

initial appearance a person's first appearance before a judge after being arrested

initiative a formal petition generated by a certain percentage of the electorate to introduce legislative change

injunction a court order to refrain from doing a specified act; less commonly, a court order to do a specified act

injurious falsehood false statements knowingly made that lead to economic loss for a plaintiff

innkeeper's lien a possessory lien placed on the luggage of hotel guests for the hotel charges that remain unpaid

innocent misrepresentation misrepresentation of a material fact without intent to deceive

in pari delicto (Latin) "equally at fault"

***in personam* jurisdiction** *see* **personal jurisdiction**

inquisitorial system legal system, found in many countries throughout the world, in which the judiciary initiates, conducts, and decides cases; the judiciary takes a more active role in developing the facts than the adversarial system (found in the United States), where the parties are responsible for developing the facts

in re (Latin) in the affair, in the matter of, concerning, regarding; the usual method of entitling a judicial proceeding in which there are no adversary parties but merely some res (thing) concerning which judicial action is to be taken (e.g., a bankrupt person's estate or an estate in probate court)

***in rem* jurisdiction** the authority of a court to take action directly against the defendant's property; jurisdiction is thus based on the location of the property (i.e., the court is in the same state or county as is the property)

insanity mental impairment sufficient to prevent a person from appreciating the nature of an agreement or the consequences of his/her actions; a defense to crimes and intentional torts

inside directors members of the board of directors also employed by the corporation as officers and/or employees; *contrast with* **outside director**

inside information confidential information not readily available to the public

insider an owner of 10% or more of the corporate stock of an issuer listed on a national stock exchange, or a director or officer of such an issuer, as well as others, including employees, consultants and tippees, with inside information about corporate affairs

insider trading buying or selling securities on the basis of information not available to the public

insolvency 1. *equitable* insolvency is the inability to pay debts as they become due, which is the test for bankruptcy 2. *balance sheet insolvency* is a financial state in which liabilities exceed assets

insolvent unable to pay debts as they fall due

instrument 1. a formal document or other writing that evinces a legal relationship (e.g., a deed, will, lease, mortgage) 2. under the UCC, a negotiable instrument, security, or other writing demonstrating a right to payment and not itself a security agreement or lease

insurable interest a legal or equitable interest in the subject matter such that the insured benefits from its preservation and/or incurs a loss if it is destroyed or damaged

insurance a contract whereby risks are transferred; the insurer issues a policy covering (paying compensation in the event of) certain occurrences (risks) that, if they occur, will result in a loss to the insured

insurance agent insurance company employee who sells insurance for only that company

insurance broker independent businessperson who buys insurance for the insured from one of many companies

insured the party who is the holder of an insurance policy

insurer the company offering the insurance policy

intangible personal property property (rights in something) that lacks physical substance (e.g., stock, intellectual property)

integrated agreement (integration) in contract law, a writing that constitutes the final written expression of one or more terms of an agreement, either complete (exclusive statement of all terms of the agreement) or partial (conclusive on some but not all issues)

integrated contract complete and total agreement as found in a written agreement. *See* **parol evidence rule.**

integrated disclosure system the system that seeks to eliminate duplicative or unnecessary disclosure requirements under the Securities Act of 1933 and the Securities Exchange Act of 1934

intellectual property protected expressions of scientific, artistic or other creative, and/or commercial endeavors; a special type of intangible personal property, arising from the creative endeavors of the human mind, generally evinced by patents, copyrights, trademarks, and/or trade names

intelligent agents semiautonomous computer programs that the user can dispatch to execute certain tasks

intended beneficiary 1. a third party for whose benefit a contract is formed and who can sue the promisor if that contract is breached 2. a person, not a party to (or otherwise in privity of) a contract, but who has rights under the contract and can enforce these rights against the contract's obligor

intent an express or implied desire to perform a particular act; a state of mind (to do the act) preceding or accompanying an act

intent to be bound the oral or written statement regarding the intention of parties to enter into a contract

intentional infliction of mental (emotional) distress an intentional tort involving disturbance of the plaintiff's peace of mind by the defendant's outrageous conduct

intentional misrepresentation *see* **fraud**

intentional tort a tort in which the tortfeasor expressly or implicitly intends to do the act(s) causing the injury

inter alia (Latin) "among other things"

inter se or *inter sese* (Latin) "among or between themselves"; used to distinguish rights or duties among two or more parties from their rights or duties to others

inter vivos gift gift of property by one living person to another that becomes irrevocable during their lifetimes

inter vivos trust a trust created by the grantor (settlor) and effective during the grantor's lifetime; a trust not established by a will

interbrand competition competition among the various brands of a product

interest fee paid by borrower to lender for the use of money; also, a legal right to use or claim real property

interest in land any right, privilege, power, or immunity in real property

interest in partnership a partner's share in the partnership's profits and surplus

interested director one who may make a profit from some action of the corporation on which he/she is entitled to vote but should recuse—i.e., excuse—himself/herself from voting on

interfamilial immunity 1. once preventing all parent/child suits for tortious conduct, now applying only to negligence; a child can now sue his/her parents for intentional torts such as assault and battery 2. for spousal claims against each other, tort immunity still applies in several states for personal injuries; that stems from the concern that a husband and wife might conspire in a fraudulent scheme to collect money under a liability insurance policy. However, interspousal tort suits for damage that one spouse inflicted on the other's *property* are now permitted in every state.

interference with business relations a business tort under which a tortfeasor attempts to interfere with the conduct of another's business affairs. *See* **interference with contract** and **interference with prospective economic advantage.**

interference with contract an intentional tort with three requirements: (a) a valid contract exists, (b) a third party knows about the contract, and (c) the third party intentionally (and unjustifiably) causes one of the contracting parties to breach the contract, or otherwise unjustifiably prevents performance of the contract

interference with prospective business advantage intentional interference by the defendant with a business relationship the plaintiff seeks to develop, which interference causes loss to the plaintiff (often it is the same as interference with prospective economic advantage)

interference with prospective economic advantage an intentional tort with essentially the same three requirements as the tort of interference with contract, except that the interference affects a prospective contract or other economic arrangement, not an existing contract

interim financing financing that a developer obtains to pay off a construction loan when it becomes due before the permanent financing is available, also called *gap financing*

interlocking directorship a violation of antitrust laws whereby the same person serves as director of two or more significantly competing companies, both of which have capital, surplus, or undivided profits altogether exceeding $12 million, competitive sales of at least 2% of the business' total sales, and competitive sales exceeding $1.2 million (the Commerce Department annually adjusts these 1994 figures in proportion with any changes in the gross national product).

interlocutory judgment a decision on some point(s) but not a final decision concerning the whole controversy; ordinarily, not an appealable decision

intermediary bank a bank in the collection process that is not the depository or payor bank

intermediate scrutiny test discrimination test for which two requirements must be met to justify the differential treatment of people: 1. an important governmental objective and 2. a substantial relationship between the means and the end

international law law governing relations between nations as well as all business or other activities—public or private—conducted beyond the boundaries of a single nation; derived from treaties, texts, past court cases, statutes, custom and all other sources used in national law

interpleader a legal proceeding used when one person (the stakeholder) possesses property or a fund in which he claims no interest but which is claimed by two or more other persons; the rival claimants must then litigate their claims to the property, and the stakeholder is relieved from potential liability for paying the wrong claimant

interrogatories a method of discovery: written questions, to be answered, in writing and under oath, by another party

intervening cause *see* **superseding (intervening) cause**

intervention procedure by which a person not originally a party to a lawsuit is permitted, on his/her own application, to join one of the original parties in maintaining a cause of action or defense, or to assert a claim against one or more of the original parties

intestacy laws state laws governing the administration and distribution of an intestate's estate

intestacy succession the order in which an intestate's estate is divided among surviving relatives

intestate (to die) without leaving a valid will; the term also is a noun, designating a person who so dies

in toto (Latin) "in whole"; altogether, wholly, completely

intoxication an impairment of the mind and will by alcohol or drugs so as to bring about contractual incapacity; if involuntary (occurring by force or mistake), it may be a defense to a crime or tort

intrabrand competition competition among retailers in the sale of a particular brand of a product

intrastate offering exemption an exempt security (no Securities Act registration necessary) because it is issued solely to in-state purchasers for the local financing of a local business

intra vires (Latin) "within the powers" (of a corporation)

intrinsic fraud fraud in which a party is unaware of the nature of the agreement into which he/she is entering, also known as *fraud in the factum* or *fraud in the execution*

intrusion a form of invasion of privacy; unreasonable and highly offensive interference with the seclusion of another

invasion of privacy an intentional tort involving interference with a person's right to be left alone

inventory goods held for sale or lease or consumed in a business

inverse condemnation government-imposed sanctions that take a significant portion of the value of one's private property and may require compensation as eminent domain

investment company a company acting on behalf of many smaller shareholders/ owners by buying a large portfolio of securities and professionally managing that portfolio

investment contract a contract that may be a "security" if it requires an investment of money in a common enterprise with the expectation of profits from the efforts solely of others

investors persons putting up cash or property in exchange for an equity interest in an enterprise

invitee person entering real property at the express or implicit invitation of the owner/ possessor, generally to engage in business (e.g., to shop, to make repairs)

invoice an itemized list of goods or services, usually specifying the price, quantities, and term of sale, that a seller furnishes a buyer

involuntary bankruptcy a proceeding initiated by one or more creditors against an insolvent debtor

involuntary dissolution dissolution by court order, creditors, bankruptcy, or administratively by the state

involuntary manslaughter taking the life of another by criminal negligence or during the course of a misdemeanor

involuntary redemption rights the permission of a corporation, at its option, to redeem the shares for a specified price either after a stated period of time or on the occurrence of a certain event

ipso facto Latin for "by the fact itself"

irrebuttable presumption a presumption that cannot be disputed even through the introduction of contrary evidence

irregular (anomalous) indorsement an indorsement that is not in the chain of title (not necessary to negotiate the instrument); in other words, an indorsement by a person who is not a holder. Such an indorsement gives notice to later holders of the indorser's accommodation status.

irrevocable letter of credit a letter of credit that cannot be amended or canceled without the consent of the beneficiary and the issuing bank

issue in negotiable instruments law, the first delivery of a negotiable instrument to a holder; to issue securities; a decedent's lineal descendants (e.g., children, grandchildren)

issued shares shares in a corporation that have been sold to shareholders

issuer a person who issues securities, and any other persons or entities acting under his/her control or as part of a plan of sale or distribution of the securities

joint and several liability liability in which all parties are concurrently liable, but each is also individually liable; a plaintiff has the option of suing one of them, some of them, or all of them (i.e., any combination)

joint and several promises promises of the same performance made by two or more parties in which the promisors bind themselves jointly as one party and also severally as separate parties

joint council a group consisting of management and union representatives that attempts to resolve disputes arising under the contract and to facilitate the collective bargaining process

joint estate property in which two or more persons have the same rights of ownership

joint liability liability in which all parties are concurrently liable and all must be sued together

joint stock company a partnership in which the capital is divided into shares so that a partner's shares are transferable without the other partner's consent

joint tenancy joint ownership of property, established when the instrument conveying the property states that the parties acquire the property as joint tenants; the co-owners must have received their property interest at the same time, from the same source, in equal interests, and with each owner having the right to possess the whole

joint tenancy with right of survivorship a situation in which two or more persons own an undivided interest in either personal or real property and, on the death of one of the joint tenants, his/her interest transfers to the remaining joint tenant, not to his/her heirs

joint tortfeasors two or more persons who commit a wrong with a common intent

joint venture an association of two or more entities to carry on a single business enterprise for profit

jointly acting together or cooperating; holding in common or interdependently, not separately; people are "jointly bound" on a bond or note when they all must be sued in one action for its enforcement (*see* **joint liability**), not either one at the election of the creditor (*see* **joint and several liability**); *compare with* **joint and several promises**

journeyman a worker who has successfully completed an apprenticeship and is entirely skilled at a craft

judgment a court's final decision on matters submitted to it; a pronouncement, holding, or decree by a court with competent jurisdiction

judgment by default the court's decision that a plaintiff with proof of a claim may recover damages against a defendant who has not responded to the action brought against him/her

judgment creditor a creditor who has obtained a judgment against his/her debtor

judgment debtor a defendant liable for a judgment that has not been satisfied

judgment *in personam* a judgment against a particular person, as distinguished from a judgment against a thing, status, or right (*in rem*)

judgment *in rem* adjudication concerning the status of some thing or right, such as a right to property

judgment lien lien granted to a creditor who has sued a debtor and obtained a judgment

judgment *non obstante veredicto (J.N.O.V.)* literally, a judgment notwithstanding the verdict; if, after the jury has rendered a verdict for one party the judge finds that there is insufficient evidence to support the jury's decision, he/she enters a judgment for the other side

judgment proof having few, if any, assets that can be reached by a judgment creditor; thus, persons against whom money judgments are of no practical effect

judgment rate interest rate set by statute and used when the parties to a negotiable instrument or a contract have failed to specify an interest rate

judicial lien a property interest obtained by court action to secure payment of a debt

judicial review a doctrine whereby courts, notably the federal courts (in particular, the U.S. Supreme Court), have the power to declare federal or state actions to be in violation of the Constitution (unconstitutional)

judicial sale when the mortgagor is in default, the customary method of foreclosure on mortgaged property: after proper notice, the sheriff or other court official takes control of the property and sells it

junk bond a bond that is ordinarily high yield but with a below-standard industry rating; the bond, usually used in a leveraged buyout, represents a promise to pay a certain amount to investors after or during a specific period but subject to a higher degree of risk than other bonds; the risk that the issuer will be unable to pay according to the terms of the bonds

jurisdiction the power of a court to hear and decide the issues in a case and to bind the parties. *See also* **appellate, concurrent, diversity, exclusive, "federal questions," general personal, *in rem*, original, personal, removal, specific personal,** and **subject-matter jurisdiction.**

jurisdictional dispute in labor law, a dispute between rival labor unions that may take the form of each claiming that particular work should be assigned to it or claiming the right to organize a class of employees

jurisprudence the science or philosophy of law

jury a body of persons charged with declaring the facts in a case and deciding (a) whether a criminal defendant is guilty, or (b) whether a civil defendant is liable; a petit jury usually has 12 members (jurors), although some states and the federal courts allow as few as six. *See also* **grand jury.**

jury charge written instructions for the jury

jury directed settlements *see* **high-low agreements**

jury instructions the judge's instructions to the jury on legal issues the jury must decide and rules the jury should apply to the case before it

jury panel a group of citizens from whom a jury is selected

just cause *see* **good cause**

just compensation clause constitutional requirement that government pay fair market value when it acquires property through eminent domain

justice the major goal of most legal systems; encompasses such ideals as impartiality, equity, and fairness

justifiable controversy an actual controversy between parties involving their legal relationship (adverse interests involving something of value such as money, property, or rights) and appropriate for a court of law to decide the outcome.

Kantian theory an ethical theory that looks to the form of an action, rather than the intended result, in examining its ethical worth. *See* **categorical imperative.**

Keiretsu Japanese cartels of vertically related firms working together in a collaborative fashion

kicker a percentage of gross or net income in a real estate transaction that is payable to the lender

kite to secure temporary use of money by negotiating or issuing worthless paper and then redeeming such paper with the proceeds of similar paper

knockoff an unauthorized counterfeit, usually an inferior copy of someone else's product and typically passed off at a much lower price than the genuine item, especially when the item is accorded intellectual property rights under copyright, patent, trademark, or trade dress law

labor relations law statutory, administrative, and case law, almost exclusively federal, dealing with labor/management relations

laches an equity concept similar to statutes of limitations but with no stated period; serves to bar recovery for a claimant who waited too long to assert his/her rights

laesio enormis a doctrine developed from language in the Code of Justinian that provided a remedy for those who sold property at less than half its just price; the seller could rescind the sale, but the buyer could keep the item purchased by paying the full price. The concept extends to overreaching contracts favoring either side in the concept, *laesio ultra dimidium vel enormis* ("loss beyond half or great"), with buyers for more than double the property's value also entitled to rescind the contract.

laissez-faire a political or legal doctrine favoring governmental restraint, if not outright abstention, from the regulation of business

landlord a lessor of real property

landlord's lien statutory lien that secures payment of rent by giving the landlord a lien upon the tenant's personal property located on the premises

land-use restrictions governmental restrictions (e.g., zoning) on the use and disposition of real property

lapse a bequest (gift) via will that is ineffective because the beneficiary has died before the testator/testatrix

lapsed offer a contract offer that can no longer be accepted (is ineffective) because of the passage of time

larceny the crime of unlawfully taking personal property with the intent to deprive the owner of it

last clear chance final opportunity to avoid an injury; used as an exception to the contributory negligence defense

lateral support, right to a right protecting a landowner by prohibiting his/her neighbors from excavating or otherwise changing their own land to such an extent that the landowner's land and/or buildings are damaged

law that which a judge will decide concerning matters properly brought before him/her; in a broader sense, any rule that society will enforce. *See also* **administrative, antitrust, commercial, criminal, environmental, employment, international, labor-relations, positive, procedural, public,** and **substantive law,** and **law merchant.**

law clerk 1. an attorney/law school graduate who works for a judge doing research and administrative functions 2. a student in a law school who works in a law firm during summer months or part-time during the school year

law journal a legal periodical containing scholarly articles on, and reviews of, the law; often published by a law school

law merchant the English system of commercial law, once enforced in special merchant courts, now merged into the common law; part of it was the basis for negotiable instruments law; broadly, it was the law of business custom and commercial practices enforced by European guilds and special merchant courts in the Middle Ages and continuing for several centuries, and now forming one of the bases for current U.S. and international commercial law

law review a law journal

lawsuit a broad, general term for an action or proceeding in a civil court

LBO initialism for a leveraged buyout

leading case a case often referred to by judges and lawyers as having established and settled a point of law

leading question a question that suggests the answer, especially one to be answered by a mere "yes" or "no"; at trial, it is usually allowed only in cross-examination

lease a transfer of possession of property (real or personal), but not title (ownership), for a period of time for a consideration (e.g., rent)

leasehold a real property estate held by a tenant, under a lease, for a set term

leasehold estate an estate in realty held by a tenant under a lease. In every leasehold estate, the tenant has a qualified right to possess and/or use the land.

legacy personal property transferred (bequeathed) by will

legal aggregate a group of individuals not having a legal existence separate from its members

legal entity an organization having a legal existence separate from that of its members

legal ethics the practices and customs among members of the legal profession concerning their professional and moral duties to society, their profession, and, especially, their clients and the courts

legal fiction a construction by the law to reach a just result

legal realism school of legal thought, started and at its apex in the 1920s and 1930s (but with a lasting imprint on American jurisprudence), it generally advocated a less abstract and more realistic approach (pragmatic and empirical) to the law, an approach that considers customary practices, the circumstances in which transactions occur, and how well the law meets the needs of society

legal reasoning a method of critical thinking and persuasion involving strategy and analysis in order to recognize and solve problems, primarily in law, but also sometimes in business or related matters

legal remedies monetary remedies, such as actual damages or punitive damages, awarded an injured party. *Contrast with* **equitable remedies.**

legal tender form of money accepted as lawful payment of debts

legatee the person to whom a legacy is given

legend language on a share certificate's reverse side and setting forth any limitations on transfer of the shares represented by that certificate

legislative history record of the passage of a bill through a legislature, beginning with the initial draft

lemon law statute or regulation requiring a product's manufacturer or dealer to make all repairs necessary to conform with the warranty (or refund the purchase price), provided the buyer reports the defects within a specified time period; if, after a reasonable number of attempts (usually four), the manufacturer or dealer fails to remedy a defect that substantially impairs the value of the product (typically, a new car), the manufacturer or dealer must replace the product or refund the purchase price—this duty to replace or refund also usually arises if a product has been out of service for 30 or more days during the statutory warranty period (often, the first year that the consumer has owned a new product)

lessee the person to whom a lease is granted

lessor the person who grants a lease to another

letter of credit (especially used in international trade) any instrument by which a drawer requests a particular person or people in general to give the bearer or a named person money or something else of value and to look for recompense from the drawer. Unlike most notes and drafts, letters of credit have no standard format; they are governed by UCC Article 5.

letter of intent an instrument entered into by the parties to real estate or other transactions for the purpose of setting forth the general terms and conditions of a sales agreement until a formal legal commitment can be executed via a formal acquisition agreement

letters of administration formal document in which a probate court appoints the administrator of an estate

letters testamentary the formal instrument of authority and appointment the court gives to an executor (personal representative); it corresponds to letters of administration granted to an administrator

leveraged buyout (LBO) a method to gain control over a corporation by buying its stock and financing its purchase with a loan based on the to-be-acquired corporation's assets

levy lawful seizure of property to obtain money owed

lex talionis (Latin) "the law of retaliation" (an eye for an eye)

liability insurance insurance covering liability to others for personal or property injuries

libel written, photographic, or otherwise recorded defamation

license 1. freely revocable permission by a landowner to use his/her land for a limited, specific purpose (e.g., camping, hunting); persons given this right of use have a nonpossessory interest in the real property 2. a revocable privilege granted by the government to do something (e.g., sell liquor, broadcast at a particular frequency) that would otherwise be illegal 3. a contractual arrangement whereby a party receives (in effect, purchases or leases) another party's right to manufacture, distribute, and/or sell goods or services

licensee a person entering real property with the permission of the owner/possessor (e.g., a guest invited to a party)

lien an encumbrance imposed on property to force payment of a debt; if the debt remains unpaid, the property (collateral) can be sold to satisfy the debt (lien). *See also* **artisan's lien, judicial lien, mechanic's lien,** and **possessory lien.**

lien creditor a creditor who has a lien on the debtor's property

lien notice written notice that property is subject to a claim by someone other than its owner for the payment of a debt

lien subordination an agreement between two secured creditors whose respective security interest, liens, or mortgages attach to the same property. The subordinating party agrees that the other creditor's lien shall have priority notwithstanding the relative priorities that the parties' liens would otherwise have under applicable law.

life estate a person's possessory interest in real property for the duration of one or more human lives as specified in the granting instrument

life estate *pur autre vie* a life estate measured by the life of a person other than the grantee (person holding the estate)

life tenant the owner of a life estate

limitation of actions *see* **statute of limitations**

limited (Ltd.) one of the words that indicate a business is incorporated (or a limited partnership)

limited guaranty a guaranty in which the maximum amount of the guarantor's liability is expressly stated in the guaranty instrument

limited jurisdiction power of a court to hear only certain kinds of cases; *compare* **general jurisdiction trial court**

limited liability liability limited to the amount invested in a business entity

limited liability company a form of business that is a partnership-corporation hybrid, with certain advantages of each form

limited liability limited partnership type of limited partnership in which the liability of all the partners, including general partners, is limited to the amount of their investments

limited liability partnership a form of partnership in which a partner (e.g., in a law firm or an accounting firm) is not liable for a negligent act committed by another partner or by an employee not under the partner's supervision—partners can take an active role in management while protected from personal liability

limited partner a partner without power to manage partnership business and with liability for partnership debts only up to the amount of his/her contribution to the business

limited partnership a partnership conforming to state statutory requirements and having one or more general partners and one or more limited partners

limited personal liability a limited partner's or corporate shareholder's liability, which is limited to the amount that a partner or a shareholder invested in the business

limited warranty a warranty expressly limited as to duration and/or effect

line agency administrative agency under the U.S. president's direct control (e.g., the Department of Labor)

line-of-business test if an officer, director, or controlling shareholder learns of an opportunity in the course of his/her business for the corporation and if the opportunity is in the corporation's line of business, a court will not permit that person to keep the opportunity for personal gain

liquid assets assets that can be used immediately to pay debts, taxes, and so on

liquidated claim a debt, the amount of which is not in dispute

liquidated damages the damages for breach of contract that are specified in the contract; these damages will be upheld in court if reasonable (not simply a penalty)

liquidated debt an undisputed debt for a known or ascertainable sum of money

liquidation 1. conversion of assets to cash, usually in order to pay creditors, the procedure followed before distribution in a Chapter 7 bankruptcy proceeding 2. in partnership law, part of the "winding up" after dissolution; collection, preservation, and sale of partnership assets

lis pendens a pending lawsuit; a legal notice that a suit is pending; under the doctrine of *lis pendens*, a court hearing a case acquires power over property involved in that lawsuit until any final judgment in the case

listing (or **listing agreement**) in real estate law, an agreement between a property owner and an agent, with the agent agreeing to obtain a buyer or tenant for a particular property at a certain price and for other terms in return for a fee or commission

litigants the parties to a lawsuit

litigation the process of filing, maintaining, and defending a lawsuit

livery of seisin medieval term denoting transferring land by the parties going to the land and the grantor's giving the grantee a clod of earth or twig to symbolize transfer of the land

living will instrument making known an individual's wishes concerning life-sustaining medical treatments

lobbying attempting to influence legislation

lobster trap defense prohibiting holders of convertible securities (stocks or bonds that can be converted into common shares) from converting the securities into common shares if the holders already own, or would own after conversion, 10 percent or more of the voting shares of stock

lockout a management tactic whereby employees are prevented from entering the work premises, generally in order for management to obtain better terms. Defensive lockout (permitted): when a single union bargains throughout an industry by striking one employer (or more), but not all employers, the struck employer responds by locking the workers out. Offensive lockout (sometimes allowed): management keeps workers out in anticipation of a strike.

lock-up when one broker or dealer has full control of selling a new issue or a series of bonds; in order to ward off a corporate raider, a favored bidder is given a good deal on the purchase of assets or stock

lock-up option an option to buy assets or stock of a target company; it is exercisable only if the recipient of the option is unsuccessful in acquiring control of the target company. Depending on how it is priced, a lock-up option can have the effect of deterring other bids.

long-arm statute a state law extending personal jurisdiction over out-of-state persons, including corporations, that do business in the state, own real property there, or have taken other relevant actions (e.g., committed an alleged tort, entered a contract) in a state

"look and feel" software a computer program or user interface that looks and acts (feels) like another copyrighted program but does not copy the actual code of the first program

loss leader items sold at or below cost to attract customers

loss of value the value of a promised performance minus the value of an actual performance

lost property personal property accidentally left somewhere; the owner does not intend to relinquish ownership

L.S. an abbreviation for *locus sigilli*, "place of the seal," that may serve as a seal

magistrate broadly, a public civil officer having some part of the legislative, executive, or judicial power given by the Constitution, with the U.S. President being the chief magistrate of the nation; more specifically, a lower judicial officer such as a justice of the peace, police judge, town recorder, and other local judicial functionary—often restricted to lesser criminal matters—or an appointed federal judicial officer who hears civil and criminal pretrial matters and who may conduct civil trials or criminal misdemeanor trials

mail fraud a scheme intended to defraud or to obtain money or property by fraudulent means through use of the mails

mailbox acceptance rule principle of contract law that, unless the offer states otherwise, an acceptance using the same method of transmission as the offer is effective when the acceptance is sent (when the offeree places it in the mailbox or otherwise relinquishes control over it)

main purpose rule the doctrine that if the promisor's or surety's goal is to provide an economic benefit for himself/herself, then his/her promise/suretyship is considered outside of the statute of frauds; also known as the main purpose exception or the leading object exception

major emitting facility under the Clean Air Act, a stationary source such as a factory, which emits or has the potential to emit 100 tons of pollutants annually

maker a person or institution that issues a promissory note or certificate of deposit (i.e., promises to pay)

mala fides bad faith

mala in se (Latin) "morally wrong"

mala prohibita (Latin) "wrong by law"

malfeasance a wrongful or unlawful act, especially by a public official; performing an act that a person ought not to do at all, hence distinguishable from "misfeasance"

malicious institution of civil proceedings the intentional tort of instigating civil proceedings against someone for an improper purpose and without good or probable cause, with those proceedings ending decisively in the defendant's favor

malicious prosecution an intentional tort involving the same factors as malicious institution of civil proceedings, except that the improperly instituted proceedings are criminal, not civil

malpractice professional misconduct or unreasonable lack of skill; the failure of a professional to use the skills and learning common to the average reputable members of the profession or those the professional claims to possess, resulting in injury, loss, or damage to those relying on the professional

malpractice suit a lawsuit alleging failure to exercise the standard of care (the skills and learning) expected of someone in a particular profession (e.g., law, medicine, accounting), that is, negligence by a professional during the course of his/her professional employment

malum in se an act that is wrong in and of itself without regard to whether it is punishable by law (e.g., murder)

malum prohibitum an act that is wrong because it is forbidden by law

manager natural person elected by the members of a limited liability company, authorized to manage and operate the business of the limited liability company

managerial employees people involved in formulating or effectuating management policies

mandamus (Latin) "we command"; a legal writ compelling a defendant to perform an action

mandatory bargaining subjects matters relating to wages, hours, terms, and conditions of employment of the members of the bargaining unit and over which the parties are required to bargain by the NLRA

manifest system in environmental and occupational safety law, the requirement that certain chemicals have documentation about their production, distribution, and disposal, to ensure proper handling and disposal of toxic substances

manslaughter unlawful taking of another's life without malice

manufacturing defect not produced according to specifications

manufacturing or processing plant franchise a type of franchise in which the franchisor transfers to the franchisee essential ingredients or the formula to make a particular product

margin the amount that must be paid in cash (not borrowed) in purchasing or investing in securities

mark the collective name for a trademark, service mark, collective mark, or certification mark; a trade symbol

market allocations division of market by customers, geographic location, or products

market concentration the percentage of a particular firm's market sales in a relevant market area

market power a firm's power to control the market price of its product, with a monopoly providing the greatest degree of market power; a firm's market share (its percentage of control of that market) is the primary measure of market or monopoly power

market price the price at which goods are currently bought and sold

marketable title free from defects, encumbrances or reasonable objections to one's ownership

marketable title acts in real property law, state statutes reducing the period of title searches by extinguishing all claims and title defects automatically after a fixed period unless they were preserved by filing a statutory notice.

market-share liability damages liability based on a defendant manufacturer's national market share for the product that caused harm to the plaintiffs

marshaling of assets in partnership law, segregating the assets and liabilities of a partnership from the assets and liabilities of the individual partners

marshals ministerial officers in the federal government's executive department, who with their deputies have the same power to enforce U.S. laws in each state as the sheriffs and their deputies of that state have in enforcing state laws

martial law law exercised by military authorities over civilians, usually in time of war, superseding civil law

master an employer. *See* **servant.**

master-of-the-offer rule a contract law doctrine allowing the offeror to dictate the terms under which the offer may be accepted, including the time, place, and manner of acceptance.

material important; in securities law, a fact that a reasonable person would consider important in his/her decision to purchase or vote shares

material alteration substantial change in one or more terms of an instrument that gives the instrument a different legal effect (e.g., changes the liability, duties, and/or rights of one or more parties to the instrument)

material misrepresentation a misrepresentation is material if either 1. a reasonable person would attach importance to the existence or nonexistence of the fact represented or 2. the person making the misrepresentation knows or should know that the other person is likely to regard the fact as important

material mistake a mistake that goes to the very heart of the agreement

materialmen's lien a lien in favor of suppliers of construction materials

maturity the date when an obligation to pay a debt (e.g., a note, a draft) becomes due

maxim a legal principle; an equity principle of fair play

mechanic's lien a lien in favor of contractors or workers; a statutory lien filed against a debtor's real property for materials or labor expended (but unpaid for) in repairing or improving that property

mediation an alternative method of dispute resolution, preceding or in lieu of litigation, whereby a third party (mediator) tries to help the disputing parties to settle their case

meeting-the-competition defense in an antitrust price discrimination case, this defense may justify selling goods or services at a lower price to some customers (than to others) in order to meet a competitor's price

member a person who joins a nonprofit corporation or a limited liability company; the equivalent of a shareholder in a business corporation

membership corporation a corporation owned by its members, such as a church or other nonstock corporation

memorandum the written evidence required by the Statute of Frauds for certain kinds of contracts

mens rea (Latin) "criminal intent"; usually a requirement for criminal liability

mercantile law *see* **law merchant**

merchant 1. under the UCC, a person who regularly deals in a particular type of goods 2. one who deals in goods or has knowledge or skill with regard to goods

merchantability fitness for the ordinary purposes for which goods of a specific class are sold

merchantable of good quality and suitable for sale, but not necessarily the best; at the very least, such as is usually sold in the market, of medium quality, and bringing the average price

merchant protection statute a law permitting merchants to stop, detain, and question suspected shoplifters without being held liable for false imprisonment if (a) there are reasonable grounds for the suspicion, (b) suspects are detained for only a reasonable time, and (c) investigations and detentions are conducted reasonably

merger concerning businesses and antitrust law, the combination of two or more business entities. Specifically, in corporate law, the combining of two corporations by a procedure under which one acquires the stock of the other. *See also* **conglomerate, horizontal,** and **vertical merger.**

merger clause a contract clause stipulating that the contract is a complete integration and the exclusive expression of the parties' agreement; this clause serves to bring the parol evidence rule into play when interpreting the contract

merger doctrine in copyright law, the doctrine that, if an idea and its expression are inseparable, the expression is not copyrightable

merger guidelines U.S. Justice Department guidelines detailing the general principles and specific standards used to determine which mergers are likely to be challenged by the government under Section 7 of the Clayton Act

merit registration a securities registration that is reviewed by state regulators for its merits rather than just for its disclosures (as federal securities regulators limit their review). The state securities commissioner decides whether the issuer's plan of business and proposed securities issuance are fair, just, and equitable.

merit regulation the power of some state securities commissions to declare a proposed securities offering "too risky" to be permitted (sold) in that state

metes and bounds a precise description of the territorial limits of a parcel of real property including measured distances and angles

minimum contacts as long as the person has sufficient minimum contacts with a state, such that it is fair to require him/her to appear in a court of that state, the state has personal jurisdiction over that person

mini-trial a private ADR proceeding that aids disputing parties in deciding whether and how to bring a case to court; each party (or his/her attorney) briefly argues the facts and law before a neutral third person who advises the parties on how a court would likely decide the case

minor in most states, a person under the age of 18

minute book a notebook of corporate records; the minutes of meetings of shareholders, directors, or committees or the written consents given in lieu of such meetings

minutes a written record of what took place at a meeting

***Miranda* warning** oral admonition advising a person under arrest of the rights he/she has under the United States Constitution, such as the right against self-incrimination and the right to have an attorney present; named for the U.S. Supreme Court holding in *Miranda v. Arizona*, 384 U.S. 436 (1966)

mirror image rule legal principle that the offer and acceptance, in order to form a contract, must mirror each other exactly (the terms must all be the same)

misappropriation the wrongful taking of a nonpublic business secret or asset from one firm and its use by another firm

misappropriation theory (securities) a securities violation occurs when a person breaches a fiduciary duty to the owner of nonpublic information by trading on that information after misappropriating it for his/her own use

misbranding false or misleading labeling prohibited by federal and state statutes (e.g., selling a prescription-required drug over the counter, claiming unsubstantiated medicinal benefits for a food)

misdemeanor a crime placed by a state's criminal code in a class less serious than the other main class of crimes, felonies, with lesser punishment than is generally accorded a felony

misfeasance a lawful act performed in a wrongful manner; more broadly, a transgression

mislaid property personal property intentionally put somewhere, but then forgotten; the owner does not intend to relinquish ownership

misrepresentation a false statement of fact

mistake in contract law, an error or misunderstanding about a material aspect of an agreement

mistake of fact in criminal law, ignorance of an important fact; this may negate *mens rea* and hence serve as a defense

mistake of law the criminal defense that a person honestly did not know that he/she was breaking the law *and* (a) the law was not published or otherwise made public, or (b) the person relied on an erroneous but official statement of the law; otherwise, ignorance of the law is no excuse

mistrial judicial holding that a trial cannot occur or must end prematurely (without a decision) because the court lacks jurisdiction, jurors have engaged in misconduct, or some other procedural failure has occurred

misuse a person's use of a product in a way that the manufacturer could not have reasonably foreseen

mitigating circumstances extenuating facts or situations that do not excuse a wrongful act but that do reduce overall culpability and thus are considered by the court in perhaps lessening the severity of criminal punishment (e.g., reducing the sentence) or, for civil cases, in deciding the amount of damages due to the plaintiff

mitigation the requirement that an injured party reduce his/her damages to a minimum

mixed transaction (or **mixed sale**) a contract that involves the provision of services and goods; the transaction is treated as a sale under UCC Article 2 if the supplying of goods is the predominant factor, or primary purpose, of the contract

mobile source under the Clean Air Act, a moving polluter such as an automobile, truck, or airplane

model in sales contracts, goods the seller shows to the buyer for inspection during the precontract negotiation to describe goods to be sold when the goods themselves are not available (UCC 2-313(1)(c))

Model Business Corporation Act (MBCA) a model state law dealing with corporations, drafted by an organization of business lawyers, which was enacted by many states

modified life insurance life insurance with gradually increasing premiums

moiety one half

money a medium of exchange issued by a government body

money laundering falsely reporting income that has been obtained through criminal activity as income obtained through a legitimate business enterprise—in effect, "laundering" the "dirty money"; federal law requires the tracking of large sums of currency to prevent the free flow of currency gained by criminal acts

monopolization the possession of monopoly power in the relative market and the willful acquisition or maintenance of the power, as distinguished from growth or development as a consequence of a superior product, business acumen, or historic accident

monopoly exclusive or practically exclusive control of the supply and/or sale of a product or service

monopoly power the ability of a monopoly to dictate what takes place in a given market

moral rights the noneconomic rights that an artist acquires simply by creating a work of art. These are rights that either affect or have the potential to affect the artist's personality and reputation (recognized in Europe more so than in the United States).

morality the body of self-imposed rules of conduct generally perceived to be right

mortgage a written agreement between a creditor (mortgagee) and debtor (mortgagor) whereby real property is given as security (mortgage) for a loan

mortgage assumption the right of a buyer to take over and be bound by an existing mortgage

mortgagee the creditor who has received a security interest in real property (a mortgage)

mortgagor the debtor who has given a security interest in real property (a mortgage)

most favored nation (MFN) status an approach to trade that if one nation gives a lower (or nonexistent) tariff rate to certain goods from one World Trade Organization (WTO) member, it must give the same rate to all WTO members

motion a request that a court take a specified action in a case; motions can concern numerous matters

motion for a directed verdict in a jury trial, a motion for the judge to take the decision out of the hands of the jury and direct a verdict for the moving party on the ground that the other party has not produced sufficient evidence to support his/her claim

motion for a new trial a motion asserting that the trial was so fundamentally flawed (because of error, newly discovered evidence, prejudice, or other reason) that a new trial is necessary to prevent a miscarriage of justice

motion for change of venue a motion to have the trial held in another geographic site, often invoked when the defense counsel alleges that the defendant cannot receive a fair trial at the original venue due to pretrial publicity or some other problem

motion in limine *see* **motion to suppress**

motion to compel a motion in which one party asks the court to order the other party to respond to the discovery requests filed by the first party

motion to dismiss a motion contending that, even if the plaintiff's allegations are true, there is no legal basis for finding the defendant liable. *See also* **demurrer.**

motion to suppress evidence or to dismiss the indictment a criminal defense motion claiming that the grounds for the charges are not sufficiently specific or that the evidence against the defendant is inadmissible because it is irrelevant, is unduly prejudicial, or was obtained illegally

multinational enterprise business engaged in transactions in which goods, information, money, people, or services cross national borders

multi-peril policy insurance combining various types of coverage with emphasis on who is insured rather than perils insured against

multiple listing a real estate listing agreement in which the real property owner's agent ("the original agent") lets other agents also try to sell the property; if an agent other than the original agent obtains a buyer, then the original agent gives this other agent a percentage of the commission or a contractually stipulated amount

murder clause a contract clause that a general contractor inserts into subcontracts that is so onerous in obligation and so open to potential conflict that it invites litigation by its very terms (e.g., unrealistic scheduling)

mutual mistake a mistake by both parties to an agreement concerning a fundamental fact

mutual rescission an agreement between the parties to a contract to terminate the contract

mutuality the reciprocal obligations of the parties to a contract, in the absence of which there is no legally binding agreement

mutuality of consideration the requirement for forming valid contracts that both parties must provide consideration

naked restraint a restraint of trade with no purpose except to suppress or eliminate competition; therefore, an unlawful restraint

national ambient air quality standards as mandated by the Clean Air Act, the maximum amount of exposure to major pollutants allowed in outdoor air

national treatment the World Trade Organization principle that once goods are legally imported into a nation, the goods must be treated the same as goods produced in that nation

nationalization 1. the forced taking of foreign assets by a host government. *See* **expropriation, confiscation.** 2. the conversion of a private business into a government-owned business

natural law the theory that law is the basic system of moral principles developed through the power of reasoning, analysis, religion, and philosophy

natural monopoly an industry with economies of scale so large that it is most efficient for one firm to supply the entire market

natural person a human being, as distinguished from an artificial person such as a corporation

necessaries goods or services considered essential to sustain existence (e.g., food, shelter) and/or to maintain a person's station in life

"necessary and proper" clause a provision in the U.S. Constitution, Article I, Section 8, granting to Congress the authority to make laws "necessary and proper" for carrying out any of the government's enumerated powers under the Constitution; hence, Congress has implied powers under this clause

negligence failure to exercise the standard of care that a reasonable person would exercise in like circumstances. To succeed in court, the plaintiff must show (a) duty of care, (b) breach of that duty, (c) causation, and (d) damages.

negligence *per se* an action or omission in violation of a statutory requirement; plaintiffs showing such an act or omission need only prove causation and damages to win a negligence action

negligent misrepresentation a tort involving essentially the same elements as fraud, except that negligence replaces *scienter* (knowledge of falsity, or reckless disregard of truth or falsity); it applies mainly to special situations involving negligent opinions by supposed experts (e.g., lawyers, title examiners, accountants)

negotiability a characteristic of negotiable instruments, documents of title, and certificated investment securities that is meant to promote their marketability and transferability by permitting transfer free of claims and defenses

negotiable capable of being transferred by indorsement or delivery so that the subsequent holder has all the rights that, and possibly more than, were held by the transferor, particularly the right to sue on the instrument in the holder's own name

negotiable document of title a document of title whose terms state that the goods are to be delivered to the bearer or to the order of a named person, or, if recognized in foreign trade, that runs to a named person or assigns

negotiable instrument a type of commercial paper; specifically, a written, signed, unconditional promise or order to pay a fixed amount of money to order or bearer either on demand or at a definite time

negotiation 1. contracts: the transaction of business; the usual setting for the formation of a contract 2. negotiable instruments: the process by which both possession of, and title to, an instrument are transferred from one party to another, with the transferee becoming a holder

net assets total assets minus total liabilities (debts)

net listing a real estate listing in which the agent agrees to sell the owner's property for at least a minimum price, with any amount over the minimum retained by the agent as his/her commission

nimble dividend a dividend to shareholders from current earnings, paid even though there are debts outstanding from previous years

no arrival, no sale a destination contract in which the goods' failure to arrive excuses the seller from liability unless the failure is the seller's fault

no-bill a grand jury's conclusion indicating there was insufficient evidence to warrant a true bill (formal charge)

Noerr-Pennington Doctrine a principle of law derived from two Supreme Court cases (*Eastern R. Presidents Conf. v. Noerr Motor Freight, Inc.,* 365 U.S. 127 (1961) and *United Mine Workers of America v. Pennington,* 381 U.S. 657 (1965)); it extends immunity from antitrust liability to private parties who petition the government for redress (e.g., for businesses who work together lobbying Congress or legislatures to pass certain laws), notwithstanding the anticompetitive purpose or consequences of their petitions

no-fault insurance insurance compensating automobile accident victims regardless of fault

nolo contendere (Latin) "I will not contest it"; a pleading by an accused criminal that does not admit guilt but is equivalent to a plea of guilt for sentencing purposes

nominal consideration a dollar or other very small sum of money used to bind a contract

nominal damages damages in the amount of $1 or some other token amount, awarded when the plaintiff has been legally wronged, but not actually injured

non obstante veredicto Latin for "notwithstanding the verdict." *See* **judgment *non obstante veredicto.***

noncompete clause *see* **restrictive covenant** (second definition)

nonconforming use preexisting use permitted under a zoning ordinance. *See also* **grandfather clause.**

noncumulative dividends payable to certain preferred stock shareholders, these dividends were not declared by the board of directors and therefore are not paid to the shareholders. Noncumulative dividends do not accumulate for payment in future years.

noncumulative preferred stock preferred stock that loses its dividend rights for years in which no dividend is declared or paid

nonexclusive jurisdiction jurisdiction by either a federal or a state court, thus not reserved exclusively to federal court

nonexempt property a debtor's property that neither state nor federal statutes protect from seizure and sale, with sale proceeds used to pay off the outstanding debts. *Contrast with* **exempt property.**

nonfeasance substantial failure, without excuse, to perform a legal duty

nonfreehold estate a legal right to possession, but not ownership, of real property (e.g., a lease)

nonliquid assets assets that cannot be used immediately to pay debts, taxes, or other expenses

nonmerchant a casual or occasional seller

nonobviousness a prerequisite to receiving a patent—the invention must be original and not obvious to others who work in or are otherwise competent in a particular field of knowledge

nonparticipating shares preferred shares entitled to receive the amount of the stated dividend preference and no more

nonpossessory security interest a security interest in personal property in which the debtor retains possession of the collateral that is subject to the security interest. *Contrast with* **pledge** (a possessory security interest).

nonprofit corporations formed under state law (sometimes for specific purposes set by statutes), these corporations are not established to earn a profit (so no exclusive distribution to its members, directors, or officers) but to meet a charitable, educational, or scientific purpose. They have no shareholders and no dividends.

nonrestrictive endorsement in negotiable instruments law, an endorsement that transfers the holder's entire interest in the instrument

nonsuit judgment against a plaintiff who failed to prosecute his action or prove his case. *See also* **default judgment.**

nontariff barriers a nation's laws and regulations other than tariffs (e.g., taxes, business rules) tending to restrict the free flow of products into that country from other nations

nontrading partnership a partnership doing business for professional purposes

no-par stock stock for which no dollar value is indicated on the share certificate; no-par stock is issued for any amount assigned by the board of directors

normal trade relations required under the World Trade Organization (WTO) rules, a nondiscrimination principle calling for equal treatment of goods exported and imported among countries that are WTO members, also called the *most favored nation principle*

noscitur a sociis (Latin) "known by association"; a rule of statutory or contract construction meaning that words occurring together in a phrase are to be defined by their common relationship or their similarity of meaning. *Compare* **eiusdem generis.**

notary public a person authorized by the government to administer oaths and to attest to the authenticity of signatures

note (also called a **promissory note**) a two-party negotiable instrument in which one person (the maker) makes an unconditional, written promise to pay another person (the payee), or a person specified by the payee, a fixed amount of money either on demand or at a particular time in the future

notice the formal presentation of information concerning matters of legal import. Notice is legally required in many situations (e.g., by service of process at the beginning of a lawsuit), regardless of whether the person receiving notice already has the information given in the notice.

notice of dishonor notice given to a secondary party orally or in writing that the primary party has refused to pay instrument

notice-and-comment rule making a procedure in agency rule making that requires 1. notice, 2. opportunity for comment, and 3. a published draft of the final rule

novation an agreement among contracting parties and an outside third party that the third party will perform the duties (and receive the rights) of one of the original parties to the contract—the new party completely substitutes for (replaces) that original party, whose contract duties are thus discharged

novel an invention is novel if it was not anticipated, i.e., if it was not previously known or used by others in the United States and was not previously patented or described in a printed publication in any country

NOW a negotiable order of withdrawal, treated the same as a check under the UCC; the federal Consumer Checking Account Equity Act (1980) permits savings and loan associations, mutual savings associations, credit unions, and banks to offer their savers NOW accounts

nudum pactum (Latin) "a naked promise"; a gratuitous promise for which there is no consideration; a promise to make a gift

nuisance the intentional tort (or crime) of substantially interfering with the plaintiff's right to use and enjoy his/her property (private nuisance) or with rights common to all (public nuisance)

null and void having no legal effect

nuncupative will an oral will made before a witness during the testator's final illness

oath oral or written promise to perform an act or speak truthfully

obiter dicta *see* **dicta**

objection in the trial of a case, the formal remonstrance made by counsel to something that has been said or done, in order to obtain the court's ruling thereon; when the court rules, either party (the objector if his/her objection is denied, and the other side if the objection is granted) may lodge an exception to preserve the issue and put it on the record for a possible appeal; *see also* **exception**

objective intent to form a contract contract law approach that intent to offer or accept is judged by reasonable interpretation of the parties' words and conduct, not by their subjective wishes

objective satisfaction contractual standard of performance based upon whether a reasonable person would be satisfied

objective theory of contracts a theory under which the intent to form a contract will be judged by outward, objective facts (what the party said when entering into the contract, how the party acted or appeared, and the circumstances surrounding the transaction) as interpreted by a reasonable person rather than by the party's own secret, subjective intentions

obligee a person to whom an obligation is owed

obligor a person who owes an obligation to another

obtaining goods or money by false pretenses the crime of obtaining title to another's property using an intentionally false statement of a past or existing fact with the intent to defraud another

obvious risk if the use of a product carries an obvious risk, the manufacturer will not be held liable for injuries that result from ignoring the risk

offenses 1. in criminal law, the least serious type of wrong, such as a minor traffic violation; sometimes called "infractions" or "violations," offenses are not even classified as crimes in some states 2. a general term for crimes, including felonies and misdemeanors

offer a proposal made by one person to another and intended to create a contract if the other party expresses his/her assent

offeree the person to whom an offer is made

offering circular information prepared by the issuer for distribution with a small public offering of securities under Regulation A of the Securities and Exchange Commission

offeror the person making an offer

officer (corporate) a person named by the board of directors to operate the corporate business

oligopoly an industry dominated by a few large firms

ombudsperson 1. a government official who investigates and reports on grievances against the government 2. a similar appointee in a nongovernmental organization (e.g., a business or university)

omnibus clause insurance for members of the insured's family and those who drive the insured's car with permission

open account purchases made, on credit, without security; sellers may permit such purchases if they deem the buyer to be creditworthy (highly unlikely to default)

open listing a real estate listing in which the broker receives a commission only if he or she procures a ready, willing, and able buyer

open listing agreement a contract in which a real estate owner hires a broker to procure a purchaser without giving the broker an exclusive right to sell; usually the owner may terminate the broker at will, with the owner's own sale of the property terminating the arrangement and the broker not entitled to a commission for such a sale; *also called a* **nonexclusive, general, or simple listing**

"open season" window *see* **contract bar rule**

open shop a business where employees are not required to join a union

open-ended credit credit one can use again and again (a series of credit transactions) until a certain prearranged borrowing limit is reached

opening statement at the beginning of a trial, each lawyer has an opportunity to tell the jury what the case is about; it is a brief statement of a party's position and what the party intends to prove at trial

operating agreement in most states, the term for a document setting forth the terms and conditions for managing a limited liability company

operation of law the method by which a right or a liability is created for a party regardless of the party's actual intent; certain consequences arise from certain facts because of legal principles that operate automatically, as contrasted with consequences that arise because of a party's voluntary actions designed to create those consequences

opinion the statement of reasons forming the basis for a court's judgment

oppression an inequality of bargaining power that results in no real negotiation and an absence of meaningful choice for one party to the contract

option contract a contract to keep an offer open for a specified time

order for relief 1. a court's grant of assistance to a complainant 2. in bankruptcy proceedings, the order relieves a debtor of the immediate obligation to pay the debts listed in the bankruptcy petition

order paper a negotiable instrument payable to a specific person or to his/her order, so that it requires the proper indorsement(s) and delivery in order to be negotiated

ordinance a law passed by a governmental body below the state level and dealing with a local concern

ordinary comparative negligence the standard in many jurisdictions that a plaintiff may recover only if he/she is less culpable than the defendant

ordinary holder one who does not qualify as a holder in due course and is subject to both real and personal defenses

organizational meeting required to be held shortly after the corporation has been incorporated, a meeting of directors intended mainly for housekeeping, including adopting bylaws, electing officers, and issuing shares of stock in the corporation; in lieu of such a meeting, the initial directors may give a unanimous written consent

organizational picketing picketing to encourage employees to join or endorse a particular union

organized crime crime committed by groups in the "business" of crime

original acquisition the method of acquiring title to unowned goods, such as wild animals and abandoned property, by reducing them to possession

original issue 1. shares of stock that a corporation issues directly to a shareholder rather than shares transferred from another shareholder or created through a stock split 2. the corporation's first sale of its stock (the selling price goes to the corporation)

original jurisdiction the authority to hear a case after it has first been filed, including holding a trial and passing judgment on the law and facts

ostensible authority *see* **apparent authority**

ostensible ownership when a seller retains sold goods, this doctrine (UCC 2-402) provides that the sale is void against the seller's creditors if the seller's retention is fraudulent according to the laws of the state where the goods are situated

otherwise qualified individual with a disability individuals who, despite their disability or with reasonable accommodation to their disability, are capable of performing the essential functions of a particular job

output contract a contract whereby the seller (usually a manufacturer) agrees to sell all or a stated amount of the seller's output or production of certain goods to a single, specific buyer

outside director 1. members of the board of directors who are not officers or employees of the corporation 2. one not employed by the company but invited to be on the board of directors because of his or her business expertise (often serving on the committee determining compensation for the corporation's executives). *Contrast with* **inside director.**

outstanding shares shares that have been issued, except those repurchased by the corporation after their original issuance

overdraft a check for more than the amount in the customer's account

overdraw to make an overdraft

override Congress' power to annul a president's veto (and thus enact a statute) by a two-thirds vote of both the House of Representatives and the Senate

overrule to make a decision in a prior case void

oversight hearings hearings held by a congressional committee to review an agency's performance

owner's risk a term in bills of lading and shipping receipts to signify that the common carrier does not assume responsibility for the safety of the goods

P.A. an abbreviation for "Professional Association," indicating a professional corporation (e.g., doctors, accountants)

palming off unfair competition when a business tries to pass its product off as being that of (or comparable to) a rival's product

par value stock stock for which a specified dollar amount is indicated on the share certificate; the par value must be set out in the charter

paralegals nonlawyers who work under the supervision of a lawyer (e.g., in a law firm)

parent corporation a corporation that owns all, or a majority of, the stock of another corporation

parol oral; in spoken words

parol evidence evidence concerning a written agreement that is not part of the writing

parol evidence rule contracts law principle that bars parol evidence contradictory to the terms of a written agreement intended to be the final and complete expression of the parties' contract

parole the conditional release of a convicted criminal from prison followed by the opportunity to serve the remainder of the prison term in the community

partially cumulative dividend a type of preferred stock dividend that is a combination of cumulative and noncumulative dividends

partially disclosed principal a principal whose identity a third party does not know, although the third party knows that the person with whom he is dealing may be an agent (acting for a principal)

partially protected speech speech that cannot be regulated by the government but can be restricted as to time and place and must be fully truthful

participating bonds where a bondholder participates in the net profits of the corporation, usually by receiving a percentage of the gains in the form of interest

participating preferred preferred stock that share in corporate profits as well as receive preferred stock dividends

participation in a breach of fiduciary duty a tort committed when the defendant induces another party to breach his/her fiduciary duty to the plaintiff

participation loan a loan in which the original lender sells shares to other parties, called participants

parties 1. in contract law, the persons who have engaged in a transaction or made an agreement 2. the plaintiffs and defendants in a lawsuit

partition a division of land demanded by a partner, joint tenant, or such partner in common so that a tenant will receive exclusive title of a portion of the land, with this portion representing the partner's or tenant's fair share

partner co-owner of a business; *see* **general partner** and **limited partner**

partnership the association of two or more persons who have expressly or implicitly agreed to carry on, as co-owners, a business for profit. *See also* **general, implied, and limited partnership.**

partnership agreement *see* **articles of partnership**

partnership at will a partnership with no set term of duration

partnership by estoppel a partnership created by law because third parties were led to the reasonable belief that a partnership existed

partnership capital the total assets (money and property) that partners contribute for a partnership's permanent use

partnership opportunity similar to a corporate opportunity, a business opportunity available to a partnership and encompassed within the purpose of the partnership; a partner who takes personal advantage of that opportunity violates his/her fiduciary duty to his/her fellow partners.

pass-through entity a business organization that is not a separate taxpayer; all its income and losses are passed through and taxed to its owners; S corporations, partnerships, and limited liability companies are pass-through entities

past consideration an action completed in the past and claimed as consideration for a present promise

patent the 20-year exclusive right, granted by the U.S. government, to make, use, and sell a new and useful design, process, machine, manufactured item, or other composition, or any new and useful improvement on it; a patentable invention must be novel, useful, and nonobvious

patent deed the official document from the U.S. Patent and Trademark Office stating that a patent has been granted

patent misuse in a patent dispute, a defense asserting that although the defendant has infringed a valid patent, the patent holder has abused its patent rights and therefore has lost, at least temporarily, its right to enforce them

patent pending when a patent has been applied for but not yet granted, this legally recognized status puts potential copycats on notice that upon the patent's issuance they could be liable for damages and subject to an injunction

pawn *see* **pledge**

payee the party to whom a negotiable instrument is made payable

payor a party (e.g., drawee) directed to make a payment, generally pursuant to a negotiable instrument

P.C. an abbreviation for "Professional Corporation"

pecuniary financial; concerning money; capable of being measured, computed, or estimated by a monetary value

pendente lite Latin, meaning, in effect, "while the litigation is pending"; *see lis pendens*

per curiam by the whole court; a court opinion written by the court as a whole instead of being authored by a named judge or justice

per stirpes system of distribution of property in an estate whereby each descendant of the testator takes a share representing a proportionate distribution of the property at each succeeding generation; so if a grandparent leaves an estate per stirpes to six grandchildren born of the grandparents' three children, one of whom had one child (A), one of whom had two children (B and C), and the third of whom had three children (D, E, and F), then A receives one-third of the estate, B and C each receive one sixth, and D, E, and F each receive one-ninth of the estate

peremptory challenge *see voir dire*

perfect tender rule the UCC rule that goods be tendered strictly in conformity with the contract

perfection *see* **perfection of security interest**

perfection of security interest a procedure whereby a secured party obtains priority over other parties that seek, or may seek, to attach or otherwise use the collateral

performance discharge of a contract by substantial completion or by the performance of all of the conditions (essentials) of the contract

periodic disclosure federal securities law requirement that issuers of most publicly held securities file monthly, quarterly, and annual reports with the Securities and Exchange Commission

periodic tenancy (lease) tenancy for a definite period of time, which automatically renews until a timely notice to the contrary is given by the lessor or lessee

perjury making a false statement after having taken an oath to be truthful

permissive bargaining subjects matters that are neither mandatory nor illegal—the parties may but are not required to bargain over such subjects under the National Labor Relations Act

permissive counterclaim a defendant's counterclaim arising out of an incident other than the one that is the subject matter of the plaintiff's action. Such a counterclaim need not be filed and can, subject to statute of limitations, be brought in a later suit.

perpetual existence for most modern corporations, the period of corporate existence

per se (Latin) "by itself"; this expression means "in and of itself, without looking (or having to look) to other persons or things"

per se **violations** agreements among competitors that are automatic violations of antitrust laws (e.g., concerning price fixing, production quotas, and some boycotts or tying arrangements)

person individual, sole proprietorship, general partnership, joint venture, limited partnership, foreign limited partnership, limited liability company, foreign limited liability company, professional limited liability company, trust, estate, corporation, custodian, trustee, executor, administrator, nominee, or entity in its own or a representative capacity

personal (limited) defense any defense not a "real" defense; generally, insufficient against holders in due course

personal jurisdiction the authority of a court to bind the parties in a case

personal property all property, tangible and intangible, except real property; generally, property without a permanent location or property that may be easily moved without damage to real estate

personal recognizance the promise of a defendant to appear at trial without a sum of money to guarantee each appearance. *Contrast with* **bail bond.**

personal representative *see* **executor**

personal service contract a contract to perform services for another; generally not delegable

persuasive authority any legal authority or source of law that a court may look to for guidance but on which it need not rely in making its decision. Persuasive authorities include cases from other jurisdictions and secondary sources of law.

petit jury *see* **jury**

petition *see* **complaint**

petitioner the plaintiff; the term is often used in equity cases

picket fencing the patenting of small improvements in another business's patent in order to erode its value; such patent applications may be denied as insufficiently novel, nonobvious, or practical

pierce the corporate veil to disregard the corporate entity, and thus hold the shareholders liable for corporate actions; this is possible under circumstances involving fraud

piracy the manufacture and sale, without permission, of goods copyrighted or trademarked by another firm

plaintiff the person who initiates a lawsuit

plaintiff in error the unsuccessful party in a trial who has then pursued a writ of error in a higher court; the appellant

plant patent a patent that may be issued to anyone who invents or discovers and asexually reproduces any distinct and new variety of plant

plat a chart or map, usually filed in the local court or records office, delineating parcels (boundaries) of real property

plea a civil defendant's answer or other pleading that responds to the complaint; a factual allegation or other pleading offered in a case; in criminal procedure, how the accused, at his/her arraignment, answers the charge(s) against him/her—generally, a formal response of "guilty," "not guilty," or "no contest" (*nolo contendere*)

plea bargain a deal between the criminal defendant and the prosecutor—typically, a trial is avoided as the defendant pleads guilty to a lesser charge; judges have the final authority over whether to approve these compromises

pleadings the papers filed in court, with copies to other parties concerned, in preparation for bringing or defending a lawsuit before the court

pledge the oldest and simplest type of secured transaction, whereby the debtor provides the creditor with physical possession of some of the debtor's property, which serves as collateral

pledgee a person to whom personal property is pledged by a pledgor

pledgor one who transfers possession of personal property as security for a debt

plenary power authority not granted (expressly or implicitly) to the federal government, and thus reserved to the states and the people, by the U.S. Constitution, Tenth Amendment

poison pill plan a defensive tactic used by a company facing an unwanted takeover bid that makes the purchase of its stock very costly

police powers 1. the general power granted state and city government to protect its citizens' health, safety, morals, and general welfare 2. state power to promote or protect public health, safety, morals, and general welfare

political speech relating to the conduct of government or—more generally—matters of public interest, discourse lying at the heart of a republic and thus deserving of the highest protections under the Constitution's freedom of speech provision in the First Amendment

polling the jury asking each juror what his or her verdict is before it is recorded

positive law the body of written law of a particular society at a particular time; the aggregate of legal precepts specifically enacted or otherwise recognized by governments, as distinguished from natural law, moral principles, customs or ideal law

positivists adherents to a school of legal thought that there can be no higher law than a nation's positive law

possession for personal property, manual control either as owner or as one having a qualified right in the property; for real property, exclusive dominion and control such as owners of like property usually exercise

possessory lien a lien in which the creditors can possess the debtor's property until the debt is paid

possibility of reverter a grantor's future right to retake real property if a specified action occurs; the right a grantor has under a fee simple subject to a condition subsequent

postdate to write on an instrument a date later than the one on which the instrument is actually executed

power of attorney an instrument authorizing a specified person to act as agent or attorney for the person executing the instrument

prayer the request for relief in a complaint

precedent a prior judicial decision relied on as authority or guide for resolving later, similar cases

predatory pricing an antitrust law violation in which prices are set below cost for the purpose of driving competitors from the market and reducing competition in the long run

preemption federal law expressly or implicitly covers a subject so completely that the states are barred from making their own laws on this subject

preemptive right the right of existing shareholders to preempt, or go ahead of, other purchasers of stock of the same class in order to protect their percentage interest in, or control of, the corporation

preexisting duty rule common law contract principle stating that a promise to perform (or the performance of) a preexisting legal or public duty does not furnish consideration to support a return promise

preference a debtor's action in paying or securing one or more of his/her creditors in a manner more favorable to them than to other creditors or to the exclusion of such other creditors; unless there is an applicable rule or statute (e.g., bankruptcy laws), a preference is valid if in good faith and not a mere subterfuge for the debtor to secure a future benefit to himself/herself or to prevent the use of his/her property to pay his/her debts

preferential transfer (preference) a transfer (of money or other property) that unfairly favors one creditor over others (i.e., the favored creditor gets more than he/she would under the bankruptcy laws); prohibited, and thus overturned, if to pay a preexisting debt and made during the 90-day period before the bankruptcy petition is filed

preferred stock the class of shares that take precedence over common shares as to (a) distribution of dividends, and (b) distribution upon liquidation

prejudgment attachment an attachment before a judgment, permitted if all statutory and constitutional (due process) requirements are met. *See also* **attachment.**

prejudgment interest the interest on the amount of an award from the date of the injury to the date of judgment

preliminary hearing a court hearing in a criminal case at which the prosecutor must produce sufficient evidence to show that a crime has been committed and that there is good cause to believe that the defendant committed it

premises liability the liability of landlords and tenants to persons injured on their premises

prenuptial agreement an agreement made before marriage that defines each partner's ownership rights in the other's property. Prenuptial agreements must be in writing to be enforceable.

prepackaged bankruptcy a workout plan approved by key creditors and the debtor before the debtor files bankruptcy; it becomes the plan of reorganization in a Chapter 11 bankruptcy

preponderance of the evidence the burden of proof necessary for civil liability

prerogative a special power, privilege, or immunity, usually used in reference to an official or his/her office

prescription *see* **easement by prescription**

presentment the giving of a draft or note to a party (e.g., a bank) that is asked to transfer to the bearer the sum stated in the instrument

presentment warranty a warranty imposed both on the person who obtains payment of a negotiable instrument and on all prior transferors; it warrants title, signature authorization, and lack of material alteration and is given to any person who, in good faith, pays or accepts the instrument

president the chief executive officer of a corporation

presumption a presumption is a rule of law, statutory or judicial, by which the finding of a basic fact gives rise to the existence of a presumed fact until presumption is rebutted. A presumption imposes on the party against whom it is directed the burden of going forward with evidence to rebut or meet the presumption but does not shift to such party the burden of proof in the sense of the risk of nonpersuasion, which remains throughout the trial upon the party on whom it was originally cast

price amendment information concerning the price of securities and underwriting arrangement filed with the Securities and Exchange Commission once the registration statement has been informally cleared by the SEC staff or the registrant receives notice that the registration statement will not be reviewed

price antidilution a provision that prevents a corporation from diluting a shareholder's interests by simply issuing shares of common stock at a price below the conversion price

price discrimination in antitrust law, charging different prices to different customers for the same product without a cost justification for the difference

price fixing an agreement by or among competitors (horizontal) or businesses at different levels of distribution (vertical) to set prices of the goods or services they sell; raising, depressing, fixing, pegging, or stabilizing prices

prima facie (Latin) "on first face" or at first blush; creates a rebuttable presumption

prima facie **case** a presumptively good case that shifts the burden of proof to the opposing party; a case strong enough to require a jury's consideration

primary benefit under the holdings in some cases, the doctrine that an accountant is liable only to the party receiving the primary benefit of his/her services and not to all those to whom he/she could foresee injury because of his/her negligence

primary party in negotiable instruments law, the maker or acceptor (the party primarily liable on the instrument)

principal 1. the person for whom an agent acts and from whom the agent derives authority 2. an amount of money borrowed or invested, as distinguished from the interest charged or earned on that amount

principal place of business physical site from which a person conducts his/her business and keeps his/her records

prior art any existing patents or patent applications or publications, throughout the world, that are relevant to an invention

prior restraint court restrictions (very rarely granted) on a person's making a particular statement

priority being earlier in time or higher in degree or rank; having precedence; holding a better right than another person

private corporation a corporation created for other than public or municipal purposes

private international law a branch of conflicts of law that determines when a domestic court should exercise jurisdiction over a case involving foreign persons or territories, when foreign rather than domestic law should apply to a case, and when judgments rendered by foreign courts should be recognized and enforced in a domestic court

private judge a "referee," a judge, usually retired, who is hired by parties to resolve a dispute because of his or her subject matter expertise in the area of the dispute

private law the law involving relationships among individuals and legal entities

private nuisance interference with a landowner's right to possession and enjoyment of the landowner's land

private offering an offering of securities to a limited number of investors

private placement memorandum a booklet offered by entrepreneurs seeking financing from private individual investors that furnishes information about themselves and their enterprise

privilege an immunity existing under law and constituting a defense in most tort cases (e.g., the privilege of self-defense can defeat the tort of battery)

privileged communication communication between two people in a confidential, protected relationship, such as an attorney-client, husband-wife (in some states), or priest-penitent relationship, that need not be revealed in a legal proceeding

privity in regard to contracts, the requirement that a person be one of the parties to a contract in order to have a legal interest in the contract. *See also* **horizontal** and **vertical privity.**

probable cause proper grounds for a search or arrest; reasonable grounds (something more than mere suspicion) to believe that a particular person committed a crime

probate a court procedure by which a will is held to be valid or invalid; broadly all matters concerning the administration of estates and guardianships

procedural due process the requirement that governmental action depriving a person of life, liberty, or property be via fair procedure

procedural law the operating rules through which cases are presented, tried, and decided

procedural unconscionability a problem in contract formation when, as a result of one party's vastly superior bargaining power, the other party lacks knowledge or understanding of the contract terms because of inconspicuous print or a lack of opportunity to read the contract or to ask questions about its meaning

procedure step-by-step methods that people bringing or defending a lawsuit or criminal prosecution must follow

proceeds consideration for the sale, exchange, or other disposition of collateral

process formal delivery of a writ, summons, or other legal notice, typically at the start of a legal matter; a summons or writ to appear or respond in court; *see also* **process, service of**

process, service of in accordance with statutory, procedural requirements, formal notification to a civil defendant that he/she is being sued

product liability the legal liability of manufacturers, sellers, and lessors of goods to consumers, users, and bystanders for injuries or damages caused by the goods

production of documents a discovery request that a party to a lawsuit produce and permit the other party to inspect and copy designated documents

professional association persons, licensed to practice a profession, that have associated themselves under the laws of a state in order to perform professional services and divide the gains therefrom as stated in the articles of association or bylaws

professional corporation a corporation created by a professional or professionals in order to gain corporate tax advantages for traditional partnership or proprietary activities

professional employee an employee who holds a position requiring advanced knowledge in a field of science or learning customarily acquired by a prolonged course of specialized intellectual instructions and study

professional limited liability company a limited liability company (LLC) organized for the sole and specific purpose of rendering a professional service and services ancillary to such professional service and that has as its members only individuals who themselves are duly licensed or otherwise duly authorized to render the same professional service as is the LLC

proffer to tender

profit the right to obtain a possessory interest in some aspects of another's land (e.g., crops, timber, minerals); the right allows one to enter on the land and remove the crops, timber, or other interest

profit a prendre a right to make use of another's soil (e.g., to mine metals); the right carries with it the right of entry and the right to remove

program trading on the large exchanges, the trading of stock based on computer programs that order trades at prespecified prices or when other conditions occur

promisee the person to whom a promise is made

promisor the person who makes a promise

promissory estoppel such reliance on the promise of another to make a gift, or on some other gratuitous promise, that the promisor is bound by his/her promise notwithstanding the absence of consideration. *See also* **estoppel.**

promissory fraud a type of fraud that occurs when one party induces another to enter into a contract by promising to do something without having the intention to carry out the promise

promissory note *see* **note**

promoter a person who conceives of, organizes, and begins a corporation

proof of claim written and verified statement setting forth a claim

property a collection of rights and interests, generally associated with the concept of ownership; anything subject to use, possession, transfer, and/or ownership. The two main types are real property and personal property. *See also* **intangible personal, intellectual, personal, real,** and **tangible personal property.**

proprietary covenant contract clause concerning ownership of patents, copyrights, marks, and work products

proprietorship *see* **sole proprietorship**

pro rata (Latin) "in proportion"; division (e.g., of assets) according to the proportionate share held by each person

prosecutor the person who represents the government in a criminal proceeding and who prepares and conducts the case against the accused. A municipal or state prosecutor is usually called a district attorney or state's attorney; a federal prosecutor is called a U.S. attorney

prospectus a statement or document describing securities to be offered or being offered; a statutory prospectus meeting the requirements of the Securities Act of 1933 must be prepared and submitted to the Securities and Exchange Commission before securities subject to the Act may be advertised or offered

pro tanto (Latin) "for so much"; to that extent; as far as it goes; to such an extent

protected class under Title VII of the 1964 Civil Rights Act, employment classifications based on race, color, religion, sex, or national origin are suspect; therefore, Title VII has been interpreted by courts to protect people grouped according to race, color, religion, sex, or national origin

protest a required event in international commercial paper transactions (but only optional in domestic transactions) signifying that a proper presentment was made and that notice of dishonor was provided

provisional application an easier, more economical process for obtaining an initial, one-year set of limited patent rights, compared to pursuing the standard patent application

proviso a statutory clause, usually preceded by the words *provided, provided that,* or *provided, however* that exempts something from the enacting clause; that qualifies, modifies, or restrains its generality; or that excludes some possible interpretations

proximate cause an essential element for almost all tort cases, consisting of causation in fact and foreseeability; a tort defense can thus be that the plaintiff's damages were not the natural and probable consequence of the defendant's acts (i.e., the damages were unforeseeable—too remote in time, distance, or chain of events)

proxy a limited power of attorney whereby a shareholder names a proxy (agent or representative) to vote his/her shares

proxy contest (proxy fight) a battle for corporate control whereby an individual, group, or entity seeking to replace the board of directors with its own candidates tries to acquire a sufficient number of shareholder votes to do so

prudent investor (prudent person) rule a principle that trustees manage trust or investment assets as a prudent investor (person) would manage his/her own property—seeking not just property preservation but also a reasonable return in the amount and frequency of income generated. Management and investment decisions concerning individual assets should be evaluated in the context of the overall portfolio, with trustees owing a fiduciary duty to beneficiaries.

public corporation a corporation formed to meet a governmental or public purpose

public defender a criminal defense lawyer, paid by public funds, who defends accused persons who cannot afford representation

public disclosure of private facts a form of invasion of privacy; it is offensive publicity given to private information about another person

public figures individuals who, because of their achievements or their success in gaining the public's attention, are in the public eye. In a defamation suit, a statement made about a public figure or public official must usually be made with actual malice (with either knowledge of its falsity or a reckless disregard for the truth) for liability to be incurred

public invitee a member of the public invited to enter or remain upon another's land for a purpose for which the land is held open to the public

public law the body of law dealing with the relationship between society (government) and individuals

public policy concepts of prevailing morality used by courts to determine the legality or illegality of contracts

public utility a private corporation created for certain public purposes, and governmentally controlled as to services and prices charged (rates)

publication communication to a third party

publicly held corporation a corporation whose shares are widely traded and are owned by a large number of people

puffing (also called puffery) exaggerated statements of value that induce a party, usually a buyer, to enter into an agreement; usually not the basis of fraud or misrepresentation in the legal sense

punitive damages damages recovered in tort (not contract) cases to punish the defendant for outrageous or malicious conduct. *See also* **exemplary damages.**

purchase money security interest a security interest that is (a) held by the seller of the collateral in order to secure all or part of the sales price, or (b) held by a person lending money or otherwise giving value that the debtor uses to acquire or use the collateral (UCC 9-107)

purchase order a document authorizing a seller to deliver goods with payment to be made later

pure comparative negligence a tort system in which the plaintiff may recover for the part of the injury (the percentage of liability) found to be due to the defendant's negligence, even if the plaintiff was found to be the more negligent party

pure notice recording statute statute under which a person who has notice that someone else has already bought the real property cannot validate his/her deed by recording the deed first; in effect, a subsequent purchase acquiring a deed in good faith—without notice of a prior deed—will have superior rights upon recording the deed

pure race recording statute statute under which the first purchaser to record an interest in real property prevails ("first in time is first in right"), even if he/she acquired the property with actual knowledge of a prior unrecorded conveyance, claim, or interest

pyramid sales scheme an illegal scheme in which participants give money or other valuables in exchange for the chance to be paid for recruiting others as participants in the scheme

qualified acceptance a conditional or modified acceptance; because formation of a contract requires acceptance of the offer substantially as made, a qualified acceptance, insofar as it involves a material difference from the offer, is no acceptance at all and the courts treat it as a counteroffer

qualified indorsement *see* **disclaimer,** 2

qualify to do business authorization obtained from another state for a corporation, limited partnership, or limited liability company to do business in that state

quantum meruit (Latin) "as much as he/she earned"; the compensation permitted by law to the performing party in a quasi contract

quash to declare invalid

quasi (Latin) "as if," "as if it were"

quasi contract a contract created by operation of law to prevent unjust enrichment

quasi in rem **jurisdiction** the authority of a court based on the location of the defendant's property, but with the case brought against the defendant personally

quasi-judicial acts a judicial act by an official who is not a judge—the public officer may investigate facts and draw conclusions from them as a basis of official action, with the fact-finding and conclusions subject to review by the courts; an action performed by a judge who is not then acting entirely in a judicial capacity

quasi-public corporation a privately owned corporation created for public purposes, such as a public utility

qui tam plaintiff a plaintiff suing on the government's behalf, often entitled to a share of the amount recovered

quid pro quo (Latin) "something for something (else)"; the thing sought; consideration

quid pro quo **harassment** harassment in which the harassed employee's response to the harassment is considered, by the harasser, in deciding whether and how to grant employee benefits

quiet enjoyment a tenant's right not to have his physical possession of the premises interfered with by the landlord

quiet period the time between filing of securities registration statement and the date the registration statement becomes effective

quiet title *see* **cloud on title**

quitclaim deed a deed containing no warranty of title; it simply conveys all of the rights in the property that the grantor has, whatever those rights may or may not be; no title is transferred if this deed is acquired after execution

quorum for corporations: a majority of the outstanding shares of a corporation; the number of shareholders required to be present to conduct business at a shareholders' meeting

quo warranto (Latin) "by what authority"; a writ (or civil proceeding) by which the government seeks to recover an office or franchise from the person or corporation in possession of it, or seeks to revoke a corporation's charter

race-notice recording statute a statute giving the better claim to the prior purchaser of real estate (over a subsequent purchaser of the same property), unless the subsequent purchaser bought in good faith (e.g., without knowing of the prior purchase) and recorded his/her deed before the prior purchaser recorded his/her deed

race statute *see* **pure race recording statute**

racketeering activity state and federal offenses involving a pattern of illegal acts, including mail and wire fraud

raider in a hostile takeover, a third party who seeks to obtain control of a corporation, called the target, over the objections of its management

ratification a person's explicit or implicit approval or adoption of a prior act that did not bind him/her

ratify to adopt the act even if it was not approved beforehand; to agree to be bound to a contract

rational basis test *see* **rational relationship test**

rational relationship test the most permissive standard for constitutionality under the equal protection clause, a requirement that legislation bear a rational relationship to a legitimate governmental interest

reaffirmation agreement a debtor's written, signed agreement, filed in bankruptcy court, in which the debtor reaffirms (again agrees to pay) a dischargeable or already discharged debt

real (universal) defenses defenses to the enforcement of an instrument that are good against anyone, including holders in due course; examples are fraud in the execution (factum), forgery, discharge in bankruptcy, statute of limitations, material alteration, and defenses (e.g., duress, illegality) that render a contract void

Real Estate Investment Trust (REIT) a tax-advantaged pool of real property

real property land, whatever is growing or built on land, and the rights associated with ownership and use thereof

reasonable accommodation the degree of workplace accommodation an employer or prospective employer must provide a disabled employee or prospective employee to perform a job

reasonable care care taken by the average person under ordinary circumstances

reasonable doubt *see* **guilt beyond a reasonable doubt**

reasonable expectation test for some product liability or warranty cases, a test that courts impose to determine if foods or beverages are merchantable—what the jury or judge determines a consumer would reasonably expect relevant to contents and quality

"reasonable person" standard a tort doctrine, used especially in negligence cases; the duty of care that a hypothetical, reasonable person would meet in the circumstances in question

rebuttal testimony directed toward the evidence produced by the opposite party; often referring to the plaintiff's calling of witnesses and presenting evidence opposing the defendant's case

receiver a fiduciary (for all parties) appointed by the court to take charge of property involved in a lawsuit and to manage and dispose of it as the court orders

recidivism repeated criminal conduct

recklessness usually a criminal law concept—a person's conscious disregard of the substantial risk that the person's actions may violate the law and cause harm

recognition picketing picketing (restricted under the National Labor Relations Act) to induce an employer to recognize a union as bargaining representative for a unit of employees

recognitional strike an unlawful strike whose purpose is to force an employer to recognize the union as the collective bargaining agent for certain of its employees

recognizance an in-court acknowledgment of indebtedness

record the oral and written evidence presented at a court trial or an administrative hearing

recording statute legislation requiring that deeds, mortgages, and other real property transactions be recorded (filed with a government official in a public office) in order to notify future purchasers, creditors, or other interest holders of an existing claim on the property; these statutes are intended to establish an orderly process for resolving claims to (title to) interests in real property

recoupment the defendant's reduction of the amount he/she owes the plaintiff by asserting claims or defenses arising out of the same contract or transaction on which the plaintiff's action is based

red herring prospectus a preliminary prospectus, tentatively reviewed by the Securities and Exchange Commission, designated in red ink as such, and required to accompany a written offer of securities during the waiting period before the securities are formally offered for sale

redeem when a corporation buys up its share of bonds

redemption *see* **equity of redemption** and **statutory period of redemption**

redemption right the right of a corporation to redeem (purchase) preferred shares, even over the objection of their owners

redress to correct or make right

referee a court-appointed person who takes testimony and decides a matter in dispute

reformation an equity action used to revise a written contract so that it will state the actual agreement of the parties

registered agent a person authorized to receive service of process for the corporation

registered limited liability partnership a partnership created and maintained by filing with the appropriate state official an annual registration and by maintaining a statutorily required amount of liability insurance, thereby usually limiting the personal liability of general partners for another partner's wrongful acts of which the first partner had no knowledge

registration rights an investor's right to require a company to register under applicable federal and state securities laws the shares of common stock into which the preferred stock is convertible

registration statement a statement filed by an issuer with the Securities and Exchange Commission under the Securities Act of 1933 and containing all relevant information about the securities to be offered for sale

reimbursement 1. the principal's duty to pay back authorized payments that an agent made on the principal's behalf 2. the principal debtor's duty to repay a surety who paid the principal debtor's obligation

rejection in contract law, the offeree's manifestation of unwillingness to accept an offer

rejoinder a party's presenting evidence and witnesses responding to the other party's rebuttal, usually referring to the defendant's response at trial to the plaintiff's rebuttal

release an agreement by one party to a contract excusing the other party from performance; a person's giving up a right, claim, or privilege that might have been enforced against or demanded from another person

relevant geographic market in analyzing the market structure to decide whether a monopoly exists, courts and other decision makers consider where the product is sold, transportation costs, and how far consumers must travel to purchase the product

relevant product market in analyzing the market structure to determine whether a monopoly exists, courts and other decision makers consider the characteristics of the product, including its substitutes

reliance damages contractual damages placing the injured party in as good a position as he would have been in had the contract not been made

remainder an estate that commences upon the termination of a prior estate; for example A gives B a life estate, with the remainder to C or C's heirs

remainderman the person entitled to a remainder

remand to return a case, by order of an appellate court, to the trial court for further action

remedy legal relief (e.g., by judicial decree or by contract) that prevents a wrong, enforces a right, or compensates a party for harm caused by a violation of his rights

remittance chain the chain of banks in the check collection process that become accountable for the amount of a check, beginning with the payor bank and ultimately ending with the depositary bank's liability to pay its customer, the check's depositor

remittitur the process (and the court order itself) by which a court reduces or proposes to reduce the damages awarded in a jury verdict

removal for cause during the jury selection process, a prospective juror's dismissal because of the juror's actual or presumed inability to be impartial or otherwise fairly assume the role of juror for that case

removal jurisdiction judicial power to remove a case from one court system to another (e.g., from state court to federal court)

rent consideration paid, usually a periodic fee, for the use/occupation of any land, building, equipment, or other property

reorganization rearrangement of a business under Chapter 11 of the Bankruptcy Code

reorganization plan in a bankruptcy case, a rehabilitation plan filed with and approved by the court that divides creditors and shareholders into classes and then designates how claimants within each class are to be treated

repatriation the process a business firm follows in transferring assets or earnings from a host nation to another nation

replacement workers employees hired on either a temporary or permanent basis to take the place of striking employees

replevin a court proceeding instituted to recover personal property wrongfully held by another person

reply the plaintiff's pleading in response to the defendant's answer

reporting company a company registered under Section 12 of the Securities Exchange Act of 1934 that subjects issuers to various reporting requirements and to certain rules and regulations concerning proxies, tender offers, and insider trading

repossession a creditor's taking possession of collateral after the debtor defaults (e.g., fails to make payments)

representation election an election to determine if the workers in a current or proposed bargaining unit will be represented by a particular labor union

repudiation 1. in contract law, words or conduct of one contracting party that unequivocally indicate his/her inability or unwillingness to perform without breach 2. refusal to accept goods that have been tendered in accordance with a sales contract

requests for admissions a method of discovery; written requests that another party admit particular facts or acknowledge the genuineness of certain documents

requests for production of documents requests for documents (e.g., medical records and personnel files) to be produced as part of the pretrial discovery process

requirements contract a contract whereby the buyer agrees to purchase all of his/her requirements of certain goods from a single, specified seller

res (Latin) "thing," "matter"; the subject matter of a legal action (e.g., the land involved in a quiet title action)

resale price maintenance a restraint of trade, generally judged by a rule of reason approach, in which manufacturers or wholesalers set the price of a good at the next level (e.g., retail)

rescind to cancel

rescission cancellation; a remedy in which a contract is terminated and the parties are returned to the positions they occupied before the contract was made

res ipsa loquitur (Latin) "the thing speaks for itself"; a torts doctrine excusing the requirement that a plaintiff prove the defendant negligent if, under certain conditions, the fact of the negligence is obvious; the defendant can rebut the inference of negligence that arises from the defendant's exclusive control over the instrument that caused the harm

resident agent a person or other entity authorized to receive service of process and other official papers for a corporation

res judicata a doctrine prohibiting subsequent litigation between parties as to a dispute between those parties that has already been adjudicated (with final judgment entered and appeals either completed or not taken)

respondeat superior (Latin) "Let the superior respond"; liability of the principal for his/her agent's torts if committed while acting within the scope of the agent's authority

respondent a term for the defendant, often used in an equity case

restitution restoring the status quo; return of property; a tort or breach of contract remedy, such as for unjust enrichment; a criminal sentence requiring repayment of the victim

restraining order a court order requiring a party to cease doing certain acts

restraint of trade in a contract, a provision unreasonably restricting a person from making a livelihood after the sale of that person's business or that person's leaving his/her employment; any number of business practices that limit competition and may violate antitrust laws

restraint on alienation in an instrument conveying property, a provision that prohibits the grantee from selling or transferring the property; many such restraints are unenforceable as against the public policy favoring freely transferable land

restricted security a security that has been issued under an exempted transaction, with further transfer being subject to limitations

restrictive covenant an express provision (e.g., placed in a deed) that attempts to restrict the transfer or use of property; also, a clause in an employment, partnership, or other agreement that limits or forbids the contracting party from performing the same or similar type of work (e.g., for a competitor) within a certain geographic area for a specified period of time after the contract ends

restrictive indorsement an indorsement that (a) is conditional, (b) attempts to prohibit further transfer of the instrument, (c) includes the words "for collection," "for deposit only," "pay any bank," or a similar term, or (d) states that it is for the benefit or use of the indorser or another person

resulting trust a trust that ensues when the person receiving property was not intended to receive it; he/she is made a resulting trustee for the intended beneficiary. This type of trust is intended to correct a mistake.

retained earnings the portion of a corporation's profits that has not been paid out as dividends to shareholders

retainer 1. a fee that a client pays to a lawyer, such as a lump sum to engage a lawyer at the start of a matter (also called an **engagement fee**), advance remuneration for a lawyer's future services (also called a **retaining fee**), or a payment to ensure the lawyer's availability during a specified period or for a particular matter 2. a client's authorization for a lawyer to act in a case

retaliation an unlawful employment practice in which the employer punishes an employee who has reported some other illegal employment practice

retaliatory eviction eviction or eviction proceedings initiated by a landlord because a tenant has complained or otherwise exercised contractual or statutory rights

revenue license a license requirement intended mainly not to regulate but for the government's charging of fees to those obtaining or renewing a license

reverse discrimination employment, education, and other types of decisions favoring women or minorities over white males in violation of the latter's constitutional and statutory protections entitling them to equal treatment

reverse stock split an amendment to corporate articles decreasing the existing number of authorized shares by combined currently issued shares

reversion in effect, a remainder retained by the grantor of an estate; for example, A gives B a life estate, with reversion to A or his heirs

reversionary interest *see* **reversion**

revocation in contract law, the offeror's withdrawal of his offer

rider an addition to a contract, usually an insurance policy

right a power, privilege, interest or immunity; a legally enforceable demand or claim; that which, upon its violation, affords one a remedy at law or in equity

right of action the right to start a lawsuit

right of contribution *see* **contribution**

right of election surviving spouse's right to avoid disinheritance; his/her right to a portion of the dead spouse's estate despite what the will says—generally one-half of the estate if there are no children or other descendants and one-third if there are

right of entry the right to take or resume possession of land by entering on it in a peaceful manner

right of first refusal a contract that provides the holder with the right to purchase property on the same terms and conditions offered by or to a third party

right of redemption *see* **statutory period of redemption**

right of survivorship *see* **survivorship, right of**

right to lateral support *see* **lateral support, right to**

right to publicity an individual's right to control the commercial use of his/her identity and likeness

right-to-sue notice a document the Equal Employment Opportunity Commission (EEOC) issues as a prerequisite to the charging party being able to file a private suit in court

right-to-work law a state statute prohibiting union shops; that is, in that state, union membership cannot be required for obtaining or retaining employment

riparian rights a landowner's rights (use, accretion, etc.) in a natural waterway within his/her property

ripeness the concept that a court will not decide a case before the necessity to decide it (i.e., will not decide a matter until it is *ripe*)

risk in insurance, a contingency, peril, or other area of potential exposure, which a policy may cover

risk of loss the allocation of loss between the seller and buyer when the goods have been damaged, destroyed, or lost

robbery larceny accomplished by using force or threats of force

rule an established standard, guideline, principle, or doctrine; in administrative law, a regulation issued by a federal, state, or local administrative agency (or court) and governing procedure or conduct in a specific field

rule against perpetuities the common law principle that no interest in property is good unless it must vest, if at all, not later than 21 years plus the period of gestation, after some life or lives in being when the interest was created; several states have abolished the rule, others apply the *cy pres* doctrine to validate contingent remainders and executory interests in some situations (in effect, these states use a "wait and see" approach), and more than half the states have adopted the Uniform Statutory Rule Against Perpetuities, which validates nonvested interests that would otherwise be void under the common law rule if that interest actually vests within 90 years after its creation (so in most states and in most circumstances potential grantors can control where their wealth goes far into the future and even perpetually in some jurisdictions)

rule making an administrative agency's process for adopting new regulations or amending old ones, which generally includes notifying the public of proposed rules or changes and receiving and considering the public's comments

rule of four a U.S. Supreme Court rule that the Court will not issue a writ of certiorari unless at least four justices vote to issue the writ

rule of reason the antitrust doctrine whereby most unintentional, reasonable restraints of trade are lawful if tied to a valid business purpose considering all facts and circumstances

runaway shop an employer's closing of a shop in one location and opening it in another location to avoid unionization

S corporation a corporation organized to meet certain Internal Revenue Code requirements and thus qualified for special federal income tax treatment; the income of an S corporation, whether or not distributed, is taxed to its shareholders, but the S corporation itself is not subject to federal income tax (in essence, the S corporation is taxed the same as a general partnership)

sale a transfer of title to goods for a consideration (a price)

sale on approval a delivery of goods for the buyer's inspection and approval; title and risk of loss remain with the seller until the buyer approves and accepts the goods

sale or return a sale in which the buyer can choose to return goods to the seller

sale with reserve an auction sale in which the auctioneer (seller) may withdraw the goods at any time prior to announcing completion of the sale (UCC 2-328)

sample in precontract negotiations, goods withdrawn from the bulk of goods in a sale and—to describe the goods to be sold—exhibited by the seller for the buyer's inspection (UCC 2-313(1)(c)). *See* **model.**

satisfaction 1. performance of the terms of a new agreement resulting from an accord 2. discharge of an obligation by paying a party what is due to him/her (e.g., on a mortgage, lien, or contract) or what a judgment has awarded to him/her

satisfactory performance a contractually stated measure of performance that is a condition of the contract if the satisfaction is subjective in nature, but is not a condition if satisfaction can be objectively tested

scab a derogatory term for workers who do not comply with a strike

scienter (Latin) "knowingly," "with guilty knowledge" (i.e., with intent to deceive); a term used in law to mean a broadly constructed form of knowledge—what one knows *or should know*; a requirement for proving fraud, scienter arises when the misrepresenting party knew or should have known that material facts have been falsely represented

scope of employment conduct of an agent in furtherance of the business of his/her principal such that, if the agent commits a tort, the principal, as well as the agent, will be liable for the tort

scrip a certificate representing the right to receive a portion of a share (an alternative to fractional shares in distributing share dividends)

seal a distinctive mark, wax impression, letters such as L.S. (*locus sigilli*), or the word "seal" itself, indicating an intention to sign a document with a seal

search concerning intellectual property, an investigation to determine if any type of intellectual property belongs to another party

search warrant a document that a judge or magistrate issues, upon a showing of probable cause, authorizing governmental officials to search a specific place and seize specific items allegedly connected to illegal activities

seasonably an action taken at or within the agreed upon time or—if no time is agreed to—at least within a reasonable time frame

secondary boycott a boycott against businesses other than the one involved in the primary labor dispute (it is intended to cause these businesses to pressure the party in the labor dispute to comply with the union's demands); like secondary picketing and secondary striking, this refusal to do business is usually an unfair labor practice

secondary liability in negotiable instruments law, a form of contract liability undertaken by the drawer of a draft and the indorser (without qualification) of any instrument; these secondary parties must pay the instrument only if the primary party does not pay and certain conditions are met. These obligations to pay are ordinarily subject to the conditions of presentment, dishonor, notice of dishonor, and sometimes protest

secondary offering a securities offering by a person other than the issuer

secondary party in negotiable instruments law, the drawer or indorser (the party secondarily liable on the instrument)

secret partner a partner whose existence is not publicly known

secured creditor generally, a creditor who has a contractually created lien in a debtor's property

secured debt a debt in which the creditor has a claim against specific property of the debtor

secured party a secured creditor

secured transaction any transaction in which a creditor acquires a security interest in personal property or fixtures of the debtor; if the debtor fails to perform, the secured creditor can use the personal property or fixtures (known as collateral) as a substitute for, or a means to collect, the debtor's performance (e.g., payment)

securities notes, stocks, bonds, debentures, evidences-of-debt or other documents, certificates, or interests that represent a share in a corporation, business, or venture, or a debt owed by a corporation, business, or venture; any instrument or interest commonly known as a security and regulated by the Securities Act of 1933. *See also* **certificated, exempt, restricted,** and **uncertified security.**

security collateral given for a loan, bond, or note

security agreement an agreement granting a security interest

security interest an interest in the debtor's personal property (or fixtures) held by the creditor as a means to ensure payment or other performance of an obligation

seisin possession of premises with the intention of asserting a claim to a freehold estate therein; as a practical matter, possession of real estate with the same rights and interests as ownership itself; at common law, a possessory interest (ownership) created by, for example, **livery of seisin**

selective disclosure a practice whereby issuers of publicly traded securities disclose material nonpublic information, such as advance warnings of earnings results, to securities analysts or selected institutional investors before making full disclosure of the same information to the general public

self-dealing directors or officers engaged in buying, selling, or leasing property or services to or from the corporation; to be lawful, the deal must be fair to the corporation and fully disclosed to all other directors, officers and, in some cases, shareholders (otherwise, the corporation may void the deal)

self-defense a defense to criminal or tort liability that permits people to use the degree of force reasonably necessary to protect themselves (or others) from criminal force

self-help when the debtor defaults, the secured creditors' remedy of repossessing the collateral without going to court

self-incrimination statements subjecting the speaker to possible criminal prosecution; the U.S. Constitution's Fifth Amendment protects against compelled self-incrimination by declaring that no person "shall be compelled in any criminal case to be a witness against himself"

self-proved will instrument recognized in states following the Uniform Probate Code, eliminating certain formalities of proof

self-proving affidavit an affidavit attached to a will executed by the testator and two witnesses before a notary, which by its very existence attests to the proper execution of the will

self-tender a corporation's offer to buy back its stock or shareholder rights for a fair price

seniority system a system granting employees employment preferences according to the employee's length of service, with each branch to be independent of and serving as a check on the other two

separation of powers allocation of powers among the legislative, executive, and judicial branches of government

sequester to remove or set apart, as in to seize property as security for a claim, or— in a trial—to remove all potential witnesses (except for parties) from observing the trial

servant an employee; subject to great control by the master (employer)

service concerning court procedures, an act or proceeding adverse to a party (ordinarily, a defendant) or a notice to that party; *see also* **process** and **process, service of**

service mark a distinctive symbol, word, letter, number, picture, or combination thereof adopted and used by a business to identify its services (distinguish them from the services of others)

service of process *see* **process, service of**

servient land subject to an easement

set fee a lawyer's fixed fee for performing a specific task (e.g., drafting a contract or registering a trademark)

set-off a counterclaim that a party asserts in reduction or elimination of another party's monetary claim

settlement conference a pre-trial hearing to foster settlement of the case

settlor *see* **trustor**

severable contract a contract with two or more promises, each of which can be enforced separately, so that failure to perform one of the promises may not mean the promisor has breached the entire contract; a contract that is not entire or indivisible, with its consideration expressly or by necessary implication apportioned; a contract may be severable according to its terms (a contract clause), or severability may be an implied term—whether the contract embraces one or more subject matters, whether the obligation is due at the same time to the same person, and whether the consideration is entire or apportioned; *see also* **severability**

severability the ability to separate a contract clause or legislative provision from the remainder of the contract or legislation, respectively (e.g., so that a court can declare the clause/provision unlawful without overturning the rest of the contract or statute)

several liability a creditor's ability to sue one of many debtors separately

severance 1. the destruction of any one of the four unities (time, title, interest, and possession) of what was a joint tenancy but now is severed 2. the cutting of crops or the separation of anything from realty

sexual harassment in employment law, when sexual favors are requested of an employee in exchange for job benefits (quid pro quo) or the employee is forced to work in a sexually hostile (offensive) work environment

sham sale a sale the seller arranges in order to benefit a buyer who purchases an item for an unreasonably low price

share (of stock) a proportionate ownership interest in a corporation or in its equity. *See also* **stock.**

share subscription a written agreement to purchase a specified number of a corporation's unissued shares, perhaps on a periodic basis and/or preceding the corporation's formation

shareholder an owner of a share of a corporation through the ownership of its stock

shareholder of record a person whose name appears on a corporation's shareholder list, as of a specified date, and thus is entitled to vote

Shari'a Islamic legal principles, predominant in some Muslim nations, based on directives that follow the teaching of the prophet Muhammad

shelf registration a single registration statement covering the future sale of securities, permitted by an SEC rule so that the company can react quickly to changing market conditions

shell corporation a corporation intentionally undercapitalized in order to be effectively judgment proof and thus a fraud upon creditors

shelter rule a doctrine of negotiable instruments law whereby, in the chain of title after a holder in due course, all transferees have the status and benefits of a holder in due course, except transferees who (a) were parties to fraud or illegality affecting the instrument, or (b) as prior holders, had notice of a claim or defense to the instrument

shipment contract a contract whereby the seller pays the cost of delivering goods to the carrier; upon delivery to the carrier, risk of loss passes to the buyer

shipment under reservation (documentary sale) a sales contract in which the seller draws a draft against the buyer for the purchase price and forwards it to the buyer's bank with a bill of lading covering the goods and with instructions not to surrender the bill of lading to the buyer until the buyer accepts or pays the draft

shop steward at a particular workplace, the union person who handles union matters (e.g., processes employee grievances, perhaps collects dues)

short-form merger a merger between a subsidiary corporation and a parent corporation that owns at least 90% of the outstanding shares of each class of stock issued by the subsidiary corporation (either corporation's approval by a shareholder vote is unnecessary)

short sale a sale of a security that the seller does not own or has not contracted for at the time of the sale and that the seller must borrow to make delivery; the seller profits from the overall transaction if the security's price drops (the seller buys securities to pay off his/her loan at a lower price than he/she received for initially selling the securities). A rise in the security's price results in a loss for the short seller.

short-swing profits profits made by an insider through the sale or other disposition of securities within 6 months after purchase

shrinkwrap license a license that customers cannot read when they purchase software but are deemed to have accepted when they open the wrapping around the envelope containing the discs. *Compare* **clickwrap agreement.**

sight draft draft payable upon proper presentment

signature in commercial law, any name, word, or mark used for the purpose of executing or authenticating a document

silent partner a partner with no voice in managing the partnership

situs location; local position; the place where a person or thing is; intangible property has no actual situs, but it may have a legal situs—as an example, for tax purposes the situs is the location of the owner, not the place where the tax is owed

slander oral defamation

slander of quality (trade libel) publication of false information about another's product, alleging that it is not what its seller claims

slander of title 1. defaming the title a person has to particular property and thus possibly preventing the sale of that property 2. publication of a statement denying or casting doubt on another's legal ownership of any property, causing financial loss to that property's owner

slander per se words that are slanderous of and by themselves, specifically that (a) a person has committed a serious crime, (b) has a loathsome disease, (c) is guilty of sexual misconduct, or (d) is not fit to conduct business or a profession

SLAPP-suits acronym for Strategic Lawsuits Against Public Participation; lawsuits (e.g., for defamation or for interference with contract) intended to persuade people to drop their opposition to particular governmental or business activities

small claims courts inferior state civil courts with jurisdiction limited by dollar amount

small offering exemption an issuer's offerings that are too small for the federal government to regulate, including some bank loans, privately negotiated securities sales to large institutional investors, and business-venture promotions by a few closely related persons

social contract theory the theory that businesses, especially large entities, must conduct commerce in a manner recognizing the impact on, and considering the views of, persons and interests beyond simply the business owners and managers; business behavior must meet, or at least reflect, society's expectations

sole proprietorship the simplest form of business, in which a sole owner and his/her business are not legally distinct entities, the owner being personally liable for business debts

solicitation an inchoate crime committed when a person, intending for a crime to be committed, asks, orders, or otherwise encourages another to commit that crime

sophisticated purchaser in tort law, a manufacturer's defense that a sophisticated buyer, such as another manufacturer, is responsible for instructing its employees about the dangers in using the product

sovereign a person, governing body, or nation in which independent and supreme authority is vested

sovereign acts doctrine a legal principle that the government cannot be held liable for breach of contract due to legislative or executive acts of general application

sovereign immunity the doctrine under which a government (sovereign) may not be sued without its consent

special agent a temporary agent for a single transaction or some other limited purpose

special damages damages peculiar to the plaintiff in the situation or circumstance in question; actual damages that would not necessarily occur, but because of special circumstances do in fact flow from an injury

special indorsement an indorsement specifying the person to whom, or to whose order, an instrument is payable. The instrument may be further negotiated only by the special indorsee's indorsement. *Compare* **blank (general) indorsement.**

special permit an administrative remedy provided for in zoning ordinances that allows a landowner to use his/her land in a manner expressly permitted by the ordinance if conditions and standards set forth in the zoning regulations are met

special verdict a verdict in which the jury responds in writing to specific written questions on factual issues. *Contrast* **general verdict.**

special warranty deed a deed that includes the general warranty deed's covenants, but warrants only against defects or encumbrances arising after the grantor acquired the property

specific intent crimes certain types of crimes (e.g., burglary, arson) requiring proof of an intent to commit that particular crime; otherwise, *mens rea* (criminal intent) can be transferred from the crime intended to the one that actually occurred

specific performance a court order to a breaching party to perform his/her contract

specific personal jurisdiction personal jurisdiction over a defendant based on the defendant's contacts with the forum state and the case's relating to issues (e.g., an accident, a contract) arising from those contacts. *Compare* **general personal jurisdiction.**

split sentence a sentence in which imprisonment is to be followed by probation

spot zoning a zoning amendment, designed primarily for the landowner's economic benefit, classifying a property or properties to a use inconsistent with the general zoning pattern of the surrounding area

staggered board a board on which the directors serve for specified terms, usually three years, with only a fraction of them up for reelection at any one time

stakeholder model *see* **stakeholders**

stakeholders shareholders, employees, customers, creditors, suppliers, communities, neighbors, local businesses, and other people affected by a corporation's activities and thereby having a stake, albeit perhaps unrecognized at law, in that corporation; the stakeholder model is premised on the supposition that a corporation has a social responsibility to (owes duties to) all stakeholders

stale check an uncertified check drawn more than six months before presentation for payment

standby letter of credit a method for securing the performance a party owes the beneficiary—an issuing bank is to pay a sum of money to the beneficiary on presentation of certain documents specified in the letter of credit, usually a brief statement (in language agreed upon by the two parties) that the other party is in default and the beneficiary is entitled to the payment

standing (to sue) requirement that a person have a sufficient stake in a dispute in order to sue. Plaintiffs generally must show that they have been either harmed or threatened with harm

stare decisis (Latin) "stand by the decision"; a requirement that a court follow its own and higher court precedents

state action constitutional protections in some amendments, or parts thereof, apply only to situations in which the government has acted

stated capital the amount of money received by a corporation upon issuance of its shares, except capital surplus

state of the art a possible defense in product liability cases when a product was made in accord with the highest level of technology that existed at the time of manufacture

statute a law passed by the U.S. Congress or a state legislature

Statute of Frauds the requirement that certain agreements be evinced by a memorandum in writing, and are not provable in court if entirely oral; based on a 1677 statute of the English Parliament and on the Uniform Commercial Code

statute of limitations a statute setting forth the period during which a lawsuit must be brought after a right to sue arises and after a person knows or should know of his/her right to sue

statute of repose a statute limiting the seller's liability to a certain number of years after the product was first sold in general, whether wholesale or retail

statutory interpretation a court's power to give meaning to legislation (a statute) by clarifying ambiguities, providing limits, and ultimately applying that statutory law to a specific fact pattern in litigation

statutory period of redemption a brief, specified time after the foreclosure sale, in which mortgagors are allowed by statute in most states to redeem (recover) the mortgaged property; the mortgagor must pay all of the amounts necessary to redeem under a presage equity of redemption, and also (in most cases) the nonrefundable expenses incurred in the foreclosure sale

stay court order to stop a proceeding

stipulation an agreement between opposing counsel in a pending action, usually required to be made in open court and entered on the record or else in writing and filed in the action, ordinarily entered into for the purpose of avoiding delay, trouble, or expense in the conduct of the action

stock a term used synonymously with "share"; also, the physical evidence of share ownership, the share certificate; also, the aggregate of corporate shares. *See also* **authorized, canceled, capital, certified, common, convertible, cumulative preferred, noncumulative preferred, no-par, par, preferred,** and **treasury stock.**

stock certificate *see* **certificate of stock**

stock dividend to transfer retained earnings to capital stock, a corporation issues to its shareholders new shares of its stock

stock option a right granted to the option holder to purchase stock at a time and price specified in the option

stock split corporate articles amendment increasing the existing number of authorized shares by dividing the currently issued and outstanding shares

stock subscription a promise to buy shares of stock at a specified price

stock warrant a certificate sold to the public and entitling the owner to buy a specified amount of stock at a specified time for a specified price (often equal to the fair market value when the warrant was issued, permitting its holder to benefit from any increase in the stock's value); similar to options (see option contract)

stockholder 1. one who owns an interest in the corporation through stock ownership 2. persons who own a corporation

stockholders agreement a closed corporation agreement, or just an agreement between shareholders in a small corporation, defining the rights of all parties

stoppage *in transitu* (Latin for "in transit") a right that the vendor of goods on credit has to recall them, or retake them, when the vendor discovers the insolvency of the vendee—the right continues so long as the carrier possesses the goods or until there has been an actual or constructive delivery to the vendee or a third party has acquired a bona fide right in the goods

stop-payment order an order, oral or written, by a depositor (drawer) directing his/her bank (drawee) not to honor a specified check

straight bankruptcy a Chapter 7 bankruptcy proceeding

straight preferred stock the usual kind of stock issued with a fixed dividend, paid quarterly, and dividends to be paid before dividends for common shares could be sold

straight voting the usual manner of election of directors in which each share of stock entitles its holder to cast one vote for as many different directors as there are vacancies being filled. Thus, if there are seven vacancies, the owner of 100 shares may vote 100 shares for each of seven persons. *Compare* **cumulative voting.**

street certificate a share certificate that has been transferred in blank, that is, without designating a transferee by name; this certificate may be further transferred by delivery only, without endorsement

strict foreclosure after default and repossession, the secured party simply retains the collateral in full satisfaction of the debt (instead of selling the collateral and applying the proceeds to the unpaid obligation)

strict liability a modern common law principle imposing liability (regardless of whether the defendant is at fault) as a matter of public policy

strict product liability a legal theory permitting a person harmed by a defective product to sue successfully the merchant seller or manufacturer of that product, without proving "fault" or lack of due care if 1. the goods were defective when they left the defendant, 2. the goods were not materially altered after they left the defendant, 3. the goods proximately caused the plaintiff harm, and, 4. in most states, the goods were unreasonably dangerous

strict scrutiny test requirement that, for legislation to successfully withstand court challenges, it must, among other things, be proven necessary to promote a compelling governmental interest

strike union action of refusing to work for a particular employer

struck-work clause a contract clause permitting employees to refuse to perform work which would have been performed by another firm's employees if those latter employees were not on strike

sub judice before a court

sub nom under the name

Subchapter S corporation *see* **S corporation**

subject-matter jurisdiction the authority of a court to decide the issues in a particular case

sublease a lessee's lease of his/her leasehold interest to a third person; a sublease is for less than the full term of the leasehold (if not, it is an assignment rather than a sublease)

submission disputing parties referring an issue to arbitration

subordinated debt instrument a document providing that a holder's right to repayment is subordinate to that of other creditors of the debtor

subpoena a court order requiring a person to appear as a witness, generally, at a deposition or at trial

subpoena *duces tecum* a court order requiring a person to appear as a witness and to bring specified documents

subrogation the right of an insurer, once it has paid the insured for a loss, to proceed against third parties responsible for that loss (exception: no subrogation on life insurance payments); a surety's or guarantor's right to reimbursement from the debtor for any amounts the surety or guarantor must pay the creditor

subscribe to agree to buy shares of stock at a specified price

subsequent purchaser a person who buys a security other than by original issue

subsidiarity the concept, supportive of federalism, that decision-making powers ought to be lodged with the smallest private or governmental unit having the information and resources to make a particular decision; under this approach, the preferred allocation of power is to the individual and to the private sector, then to local communities, and only then to provinces/states, national governments, or (very rarely) international organizations

subsidiary corporation a corporation controlled by another corporation, called the "parent corporation"

substantial evidence evidence that a reasonable person might accept as adequate to support a conclusion

substantial evidence standard in reviewing agency decisions, the court is to follow the agency's fact findings as long as there is substantial evidence to support the findings

substantial performance doctrine that a contract performance slightly deviating from a contract's terms still entitles the performing party to the contract price, less any damages caused by the slight deviation

substantive due process a constitutional theory focusing on the content, or substance, of legislation; if a law or other governmental action limits a fundamental right, such as to vote or to travel, it violates substantive due process unless it promotes a compelling or overriding state interest

substantive law a body of law defining rights and obligations within a single area, such as contracts or torts

substituted contract the parties' agreement to rescind their old contract and replace it with a new contract

subtenant person to whom a portion of a lease term is transferred

subterranean rights the exclusive rights of a landowner to oil, minerals, and other substances found beneath his/her land, including reasonable use of percolating (subsurface) waters. (This last right is also often considered a riparian right.)

successor liability individuals or entities that acquire an interest in a business or in real property may be held liable for personal injury and property or environmental damage resulting from acts (including sale of products) of the previous owner

sue to begin a lawsuit in a court

sui generis unique; of its own kind; peculiar to itself

suit a lawsuit

summary judgment a pretrial judgment on behalf of a civil plaintiff or civil defendant; awarded if the judge decides that (a) there is no genuine issue as to material (potentially determinative) facts, and (b) when the law is applied to these facts, one party is clearly entitled to a judgment in his/her favor. Summary judgment is generally granted or denied in response to a motion for it; it may be awarded on all or just part of a lawsuit.

summary jury trial a form of alternative dispute resolution (ADR); an abbreviated trial process in which the jury's verdict is non-binding and is meant as a guide to help parties settle their dispute rather than proceed to a full trial later

summary proceedings proceedings, usually statutory, during which many formalities are not used, although there still must be notice to the parties, a proper investigation of the facts, and an opportunity to be heard by the person alleged to have committed a wrongful act or whose property or other legally protected interests may be affected

summons a document served on the defendant, along with the complaint, and notifying the defendant that he/she must file an answer or other response to the complaint within a certain time period (e.g., 30 days) or else be subject to a default judgment

sunset law a statute requiring periodic review of an administrative agency (or other governmental function) and whether it should continue; the legislature must act to "renew" the agency by a certain date or it ceases to exist

super discharge a type of bankruptcy discharge under Bankruptcy Code Chapter 13 that extinguishes otherwise nondischargeable debts such as claims for fraud, theft, willful and malicious injury, or drunk driving but not spousal or child support

superseding (intervening) cause a tort of negligence defense based on the lack of either causation in fact or proximate cause forseeability; an intervening cause, subsequent to and not resulting from the defendant's conduct, that breaks the causal connection between the defendant's acts and the plaintiff's damages

supervisor a person with authority to hire, direct, discipline, and fire employees in the interest of the employer

supplementary proceeding concerning enforcement of judgments, a court proceeding occurring after a judgment has been entered, aimed at determining the extent and whereabouts of the judgment debtor's money and property

supra above mentioned; above (used to designate a previous reference in a court opinion, a law journal article, a pleading, or other legal writings)

"supremacy" clause a provision in the U.S. Constitution, Article VI, Section 2, stating that the federal Constitution, laws made in pursuit of the Constitution, and treaties are "the supreme law of the land"

surety a person who has expressly or implicitly agreed to be liable for another's debts even if the creditor has not exhausted all remedies for collection; the surety is primarily, not secondarily, liable (as is a guarantor)

surety bond a bail bond in which a second person promises to pay (guarantees payment) if the defendant fails to appear for trial

surplus an excess of net assets over stated capital; capital surplus may be used in the calculation of dividends

surviving corporation in a merger of two corporations, the corporation that maintains its corporate existence is the surviving corporation

survivorship, right of in certain types of joint ownership (e.g., joint tenancy, tenancy by the entireties), when a co-owner dies his/her interest passes equally to the surviving co-owner(s), who have a right of survivorship

suspended sentence a sentence under which a convicted defendant may stay in society under probation and, if the defendant violates terms of that probation, the defendant goes immediately to prison for the duration of the sentence

sustainability a principle of law and ethics that regulators, businesses, and consumers must create and maintain the conditions for meeting humanity's current and future needs (social, economic, and ecological) in harmony with a thriving, resilient natural environment

symbolic speech nonverbal expressions of beliefs, including gestures, movements, and articles of clothing, strongly (but not absolutely) protected under the U.S. Constitution's First Amendment (free speech)

sympathy strike a strike called, not to gain benefits for the strikers, but to assist other workers and/or unions

syndicate 1. an underwriting group in a public offering; each member agrees to purchase a certain number of the securities of the issuer once the offering is declared effective by the Securities and Exchange Commission 2. a combination of individuals or corporations formed to carry out a commercial undertaking, especially one requiring a large capital investment; any group of persons joined together to promote or continue an enterprise

syndicated loan lenders have concurrent direct obligations with the borrower to make a loan, typically on a pro rata basis, with a lead lender serving as agent for all the lenders in disbursing the funds, collecting payments of interest and principal, and administering/enforcing the loan

t/a trading as, indicating the use of a trade name

tacking adding periods of occupancy by various owners to determine if title has been obtained by adverse possession

takeover acquiring control of a corporation through a merger, consolidation, or purchase of a substantial number of voting shares or the assets of a corporation

taking the government's taking of private property for public use. Under the U.S. Constitution's Fifth Amendment, the government may not take private property for public use without "just compensation"

takings clause *see* **just compensation clause**

tangible personal property personal property that may be physically possessed

target corporation a corporation to whose shareholders a tender offer is submitted or that otherwise is the target of a corporate takeover

tariff a custom or duty imposed on foreign merchandise imported into a country

technology licensing allowing others to use and profit from intellectual property (e.g., patents, copyrights, trademarks, and innovative products or processes) for consideration. In international business transactions, technology licensing is sometimes an attractive alternative to establishing foreign production facilities

teller's check a draft drawn by a bank on another bank or payable at or through a bank

temporary insiders outside attorneys, accountants, consultants, or investment bankers who are not directly employed by a corporation but who acquire confidential information through performance of professional services

temporary restraining order a person is ordered for a temporary time to refrain from an activity

tenancy 1. the right to possess, and/or actual possession of, real property (a lease) without having title (ownership) 2. a form of co-ownership of property. *See also* **joint** and **periodic tenancy.**

tenancy at sufferance (lease) tenancy continuing after a lease has expired, with most states holding that the leasehold implicitly becomes a periodic tenancy.

tenancy at will (lease) tenancy which either lessor or lessee may end at any time, although most states require a termination notice

tenancy by the entirety (co-ownership) no longer recognized in many states, tenancy held by a married couple; similar to a joint tenancy with a right of survivorship and the four unities (owners received their interest at the same time, from the same source and in equal interests (e.g., amounts), with each having a right to possess the whole); however, unlike a joint tenancy, can be terminated only by death, divorce, or agreement by both owners

tenancy for years tenancy for a fixed period

tenancy from period to period a nonfreehold estate created by a lease that does not specify length of time but states that rent is to be paid at certain intervals

tenancy in common (co-ownership) tenancy in which each of two or more co-owners has a right to possess the whole; the three other unities (same time, same source, equal interests) are not required, and there is no right of survivorship (interests pass to one's heirs); if unclear, a conveyance to two or more persons is treated as creating this tenancy, not a joint tenancy

tenancy in partnership type of joint ownership that determines partners' rights in specific partnership property

tenant 1. a person with a right to possess, and/or actual possession of, real property without having title (ownership); a lessee of real property 2. a co-owner of property owned by more than one person

tender to proffer or make available

tender of delivery to offer or make available goods conforming to a contract of sale

tender of performance in contract law, actual performance of the contract or an offer of performance coupled with the manifested present ability to do so

tender offer a corporate takeover bid; a general invitation from the bidding party to all shareholders of the targeted corporation that they sell their shares to the bidding party at a specified price; *see* **target corporation**

tenement a word usually referring exclusively to real property; a term commonly used in deeds that transfers not only land and other inheritances but also offices, rents, commons, and profits arising from lands

tenor an exact copy of an instrument; the exact words of a legal document, especially as cited in a pleading; a legal document's meaning; an indictment for forgery typically must, for example, state the tenor of the forged instrument—precisely all that was in the instrument, including its exact words and figures

tenure 1. a right, term, or manner of holding land in subordination to a superior 2. the status afforded academic professionals and others as a protection against summary dismissal without sufficient cause 3. generally, the legal protection of a long-term relationship (e.g., employment)

termination in sales contracts, an event occurring when either party pursuant to a power created by an agreement or law puts an end to the contract otherwise than for its breach

termination statement in secured transactions, a statement filed in an appropriate public office indicating that a financing arrangement has been terminated

testamentary capacity knowing the value of one's business and property, understanding which persons are the natural objects of one's bequest, and comprehending how one's property is to be distributed

testamentary gift a gift specified in a will, but effective (property is transferred) only upon death; hence, as with the will itself, this gift is revocable until death of the testator

testamentary trust a trust established according to the terms of a will

testator a man who has executed a will

testatrix a woman who has executed a will

testimony a witness's evidence, at trial or a deposition, given under oath (generally, by answering questions that lawyers have posed)

theft the unlawful taking of a person's property without the use of force and with the intent of permanently depriving the person of the property

theft of services obtaining or attempting to obtain services without paying for them

theft of trade secrets the unlawful acquisition of information vital to a business (e.g., stealing confidential information)

third party in contract law, anyone other than the contracting parties who may be affected by or have rights under the contract; generally, anyone other than the parties

third-party beneficiary a person, not a party to a contract, who receives a benefit from the contractual promise

third-party claim a claim bringing a third party into an existing lawsuit; for example, A has sued B, who files a third-party claim against C for all or part of the damages A claims from B

third-party complaint *see* **third-party claim**

time draft in negotiable instruments law, a draft payable at some fixed or determinable future time

time instrument in negotiable instruments law, an instrument calling for future (other than demand) payment

time is of the essence a contract clause allowing a court to deem late performance a material breach unless the penalty on the promisor would be unjust; a court may infer that time is of the essence if late performance would be of little or no value to the promisee

time-price doctrine principle of law permitting sellers to have different prices for cash sales and credit sales

time-sharing the right to use a certain property for a specific period of time each year

tip the disclosure of a fact to an individual (a tippee) and withheld from the general public

tippee a person who receives special information about corporate affairs from an insider so that he/she may invest in its securities

tipper a person who provides another person (the tippee) material information about a security that could be used for insider trading

title 1. a section of a code devoted to a single subject matter 2. legal, formal ownership rights—broadly, the right to possess, control, and benefit from property; other types of title (ownership) are more limited in scope

title closing (settlement) performance of a real estate contract in which the seller of property conveys the property by delivering a deed to the buyer and the buyer pays the purchase price

title insurance insurance against defects in title to real property

title search 1. examination of public records to determine if title to real property is clear 2. tracing a chain of grantors and grantees of a property

tolling *see* **equitable tolling**

tombstone advertisement a limited informational notice of anticipation concerning an issuance of securities

tort a private wrong against a person or his/her property. Aside from certain limited circumstances, all torts arise from either an intentional, wrongful action or a negligent action.

tortfeasor a person who commits a tort

tortious wrongful; injurious; having the nature of a tort

tortious interference with contract *see* **interference with contract**

total-activity test a test used to determine where a company engaged in multistate operations is domiciled, it considers all aspects of the corporate entity, including the nature and scope of the company's activities

Totten trust a special trust consisting of a bank account controlled by the trust's creator, who is also the trustee; the trust is revocable (the trustee may withdraw the funds), but any funds on deposit when the trustee dies automatically pass to the trust's beneficiary

trade acceptance draft drawn by a seller of goods and presented to the buyer for his/her signature (acceptance)—its signing effectively makes the instrument a note receivable of the seller and a note payable of the buyer

trade association subject to antitrust laws, an organized group of competitors pursuing a common interest, such as dissemination of information, advertising campaigns, and codes of conduct

trade dress the image and overall appearance of a product (e.g., the distinctive decor, menu, layout, and style of service of a particular restaurant), subject to the same protection as trademarks

trade fixture a fixture placed on leased premises by a tenant for use in his/her business; unlike the situation with other fixtures, the tenant can continue to treat a trade fixture as personal property

trade libel *see* **disparagement**

trade name a name that, while it may act as a trademark or service mark, is used in business and generally serves to designate the business entity itself

Trade-Related Intellectual Property Issues (TRIPs) provisions in international agreements that affect patent, copyright, and trademark maintenance, protection, and prosecution

trade secret any formula, process, or method of operation used in the production of goods or services, needed by an employee to perform his/her job, and meant to be held in the employee's confidence

trademark a distinctive symbol, word, letter, number, picture, or a combination thereof adopted and used by a merchant or manufacturer to identity his/her goods (e.g., in the minds of consumers and potential consumers)

trademark infringement use of a trademark without the owner's permission, thereby selling goods and services in a way likely to confuse consumers about the goods' or services' genuine source

traditional shelf offerings the registration of 1. securities offered pursuant to employee benefit plans; 2. securities offered or sold pursuant to dividend or interest reinvestment plans; 3. warrants, rights, or securities to be issued upon conversion of other outstanding securities; 4. mortgage-related securities; and 5. securities issued in connection with business combination transactions. *See* **shelf registration.**

transactional immunity the prohibition from prosecution granted a witness that relates to any matter discussed in that person's testimony

transfer warranty *see* **warranty on transfer**

transferee the party to whom an instrument or other property or right has been transferred

transferor the party who has transferred to another an instrument or other property or right

transit check in bank deposit and collection, a check deposited in one bank but payable at or through another bank

traveler's check similar to a cashier's check (the same bank is both drawer and drawee); a negotiable instrument signed by the purchaser when obtained from the bank and later used as cash upon a second signature (indorsement) by the purchaser

treason the only crime defined in the U.S. Constitution: "treason against the United States shall consist only in levying war against them, or in adhering to their enemies, giving them aid and comfort" (Article III, Section 3)

treasure trove rule a common law principle, followed in most states, that a non-trespassing finder has title to money or other treasure buried for so long a time that it is unlikely a prior owner will return. (Otherwise, the landowner usually has the rightful claim.)

treasury stock shares issued and later repurchased by a corporation

treaty an agreement between or among independent nations

treble damages three times the actual loss; in antitrust law and some other subject areas, a winning plaintiff may be entitled to a treble damages award

trespass any wrongful encroachment on, or other offense against, real or personal property

trespass to chattels when personal property is interfered with but not taken, destroyed, or substantially altered (i.e., not converted), also called *trespass to personal property*

trespass to personal property the intentional tort (and often a crime: e.g., conversion or criminal trespass) of unjustifiably interfering with the plaintiffs possessory interest (e.g., use) in personal property; not generally as serious as the intentional tort of conversion

trespass to real property the intentional tort (and usually a crime) of unauthorized entry onto, above, or below the surface of the plaintiff's land, either by a person or by something the person caused to enter the land; also occurs when presence on the plaintiffs land becomes unauthorized, but continues

trial the proceedings before a competent tribunal in which a civil or criminal case is heard and adjudicated

trier of fact the decision maker as to the facts of a case; it is the jury during jury trials and the judge when there is no jury for that case (a **bench trial**)

triple bottom line model the broad approach to traditional, ecological, and social responsibility measures of corporate performance that requires decision makers to consider the profits, the planet, and people ("the 3 P's")

trover a court action to recover damages for wrongfully converted property

trust 1. a relationship requiring a high degree of loyalty 2. an arrangement whereby property is transferred to a trustee, who administers it for the benefit of another party, the beneficiary. Trusts can be *inter vivos* (taking effect during the trust creator's lifetime) or by will (a testamentary trust). In a business trust (one for profit), corporate shareholders have transferred their voting powers to a committee or board that controls the organization. *See also* **constructive, resulting, Totten,** and **voting trust.**

trustee 1. a person who administers property for the benefit of another party 2. a person occupying a position of trust; a fiduciary 3. in bankruptcy, a person who acquires title to the debtor's property (the estate) and administers the estate by collecting and liquidating assets, as well as deciding claims; the trustee has numerous powers and is in charge of distributing the estate to creditors

trustee in bankruptcy the trustee of a debtor's property in a bankruptcy liquidation who locates and collects the debtor's property, converts the assets to cash, and distributes the proceeds to creditors who have filed claims against the estate. The trustee represents the debtor's general unsecured creditors

trustor a transferor of property to a trustee for the benefit of a third party. Also called a "settler" or "creator."

twenty-four-hour silent period the 24-hour period before the representation election, during which the parties must refrain from formal campaign meetings, such as union rallies or captive-audience speeches; those meetings would constitute unfair labor practices

tying arrangement an agreement requiring the purchase of one product (the tied product) in order to purchase another product (the tying product); often a violation of antitrust laws

ultrahazardous activity a tort doctrine imposing strict liability for harm caused by activities (e.g., using explosives or toxic substances) that necessarily involve a risk of serious harm

ultra vires (Latin) "beyond the powers" (of a corporation)

unaccredited investors investors likely to need protection when making investments. *Compare* **accredited investors.**

unauthorized completion in negotiable instruments law, the completion of an instrument on which the signature of the maker or drawer is genuine or authorized but on which other essential terms, such as the payee and amount, are completed in an unauthorized manner

unauthorized signature a signature indicating that the signer has authority to bind another person when such is not the case

uncertified security a security for which no certificate has been issued

uncertified share a share for which no certificate has been issued, but the ownership is shown on stock books maintained for that purpose by the issuer

unconscionability gross unfairness in favor of, and brought about because of, the superior position of one of the parties to the contract

unconscionable contract a grossly unfair contract brought about by the superior position of one of the parties

unconstitutional legislation, rules, or actions that conflict with the U.S. Constitution or a state constitution

underwriter one who provides an outlet for the stock of an issuer and who may guarantee to furnish a definite sum of money by a definite date for an issue of bonds or stock; more than just someone whose sole interest in the sale of stock is an ordinary commission, the underwriter acquires securities intending their overall distribution. In insurance law, the insurer.

undisclosed principal a principal/agency relationship in which neither the fact of agency, nor the identity of the principal, is disclosed to third parties acting in the belief that the agent is the real party in interest

undivided property interest characteristic of concurrent ownership arrangements (e.g., joint tenancy and tenancy in common), with each co-tenant having a simultaneous, proportionate share of the entire property but no separate interest in any particular or identifiable portion of it

undue influence taking advantage of another by reason of a position of trust in a close or confidential relationship

unemployment compensation benefits paid to employees out of work through no fault of their own and who are on hand for suitable work if and when it becomes available

unenforceable contract an agreement that, for some legal reason, is not enforceable in a court of law

unfair competition broadly, an intentional tort encompassing such activities as infringement of intellectual property and interference with contracts or prospective economic advantage; more narrowly, the intentional tort of trying to "pass off" goods or services upon the public as if they were the goods or services of another, more reputable business or product; also, usually a crime

unfair labor practice any activity by a labor union or management that is prohibited by the National Labor Relations Act or an amendment to that act

unfair labor practices strike a strike to protest employer unfair practices; *compare* **economic strike**

Uniform Commercial Code a comprehensive uniform law covering most commercial transactions (e.g., banking, sale of goods)

uniform laws laws uniformly enacted in several, most, or all states; and designed to eliminate or at least to reduce (a) uncertainty about the law of other states, and (b) differing interpretations and enforcement of the law. An example is the Uniform Commercial Code.

unilateral contract a contract based on the exchange of a promise by one party for an action of the other

unilateral mistake a mistake by one of the parties, but not by both parties, to a contract; not grounds for rescission or cancellation

unincorporated association an association of two or more persons to pursue a common objective. Unlike a partnership or corporation, there is no particular form of organization.

uninsured motorist insurance insurance for injuries caused by a driver who has no insurance or by a hit-and-run driver

union a worker association authorized to represent the workers in bargaining with their employers

union authorization card generally, a card containing a statement that the individual signing it wishes to be represented for purposes of collective bargaining by a certain union

union shop a business entity that requires (e.g., because of union "rules") that a worker, in order to remain employed, become a union member within a specified period of time after being hired. Some states outlaw union shops. *See also* **right-to-work law.**

unitary system a system of governance; a centralized governmental system in which local or subdivisional governments exercise only those powers given to them by the central government; *compare with* **federalism**

United States Attorney the attorney appointed by the president upon Senate confirmation for a term of four years; reports to the attorney general; he/she is the head prosecutor in a particular federal district court region

United States Code (U.S.C.) a compilation or codification of all federal statutes

universal defenses *see* **real defenses**

unjust enrichment a benefit received by chance, mistake, or at someone else's expense; the doctrine under which one party unfairly receives a benefit and must therefore furnish an equitable remedy to the person who provided the benefit

unlawful boycott 1. *see* **secondary boycott** 2. a *per se* violation of antitrust laws: an agreement among supposed competitors that excludes other businesses from dealing in their product(s)

unliquidated claim a claim that is not fixed in amount

unliquidated debt debt about which there is a good faith dispute as to the amount due; an obligation not reduced to a specific amount due

unpaid seller's lien the right of an unpaid seller to retain goods sold to an insolvent buyer until those goods are paid for in cash

unprotected speech speech not protected by the U.S. Constitution's First Amendment, including fighting words, speech that incites violence or revolution, defamatory speech, and obscenity

unreasonably dangerous in product liability law, a product that (a) endangers health and safety beyond the expectations of the ordinary consumer or (b) was manufactured even though it was economically feasible to make a less dangerous alternative product

unrestricted indorsement an indorsement that does not attempt to restrict the rights of the indorsee

unsecured bonds bonds that have no specific collateral other than the general assets of the company

unsecured credit credit based solely on the borrower's pledge to pay

unsecured creditor a creditor without security for a debt who has only the debtor's express or implied promise to pay

unsecured debt debt based solely on the debtor's promise to pay

upstream guaranty a guaranty whereby subsidiaries guarantee the parent corporation's debt or pledge their assets as security for the parent corporation's debt

usage of trade a regular practice or method of dealing, observed with such frequency as to become part of the transaction or contract of the parties

useful article doctrine the principle that pictorial, graphic, and sculptural works, including works of artistic craftsmanship, are copyrightable as to their form but not their mechanical or utilitarian aspects

usury a charge of interest in excess of the rate allowed by law

utilitarianism a philosophical and economic doctrine that ethically correct behavior is not related to any absolute moral values but to an evaluation of the consequences of a given action on those who will be affected by it; thus, as consequentialists, utilitarians find that the best social policy leads to the greatest good for the greatest number of people

utility easement the specified use of land for utilities

utility patent a patent that protects any novel, useful, and nonobvious process, machine, manufacture, or composition of matter; or any novel, useful, and nonobvious improvement of such process, machine, manufacture, or composition of matter

utter to offer in payment a counterfeit instrument; in the law of counterfeiting, to utter and publish is to declare or assert, directly or indirectly, by words or action, that the money or note is good

valid effective; operative; not void; sufficient in law

valid contract 1. an agreement that meets all of the legal requirements for a contract and is enforceable by either party in a court of law 2. a contract containing all the essential elements

value under UCC 1-201(44), the performance of legal consideration, the forgiveness of an antecedent debt, the giving of a negotiable instrument, or the making of an irrevocable commitment to a third party

variance a use different from that provided in a zoning ordinance but allowed in order to avoid undue hardship

veil of ignorance a concept developed by philosopher John Rawls; as a method to attain a just distribution of societal resources, Rawls argued that the fairest way to formulate laws is to make them without consideration of one's own situation—this "veil of ignorance" about personal characteristics makes lawmakers more likely to favor policies fostering equal access to opportunities and rights

vendee a person to whom something is sold; a buyer

vendor a person who sells something; a seller

venire a panel of people selected for jury duty and from among whom the jurors are to be impaneled

venire facias (often shortened to *venire*) a writ directing a sheriff or other official to summon (assemble) a jury

venue the geographic district (e.g., a county) in which an action is tried and from which jurors are chosen

verbal in words, oral or written

verbatim word for word

verdict the formal decision reached by a jury in a civil or criminal case

vertical agreement (vertical restraint) an agreement between firms that operate at different levels of production of distribution

vertical market division an agreement between a company and a dealer or distributor that prevents the dealer or the distributor from selling outside a certain territory or to a certain class of customer

vertical merger a merger in which the merged business entities operated the same type of business, but at different levels (e.g., a manufacturer merges with his/her supplier of raw materials); generally permitted under antitrust law

vertical privity privity among persons up and down, that is, on different levels, of the chain of distribution or consumption

vertically integrated firm a firm that carries out two or more functional phases (manufacture, distribution, retailing, and so on) of a product

vest to confer upon a person the ownership of (full title to) property; to give an immediate fixed right of present or future enjoyment

vested settled; accrued; fixed; definite; more than an expectation based on a contingency; a present right or interest that is or will be definitely enforceable

vested remainder an unconditional remainder that is a fixed present interest to be enjoyed in the future

vicarious liability responsibility for another party's actions because of the relationship between the two parties (the acting party and the vicariously liable party). *Respondeat superior* is the most important type of vicarious liability.

"victimless" crime a crime sometimes considered to have no specific victims, just society as a whole (e.g., prostitution, gambling)

view easement an easement holder's interest in another's real property—the holder is guaranteed that the landowner will not obstruct the holder's view by making changes to the property

virtual courthouse *see* **e-court**

virtual property property that, in the context of cyberspace, is conceptual, as opposed to physical; intellectual property that exists on the Internet is virtual property

void of no legal effect from the very beginning; not even susceptible to ratification

void contract an agreement having no legal force or effect; null from the very beginning

voidable capable of being made void; a voidable thing may have some validity until an appropriate action is taken declaring the thing to be void

voidable contract an agreement subject to being declared of no legal effect as a result of action (e.g., rescission, a lawsuit) by one of the parties

voidable preference *see* **preferential transfer**

voidable title a title received by a buyer subject to cancellation by the seller

voir dire a jury selection process in which the judge and/or the attorneys for both sides question prospective jurors; the information provided may be used to determine whether persons can be kept off the panel "for cause" (e.g., bias) and whether a peremptory challenge (rejecting a potential juror without offering a reason) should be exercised; also, sometimes it is an attorney's motion to have a special hearing to determine whether a piece of evidence or testimony should be admitted at trial, *or* an attorney's special cross-examination of an opponent's expert witness to examine and perhaps challenge his/her expertise

voluntary resulting from free choice; especially in statutes, often implying knowledge of essential facts

voluntary bankruptcy proceedings initiated by the debtor under Chapter 7, 9, 11, or 13 of the Bankruptcy Code

voluntary intoxication *see* **intoxication.** Generally, not a defense to crimes or torts

voting agreement pursuant to an agreement that must be in writing and on file with the corporation, an arrangement by which certain shareholders agree to vote their shares as a block (it may create a voting trust)

voting trust a combination of shareholders accomplished through transfer of shares to a voting trustee for the limited purpose of voting on matters to come before a shareholders' meeting

voting trustee the person to whom shares are transferred, pursuant to the creation of a voting trust, in order to be voted together pursuant to a voting agreement

voucher a receipt

wage assignment an employee's assignment to a creditor of a set amount of the employee's wages so that this amount is transferred to the creditor before the wages are paid to the employee

wager *see* **gambling**

waiting period the period between the filing of the registration statement and the date the registration statement becomes effective with the SEC; also called the quiet period

waive to refrain from exercising certain rights

waiver voluntary relinquishment of one or more of a person's known rights (e.g., rights in a contract). A written waiver does not require consideration; other waivers may. *See also* **estoppel.**

ward a legal infant or insane person that the law has placed under the care of a guardian

warehouse receipt 1. a form issued by a bailee for the storage of personal property 2. a receipt issued by a person storing goods

warehouseman a person engaged in the business of receiving and storing goods for hire (UCC Article 7)

warehouser a storer of goods for compensation

warrant court order, such as a search or arrest warrant; *see also* **stock warrant**

warranty a guarantee. *See also* **implied, limited,** and **presentment warranty.**

warranty against infringement a merchant seller's warranty that goods will be delivered free of any third-party claim of intellectual property infringement

warranty deed a deed in which the grantor warrants good, clear title to the grantee. The usual covenants are possession, quiet enjoyment, right to convey, freedom from encumbrances, and defense of title as to all claims.

warranty disclaimer a contract term that limits, modifies, or excludes a warranty liability

warranty liability a warranty applied to (with liability for its breach) those persons who transfer an instrument or receive payment or acceptance

warranty of fitness an implied warranty that goods being sold are fit for the buyer's use or purpose

warranty of habitability the landlord's implied promise that a property is fit for human habitation and free of hazardous conditions

warranty of merchantability an implied warranty that goods being sold are fit for the ordinary purpose for which goods of that class or kind are sold

warranty of title a guarantee that one has conveyed a right to ownership (good title) without any lien

warranty on transfer a warranty made by any person who transfers a negotiable instrument and receives consideration; it covers title, signature genuineness, and authorization, lack of material alteration, lack of knowledge of insolvency proceedings (against maker, acceptor or—for unaccepted drafts—drawer), and lack of good defenses against the transferor (the last one can be qualified); it is given to the immediate transferee and, if the transfer is by indorsement, any subsequent holder who takes the instrument in good faith

waste property damage beyond ordinary wear and tear by a person in rightful possession of the property; the damage harms another with an interest in the property (e.g., a landlord, a co-owner)

watered stock stock issued without consideration or for cash, property, or services less than par value

Weingarten rights named after the Supreme Court case, *NLRB v. Weingarten*, 420 U.S. 251 (1975), establishing these rights, an employee of a unionized workforce is entitled to have a representative of his/her choice present at meetings that may result in disciplinary action against the employee

whipsaw strike a selective strike against one firm in an industry, with the striking union attempting to pit the struck firm against its competitors, who have gained an advantage over the struck firm; the struck firm is under great pressure to accede to union demands in order to get back to full production and regain lost business—once that firm capitulates, then the union can repeat the process against other firms

whistleblowing an employee's disclosure to government or the press that his/her employer is engaged in dangerous, illegal, or improper activities

white-collar crime a nonviolent crime, perpetrated by a person in a position of trust, against a business or government

white knight a favorite to take over a corporation (e.g., an outside business that management favors as opposed to another business attempting a hostile takeover)

wildcat strike a strike by union members that the union has not authorized

will an instrument, executed by a testator/testatrix according to the formalities required by state statute, setting forth how that person's estate is to be distributed after his/her death

willful knowing or conscious

winding up 1. action by the corporation, after dissolution, to liquidate assets and distribute the proceeds—first, to creditors; second, to preferred shareholders (if any); finally to common shareholders 2. in partnership law, the liquidation and termination process for a dissolved partnership. *See* **liquidation, 2.**

wire fraud a scheme intended to defraud or to obtain money or property by fraudulent means through the use of telephone systems

with cause having good legal reason to do something; for example, to discipline or terminate an employee with just cause

without cause without legal reason to do something; for example, to terminate or suspend an employee unlawfully

without recourse indorsement *see* **disclaimer, 2**

with reserve the item owner's right at an auction to withdraw that sold item before its sale is declared final

without reserve the stipulation that an auctioneer may not withdraw goods from the auction

work for hire when an employee or independent contractor creates a work while "on the job" and thus allows someone else (the employer or hirer) to own the copyright

work letter agreement an agreement between a tenant and a landlord, often an exhibit to a lease, that covers issues concerning the tenant's improvements to a rented space

work made for hire a copyrightable work that 1. an employee created within the scope of his/her employment 2. is in one of nine listed categories and is specially commissioned through a signed writing stating that the work is a work made for hire

workers' compensation statute a law, found in all states, requiring many types of employees to relinquish their right to sue their employers for accidental death, injury, or disease arising from or during the course of their employment; in exchange, the employees gain the right to receive financial benefits (according to a statutory schedule of amounts) regardless of fault

working capital a business firm's investment in current assets, such as cash, accounts receivable, inventory, materials, and supplies ordinarily required in day-to-day operations; working capital should meet current expenses and such contingencies as often occur

workout a common law or bankruptcy out-of-court negotiation in which the debtor enters into an agreement with one or more creditors for a payment plan to discharge the debtor's debt

writ a written court order requiring the performance of an act or giving authority to have it done

writ of attachment *see* **attachment**

writ of *certiorari* *see* ***certiorari,*** **writ of**

writ of execution after a judgment against the debtor, a court order that a sheriff or other authorized official seize and sell the debtor's nonexempt property

wrongful boycott *see* **unlawful boycott, 2**

wrongful discharge *see* **abusive discharge**

wrongful dishonor dishonoring, by a bank, of a customer's check without good cause (e.g., insufficient funds, improper or missing endorsements)

yellow dog contract an unlawful agreement in which the employee, as a condition of employment, agrees not to join or remain a member of a union

zero sum negotiations negotiations in which the only issue is the distribution of the fixed pie, also called *distributive negotiations*

zone of danger the area in which an individual is physically close enough to an accident victim as to also be in personal danger and, therefore, also owed a duty of care by the defendant

zoning legislative action, usually at the municipal level, regulating the use of real property, including the types of construction permitted within different zoning districts

INDEX